**Prentice Hall Series in
Computer Networking and Distributed Systems**

Kaufman, Perlman, and Speciner *Network Security:*
Private Communication in a Public World

NETWORK SECURIT

PRIVATE Communication in a PUBLIC Wor

NETWORK SECURITY
PRIVATE Communication in a PUBLIC World

CHARLIE KAUFMAN

RADIA PERLMAN

MIKE SPECINER

PTR Prentice Hall
Englewood Cliffs, New Jersey 07632

Editorial/production supervision: *Camille Trentacoste*
Cover design: *Gryphon Three Design*
Cover illustration: *Tom Post*
Back cover design: *Anthony Gemmellaro*
Manufacturing manager: *Alexis R. Heydt*
Acquisitions editor: *Mary Franz*
Editorial Assistant: *Noreen Regina*

The publisher offers discounts on this book when ordered in bulk quantities.
For more information, contact:

Corporate Sales Department
Prentice Hall PTR
113 Sylvan Avenue
Englewood Cliffs, NJ 07632
Phone: 800-382-3419 Fax: 201-592-2249
E-mail: dan_rush@prenhall.com

All product names mentioned herein are the trademarks of their respective owners.

Printed in the United States of America
10 9 8 7 6 5 4 3 2 1

ISBN 0-13-061466-1

Prentice-Hall International (UK) Limited, *London*
Prentice-Hall of Australia Pty. Limited, *Sydney*
Prentice-Hall Canada Inc., *Toronto*
Prentice-Hall Hispanoamericana, S.A., *Mexico*
Prentice-Hall of India Private Limited, *New Delhi*
Prentice-Hall of Japan, Inc., *Tokyo*
Simon & Schuster Asia Pte. Ltd., *Singapore*
Editora Prentice-Hall do Brasil, Ltda., *Rio de Janeiro*

Si spy net work, big fedjaw iog link kyxogy

CONTENTS

AUTHENTICATION

ACKNOWLEDGMENTS

Despite the controversies that crop up around security issues, it has been our experience that people in the security community are generally generous with their wisdom and time. It's always a little scary thanking specific people, for fear we'll leave someone out, but leaving everyone out seems wrong. It's not even the fair thing to do, since some people would be more egregiously wronged by being left out than others.

Jeff Schiller has always been an inspiration. The too brief and rare occasions when we get to spend time with him are always highly informative as well as entertaining. Bert Kaliski, Tony Lauck, and Phil Karn also stand out as people that have always been helpful to us and from whom we've learned a great deal.

Which brings us to our reviewers. Thank you, Tony Lauck and Joe Tardo, for reading the whole book and giving us enthusiastic and helpful feedback. Ron Rivest, Steve Crocker, and John Linn also did thorough reviews of significant portions and their comments were valuable and inspiring. Other helpful reviewers include Hilarie Orman, Jim Bidzos, Ted Ts'o, Matthew Barnes, Keith McCloughrie, Jeffrey Case, Kathrin Winkler, Philippe Auphelle, Sig Handelman, and Uri Blumenthal.

We could not have done the final chapter without help from the various companies involved, since for the most part the security systems were previously undocumented. We'd like to thank Al Eldridge from Iris (Lotus Notes^{TM}), Amir Herzberg and Mark Davis from IBM (KryptoKnight), Walt Tuvell from OSF, and Cliff Van Dyke from Microsoft (LAN Manager^{TM} and Windows NT^{TM} security) for explaining to us how their systems worked, doing timely reviews of what we wrote, and being enthusiastic and supportive of the project. Although nearly 67% of us work for companies that have products in this area, the opinions we offer are ours alone, and not those of our companies.

Mary Franz, our editor at Prentice Hall, has been enthusiastic and optimistic and patient with us throughout. She's shown good judgment about when to be helpful, when to keep out of the way, when to nag, and when to just look soulful so we feel guilty enough to meet a deadline. Camille Trentacoste, our production manager, has been ambitious about hurrying us along and has a great sense of humor.

Despite the fact that this book has kept both of his parents busy for a significant part of his life, Ray Perlner has kept us inspired with his wholehearted and unselfish enthusiasm for the project. He's shown genuine interest in the subject matter, offered useful advice during interauthor arguments, helped search for quotes, reviewed part of the book, and particularly liked the subscripted pronouns. If we overdo those, it's just because it's fun to see him giggle.

And of course we thank you, our reader. We welcome your comments and suggestions, and hope to update the book periodically. If there are topics you wish we'd covered or errors you'd like us to correct, let us know. Compliments are always welcome. Our current email addresses are charlie_kaufman@iris.com, perlman@novell.com, and ms@color-age.com. But we've found that email is not always reliable and email addresses change. If all else fails, you can contact the publisher Prentice Hall, particularly our editor Mary Franz (mfranz@prenhall.com), and find out our current addresses.

We wish to thank the following for their permission to use their quotes in this book:

- Quote on page 8 from *The Hollywood Book of Quotes*, Omnibus Press.

- Quotes on page 13 and page 24 Copyright © 1994 Newsweek, Inc. All rights reserved. Reprinted by permission.

- Quote on page 41 reprinted by permission of Singer Media Corporation.

- Quote on page 18 reprinted by permission of Turner Entertainment.

- Quote on page 101 courtesy of Donald Knuth.

- Quote on page 221 reprinted by permission of *The Wall Street Journal*, Copyright © 1992 Dow Jones & Company, Inc.

INTRODUCTION

It was a dark and stormy night. Somewhere in the distance a dog howled. A shiny object caught Alice's eye. A diamond cufflink! Only one person in the household could afford diamond cufflinks! So it was the butler, after all! Alice had to warn Bob. But how could she get a message to him without alerting the butler? If she phoned Bob, the butler might listen on an extension. If she sent a carrier pigeon out the window with the message taped to its feet, how would Bob know it was Alice that was sending the message and not Trudy attempting to frame the butler because he spurned her advances?

That's what this book is about. Not much character development for Alice and Bob, we're afraid; nor do we really get to know the butler. But we do discuss how to communicate securely over an insecure medium.

What do we mean by communicating securely? Alice should be able to send a message to Bob that only Bob can understand, even though Alice can't avoid having others see what she sends. When Bob receives a message, he should be able to know for certain that it was Alice who sent the message, and that nobody tampered with the contents of the message in the time between when Alice launched the message and Bob received it.

What do we mean by an insecure medium? Well, in some dictionary or another, under the definition of "insecure medium" should be a picture of the Internet. The world is evolving towards interconnecting every computer, and people talk about connecting household appliances as well, all into some wonderful global internetwork. How wonderful! You'd be able to send electronic mail to anyone in the world. You'd also be able to control your nuclear power plant with simple commands sent across the network while you were vacationing in Fiji. Or sunny Libya. Or historic Iraq. Inside the network the world is scary. There are links that eavesdroppers can listen in on. Information needs to be forwarded through packet switches, and these switches can be reprogrammed to listen to or modify data in transit.

The situation might seem hopeless, but we may yet be saved by the magic of mathematics, and in particular cryptography, which can take a message and transform it into a bunch of numbers known as ciphertext. The ciphertext is unintelligible gibberish except to someone who knows the secret to reversing the transformation. Cryptography allows us to disguise our data so that eavesdroppers gain no information from listening to the information as transmitted. Cryptography also allows us to create an unforgeable message and protect it from being modified in transit. One method of accomplishing this is with a **digital signature**, a number associated with a message and its sender that can be verified as authentic by others, but can only be generated by the sender. This should seem astonishing. How can there be a number which you can verify but not generate? A person's handwritten signature can (more or less) only be generated by that person, though it can be verified by others. But it would seem as if a number shouldn't be hard to generate, especially if it can be verified. Theoretically, you could generate someone's signature by trying lots of numbers and testing each one until one passed the verification test. But with the size of the numbers used, it would take too much compute time (for instance, several universe lifetimes) to generate the signature that way. So a digital signature has the same property as a handwritten signature, in that it can only be generated by one person. But a digital signature does more than a handwritten signature. Since the digital signature depends on the contents of the message, if someone alters the message the signature will no longer be correct and the tampering will be detected. This will all become clear if you read Chapter 2 *Introduction to Cryptography*.

Cryptography is a major theme in this book, not because cryptography is intrinsically interesting (which it is), but because the security features people want in a computer network can best be provided through cryptography.

1.1 ROADMAP TO THE BOOK

The book is divided into three main sections.

- **Part 1 CRYPTOGRAPHY**   Chapter 2 *Introduction to Cryptography* is the only part of the cryptography section of the book essential for understanding the rest of the book, since it explains the generic properties of secret key, message digest, and public key algorithms, and how each is used. We've tried our best to make the descriptions of the actual cryptographic algorithms nonthreatening yet thorough, and to give intuition into why they work. It's intended to be readable by anyone, not just graduate students in mathematics. Never once do we use the term *lemma*. We do hope you read Chapter 3 *Secret Key Cryptography*, Chapter 4 *Hashes and Message Digests*, and Chapter 5 *Public Key Algorithms* which give the details of the popular standards, but it's also OK to skip them and save them for later, or just for reference. Chapter 6 *Number Theory* gives a deeper treatment of the mathematics behind the cryptography.

- **Part 2 AUTHENTICATION**   Chapter 7 *Authentication Systems* introduces the general issues involved in proving your identity across a network. Chapter 8 *Authentication of People* deals with the special circumstances when the device proving its identity is a human being. Chapter 9 *Security Handshake Pitfalls* deals with the details of authentication handshakes.

There are many security flaws that keep getting designed into protocols. This chapter attempts to describe variations of authentication handshakes and their relative security and performance strengths. We end the chapter with a checklist of security attacks so that someone designing a protocol can specifically check their protocol for these flaws. Chapter 10 *Kerberos V4* and Chapter 11 *Kerberos V5* describe the details of those authentication systems.

- **Part 3 ELECTRONIC MAIL**   Chapter 12 *Electronic Mail Security* describes the various types of security features one might want, and how they might be provided. Chapter 13 *Privacy Enhanced Mail (PEM)*, Chapter 14 *PGP (Pretty Good Privacy)*, and Chapter 15 *X.400* describe three mail standards which are compared in Chapter 16 *A Comparison of PEM, PGP, and X.400.*

There are two chapters that aren't in any of the three main sections. The first chapter (the one you're reading now) gives a whirlwind tour of computer networking and computer security to set the stage for the main focus of the book—computer network security. The final chapter, Chapter 17 *More Security Systems*, describes a variety of security systems, including Novell NetWare® (Versions 3 and 4), Lotus Notes®, DCE, KryptoKnight/NetSP, Clipper, SNMP, DASS/SPX, Microsoft (LAN Manager™ and Windows NT™), and sabotage-proof routing protocols.

1.2 WHAT TYPE OF BOOK IS THIS?

We believe the reason most computer science is hard to understand is because of jargon and irrelevant details. When people work with something long enough they invent their own language, come up with some meta-architectural framework or other, and forget that the rest of the world doesn't talk or think that way. We intend this book to be reader-friendly. We try to extract the concepts and ignore the meta-architectural framework, since whatever a meta architectural framework is, it's irrelevant to what something does and how it works.

We believe someone who is a relative novice to the field ought to be able to read this book. But readability doesn't mean lack of technical depth. We try to go beyond the information one might find in specifications. The goal is not just to describe exactly how the various standards and de facto standards work, but to explain why they are the way they are, why some protocols designed for similar purposes are different, and the implications of the design decisions. Sometimes engineering tradeoffs were made. Sometimes the designers could have made better choices (they are human after all), in which case we explain how the protocol could have been better. This analysis should make it easier to understand the current protocols, and aid in design of future protocols.

The primary audience for this book is engineers, especially those who might need to evaluate the security of or add security features to a distributed system, but the book is also intended to be useable as a textbook, either on the advanced undergraduate or graduate level. Most of the chapters have homework problems at the end.

1.3 TERMINOLOGY

Computer science is filled with ill-defined terminology used by different authors in conflicting ways, often by the same author in conflicting ways. We apologize in advance for probably being guilty sometimes ourselves. Some people take terminology very seriously, and once they start to use a certain word in a certain way, are extremely offended if the rest of the world does not follow.

> *When I use a word, it means just what I choose it to mean—neither more nor less.* —Humpty Dumpty (in *Through the Looking Glass*)

Some terminology we feel fairly strongly about. We do *not* use the term *hacker* to describe the vandals that break into computer systems. These criminals call themselves hackers, and that is how they got the name. But they do not deserve the name. True hackers are master programmers, incorruptably honest, unmotivated by money, and careful not to harm anyone. The criminals termed "hackers" are not brilliant and accomplished. It is really too bad that they not only steal money, people's time, and worse, but they've also stolen a beautiful word that had been used to describe some remarkable and wonderful people. We instead use words like *intruder*, *bad guy*, and *impostor*. When we need a name for a bad guy, we usually choose *Trudy* (since it sounds like *intruder*).

We grappled with the terms *secret key* and *public key* cryptography. Often in the security literature the terms *symmetric* and *asymmetric* are used instead of *secret* and *public*. We found the terms *symmetric* and *asymmetric* intimidating and sometimes confusing, so opted instead for *secret key* and *public key*. We occasionally regretted our decision to avoid the words *symmetric* and *asymmetric* when we found ourselves writing things like *secret key based interchange keys* rather than *symmetric interchange keys*.

We use the term *privacy* when referring to the desire to keep communication from being seen by anyone other than the intended recipients. Some people in the security community avoid the term *privacy* because they feel its meaning has been corrupted to mean *the right to know*, because in some countries there are laws known as *privacy laws* which state that citizens have the right to see records kept about themselves. The security community also avoids the use of the word *secrecy*, because *secret* has special meaning within the military context, and they feel it would be confusing to talk about the secrecy of a message that was not actually labeled top secret or secret. The term most commonly used in the security community is *confidentiality*. We find that strange because *confidential*, like *secret*, is a security label, and the security community should have scorned use of *confidential*, too. We chose not to use *confidentiality* because we felt it had too many syllables, and saw no reason not to use *privacy*.

> Speaker: *Isn't it terrifying that on the Internet we have no privacy?*
> Heckler$_1$: *You mean* confidentiality. *Get your terms straight.*
> Heckler$_2$: *Why do security types insist on inventing their own language?*
> Heckler$_3$: *It's a denial of service attack.*
> —Overheard at recent gathering of security types

We often refer to things involved in a conversation by name, for instance, *Alice* and *Bob*, whether the things are people or computers. This is a convenient way of making things unambiguous with relatively few words, since the pronoun *she* can be used for Alice and *he* can be used for Bob. It also avoids lengthy inter- (and even intra-) author arguments about whether to use the politically incorrect *he*, a confusing *she*, an awkward *he/she* or *(s)he*, an ungrammatical *they*, an impersonal *it*, or an incredibly awkward rewriting to avoid the problem. We remain slightly worried that people will assume when we've named things with human names that we are referring to people. Assume Alice, Bob, and the rest of the gang may be computers unless we specifically say something like *the user Alice*, in which case we're talking about a human.

> *With a name like yours, you might be any shape, almost.*
> —Humpty Dumpty to Alice (in *Through the Looking Glass*)

Occasionally, one of the three of us authors will want to make a personal comment. In that case we use *I* or *me* with a subscript. When it's a comment that we all agree with, or that we managed to slip past me$_3$ (the rest of us are wimpier), we use the term *we*.

1.4 NOTATION

We use the symbol $\oplus$ (pronounced *ex-or*) for the bitwise exclusive or operation. We use the symbol | for concatenation. We denote secret key encryption with curly brackets preceded by the key with which something was encrypted, as in $K\{message\}$, which means *message* is secret key encrypted with K. Public key encryption we denote with curly braces, and the name of the owner of the public key subscripting the close brace, as in $\{message\}_{\text{Bob}}$. Signing (which means using the private key), we denote with square brackets, with the name of the owner of the key subscripting the close bracket, as in [*message*]$_{Bob}$.

Table of Notation

$\oplus$	bitwise exclusive or (pronounced *ex-or*)
|	concatenation (pronounced *concatenated with*)
$K\{message\}$	*message* encrypted with secret key K
$\{message\}_{Bob}$	*message* encrypted with Bob's public key
$[message]_{Bob}$	*message* signed with Bob's private key

1.5 PRIMER ON NETWORKING

You have to know something about computer networks to understand computer network security, so we're including this primer. For a more detailed understanding, we recommend [PERL92, TANE88, PISC93, COME88].

Networks today need to be very easy to use and configure. Networks are no longer an expensive and educational toy for researchers, but instead are being used by real people. Most sites with networks will not be able to hire a full-time person with networking expertise to start and keep the network running.

1.5.1 OSI Reference Model

Somehow, a book about computer networks would seem incomplete without a picture of the OSI (Open Systems Interconnection) Reference Model, so here it is.

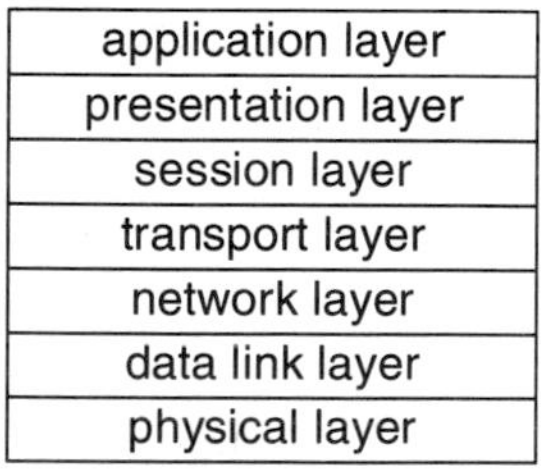

application layer
presentation layer
session layer
transport layer
network layer
data link layer
physical layer

Figure 1-1. OSI Reference Model

The OSI Reference Model is useful because it gives some commonly used terminology, though it might mislead you into thinking that there is only one way to construct a network. The reference model was designed by an organization known as the International Standards Organization (ISO). ISO decided it would be a good idea to standardize computer networking. Since that was too big a task for a single committee, they decided to subdivide the problem among several committees. They somewhat arbitrarily chose seven, each responsible for one layer. The basic idea is that each layer uses the services of the layer below, adds functionality, and provides a service to the layer above. When you start looking at real networks, they seldom neatly fit into the seven-layer model, but for basic understanding of networking, the OSI Reference Model is a good place to start.

1. **physical layer**. This layer delivers an unstructured stream of bits across a link of some sort.

2. **data link layer**. This layer delivers a piece of information across a single link. It organizes the physical layer's bits into packets and controls who on a shared link gets each packet.

3. **network layer**. This layer computes paths across an interconnected mesh of links and packet switches, and forwards packets over multiple links from source to destination.

4. **transport layer**. This layer establishes a reliable communication stream between a pair of systems across a network by putting sequence numbers in packets, holding packets at the destination until they can be delivered in order, and retransmitting lost packets.

5. **session layer**. The OSI session layer adds extra functions to the reliable pair-wise communication provided by the transport layer. Most network architectures do not have or need the functionality in this layer, and it is not of concern to security, so for the purposes of this book we can ignore it.

6. **presentation layer**. This layer encodes application data into a canonical (system-independent) format.

7. **application layer**. This is where the applications, such as file transfer and electronic mail, reside. These are the applications that use the network.

A layer communicates with the equivalent layer in a different node. In order to get data to a peer layer, though, the layer at the transmitting node gives the data to the layer below it (on the same node), which adds a header containing additional information if necessary, and that layer in turn gives it to the layer below. As the packet is received by the destination node, each layer reads and strips off its own header, so that the packet received by layer n looks to that layer just like it did when it was sent down to layer $n-1$ for transmission.

1.5.2 Directory Service

Having a telephone line into your house means you can access any phone in the world, if you know the telephone number. The same thing is true, more or less, in computer networks. If you know the network layer address of a node on the network, you should be able to communicate with that node. (This isn't always true because of security gateways, which we'll discuss in §1.7 *Firewalls/Security Gateways*). But how do you find out another node's network layer address? Network layer addresses are not the kind of things that people will be able to remember, or type. People instead will want to access something using a name such as File-Server-3.

This is a similar problem to finding someone's telephone number. Typically you start out by knowing the name of the person or service you want to talk to, and then look the name up in a telephone book. In a computer network there is a service known as the **directory service**, which stores information about a name, including its network layer address. Anything that needs to be found is listed in the directory service. Anything that needs to find something searches the directory service.

Rather than keeping all names in one directory, the directory service is typically structured as a tree of directories. Usually a name is hierarchical, so that the directory in which the name can be found is obvious from the name. For example, an internet name looks like leno@nbc.ge.com. The top level consists of pointers to the directories com for commercial enterprises, edu for educational institutions, gov for U.S. government, and various country names. Under com, there are various company names.

Having multiple directories rather than keeping all names in one directory serves two purposes. One is to prevent the directory from getting unreasonably large. The other reason is to reduce name collisions (more than one object with the same name). For instance, when you're looking up a telephone number for your friend John Smith, it's bad enough trying to figure out which John Smith is the one you want if you know which town he lives in and the telephone company has separate directories for each town, but imagine if the telephone company didn't have separate books for each town and simply had a list of names and telephone numbers!

Ideally, with a hierarchy of directories, name collisions could be prevented. Once a company hired one Radia Perlman, they just wouldn't hire another. I_2 think that's reasonable, but someone with a name like John Smith might start having problems finding a company that could hire him.

> *Now why did you name your baby* John*? Every Tom, Dick, and Harry is named* John.
>
> —Sam Goldwyn

For electronic mail addresses, conflicts must be prevented. Typically, companies let the first John Smith use the name John@companyname for his email address, and then perhaps the next one will be Smith@companyname, and the next one JSmith@companyname, and the next one has to start using middle initials. But for directories of names, there is usually no way to avoid name collisions within a directory. In other words, both John Smiths will use the same name within the company. Then, just like with a telephone book and multiple John Smiths, you have to do the best you can to figure out which one you want based on various attributes (such as in the telephone directory, using the street address). And just like in "real life", there will be lots of confusion where one John Smith gets messages intended for a different John Smith.

The directory service is very important to security. It is assumed to be widely available and convenient to access—otherwise large-scale networking really is too inconvenient to be practical. The directory service is a convenient place to put information, such as a user's public cryptographic key. But the directory service, although convenient, is not likely to be very secure. An intruder might tamper with the information. The magic of cryptography will help us detect such tampering so that it will not be necessary to physically secure all locations that store directory service information. If the information is tampered with, it might prevent good guys from accessing the network, but it will not allow bad guys to access things they are not authorized to access.

1.5.3 Replicated Services

Sometimes it is convenient to have two or more computers performing the same function. One reason is performance. A single server might become overloaded, or might not be sufficiently close to all users on a large network. Another reason is availability. If the service is replicated, it does not matter if some of the replicas are down or unavailable. When someone wants to access the service provided, it doesn't matter which of the computers they reach. Often the fact that the service is replicated is transparent to the user, meaning that the user does not know whether there's a single copy of the service or there are replicas.

What are the security issues with a replicated service? You'd want the user to have the same authentication information regardless of which replica was authenticating the user. If authentication information is stored at each replica, then coordinating the databases, for example after a *change password* command, can be tricky. And if the identical exchange will work with any of the replicas, then having an eavesdropper repeat the authentication handshake with a different replica might be a security problem.

1.5.4 Packet Switching

A really naive assumption would be that if people wanted computer A to talk to computer B, they'd string a wire between A and B. This doesn't work if networks get large, either in number of nodes (n^2 wires) or physical distance (it takes a lot of wire to connect each of 10000 nodes in North America with each of 10000 nodes in Asia). So in a network, messages do not go directly from sender to recipient, but rather have to be forwarded by various computers along the way. These message forwarders are referred to as packet switches, routers, gateways, bridges, and probably lots of other names as well.

A message is generally broken into smaller chunks as it is sent through the network. There are various reasons for this, all irrelevant for the purposes of this book, but we'll mention some of them anyway.

- Messages from various sources can be interleaved on the same link. You wouldn't want your message to have to wait until someone else finished sending a huge message, so messages are sent a small chunk at a time. If the link is in the process of sending the huge message when your little single-chunk message arrives, your message only has to wait until the link finishes sending a single chunk of the large message.

- Error recovery is done on the transmission unit. If you find out that one little chunk got mangled in transmission, only that chunk needs to be retransmitted.

- Buffer management in the routers is simpler if the size of packets has a reasonable upper limit.

Encryption and integrity protection are sometimes done end-to-end on the original message or hop-by-hop, on each chunk of the message.

1.5.5 Network Components

The network is a collection of packet switches (usually called routers) and links. A link can either be a wire between two computers or a multi-access link such as a LAN (local area network). A multi-access link has interesting security implications. Whatever is transmitted on the link can be seen by all the other nodes on that link. Multi-access links with this property are Ethernet (also known as CSMA/CD), token rings, and packet radio networks.

Connected to the backbone of the network are various types of nodes. A common categorization of the nodes is into *clients*, which are workstations that allow humans to access the resources on the network, and *servers*, which are typically dedicated machines that provide services such as file storage and printing. It should be possible to deploy a new service and have users be able to conveniently find the service. Users should be able to access the network from various locations, such as a public workstation a company makes available for visitors. If a person has a dedicated workstation located in one location, such as an office, it should be possible with a minimum of configuration for the user to plug the workstation into the network.

Another method for users to access a network is through a *dumb terminal*. A dumb terminal is not a general-purpose computer and does not have the compute power to do cryptographic operations. Usually a dumb terminal hooks directly into a host machine, or into a *terminal server* which relays the terminal's keystrokes via a network protocol across the network to the host machine (the machine the user logs into).

1.5.6 Destinations: Ultimate and Intermediate

A network is something to which multiple systems can attach. We draw it as a cloud since, from the point of view of the systems connected to it, exactly what goes on inside is not relevant. If you want to send a message to a system, and you are both connected to the same cloud, you hand your message to the cloud, together with a header that contains your address (the source address) and the address of the desired recipient (the destination address).

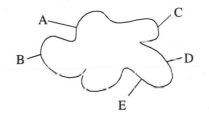

Figure 1-2. A Network

But how do you connect to the network? With a point-to-point link to a packet switch inside the network, things are reasonably simple. If A wants to send a message to B, A will put A as source address and B as destination address and send the message on the point-to-point link. But what if A is connected on a LAN? In that case, in order to transmit the packet through the network, A has to specify which of its neighbors should receive the message. For example:

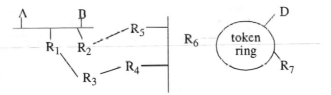

Figure 1-3. Network Connections

If A wants to send a message to D it has to know (somehow—if you care you can read my[2] book [PERL92]) that the appropriate neighbor for forwarding the packet is R_2. So when A transmits the message there are two destinations: R_2 as the next recipient and D as the ultimate recipient. A reasonably simple way of thinking about this is that the data link layer worries about transmission across a single link. The data link header has a source address and a destination address which indicate the transmitter on that link and the receiver on that link. The network layer worries about transmission across a multi-hop network. It has a header that carries the original source and ultimate destination. The data link header is removed each time a message is received, and a new data link header is tacked onto the message when it is forwarded to the next hop.

When A transmits the packet, the network header has source A, destination D. The data link header has source A, destination R_2. R_2 forwards the packet to R_5. Since R_2 is connected to R_5 with a point-to-point link, the data link header will not have addresses. But when R_5 forwards the packet to R_6 across the LAN, the network layer header will (still) be source A, destination D. The data link header will be source R_5, destination R_6. When R_6 forwards it (across the token ring LAN) the network header is still the same, and the data link header has source R_6, destination D.

Most likely A's data link address will look different from its network layer address, so it's a bit sloppy to say source A in both the data link header and network header. But this is all irrelevant to security. Fascinating in its own right, but irrelevant to this book.

The network layer header can be thought of as an envelope for the message. The data link header is an outer envelope. We've described the case of two envelopes—a network header inside a data link header. The world can be even more complicated than this. In fact, the "data link layer" might be a multi-hop network with multi-hop networks inside it as well. So a message might wind up with several envelopes. Again this is fascinating stuff but irrelevant to this book.

1.5.7 Address Structure

What do addresses look like? In terms of security, the main issue is how difficult it is to forge a source address, and how easy it is to arrange for the network to deliver packets to you when they are addressed to someone other than you. For instance, think of a letter as having a source address (the return address, it's called in paper mail) and a destination address. It's easy to send a letter to anyone and put **President, White House, USA** as the source address. It's harder to arrange to receive mail sent to **President, White House, USA** if you are not the U.S. President, especially if you don't live in the White House, and most likely more difficult the further you live from the address you'd like to impersonate. Addresses are usually hierarchical, just like a postal address. If we think of the address as specifying country/state/city/person, then in general it will be easier to arrange to receive someone else's messages if you reside in the same city (for instance by bribing a postal employee), and most difficult if they're in a different country.

Forging source addresses is easy in most network layers today. Routers could be built more defensively and do a sanity check on the source address, based on where they receive the packet from, but routers in general do not do this. Sometimes security gateways (also known as firewalls) have such features.

1.6 TEMPEST

One security concern is having intruders tap into a wire, giving them the ability to eavesdrop and possibly modify or inject messages. Another security concern is electronic emanation, whereby through the magic of physics, the movement of electrons can be measured from a surprising distance away. This means that intruders can sometimes eavesdrop without even needing to physically access the link. The U.S. military Tempest program measures how far away an intruder must be before eavesdropping is impossible. That distance is known as the device's **control zone**. The control zone is the region that must be physically guarded to keep out intruders that might be attempting to eavesdrop. A well-shielded device will have a smaller control zone. I_1 remember being told in 1979 of a tape drive that had a control zone over two miles. Unfortunately, most control zone information is classified, and I_2 couldn't get me_1 to be very specific about them, other than that they're usually expressed in metric. Since it is necessary to keep intruders away from the control zone, it's certainly better to have something with a control zone on the order of a few inches rather than a few miles (oh yeah, kilometers).

> *CIA eavesdroppers could not intercept the radio transmissions used by Somali warlord Mohammed Farah Aidid; his radios, intelligence officials explained, were too "low tech."*
> —Douglas Waller & Evan Thomas, *Newsweek*, October 10, 1994, page 32

1.7 FIREWALLS/SECURITY GATEWAYS

> *Firewalls are the wrong approach. They don't solve the general problem, and they make it very difficult or impossible to do many things. On the other hand, if I were in charge of a corporate network, I'd never consider hooking into the Internet without one. And if I were looking for a likely financially successful security product to invest in, I'd pick firewalls.*
> —Charlie Kaufman

A **firewall** (see Figure 1-4) is a computer that sits between your internal network and the rest of the network and filters packets as they go by, according to various criteria you can configure. It is sometimes called other things, like a security gateway, or various more colorful names thought up by frustrated network users.

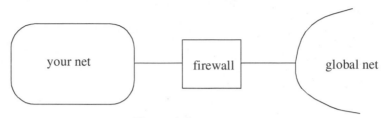

Figure 1-4. Firewall

Why is a firewall needed? It isn't, if security is done right, meaning that every system in the network has sophisticated authentication, the ability to do integrity-protected and encrypted communication, and is well-managed (when users rely on passwords, they choose good passwords, system accounts are not left with no password or a default password, etc.). The dilemma is that most corporate networks are not designed for security, and yet it is desirable to have some connectivity to a global network. You want to be able to send mail to anyone. You want to occasionally share files. You want to communicate with publicly available services. But a large global network is a scary place. There will be spies from unfriendly countries, users from competing companies, playful undergraduates, press people eager for a juicy scoop, criminals anxious to steal information for profit, and disgruntled ex-employees.

1.7.1 Packet Filters

The simplest form of firewall selectively discards packets based on things it can be configured to look for, such as the network address. For example, it might be configured to only allow some systems on your network to communicate outside, or some addresses outside your network to communicate into your network. For each direction, the firewall might be configured with a set of legal source and destination addresses, and it drops any packets that don't conform. This is known as **address filtering**. Address filtering has the problem that it is often easy to forge a network address.

1.7.2 Application Level Gateway

Another strategy for protecting your vulnerable network is an application level gateway. This can be accomplished with three boxes (see Figure 1-5). The two firewalls are routers that refuse to forward anything unless it's to or from the gateway. Firewall F_2 refuses to forward anything from the global net unless the destination address is the gateway, and refuses to forward anything to the global net unless the source is the gateway. Firewall F_1 refuses to forward anything from your network unless the destination address is the gateway, and refuses to forward anything to your network

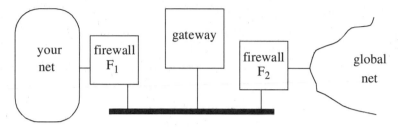

Figure 1-5. Application Level Gateway

unless the source address is the gateway. To transfer a file from your network to the global network you need to have someone from inside transfer the file to the gateway machine, and then the file is accessible to be read by the outside world. Similarly, to read a file into your network a user has to arrange for it to first get copied to the gateway machine. To log into a machine in the global network you first log into the gateway machine, and from there you can access machines in the remote network.

The gateway machine need not support every possible application. A common strategy is to allow only electronic mail to pass between your corporate network and the outside world. The intention is to specifically disallow file transfer and remote login. But electronic mail can certainly be used to transfer files. Sometimes a firewall might specifically disallow very large electronic mail messages, on the theory that this will limit the ability to transfer files. But often large electronic mail messages are perfectly legitimate, and any file can be broken down into small pieces. Because of such firewalls, many applications that post data for public retrieval on the Internet have automatic mail responders to which you can send an email message requesting the file, and the file will be sent back as an email message—several email messages, in fact, since such applications also realize that email messages have to be kept small in order to make it through the firewall. It is slow and painful for legitimate users to get files that way. Typically, the file arrives in several pieces. Each piece has to be extracted from the received email (to get rid of email headers). Then the pieces must be rearranged into proper order (since email tends to get out of order) and assembled into a file.

1.7.3 Encrypted Tunnels

A tunnel is a point-to-point connection in which the actual communication occurs across a network. This becomes a useful concept when you are thinking about your communication path as a sequence of links, some of which are secure and some of which aren't. The right way to ensure secure communication is end-to-end, i.e. where the two communicating parties do all the security work and assume that the medium over which they are communicating is insecure. But the parties may not be capable of providing security, which is okay if the links themselves are secure. When some of the links are subject to eavesdropping, you can encrypt over those links. Only the routers on those links need to do encryption and decryption.

Suppose the only reasons you've hooked into a public internet is to connect disconnected pieces of your own network to each other and to allow your off-site users to connect to your network. You don't care about making internet resources available to the users inside your corporate network.

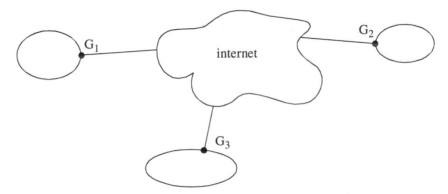

Figure 1-6. Connecting a Private Network over a Public Internet

The typical solution for this is to have G_1, G_2, and G_3 treat the internet just as if it's some sort of insecure wire. G_1, G_2, and G_3 are configured with security information about each other. All information between them is cryptographically protected.

You might want your users to be able to access the corporate network from across the internet as well. Suppose X is some sort of workstation that can attach to the internet in any location. To do this, X would create a tunnel with one of the G's.

1.8 KEY ESCROW FOR LAW ENFORCEMENT

The U.S. government has proposed technology to preserve its ability to wiretap otherwise secure communication. To do this it must either prevent use of encryption, break the codes used for encryption (as it did in a military context during World War II), or somehow learn everyone's cryptographic keys. The proposed technology takes the last option. It allows the Government to reconstruct your key (only upon court order and with legitimate cause of course). This is made possible through the use of a device known as the Clipper chip. A lot about Clipper is classified by the government as secret (and classified by a lot of other people as evil). We describe the basic technical design of Clipper in §17.10 *Clipper*. The simple concept is that encryption is done with a special chip (the Clipper chip). Each chip manufactured has a unique key, and the government keeps a record of the serial number/encryption key correspondence of every chip manufactured. Because not all people have complete trust in the government, rather than keeping the key in one place, each key is broken into two quantities which must be ⊕'d in order to obtain the actual key. Each piece is completely useless without the other. Since each piece is kept with a separate government agency, it would require two U.S. government agencies to cooperate in order to cheat and obtain the key for your Clipper chip without a valid court order. The government assures us, and evidence of past experience supports its claim, that cooperation between U.S. government agencies is unlikely.

The Clipper proposal is controversial, starting with its name. The name will certainly change, since it violates someone's trademark on something unrelated. But since everyone calls the proposal Clipper, we will too, especially since the new name has not been chosen.

Why would anyone use Clipper when alternative methods should be cheaper and more secure? The reason alternatives would be cheaper is that enforcing the ability of the U.S. government to wiretap will add a lot of complexity. Proponents of Clipper have given several answers to this question:

- The government will buy a lot of Clipper chips, bringing the cost down because of volume production, so Clipper will wind up being the most cost-effective solution.

- Encryption technology is only useful if both parties have compatible equipment. If you want to talk securely to the U.S. government, you will have to use Clipper. So any other mechanism would have to be implemented *in addition* to Clipper.

- Again, since encryption technology is only useful if both parties have compatible equipment, if Clipper takes over enough market share, it will essentially own the market (just like VHS, a technically inferior standard supposedly, beat out Beta in the VCR marketplace). Since Clipper will be one of the earliest standards, it might take over the marketplace before any other standards have an opportunity to become entrenched. Most people won't care that Clipper enables wiretapping, because they'll assume they have nothing to fear from the U.S. government wiretapping them.

- The government claims that the cryptographic algorithm in Clipper is stronger than you'll be able to get from a commercial source.

Civil libertarians fear Clipper is a first step towards outlawing untappable cryptography. Clipper proponents say it is not. It's true that outlawing alternatives is not part of the Clipper proposal. However, there have been independent efforts to outlaw cryptography. Those efforts have been thwarted in part with the argument that industry needs security. But if Clipper is deployed, that argument goes away.

Clipper is designed for telephones, fax, and other low-speed applications, and in some sense is not relevant to computer networking. Many people regard it, however, as a first step and a model for taking the same approach for computer networks.

1.9 KEY ESCROW FOR CARELESS USERS

It is prudent to keep your key in a safe place so that when you misplace your own key you can retrieve a copy of the key rather than conceding that all your encrypted files are irretrievably lost. It would be a security risk to have all users' keys stored unencrypted somewhere. The database of keys could be stored encrypted with a key known to the server that was storing the database, but this would mean that someone who had access to that machine could access all the user keys. Another possibility is to encrypt the key in a way that can only be reconstructed with the cooperation of several independent machines. This is feasible, and we'll discuss it more in §17.10.1 *Key Escrow*.

Some applications don't require recoverable keys. An example of such an application is login. If a user loses the key required for login, the user can be issued a new key. A user may therefore want different keys for different uses, where only some of the keys are escrowed. For applications that do require recoverable keys, protection from compromise can be traded off against protection from loss.

1.10 VIRUSES, WORMS, TROJAN HORSES

> *Lions and tigers and bears, oh my!*
> —Dorothy (in the movie *The Wizard of Oz*)

People like to categorize different types of malicious software and assign them cute biological terms (if one is inclined to think of worms as cute). We don't think it's terribly important to distinguish between these things, but will define some of the terms that seem to be infecting the literature.

- **Trojan horse**—instructions hidden inside an otherwise useful program that do bad things. Usually the term Trojan horse is used when the malicious instructions are installed at the time the program is written (and the term *virus* is used if the instructions get added to the program later).

- **virus**—a set of instructions that, when executed, inserts copies of itself into other programs.

- **bacterium**—a free-standing program that replicates itself, causing harm by consuming resources.

- **worm**—a program that replicates itself by installing copies of itself on other machines across a network. Similar to a bacterium, but it replicates over a network whereas a bacterium tends to stay confined to one machine.

- **trapdoor**—an undocumented entry point intentionally written into a program, often for debugging purposes, which can be exploited as a security flaw.

- **logic bomb**—malicious instructions that trigger on some event in the future, such as a particular time occurring.

We do not think it's useful to take these categories seriously. As with most categorizations (e.g., plants vs. animals, intelligence vs. instinct), there are things that don't fit neatly within these categories. So we'll refer to all kinds of malicious software generically as **digital pests**.

1.10.1 Where Do They Come From?

Where do these nasties come from? Except for trapdoors, which may be intentionally installed to facilitate troubleshooting, they are written by bad guys with nothing better to do with their lives than annoy people.

How could an implementer get away with writing a digital pest into a program? Wouldn't someone notice by looking at the program? One of the most famous results in computer science is that it is provably impossible to be able to tell what an arbitrary program will do by looking at it[1], so certainly it would be impossible to tell, in general, whether the program had any unpleasant side effects besides its intended purpose. But that's not the real problem. The real problem is that nobody looks. Often when you buy a program you do not have access to the source code, and even if you did, you probably wouldn't bother reading it all, or reading it very carefully. Many programs that run have never been reviewed by anybody. If it were possible to examine source code to see if it did anything other than its intended purpose, nobody would have an excuse for shipping software with bugs.

What does a virus look like? A virus can be installed in just about any program by doing the following:

---

1. This is known in the literature as *the halting problem*, which states that it is impossible in general to tell whether a given program will halt or not. In fact it is impossible in general to discern any nontrivial property of a program.

- replace any instruction, say the instruction at location *x*, by a jump to some free place in memory, say location *y*; then

- write the virus program starting at location *y*; then

- place the instruction that was originally at location *x* at the end of the virus program, followed by a jump to *x*+1.

Besides doing whatever damage the virus program does, it might replicate itself by looking for any executable files in any directory and infecting them. Once an infected program is run, the virus is executed again, to do more damage and to replicate itself to more programs. Most viruses spread silently until some triggering event causes them to wake up and do their dastardly deeds. If they did their dastardly deeds all the time, they wouldn't spread as far.

How does a digital pest originally appear on your computer? All it takes is running a single infected program. A program posted on a bulletin board might certainly be infected. But even a program bought legitimately might conceivably have a digital pest. It might have been planted by a disgruntled employee or a saboteur who had broken into the computers of the company and installed the pest into the software before it was shipped. There have been cases where commercial programs were infected because some employee ran a program gotten from a friend or a bulletin board.

Often at holiday times people send email messages that are programs, with the instruction that you extract the mail message and run it. Often the result is some sort of cute holiday-specific thing, like displaying a picture of a turkey or playing a Christmas carol. It could certainly also contain a virus. Few people will scan the program before running it, especially if the message arrives from a friend. And if you were to run such a program and it did something cute, you might very well forward it to a friend, not realizing that in addition to doing the cute thing it might very well have installed a virus that will start destroying your directory a week after the virus is first run. A good example of a Christmas card email message is a program written by Ian Phillipps, which was a winner of the 1988 International Obfuscated C Code Contest. It is delightful as a Christmas card. It does nothing other than its intended purpose (I_1 have analyzed the thing carefully and I_2 have complete faith in me_1), but we doubt many people would take the time to understand this program before running it (see Figure 1-7).

Sometimes you don't realize you're running a program. PostScript[1] is a complete programming language. It is possible to embed a Trojan horse into a PostScript file that infects files with viruses and does other damage. Someone could send you a file and tell you to display it. You wouldn't realize you were running a program by merely displaying the file. And if there was any hope of scanning a C program to find suspicious instructions, there are very few people who could

---

1. PostScript[®] is a registered trademark of Adobe Systems Inc.

```
/* Have yourself an obfuscated Christmas! */
#include <stdio.h>
main(t,_,a)
char *a;
{
return!0<t?t<3?main(-79,-13,a+main(-87,1-_,main(-86,0,a+1)+a)):
1,t<_?main(t+1,_,a):3,main(-94,-27+t,a)&&t==2?_<13?
main(2,_+1,"%s %d %d\n"):9:16:t<0?t<-72?main(_,t,
"@n'+,#'/*{}w+/w#cdnr/+,{}r/*de}+,/*{*+,/w{%+,/w#q#n+,/#{l,+,/n{n+,/+#n+,/#\
;#q#n+,/+k#;*+,/'r :'d*'3,}{w+K w'K:'+}e#';dq#'l \
q#'+d'K#!/+k#;q#'r}eKK#}w'r}eKK{nl]'/#;#q#n')(){)#}w')(){nl]'/+#n';d}rw' i;# \
){nl]!/n{n#'; r{#w'r nc{nl]'/#{l,+'K {rw' iK{;[{nl]'/w#q#n'wk nw' \
iwk{KK{nl]!/w{%'l##w#' i; :{nl]'/*{q#'ld;r'}{nlwb!/*de}'c \
;;{nl'-{}rw]'/+,}##'*}#nc,',#nw]'/+kd'+e}+;#'rdq#w! nr'/ ') }+}{rl#'{n' ')# \
}'+}##(!!/")
:t<-50?_==*a?putchar(31[a]):main(-65,_,a+1):main((*a=='/')+t,_,a+1)
:0<t?main(2,2,"%s"):*a=='/'||main(0,main(-61,*a,
"!ek;dc i@bK'(q)-[w]*%n+r3#l,{}:\nuwloca-O;m .vpbks,fxntdCeghiry"),a+1);
}
```

Figure 1-7. Christmas Card?

scan a PostScript file and look for suspicious PostScript commands. PostScript is, for all practical purposes, a write-only language.

As mail systems get more clever in their attempt to make things more convenient for users, the risk becomes greater. If you receive a PostScript file and you are running a non-clever mail program, you will see delightful crud like:

```
%!PS-Adobe-3.0
%%Creator: Windows PSCRIPT
%%Title: c:\book\spcaut.doc
%%BoundingBox: 18 9 593 784
%%DocumentNeededResources: (atend)
%%DocumentSuppliedResources: (atend)
%%Pages: (atend)
%%BeginResource: procset Win35Dict 3 1
/Win35Dict 290 dict def Win35Dict begin/bd{bind def}bind def/in{72
mul}bd/ed{exch def}bd/ld{load def}bd/tr/translate ld/gs/gsave ld/gr
/grestore ld/M/moveto ld/L/lineto ld/rmt/rmoveto ld/rlt/rlineto ld
/rct/rcurveto ld/st/stroke ld/n/newpath ld/sm/setmatrix ld/cm/currentmatrix
ld/cp/closepath ld/ARC/arcn ld/TR{65536 div}bd/lj/setlinejoin ld/lc
/setlinecap ld/ml/setmiterlimit ld/sl/setlinewidth ld/scignore false
def/sc{scignore{pop pop pop}{0 index 2 index eq 2 index 4 index eq
and{pop pop 255 div setgray}{3{255 div 3 1 roll}repeat setrgbcolor}ifelse}ifelse}bd
```

Figure 1-8. Typical PostScript Code

If you wanted to display the file, you'd have to extract the mail message and send it to the printer, or input it into a special program that displays PostScript on your screen. However, a clever mail program might look at the message, recognize that it was PostScript, and automatically run the

PostScript code to display the message. Although this is convenient, it is dangerous, since no matter how clever your vendor claims their mail product is, we can assure you it won't scan the PostScript for Trojan horses before displaying the message.

There are various other clever features being added to mail programs. Some mail programs allow the sender to send a program along with the mail message. Usually the mail message will arrive and display some sort of icon. If the receiver clicks on the icon, the transmitted program is executed. Someone, to illustrate this point, sent such a mail message. It displayed only as a button that said *push me*. When the person who received the message clicked on the box, it came up with a message that said, *I could have just reformatted your hard drive*.

Before the technology for clever mail goes much further, we ought to consider how we can reap the benefits of such cleverness while minimizing the security risks.

There are dangers associated with booting from floppy disks. Even if system software becomes sophisticated about security, it won't be able to protect against Trojan horses on the boot device, and people still commonly boot from floppies. When you turn the machine on with a floppy disk inserted into the drive, the machine executes the code on the floppy. If there is a virus in that code, it can stay resident in memory, and infect any new floppies inserted into the drive (unless the machine is powered off between floppies). Even machines with hard drives allow booting off floppies. If the hard drive were completely wiped clean, there has to be some way to come up again, so machines provide the feature that if there is a floppy in the drive when the machine is powered on, the machine boots off the floppy. Often it is convenient to boot off a floppy. It is common to run games by booting off the floppy containing the game. Once you run code on a floppy, the code can do anything, so if it contains a virus it can destroy or infect all the files on the hard disk.

1.10.2 Spreading Pests from Machine to Machine

How might a virus or worm spread from machine to machine? An infected program might be copied to a floppy and moved to another machine. Or, as we said, a mail message might carry the infection. But it is also possible for the pest to explore the network and send itself to other machines, once it is running in one machine on a network. Such a pest is called a worm.

One method a worm can employ to transmit itself to another machine is to actually log into the other machine. It can do this by guessing passwords. Sometimes things are set up to make it really easy; for instance, account name/password pairs might be stored in script files so that a naive user can access remote resources automatically. If the worm manages to find that information, it can easily log into other machines and install itself. Sometimes machines have trapdoor debugging features, such as the ability to run a command remotely. Sometimes it isn't even necessary to log in in order to run such a command. And if intruders can execute commands, they can do anything.

*The only reason all the computers in the world haven't crashed at the same
time is that they're not all connected together yet.*   —Dave Cheriton

One Christmas-card-type email message displayed a pretty animated tree on the screen, but
also scanned the user's directory for all possible correspondents, including distribution lists, and
mailed itself to them. Each time a recipient read a copy of the message, it sprang into life and
mailed itself off to all the mailboxes it could locate from that node. Although this program did not
destroy data, like a classic worm it completely disabled the corporation's electronic mail.

1.10.3   Virus Checkers

How can a program check for viruses? There's rather a race between the brave and gallant
people who analyze the viruses and write clever programs to detect and eliminate the known
viruses, and the foul-smelling scum who devise new types of viruses that will escape detection by
all the current virus checkers.

The most common form of virus checker knows the instruction sequence for lots of types of
viruses, checks all the files on disk and instructions in memory for those patterns of commands, and
raises a warning if it finds a match hidden somewhere inside some file. Once you own such a virus
checker, you need to periodically get updates of the patterns file that includes the newest viruses.
To evade detection of their viruses, virus creators have devised what is known as a **polymorphic
virus** which changes the order of its instructions, or changes to functionally similar instructions,
each time it copies itself. Such a virus may still be detectable, but it takes more work and typically
requires a coding change and not just a new pattern file.

Another type of virus checker takes a snapshot of disk storage by recording the information
in the directories, such as file lengths. It might even take message digests of the files. It is designed
to run, store the information, and then run again at a future time. It will warn you if there are suspicious changes. One type of virus, wary of changing the length of a file by adding itself to the program, compressed the program so that the infected program would wind up being the same length
as the original. When the program was executed, the uncompressed portion containing the virus
decompressed the rest of the program, so (other than the virus portion) the program could run normally.

1.10.4   What Can We Do Today?

The world was a scary place before computer viruses came along, and will most likely continue to be scary. How can you know whether you can trust a program not to do bad things when
you run it? Wouldn't it be nice to have the equivalent of a lie-detector test for programs?

> *Ames slipped by a lie-detector test because no one had told the polygra-*
> *pher he was under suspicion.* —Douglas Waller & Evan Thomas
> *Newsweek* article on CIA and traitor Aldrich Ames, October 10, 1994

Given that there is no infallible method to test a program for hidden bad side effects, we can't be completely safe, but there are some precautions that are worth taking:

- Don't run software from suspicious sources, like bulletin boards or people who aren't as careful as you are.

- Frequently run virus checkers. Have the industry employ people whose job it is to keep up with virus technology and come up with vaccines.

- Try to run programs in the most limited possible environments. For instance, if you have a PC in order to get real work done, and you also want to play games, sometimes using shareware or games copied from bulletin boards, have two machines. If you run a game with a virus, you'll only wipe out your games.

- Do frequent backups, and save old backups for a long time.

- Don't boot off floppies, except in an extreme circumstance, such as the first time you unpack your machine and turn it on. In those circumstances, be extremely careful about what floppy you boot from.

But mostly, the situation is pretty bleak, given the design of the operating systems for PCs. Maybe in the future, some of our suggestions in the next section might be implemented.

1.10.5 Wish List for the Future

I_2 always assumed computers were designed in such a way that no program that ran on the machine could possibly injure the machine. Likewise, it should not be possible to send a piece of information to a machine that might damage the machine. People are designed properly that way, aren't they?

> *Sticks and stones may break my bones but words will never hurt me.*
> [chant designed to encourage bullies to get physical]

But one of my$_2$ first programs consisted of something that just sat around and waited for interrupts, and processed the interrupts. The program itself, not counting the instructions for processing the interrupts, was `HERE: JUMP HERE` (that's not the exact instruction because I'm attempting not to divulge the computer brandname). I_2 discovered (the hard way) that you weren't supposed to do that, because it burned out core at the instruction that kept getting executed over and over. Gerry Sussman, while a high school student, wrote a program that broke magnetic tapes. The guru who guarded and ran the mainframe didn't believe Gerry when he boasted that he could write a program to break tapes, so Gerry wrote his program to go down the entire row of tape drives, breaking the tape in each one. Another example was a machine designed with a small amount of nonvolatile memory, but the type that wore out after a finite number of writes, say 10000. That kind of memory is fine for something like saving terminal settings, since a human has to type the key sequence to cause a write, and a human won't do it very often. But if the same kind of message is used for storing parameter settings received by a network management message, then it is possible to break the machine within seconds by sending it parameter settings over and over.

In an ideal world, it should be possible to load a floppy and examine the contents without fear. You should be able to receive any email message without fear. If it is a multimedia message, it should be possible to play the audio, display the video, print the text, or waft the odors without damage to either the machine or files stored on the machine. A file is just a bunch of bits. If the file claims to be audio, it should be possible, without risk of any type of harm, to play the file. Likewise, if the file claims to be something worthy of printing, it should not cause any harm to print the file.

Programs are a bit trickier. It should be possible to run a program and not have it affect the files stored on your machine or the basic integrity of the operating system.

We know none of these "shoulds" are true today. The files on your machine can be virus-infected through email, by displaying a PostScript file, or simply by inserting a floppy disk (on some machines). How could systems be designed more defensively?

One simple feature would be a write-protect switch on your hard disk. Sometimes you run programs that you know should not be writing to your hard disk. A game program shouldn't be writing to your hard disk. Perhaps it wants to record highest score, but consumers might be willing to do without that frill, if it means that they can run any game they want without fear of wiping out their life's work. Legitimate game manufacturers could design their games to work with write-protected hard disks. Even the social misfits who design games that spread viruses could design their games to work with write-protected hard disks, but just have their program check to see if some user has forgotten to write-protect the disk, and then launch the virus.

Timesharing systems used to be much more defensive. You could not run a program that would write into some other user's memory, or modify any portion of the disk that you were not authorized to write into. But PCs make the assumption that there is only one human on the machine at a time, and that human ought to be able to do anything it wants. To make matters worse, to enable snazzy maximally flexible features, there are all sorts of surprising places where someone can insert a program that will be executed.

The operating system ought to be built more defensively. PCs should have accounts just like timesharing systems so that you can set up a game account that can't affect the rest of the system.

Likewise, your normal account shouldn't be able to alter system software. The world is moving in this direction, but progress is slow.

Booting off a floppy is unavoidably dangerous, since it involves loading the operating system itself. Since a program that is supposed to be the operating sytem will certainly be allowed to do anything it wants, there's no way to prevent polluted software on a floppy from destroying the world, if you boot off that floppy. At least, one should only boot off the floppy that came with the machine, rather than using the boot feature to more conveniently run games. One game I_1 ran recently ran out of memory, and with the error message giving the bad news, offered to make a special floppy that could run the game, finding extra memory by avoiding loading anything that wasn't essential to the running of the game. That was a very helpful suggestion, but it means that people still, for various reasons, will be tempted to boot off floppies of suspicious heritage.

1.11 THE MILITARY MODEL OF SECURITY

The main concern in the military model of security is keeping data secret. It involves worrying about arcane threats such as covert channels, and creating cumbersome mechanisms such as mandatory access controls for keeping secret data from leaking out.

1.11.1 Mandatory (Nondiscretionary) Access Controls

> *O negligence! ... what cross devil made me put this main secret in the*
> *packet I sent the king? Is there no way to cure this? No new device to beat*
> *this from his brains?*   —Shakespeare's *King Henry VIII*, act 3, scene 2

Discretionary means that someone who owns a resource can make a decision as to who is allowed to use (access) it. **Nondiscretionary access controls** are where strict rules are automatically enforced about who is allowed access to certain resources, and even the owners of the resources cannot change the attributes of a resource.

The basic philosophy behind discretionary controls is that the users and the programs they run are the good guys, and it is up to the operating system to trust them and protect each user from outsiders and other users. The basic philosophy behind nondiscretionary controls is that everything would be fine except for the pesky human beings who unfortunately have to be allowed to use the system. The system must be ever vigilant to prevent the users from accidentally or intentionally giving information to someone who shouldn't have it. This philosophy does not necessarily imply that the users are expected to be evil, but it does expect them to be careless, and possibly run programs with digital pests. Careless users might accidentally type the wrong file name when including a file in a mail message, or might leave a message world-readable.

Nondiscretionary access controls grew out of the military mindset. The primary concern is secret data getting leaked to the enemy. The concept is to confine information within a **security perimeter**, and not allow any information to move from a more secure environment to a less secure environment.

Now of course, if you allow the users out of the building there is an avenue for information to leak out of a secure environment, since a user can remember the information and tell someone once the user gets out of the security perimeter. But the designers of these controls weren't primarily worried about the authorized users selling secrets. There really is no way for a computer system to prevent that. But they wanted to ensure that no Trojan horse in software could transmit any information out of the perimeter, and they wanted to make sure that nothing inadvertent a user did could leak information.

1.11.2 Levels of Security

What does it mean for something to be "more sensitive" than something else? We will use a somewhat simplified description of the U.S. Department of Defense (DoD) definitions of levels of security as an example. It is a reasonably general model and similar to what is done in other contexts. It is sufficient to understand the security mechanisms we'll describe.

The security label of something consists of two components:

- A **security level** which might be an integer in some range, but in the U.S. DoD consists of one of the four ratings unclassified, confidential, secret, and top secret, where unclassified < confidential < secret < top secret.

- A set of zero or more **categories** (also known as **compartments**) which describe kinds of information. For instance, the name CRYPTO might mean information about cryptographic algorithms, INTEL might mean information about military intelligence, COMSEC might mean information about communications security, or NUCLEAR might mean information about types of families.

Documents (or computer files) are marked with a security label saying how sensitive the information is, and people are issued security clearances according to how trustworthy they are perceived to be and for which they have demonstrated a "need to know".

A clearance might therefore be (SECRET;{COMSEC,CRYPTO}), which would mean someone was allowed to know information classified unclassified, confidential, or secret (but not top secret) dealing with cryptographic algorithms or communications security.

Given two security labels, (X,S_1) and (Y,S_2), (X,S_1) is defined as being "at least as sensitive as" (Y,S_2) iff $X \geq Y$ and $S_2 \subseteq S_1$. For example,

(TOP SECRET, {CRYPTO, COMSEC}) > (SECRET, {CRYPTO})

where ">" means "more sensitive than".

It is possible for two labels to be incomparable, in the sense that neither is more sensitive than the other. For example, neither of the following are comparable to each other:

(TOP SECRET, {CRYPTO, COMSEC})

(SECRET, {NUCLEAR, CRYPTO})

1.11.3 Mandatory Access Control Rules

Every person, process, and piece of information has a security label. A person cannot run a process with a label higher than the person's label, but may run one with a lower label. Information is only allowed to be read by a process that has at least as high a rating as the information. The terminology used for having a process read something with a higher rating than the process is **read-up**. Read-up is illegal and must be prevented. A process cannot write a piece of information with a rating lower than the process's rating. The terminology used for a process writing something with a lower rating than the process is **write-down**. Write-down is illegal and must be prevented.

The rules are:

- A human can only run a process which has a security label below or equal to that of the human's label.

- A process can only read information marked with a security label below or equal to that of the process.

- A process can only write information marked with a security label above or equal to that of the process. Note that if a process writes information marked with a security label above that of the process, the process can't subsequently read that information.

The prevention of read-up and write-down is the central idea behind mandatory access controls. The concepts of confinement within a security perimeter and a generalized hierarchy of security classes were given a mathematical basis by Bell and La Padula in 1973 [BELL74]. There is significant complexity associated with the details of actually making them work.

1.11.4 Covert Channels

A covert channel is a method for a Trojan horse to circumvent the automatic prevention of information outside a security domain. Let's assume an operating system has enforced the rules in the previous section. Let's assume also that a bad guy has successfully tricked someone inside a security perimeter into running a program with a Trojan horse. The program has access to some sensitive data, and wants to pass the data to a process outside the security perimeter. We're assuming the operating system prevents the process from doing this straightforwardly, but there are diabolical methods that theoretically could be employed to get information out. These are known as **covert channels**.

The Trojan horse program cannot directly pass data, but all it needs is for there to be anything it can do that can be detected by something outside the security perimeter. As long as information can be passed one bit at a time, anything can be transmitted, given enough time.

One possible covert channel is a **timing channel**. The Trojan horse program alternately loops and waits, in cycles of, say one minute per bit. When the next bit is a 1, the program loops for one minute. When the next bit is a 0, the program waits for a minute. The program outside the perimeter constantly tests the loading of the system. If the system is sluggish, its conspirator inside the perimeter is looping, and therefore transmitting a 1. Otherwise the conspirator is waiting, and therefore transmitting a 0.

This assumes those two processes are the only ones running on the machine. What happens if there are other processes running and stopping at seemingly random times (from the point of view of the program trying to read the covert channel)? That introduces noise into the channel. But communications people can deal with a noisy channel; it just lowers the potential bandwidth, depending on the signal to noise ratio.

Another example of a covert channel involves the use of shared resources other than processor cycles. For instance, suppose there were a queue of finite size, say the print queue. The Trojan horse program could fill the queue to transmit a 1, and delete some jobs to transmit a 0. The covert channel reader would attempt to print something and note whether the request was accepted. Other possible shared resources that might be exploited for passing information include physical memory, disk space, and I/O buffers.

Yet another example depends on how clever the operating system is about not divulging information in error messages. For instance, suppose the operating system says file does not exist when a file really does not exist, but says insufficient privilege for requested operation when the file does exist, but inside a security perimeter off limits to the process requesting to read the file. Then the Trojan horse can alternately create and delete a file of some name known to the other process. The conspirator process periodically attempts to read the file and uses the information about which error message it gets to determine the setting of the next bit of information.

There is no general way to prevent all covert channels. Instead, people imagine all the different ways they can think of, and specifically attempt to plug those holes. For instance, the timing channel can be eliminated by giving each security perimeter a fixed percentage of the processor cycles. This is wasteful, and impractical in general because there can be an immense number of distinct classifications (in our model of (*one of four levels*, {*categories*})), the number of possible security perimeters is $4 \cdot 2^n$, where n is the number of categories.

Most covert channels have very low bandwidth. In many cases, instead of attempting to eliminate a covert channel, it is more practical to introduce enough noise into the system so that the bandwidth becomes too low to be useful to an enemy. It's also possible to look for jobs that appear to be attempting to exploit covert channels (a job that alternately submitted enough print jobs to fill the queue and then deleted them would be suspicious indeed if someone knew to watch). If the bandwidth is low *and* the secret data is large, and knowing only a small subset of the secret data is not of much use to an enemy, the threat is minimized.

How much secret data must be leaked before serious damage is done can vary considerably. For example, assume there is a file with 100 megabytes of secret data. The file has been transmitted, encrypted, on an insecure network. The enemy therefore has the ciphertext, but the cryptographic algorithm used makes it impossible for the enemy to decrypt the data without knowing the key. A Trojan horse with access to the file and a covert channel with a bandwidth of 1 bit every 10 seconds would require 250 years to leak the data (by which time it's hard to believe the divulging of the information could be damaging to anyone). However, if the Trojan horse had access to the 56-bit key, it could leak that information across the covert channel in less than 10 minutes. That information would allow the enemy to decrypt the 100-megabyte file. For this reason, many secure systems go to great pains to keep cryptographic keys out of the hands of the programs that use them.

1.11.5 The Orange Book

The National Computer Security Center (NCSC) (an agency of the U.S. Government) has published an official standard called "Trusted Computer System Evaluation Criteria", universally known as "the Orange Book" (guess what color the cover is). The Orange Book defines a series of ratings a computer system can have based on its security features and the care that went into its design. This rating system is intended to give government agencies and commercial enterprises an objective assessment of a system's security and to goad computer manufacturers into placing more emphasis on security.

The official categories are D, C1, C2, B1, B2, B3, and A1, which range from least secure to most secure. In reality, of course, there is no way to place all the possible features in a linear scale. Different threats are more or less important in different environments. The authors of the Orange Book made an attempt to linearize these concerns given their priorities. But the results can be misleading. An otherwise A1 system that is missing some single feature might have a D rating. Systems not designed with the Orange Book in mind are likely to get low ratings even if they are in fact very secure.

The other problem with the Orange Book rating scheme is that the designers focused on the security priorities of military security people—keeping data secret. In the commercial world, data integrity is at least as important as data confidentiality. Mandatory access controls, even if available, are not suitable for most commercial environments because they make the simplest operations incredibly cumbersome, operations such as having a highly privileged user send mail to an unprivileged user.

With the Orange Book ratings, high ratings will not protect the system from infection by viruses. The fancy mandatory access controls required for high ratings allow write-up, so if some unprivileged account became infected by having someone carelessly run, say, a game program loaded from a bulletin board, the virus could infect more secure areas. Ironically, if it was a very secure area that first got infected, the mandatory access control features would prevent the infection from spreading to the less secure environments.

The following is a summary of what properties a system must have to quality for each rating.

D – Minimal Protection. This simply means the system did not qualify for any of the higher ratings; it might actually be very secure. No system is ever going to brag about the fact that it was awarded a D rating.

C1 – Discretionary Security Protection. The requirements at this level correspond roughly to what one might expect from a classic timesharing system. It requires:

- The operating system must prevent unprivileged user programs from overwriting critical portions of its memory. (Note that most PC operating systems do not satisfy this condition.)

- Resources must be protected with access controls. Those access controls need not be sophisticated; classic owner/group/world controls would be sufficient.

- The system must authenticate users by a password or some similar mechanism, and the password database must be protected so that it cannot be accessed by unauthorized users.

There are additional requirements around testing and documentation, which become more detailed at each successive rating.

C2 – Controlled Access Protection. This level corresponds roughly to a timesharing system where security is an important concern but users are responsible for their own fates; an example might be a commercial timesharing system. The additional requirements (over those required for C1) for a C2 rating are:

- access control at a per user granularity—It must be possible to permit access to any selected subset of the user community, probably via ACLs. An **ACL** is a data structure attached to a resource that specifies the resource's authorized users.

- clearing of allocated memory—The operating system must ensure that freshly allocated disk space and memory does not contain "left-over" data deleted by some previous user. It can do that by writing to the space or by requiring processes to write to the space before they can read it.

- auditing—The operating system must be capable of recording security-relevant events, including authentication and object access. The audit log must be protected from tampering and must record date, time, user, object, and event. Auditing must be selective based on user and object.

It is reasonable to expect that C2-rateable systems will become ubiquitous, since they contain features that are commonly desired and do not represent an unacceptable overhead. It is somewhat surprising that such systems are not the norm.

B1 – Labeled Security Protection. Additional requirements at this level are essentially those required to implement Mandatory Access Controls for secrecy (not integrity) except that little attention is given to covert channels. Requirements for B1 above those for C2 include:

- Security Labels: Sensitivity labels must be maintained for all users, processes, and files, and read-up and write-down must be prevented by the operating system.

- Attached devices must either themselves be labeled as accepting only a single level of information, or they must accept and know how to process security labels.

- Attached printers must have a mechanism for ensuring that there is a human-readable sensitivity label printed on the top and bottom of each page corresponding to the sensitivity label of the information being printed. The operating system must enforce this correspondence.

B2 – Structured Protection. Beyond B1, there are few new features introduced; rather, the operating system must be structured to greater levels of assurance that it behaves correctly (i.e. has no bugs). Additional requirements for B2 include:

- trusted path to user—There must be some mechanism to allow a user at a terminal to reliably distinguish between talking to the legitimate operating system and talking to a Trojan horse password-capturing program.

- security level changes—A terminal user must be notified when any process started by that user changes its security level.

- security kernel—The operating system must be structured so that only a minimal portion of it is security-sensitive, i.e. that bugs in the bulk of the O/S cannot cause sensitive data to leak. This is typically done by running the bulk of the O/S in the processor's user mode and having a secure-kernel mini-O/S which enforces the mandatory access controls.

- Covert channels must be identified and their bandwidth estimated, but there is no requirement that they be eliminated.

- Strict procedures must be used in the maintenance of the security-sensitive portion of the operating system. For instance, anyone modifying any portion must document what they changed, when they changed it, and why, and some set of other people should compare the updated section with the previous version.

B3 – Security Domains. Additional requirements for B3 mostly involve greater assurance that the operating system will not have bugs that might allow something to circumvent mandatory access controls. Additional requirements include:

- ACLs must be able to explicitly deny access to named individuals even if they are members of groups that are otherwise allowed access. It is only at this level that ACLs must be able to separately enforce modes of access (i.e. read vs. write) to a file.

- active audit—There must be mechanisms to detect selected audited events or thresholds of audited events and immediately trigger notification of a security administrator.

- secure crashing—The system must ensure that the crashing and restarting of the system introduces no security policy violations.

A1 – Verified Design. There are no additional features in an A1 system over a B3 system. Rather, there are formal procedures for the analysis of the design of the system and more rigorous controls on its implementation.

1.12 LEGAL ISSUES

The legal aspects of cryptography are fascinating, but the picture changes quickly, and we are certainly not experts in law. Although it pains us[1,2] to say it, if you're going to do anything involving cryptography, talk to a lawyer.

1.12.1 Patents

One legal issue that affects the choice of security mechanisms is patents. Most cryptographic techniques are covered by patents. DES (see §3.3 *Data Encryption Standard (DES)*), the most popular cryptographic algorithm, is patented but royalty-free. IDEA (see §3.4 *International Data Encryption Algorithm (IDEA)*) is patented and royalty-free for non-commercial use. All public key algorithms are patented, and most of the important patents have been acquired by Public Key Partners (PKP). Most people who wish to use public key algorithms do so by licensing software from a related company called RSA Data Security, Inc. (RSADSI). Neither of these companies is careless about collecting license fees where applicable.

The most popular public key algorithm is RSA (see §5.3 *RSA*). RSA was developed at MIT, and under the terms of MIT's funding at the time there are no license fees for U.S. government use. It is only patented in the U.S., but PKP claims that the Hellman-Merkle patent also covers RSA, and that patent is international. Interpretation of patent rights varies by country, so the legal issues are complex. At any rate, the last patent on RSA runs out on September 20, 2000. A good time for a party.

The U.S. government is advocating a digital signature standard (see §5.5 *Digital Signature Standard (DSS)*). Although in most respects DSS is technically inferior to RSA, when first announced it was advertised that DSS would be freely licensable, i.e., it would not be necessary to reach agreement with RSADSI or PKP. But PKP claims Hellman-Merkle covers all public key cryptography, and strengthened its position by acquiring rights to a patent by Schnorr that is closely related to DSS.

So at this point PKP claims that DSS is not freely licensable. NIST, which has patented DSS, disagrees. Lawsuits loom, and the situation is still murky.

> *"I don't know what you mean by* your *way," said the Queen: "all the ways about here belong to* me*..."*   —*Through the Looking Glass*

Some of the relevant patents are:

- Diffie-Hellman: Patent #4,200,770, issued 1980, expires on April 29, 1997. This covers the Diffie-Hellman key exchange described in §5.4 *Diffie-Hellman*.

- Hellman-Merkle: Patent #4,218,582, issued 1980, expires on August 19, 1997. This is claimed to cover all public key systems. There is some controversy over whether this patent should be valid. The specific public key mechanisms described in the patent (*knapsack* systems) were subsequently broken.

- Rivest-Shamir-Adleman: Patent #4,405,829, issued 1983, expires on September 20, 2000. This covers the RSA algorithm described in §5.3 *RSA*.

- Hellman-Pohlig: Patent #4,424,414, issued 1984, expires on January 3, 2001. This is related to the Diffie-Hellman key exchange.

- Schnorr: Patent #4,995,082, issued 1991, expires on February 19, 2008. This is what the DSS algorithm is directly based upon.

- Kravitz: Patent #5,231,668, issued 1993, expires on July 27, 2008. This is the actual DSS algorithm.

1.12.2 Export Controls

The three golden rules of export control:
1. *The rules don't make any sense.*
2. *If you get it wrong you go to jail.*
3. *The boys on the hill don't have a sense of humor.*

—anonymous

The U.S. government considers encryption to be a dangerous technology, like germ warfare and nuclear weapons. If a U.S. corporation would like to sell to other countries (and the proceeds are not going to be funding the Contras), it needs export approval. The export control laws around encryption are not clear, and their interpretation changes over time. The general principle is that the U.S. government does not want you to give out technology that would make it more difficult for them to spy. Sometimes companies get so discouraged that they leave encryption out of their products altogether. Sometimes they generate products that, when sold overseas, have the encryption mechanisms removed. It is usually possible to get export approval for encryption if the key lengths are short enough for the government to brute-force check all possible keys to decrypt a message. So sometimes companies just use short keys, or sometimes they have the capability of varying the key length, and they fix the key length to be shorter when a system is sold outside the U.S.

Even if you aren't in the business of selling software abroad, you can run afoul of export controls. If you install encryption software on your laptop and take it along with you on an international trip, you may be breaking the law. If you distribute encryption software within the U.S. without adequate warnings, you are doing your customers a disservice. And the legality of posting encryption software on a public network is questionable.

PART 1

CRYPTOGRAPHY

2 INTRODUCTION TO CRYPTOGRAPHY

2.1 WHAT IS CRYPTOGRAPHY?

The word *cryptography* comes from the Greek words κρυπτο (*hidden* or *secret*) and γραφη (*writing*). Oddly enough, cryptography is the art of secret writing. More generally, people think of cryptography as the art of mangling information into apparent unintelligibility in a manner allowing a secret method of unmangling. The basic service provided by cryptography is the ability to send information between participants in a way that prevents others from reading it. In this book we will concentrate on the kind of cryptography that is based on representing information as numbers and mathematically manipulating those numbers. This kind of cryptography can provide other services, such as

- integrity checking—reassuring the recipient of a message that the message has not been altered since it was generated by a legitimate source

- authentication—verifying someone's (or something's) identity

But back to the traditional use of cryptography. A message in its original form is known as **plaintext** or **cleartext**. The mangled information is known as **ciphertext**. The process for producing ciphertext from plaintext is known as **encryption**. The reverse of encryption is called **decryption**.

$$\text{plaintext} \xrightarrow{\text{encryption}} \text{ciphertext} \xrightarrow{\text{decryption}} \text{plaintext}$$

While cryptographers invent clever secret codes, cryptanalysts attempt to break these codes. These two disciplines constantly try to keep ahead of each other. Ultimately, the success of the cryptographers rests on the

Fundamental Tenet of Cryptography

If lots of smart people have failed to solve a problem,
then it probably won't be solved (soon).

Cryptographic systems tend to involve both an algorithm and a secret value. The secret value is known as the **key**. The reason for having a key in addition to an algorithm is that it is difficult to keep devising new algorithms that will allow reversible scrambling of information, and it is difficult to quickly explain a newly devised algorithm to the person with whom you'd like to start communicating securely. With a good cryptographic scheme it is perfectly OK to have everyone, including the bad guys (and the cryptanalysts) know the algorithm because knowledge of the algorithm without the key does not help unmangle the information.

The concept of a key is analogous to the combination for a combination lock. Although the concept of a combination lock is well known (you dial in the secret numbers in the correct sequence and the lock opens), you can't open a combination lock easily without knowing the combination.

2.1.1 Computational Difficulty

It is important for cryptographic algorithms to be reasonably efficient for the good guys to compute. The good guys are the ones with knowledge of the keys.[1] Cryptographic algorithms are not impossible to break without the key. A bad guy can simply try all possible keys until one works. The security of a cryptographic scheme depends on how much work it is for the bad guy to break it. If the best possible scheme will take 10 million years to break using all of the computers in the world, then it can be considered reasonably secure.

Going back to the combination lock example, a typical combination might consist of three numbers, each a number between 1 and 40. Let's say it takes 10 seconds to dial in a combination. That's reasonably convenient for the good guy. How much work is it for the bad guy? There are 40^3 possible combinations, which is 64000. At 10 seconds per try, it would take a week to try all combinations, though on average it would only take half that long (even though the right number is always the last one you try!).

Often a scheme can be made more secure by making the key longer. In the combination lock analogy, making the key longer would consist of requiring four numbers to be dialed in. This would make a little more work for the good guy. It might now take 13 seconds to dial in the combination. But the bad guy has 40 times as many combinations to try, at 13 seconds each, so it would take a year to try all combinations. (And if it took that long, he might want to stop to eat or sleep).

---

1. We're using the terms *good guys* for the cryptographers, and *bad guys* for the cryptanalysts. This is a convenient shorthand and not a moral judgment—in any given situation, which side you consider *good* or *bad* depends on your point of view.

With cryptography, computers can be used to exhaustively try keys. Computers are a lot faster than people, and they don't get tired, so thousands or millions of keys can be tried per second. Also, lots of keys can be tried in parallel if you have multiple computers, so time can be saved by spending money on more computers.

Sometimes a cryptographic algorithm has a variable-length key. It can be made more secure by increasing the length of the key. Increasing the length of the key by one bit makes the good guy's job just a little bit harder, but makes the bad guy's job up to twice as hard (because the number of possible keys doubles). Some cryptographic algorithms have a fixed-length key, but a similar algorithm with a longer key can be devised if necessary. If computers get 1000 times faster, so that the bad guy's job becomes reasonably practical, making the key 10 bits longer will make the bad guy's job as hard as it was before the advance in computer speed. However, it will be much easier for the good guys (because their computer speed increase far outweighs the increment in key length). So the faster computers get, the better life gets for the good guys.

Keep in mind that breaking the cryptographic scheme is often only one way of getting what you want. For instance, a bolt cutter works no matter how many digits are in the combination.

> *You can get further with a kind word and a gun than you can with a kind*
> *word alone.* —Willy Sutton, bank robber

2.1.2 To Publish or Not to Publish

Some people believe that keeping a cryptographic algorithm as secret as possible will enhance its security. Others argue that publishing the algorithm, so that it is widely known, will enhance its security. On the one hand, it would seem that keeping the algorithm secret must be more secure—it makes for more work for the cryptanalyst to try to figure out what the algorithm is.

The argument for publishing the algorithm is that the bad guys will probably find out about it eventually anyway, so it's better to tell a lot of nonmalicious people about the algorithm so that in case there are weaknesses, a good guy will discover them rather than a bad guy. A good guy who discovers a weakness will warn people that the system has a weakness. Publication provides an enormous amount of free consulting from the academic community as cryptanalysts look for weaknesses so they can publish papers about them. A bad guy who discovers a weakness will exploit it for doing bad-guy things like embezzling money or stealing trade secrets.

It is difficult to keep the algorithm secret because if an algorithm is to be widely used, it is highly likely that determined attackers will manage to learn the algorithm by reverse engineering whatever implementation is distributed, or just because the more people who know something the more likely it is for the information to leak to the wrong places. In the past, "good" cryptosystems were not economically feasible, so keeping the algorithms secret was needed extra protection. We believe (we hope?) today's algorithms are sufficiently secure that this is not necessary.

Common practice today is for most commercial cryptosystems to be published and for military cryptosystems to be kept secret. If a commercial algorithm is unpublished today, it's probably for trade secret reasons or because this makes it easier to get export approval rather than to enhance its security. We suspect the military ciphers are unpublished mainly to keep good cryptographic methods out of the hands of the enemy rather than to keep them from cryptanalyzing our codes.

2.1.3 Secret Codes

We use the terms *secret code* and *cipher* interchangeably to mean any method of encrypting data. Some people draw a subtle distinction between these terms that we don't find useful.

The earliest documented cipher is attributed to Julius Caesar. The way the **Caesar cipher** would work if the message were in English is as follows. Substitute for each letter of the message, the letter which is 3 letters later in the alphabet (and wrap around to A from Z). Thus an A would become a D, and so forth. For instance, DOZEN would become GRCHQ. Once you figure out what's going on, it is very easy to read messages encrypted this way (unless, of course, the original message was in Greek).

A slight enhancement to the Caesar cipher was distributed as a premium with Ovaltine in the 1940s as *Captain Midnight Secret Decoder rings*. (Were this done today, Ovaltine would probably be in violation of export controls for distributing cryptographic hardware!) The variant is to pick a secret number n between 1 and 25, instead of always using 3. Substitute for each letter of the message, the letter which is n higher (and wrap around to A from Z of course). Thus if the secret number was 1, an A would become a B, and so forth. For instance HAL would become IBM. If the secret number was 25, then IBM would become HAL. Regardless of the value of n, since there are only 26 possible ns to try, it is still very easy to break this cipher if you know it's being used and you can recognize a message once it's decrypted.

The next type of cryptographic system developed is known as a **monoalphabetic cipher**, which consists of an arbitrary mapping of one letter to another letter. There are 26! possible pairings of letters, which is approximately 4×10^{26}. [Remember, $n!$, which reads "n factorial", means $n(n-1)(n-2)\cdots 1$.] This might seem secure, because to try all possibilities, if it took 1 microsecond to try each one, would take about 10 trillion years. However, by statistical analysis of language (knowing that certain letters and letter combinations are more common than others), it turns out to be fairly easy to break. For instance, many daily newspapers have a daily cryptogram, which is a monoalphabetic cipher, and can be broken by people who enjoy that sort of thing during their subway ride to work. An example is

Cf lqr'xs xsnyctm n eqxxqgsy iqul qf wdcp eqqh, erl lqrx qgt iqul!

Computers have made much more complex cryptographic schemes both necessary and possible. Necessary because computers can try keys at a rate that would exhaust an army of clerks; and possible because computers can execute the complex algorithms quickly and without errors.

2.2 BREAKING AN ENCRYPTION SCHEME

What do we mean when we speak of a bad guy Fred *breaking* an encryption scheme? The three basic attacks are known as **ciphertext only**, **known plaintext**, and **chosen plaintext**.

2.2.1 Ciphertext Only

In a ciphertext only attack, Fred has seen (and presumably stored) some ciphertext that he can analyze at leisure. Typically it is not difficult for a bad guy to obtain ciphertext. (If a bad guy can't access the encrypted data, then there would have been no need to encrypt the data in the first place!)

How can Fred figure out the plaintext if all he can see is the ciphertext? One possible strategy is to search through all the keys. Fred tries the decrypt operation with each key in turn. It is essential for this attack that Fred be able to recognize when he has succeeded. For instance, if the message was English text, then it is highly unlikely that a decryption operation with an incorrect key could produce something that looked like intelligible text. Because it is important for Fred to be able to differentiate plaintext from gibberish, this attack is sometimes known as a **recognizable plaintext** attack.

It is also essential that Fred have enough ciphertext. For instance, using the example of a monoalphabetic cipher, if the only ciphertext available to Fred were XYZ, then there is not enough information. There are many possible letter substitutions that would lead to a legal three-letter English word. There is no way for Fred to know whether the plaintext corresponding to XYZ is THE or CAT or HAT. As a matter of fact, in the following sentence, any of the words could be the plaintext for XYZ:

The hot cat was sad but you may now sit and use her big red pen.

[Don't worry—we've found a lovely sanatorium for the coauthor who wrote that.

—the other coauthors]

Often it isn't necessary to search through a lot of keys. For instance, the authentication scheme Kerberos (see §10.4 *Logging Into the Network*) assigns to user Alice a DES key derived from Alice's password according to a straightforward, published algorithm. If Alice chooses her password unwisely (say a word in the dictionary), then Fred does not need to search through all 2^{56} possible DES keys—instead he only needs to try the derived keys of the 10000 or so common English words.

A cryptographic algorithm has to be secure against a ciphertext only attack because of the accessibility of the ciphertext to cryptanalysts. But in many cases cryptanalysts can obtain additional information, so it is important to design cryptographic systems to withstand the next two attacks as well.

2.2.2 Known Plaintext

Sometimes life is easier for the attacker. Suppose Fred has somehow obtained some ⟨plaintext, ciphertext⟩ pairs. How might he have obtained these? One possibility is that secret data might not remain secret forever. For instance, the data might consist of specifying the next city to be attacked. Once the attack occurs, the plaintext to the previous day's ciphertext is now known.

With a monoalphabetic cipher, a small amount of known plaintext would be a bonanza. From it, the attacker would learn the mappings of a substantial fraction of the most common letters (every letter that was used in the plaintext Fred obtained). Some cryptographic schemes might be good enough to be secure against ciphertext only attacks but not good enough against known plaintext attacks. In these cases, it becomes important to design the systems that use such a cryptographic algorithm to minimize the possibility that a bad guy will ever be able to obtain ⟨plaintext, ciphertext⟩ pairs.

2.2.3 Chosen Plaintext

On rare occasions, life may be easier still for the attacker. In a "chosen plaintext" attack, Fred can choose any plaintext he wants, and get the system to tell him what the corresponding ciphertext is. How could such a thing be possible?

Suppose the telegraph company offered a service in which they encrypt and transmit messages for you. Suppose Fred had eavesdropped on Alice's encrypted message. Now he'd like to break the telegraph company's encryption scheme so that he can decrypt Alice's message.

He can obtain the corresponding ciphertext to any message he chooses by paying the telegraph company to send the message for him, encrypted. For instance, if Fred knew they were using a monoalphabetic cipher, he might send the message

The quick brown fox jumps over the lazy dog.

knowing that he would thereby get all the letters of the alphabet encrypted and then be able to decrypt with certainty any encrypted message.

It is possible that a cryptosystem secure against ciphertext only and known plaintext attacks might still be susceptible to chosen plaintext attacks. For instance, if Fred knows that Alice's message is either Surrender or Fight on, then no matter how wonderful an encryption scheme the telegraph company is using, all he has to do is send the two messages and see which one looks like the encrypted data he saw when Alice's message was transmitted.

A cryptosystem should resist all three sorts of attacks. That way its users don't need to worry about whether there are any opportunities for attackers to know or choose plaintext. Like wearing both a belt and suspenders, many systems that use cryptographic algorithms will also go out of their way to prevent any chance of chosen plaintext attacks.

2.3 TYPES OF CRYPTOGRAPHIC FUNCTIONS

There are three kinds of cryptographic functions: hash functions, secret key functions, and public key functions. We will describe what each kind is, and what it is useful for. Public key cryptography involves the use of two keys. Secret key cryptography involves the use of one key. Hash functions involve the use of zero keys! Try to imagine what that could possibly mean, and what use it could possibly have—an algorithm everyone knows with no secret key, and yet it has uses in security.

Since secret key cryptography is probably the most intuitive, we'll describe that first.

2.4 SECRET KEY CRYPTOGRAPHY

Secret key cryptography involves the use of a single key. Given a message (called plaintext) and the key, encryption produces unintelligible data (called an IRS Publication—no! no! that was just a finger slip, we meant to say "ciphertext"), which is about the same length as the plaintext was. Decryption is the reverse of encryption, and uses the same key as encryption.

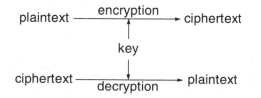

Secret key cryptography is sometimes referred to as **conventional cryptography** or **symmetric cryptography**. The Captain Midnight code and the monoalphabetic cipher are both examples of secret key algorithms, though both are easy to break. In this chapter we describe the functionality of cryptographic algorithms, but not the details of particular algorithms. In Chapter 3 *Secret Key Cryptography* we describe the details of two secret key cryptographic algorithms (DES and IDEA) in current use.

2.4.1 Security Uses of Secret Key Cryptography

The next few sections describe the types of things one might do with secret key cryptography.

2.4.2 Transmitting Over an Insecure Channel

It is often impossible to prevent eavesdropping when transmitting information. For instance, a telephone conversation can be tapped, a letter can be intercepted, and a message transmitted on a LAN can be received by unauthorized stations.

If you and I agree on a shared secret (a key), then by using secret key cryptography we can send messages to one another on a medium that can be tapped, without worrying about eavesdroppers. All we need to do is for the sender to encrypt the messages and the receiver to decrypt them using the shared secret. An eavesdropper will only see unintelligible data.

. This is the classic use of cryptography.

2.4.3 Secure Storage on Insecure Media

If I have information I want to preserve but which I want to assure no one else can look at, I have to be able to store the media where I am sure no one can get it. Between clever thieves and court orders, there are very few places that are truly secure, and none of these is convenient. If I invent a key and encrypt the information using the key, I can store it anywhere and it is safe so long as I can remember the key. Of course, forgetting the key makes the data irrevocably lost, so this must be used with great care.

2.4.4 Authentication

In spy movies, when two agents who don't know each other must rendezvous, they are each given a password or pass phrase that they can use to recognize one another. This has the problem that anyone overhearing their conversation or initiating one falsely can gain information useful for replaying later and impersonating the person to whom they are talking.

The term **strong authentication** means that someone can prove knowledge of a secret without revealing it. Strong authentication is possible with cryptography. Strong authentication is particularly useful when two computers are trying to communicate over an insecure network (since few people can execute cryptographic algorithms in their heads). Suppose Alice and Bob share a key K_{AB} and they want to verify they are speaking to each other. They each pick a random number, which is known as a **challenge**. Alice picks r_A. Bob picks r_B. The value x encrypted with the key K_{AB} is known as the **response** to the challenge x.

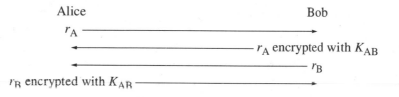

If someone, say Fred, were impersonating Alice, he could get Bob to encrypt a value for him (though Fred wouldn't be able to tell if the person he was talking to was *really* Bob), but this information would not be useful later in impersonating Bob to the real Alice because the real Alice would pick a different challenge. If Alice and Bob complete this exchange, they have each proven to the other than they know K_{AB} without revealing it to an impostor or an eavesdropper. Note that in this particular protocol, there is the opportunity for Fred to obtain some ⟨chosen plaintext, ciphertext⟩ pairs, since he can claim to be Bob and ask Alice to encrypt a challenge for him. For this reason, it is essential that challenges be chosen from a large enough space, say 2^{64} values, so that there is no significant chance of using the same one twice.

That is the general idea of a cryptographic authentication algorithm, though this particular algorithm has a subtle problem that would prevent it from being useful in most computer-to-computer cases. (We would have preferred not bringing that up, but felt we needed to say that so as not to alarm people who already know this stuff and who would realize the protocol was not secure. Details on fixing this authentication protocol are discussed in Chapter 9 *Security Handshake Pitfalls.*)

2.4.5 Integrity Check

A secret key scheme can be used to generate a fixed-length cryptographic checksum associated with a message. This is a rather nonintuitive use of secret key technology.

What is a checksum? An ordinary (noncryptographic) checksum protects against accidental corruption of a message. The original derivation of the term *checksum* comes from the operation of breaking a message into fixed-length blocks (for instance, 32-bit words) and adding them up. The sum is sent along with the message. The receiver similarly breaks up the message, repeats the addition, and *checks the sum*. If the message had been garbled en route, the sum will not match the sum sent and the message is rejected, unless, of course, there were two or more errors in the transmission that canceled one another. It turns out this is not terribly unlikely, given that if flaky hardware turns a bit off somewhere, it is likely to turn a corresponding bit on somewhere else. To protect against such "regular" flaws in hardware, more complex checksums called CRCs were devised. But these still only protect against faulty hardware and not an intelligent attacker. Since CRC algorithms are published, an attacker who wanted to change a message could do so, compute the CRC on the new message, and send that along.

To provide protection against malicious changes to a message, a *secret* checksum algorithm is required, such that an attacker not knowing the algorithm can't compute the right checksum for the message to be accepted as authentic. As with encryption algorithms, it's better to have a common (known) algorithm and a secret key. This is what a cryptographic checksum does. Given a key and a message, the algorithm produces a fixed-length message integrity code (MIC) that can be sent with the message.

If anyone were to modify the message, and they didn't know the key, they would have to guess a MIC and the chance of getting it right depends on the length. A typical MIC is at least 48 bits long, so the chance of getting away with a forged message is only one in 280 trillion (or about the chance of going to Las Vegas with a dime and letting it ride on red at the roulette table until you have enough to pay off the U.S. national debt).

Such message integrity codes have been in use to protect the integrity of large interbank electronic funds transfers for quite some time. The messages are not kept secret from an eavesdropper, but their integrity is ensured.

2.5 PUBLIC KEY CRYPTOGRAPHY

Public key cryptography is sometimes also referred to as **asymmetric cryptography**.

Public key cryptography is a relatively new field, invented in 1975 [DIFF76b] (at least that's the first published record—it is rumored that NSA or similar organizations may have discovered this technology earlier). Unlike secret key cryptography, keys are not shared. Instead, each individual has two keys: a private key that need not be revealed to anyone, and a public key that is preferably known to the entire world.

Note that we call the private key a *private key* and not a *secret key*. This convention is an attempt to make it clear in any context whether public key cryptography or secret key cryptography is being used. There are people in this world whose sole purpose in life is to try to confuse people.

They will use the term *secret key* for the private key in public key cryptography, or use the term *private key* for the secret key in secret key technology. One of the most important contributions we can make to the field is to convince people to feel strongly about using the terminology correctly—the term *secret key* refers only to the single secret number used in secret key cryptography. The term *private key* MUST be used when referring to the key in public key cryptography that must not be made public. (Yes, when we speak we sometimes accidentally say the wrong thing, but at least we feel guilty about it.)

There is something unfortunate about the terminology *public* and *private*. It is that both words begin with *p*. We will sometimes want a single letter to refer to one of the keys. The letter *p* won't do. We will use the letter *e* to refer to the public key, since the public key is used when encrypting a message. We'll use the letter *d* to refer to the private key, because the private key is used to decrypt a message. Encryption and decryption are two mathematical functions that are inverses of each other.

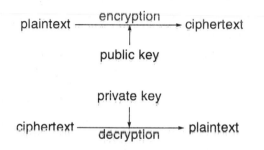

There is an additional thing one can do with public key technology, which is to generate a **digital signature** on a message. A digital signature is a number associated with a message, like a

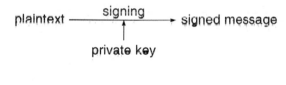

checksum or the MIC (message integrity code) described in §2.4.5 *Integrity Check*. However, unlike a checksum, which can be generated by anyone, a digital signature can only be generated by someone knowing the private key. A public key signature differs from a secret key MIC because verification of a MIC requires knowledge of the same secret as was used to create it. Therefore anyone who can verify a MIC can also generate one, and so be able to substitute a different message and corresponding MIC. In contrast, verification of the signature only requires knowledge of the public key. So Alice can sign a message by generating a signature only she can generate, and other people can verify that it is Alice's signature, but cannot forge her signature. This is called a signature because it shares with handwritten signatures the property that it is possible to be able to recognize a signature as authentic without being able to forge it.

2.5.1 Security Uses of Public Key Cryptography

Public key cryptography can do anything secret key cryptography can do, but the known public key cryptographic algorithms are orders of magnitude slower than the best known secret key cryptographic algorithms and so are usually only used for things secret key cryptography can't do. Public key cryptography is very useful because network security based on public key technology tends to be more secure and more easily configurable. Often it is mixed with secret key technology. For example, public key cryptography might be used in the beginning of communication for authentication and to establish a temporary shared secret key, then the secret key is used to encrypt the remainder of the conversation using secret key technology.

For instance, suppose Alice wants to talk to Bob. She uses his public key to encrypt a secret key, then uses that secret key to encrypt whatever else she wants to send him. Only Bob can decrypt the secret key. He can then communicate using that secret key with whoever sent that message. Notice that given this protocol, Bob does not know that it was Alice who sent the message. This could be fixed by having Alice digitally sign the encrypted secret key using her private key.

Now we'll describe the types of things one might do with public key cryptography.

2.5.2 Transmitting Over an Insecure Channel

Suppose Alice's ⟨public key, private key⟩ pair is $\langle e_A, d_A \rangle$. Suppose Bob's key pair is $\langle e_B, d_B \rangle$. Assume Alice knows Bob's public key, and Bob knows Alice's public key. Actually, accurately learning other people's public keys is one of the biggest challenges in using public key cryptography and will be discussed in detail in §7.7.2 *Certification Authorities (CAs)*. But for now, don't worry about it.

Alice		Bob
encrypt m_A using e_B	⟶	decrypt to m_A using d_B
decrypt to m_B using d_A	⟵	encrypt m_B using e_A

2.5.3 Secure Storage on Insecure Media

This is really the same as what one would do with secret key cryptography. You'd encrypt the data with your public key. Then nobody can decrypt it except you, since decryption will require the use of the private key. It has the advantage over encryption with secret key technology that you don't have to risk giving your private key to the machine that is going to encrypt the data for you. As with secret key technology, if you lose your private key, the data is irretrievably lost. If you are worried about that, you can encrypt an additional copy of the data under the public key of someone you trust, like your lawyer.

2.5.4 Authentication

Authentication is an area in which public key technology potentially gives a real benefit. With secret key cryptography, if Alice and Bob want to communicate, they have to share a secret. If Bob wants to be able to prove his identity to lots of entities, then with secret key technology he will need to remember lots of secret keys, one for each entity to which he would like to prove his identity. Possibly he could use the same shared secret with Alice as with Carol, but that has the disadvantage that then Carol and Alice could impersonate Bob to each other.

Public key technology is much more convenient. Bob only needs to remember a single secret, his own private key. It is true that if Bob wants to be able to verify the identity of thousands of entities, then he will need to know thousands of public keys, but in general the entities verifying identities are computers which don't mind remembering thousands of things, whereas the entities proving their identities are often humans, which do mind remembering things.

Here's an example of how Alice can use public key cryptography for verifying Bob's identity assuming Alice knows Bob's public key. Alice chooses a random number r, encrypts it using Bob's public key e_B, and sends the result to Bob. Bob proves he knows d_B by decrypting the message and sending r back to Alice.

                Alice   Bob

encrypt r using e_B ⟶ decrypt to r using d_B

                        ⟵———————————— r

Another advantage of public key authentication is that Alice does not need to keep any secret information. For instance, Alice might be a computer system in which backup tapes are unencrypted and easily stolen. With secret key based authentication, if Carol stole a backup tape and read the key that Alice shares with Bob, she could then trick Bob into thinking she was Alice. In contrast, with public key based authentication, the only information on Alice's backup tapes is public key information, and that cannot be used to impersonate Bob.

In large-scale systems, like computer networks with thousands of users and services, authentication is usually done with trusted intermediaries. As we'll see in §7.7 *Trusted Intermediaries*, public key based authentication using intermediaries has several important advantages over secret key based authentication.

2.5.5 Digital Signatures

> *Forged in USA*
> > engraved on a screwdriver claiming to be of brand *Craftsman*

It is often useful to prove that a message was generated by a particular individual, especially if the individual is not necessarily around to be asked about authorship of the message. This is easy with public key technology. Bob's signature for a message *m* can only be generated by someone with knowledge of Bob's private key. And the signature depends on the contents of *m*. If *m* is modified in any way, the signature no longer matches. So digital signatures provide two important functions. They prove who generated the information, and they prove that the information has not been modified in any way by anyone since the message and matching signature were generated.

An important example of a use of a signature is in electronic mail to verify that a mail message really did come from the claimed source.

Digital signatures offer an important advantage over secret key based cryptographic checksums—**non-repudiation**. Suppose Bob sells widgets and Alice routinely buys them. Alice and Bob might agree that rather than placing orders through the mail with signed purchase orders, Alice will send electronic mail messages to order widgets. To protect against someone forging orders and causing Bob to manufacture more widgets than Alice actually needs, Alice will include a message integrity code on her messages. This could be either a secret key based MIC or a public key based signature. But suppose sometime after Alice places a big order, she changes her mind (the bottom fell out of the widget market). Since there's a big penalty for canceling an order, she doesn't fess up that she's canceling, but instead denies that she ever placed the order. Bob sues. Bob knows Alice really placed the order because it was cryptographically signed. But if it was signed with a secret key algorithm, he can't prove it to anyone! Since he knows the same secret key that Alice used to sign the order, he could have forged the signature on the message himself and he can't prove to the judge that he didn't! If it was a public key signature on the other hand, he can show the signed message to the judge and the judge can verify that it was signed with Alice's key. Alice can still claim of course that someone must have stolen and misused her key (it might even be true!), but the contract between Alice and Bob could reasonably hold her responsible for damages caused by her inadequately protecting her key. Unlike secret key cryptography, where the keys are shared, you can always tell who's responsible for a signature generated with a private key.

Public key algorithms are discussed further in Chapter 5 *Public Key Algorithms*.

2.6 HASH ALGORITHMS

Hash algorithms are also known as **message digests** or **one-way transformations**.

A cryptographic hash function is a mathematical transformation that takes a message of arbitrary length (transformed into a string of bits) and computes from it a fixed-length (short) number. We'll call the hash of a message m, $h(m)$. It has the following properties:

- For any message m, it is relatively easy to compute $h(m)$. This just means that in order to be practical it can't take a lot of processing time to compute the hash.

- Given $h(m)$, there is no way to find an m that hashes to $h(m)$ in a way that is substantially easier than going through all possible values of m and computing $h(m)$ for each one.

- Even though it's obvious that many different values of m will be transformed to the same value $h(m)$ (because there are many more possible values of m), it is *computationally infeasible* to find two values that hash to the same thing.

An example of the sort of function that might work is taking the message m, treating it as a number, adding some large constant, squaring it, and taking the middle n digits as the hash. You can see that while this would not be difficult to compute, it's not obvious how you could find a message that would produce a particular hash, or how one might find two messages with the same hash. It turns out this is not a particularly good message digest function—we'll give examples of secure message digest functions in Chapter 4 *Hashes and Message Digests*. But the basic idea of a message digest function is that the input is mangled so badly the process cannot be reversed.

2.6.1 Password Hashing

When a user types a password, the system has to be able to determine whether the user got it right. If the system stores the passwords unencrypted, then anyone with access to the system storage or backup tapes can steal the passwords. Luckily, it is not necessary for the system to know a password in order to verify its correctness. (A proper password is like pornography. You can't tell what it is, but you know it when you see it.)

Instead of storing the password, the system can store a hash of the password. When a password is supplied, it computes the password's hash and compares it with the stored value. If they match, the password is deemed correct. If the hashed password file is obtained by an attacker, it is not immediately useful because the passwords can't be derived from the hashes. Historically, some systems made the password file publicly readable, an expression of confidence in the security of the hash. Even if there are no cryptographic flaws in the hash, it is possible to guess passwords and hash them to see if they match. If a user is careless and chooses a password that is guessable (say, a word that would appear in a 50000-word dictionary or book of common names), an exhaustive search would "crack" the password even if the encryption were sound. For this reason, many systems hide the hashed password list (and those that don't should).

2.6.2 Message Integrity

Cryptographic hash functions can be used to generate a MIC to protect the integrity of messages transmitted over insecure media in much the same way as secret key cryptography.

If we merely sent the message and used the hash of the message as a MIC, this would not be secure, since the hash function is well-known. The bad guy can modify the message and compute a new hash for the new message, and transmit that.

However, if Alice and Bob have agreed on a password, Alice can use a hash to generate a MIC for a message to Bob by taking the message, concatenating the password, and computing the hash of *message|password*. Alice then sends the hash and the message (without the password) to Bob. Bob concatenates the password to the received message and computes the hash of the result. If that matches the received hash, Bob can have confidence the message was sent by someone knowing the password. [Note: there are some cryptographic subtleties to making this actually secure; see §4.2.2 *Computing a MIC with a Hash*].

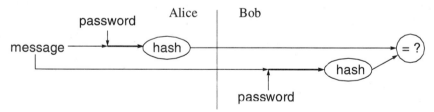

2.6.3 Message Fingerprint

If you want to know whether some large data structure (e.g. a program) has been modified from one day to the next, you could keep a copy of the data on some tamper-proof backing store and periodically compare it to the active version. With a hash function, you can save storage: you simply save the message digest of the data on the tamper-proof backing store (which because the hash is small could be a piece of paper in a filing cabinet). If the message digest hasn't changed, you can be confident none of the data has.

A note to would-be users—if it hasn't already occurred to you, it has occurred to the bad guys—the program that computes the hash must also be independently protected for this to be secure. Otherwise the bad guys can change the file but also change the hashing program to report the checksum as though the file were unchanged!

2.6.4 Downline Load Security

It is common practice to have special-purpose devices connected to a network, like routers or printers, that do not have the nonvolatile memory to store the programs they normally run. Instead, they keep a bootstrap program smart enough to get a program from the network and run it. This scheme is called **downline load**.

Suppose you want to downline load a program and make sure it hasn't been corrupted (whether intentionally or not). If you know the proper hash of the program, you can compute the hash of the loaded program and make sure it has the proper value before running the program.

2.6.5 Digital Signature Efficiency

The best-known public key algorithms are sufficiently processor-intensive that it is desirable to compute a message digest of the message and sign that, rather than to sign the message directly. The message digest algorithms are much less processor intensive, and the message digest is much shorter than the message.

2.7 HOMEWORK

1. Random J. Programmer discovers a much faster method of generating a 64-bit signature for a message using secret key technology. The idea is to simply encrypt the first 64 bits of the message, and use that as the signature. What's wrong with this idea?

2. What's wrong with adding up the words of a message and using the result as a hash of the message?

3. Random J. Protocol-Designer has been told to design a scheme to prevent messages from being modified by an intruder. Random J. decides to append to each message a hash of that

message. Why doesn't this solve the problem? (We know of a protocol that uses this technique in an attempt to gain security.)

SECRET KEY CRYPTOGRAPHY

3.1 INTRODUCTION

This chapter describes how secret key cryptographic algorithms work. It describes in detail the DES and IDEA algorithms. These algorithms take a fixed-length block of message (64 bits in the case of both DES and IDEA), a fixed-length key (56 bits for DES and 128 bits for IDEA) and generate a block of output (the same length as the input). In general, a message won't happen to be 64 bits long. In §3.6 *Encrypting a Large Message* we'll discuss how to convert the basic fixed-length block encryption algorithm into a general message encryption algorithm.

3.2 GENERIC BLOCK ENCRYPTION

A cryptographic algorithm converts a plaintext block into an encrypted block. It's fairly obvious that if the key length is too short (for instance, 4 bits), the cryptographic scheme would not be secure because it would be too easy to search through all possible keys. There's a similar issue with the length of the block of plaintext to be encrypted. If the block length is too short (say one byte, as in a monoalphabetic cipher), then if you ever had some paired ⟨plaintext, ciphertext⟩, you could construct a table to be used for decryption. It might be possible to obtain such pairs because messages might only remain secret for a short time, perhaps because the message says where the army will attack the next day.

Having a block length too long is merely inconvenient—unnecessarily complex and possibly having performance penalties. 64 bits is probably the right length, in that you are unlikely to get that many blocks of ⟨plaintext, ciphertext⟩ pairs, and even if you did, it would take too much space to store the table (2^{64} entries of 64 bits each) or too much time to sort it for efficient searching.

The most general way of encrypting a 64-bit block is to take each of the 2^{64} input values and map it to a unique one of the 2^{64} output values. (It is necessary that the mapping be **one-to-one**, i.e.

only one input value maps to any given output value, since otherwise decryption would not be possible. For instance, suppose all values mapped to zero! Only ESP could decrypt that one!)

Suppose Alice and Bob (who happen to speak a language in which all sentences are 64 bits long) want to decide upon a mapping that they can use for encrypting their conversations. How would they specify one? To specify a monoalphabetic cipher with English letters takes 26 specifications of 26 possible values, approximately. For instance,

$$a \to q \quad b \to d \quad c \to w \quad d \to x \quad e \to a \quad f \to f \quad g \to z \quad h \to b \quad \text{etc.}$$

How would you specify a mapping of all possible 64-bit input values? Well, let's start:

$$0000000000000000 \to 8ad1482703f217ce$$
$$0000000000000001 \to b33dc8710928d701$$
$$0000000000000002 \to 29e856b28013fa4c$$

Hmm, we probably don't want to write this all out. There are 2^{64} possible input values and for each one we have to specify a 64-bit output value. This would take 2^{70} bits. (Actually, nitpickers might note that there aren't quite 2^{70} bits of information since the mapping has to be a **permutation**, i.e., each output value is used exactly once, so for instance the final output value does not need to be explicitly specified—it's the one that's left over. However, there are $2^{64}!$ different possible permutations of 2^{64} values, which would take more than 2^{69} bits to represent.) [Remember $n!$ (read "n factorial") is $n \cdot (n-1) \cdot (n-2) \cdot (n-3) \cdots 3 \cdot 2 \cdot 1$. It can be approximated by Stirling's formula: $n! \approx n^n e^{-n} \sqrt{2\pi n}$]

So let's say it would take 2^{69} bits to specify the mapping. That 2^{69} bit number would act like a secret key that Alice and Bob would share. But it is doubtful that they could remember a key that large, or even be able to say it to each other within a lifetime, or store it on anything. So this is not particularly practical.

Secret key cryptographic systems are designed to take a reasonable-length key (i.e., more like 64 bits than 2^{64} bits) and generate a one-to-one mapping that looks, to someone who does not know the key, completely random. **Random** means that it should look, to someone who doesn't know the key, as if the mapping from an input value to an output value were generated by using a random number generator. (To get the mapping from input i to output o, flip a 2^{64}-sided coin to choose the value of o—or if such a coin is not readily available, a single coin could be flipped 64 times. Since the mapping must be one-to-one, you'll have to start over again choosing o if the value selected by the coin has been previously used.) If the mapping were truly random, any single bit change to the input will result in a totally independently chosen random number output. The two different output numbers should have no correlation, meaning that about half the bits should be the same and about half the bits should be different. For instance, it can't be the case that the 3rd bit of output always changes if the 12th bit of input changes. So the cryptographic algorithms are designed to *spread bits* *around*, in the sense that a single input bit should have influence on all the bits of the output, and be able to change any one of them with a probability of about 50% (depending on the values of the other 63 bits of input).

There are two kinds of simple transformations one might imagine on a block of data, and they are named in the literature as *substitutions* and *permutations* (which is the only reason we are using those names—we would have chosen different words, perhaps the term *bit shuffle* instead of *permutation*). Let's assume we are encrypting k-bit blocks:

A **substitution** specifies, for each of the 2^k possible values of the input, the k-bit output. As noted above, this would be impractical to build for 64-bit blocks, but would be possible with blocks of length, say, 8 bits. To specify a completely randomly chosen substitution for k-bit blocks would take about $k \cdot 2^k$ bits.

A **permutation** specifies, for each of the k input bits, the output position to which it goes. For instance, the 1st bit might become the 13th bit of output, the 2nd bit would become the 61st bit of output, and so on. To specify a completely randomly chosen permutation of k bits would take about $k \log_2 k$ bits (for each of the k bits, one has to specify which bit position it will be in the output, and it only takes $\log_2 k$ bits to specify k values).

A permutation is a special case of a substitution in which each bit of the output gets its value from exactly one of the bits of the input. The number of permutations is sufficiently small that it is possible to specify and build an arbitrary 64-bit permuter.

One possible way to build a secret key algorithm is to break the input into manageable-sized chunks (say 8 bits), do a substitution on each small chunk, and then take the outputs of all the substitutions and run them through a permuter that is as big as the input, which shuffles the bits around. Then the process is repeated, so that each bit winds up as input to each of the substitutions. (See Figure 3-1.)

Each time through is known as a **round**. If we do only a single round, then a bit of input can only affect 8 bits of output, since each input bit goes into only one of the substitutions. On the second round, the 8 bits affected by a particular input bit get spread around due to the permutation, and assuming each of those 8 bits goes into a different substitution, then the single input bit will affect all the output bits. Just as when shuffling a deck of cards, there is an optimal number of rounds (shuffles). Once the cards are sufficiently randomized, extra shuffles just waste time. Part of the design of an algorithm is determining the best number of rounds (for optimal security, at least enough rounds to randomize as much as possible; for efficiency reasons no more rounds than necessary).

Another important feature of an encryption mechanism is it must be efficient to reverse, given the key. An algorithm like the one above would take the same effort to decrypt as to encrypt, since each of the steps can be run as efficiently backwards as forwards.

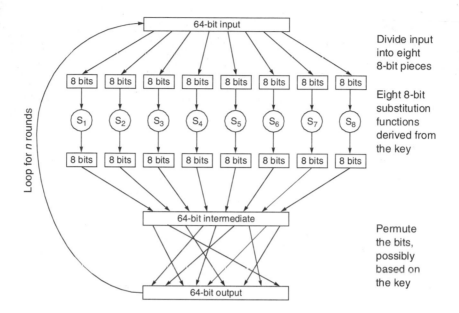

Figure 3-1. Example of Block Encryption

3.3 DATA ENCRYPTION STANDARD (DES)

DES was published in 1977 by the National Bureau of Standards for use in commercial and unclassified (hmm...) U.S. Government applications. It was based on an algorithm known as the *Lucifer cipher* designed by IBM. DES uses a 56-bit key, and maps a 64-bit input block into a 64-bit output block. The key actually looks like a 64-bit quantity, but one bit in each of the 8 bytes is used for odd parity on each byte. Therefore, only 7 of the bits in each byte are actually meaningful as a key.

DES is efficient to implement in hardware but relatively slow if implemented in software. Although making software implementations difficult was not a documented goal of DES, people have asserted that DES was specifically designed with this in mind, perhaps because this would limit its use to organizations that could afford hardware-based solutions, or perhaps because it made it easier to control access to the technology. At any rate, advances in CPUs have made it feasible to do DES in software. For instance, a 50-MIP CPU can encrypt at about 300 Kbytes per second (and perhaps more depending on the details of the CPU design and the cleverness of the implementation). This is adequate for many applications.

Why 56 bits?

Use of a 56-bit key is one of the most controversial aspects of DES. Even before DES was adopted, people outside of the intelligence community complained that 56 bits provided inadequate security [DENN82, DIFF76a, DIFF77, HELL79]. So why were only 56 of the 64 bits of a DES key used in the algorithm? The disadvantage of using 8 bits of the key for parity checking is that it makes DES considerably less secure (256 times less secure against exhaustive search).

OK, so what is the advantage of using 8 bits of the key for parity? Well, uh, let's say you receive a key electronically, and you want to sanity-check it to see if it could actually be a key. If you check the parity of the quantity, and it winds up not having the correct parity, then you'll know something went wrong.

There are two problems with this reasoning. One is that there is a 1 in 256 chance (given the parity scheme) that even if you were to get 64 bits of garbage, that the result will happen to have the correct parity and therefore look like a key. That is way too large a possibility of error for it to afford any useful protection to any application. The other problem with the reasoning is that there is nothing terribly bad about getting a bad key. You'll discover the key is bad when you try to use it for encrypting or decrypting.

The key, at 56 bits, is pretty much universally acknowledged to be too small to be secure. Perhaps one might argue that a smaller key is an advantage because it saves storage— but that argument doesn't hold since nobody does data compression on the 64-bit keys in order to fit them into 56 bits. So what benefits are there to usurping 8 bits for parity that offset the loss in security?

People (not us, surely!) have suggested that our government consciously decided to weaken the security of DES just enough so that NSA would be able to break it. We would like to think there is an alternative explanation, but we have never heard a plausible one proposed. Ten years ago, 56 bits were probably just secure enough so that only an organization like NSA might be able to afford the compute power to break DES, but now that prices have fallen, a brute force DES-breaking device is within the budgets of small governments and drug dealers, though there is no reported instance of anyone building one.

Advances in semiconductor technology make the key length issue more critical. Chip speeds have caught up so that DES keys can be broken with a bit of cleverness and exhaustive search. Perhaps a 64-bit key might have extended its useful lifetime by a few years. Given hardware price/performance improving about 40% per year, keys must grow by about 1 bit every 2 years. Assuming 56 bits was just sufficient in 1979 (when DES was standardized), 64 bits would be about right in 1993, and 128 bits would suffice until 2121.

How secure is DES?

Suppose you have a single block of ⟨plaintext, ciphertext⟩. *Breaking* DES in this case would mean finding a key that maps that plaintext to that ciphertext. With DES implemented in software, it would take on the order of half a million MIP-years, through brute force, to find the key. (Is it possible to find the "wrong" key, given a particular pair? Might two different keys map the same plaintext to the same ciphertext? How many keys on the average map a particular pair? See Homework Problem 3).

Often the attacker does not have a ⟨plaintext, ciphertext⟩ block. Instead the attacker has a reasonable amount of ciphertext only. It might be known, for example, that the encrypted data is likely to be 7-bit ASCII. In that case, it is still just about as efficient to do brute-force search. The ciphertext is decrypted with the guessed key, and if all the 8th bits are zero (which will happen with an incorrect key with probability 1 in 256), then another block is decrypted. After several (say 10) blocks are decrypted, and the result always appears to be 7-bit ASCII, the key has a high probability of being correct.

Current DES chips do not lend themselves to doing exhaustive key search—they allow encrypting lots of data with a particular key. The relative speed of key loading is much less than the speed of encrypting data. It would be straightforward to design and manufacture a key-searching DES chip, but it is luckily outside the resources of a hobbyist, and probably even an embezzler. It would be difficult to do in secret and suspicious to do publicly.

In 1977 [DIFF77], Diffie and Hellman did a detailed analysis of what it would cost to build a DES-breaking engine and concluded that for twenty million dollars you could build a million-chip machine that could find a DES key in twelve hours (given a ⟨plaintext, ciphertext⟩ pair). In 1995, we estimate that advances in chip densities and speeds would permit a several-thousand-chip machine to do the same job at a cost of well under a million dollars. Furthermore, design would be a substantial fraction of the cost, so additional capacity (in DES keys broken per day) would be relatively cheap. That cost will continue to drop.

There are published papers [BIHA93] claiming that less straightforward attacks can break DES faster than simply searching the key space. However, these attacks involve the premise, unlikely in real-life situations, that the attacker can choose lots of plaintext and obtain the corresponding ciphertext.

The reality is that, at least in 1995, DES is perfectly adequate for most applications. The cost of a DES-breaking machine is still prohibitive for hobbyists. Organized crime could most likely afford a DES-breaking machine, but there are easier ways of robbing banks. Most likely the NSA has built a DES-breaking machine, in fact one could probably even say they'd be derelict in their duties if they hadn't built such a device, but the NSA's budget is sufficient that they do not need to resort to robbing banks. The NSA isn't a law enforcement agency, so most likely even criminal uses of DES are safe. And although a DES-breaking machine is probably within the budget of other government agencies (for instance, the FBI), it would be unlikely that such agencies could construct such a device in secret.

Also, if it ever does get too easy to break DES, it is possible to encrypt multiple times with different keys (see §3.8 *Multiple Encryption DES*). It is generally believed that DES with triple encryption is 2^{56} times as difficult to crack and therefore will be secure for the forseeable future.

3.3.1 DES Overview

DES is quite understandable, and has some very elegant tricks. Let's start with the basic structure of DES (Figure 3-2).

The 64-bit input is subjected to an initial permutation to obtain a 64-bit result (which is just the input with the bits shuffled). The 56-bit key is used to generate sixteen 48-bit per-round keys, by taking a different 48-bit subset of the 56 bits for each of the keys. Each round takes as input the 64-bit output of the previous round, and the 48-bit per-round key, and produces a 64-bit output. After the 16th round, the 64-bit output is subjected to another permutation, which happens to be the inverse of the initial permutation.

That is the overview of how encryption works. Decryption works by essentially running DES backwards. To decrypt a block, you'd first run it through the initial permutation to undo the final permutation (the initial and final permutations are inverses of each other). You'd do the same key generation, though you'd use the keys in the opposite order (first use K_{16}, the key you generated last). Running a round backwards is quite interesting and not so straightforward. That will be explained when we explain what happens during a round. After 16 rounds of decryption, the output will be subjected to the final permutation (to undo the initial permutation).

To fully specify DES, we need to specify the initial and final permutations, how the per round keys are generated, and what happens during a round. Let's start with the initial and final permutations of the data.

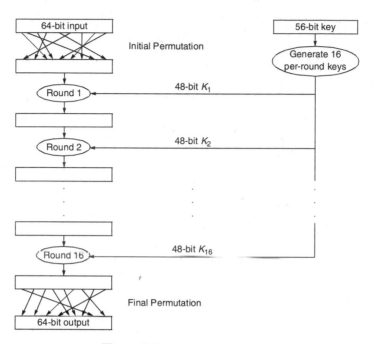

Figure 3-2. Basic Structure of DES

3.3.2 The Permutations of the Data

DES performs an initial and final permutation on the data, which do essentially nothing to enhance DES's security (see *Why permute?* on page 66). The most plausible reason for these permutations is to make DES less efficient to implement in software.

The way the permutations are specified in the DES spec is as follows:

Initial Permutation (IP)								Final Permutation (IP^{-1})							
58	50	42	34	26	18	10	2	40	8	48	16	56	24	64	32
60	52	44	36	28	20	12	4	39	7	47	15	55	23	63	31
62	54	46	38	30	22	14	6	38	6	46	14	54	22	62	30
64	56	48	40	32	24	16	8	37	5	45	13	53	21	61	29
57	49	41	33	25	17	9	1	36	4	44	12	52	20	60	28
59	51	43	35	27	19	11	3	35	3	43	11	51	19	59	27
61	53	45	37	29	21	13	5	34	2	42	10	50	18	58	26
63	55	47	39	31	23	15	7	33	1	41	9	49	17	57	25

The numbers in the above tables specify the bit numbers of the input to the permutation. The order of the numbers in the tables corresponds to the output bit position. So for example, the initial permutation moves input bit 58 to output bit 1 and input bit 50 to output bit 2.

The permutation is not a random-looking permutation. Figure 3-3 pictures it. The arrows indicate the initial permutation. Reverse the arrows to get the final permutation. We hope you

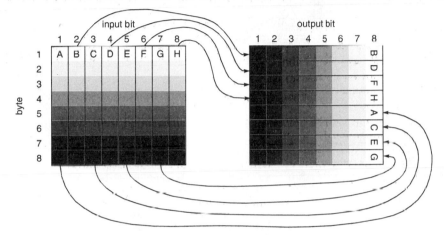

Figure 3-3. Initial Permutation of Data Block

appreciate the time we spent staring at the numbers and discovering this completely useless structure.

The input is 8 bytes. The output is 8 bytes. The bits in the first byte of input get spread into the 8th bits of each of the bytes. The bits in the second byte of input get spread into the 7th bits of all the bytes. And in general, the bits of the ith byte get spread into the $(9-i)^{th}$ bits of all the bytes. The pattern of spreading of the 8 bits in byte i of the input among the output bytes is that the even-numbered bits go into bytes 1–4, and the odd-numbered bits go into bytes 5–8. Note that if the data happens to be 7-bit ASCII, with the top bit set to zero, then after the permutation the entire 5th byte will be zero. Since the permutation appears to have no security value, it seems nearly certain that there is no security significance to this particular permutation.

3.3.3 Generating the Per-Round Keys

Next we'll specify how the sixteen 48-bit per-round keys are generated from the DES key. The DES key looks like it's 64 bits long, but 8 of the bits are parity. Let's number the bits of the DES key from left to right as 1, 2,…64. Bits 8, 16,…64 are the parity bits. DES performs a function, which we are about to specify, on these 64 bits to generate sixteen 48-bit keys, which are K_1, K_2,…K_{16}.

Why permute?

Why can't the initial and final permutations of the data be of security value? Well, suppose they were important, i.e., if DES did not have them it would be possible to break DES. Let's call a modified DES that does not have the initial and final permutation **EDS**. Let's say we can break EDS, i.e., given a ⟨plaintext, ciphertext⟩ EDS pair, we can easily calculate the EDS key that converts the plaintext into the ciphertext. In that case, we can easily break DES as well. Given a DES ⟨plaintext, ciphertext⟩ pair ⟨m,c⟩, we simply do the inverse of the initial permutation (i.e. the final permutation) on m to get m', and the inverse of the final permutation (i.e. the initial permutation) on c to get c', and feed ⟨m',c'⟩ to our EDS-breaking code. The resulting EDS key will work as the DES key for ⟨m,c⟩.

Note that when multiple encryptions of DES are being performed, the permutation might have some value. However, if encryption with key_1 is followed by encryption with key_2, then the final permutation following encryption with key_1 will cancel the initial permutation for key_2. That is one of the reasons people discuss alternating encrypt operations with decrypt operations (see §3.8 *Multiple Encryption DES*).

In §3.3.3 *Generating the Per-Round Keys*, we'll see there is also a permutation of the key. It also has no security value (by a similar argument).

First it does an initial permutation on the 56 useful bits of the key, to generate a 56-bit output, which it divides into two 28-bit values, called C_0 and D_0. The permutation is specified as

			C_0								D_0			
57	49	41	33	25	17	9		63	55	47	39	31	23	15
1	58	50	42	34	26	18		7	62	54	46	38	30	22
10	2	59	51	43	35	27		14	6	61	53	45	37	29
19	11	3	60	52	44	36		21	13	5	28	20	12	4

The way to read the table above is that the leftmost bit of the output is obtained by extracting bit 57 from the key. The next bit is bit 49 of the key, and so forth, with the final bit of D_0 being bit 4 of the key. Notice that none of the parity bits (8, 16,…64) is used in C_0 or D_0.

This permutation is not random. Figure 3-4 pictures it. Feel free to draw in any arrows or other graphic aids to make it clearer.

The initial and final permutations of the bits in the key have no security value (just like the initial and final permutations of the data), so the permutations didn't have to be random—the identity permutation would have done nicely.

1	2	3	4	5	6	7
9	10	11	12	13	14	15
17	18	19	20	21	22	23
25	26	27	28	29	30	31
33	34	35	36	37	38	39
41	42	43	44	45	46	47
49	50	51	52	53	54	55
57	58	59	60	61	62	63

$\Rightarrow$

57	49	41	33	25	17	9
1	58	50	42	34	26	18
10	2	59	51	43	35	27
19	11	3	60	52	44	36
63	55	47	39	31	23	15
7	62	54	46	38	30	22
14	6	61	53	45	37	29
21	13	5	28	20	12	4

Figure 3-4. Initial Permutation of Key

Now the generation of the K_i proceeds in 16 rounds (see Figure 3-5). The number of bits

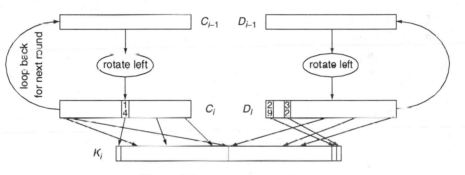

Figure 3-5. Round i for generating K_i

shifted is different in the different rounds. In rounds 1, 2, 9, and 16, it is a single-bit rotate left (with the bit shifted off the left end carried around and shifted into the right end). In the other rounds, it is a two-bit rotate left.

The permutations in this case are likely to be of some security value.

The permutation of C_i that produces the left half of K_i is the following. Note that bits 9, 18, 22, and 25 are discarded.

permutation to obtain the left half of K_i:

14	17	11	24	1	5
3	28	15	6	21	10
23	19	12	4	26	8
16	7	27	20	13	2

The permutation of the rotated D_{i-1} that produces the right half of K_i is as follows (where the bits of the rotated D_{i-1} are numbered 29, 30,…56, and bits 35, 38, 43, and 54 are discarded).

permutation to obtain the right half of K_i:

41	52	31	37	47	55
30	40	51	45	33	48
44	49	39	56	34	53
46	42	50	36	29	32

Each of the halves of K_i is 24 bits, so K_i is 48 bits long.

3.3.4 A DES Round

Now let's look at what a single round of DES does. Figure 3-6 shows both how encryption and decryption work.

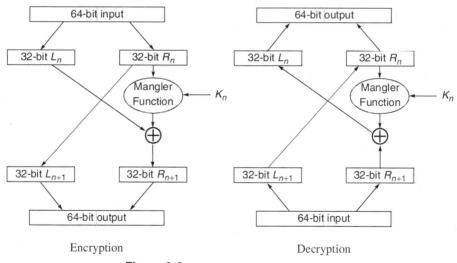

Figure 3-6. DES Encryption and Decryption

In encryption, the 64-bit input is divided into two 32-bit halves called L_n and R_n. The round generates as output 32-bit quantities L_{n+1} and R_{n+1}. The concatenation of L_{n+1} and R_{n+1} is the 64-bit output of the round.

L_{n+1} is simply R_n. R_{n+1} is obtained as follows. First R_n and K_n are input to what we call a *mangler function*, which outputs a 32-bit quantity. That quantity is $\oplus$'d with L_n to obtain the new R_{n+1}. The mangler takes as input 32 bits of the data plus 48 bits of the key to produce a 32-bit output.

Given the above, suppose you want to run DES backward, i.e. to decrypt something. Suppose you know L_{n+1} and R_{n+1}. How do you get L_n and R_n?

Well, R_n is just L_{n+1}. Now you know R_n, L_{n+1}, R_{n+1} and K_n. You also know that R_{n+1} equals $L_n \oplus \text{mangler}(R_n, K_n)$. You can compute $\text{mangler}(R_n, K_n)$, since you know R_n and K_n. Now $\oplus$ that with R_{n+1}. The result will be L_n. Note that the mangler is never run backwards. DES is elegantly designed to be reversible without constraining the mangler function to be reversible. Theoretically the mangler could map all values to zero, and it would still be possible to run DES backwards, but having the mangler function map all functions to zero would make DES pretty unsecure (see Homework Problem 5).

So you can reverse all the steps, one by one, to get back to the original message, i.e. the decrypted value.

3.3.5 The Mangler Function

The mangler function takes as input the 32-bit R_n, which we'll simply call R, and the 48-bit K_n, which we'll call K, and produces a 32-bit output which, when $\oplus$'d with L_n, produces R_{n+1} (the next R).

The mangler function first expands R from a 32-bit value to a 48-bit value. It does this by breaking R into eight 4-bit chunks and then expanding each of those chunks to 6 bits by taking the adjacent bits and concatenating them to the chunk. The leftmost and rightmost bits of R are considered adjacent.

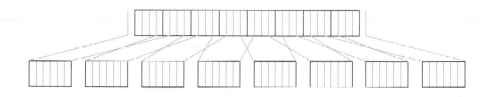

Figure 3-7. Expansion of R to 48 bits

The 48-bit K is broken into eight 6-bit chunks. Chunk i of the expanded R is $\oplus$'d with chunk i of K to yield a 6-bit output. That 6-bit output is fed into an **S box**, a substitution which produces a 4-bit output for each possible 6-bit input. Since there are 64 possible input values (6 bits) and only 16 possible output values (4 bits), the S box clearly maps several input values to the same output value. As it turns out, there are exactly four input values that map to each possible output value. There's even more pattern to it than that. Each S box could be thought of as four separate 4-bit to 4-

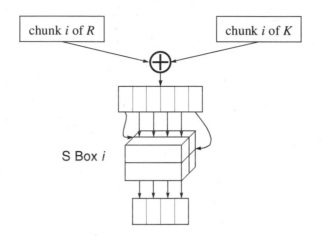

Figure 3-8. Chunk Transformation

bit S boxes, with the inner 4 bits of the 6-bit chunk serving as input, and the outer 2 bits selecting which of the four 4-bit S boxes to use. The S boxes are specified as follows:

Input bits 1 and 6   Input bits 2 thru 5

↓	0000	0001	0010	0011	0100	0101	0110	0111	1000	1001	1010	1011	1100	1101	1110	1111
00	1110	0100	1101	0001	0010	1111	1011	1000	0011	1010	0110	1100	0101	1001	0000	0111
01	0000	1111	0111	0100	1110	0010	1101	0001	1010	0110	1100	1011	1001	0101	0011	1000
10	0100	0001	1110	1000	1101	0110	0010	1011	1111	1100	1001	0111	0011	1010	0101	0000
11	1111	1100	1000	0010	0100	1001	0001	0111	0101	1011	0011	1110	1010	0000	0110	1101

Figure 3-9. Table of 4-bit outputs of S Box 1 (bits 1 thru 4)

Input bits 7 and 12   Input bits 8 thru 11

↓	0000	0001	0010	0011	0100	0101	0110	0111	1000	1001	1010	1011	1100	1101	1110	1111
00	1111	0001	1000	1110	0110	1011	0011	0100	1001	0111	0010	1101	1100	0000	0101	1010
01	0011	1101	0100	0111	1111	0010	1000	1110	1100	0000	0001	1010	0110	1001	1011	0101
10	0000	1110	0111	1011	1010	0100	1101	0001	0101	1000	1100	0110	1001	0011	0010	1111
11	1101	1000	1010	0001	0011	1111	0100	0010	1011	0110	0111	1100	0000	0101	1110	1001

Figure 3-10. Table of 4-bit outputs of S Box 2 (bits 5 thru 8)

Input bits 13 and 18　　　　　Input bits 14 thru 17

↓	0000	0001	0010	0011	0100	0101	0110	0111	1000	1001	1010	1011	1100	1101	1110	1111
00	1010	0000	1001	1110	0110	0011	1111	0101	0001	1101	1100	0111	1011	0100	0010	1000
01	1101	0111	0000	1001	0011	0100	0110	1010	0010	1000	0101	1110	1100	1011	1111	0001
10	1101	0110	0100	1001	1000	1111	0011	0000	1011	0001	0010	1100	0101	1010	1110	0111
11	0001	1010	1101	0000	0110	1001	1000	0111	0100	1111	1110	0011	1011	0101	0010	1100

Figure 3-11. Table of 4-bit outputs of S Box 3 (bits 9 thru 12)

Input bits 19 and 24　　　　　Input bits 20 thru 23

↓	0000	0001	0010	0011	0100	0101	0110	0111	1000	1001	1010	1011	1100	1101	1110	1111
00	0111	1101	1110	0011	0000	0110	1001	1010	0001	0010	1000	0101	1011	1100	0100	1111
01	1101	1000	1011	0101	0110	1111	0000	0011	0100	0111	0010	1100	0001	1010	1110	1001
10	1010	0110	1001	0000	1100	1011	0111	1101	1111	0001	0011	1110	0101	0010	1000	0100
11	0011	1111	0000	0110	1010	0001	1101	1000	1001	0100	0101	1011	1100	0111	0010	1110

Figure 3-12. Table of 4-bit outputs of S Box 4 (bits 13 thru 16)

Input bits 25 and 30　　　　　Input bits 26 thru 29

↓	0000	0001	0010	0011	0100	0101	0110	0111	1000	1001	1010	1011	1100	1101	1110	1111
00	0010	1100	0100	0001	0111	1010	1011	0110	1000	0101	0011	1111	1101	0000	1110	1001
01	1110	1011	0010	1100	0100	0111	1101	0001	0101	0000	1111	1010	0011	1001	1000	0110
10	0100	0010	0001	1011	1010	1101	0111	1000	1111	1001	1100	0101	0110	0011	0000	1110
11	1011	1000	1100	0111	0001	1110	0010	1101	0110	1111	0000	1001	1010	0100	0101	0011

Figure 3-13. Table of 4-bit outputs of S Box 5 (bits 17 thru 20)

Input bits 31 and 36　　　　　Input bits 32 thru 35

↓	0000	0001	0010	0011	0100	0101	0110	0111	1000	1001	1010	1011	1100	1101	1110	1111
00	1100	0001	1010	1111	1001	0010	0110	1000	0000	1101	0011	0100	1110	0111	0101	1011
01	1010	1111	0100	0010	0111	1100	1001	0101	0110	0001	1101	1110	0000	1011	0011	1000
10	1001	1110	1111	0101	0010	1000	1100	0011	0111	0000	0100	1010	0001	1101	1011	0110
11	0100	0011	0010	1100	1001	0101	1111	1010	1011	1110	0001	0111	0110	0000	1000	1101

Figure 3-14. Table of 4-bit outputs of S Box 6 (bits 21 thru 24)

Input bits 37 and 42   Input bits 38 thru 41

↓	0000	0001	0010	0011	0100	0101	0110	0111	1000	1001	1010	1011	1100	1101	1110	1111
00	0100	1011	0010	1110	1111	0000	1000	1101	0011	1100	1001	0111	0101	1010	0110	0001
01	1101	0000	1011	0111	0100	1001	0001	1010	1110	0011	0101	1100	0010	1111	1000	0110
10	0001	0100	1011	1101	1100	0011	0111	1110	1010	1111	0110	1000	0000	0101	1001	0010
11	0110	1011	1101	1000	0001	0100	1010	0111	1001	0101	0000	1111	1110	0010	0011	1100

Figure 3-15. Table of 4-bit outputs of S Box 7 (bits 25 thru 28)

Input bits 43 and 48   Input bits 44 thru 47

↓	0000	0001	0010	0011	0100	0101	0110	0111	1000	1001	1010	1011	1100	1101	1110	1111
00	1101	0010	1000	0100	0110	1111	1011	0001	1010	1001	0011	1110	0101	0000	1100	0111
01	0001	1111	1101	1000	1010	0011	0111	0100	1100	0101	0110	1011	0000	1110	1001	0010
10	0111	1011	0100	0001	1001	1100	1110	0010	0000	0110	1010	1101	1111	0011	0101	1000
11	0010	0001	1110	0111	0100	1010	1000	1101	1111	1100	1001	0000	0011	0101	0110	1011

Figure 3-16. Table of 4-bit outputs of S Box 8 (bits 29 thru 32)

The 4-bit output of each of the eight S boxes is combined into a 32-bit quantity whose bits are then permuted. A permutation at this point is of security value to DES in order to ensure that the bits of the output of an S box on one round of DES affects the input of multiple S boxes on the next round. Without the permutation, an input bit on the left would mostly affect the output bits on the left.

The actual permutation used is very random looking (we can't find any nice patterns to make the permutation easy to visualize—it's possible a non-random looking permutation would not be as secure).

| 16 | 7 | 20 | 21 | 29 | 12 | 28 | 17 | 1 | 15 | 23 | 26 | 5 | 18 | 31 | 10 | 2 | 8 | 24 | 14 | 32 | 27 | 3 | 9 | 19 | 13 | 30 | 6 | 22 | 11 | 4 | 25 |

Figure 3-17. Permutation of the 32 bits from the S boxes

The way to read this is that the 1st bit of output of the permutation is the 16th input bit, the 2nd output bit is the 7th input bit,…the 32nd output bit is the 25th input bit.

3.3.6 Weak and Semi-Weak Keys

We include this section mainly for completeness. There are sixteen DES keys that the security community warns people against using, because they have strange properties. But the probability of randomly generating one of these keys is only $16/2^{56}$, which in our opinion is nothing to worry about. It's probably equally insecure to use a key with a value less than a thousand, since an attacker might be likely to start searching for keys from the bottom.

Remember from §3.3.3 *Generating the Per-Round Keys* that the key is subjected to an initial permutation to generate two 28-bit quantities, C_0 and D_0. The sixteen suspect keys are ones for which C_0 and D_0 are one of the four values: all ones, all zeroes, alternating ones and zeroes, alternating zeroes and ones. Since there are four possible values for each half, there are sixteen possibilities in all. The four **weak keys** are the ones for which each of C_0 and D_0 are all ones or all zeroes. Weak keys are their own inverses.[1] The remaining twelve keys are the **semi-weak keys**. Each is the inverse of one of the others.

3.3.7 What's So Special About DES?

DES is actually quite simple, as is IDEA (which we'll explain next). One gets the impression that anyone could design a secret key encryption algorithm. Just take the bits, shuffle them, shuffle them some more, and you have an algorithm. In fact, however, these things are very mysterious. For example, the S boxes seem totally arbitrary. Did anyone put any thought into exactly what substitutions each S box should perform? Well, Biham and Shamir [BIHA91] have shown that with an incredibly trivial change to DES consisting of swapping S box 3 with S box 7, DES is about an order of magnitude less secure in the face of a specific (admittedly not very likely) attack.

It is unfortunate that the design process for DES was not more public. We don't know if the particular details were well-chosen for strength, whether someone flipped coins, for instance, to construct the S boxes, or even whether the particular details were well-chosen to have some sort of weakness that could only be exploited by someone involved in the design process. The claim for why the design process was kept secret, and it is a plausible claim, is that the DES designers knew about many kinds of cryptanalytic attacks, and that they specifically designed DES to be strong against all the ones they knew about. If they publicized the design process, they'd have to divulge all the cryptanalytic attacks they knew about, which would then further educate potential bad guys, which might make some cryptographic standards that were designed without this knowledge vulnerable.

In the hash algorithms designed by Ron Rivest (MD2, MD4, MD5), in order to eliminate the suspicion that they might be specifically chosen to have secret weaknesses, constants that should be reasonably random were chosen through some demonstrable manner, for instance by being the digits of an irrational number such as $\sqrt{2}$.

---

1. Two keys are inverses if encrypting with one is the same as decrypting with the other.

3.4 INTERNATIONAL DATA ENCRYPTION ALGORITHM (IDEA)

IDEA (International Data Encryption Algorithm) was originally called IPES (Improved Proposed Encryption Standard). It was developed by Xuejia Lai and James L. Massey of ETH Zuria.

IDEA was designed to be efficient to compute in software. It encrypts a 64-bit block of plaintext into a 64-bit block of ciphertext using a 128-bit key. It's relatively new (1991), but sufficiently published that cryptanalysts have had some amount of time to find weaknesses. So far none has been found, at least by the good guys (the ones who would publish their results).

IDEA is similar to DES in some ways. Both of them operate in rounds, and both have a complicated mangler function that does not have to be reversible in order for decryption to work. Instead, the mangler function is run in the same direction for encryption as decryption, in both IDEA and DES. In fact, both DES and IDEA have the property that encryption and decryption are identical except for key expansion. With DES, the same keys are used in the reverse order; with IDEA, the encryption and decryption keys are related in a more complex manner.

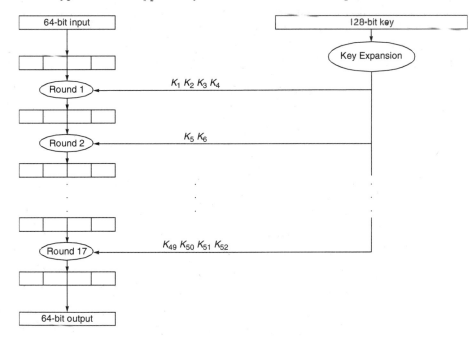

Figure 3-18. Basic Structure of IDEA

3.4.1 Primitive Operations

Each primitive operation in IDEA maps two 16-bit quantities into a 16-bit quantity. (In contrast, each DES S box maps a 6-bit quantity into a 4-bit quantity.) IDEA uses three operations, all easy to compute in software, to create a mapping. Furthermore, the operations are all reversible, which is important in order to run IDEA backwards (i.e., to decrypt).

The operations are bitwise exclusive or ($\oplus$), a slightly modified add (+), and a slightly modified multiply ($\otimes$). The reason add and multiply can't be used in the ordinary way is that the result has to be 16 bits, which won't always be the case when adding or multiplying two 16-bit quantities. Addition in IDEA is done by throwing away carries, which is equivalent to saying addition is mod 2^{16}. Multiplication in IDEA is done by first calculating the 32-bit result, and then taking the remainder when divided by $2^{16}+1$ (which can be done in a clever efficient manner). Multiplication mod $2^{16}+1$ is reversible, in the sense that every number x between 1 and 2^{16} has an inverse y (i.e., a number in the range 1 to 2^{16} such that multiplication by y will "undo" multiplication by x), because $2^{16}+1$ happens to be prime. There is one subtlety, though. The number 0, which can be expressed in 16 bits, would not have an inverse. And the number 2^{16}, which is in the proper range for mod $2^{16}+1$ arithmetic, cannot be expressed in 16 bits. So both problems are solved by treating 0 as an encoding for 2^{16}.

How are these operations reversible? Of course the operations are not reversible if all that is known is the 16-bit output. For instance, if we have inputs A and B, and perform $\oplus$ to obtain C, we can't find A and B from C alone. However, when running IDEA backwards we will have C and B, and will use that to obtain A. $\oplus$ is easy. If you know B and C, then you can simply do $B \oplus C$ to get A. B is its own inverse with $\oplus$. + is easy, too. You compute $-B$ (mod 2^{16}). If you know C and $-B$, then you can find A by doing $C + -B$. With $\otimes$ you find B^{-1} (mod $2^{16}+1$) using Euclid's algorithm—see §6.4 *Euclid's Algorithm*, and you perform $C \otimes B^{-1}$ to get A.

The only part of IDEA that isn't necessarily reversible is the mangler function, and it is truly marvelous to note how IDEA's design manages not to require a reversible mangler function (see §3.4.3.2 *Even Round*).

3.4.2 Key Expansion

The 128-bit key is expanded into 52 16-bit keys, $K_1, K_2, ...K_{52}$. The key expansion is done differently for encryption than for decryption. Once the 52 keys are generated, the encryption and decryption operations are the same.

The 52 encryption keys are generated by writing out the 128-bit key and, starting from the left, chopping off 16 bits at a time. This generates eight 16-bit keys (see Figure 3-19).

The next eight keys are generated by starting at bit 25, and wrapping around to the beginning when the end is reached (see Figure 3-20).

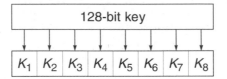

Figure 3-19. Generation of keys 1 through 8

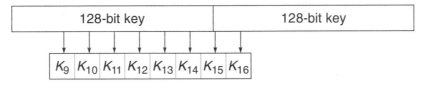

Figure 3-20. Generation of keys 9 through 16

The next eight keys are generated by offsetting 25 more bits, and so forth, until 52 keys are generated. The last offset starts at bit 23 and only needs 4 keys, so bits 1 thru 22 and bits 87 thru 128 get used in keys once less than bits 23 thru 86.

Warning! If you're actually going to implement this, we lied a bit above because there's a strange quirk in IDEA. Possibly due to someone mixing up the labels on a diagram of IDEA, the keys K_{50} and K_{51} are swapped. That means that an implementation has to swap encryption keys K_{50} and K_{51} after generating them as described above.

We'll discuss how to generate the 52 decryption keys after we finish describing IDEA.

3.4.3 One Round

Like DES, IDEA is performed in rounds. It has 17 rounds, where the odd-numbered rounds are different from the even-numbered rounds. (Note that in other descriptions of IDEA, it is described as having 8 rounds, where those rounds do the work of two of our rounds. Our explanation is functionally equivalent. It's just that we think it's clearer to explain it as having 17 rounds.)

Each round takes the input, a 64-bit quantity, and treats it as four 16-bit quantities, which we'll call X_a, X_b, X_c, and X_d. Mathematical functions are performed on X_a, X_b, X_c, X_d to yield new versions of X_a, X_b, X_c, X_d.

The odd rounds use four of the K_i, which we'll call K_a, K_b, K_c, and K_d. The even rounds use two K_i, which we'll call K_e and K_f. So round one uses K_1, K_2, K_3, K_4 (i.e., in round 1, $K_a = K_1$,

$K_b = K_2$, $K_c = K_3$, $K_d = K_4$). Round 2 uses K_5 and K_6 (i.e., in round 2, $K_e = K_5$ and $K_f = K_6$). Round 3 uses K_7, K_8, K_9, K_{10} ($K_a = K_7$ etc). Round 4 uses K_{11} and K_{12}, and so forth.

An odd round, therefore has as input X_a, X_b, X_c, X_d and keys K_a, K_b, K_c, K_d. An even round has as input X_a, X_b, X_c, X_d and keys K_e and K_f.

3.4.3.1 Odd Round

The odd round is simple. X_a is replaced by $X_a \otimes K_a$. X_d is replaced by $X_d \otimes K_d$. X_c is replaced by $X_b + K_b$. X_b is replaced by $X_c + K_c$.

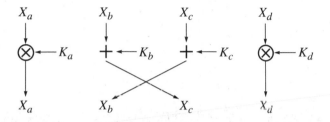

Figure 3-21. IDEA Odd Round

Note that this is easily reversible. To get from the new X_a to the old X_a, we perform $\otimes$ with the multiplicative inverse of K_a, mod $2^{16}+1$. Likewise with X_d. To get the old X_b, given the new X_c, we add the additive inverse of K_b, i.e., we subtract K_b.

So when decrypting, the odd rounds run as before, but with the mathematical inverses of the keys. This will undo the work that was done during that round in encryption.

3.4.3.2 Even Round

The even round is a little more complicated. Again, we have X_a, X_b, X_c, and X_d. We have two keys, K_e and K_f. We're going to first compute two values, which we'll call Y_{in} and Z_{in}. We'll do a function, which we'll call the *mangler function*, which takes as input Y_{in}, Z_{in}, K_e, and K_f and produces what we'll call Y_{out} and Z_{out}. We'll use Y_{out} and Z_{out} to modify X_a, X_b, X_c, and X_d.

$$Y_{in} = X_a \oplus X_b \qquad Z_{in} = X_c \oplus X_d$$

$$Y_{out} = ((K_e \otimes Y_{in}) + Z_{in}) \otimes K_f \qquad Z_{out} = (K_e \otimes Y_{in}) + Y_{out}$$

Now we compute the new X_a, X_b, X_c, and X_d.

$$\text{new } X_a = X_a \oplus Y_{out} \qquad \text{new } X_b = X_b \oplus Y_{out}$$

$$\text{new } X_c = X_c \oplus Z_{out} \qquad \text{new } X_d = X_d \oplus Z_{out}$$

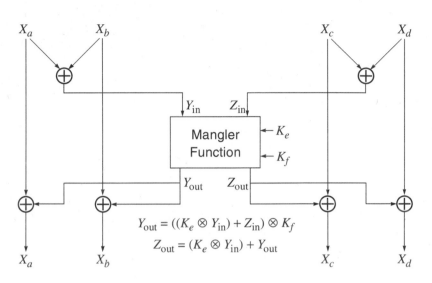

Figure 3-22. IDEA Even Round

How is the work of an even round reversed? This is truly spectacular (we don't get out much). The even round is its own inverse! When performing decryption, the same keys are used as when performing encryption (not the mathematical inverses of the keys, as in the odd rounds).

The even round takes as input the four quantities X_a, X_b, X_c, and X_d, together with keys K_e and K_f, and produces new X_a, new X_b, new X_c, and new X_d. If new X_a, new X_b, new X_c, and new X_d (with the same K_e and K_f) are fed into the even round, the output is the old X_a, X_b, X_c, and X_d. Why is this true?

Note that new $X_a = X_a \oplus Y_{\text{out}}$ and new $X_b = X_b \oplus Y_{\text{out}}$. In the beginning of the round, X_a and X_b are $\oplus$'d together, and the result is Y_{in}, the input to the mangler function. What if we use new X_a and new X_b instead of X_a and X_b? (new X_a) $\oplus$ (new X_b) = $(X_a \oplus Y_{\text{out}}) \oplus (X_b \oplus Y_{\text{out}}) = X_a \oplus X_b$. So Y_{in} will be the same, whether X_a and X_b are the inputs, or new X_a and new X_b are the inputs. The same is true for X_c and X_d. (Z_{in} is the same value whether the inputs X_c and X_d are used, or inputs new X_c and new X_d are used.) So we've shown that the input to the mangler function is the same whether the input is X_a, X_b, X_c, and X_d or whether the input is new X_a, new X_b, new X_c, and new X_d.

That means the output of the mangler function will be the same whether you're doing encryption (starting with X_a, etc) or decryption (starting with new X_a, etc). We called the outputs of the mangler function Y_{out} and Z_{out}. To get the first output of the round (new X_a, in the case of encryption), we take the first input (X_a) and $\oplus$ it with Y_{out}. We're going to show that with inputs of new X_a, new X_b, new X_c, and new X_d, the output of the round is X_a, X_b, X_c, and X_d, i.e., that running the round with the output results in getting the input back.

We'll use as inputs new X_a, new X_b, new X_c, and new X_d, and we know that Y_{out} and Z_{out} are the same as they would have been with inputs of X_a, X_b, X_c, and X_d. What happens in the round? The first output of the round is computed by taking the first input and $\oplus$ing it with Y_{out}. We also know (from the encryption round) that new $X_a = X_a \oplus Y_{out}$.

$$\text{first output} = \text{first input} \oplus Y_{out}$$

$$\text{first output} = (\text{new } X_a) \oplus Y_{out}$$

$$\text{first output} = (X_a \oplus Y_{out}) \oplus Y_{out} = X_a$$

Magic! With an input of new X_a, we get an output of X_a.

3.4.4 Inverse Keys For Decryption

IDEA is cleverly designed so that the same code (or hardware) can perform either encryption or decryption given different expanded keys. We want to compute inverse keys such that the encryption procedure, unmodified, will work as a decryption procedure. The basic idea is to take the inverses of the encryption keys and use them in the opposite order (use the inverse of the last-used encryption key as the first key used when doing decryption).

Remember that for encryption, we generated 52 keys, K_1 through K_{52}. We use four of them in each of the odd rounds, and two of them in each of the even rounds. And since we are working backwards, the first decryption keys should be inverses of the last-used encryption keys. Given that the final keys used are K_{49}, K_{50}, K_{51}, and K_{52}, in an odd round, the first four decryption keys will be inverses of the keys K_{49}–K_{52}. K_{49} is used in $\otimes$, so the decryption key K_1 will be the multiplicative inverse of K_{49} mod $2^{16}+1$. And the decryption key K_4 is the multiplicative inverse of K_{52}. Decryption keys K_2 and K_3 are the additive inverses of K_{50} and K_{51} (meaning negative K_{50} and K_{51}).

In the even rounds, as we explained, the keys do not have to be inverted. The same keys are used for encryption as decryption.

3.4.5 Does IDEA Work?

The definition of "working" is that decryption really does undo encryption, and that is easy to see. Whether it is secure or not depends on the Fundamental Tenet of Cryptography, as nobody has yet published results on how to break it. Certainly, breaking IDEA by exhaustive search for the 128-bit key requires currently unbelievable computing resources.

3.5 USING SECRET KEY CRYPTOGRAPHY IN PROTOCOLS

We've covered how to encrypt a 64-bit block with DES or IDEA, but that doesn't really tell how to use these algorithms. For instance, sometimes messages to be encrypted don't happen to be 64 bits long. We also mentioned in §2.4.5 *Integrity Check* that it was possible, using a secret key encryption scheme, to generate a MIC (message integrity code). The rest of this chapter will attempt to tie up these various loose ends.

3.6 ENCRYPTING A LARGE MESSAGE

How do you encrypt a message larger than 64 bits? There are several schemes defined in [DES81]. These schemes would be equally applicable to IDEA or any secret key scheme that encrypted fixed-length blocks, and no doubt one could come up with variant schemes as well. The ones defined in [DES81], and which we'll describe in detail, are:

1. Electronic Code Book (ECB)

2. Cipher Block Chaining (CBC)

3. *k*-Bit Cipher Feedback Mode (CFB)

4. *k*-Bit Output Feedback Mode (OFB)

3.6.1 Electronic Code Book (ECB)

This mode consists of doing the obvious thing, and it is usually the worst method. You break the message into 64-bit blocks (padding the last one out to a full 64 bits), and encrypt each block with the secret key (see Figure 3-23). The other side receives the encrypted blocks and decrypts each block in turn to get back the original message (see Figure 3-24).

There are a number of problems with this approach that don't show up in the single-block case. First, if a message contains two identical 64-bit blocks, the corresponding two blocks of ciphertext will be identical. This will give an eavesdropper some information. Whether it is useful or not depends on the context. We'll give an example where ECB would have a problem. Suppose that the eavesdropper knows that the plaintext is an alphabetically sorted list of employees and salaries being sent from management to payroll, tabularly arranged (see Figure 3-25).

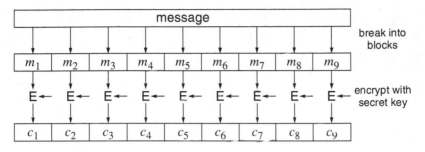

Figure 3-23. Electronic Code Book Encryption

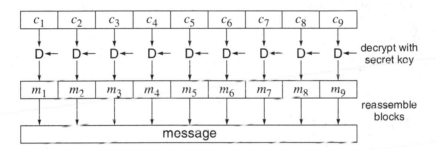

Figure 3-24. Electronic Code Book Decryption

Name	Position	Salary
Adams, John	President	78,964.31
Bush, Neil	Accounting Clerk	623,321.16
Hoover, J. Edgar	Wardrobe Consultant	34,445.22
Stein, Howard	Affirmative Action Officer	38,206.51
Woods, Rosemary	Audiovisual Supervisor	21,489.15

Block boundaries

Figure 3-25. Payroll Data

Further suppose that, as luck would have it, each line is exactly 64 bytes long, and the blocks happen to be divided in the salary field between the 1,000's and the 10,000's digit. Since identical plaintext blocks produce identical ciphertext blocks, not only can an eavesdropper figure out which sets of employees have identical salaries, but also which sets of employees have salaries in the same $10,000 ranges. If he can guess a few relative salaries, he will have a pretty good idea of what all the salaries are from this "encrypted" message.

Furthermore, if the eavesdropper is one of the employees, he can alter the message to change his own salary to match that of any other employee by copying the ciphertext blocks from that employee to the corresponding blocks of his own entry. Even a human looking at the resulting message would see nothing awry.

So, ECB has two serious flaws. Someone seeing the ciphertext can gain information from repeated blocks, and someone can rearrange blocks or modify blocks to his own advantage. As a result of these flaws, ECB is rarely used to encrypt messages.

3.6.2 Cipher Block Chaining (CBC)

CBC is a method of avoiding some of the problems in ECB. Using CBC, even if the same block repeats in the plaintext, it will not cause repeats in the ciphertext.

First we'll give an example of how this might be accomplished. Our example is not CBC, but it helps for understanding CBC.

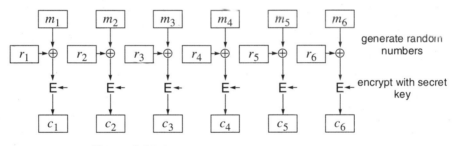

Figure 3-26. Randomized Electronic Code Book Encryption

Generate a 64-bit random number r_i for each plaintext block m_i to be encrypted. $\oplus$ the plaintext block with the random number, encrypt the result, and transmit both the unencrypted random number r_i and the ciphertext block c_i (see Figure 3-26). To decrypt this, you'd decrypt all the c_is, and for each c_i, after decrypting it, you'd $\oplus$ it with the random number r_i.

The main problem with this scheme is efficiency. It causes twice as much information to be transmitted, since a random number has to be transmitted along with each block of ciphertext. Another problem with it is that an attacker can rearrange the blocks and have a predictable effect on the resulting plaintext. For instance, if $r_2|c_2$ were removed entirely it would result in m_2 being absent in the decrypted plaintext. Or if $r_2|c_2$ were swapped with $r_7|c_7$, then m_2 and m_7 would be swapped in the result. Worse yet, an attacker knowing the value of any block m_n can change it in a predictable way by making the corresponding change in r_n.

Now we can explain CBC. CBC generates its own "random numbers". It uses c_i as r_{i+1}. In other words, it takes the previous block of ciphertext and uses that as the random number that will be $\oplus$'d into the next plaintext. To avoid having two plaintext messages that start the same wind up with the same ciphertext in the beginning, CBC does select one random number, which gets $\oplus$'d into the first block of plaintext, and transmits it along with the data. This initial random number is known as an **IV** (**initialization vector**).

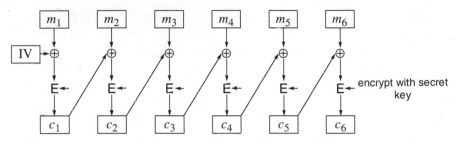

Figure 3-27. Cipher Block Chaining Encryption

Decryption is simple because $\oplus$ is its own inverse.

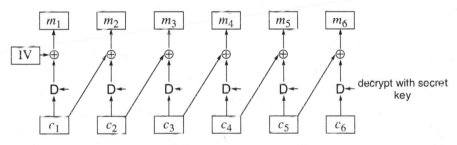

Figure 3-28. Cipher Block Chaining Decryption

Since the cost of the $\oplus$ is trivial compared to the cost of an encryption, CBC encryption has the same performance as ECB encryption except for the cost of generating and transmitting the IV.

In many cases the security of CBC would not be adversely affected by omitting the IV (or, equivalently, using the value 0 as the IV). However, we'll give one example where it would matter. Suppose the encrypted file of employees and salaries is transmitted weekly. If there were no IV, then an eavesdropper could tell where the ciphertext first differed from the previous week, and therefore perhaps determine the first person whose salary had changed.

Another example is where a general sends information each day saying continue holding your position. The ciphertext will be the same every day, until the general decides to send something else, like start bombing. Then the ciphertext would suddenly change, alerting the enemy.

A randomly chosen IV guarantees that even if the same message is sent repeatedly, the ciphertext will be completely different each time.

Finally, a randomly chosen IV prevents attackers from supplying chosen plaintext to the underlying encryption algorithm even if they can supply chosen plaintext to the CBC.

3.6.2.1 CBC Threat 1—Modifying Ciphertext Blocks

Using CBC does not eliminate the problem of someone modifying the message in transit; it does change the nature of the threat. Attackers can no longer see repeated values and simply copy or move ciphertext blocks in order to, say, swap the janitor's salary with the salary of the VP of marketing. But they certainly can still modify the ciphertext. What would happen if they changed a block of the ciphertext, say the value of ciphertext block c_n? c_n gets $\oplus$'d with the decrypted c_{n+1} to yield m_{n+1}, so changing c_n has a predictable effect on m_{n+1}. For instance, changing bit 3 of c_n changes bit 3 of m_{n+1}. c_n also gets decrypted, and then $\oplus$'d with c_{n-1} to produce m_n. Our attacker cannot know what a particular new value of c_n would decrypt to, so changing c_n will most likely garble m_n to some random 64-bit value.

For example, let's say our attacker knows that the plaintext corresponding to a certain byte range in the ciphertext is her personnel record:

```
   Tacker, Jo A          System Security Officer          54,122.10
   |         |         |         |         |         |         |         |
```

Let's say Jo wants to increase her salary by 20K. In this case she knows that the final byte of m_7 is the ten-thousands digit of her salary. The bottom three bits of the ASCII for 5 is 101. To give herself a raise of 20K, she merely has to flip the penultimate bit of c_6. Since c_6 gets $\oplus$'d into the decrypted c_7 (c_7 has not been modified, so the decrypted c_7 will be the same), the result will be the same as before, i.e. the old m_7, but with the penultimate bit flipped, which will change the ASCII 5 into a 7.

Unfortunately for Jo, as a side-effect a value she will not be able to predict will appear in her department field, since she cannot predict what the modified c_6 will decrypt to, which will affect m_6:

```
   Tacker, Jo A          System Security Of#f8Ts9(*          74,122.10
   |         |         |         |         |         |         |         |
```

A human who reads this report and issues checks is likely to suspect something is wrong; however, if it's just a program, it would be perfectly happy with it. And a bank would most likely take the check even if some unorthodox information appeared in what to them is a comment field.

In the above example, Jo made a change she could control in one block at the expense of getting a value she could neither control nor predict in the preceding block.

3.6.2.2 CBC Threat 2—Rearranging Ciphertext Blocks

Suppose Jo knows the plaintext and corresponding ciphertext of some message. So she knows $m_1, m_2,...m_n$. And she knows IV, c_1, $c_2,...c_n$. She will also know what each of the c_i decrypt to, since the decrypted version of c_i is $c_{i-1} \oplus m_i$ (see Figure 3-29).

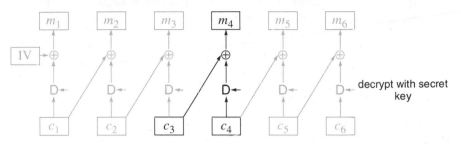

Figure 3-29. Cipher Block Chaining Decryption

Given this knowledge, she can consider each of the c_i as a *building block* and construct a ciphertext stream using any combination of c_i and she will be able to calculate what the corresponding plaintext would be.

How could this be useful? Well, admittedly it's stretching a bit, though people in the security field enjoy stretching. One of the ways to combat threat 1 is to attach a CRC to the plaintext before encrypting it with CBC. That way if Jo modifies any of the ciphertext blocks, the CRC will not match the message and a computer can verify that the message has been tampered with.

Still following? Well, suppose a 32-bit CRC is chosen. Then there is a 1 in 2^{32} chance that the CRC will happen to be correct after the message is tampered with. Suppose Jo doesn't care what she garbles the message to. She just wants the garbage accepted by the computer on the other side, knowing that it will check the CRC. Jo can try constructing lots of ciphertext streams out of c_1, $c_2,...c_n$, calculate the resulting plaintext from each one, and then test the resulting plaintext to see if the CRC comes out correct. On the average she will only have to try 2^{31} arrangements before being able to find a message that will have a correct CRC.

What harm could Jo do by garbling a message into something she could not control the contents of, but would be accepted by the computer on the other side? Perhaps Jo is just being malicious, and wants to destroy some data being loaded across the network. But there is a subtle way in which Jo can actually control the garbling of the message to a small extent. Suppose she moves contiguous blocks; for instance, she might move c_n and c_{n+1} to some other place. Then the original m_{n+1} will appear in that other position. Perhaps if m_{n+1} contains the president's salary, Jo can swap blocks so that her salary will be changed to his, but then she'll be forced to pretty much totally garble the entire rest of the file in order to find an arrangement of blocks that will result in a correct CRC.

To prevent Jo from being able to rearrange blocks to find something that will have a correct CRC, a 64-bit CRC could be used. This would certainly suffice if the only attack on the CRC inside CBC encoding was a brute force attack such as we described. There have been some interesting attacks suggested in the theoretical community [JUEN84] but these attacks are not practical. So not surprisingly, CBC is a popular way to encrypt messages, and people are not overly concerned with these threats (the second threat would be solved by using a message digest instead of a CRC—see Chapter 4 *Hashes and Message Digests*).

3.6.3 Output Feedback Mode (OFB)

Output feedback mode acts like a pseudorandom number generator. A message is encrypted by ⊕ing it with the pseudorandom stream generated by OFB.

Let's assume that the stream is created 64 bits at a time. To start, a random 64-bit number is generated, known as the IV (as in CBC mode). Let's call that b_0. Then b_0 is encrypted (using the secret key) to get b_1, which is in turn encrypted to get b_2, and so forth. The resulting pseudorandom stream is $b_0|b_1|b_2|b_3|\dots$.

To encrypt a message, merely ⊕ it with as many bits of $b_0|b_1|b_2|b_3|\dots$ as necessary. The result is transmitted along with the IV. The recipient computes the same pseudorandom stream based on knowledge of the secret key and the IV. To decrypt the message, the recipient merely ⊕s it with as many bits of $b_0|b_1|b_2|b_3|\dots$ as necessary.

A long random (or pseudorandom string) used to encrypt a message with a simple ⊕ operation is known as a **one-time pad**. The advantages of a system like this are:

1. The one-time pad can be generated in advance, before the message to be encrypted is known. When the message arrives to be encrypted, no costly cryptographic operations are needed. Instead only ⊕ is required, and ⊕ is extremely fast.

2. If some of the bits of the ciphertext get garbled, only those bits of plaintext get garbled, as opposed to in CBC mode where if c_n is garbled then m_n will be completely garbled and the same portion of m_{n+1} as was garbled in c_n will be garbled.

3. A message can arrive in arbitrary-sized chunks, and each time a chunk appears, the associated ciphertext can be immediately transmitted. In contrast, with CBC, if the message is arriving a byte at a time, it cannot be encrypted until an entire 64-bit block of plaintext is available for encryption. This results in either waiting until 7 more bytes arrive, or padding the plaintext to a multiple of 8 bytes before encrypting it, which yields more ciphertext to be transmitted and decrypted.

The disadvantages of OFB are:

1. If the plaintext and ciphertext are known by a bad guy, he can modify the plaintext into any-thing he wants by simply ⊕ing the ciphertext with the known plaintext, and ⊕ing the result with whatever message the bad guy wants to transmit.

The FIPS document specifies OFB as being capable of being generated in k-bit chunks. The description above would be equivalent to 64-bit OFB as documented in [DES81]. The way k-bit OFB (see Figure 3-30) works is as follows. The input to the DES encrypt function is initialized to some IV. If the IV is less than 64 bits long, it is padded with 0's on the left (most significant portion). The output will be a 64-bit quantity. Only k bits are used, which happen to be specified in [DES81] as the most significant k bits. Cryptographically, any k bits would do, though it is nice to standardize which bits will be selected so that implementations will interoperate. So, we've generated the first k bits of the one-time pad. Now the same k bits are shifted into the rightmost portion of the input, and what was in that register is shifted k bits to the left. Now k more bits of one-time pad are selected, as before.

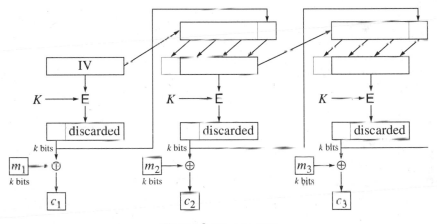

Figure 3-30. k-bit OFB

3.6.4 Cipher Feedback Mode (CFB)

CFB (see Figure 3-31) is very similar to OFB, in that k bits at a time are generated and ⊕'d with k bits of plaintext. In OFB the k bits that are shifted into the register used as the input to the DES encrypt are the output bits of the DES encrypt from the previous block. In contrast, in CFB, the k bits shifted in are the k bits of ciphertext from the previous block. So in CFB the one-time pad cannot be generated before the message is known (as it can be in OFB).

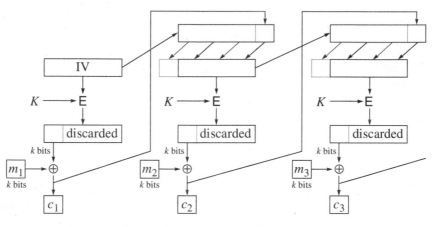

Figure 3-31. k-bit CFB

It is sensible to have k-bit CFB with k something other than 64, and in particular $k = 8$ makes sense. With OFB or CBC, if characters are lost in transmission, or extra characters are added to the ciphertext stream, the entire rest of the transmission is garbled. With 8-bit CFB, as long as the error is an integral number of bytes, things will resynchronize. If a byte is lost in transmission, one byte of plaintext will be lost and the next 8 bytes will be garbled. However, after that, the plaintext will decrypt properly. If a byte is added to the ciphertext stream, then a byte of garbage will be added to the plaintext stream, and the following 8 bytes of plaintext will be garbled, but after that it will decrypt properly. It does have the disadvantage that every byte of input requires a DES operation.

CFB-encrypted messages are somewhat less subject to tampering than either CBC or OFB. With 8-bit CFB it is possible for an attacker to change any individual byte of plaintext in a predictable way at the cost of unpredictably garbling the next 8 bytes. With 64-bit CFB it is possible for an attacker to modify any 64-bit block in a predictable way at the cost of unpredictably garbling the next 64-bit block. There is no block-rearranging attack as with CBC, though whole sections of the message can be rearranged at the cost of garbling the splice points.

In principle, CFB need not be used on a byte boundary. It could iterate for any integer number of bits up to a full block. In practice, it's only used on byte boundaries or as a full block. When done in full-block mode, it has performance comparable to ECB, CBC, and OFB; it has the OFB advantage of being able to encrypt and send each byte as it is known; it lacks OFB's ability to compute a substantial amount of pad ahead; and it detects alterations better than OFB but not as well as CBC.

3.7 GENERATING MICS

A secret key system can be used to generate a cryptographic checksum known as a MIC (message integrity code). While CBC, CFB, and OFB, when properly used, all offer good protection against an eavesdropper deciphering a message, none offers good protection against an eavesdropper who already knows the contents of the plaintext message modifying it undetected.

A standard way for protecting against undetected modifications is to compute the CBC but send only the last block along with the plaintext message. This last block is called the **CBC residue**. In order to compute the CBC residue, you have to know the secret key. If an attacker modifies any portion of a message, the residue will no longer be the correct value (except with probability 1 in 2^{64}). And the attacker will not be able to compute the residue for the modified message without knowing the secret key.

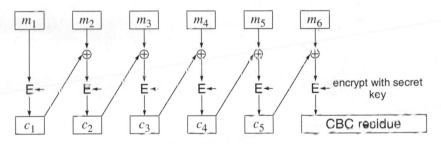

Figure 3-32. Cipher Block Chaining Residue

In this case, the picture for the recipient of the message is the same as for the sender. The recipient computes the CBC residue based on the plaintext message and sees whether it matches the one sent. If it does, someone who knew the key computed the MIC on that message.

In many contexts, messages are not secret but their integrity must be assured. In such contexts it is perfectly appropriate to transmit unencrypted data, plus a CBC residue. Interbank transfers are a traditional example (there may be a desire for secrecy as well, but it is dwarfed by the requirement for accuracy). But more commonly, there is a desire to encrypt messages for both privacy and integrity. This can be done with a single encryption operation if the message is a single block. What is the equivalent transformation on a multiblock message? (Keep reading to find out!)

3.7.1 Ensuring Privacy and Integrity Together

To summarize, if we have a message and we want to ensure its privacy, we can CBC-encrypt the message. If we have a message and we want to ensure its integrity, then we can send the CBC residue along with the message. It is natural to assume that if we want to be secure against both modification and eavesdropping that we ought to be able to do something like Figure 3-33.

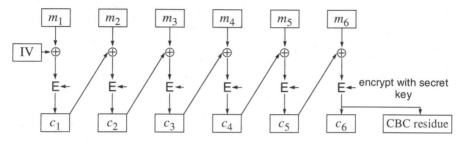

Figure 3-33. Cipher Block Chaining Encryption plus CBC Residue

Well, that can't be right. That consists of sending the CBC encrypted message and just repeating the final block. Anyone tampering with the CBC encrypted message could simply take the value of the final block they wanted to send, and send it twice. So sending the CBC residue in addition to the CBC encrypted message can't enhance security. Maybe simply sending the CBC encrypted message gives privacy and integrity protection. Well, when we say **integrity protection** we mean we'd like the receiving computer to automatically be able to tell if the message has been tampered with. With CBC alone there is no way to detect tampering automatically, since CBC is merely an encryption technique. Any random string of bits will decrypt into something, and the final 64 bits of that random string will be a "correct" CBC residue. So it is easy for anyone to modify the ciphertext, and a computer on the other side will decrypt the result, come up with garbage, but have no way of knowing that the result is garbage. If the message was an English message, and a human was going to look at it, then modification of the ciphertext would probably get detected, but if it is a computer merely loading the bits onto disk, there is no way for the computer to know, with this scheme, that the message has been modified.

OK, how about computing the CBC residue, attaching that to the plaintext, and then doing a CBC encryption of the concatenated quantity?

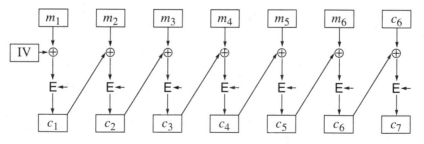

Figure 3-34. Cipher Block Chaining Encryption of Message with CBC Residue

It turns out that that doesn't work either. The last block is always the encryption of zero, since the $\oplus$ of anything with itself is always zero. An extra block that doesn't depend on the message can't offer any integrity protection.

So, what can we do? It is generally accepted as secure to protect the privacy of a message with CBC encryption and integrity with a CBC residue as long as the two are computed with different keys. Unfortunately, this requires twice the cryptographic power of encryption alone. Various shortcuts have been proposed and even deployed, but generally they have subtle cryptographic flaws. Whether those flaws are serious depends on the application and the cleverness of the attacker. It's instructive to look at some of the techniques.

3.7.2 CBC with a Weak Cryptographic Checksum

Jueneman proposed [JUEN84, JUEN85] that since using non-cryptographic checksums inside CBC did not appear to be secure, and since quality cryptographic checksums were expensive to compute, perhaps a "weak" cryptographic checksum inside a CBC would provide good security on the basis that the computational complexity of breaking the weak checksum would be multiplied by the limitations of having to do it under the constraints of the CBC. He proposed a weak cryptographic checksum for this use.

There is no reason to believe that this approach would not be effective, but it has not caught on. Ironically, Kerberos V4 (see §10.10 *Encryption for Integrity Only*) uses a variant of his weak checksum for integrity protection outside of an encrypted message, and there is no evidence that anyone has broken it.

3.7.3 CBC with a Cryptographic Hash

An approach gaining favor recently is to put a cryptographic hash of the message—typically 128 bits—inside and CBC encrypt the whole thing. This is probably secure (though it hasn't withstood the test of time), but it requires two cryptographic passes (just like doing CBC encryption and CBC residue with different keys). For software implementations, using a cryptographic hash for a MIC instead of a DES CBC residue has an advantage because DES was specifically designed to be inefficient when done in software while the currently favored message digest functions (MD2, MD4, MD5, SHS) were all designed to be efficient when done in software.

3.7.4 CBC Encryption and CBC Residue with Related Keys

It is generally accepted as secure to compute a message integrity code by computing a CBC residue and then encrypting the message using an independently chosen key. A trick used by Kerberos V5 is to use a modified version of the key for one of the operations. (Switching one bit should be sufficient, but Kerberos instead ⊕s the key with the constant $F0F0F0F0F0F0F0F0_{16}$. This has the nice properties of preserving key parity and never transforming a non-weak key into a weak key. See §3.3.6 *Weak and Semi-Weak Keys*.)

There are no known weaknesses in the approach of having one key be mathematically related to the other (as opposed to simply picking two random numbers for keys), but few advantages either. In general it's no harder to distribute a pair of keys than a single one, and having the keys be mathematically related saves no computational effort. The only advantage of deriving one key from the other is to get both privacy and integrity protection when a mechanism is in place for distributing only a single key.

3.8 MULTIPLE ENCRYPTION DES

The generally accepted method of making DES more secure through multiple encryptions is known as EDE (for encrypt–decrypt–encrypt).

Actually, any encryption scheme might be made more secure through multiple encryptions. Multiple encryption, though, has specifically been discussed in the industry in order to arrive at a "standard" means of effectively increasing DES's key length. EDE could as easily be done with, say, IDEA. It is more important with DES than with IDEA, though, because of DES's key length (or lack thereof).

Remember that a cryptographic scheme has two functions, known as *encrypt* and *decrypt*. The two functions are inverses of each other, but in fact each one takes an arbitrary block of data and garbles it in a way that is reversed by the other function. So it makes sense to perform decrypt on the plaintext as a method of encrypting it, and then perform encrypt on the result as a method of getting back to the plaintext again. It might be confusing to say something like *encrypt with decryption*, so we'll just refer to the two functions as E and D.

How to do multiple encryption is not completely obvious, especially since there is also the problem of turning block encryption into stream encryption. A common method of using EDE is:

1. Two keys are used: K_1 and K_2.

2. Each block of plaintext is subjected to E with K_1, then D with K_2, and then E with K_1. The result is simply a new secret key scheme—a 64-bit block is mapped to another 64-bit block.

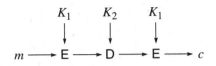

Decryption simply reverses the operation.

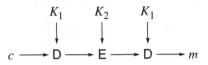

3. CBC is used to turn the block encryption scheme resulting from step 2 into a stream encryption (Figure 3-35).

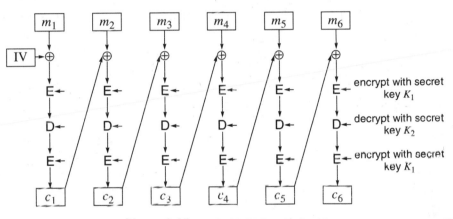

Figure 3-35. EDE with CBC on the Outside

Now we'll discuss why EDE is defined this way. There are various choices that could have been made:

1. Three encryptions were chosen. It could have been 2 or 714. Is three the right number?

2. Why are the functions EDE rather than, say, EEE or EDD?

3. Why is the cipher block chaining done on the outside rather than on the inside? Doing CBC on the **inside** (Figure 3-36) means completely encrypting the message with CBC, then completely decrypting the result with CBC using a second key, and then completely CBC-encrypting the message again. Doing CBC on the **outside** (Figure 3-35) means performing the DES encryptions and decryption on each block, but only doing the CBC once.

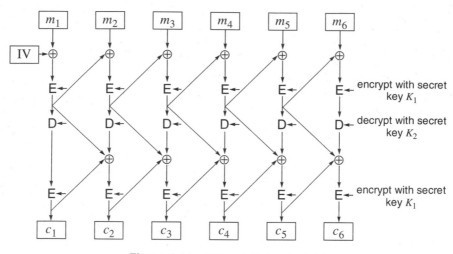

Figure 3-36. EDE with CBC on the Inside

3.8.1 How Many Encryptions?

Let's assume that the more times the block is encrypted, the more secure it is. So encrypting 749 times would therefore be some amount more secure than encrypting 3 times. The problem is, it is expensive to do an encryption. We don't want to do any more encryptions than are necessary for the scheme to be really secure.

3.8.1.1 Encrypting Twice with the Same Key

Suppose we didn't want to bother reading in two keys. Would it make things more secure if we encrypted twice in a row with the same key?

$$\text{plaintext} \xrightarrow{\quad K \quad} \xrightarrow{\quad K \quad} \text{ciphertext}$$

This turns out not to be much more secure than single encryption with K, since exhaustive search of the keyspace still requires searching only 2^{56} keys. Each step of testing a key is twice as much work, since the attacker needs to do double encryption, but a factor of two for the attacker is not considered much added security, especially since the good guys have their work doubled with this scheme as well.

(How about E followed by D using the same key? That's double the work for the good guy and no work for the bad guy, so that's generally not considered good cryptographic form.)

3.8.1.2 Encrypting Twice with Two Keys

If encrypting twice, using two different keys, were as secure as a DES-like scheme with a key length of 112 bits, then encrypting twice would have sufficed. However, it isn't, as we will show.

We'll use two DES keys, K_1 and K_2, and encrypt each block twice, first using key K_1 and then using key K_2. For the moment, let's ignore any block chaining schemes and assume we're just doing block encryption.

$$\text{plaintext} \xrightarrow{\ K_1\ } \xrightarrow{\ K_2\ } \text{ciphertext}$$

Is this as cryptographically strong as using a double-length secret key (112 bits)? The reason you might think it would be as strong as a 112-bit key is that the straightforward brute force attack would have to guess both K_1 and K_2 in order to determine if a particular plaintext block encrypted to a particular ciphertext block.

However, there is a less straightforward attack that breaks double-encryption DES in roughly twice the time of a brute-force breaking of single-encryption DES. The attack is not particularly practical, but the fact that it exists makes double encryption sufficiently suspect that it's not generally done.

The threat involves the following steps:

1. Assume you have a few ⟨plaintext, ciphertext⟩ pairs ⟨m_1,c_1⟩, ⟨m_2,c_2⟩, ⟨m_3,c_3⟩ where c_i was derived from doubly encrypting m_i with K_1 and K_2. You want to find K_1 and K_2.

2. First make Table A with 2^{56} entries, where each entry consists of a DES key K and the result r of applying that key to encrypt m_1. Sort the table in numerical order by r.

3. Now make Table B with 2^{56} entries, where each entry consists of a DES key K and the result r of applying that key to decrypt c_1. Sort the table in numerical order by r.

4. Search through the sorted lists to find matching entries, ⟨K_A,r⟩ from table A and ⟨K_B,r⟩ from Table B. Each match provides K_A as a candidate K_1 and K_B as a candidate K_2 because K_A encrypts m_1 to r and K_B encrypts r to c_1.

5. If there are multiple intermediate values (which there almost certainly will be), test the candidate K_1 and K_2 against m_2 and c_2. If you've tested all the candidate ⟨K_1,K_2⟩ pairs and multiple of them work on m_2 and c_2, then try m_3 and c_3. The correct pair will always work, of course, and an incorrect pair will almost certainly fail to work on any particular ⟨m_i,c_i⟩ pair. (See below for exact numbers, if you care.)

This attack is not really practical, since a table of size 2^{56} is a bit daunting. The existence of the attack, though, is enough reason to bother doing triple DES encryption. It may be that double encryption would be good enough, but since triple encryption isn't that much harder, it will save you from defending yourself to management when they ask you why you're doing double encryption when they've heard that double encryption isn't secure.

How many matches should you expect to find after searching the two tables? Well, there are 2^{64} possible blocks, and only 2^{56} table entries (because there are only 2^{56} keys). Therefore each 64-bit block has only a 1 in 256 chance of appearing in one of the tables. Of the 2^{56} blocks that appear in Table A, only 1/256 of them also appear in Table B. That means that there should be about 2^{48} entries which appear in both tables. One of those corresponds to the correct $\langle K_1, K_2 \rangle$ pair and the others are imposters. We'll test them against $\langle m_2, c_2 \rangle$. If $\langle K_1, K_2 \rangle$ is an imposter, the probability that $D(c_2, K_2)$ will equal $E(m_2, K_1)$ is about $1/2^{64}$. There are about 2^{48} imposters, so the probability of one of them satisfying $D(c_2, K_2) = E(m_2, K_1)$ is about $2^{48}/2^{64}$, or roughly 1 in 2^{16}. Each test against an additional $\langle m_i, c_i \rangle$ reduces the probability by a factor of 2^{64}, so the probability that there will still be false matches after trying three $\langle m, c \rangle$ pairs is about $1/2^{80}$.

3.8.1.3 Triple Encryption

EDE does triple encryption. Why does EDE use only two keys? Presumably, security cannot possibly be enhanced because K_1 is used twice rather than using a third key. People assume using K_1 twice in this way is sufficiently secure that there's no reason to bother generating, transmitting, and storing a third key. For avoiding the brute-force exhaustive key space attack, 112 bits of key is considered sufficient, and no attacks other than the straightforward brute-force search is known for EDE.

An esoteric reason for using only two keys is that in some applications (like §4.2.4.1 *UNIX Password Hash*) an important property of a cryptosystem is that given a $\langle$plaintext, ciphertext$\rangle$ pair, it is impractical to find any key that maps the plaintext to the ciphertext. (With 64-bit blocks and 112-bit keys, there will be lots of such keys.) Using EDE with three keys, it is straightforward to find a triple of keys that maps a given plaintext to a given ciphertext (Homework Problem 14). There is no known practical way of finding such a triple with $K_1 = K_3$.

Why is K_2 used in decrypt mode? Admittedly, it is no more trouble to run DES in either mode, and either way gives a mapping. DES would be just as good always done backwards (i.e., change the meaning of *encrypt* and *decrypt*). One reason for the choice of EDE is that an EDE system with $K_1 = K_2$ is equivalent to simple DES, so that such a system can interoperate with a simple DES system. Another reason to do EDE rather than EEE is that if E is followed by E, then the initial permutation before the second E will reverse the final permutation after the first E. As we said in §3.3.2 *The Permutations of the Data*, there is no security value in the initial or final permutation, at least when a single encryption is done. However, there might conceivably be some security gained by having a permutation done between encryption steps. Doing E followed by D results in doing the final permutation twice, once after E and once at the beginning of D. Doing the final permutation twice results in some permutation (Homework Problem 17). Likewise, doing D followed by E results in doing the initial permutation twice.

3.8.2 CBC Outside vs Inside

To review, the EDE commonly used in the industry (and defined in §3.8 *Multiple Encryption DES*) does CBC on the outside, which means that each block is triply encrypted, and the CBC is done on the triply encrypted block (see Figure 3-35). The alternative would be to completely encrypt the message with K_1 and CBC, and then take the result and completely decrypt it with K_2 and CBC, and then take the result and completely encrypt it with K_1 (see Figure 3-36).

What are the implications of this choice?

As shown in §3.6.2.1 *CBC Threat 1—Modifying Ciphertext Blocks*, with CBC it is possible to make a predictable change to plaintext block n, for instance flipping bit x, by flipping bit x in ciphertext block $n-1$. There is a side-effect, though, of completely garbling plaintext block $n-1$. Whether an attacker can use this for nefarious purposes depends on the exact application.

With CBC done on the outside, an attacker can still do the same attack. The fact that the encryption scheme involves triple use of DES does not change the effects of CBC. An attacker that flips bit x in ciphertext block $n-1$ will completely and unpredictably (to the attacker) garble plaintext block $n-1$. However, plaintext block n will have bit x flipped. And all plaintext blocks other than $n-1$ and n will be unaffected.

With CBC done on the inside, any change to ciphertext block n completely and unpredictably garbles all plaintext blocks from n to the end of the message. This makes CBC done on the inside more secure, and perhaps would therefore have been a better choice. However, sometimes people would prefer if garbling of a ciphertext block did not garble the entire rest of the message. They'd prefer that the encryption scheme be **self-synchronizing**, which means that after some small number of garbled blocks, the plaintext will start decrypting properly again.

Another advantage of CBC on the inside is performance. With CBC on the inside it is possible to use three times as much hardware and pipeline the encryptions so that it is as fast as single encryption. With CBC on the outside, this is not possible.

One reason that people choose CBC on the outside despite its disadvantages is that EDE encryption can be considered a new secret key block encryption scheme that uses a 112-bit key. This can then be used with any of the chaining methods (OFB, ECB, CFB, as well as CBC).

3.9 HOMEWORK

1. Come up with as efficient an encoding as you can to specify a completely general one-to-one mapping between 64-bit input values and 64-bit output values.

2. Security Dynamics makes a device that displays a number that changes frequently. Each such device has a unique secret key. A human can prove possession of a particular such device by

entering the displayed number into a computer system. The computer system knows the secret keys of each authorized device. How would you design such a device?

3. How many DES keys, on the average, encrypt a particular plaintext block to a particular ciphertext block?

4. Make an argument as to why the initial permutation of the bits of the key cannot have any security value.

5. Suppose the DES mangler function mapped every 32-bit value to zero, regardless of the value of its input. What function would DES then compute?

6. Are all the 56 bits of the DES key used an equal number of times in the K_i? Specify, for each of the K_i, which bits are not used.

7. What would change in the DES description if keys were input as 56-bit quantities rather than 64-bit quantities?

8. Why is a DES weak key (see §3.3.6 *Weak and Semi-Weak Keys*) its own inverse? Hint: DES encryption and decryption are the same once the per-round keys are generated.

9. Why is each DES semi-weak key the inverse of another semi-weak key?

10. What pseudo-random block stream is generated by 64-bit OFB with a weak DES key?

11. Class project: design and implement an efficient DES breaking computer. (Hint: to get an answer within your lifetime you will probably need to design a custom chip that takes as input a ⟨plaintext, ciphertext⟩ pair and a starting key number, and searches from that starting key number for a DES key that will map the plaintext into that ciphertext.) Use your computer to tell us what DES key mapped 0 to $5761b9ab9858b34b_{16}$. Free T-shirts to the first ten correct answers.

12. The pseudo-random stream of blocks generated by 64-bit OFB must eventually repeat (since at most 2^{64} different blocks can be generated). Will the IV necessarily be the first block to be repeated?

13. Let's assume you do DES double encryption by encrypting with K_1 and doing DES in decrypt mode with K_2. Does the same attack work as with double encryption with K_1 and K_2? If not, how could it be made to work?

14. What is a practical method for finding a triple of keys that maps a given plaintext to a given ciphertext using EDE? Hint: It is like the meet-in-the-middle attack of §3.8.1.2 *Encrypting Twice with Two Keys*.

15. Let's assume that someone does triple encryption by using EEE with CBC on the inside. Suppose an attacker modifies bit x of ciphertext block n. How does this affect the decrypted plaintext?

16. Consider the following alternative method of encrypting a message. To encrypt a message, use the algorithm for doing a CBC decrypt. To decrypt a message, use the algorithm for doing a CBC encrypt. Would this work? What are the security implications of this, if any, as contrasted with the "normal" CBC?

17. Give the first 16 values of the permutation formed by doing the initial permutation twice (as happens when ED is performed).

4 HASHES AND MESSAGE DIGESTS

4.1 INTRODUCTION

Random numbers should not be generated with a method chosen at random.
—Donald Knuth

A hash (also known as a **message digest**) is a **one-way function**. It is considered a **function** because it takes an input message and produces an output. It is considered **one-way** because it's not practical to figure out what input corresponds to a given output. For a message digest function to be considered cryptographically secure, it must be computationally infeasible to find a message that has a given prespecified message digest, and it similarly should be impossible to find two messages that have the same message digest. Also (which follows from the previous properties), given a message it should be impossible to find a different message with the same message digest.

We will use the terms *hash* and *message digest* interchangeably. The NIST proposed message digest function is called **SHA**, which stands for **secure hash algorithm**, whereas the *MD* in the MD2, MD4, and MD5 algorithms stands for *message digest*. All of the digest/hash algorithms do basically the same thing, which is to take an arbitrary-length message and wind up with a fixed-length quantity.

There's an intuitive notion of **randomness** that is important to the understanding of message digest functions. We are not trying to create a math book, so our description will be mathematically imprecise. We are merely trying to capture the intuition. We explained before that with secret key cryptography, it is desirable for the mapping from input to output to appear randomly chosen. In other words, it should look (to someone who does not know the secret key) like someone flipped coins to determine, for each possible input, what the output should be. Examples of what this means are:

- If 1000 inputs are selected at random, any particular bit in the 1000 resulting outputs should be on about half the time.

- Each output should have, with high probability, about half the bits on.

- Any two outputs should be completely uncorrelated, no matter how similar the inputs are. So for instance, two inputs that differ by only one bit should have outputs that look like completely independently chosen random numbers. About half the bits in the two outputs should differ.

This sort of randomness is important for message digests as well. It is true that someone who knows the message digest function can calculate the output, and therefore the output is certainly provably not generated by flipping coins. But ignoring that, the output should look random. It should not be possible, other than by computing the message digest, to predict any portion of the output. And in particular it should be true that, for any subset of bits in the message digest, the only way of obtaining two messages with the same value in those bits would be to try messages at random and compute the message digest of each until two happened to have the same value. Given this property, a secure message digest function with n bits should be derivable from a message digest function with more than n bits merely by taking any particular subset of n bits from the larger message digest.

There certainly will be many messages that yield the same message digest, because a message can be of arbitrary length and the message digest will be some fixed length, for instance 128 bits. For instance, for 1000-bit messages and a 128-bit message digest, there are on the average 2^{872} messages that map to any one particular message digest. So certainly, by trying lots of messages, one would eventually find two that mapped to the same message digest. The problem is that "lots" is so many that it is essentially impossible. Assuming a good 128-bit message digest function, it would take trying approximately 2^{128} possible messages before one would find a message that mapped to a particular message digest, or approximately 2^{64} messages before finding two that had the same digest (see *The Birthday Problem*, below).

An example use of a message digest is to **fingerprint** a program or document to detect modification of it. If you know the message digest of the program (and store the message digest securely so that it can't be modified, and compute the message digest of the program before running it, and check to make sure that it matches the stored value), then nobody will be able to modify the program without being detected, because they will not be able to find a different program with the same message digest.

How many bits does the output of a message digest function have to be in order to prevent someone from being able to find two messages with the same message digest? Well, if the message digest has m bits, then it would take only about $2^{m/2}$ messages, chosen at random, before one would find two with the same value. So if there were a 64-bit message digest function, it would only take searching 2^{32} messages before one could find two with the same value, and it is feasible to search 2^{32} messages. That is why message digest functions have outputs of at least 128 bits, because it is not considered feasible to search 2^{64} messages given the current state of the art.

The Birthday Problem

If there are 23 or more people in a room, the odds are better than 50% that two of them will have the same birthday. Analyzing this parlor trick can give us some insight into cryptography. We'll assume that a birthday is basically an unpredictable function taking a human to one of 365 values (yeah yeah, 366 for you nerds).

Let's do this in a slightly more general way. Let's assume n inputs (which would be humans in the birthday example) and k possible outputs, and an unpredictable mapping from input to output. With n inputs, there are $n(n-1)/2$ pairs of inputs. For each pair there's a probability of $1/k$ of both inputs producing the same output value, so you'll need about $k/2$ pairs in order for the probability to be about 50% that you'll find a matching pair. That means that if n is greater than $\sqrt{k}$, there's a good chance of finding a matching pair.

If cryptographers were happy with message digest functions that merely made it infeasible to find a message with a particular prespecified digest (rather than being worried about being able to find any pair with the same digest), then a 64-bit digest would suffice.

Why are we worried about someone being able to find any two messages with the same message digest, instead of only worrying about finding a message with a particular prespecified message digest? In most applications, to subvert a system an attacker has to find a misleading message whose message digest matches that of a pre-existing message. However, there are cases where being able to find two messages with the same message digest is a threat to the security of the system.

Suppose Alice wants to fire Fred, and asks her diabolical secretary, Bob, who happens to be Fred's friend, to compose a letter explaining that Fred should be fired, and why. After Bob writes the letter, Alice will read it, compute a message digest, and cryptographically sign the message digest using her private key. Bob would like to instead write a letter saying that Bob is wonderful and his salary ought to be doubled. However, Bob cannot generate a message digest signed with Alice's key. If he can find two messages with the same message digest, one that Alice will look at and agree to sign because it captures what she'd like it to say, and one that says what Bob would like it to say, then Bob can substitute his own message after Alice generates the signed message digest.

Suppose the message digest function has only 64 bits, and is a good message digest function in the sense of its output looking random. Then the only way to find two messages with the same message digest would be by trying enough messages so that by the birthday problem two would have the same digest.

If Bob started by writing a letter that Alice would approve of, found the message digest of that, and then attempted to find a different message with that message digest, he'd have to try 2^{64}

different messages. However, suppose he had a way of generating lots of messages of each type (type 1—those that Alice would be willing to sign; type 2—those that Bob would like to send). Then by the birthday problem he'd only have to try about 2^{32} messages of each type before he found two that matched. (See Homework Problem 3.)

How can Bob possibly generate that many letters, especially since they'd all have to make sense to a human? Well, suppose there are 2 choices of wording in each of 32 places in the letter. Then there are 2^{32} possible messages he can generate. For example:

Type 1 message

I am writing {this memo | } to {demand | request | inform you} that {Fred | Mr. Fred Jones} {must | } be {fired | terminated} {at once | immediately}. As the {July 11 | 11 July} {memo | memorandum} {from | issued by} {personnel | human resources} states, to meet {our | the corporate} {quarterly | third quarter} budget {targets | goals}, {we must eliminate all discretionary spending | all discretionary spending must be eliminated}.

{Despite | Ignoring} that {memo | memorandum | order}, Fred {ordered | purchased} {PostIts | nonessential supplies} in a flagrant disregard for the company's {budgetary crisis | current financial difficulties}.

Type 2 message

I am writing {this letter | this memo | this memorandum | } to {officially | } commend Fred {Jones | } for his {courage and independent thinking | independent thinking and courage}. {He | Fred} {clearly | } understands {the need | how} to get {the | his} job {done | accomplished} {at all costs | by whatever means necessary}, and {knows | can see} when to ignore bureaucratic {nonsense | impediments}. I {am hereby recommending | hereby recommend} {him | Fred} for {promotion | immediate advancement} and {further | } recommend a {hefty | large} {salary | compensation} increase.

There are enough computer-generatable variants of the two letters that Bob can compute message digests on the various variants until he finds a match. It is within computational feasibility to generate and test on the order of 2^{32} messages, whereas it would not be feasible to deal with 2^{64} messages.

As we will see in Chapter 5 *Public Key Algorithms*, the math behind RSA and other public key cryptographic algorithms is quite understandable. In contrast, message digest functions are like alchemy. It's a bunch of steps that each mangle the message more and more. The functions sound like a bunch of people got together and each person had some idea for mangling the message further. "And now let's swap every bit with the complement of the bit 11 bits to the right!" "How about let's multiply every set of 12 adjacent bits by the constant 384729?" "How about we throw in *I(newt)*?" And every suggestion is adopted by the group. It is possible to follow all the steps, but the incomprehensible part is why this particular shuffling of the message is done, and why it couldn't be simpler and yet just as secure.

A plausible way of constructing a message digest function is to combine lots of perverse operations into a potential message digest function, and then play with it. If any patterns are detected in the output the function is rejected, or perhaps more perverse operations are folded into it.

Ideally, the message digest function should be easy to compute. One wonders what the "minimal" secure message digest function might be. It is safer for a function to be overkill, in the sense of shuffling beyond what it necessary, but then it is harder to compute than necessary. The designers would rather waste computation than discover later that the function was not secure. Just as with secret key algorithms, the digest algorithms tend to be computed in rounds. It is likely that the designers find the smallest number of rounds necessary before the output passes various randomness tests, and then do a few more just to be safe.

There is an interesting bit of folklore in the choice of constants in cryptographic algorithms. Often a "random number" is needed. If the designer of the algorithm chooses a specific number without explanation as to where that number came from, people are suspicious that there might be some hidden flaw that the designer of the algorithm wishes to exploit, and will be able to because the designer knows some hidden properties of that choice of number. Therefore, often the algorithm designers specify how they chose a particular random number. It is often done based on the digits of π or some other irrational number. There was also a book published in the 1930s of random numbers generated from a mechanically random source. People have used some of the numbers in that as well on the theory that cryptography was not well understood then so it is inconceivable that someone could have planted special numbers.

At the end of this chapter we'll describe the major hash functions which have been proposed as standards. Ron Rivest designed MD2, MD4, and MD5. These are all documented in RFCs (1319, 1320, and 1321). In MD2 all operations are done with bytes (the microprocessors at the time operated on bytes), whereas the other standards operate on 32-bit words (today's microprocessors efficiently compute with 32-bit quantities). In fact, now that there are 64-bit microprocessors, it's quite possible a new MD algorithm optimized for that architecture will be developed.

4.2 NIFTY THINGS TO DO WITH A HASH

Before we look at the details of several popular hash algorithms, let's look at some interesting uses of hash algorithms. Surprisingly, if there is a shared secret, the hash algorithms can be used in all the ways that secret cryptography is used. It is a little confusing calling the schemes in the next few sections "message digest" schemes, since they do involve a shared secret. By our definition in

Why are there so many message digest functions?

Surprisingly, the drive for message digest algorithms started with public key cryptography. RSA was invented, which made possible digital signatures on messages, but computing a signature on a long message with RSA was sufficiently slow that RSA would not have been practical by itself. A cryptographically secure message digest function with high performance would make RSA much more useful. Instead of having to compute a signature over a whole long message, the message could be compressed into a small size by first performing a message digest and then computing the RSA signature on the digest. So MD and MD2 were created. MD was proprietary and never published. It is used in some of RSADSI's secure mail products. MD2 is documented in RFC 1319.

Then Ralph Merkle of Xerox developed a message digest algorithm called SNEFRU [MERK90] that was several times faster than MD2. This prodded Ron Rivest into developing MD4 (RFC 1320), a digest algorithm that took advantage of the fact the newer processors could do 32-bit operations, and was therefore able to be even faster than SNEFRU. Then SNEFRU was broken [BIHA92] (the cryptographic community considered it broken because someone was able to find two messages with the same SNEFRU digest). Independently, [DENB92] found weaknesses in a version of MD4 with two rounds instead of three. This did not officially break MD4, but it made Ron Rivest sufficiently nervous that he decided to strengthen it, and create MD5 (RFC 1321), which is a little slower than MD4. NIST subsequently proposed SHS, which is very similar to MD5, but even more strengthened, and also a little slower. Not satisfied with the SHS proposal, NIST revised it at the twelfth hour in an effort to make it more secure (see §4.6.3 *SHS Operation on a 512-bit Block*).

Yes, Virginia, there was an MD3, but it was superseded by MD4 before it was ever published or used.

§2.3 *Types of Cryptographic Functions* in which we said something that had a single shared secret was a secret key algorithm, these might be considered secret key algorithms. Never take definitions too seriously. The significant difference between a secret key algorithm and a message digest algorithm is that a secret key algorithm is designed to be reversible and a message digest algorithm is designed to be impossible to reverse. In this section we'll use MD as a "generic" message digest (cryptographic hash) algorithm.

4.2.1 Authentication

In §2.4.4 *Authentication* we discussed how to use a secret key algorithm for authentication. A challenge is transmitted, and the other side has to encrypt the challenge with the shared key.

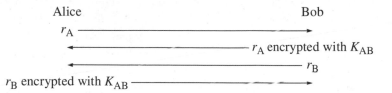

Imagine a world without secret key cryptography, but with cryptographic hash functions. So we can't use an algorithm like DES in the above example. Could we use a message digest function in some sort of way to accomplish the same thing? Bob and Alice will still need to share a secret. Message digest algorithms aren't reversible, so it can't work quite the same way. In the above example, in which secret key cryptography is used for authentication, Bob encrypts something, and Alice decrypts it to make sure Bob encrypted the quantity properly. A hash function will do pretty much the same thing. Alice still sends a challenge. Bob then concatenates the secret he shares with Alice with the challenge, takes a message digest of that, and transmits that message digest. Alice can't "decrypt" the result. However, she can do the same computation, and check that the result matches what Bob sends.

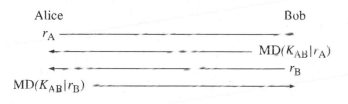

4.2.2 Computing a MIC with a Hash

In §3.7 *Generating MICs* we described how to compute a MIC (message integrity code) with a secret key algorithm. Again, let's assume that for some reason no secret key algorithms are available. Can we still compute a MIC, using a hash function instead of something like DES?

The obvious thought is that $MD(m)$ is a MIC for message m. But it isn't. Anyone can compute $MD(m)$. The point of the MIC is to send something that only someone knowing the secret can compute (and verify). For instance, if Alice and Bob share a secret, then Alice can send m, plus MIC, and since nobody except Alice and Bob can compute a MIC with their shared key, nobody but Alice or Bob would be able to send a message to Bob with an appropriate MIC. If we just simply used MD, then anyone can send any message m' together with MD(m'). So we do roughly the same trick for the MIC as we did for authentication. We concatenate a shared secret K_{AB} with the message m, and use MD($K_{AB}|m$) as the MIC.

This scheme almost works, except for some idiosyncracies of most of the popular message digest algorithms, which would allow an attacker to be able to compute a MIC of a different message, given message m and the correct MIC for m.

Assume MD is one of MD4, MD5, or SHS. The way these algorithms work is that the message is padded to a multiple of 512 bits with a pad that includes the message length. The padded message is then digested from left to right in 512-bit chunks. In order to compute the message digest through chunk n, all that you need to know is the message digest through chunk $n-1$, plus the value of chunk n of the padded message.

Let's assume Carol would like to send a different message to Bob, and have it look like it came from Alice. Let's say that Carol doesn't care what's in the message. She only cares that at the end the message says **P.S. Give Carol a promotion and triple her salary**. Alice has transmitted some message m, and MD($K_{AB}|m$). Carol can see both of those quantities. She concatenates the padding and then whatever she likes to the end of m, and initializes the message digest computation with MD($K_{AB}|m$). She does not need to know the shared secret in order to compute the MIC.

How can we avoid this flaw? There are two methods:

- Put the secret at the end of the message instead of at the beginning. This will work. This method is sometimes criticized for an extremely unlikely security flaw. The complaint is that if the MD algorithm were weak, and it was therefore possible to reverse a single block, then the final block would be the easiest block to find, and that could expose the secret. We feel that if the MD algorithm has such a serious security flaw, most likely all your cryptographic-based security is useless, so worrying about this is a waste of perfectly good brain cells. If you can't trust your MD algorithm, what can you trust? But, if you want to be paranoid, you can do the next solution, which is actually quite slick and even saves 64 bits.

  Actually, we're assuming you're using one of the message digest algorithms that are in the public domain (like MD2, MD4, MD5, or SHS) which have been published for years and withstood scrutiny by hoards of cryptanalysts. If, despite the availability of these algorithms, you for some reason decide to design and use your own message digest algorithm, then you might as well have faith in it, since if you don't think you can do a good job, we can't imagine what the excuse is for designing your own algorithm.

- Use only half the bits of the message digest as the MIC. For instance, take the low-order 64 bits of the MD5 digest. This gives an attacker no information with which to continue the message digest (well, the attacker has a 1 in 2^{64} chance of guessing the rest of the message digest correctly—I assume you're not going to worry about that risk). Having only 64 bits of MIC (rather than using all 128 bits of the MD) is not any less secure, since there is no way that an attacker can generate messages and test the resulting MIC. Without knowing the secret, there is no way for the attacker to calculate the MIC. The best that can be done is to generate a random 64-bit MIC for the message you'd like to send and hope that you'll be really really lucky.

4.2.3 Encryption with a Message Digest

"Encryption with a message digest algorithm is easy!" you say. "But let me see you do decryption!"

Message digest algorithms are not reversible, so the trick is to design a scheme in which both encryption and decryption run the message digest algorithm in the forward direction.

The schemes we'll describe are reminiscent of the chaining methods of using DES.

4.2.3.1 Generating a One-Time Pad

Just as OFB (§3.6.3 *Output Feedback Mode (OFB)*) generates a pseudorandom bit stream which then encrypts a message by simply being ⊕ed with the message, we can use a message digest algorithm to generate a pseudorandom bit stream.

Again, Alice and Bob need a shared secret, K_{AB}. Alice wants to send Bob a message. She computes $MD(K_{AB})$. That gives the first block of bit stream, b_1. Then she computes $MD(K_{AB}|b_1)$ and uses that as b_2, and in general b_i is $MD(K_{AB}|b_i)$.

Alice and Bob can do this in advance, before the message is known. Then when Alice wishes to send the message, she ⊕s it with as much of the generated bit stream as necessary. Similarly, Bob decrypts the ciphertext by ⊕ing it with the bit stream he has calculated.

It is not secure to use the same bit stream twice, so, as with OFB, Alice starts with an IV. The first block is then $MD(K_{AB}|IV)$. She must transmit the IV to Bob. Alice can generate the bit stream in advance of encrypting the message, but Bob cannot generate the bit stream until he sees the IV.

4.2.3.2 Mixing In the Plaintext

One-time pad schemes have the problem that if you are able to guess the plaintext, you can ⊕ the guessed text with the ciphertext, and then ⊕ any message you like. This is not too much of a problem. We just need to recognize that a one-time pad scheme gives privacy only, and integrity must be gained through a scheme such as using a MIC.

However, in a scheme similar to CFB (§3.6.4 *Cipher Feedback Mode (CFB)*), we can mix the plaintext into the bit stream generation. For instance, break the message into MD-length chunks p_1,

$p_2, \ldots$. We'll call the ciphertext blocks $c_1, c_2, \ldots$. And we'll need intermediate values $b_1, b_2, \ldots$ from which we'll compute each ciphertext block.

$$b_1 = \mathrm{MD}(K_{AB}|IV) \qquad\qquad c_1 = p_1 \oplus b_1$$
$$b_2 = \mathrm{MD}(K_{AB}|c_1) \qquad\qquad c_2 = p_2 \oplus b_2$$
$$\vdots \qquad\qquad\qquad\qquad \vdots$$
$$b_i = \mathrm{MD}(K_{AB}|c_{i-1}) \qquad\qquad c_i = p_i \oplus b_i$$
$$\vdots \qquad\qquad\qquad\qquad \vdots$$

Decryption is straightforward. We leave it as Homework Problem 18.

4.2.4 Using Secret Key for a Hash

In case the previous sections make the secret key algorithms nervous about job security since they can be replaced by hash algorithms, we'll show that a hash algorithm can be replaced by a secret key algorithm. What we want to generate is a function with the properties of a hash algorithm. It should not require a secret. It should be publishable. It should be noninvertible.

4.2.4.1 UNIX Password Hash

UNIX uses a secret key algorithm to compute the hash of a password, which it then stores. It never has to reverse the hash to obtain a password. Instead, when the user types a password, UNIX uses the same algorithm to hash the typed quantity and compares the result with the stored quantity.

The hashing algorithm first converts the password into a secret key. This key is then used, with a DES-like algorithm, to encrypt the number 0. The method of turning a text string into a secret key is simply to pack the 7-bit ASCII associated with each of the first 8 characters of the password into a 56-bit quantity into which DES parity is inserted. (UNIX passwords can be longer than 8 characters, but the remaining bytes are ignored.)

A 12-bit random number, known as *salt*, is stored with the hashed password. For an explanation of why salt is useful, see §8.3 *Off-Line Password Guessing*. A modified DES is used instead of standard DES to prevent hardware accelerators designed for DES from being used to reverse the password hash. The salt is used to modify the DES data expansion algorithm. The value of the salt determines which bits are duplicated when expanding R from 32 to 48 bits (see §3.3.5 *The Mangler Function*).

To summarize, each time a password is set, a 12-bit number is generated. The password is converted into a secret key. The 12-bit number is used to define a modified DES algorithm. The modified DES algorithm is used with the secret key as input to encrypt the constant 0. The result is stored along with the 12-bit number as the user's hashed password.

4.2.4.2 Hashing Large Messages

The UNIX password hash is a method of doing a message digest of a very short message (maximum length is the length of the secret key). Here's a method of converting a secret key algorithm into a message digest algorithm for arbitrary messages (see Figure 4-1).

A secret key algorithm has a key length, say k bits. It has a message block length, say b bits. In the case of DES, $k = 56$ and $b = 64$. In the case of IDEA, $k = 128$ and $b = 64$.

Divide the message into k-bit chunks m_1, m_2,.... Use the first block of the message as a key to encrypt a constant. The result is a b-bit quantity. Use the second k-bit chunk of the message to encrypt the b-bit quantity to get a new b-bit quantity. Keep doing this until you run out of k-bit blocks of the message. Use the final b-bit result as the message digest.

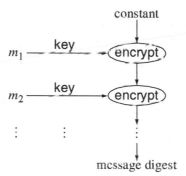

Figure 4-1. Message Digest Using Secret Key Cryptography

There's a serious problem with this, which is that the typical message block length b is 64 bits, which is too short to use as a message digest. To obtain two messages with the same message digest using this technique (and remembering the birthday problem), we'd only have to try about 2^{32} messages before finding two that had the same digest. And furthermore, if we want to find a message with a particular message digest, a technique similar to the one in §3.8.1.2 *Encrypting Twice with Two Keys* could find a message with a particular 64-bit message digest in about 2^{33} iterations.

One technique that has been recommended in order to generate 128 bits of message digest is to generate two 64-bit quantities. The first 64-bit quantity is generated as we just described—the message is broken into key-length chunks b_1, b_2,... and the chunks are used for encryption in that order. The second 64-bit quantity is generated by using the chunks in reverse order.

That technique works (though see Homework Problem 4), but it's a little inconvenient to do two passes on the message. We'd recommend instead processing the message twice in the forward direction, and just starting with two different constants.

4.3 MD2

MD2 takes a message equal to an arbitrary number of 8-bit bytes and produces a 128-bit message digest. It cannot handle a message that is not an integral number of bytes, though it would be simple to modify MD2 (see Homework Problem 5), or to have a convention for bit-padding a message before feeding it to MD2.

The basic idea behind MD2 is as follows:

1. The input to MD2 is a message whose length is an arbitrary number of bytes.

2. The message is padded, according to specified conventions, to be a multiple of 16 bytes.

3. A 16-byte quantity, which MD2 calls a **checksum**, is appended to the end. This checksum is a strange function of the padded message defined specifically for MD2.

4. Final pass—The message is processed, 16 bytes at a time, each time producing an intermediate result for the message digest. Each intermediate value of the message digest depends on the previous intermediate value and the value of the 16 bytes of the message being processed.

Note that we describe the algorithm as if the message is processed three times, first to pad it, next to compute the checksum, and then to compute the actual message digest. However, it is possible to digest a message in a single pass. This is important for machines with limited memory.

4.3.1 MD2 Padding

The padding function (see Figure 4-2) is very simple. There must always be padding, even if the message starts out being a multiple of 16 bytes. If the message starts out being a multiple of 16 bytes, 16 bytes of padding are added. Otherwise, the number of bytes (1–15) necessary to make the message a multiple of 16 bytes is added. Each pad byte specifies the number of bytes of padding that was added.

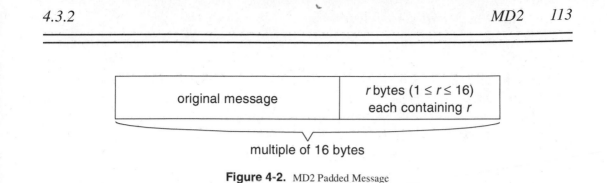

Figure 4-2. MD2 Padded Message

4.3.2 MD2 Checksum Computation

The checksum is a 16-byte quantity. It is almost like a message digest, but it is not crypto-graphically secure by itself. The checksum is appended to the message, and then MD2 processes the concatenated quantity to obtain the actual message digest.

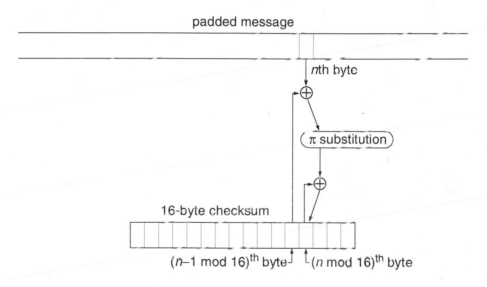

Figure 4-3. MD2 Checksum Calculation

The checksum starts out initialized to 0. Because of the padding mentioned in the previous section, the message is a multiple of 16 bytes, say $k \times 16$ bytes. The checksum calculation processes the padded message a byte at a time, so the calculation requires $k \times 16$ steps. Each step looks at one byte of the message and updates one byte of the checksum. After byte 15 of the checksum is updated, the next step starts again on byte 0 of the checksum. Therefore, each byte of the checksum will have been updated k times by the time the checksum computation terminates. At step n, byte $(n \bmod 16)$ of the checksum is computed, but for simplicity we'll call it byte n of the checksum.

Byte *n* of the checksum depends on byte *n* of the message, byte *(n−1)* of the checksum, and the previous value of byte *n* of the checksum (what it was updated to be in step *n−16*). (Think of the checksum as "wrapping around", so if *n* = 0, byte *n−1* is byte 15.)

First, byte *n* of the message and byte *(n−1)* of the checksum are ⊕'d together. This produces a byte having a value between 0 and 255. Then a substitution is done and the result is ⊕'d into the previous value of byte *n* of the checksum.

The substitution is specified by the following table. The first entry is 41, indicating that the value 0 is mapped to 41. The next is 46, indicating that the value 1 is mapped to 46.

41	46	67	201	162	216	124	1	61	54	84	161	236	240	6	19
98	167	5	243	192	199	115	140	152	147	43	217	188	76	130	202
30	155	87	60	253	212	224	22	103	66	111	24	138	23	229	18
190	78	196	214	218	158	222	73	160	251	245	142	187	47	238	122
169	104	121	145	21	178	7	63	148	194	16	137	11	34	95	33
128	127	93	154	90	144	50	39	53	62	204	231	191	247	151	3
255	25	48	179	72	165	181	209	215	94	146	42	172	86	170	198
79	184	56	210	150	164	125	182	118	252	107	226	156	116	4	241
69	157	112	89	100	113	135	32	134	91	207	101	230	45	168	2
27	96	37	173	174	176	185	246	28	70	97	105	52	64	126	15
85	71	163	35	221	81	175	58	195	92	249	206	186	197	234	38
44	83	13	110	133	40	132	9	211	223	205	244	65	129	77	82
106	220	55	200	108	193	171	250	36	225	123	8	12	189	177	74
120	136	149	139	227	99	232	109	233	203	213	254	59	0	29	57
242	239	183	14	102	88	208	228	166	119	114	248	235	117	75	10
49	68	80	180	143	237	31	26	219	153	141	51	159	17	131	20

Figure 4-4. MD2 π Substitution Table

The designers of MD2, anxious to display that they had designed no sneaky trapdoors into MD2 by having carefully chosen a particular mapping function, specified that they chose the mapping based on the digits of π. One way that they could base a substitution on the digits of π was to look at the binary representation of π a byte at a time, using the value of that byte as the next substitution value, unless it was already used, in which case they skipped it and went on to the next byte. We checked, and that isn't how they did it. We're willing to just take their word for it that somehow the numbers are based on the digits of π. We wonder whether anyone has ever bothered to verify their claim. We certainly hope none of you waste as much time as we did trying to figure out how the digits of π relate to the substitution. We could have asked the designers, but that seemed like cheating.

4.3.3 MD2 Final Pass

The final pass of the message digest computation is somewhat similar to the checksum computation. The message with padding and checksum appended is processed in chunks of 16 bytes. Each time a new 16-byte chunk of the message is taken, a 48-byte quantity is constructed consisting of the (16-byte) current value of the message digest, the chunk of the message, and the $\oplus$ of those two 16-byte quantities. The 48-byte quantity is massaged byte by byte. After 18 passes over the 48-byte quantity, the first 16 bytes of the 48-byte quantity are used as the next value of the message digest.

The message digest is initialized to 16 bytes of 0.

At each stage, the next 16 bytes of the message are taken to be processed. A 48-byte quantity is formed by appending the message bytes to the current message digest, then appending the $\oplus$ of these two 16-byte quantities.

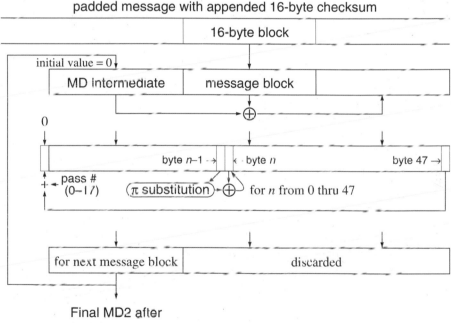

Figure 4-5. MD2 Final Pass

18 passes are made over the 48-byte quantity, and during a pass each step processes one byte, which means that 18×48 steps are made. It is necessary to know which pass is being made, since

the pass number is used in the computation. Both passes and steps are numbered starting at zero. A phantom byte −1 appears before the first byte (byte 0) of the 48-byte quantity.

At the beginning of pass 0, byte −1 is set to 0. In step *n* of each pass we take byte *n*−1 and run it through the same substitution used for the checksum, then ⊕ the result into byte *n*. After step 47 of each pass, there is a step 48 which sets byte −1 to the mod 256 sum of byte 47 and the pass number. When we have completed pass 17, the first 16 bytes of the 48-byte quantity are used as the value of the message digest for the next stage, and the next 16 bytes of the message are processed. (So in pass 17, steps 16 through 48 are useless.)

After the entire message is processed, the 16 bytes that come out of the last stage is the message digest value. The calculation requires only 16 bytes (for the checksum) plus 48 bytes of volatile memory plus a few indices and makes a single pass over the data. This is ideal for computation in a smart card (see §8.8 *Authentication Tokens*).

4.4 MD4

MD4 was designed to be 32-bit-word-oriented so that it can be computed faster on 32-bit CPUs than a byte-oriented scheme like MD2. Also, MD2 requires the message to be an integral number of bytes. MD4 can handle messages with an arbitrary number of bits. Like MD2 it can be computed in a single pass over the data, though MD4 needs more intermediate state.

4.4.1 MD4 Message Padding

The message to be fed into the message digest computation must be a multiple of 512 bits (sixteen 32-bit words). The original message is padded by adding a 1 bit, followed by enough 0 bits to leave the message 64 bits less than a multiple of 512 bits. Then a 64-bit quantity representing the number of bits in the unpadded message, mod 2^{64}, is appended to the message.

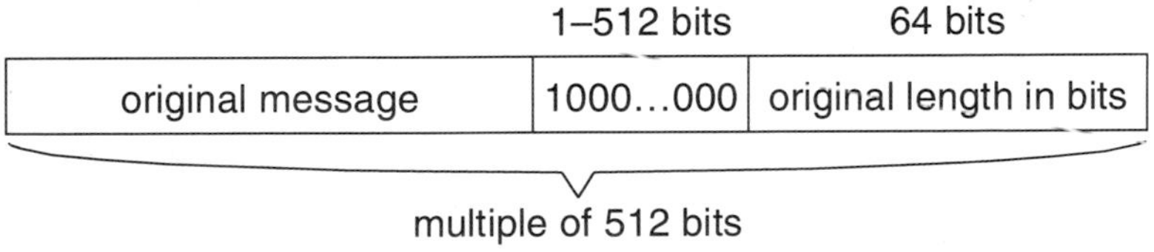

Figure 4-6. Padding for MD4, MD5, SHS

4.4.2 Overview of MD4 Message Digest Computation

The message digest to be computed is a 128-bit quantity (four 32-bit words). The message is processed in 512-bit (sixteen 32-bit words) blocks. The message digest is initialized to a fixed value, and then each stage of the message digest computation takes the current value of the message digest and modifies it using the next block of the message. The final result is the message digest for the entire message.

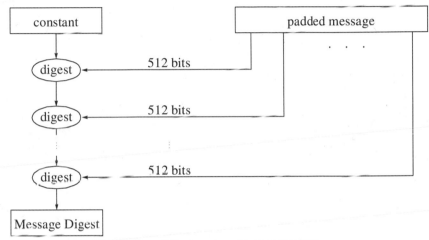

Figure 4-7. Overview of MD4, MD5, SHS

Each stage makes three passes over the message block. Each pass has a slightly different method of mangling the message digest. At the end of the stage, each word of the mangled message digest is added to its pre-stage value to produce the post-stage value (which becomes the pre-stage value for the next stage). Therefore, the current value of the message digest must be saved at the beginning of the stage so that it can be added in at the end of the stage.

Each stage starts with a 16-word message block and a 4-word message digest value. The message words are called $m_0, m_1, m_2, \ldots m_{15}$. The message digest words are called d_0, d_1, d_2, d_3. Before the first stage the message digest is initialized to $d_0 = 01234567_{16}$, $d_1 = 89\text{abcdef}_{16}$, $d_2 = \text{fedcba98}_{16}$, and $d_3 = 76543210_{16}$.

Each pass modifies d_0, d_1, d_2, d_3 using $m_0, m_1, m_2, \ldots m_{15}$. We will describe what happens in each pass separately.

The computations we are about to describe use the following operations:

- $\lfloor x \rfloor$ is the *floor* of the number x, i.e., the greatest integer not greater than x.

- $\sim x$ is the *bitwise complement* of the 32-bit quantity x.

- $x \wedge y$ is the *bitwise and* of the 32-bit quantities x and y.

- $x \vee y$ is the *bitwise or* of the two 32-bit quantities x and y.

- $x \oplus y$ is the *bitwise exclusive or* of the 32-bit quantities x and y.

- $x+y$ is the *binary sum* of the two 32-bit quantities x and y, with the carry out of the high order bit discarded.

- $x \llcorner y$ is the 32-bit quantity produced by taking the 32 bits of x and shifting them one position left y times, each time taking the bit shifted off the left end and placing it as the rightmost bit. This operation is known as a **left rotate**.

4.4.3 MD4 Message Digest Pass 1

A function $F(x,y,z)$ is defined as $(x \wedge y) \vee (\sim x \wedge z)$. This function takes three 32-bit words x, y, and z, and produces an output 32-bit word. This function is sometimes known as the **selection function**, because if the nth bit of x is a 1 it selects the nth bit of y for the nth bit of the output. Otherwise (if the nth bit of x is a 0) it selects the nth bit of z for the nth bit of the output.

A separate step is done for each of the 16 words of the message. For each integer i from 0 through 15,

$$d_{(-i) \wedge 3} = (d_{(-i) \wedge 3} + F(d_{(1-i) \wedge 3}, d_{(2-i) \wedge 3}, d_{(3-i) \wedge 3}) + m_i) \llcorner S_1(i \wedge 3)$$

where $S_1(i) = 3 + 4i$, so the $\llcorner$s cycle over the values 3, 7, 11, 15.

If you don't find the previous sentence intimidating, you may go on to the next section. However, if you are a mere mortal, we'll explain, but just this once. The other passes in MD4 and MD5 are extremely similar, and we'll assume you'll understand their description with no further explanation.

The "$\wedge 3$" that appears several times in the above equation means that only the bottom two bits are used (because we're doing a *bitwise and* with 11_2). So $i \wedge 3$ cycles 0, 1, 2, 3, 0, 1, 2, 3, ... while $(-i) \wedge 3$ cycles 0, 3, 2, 1, 0, 3, 2, 1,... and $(1-i) \wedge 3$ cycles 1, 0, 3, 2, 1, 0, 3, 2,.... We can write out the first few steps of the pass as follows:

$$d_0 = (d_0 + F(d_1, d_2, d_3) + m_0) \llcorner 3$$
$$d_3 = (d_3 + F(d_0, d_1, d_2) + m_1) \llcorner 7$$
$$d_2 = (d_2 + F(d_3, d_0, d_1) + m_2) \llcorner 11$$
$$d_1 = (d_1 + F(d_2, d_3, d_0) + m_3) \llcorner 15$$
$$d_0 = (d_0 + F(d_1, d_2, d_3) + m_4) \llcorner 3$$

4.4.4 MD4 Message Digest Pass 2

A function $G(x, y, z)$ is defined as $(x \wedge y) \vee (x \wedge z) \vee (y \wedge z)$. This function is sometimes known as the **majority function**, because the nth bit of the output is a 1 iff at least two of the three input words' n^{th} bits are a 1. As for pass 1, we'll write out each of the 16 steps. Note that in pass 2 (and pass 3 as well), the words of the message are not processed in order. Also note that there's a strange constant thrown in. To show that the designers didn't purposely choose a diabolical value of the constant, the constant is based on the square root of 2. The constant is $\lfloor 2^{30} \sqrt{2} \rfloor = 5a827999_{16}$.

A separate step is done for each of the 16 words of the message. For each integer i from 0 through 15,

$$d_{(-i) \wedge 3} = (d_{(-i) \wedge 3} + G(d_{(1-i) \wedge 3}, d_{(2-i) \wedge 3}, d_{(3-i) \wedge 3}) + m_{X(i)} + 5a827999_{16}) \lrcorner S_2(i \wedge 3)$$

where $X(i)$ is the 4-bit number formed by exchanging the low order and high order pairs of bits in the 4-bit number i (so $X(i) = 4i - 15 \lfloor i/4 \rfloor$), and $S_2(0) = 3$, $S_2(1) = 5$, $S_2(2) = 9$, $S_2(3) = 13$, so the $\lrcorner$s cycle over the values 3, 5, 9, 13. We can write out the first few steps of the pass as follows:

$$d_0 = (d_0 + G(d_1, d_2, d_3) + m_0 + 5a827999_{16}) \lrcorner 3$$
$$d_3 = (d_3 + G(d_0, d_1, d_2) + m_4 + 5a827999_{16}) \lrcorner 5$$
$$d_2 = (d_2 + G(d_3, d_0, d_1) + m_8 + 5a827999_{16}) \lrcorner 9$$
$$d_1 = (d_1 + G(d_2, d_3, d_0) + m_{12} + 5a827999_{16}) \lrcorner 13$$
$$d_0 = (d_0 + G(d_1, d_2, d_3) + m_1 + 5a827999_{16}) \lrcorner 3$$

4.4.5 MD4 Message Digest Pass 3

A function $H(x, y, z)$ is defined as $x \oplus y \oplus z$. Pass 3 has a different strange constant based on the square root of 3. The constant is $\lfloor 2^{30} \sqrt{3} \rfloor = 6ed9eba1_{16}$.

A separate step is done for each of the 16 words of the message. For each integer i from 0 through 15,

$$d_{(-i) \wedge 3} = (d_{(-i) \wedge 3} + H(d_{(1-i) \wedge 3}, d_{(2-i) \wedge 3}, d_{(3-i) \wedge 3}) + m_{R(i)} + 6ed9eba1_{16}) \lrcorner S_3(i \wedge 3)$$

where $R(i)$ is the 4-bit number formed by reversing the order of the bits in the 4-bit number i (so $R(i) = 8i - 12 \lfloor i/2 \rfloor - 6 \lfloor i/4 \rfloor - 3 \lfloor i/8 \rfloor$), and $S_3(0) = 3$, $S_3(1) = 9$, $S_3(2) = 11$, $S_3(3) = 15$, so the $\lrcorner$s cycle over the values 3, 9, 11, 15. We can write out the first few steps of the pass as follows:

$$d_0 = (d_0 + H(d_1, d_2, d_3) + m_0 + 6ed9eba1_{16}) \lrcorner 3$$
$$d_3 = (d_3 + H(d_0, d_1, d_2) + m_8 + 6ed9eba1_{16}) \lrcorner 9$$
$$d_2 = (d_2 + H(d_3, d_0, d_1) + m_4 + 6ed9eba1_{16}) \lrcorner 11$$
$$d_1 = (d_1 + H(d_2, d_3, d_0) + m_{12} + 6ed9eba1_{16}) \lrcorner 15$$
$$d_0 = (d_0 + H(d_1, d_2, d_3) + m_2 + 6ed9eba1_{16}) \lrcorner 3$$

4.5 MD5

MD5 was designed to be somewhat more "conservative" than MD4 in terms of being less concerned with speed and more concerned with security. It is very similar to MD4. The major differences are:

1. MD4 makes three passes over each 16-byte chunk of the message. MD5 makes four passes over each 16-byte chunk.

2. The functions are slightly different, as are the number of bits in the shifts.

3. MD4 has one constant which is used for each message word in pass 2, and a different constant used for all of the 16 message words in pass 3. No constant is used in pass 1.

MD5 uses a different constant for each message word on each pass. Since there are 4 passes, each of which deals with 16 message words, there are 64 32-bit constants used in MD5. We will call them T_1 through T_{64}. T_i is based on the sine function. Indeed, for any inquiring minds out there, $T_i = \lfloor 2^{32} |\sin i| \rfloor$. The 64 values (in hex) are:

T_1 = d76aa478	T_{17} = f61e2562	T_{33} = fffa3942	T_{49} = f4292244
T_2 = e8c7b756	T_{18} = c040b340	T_{34} = 8771f681	T_{50} = 432aff97
T_3 = 242070db	T_{19} = 265e5a51	T_{35} = 6d9d6122	T_{51} = ab9423a7
T_4 = c1bdceee	T_{20} = e9b6c7aa	T_{36} = fde5380c	T_{52} = fc93a039
T_5 = f57c0faf	T_{21} = d62f105d	T_{37} = a4beea44	T_{53} = 655b59c3
T_6 = 4787c62a	T_{22} = 02441453	T_{38} = 4bdecfa9	T_{54} = 8f0ccc92
T_7 = a8304613	T_{23} = d8a1e681	T_{39} = f6bb4b60	T_{55} = ffeff47d
T_8 = fd469501	T_{24} = e7d3fbc8	T_{40} = bebfbc70	T_{56} = 85845dd1
T_9 = 698098d8	T_{25} = 21e1cde6	T_{41} = 289b7ec6	T_{57} = 6fa87e4f
T_{10} = 8b44f7af	T_{26} = c33707d6	T_{42} = eaa127fa	T_{58} = fe2ce6e0
T_{11} = ffff5bb1	T_{27} = f4d50d87	T_{43} = d4ef3085	T_{59} = a3014314
T_{12} = 895cd7be	T_{28} = 455a14ed	T_{44} = 04881d05	T_{60} = 4e0811a1
T_{13} = 6b901122	T_{29} = a9e3e905	T_{45} = d9d4d039	T_{61} = f7537e82
T_{14} = fd987193	T_{30} = fcefa3f8	T_{46} = e6db99e5	T_{62} = bd3af235
T_{15} = a679438e	T_{31} = 676f02d9	T_{47} = 1fa27cf8	T_{63} = 2ad7d2bb
T_{16} = 49b40821	T_{32} = 8d2a4c8a	T_{48} = c4ac5665	T_{64} = eb86d391

4.5.1 MD5 Message Padding

The padding in MD5 is identical to the padding in MD4.

4.5.2   Overview of MD5 Message Digest Computation

Like MD4, in MD5 the message is processed in 512-bit blocks (sixteen 32-bit words). (See Figure 4-7.) The message digest is a 128-bit quantity (four 32-bit words). Each stage consists of computing a function based on the 512-bit message chunk and the message digest to produce a new intermediate value for the message digest. The value of the message digest is the result of the output of the final block of the message.

Each stage in MD5 takes four passes over the message block (as opposed to three for MD4). As with MD4, at the end of the stage, each word of the modified message digest is added to the corresponding pre-stage message digest value. And as in MD4, before the first stage the message digest is initialized to $d_0 = 01234567_{16}$, $d_1 = 89abcdef_{16}$, $d_2 = fedcba98_{16}$, and $d_3 = 76543210_{16}$.

As with MD4, each pass modifies d_0, d_1, d_2, d_3 using m_0, m_1, m_2, ... m_{15}. We will describe what happens in each pass separately.

4.5.3   MD5 Message Digest Pass 1

As in MD4, $F(x,y,z)$ is defined as the selection function $(x \wedge y) \vee (\sim x \wedge z)$. A separate step is done for each of the 16 words of the message. For each integer i from 0 through 15,

$$d_{(-i) \wedge 3} = (d_{(-i) \wedge 3} + F(d_{(1-i) \wedge 3}, d_{(2-i) \wedge 3}, d_{(3-i) \wedge 3}) + m_i + T_{i+1}) \lrcorner S_1(i \wedge 3)$$

where $S_1(i) = 7 + 5i$, so the ↵s cycle over the values 7, 12, 17, 22. This is a different S_1 from that in MD4. We can write out the first few steps of the pass as follows:

$$d_0 = (d_0 + F(d_1, d_2, d_3) + m_0 + T_1) \lrcorner 7$$
$$d_3 = (d_3 + F(d_0, d_1, d_2) + m_1 + T_2) \lrcorner 12$$
$$d_2 = (d_2 + F(d_3, d_0, d_1) + m_2 + T_3) \lrcorner 17$$
$$d_1 = (d_1 + F(d_2, d_3, d_0) + m_3 + T_4) \lrcorner 22$$
$$d_0 = (d_0 + F(d_1, d_2, d_3) + m_4 + T_5) \lrcorner 7$$

4.5.4   MD5 Message Digest Pass 2

A function $G(x,y,z)$ is defined as $(x \wedge z) \vee (y \wedge \sim z)$. Whereas the function F was the same in MD5 as in MD4, the function G is different in MD5 than the G function in MD4. In fact, MD5's G is rather like F—the nth bit of z is used to select the nth bit in x or the nth bit in y.

A separate step is done for each of the 16 words of the message. For each integer i from 0 through 15,

$$d_{(-i) \wedge 3} = (d_{(-i) \wedge 3} + G(d_{(1-i) \wedge 3}, d_{(2-i) \wedge 3}, d_{(3-i) \wedge 3}) + m_{(5i+1) \wedge 15} + T_{i+17}) \lrcorner S_2(i \wedge 3)$$

where $S_2(i) = i(i+7)/2 + 5$, so the ↵s cycle over the values 5, 9, 14, 20. This is a different S_2 from that in MD4. We can write out the first few steps of the pass as follows:

$$d_0 = (d_0 + G(d_1, d_2, d_3) + m_1 + T_{17}) \lrcorner 5$$
$$d_3 = (d_3 + G(d_0, d_1, d_2) + m_6 + T_{18}) \lrcorner 9$$
$$d_2 = (d_2 + G(d_3, d_0, d_1) + m_{11} + T_{19}) \lrcorner 14$$
$$d_1 = (d_1 + G(d_2, d_3, d_0) + m_0 + T_{20}) \lrcorner 20$$
$$d_0 = (d_0 + G(d_1, d_2, d_3) + m_5 + T_{21}) \lrcorner 5$$

4.5.5 MD5 Message Digest Pass 3

A function $H(x,y,z)$ is defined as $x \oplus y \oplus z$. This is the same H as in MD4.

A separate step is done for each of the 16 words of the message. For each integer i from 0 through 15,

$$d_{(-i) \wedge 3} = (d_{(-i) \wedge 3} + H(d_{(1-i) \wedge 3}, d_{(2-i) \wedge 3}, d_{(3-i) \wedge 3}) + m_{(3i+5) \wedge 15} + T_{i+33}) \lrcorner S_3(i \wedge 3)$$

where $S_3(0) = 4$, $S_3(1) = 11$, $S_3(2) = 16$, $S_3(3) = 23$, so the $\lrcorner$s cycle over the values 4, 11, 16, 23. This is a different S_3 from MD4. We can write out the first few steps of the pass as follows:

$$d_0 = (d_0 + H(d_1, d_2, d_3) + m_5 + T_{33}) \lrcorner 4$$
$$d_3 = (d_3 + H(d_0, d_1, d_2) + m_8 + T_{34}) \lrcorner 11$$
$$d_2 = (d_2 + H(d_3, d_0, d_1) + m_{11} + T_{35}) \lrcorner 16$$
$$d_1 = (d_1 + H(d_2, d_3, d_0) + m_{14} + T_{36}) \lrcorner 23$$
$$d_0 = (d_0 + H(d_1, d_2, d_3) + m_1 + T_{37}) \lrcorner 4$$

4.5.6 MD5 Message Digest Pass 4

A function $I(x,y,z)$ is defined as $y \oplus (x \vee \sim z)$. A separate step is done for each of the 16 words of the message. For each integer i from 0 through 15,

$$d_{(-i) \wedge 3} = (d_{(-i) \wedge 3} + I(d_{(1-i) \wedge 3}, d_{(2-i) \wedge 3}, d_{(3-i) \wedge 3}) + m_{(7i) \wedge 15} + T_{i+49}) \lrcorner S_4(i \wedge 3)$$

where $S_4(i) = (i+3)(i+4)/2$, so the $\lrcorner$s cycle over the values 6, 10, 15, 21. We can write out the first few steps of the pass as follows:

$$d_0 = (d_0 + I(d_1, d_2, d_3) + m_0 + T_{49}) \lrcorner 6$$
$$d_3 = (d_3 + I(d_0, d_1, d_2) + m_7 + T_{50}) \lrcorner 10$$
$$d_2 = (d_2 + I(d_3, d_0, d_1) + m_{14} + T_{51}) \lrcorner 15$$
$$d_1 = (d_1 + I(d_2, d_3, d_0) + m_5 + T_{52}) \lrcorner 21$$
$$d_0 = (d_0 + I(d_1, d_2, d_3) + m_{12} + T_{53}) \lrcorner 6$$

4.6　SHS

SHS (**Secure Hash Standard**) was proposed by NIST as a message digest function. SHS takes a message of length at most 2^{64} bits and produces a 160-bit output. It is similar to the MD5 message digest function, but it is a little slower to execute and presumably more secure. MD4 made three passes over each block of data; MD5 made four; SHS makes five. It also produces a 160-bit digest as opposed to the 128 of the MDs.

4.6.1　SHS Message Padding

SHS pads messages in the same manner as MD4 and MD5, except that SHS is not defined for a message that is longer than 2^{64} bits. We don't consider that a problem. If there were such a message it would take several hundred years to transmit it at 10 Gigabits per second, and it would take even longer (in the hundreds of centuries) to compute the SHS message digest for it at 100 MIPS. As our grandmothers would surely have said, had the occasion arisen,

If you can't say something in less that 2^{64} bits, you shouldn't say it at all.

4.6.2　Overview of SHS Message Digest Computation

Just like MD4 and MD5, SHS operates in stages (see Figure 4-7). Each stage mangles the pre-stage message digest by a sequence of operations based on the current message block. At the end of the stage, each word of the mangled message digest is added to its pre-stage value to produce the post stage value (which becomes the pre-stage value for the next stage). Therefore, the current value of the message digest must be saved at the beginning of the stage so that it can be added in at the end of the stage.

The 160-bit message digest consists of five 32-bit words. Let's call them A, B, C, D, and E. Before the first stage they are set to $A = 67452301_{16}$, $B = \text{efcdab89}_{16}$, $C = 98\text{badcfe}_{16}$, $D = 10325476_{16}$, $E = \text{c3d2e1f0}_{16}$. After the last stage, the value of $A|B|C|D|E$ is the message digest for the entire message.

SHS is extremely similar in structure to MD4 and MD5, even more so than their descriptions might indicate (see Homework Problem 7).

4.6.3 SHS Operation on a 512-bit Block

At the start of each stage, the 512-bit message block is used to create a 5×512-bit chunk (see Figure 4-8). The first 512 bits of the chunk consist of the message block. The rest gets filled in, a 32-bit word at a time, according to the bizarre rule that the nth word (starting from word 16, since words 0 through 15 consist of the 512-bit message block) is the $\oplus$ of words $n-3$, $n-8$, $n-14$, and $n-16$. In the revised version of SHS, the $\oplus$ of words $n-3$, $n-8$, $n-14$, and $n-16$ is rotated left one bit before being stored as word n; this is the only modification to the original SHS.

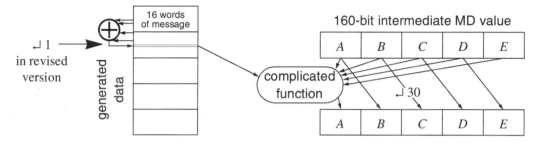

Figure 4-8. Inner Loop of SHS—80 Iterations per Block

Now we have a buffer of eighty 32-bit words (5×512 bits). Let's call the eighty 32-bit words W_0, W_1, ...W_{79}. Now, a little program:

For $t = 0$ through 79, modify A, B, C, D, and E as follows:

$$B = \text{old } A \qquad C = \text{old } B \lrcorner 30 \qquad D = \text{old } C \qquad E = \text{old } D$$

"Hmm," you're thinking. "This isn't too hard to follow." Well, we haven't yet said what the new A is! Since the new A depends on the old A, B, C, D, and E, a programmer would first compute the new A into a temporary variable V, and then after computing the new values of B, C, D, and E, set the new A equal to V. For clarity we didn't bother. In the following computation, everything to the right of the equal refers to the old values of A, B, C, D, and E:

$$A = E + (A \lrcorner 5) + W_t + K_t + f(t,B,C,D)$$

Let's look at each of the terms. E and $A\lrcorner 5$ are easy. W_t is the tth 32-bit word in the 80-word block. K_t is a constant, but it varies according to which word you're on (do you like the concept of a variable constant?):

$$K_t = \lfloor 2^{30} \sqrt{2} \rfloor = \text{5a827999}_{16} \qquad (0 <= t <= 19)$$
$$K_t = \lfloor 2^{30} \sqrt{3} \rfloor = \text{6ed9eba1}_{16} \qquad (20 <= t <= 39)$$
$$K_t = \lfloor 2^{30} \sqrt{5} \rfloor = \text{8f1bbcdc}_{16} \qquad (40 <= t <= 59)$$
$$K_t = \lfloor 2^{30} \sqrt{10} \rfloor = \text{ca62c1d6}_{16} \qquad (60 <= t <= 79)$$

$f(t,B,C,D)$ is a function that varies according to which of the eighty words you're working on:

$$f(t,B,C,D) = (B \wedge C) \vee (\sim B \wedge D) \qquad (0 <= t <= 19)$$
$$f(t,B,C,D) = B \oplus C \oplus D \qquad (20 <= t <= 39)$$
$$f(t,B,C,D) = (B \wedge C) \vee (B \wedge D) \vee (C \wedge D) \quad (40 <= t <= 59)$$
$$f(t,B,C,D) = B \oplus C \oplus D \qquad (60 <= t <= 79)$$

4.7 HOMEWORK

1. Doing a signature with RSA alone on a long message would be too slow (presumably using cipher block chaining). Suppose we could do division quickly. Would it be reasonable to compute an RSA signature on a long message by first finding what the message equals, mod n, and signing that?

2. Message digests are reasonably fast, but here's a much faster function to compute. Take your message, divide it into 128-bit chunks, and $\oplus$ all the chunks together to get a 128-bit result. Do the standard message digest on the result. Is this a good message digest function?

3. In §4.1 *Introduction* we discuss the devious secretary Bob having an automatic means of generating many messages that Alice would sign, and many messages that Bob would like to send. By the birthday problem, by the time Bob has tried a total of 2^{32} messages, he will probably have found two with the same message digest. The problem is, both may be of the same type, which would not do him any good. How many messages must Bob try before it is probable that he'll have messages with matching digests, and that the messages will be of opposite types?

4. In §4.2.4.2 *Hashing Large Messages*, we described a hash algorithm in which a constant was successively encrypted with blocks of the message. We showed that you could find two messages with the same hash value in about 2^{32} operations. So we suggested doubling the hash size by using the message twice, first in forward order to make up the first half of the hash, and then in reverse order for the second half of the hash. Assuming a 64-bit encryption block, how could you find two messages with the same hash value in about 2^{32} iterations? Hint: consider blockwise palindromic messages.

5. Design a modification to MD2 to handle messages which are not an integral number of bytes. Design it so that messages that are an integral number of bytes have the same digest value as with the existing MD2.

6. Why do MD4, MD5, and SHS require padding of messages that are already a multiple of 512 bits?

7. Modify the specification of SHS so that it looks a lot more like MD4 and MD5. Do this by having each of the words A, B, C, D, and E modified in place rather than (as SHS specifies it) modifying A and then basically rotating the words. Alternatively, modify the specifications of MD4 and MD5 to make them look more like SHS. How would you choose which specification to base an implemention on in a particular underlying architecture?

8. Open-ended project: Implement one or more of the message digest algorithms and test how "random" the output appears. For example, test the percentage of 1 bits in the output, or test how many bits of output change with minor changes in the input. Also, design various simplifications of the message digest functions (such as reducing the number of rounds) and see how these change things.

9. What are the minimal and maximal amounts of padding that would be required in each of the message digest functions?

10. Assume $\wedge$, $\vee$, $\oplus$, $+$, $\sim$, and $\lrcorner$ all take about the same amount of time. Estimate the relative performance of MD2, MD4, MD5, and SHS.

11. Show that the checksum function in MD2 would not be a good message digest function by showing how to generate a message with a given checksum.

12. Assume a good 128-bit message digest function. Assume there is a particular value, d, for the message digest and you'd like to find a message that has a message digest of d. Given that there are many more 2000-bit messages that map to a particular 128-bit message digest than 1000-bit messages, would you theoretically have to test fewer 2000-bit messages to find one that has a message digest of d than if you were to test 1000-bit messages?

13. Why do we expect that a randomly chosen 100-bit number will have about the same number of 1 bits and 0 bits? (For you statistics fans, calculate the mean and standard deviation of the number of 1 bits.)

14. For purposes of this exercise, we will define **random** as having all elements equally likely to be chosen. So a function that selects a 100-bit number will be random if every 100-bit number is equally likely to be chosen. Using this definition, if we look at the function "+" and we have two inputs, x and y, then the output will be random if at least one of x and y are random. For instance, y can always be 51, and yet the output will be random if x is random. For the following functions, find sufficient conditions for x, y, and z under which the output will be random:

$\sim x$

$x \oplus y$

$x \vee y$

$x \wedge y$

$(x \wedge y) \vee (\sim x \wedge z)$ [the selection function]

$(x \wedge y) \vee (x \wedge z) \vee (y \wedge z)$ [the majority function]

$x \oplus y \oplus z$

$y \oplus (x \vee \sim z)$

15. Prove that the function $(x \wedge y) \oplus (x \wedge z) \oplus (y \wedge z)$ and the function $(x \wedge y) \vee (x \wedge z) \vee (y \wedge z)$ are equivalent. (Sorry—this isn't too relevant to cryptography, but we'd stumbled on two different versions of this function in different documentation and we had to think about it for a bit to realize they were the same. We figured you should have the same fun.)

16. We mentioned in §4.2.2 *Computing a MIC with a Hash* that using $MD4(K_{AB}.m)$ as a MIC is not secure. This is not a problem if MD2 is used instead of MD4. Why is that the case?

17. In §4.2.3.1 *Generating a One-Time Pad*, we generate a pseudo-random stream of MD-sized blocks. This stream must eventually repeat (since only $2^{MD\text{-size}}$ different blocks can be generated). Will the first block necessarily be the first to be repeated? How does this compare to OFB (see Chapter 3 *Secret Key Cryptography* Homework Problem 12)?

18. How do you decrypt the encryption specified in §4.2.3.2 *Mixing In the Plaintext*?

19. Can you modify the encryption specified in §4.2.3.2 *Mixing In the Plaintext* so that instead of $b_i = MD(K_{AB}|c_{i-1})$ we use $b_i = MD(K_{AB}|p_{i-1})$? How do you decrypt it? Why wouldn't the modified scheme be as secure? (Hint—what would happen if the plaintext consisted of all zeroes?)

5 PUBLIC KEY ALGORITHMS

5.1 INTRODUCTION

This chapter describes public key cryptography. To really understand how and why the public key algorithms work, it is necessary to know some number theory. In this chapter we'll describe the number theory concepts necessary to understand the public key algorithms, but only in sufficient detail for an intuitive understanding. For instance, we won't give proofs, though we will explain things. And in the case of complex algorithms (like Euclid's algorithm), we'll merely state that the algorithm exists and what it does, rather than describing the algorithm in this chapter. Those desiring a more complete treatment of the subject matter can read Chapter 6 *Number Theory*.

Public key algorithms are a motley crew. All the hash algorithms do the same thing—they take a message and perform an irreversible transformation on it. All the secret key algorithms do the same thing—they take a block and encrypt it in a reversible way, and there are chaining methods to convert the block ciphers into message ciphers. But public key algorithms look very different from each other, not only in how they perform their functions, but in what functions they perform. We'll describe:

- RSA, which does encryption and digital signatures

- El Gamal and DSS, which do digital signatures but not encryption

- Diffie-Hellman, which allows establishment of a shared secret but doesn't have any algorithms that actually use the secret (it would be used, for instance, together with a secret key scheme in order to actually use the secret for something like encryption)

- zero knowledge proof systems, which only do authentication

The thing that all public key algorithms have in common is the concept of a pair of related quantities, one secret and one public, associated with each principal. (A **principal** is anything or anyone participating in cryptographically protected communication.)

5.2 MODULAR ARITHMETIC

There was a young fellow named Ben
Who could only count modulo ten.
He said, "When I go
Past my last little toe
I shall have to start over again."

—Anonymous

Most of the public key algorithms are based on modular arithmetic. Modular arithmetic uses the non-negative integers less than some positive integer n, performs ordinary arithmetic operations such as addition and multiplication, and then replaces the result with its remainder when divided by n. The result is said to be **modulo** n or **mod** n. When we write "x mod n", we mean the remainder of x when divided by n. Sometimes we'll leave out "mod n" when it's clear from context.

5.2.1 Modular Addition

Let's look at mod 10 addition. $3 + 5 = 8$, just like in regular arithmetic. The answer is already between 0 and 9. $7 + 6 = 13$ in regular arithmetic, but the mod 10 answer is 3. Basically, one can perform mod 10 arithmetic by using the last digit of the answer. For example,

$$5 + 5 = 0$$

$$3 + 9 = 2$$

$$2 + 2 = 4$$

$$9 + 9 = 8$$

Let's look at the mod 10 addition table (Figure 5-1). Addition of a constant mod 10 can be used as a scheme for encrypting digits, in that it maps each decimal digit to a different decimal digit in a way that is reversible; the constant is our secret key. It's not a *good* cipher, of course, but it is a cipher. (It's actually a Caesar cipher.) Decryption would be done by subtracting the secret key modulo 10, which is an easy operation—just do ordinary subtraction and if the result is less than 0, add 10.

Just like in regular arithmetic, subtracting x can be done by adding $-x$, also known as x's **additive inverse**. An additive inverse of x is the number you'd have to add to x to get 0. For example, 4's inverse will be 6, because in mod 10 arithmetic $4 + 6 = 0$. If the secret key were 4, then to encrypt we'd add 4 (mod 10), and to decrypt we'd add 6 (mod 10).

+	0	1	2	3	4	5	6	7	8	9
0	0	1	2	3	4	5	6	7	8	9
1	1	2	3	4	5	6	7	8	9	0
2	2	3	4	5	6	7	8	9	0	1
3	3	4	5	6	7	8	9	0	1	2
4	4	5	6	7	8	9	0	1	2	3
5	5	6	7	8	9	0	1	2	3	4
6	6	7	8	9	0	1	2	3	4	5
7	7	8	9	0	1	2	3	4	5	6
8	8	9	0	1	2	3	4	5	6	7
9	9	0	1	2	3	4	5	6	7	8

Figure 5-1. Addition Modulo 10

5.2.2 Modular Multiplication

Now let's look at the mod 10 multiplication table (Figure 5-2). Multiplication by 1, 3, 7, or 9

·	0	1	2	3	4	5	6	7	8	9
0	0	0	0	0	0	0	0	0	0	0
1	0	1	2	3	4	5	6	7	8	9
2	0	2	4	6	8	0	2	4	6	8
3	0	3	6	9	2	5	8	1	4	7
4	0	4	8	2	6	0	4	8	2	6
5	0	5	0	5	0	5	0	5	0	5
6	0	6	2	8	4	0	6	2	8	4
7	0	7	4	1	8	5	2	9	6	3
8	0	8	6	4	2	0	8	6	4	2
9	0	9	8	7	6	5	4	3	2	1

Figure 5-2. Multiplication Modulo 10

works as a cipher, because it performs a one-to-one substitution of the digits. But multiplication by any of the other numbers will not work as a cipher. For instance, if you tried to encrypt by multiplying by 5, half the numbers would encrypt to 0 and the other half would encrypt to 5. You've lost information. You can't decrypt the ciphertext 5, since the plaintext could be any of {1, 3, 5, 7, 9}. So multiplication mod 10 can be used for encryption, provided that you choose the multiplier wisely. But how do you decrypt? Well, just like with addition, where we undid the addition by adding the additive inverse, we'll undo the multiplication by multiplying by the multiplicative inverse. In ordinary arithmetic, x's multiplicative inverse is $1/x$. If x is an integer, then its multiplicative inverse is a fraction. In modular arithmetic though, the only numbers that exist are integers. The **multiplicative inverse** of x (written x^{-1}) is the number by which you'd multiply x to get 1. Only the numbers {1, 3, 7, 9} have multiplicative inverses mod 10. For example, 7 is the multiplicative inverse of 3. So encryption could be performed by multiplying by 3, and decryption could be performed by multiplying by 7. 9 is its own inverse. And 1 is its own inverse. Multiplication mod n is not a secure cipher, but it works, in the sense that we can scramble the digits by multiplying by x and get back to the original digits by multiplying by x^{-1}.

It is by no means obvious how you find a multiplicative inverse in mod n arithmetic, especially if n is very large. For instance if n was a 100-digit number, you would not be able to do a brute-force search for an inverse. But it turns out there is an algorithm that will efficiently find inverses mod n. It is known as Euclid's algorithm. §6.4 *Euclid's Algorithm* gives the details of the algorithm. For here, all you need to know to know is what it does. Given x and n, it finds the number y such that $x \cdot y$ mod $n = 1$ (if there is one).

What's special about the numbers {1, 3, 7, 9}? Why is it they're the only ones, mod 10, with multiplicative inverses? The answer is that those numbers are all relatively prime to 10. **Relatively prime** means they do not share any common factors other than 1. For instance, the largest integer that divides both 9 and 10 is 1. The largest integer that divides both 7 and 10 is 1. In contrast, 6 is not one of {1, 3, 7, 9}, and it does not have a multiplicative inverse mod 10. It's also not relatively prime to 10 because 2 divides both 10 and 6. In general, when we're working mod n, all the numbers relatively prime to n will have multiplicative inverses, and none of the other numbers will. And mod n multiplication by any number x relatively prime to n will work as a cipher because we can multiply by x to encrypt, and then multiply by x^{-1} to decrypt. (Again let us hasten to reassure you that we're not claiming it's a *good* cipher, in the sense of being secure. What we mean by its being a cipher is that we can modify the information through one algorithm (multiplication by x mod n) and then reverse the process (by multiplying by x^{-1} mod n).

How many numbers less than n are relatively prime to n? Why would anyone care? Well, it turns out to be so useful that it's been given its own notation—$\phi(n)$. ϕ is called the **totient function**, supposedly from *total* and *quotient*. How big is $\phi(n)$? If n is prime, then all the integers {1, 2, ... $n-1$} are relatively prime to n, so $\phi(n) = n-1$. If n is a product of two distinct primes, say p and q, then there are $(p-1)(q-1)$ numbers relatively prime to n, so $\phi(n) = (p-1)(q-1)$. Why is that? Well, there are $n = pq$ total numbers in {0, 1, 2, ... $n-1$}, and we want to exclude those numbers that aren't relatively prime to n. Those are the numbers that are either multiples of p or of q. There are p multiples of q less than pq and q multiples of p less than pq. So there are $p+q-1$ numbers less than

pq that aren't relatively prime to pq (we can't count 0 twice!). Thus $\phi(pq) = pq - (p+q-1) = (p-1)(q-1)$.

5.2.3 Modular Exponentiation

Modular exponentiation is again just like ordinary exponentiation. Once you get the answer, you divide by n and get the remainder. For instance, $4^6 = 6 \bmod 10$ because $4^6 = 4096$ in ordinary arithmetic, and $4096 = 6 \bmod 10$. Let's look at the exponentiation table mod 10. We are purposely putting in extra columns because in exponentiation, $x^y \bmod n$ is not the same as $x^{y+n} \bmod n$. For instance, $3^1 = 3 \bmod 10$, but $3^{11} = 7 \bmod 10$ (it's 177147 in ordinary arithmetic).

Let's look at mod 10 exponentiation (Figure 5-3). Note that exponentiation by 3 would act as

x^y	0	1	2	3	4	5	6	7	8	9	10	11	12
0		0	0	0	0	0	0	0	0	0	0	0	0
1	1	1	1	1	1	1	1	1	1	1	1	1	1
2	1	2	4	8	6	2	4	8	6	2	4	8	6
3	1	3	9	7	1	3	9	7	1	3	9	7	1
4	1	4	6	4	6	4	6	4	6	4	6	4	6
5	1	5	5	5	5	5	5	5	5	5	5	5	5
6	1	6	6	6	6	6	6	6	6	6	6	6	6
7	1	7	9	3	1	7	9	3	1	7	9	3	1
8	1	8	4	2	6	8	4	2	6	8	4	2	6
9	1	9	1	9	1	9	1	9	1	9	1	9	1

Figure 5-3. Exponentiation Modulo 10

an encryption of the digits, in that it rearranges all the digits. Exponentiation by 2 would not, because both 2^2 and 8^2 are 4 mod 10. How would you decrypt? Is there an exponentiative inverse like there is a multiplicative inverse? Just like with multiplication, the answer is *sometimes*. (I bet people are going to hate our inventing the word *exponentiative*, but it's a useful word.)

Now we'll throw in an amazing fact about $\phi(n)$. Looking at the exponentiation table, we notice that columns 1 and 5 are the same, and 2 and 6 are the same, and 3 and 7 are the same. It turns out that $x^y \bmod n$ is the same as $x^{(y \bmod \phi(n))} \bmod n$. In the case of 10, the numbers relatively prime to 10 are $\{1, 3, 7, 9\}$, so $\phi(n) = 4$. So that's why the ith column is the same as the $i+4^{th}$ column. (Note for picky mathematicians—this fact isn't true for all n, but it's true for all n we care about. It's true for primes and it's true for any product of distinct primes, i.e. it's true for any n that doesn't have p^2 as a factor for any prime p—such an n is known as **square free**.)

What we'll find important is the special case of this where $y = 1 \bmod \phi(n)$, i.e. if $y = 1 \bmod \phi(n)$, then for any number x, $x^y = x \bmod n$. Armed with this knowledge, let's look at RSA.

5.3 RSA

RSA is named after its inventors, Rivest, Shamir, and Adleman. It is a public key cryptographic algorithm that does encryption as well as decryption. The key length is variable. Anyone using RSA can choose a long key for enhanced security, or a short key for efficiency. The most commonly used key length for RSA is 512 bits.

The block size in RSA (the chunk of data to be encrypted) is also variable. The plaintext block must be smaller than the key length. The ciphertext block will be the length of the key. RSA is much slower to compute than popular secret key algorithms like DES and IDEA. As a result, RSA does not tend to get used for encrypting long messages. Mostly it is used to encrypt a secret key, and then secret key cryptography is used to actually encrypt the message.

5.3.1 RSA Algorithm

First, you need to generate a public key and a corresponding private key. Choose two large primes p and q (probably around 256 bits each). Multiply them together, and call the result n. The factors p and q will remain secret. (You won't tell anybody, and it's practically impossible to factor numbers that large.)

To generate your public key, choose a number e that is relatively prime to $\phi(n)$. Since you know p and q, you know $\phi(n)$—it's $(p-1)(q-1)$. Your public key is $\langle e,n \rangle$.

To generate your private key, find the number d that is the multiplicative inverse of e mod $\phi(n)$. $\langle d,n \rangle$ is your private key.

To encrypt a message m ($< n$), someone using your public key should compute ciphertext $c = m^e \bmod n$. Only you will be able to decrypt c, using your private key to compute $m = c^d \bmod n$. Also, only you can sign a message m ($< n$) with signature $s = m^d \bmod n$ based on your private key. Anyone can verify your signature by checking that $m = s^e \bmod n$.

That's all there is to RSA. Now there are some questions we should ask.

- Why does it work? (E.g., will decrypting an encrypted message get the original message back?)

- Why is it secure? (E.g., given e and n, why can't someone easily compute d?)

- Are the operations encryption, decryption, signing, and verifying signatures all sufficiently efficient to be practical?

- How do we find big primes?

5.3.2 Why Does RSA Work?

RSA does arithmetic mod n, where $n = pq$. We know that $\phi(n) = (p-1)(q-1)$. We've chosen d and e such that $de = 1 \bmod \phi(n)$. Therefore, for any x, $x^{de} = x \bmod n$. An RSA encryption consists of taking x and raising it to e. If we take the result and raise it to the d (i.e., perform RSA decryption), we'll get $(x^e)^d$, which equals x^{ed}, which is the same as x. So we see that decryption reverses encryption.

In the case of signature generation, x is first raised to the d power to get the signature and then the signature is raised to the e power for verification; the result, x^{de}, will equal x.

5.3.3 Why Is RSA Secure?

We don't know for sure that RSA is secure. We can only depend on the Fundamental Tenet of Cryptography—lots of smart people have been trying to figure out how to break RSA, and they haven't come up with anything yet.

The real premise behind RSA's security is the assumption that factoring a big number is hard. The best known factoring methods are really slow. To factor a 512-bit number with the best known techniques would take about a half million MIPS-years. We suspect that a better technique is to wait three hundred years and *then* use the best known technique.

If you can factor quickly, you can break RSA. Suppose you are given Alice's public key $\langle e,n \rangle$. If you could find e's exponentiative inverse mod n, then you'd have figured out Alice's private key $\langle d,n \rangle$. How can you find e's exponentiative inverse? Alice did it by knowing the factors of n, allowing her to compute $\phi(n)$. She found the number that was e's multiplicative inverse mod $\phi(n)$. She didn't have to factor n—she started with primes p and q and multiplied them together to get n. You can do what Alice did if you can factor n to get p and q.

We do not know that factoring n is the only way of breaking RSA. We know that breaking RSA (for example, having an efficient means of finding d, given e and n) is no more difficult than factoring [CORM91], but there might be some other means of breaking RSA.

Note that it's possible to misuse RSA. For instance, let's say I'm going to send Alice a message divulging the name of the Cabinet member who allegedly once hired a kid to mow his/her lawn, and didn't fill out all the proper IRS forms. Bob knows that's what I'm going to transmit. I'll encrypt the text string which is the guilty person's name using Alice's public key. Bob can't possibly decrypt it, because we believe RSA is secure. So what can Bob learn from eavesdropping on the encrypted data?

Well, Bob can't decrypt, but he can encrypt. He knows I'm sending one of fourteen possible messages. He takes each Cabinet member's name and encrypts it with Alice's public key. One of them will match my message—unless I use RSA properly. In §5.3.6 *Public-Key Cryptography Standard (PKCS)* we'll discuss how to use RSA properly. For now, a simple thing I can do to prevent Bob from guessing my message, encrypting with Alice's public key, and checking the result, is to concatenate the name with a large random number, say 64 bits long. Then instead of fourteen possible messages for Bob to check, there are 14×2^{64}, and checking that many messages is computationally infeasible.

5.3.4 How Efficient Are the RSA Operations?

The operations that need to be routinely performed with RSA are encryption, decryption, generating a signature, and verifying a signature. These need to be very efficient, because they will be used a lot. Finding an RSA key (which means picking appropriate n, d, and e) also needs to be reasonably efficient, but it isn't as critical as the other operations, since it is done less frequently. As it turns out, finding an RSA key is substantially more computationally intensive than using one.

5.3.4.1 Exponentiating With Big Numbers

Encryption, decryption, signing, and verifying signatures all involve taking a large number, raising it to a large power, and finding the remainder mod a large number. For the sizes the numbers have to be for RSA to be secure, these operations would be prohibitively expensive if done in the most straightforward way. The following will illustrate some tricks for doing the calculation faster.

Suppose you want to compute 123^{54} mod 678. The straightforward thing to do (assuming your computer has a multiple-precision arithmetic package) is to multiply 123 by itself 54 times, getting a really big product (about 100 digits), and then to divide by 678 to get the remainder. A computer could do this with ease, but for RSA to be secure, the numbers must be on the order of 150 digits. Raising a 150-digit number to a 150-digit power by this method would exhaust the capacity of all existing computers for more than the expected life of the universe, and thus would not be cost-effective.

Luckily, you can do better than that.

If you do the modular reduction after each multiply, it keeps the number from getting really ridiculous. To illustrate:

$$123^2 = 123 \cdot 123 = 15129 = 213 \text{ mod } 678$$

$$123^3 = 123 \cdot 213 = 26199 = 435 \bmod 678$$
$$123^4 = 123 \cdot 435 = 53505 = 621 \bmod 678$$

This reduces the problem to 54 small multiplies and 54 small divides, but it would still be unacceptable for exponents of the size used with RSA.

However, there is a much more efficient method. To raise a number x to an exponent which is a power of 2, say 32, you could multiply by x 32 times, which is reasonable if you have nothing better to do with your time. A much better scheme is to first square x, then square the result, and so on. Then you'll be done after 5 squarings (5 multiplies and 5 divides):

$$123^2 = 123 \cdot 123 = 15129 = 213 \bmod 678$$
$$123^4 = 213 \cdot 213 = 45369 = 621 \bmod 678$$
$$123^8 = 621 \cdot 621 = 385641 = 537 \bmod 678$$
$$123^{16} = 537 \cdot 537 = 288369 = 219 \bmod 678$$
$$123^{32} = 219 \cdot 219 = 47961 = 501 \bmod 678$$

What if you're not lucky enough to be raising something to a power of 2?

First note that if you know what 123^x is, then it's easy to compute 123^{2x}—you get that by squaring 123^x. It's also easy to compute 123^{2x+1}—you get that by multiplying 123^{2x} by 123. Now you use this observation to compute 123^{54}.

Well, 54 is 110110_2 (represented in binary). You'll compute 123 raised to a sequence of powers—1_2, 11_2, 110_2, 1101_2, 11011_2, 110110_2. Each successive power concatenates one more bit of the desired exponent. And each successive power is either twice the preceding power or one more than twice the preceding power:

$$123^2 = 123 \cdot 123 = 15129 = 213 \bmod 678$$
$$123^3 = 123^2 \cdot 123 = 213 \cdot 123 = 26199 = 435 \bmod 678$$
$$123^6 = (123^3)^2 = 435^2 = 189225 = 63 \bmod 678$$
$$123^{12} = (123^6)^2 = 63^2 = 3969 = 579 \bmod 678$$
$$123^{13} = 123^{12} \cdot 123 = 579 \cdot 123 = 71217 = 27 \bmod 678$$
$$123^{26} = (123^{13})^2 = 27^2 = 729 = 51 \bmod 678$$
$$123^{27} = 123^{26} \cdot 123 = 51 \cdot 123 = 6273 = 171 \bmod 678$$
$$123^{54} = (123^{27})^2 = 171^2 = 29241 = 87 \bmod 678$$

In other words, raising 123 to the 54 can be done by repeated squaring, together with sporadic multiplication by 123 for the bits that are 1:

$$54 = (((((1)2+1)2)2+1)2+1)2, \qquad \text{so}$$
$$123^{54} = (((((123)^2 123)^2)^2 123)^2 123)^2 = 87 \bmod 678.$$

The idea is that squaring is the same as multiplying the exponent by two, which in turn is the same as shifting the exponent left by one bit. And multiplying by the base is the same as adding one to the exponent.

In general, to perform exponentiation of a base to an exponent, you start with your value set to 1. As you read the exponent in binary bit by bit from high-order bit to low-order bit, you square your value, and if the bit is a 1 you then multiply by the base. You perform modular reduction after each operation to keep the intermediate results small.

By this method you've reduced the computation of 123^{54} to 8 multiplies and 8 divides. More importantly, the number of multiplies and divides rises linearly with the length of the exponent in bits rather than with the value of the exponent itself.

RSA operations using this technique are sufficiently efficient to be practical.

5.3.4.2 Generating RSA Keys

Most uses of public key cryptography do not require frequent generation of RSA keys. If generation of an RSA key is only done, for instance, when an employee is hired, then it need not be as efficient as the operations that use the keys. However, it still has to be reasonably efficient.

5.3.4.2.1. Finding Big Primes p and q

There is an infinite supply of primes. However, they thin out as numbers get bigger and bigger. The probability of a randomly chosen number n being prime is approximately $1/\ln n$. The natural logarithm function, ln, rises linearly with the size of the number represented in digits or bits. For a ten-digit number, there is about one chance in 23 of it being prime. For a hundred-digit number (a size that would be useful for RSA), there is about one chance in 230.

So, we'll choose a random number, and test if it is prime. On the average, we'll only have to try 230 of them before we find one that is a prime. So, how do we test if a number n is prime?

One naive method is to divide n by all numbers $\leq \sqrt{n}$ and see if the division comes out even. The problem is, that would take several universe lifetimes for each candidate prime. We said finding p and q didn't need to be as easy as generating or verifying a signature, but forever is too long.

It turns out there is no known practical way for absolutely determining that a number of this size is prime. Fortunately, there is a test for determining that a number is probably prime, and the more time we spend testing a number the more assured we can be that the number is prime.

We'll use Euler's Theorem: For any a relatively prime to n, $a^{\phi(n)} = 1 \bmod n$. (See §6.8 *Euler's Theorem* for a proof.)

In the case where n is a prime, $\phi(n) = n - 1$. The theorem then takes on a simpler form and in fact another name:

> Fermat's Theorem: If p is prime and $0 < a < p$, $a^{p-1} = 1 \bmod p$.

You might ask the question (somebody did)—does $a^{n-1} = 1 \bmod n$ hold even when n is not prime? The answer is—usually not! A primality test, then, for a number n is to pick a number $a < n$, compute $a^{n-1} \bmod n$, and see if the answer is 1. If it is not 1, n is certainly not prime. If it is 1, n may or may not be prime. If n is a randomly generated number of about a hundred digits, the probability that n isn't prime but $a^{n-1} \bmod n = 1$ is about 1 in 10^{13} [POME81, CORM91]. Most people would decide they could live with that risk of falsely assuming n was prime when it wasn't. The cost of such a mistake would be that (1) RSA might fail—they could not decrypt a message addressed to them, or (2) someone might be able to compute their private exponent with less effort than anticipated. There aren't many applications where a risk of failure of 1 in 10^{13} is a problem.

But if the risk of 1 in 10^{13} is unacceptable, the primality test can be made more reliable. A likely thing to try is using multiple values of a. If for any given n, each value of a had a probability of 1 in 10^{13} of falsely reporting primality, a few tests would assure even the most paranoid person. Unfortunately, there exist numbers n which are not prime, but which satisfy $a^{n-1} = 1 \bmod n$ for all values of a. They are called **Carmichael numbers**. Carmichael numbers are sufficiently rare that the chance of selecting one at random is nothing to lose sleep over. Nevertheless, mathematicians have come up with an enhancement to the above primality test that will detect non-primes (even Carmichael numbers) with high probability and negligible additional computation, so we may as well use it.

The method of choice for testing whether a number is prime is due to Miller and Rabin [RABI80]. We can always express $n-1$ as a power of two times an odd number, say $2^b c$. We can then compute $a^{n-1} \bmod n$ by computing $a^c \bmod n$ and then squaring the result b times. If the result is not 1, then n is not prime and we're done. If the result is 1, we can go back and look at those last few intermediate squarings. (If we're really clever, we'll be checking the intermediate results as we compute them.) If $a^c \bmod n$ is not 1, then one of the squarings took a number that was not 1 and squared it to produce 1. That number is a mod n square root of 1. It turns out that if n is prime, then the only mod n square roots of 1 are 1 and -1 (also known as $n-1$). Further, if n is not a power of a prime, then 1 has many square roots, and all are equally likely to be found by this test. For more on why, see §6.5 *Chinese Remainder Theorem*. So if the Miller-Rabin test finds a square root of 1 that is not ±1, then n is not prime. Furthermore, if n is not prime (even if it is a Carmichael number), at least ¾ of all possible values of a will show n to be composite. By trying many values for a, we can make the probability of falsely identifying n as prime inconceivably small. In actual implementations, how many values of a to try is a trade-off between performance and paranoia.

To summarize, an efficient method of finding primes is:

1. Pick an odd random number n in the proper range.

2. Test n's divisibility by small primes and go back to step 1 if you find a factor. (Obviously, this step isn't necessary, but it's worth it since it has a high enough probability of catching some non-primes and is much faster than the next step).

3. Repeat the following until n is proven not prime (in which case go back to step 1) or as many times as you feel necessary to show that n is probably prime:

   Pick an a at random and compute $a^c \bmod n$ (where c is the odd number for which $n-1 = 2^b c$). During the computation of $a^c \bmod n$, each time mod n squaring is performed, check if the result is 1; if so, check if the number that was squared (which is a square root of 1) is ± 1; if not, n is not prime.
   Next, if the result of the computation of $a^c \bmod n$ is ± 1, n passes the primality test for this a. Otherwise, at most $b-1$ times, replace the result by its square and check if it is ± 1. If it is 1, n is not prime (because the previous result is a square root of 1 different from ± 1). If it is -1, n passes the primality test for this a. If you've done the squaring $b-1$ times, n is not prime (because $a^{(n-1)/2}$ is not ± 1).

5.3.4.2.2. Finding d and e

How do we find d and e given p and q? As we said earlier, for e we can choose any number that is relatively prime to $(p-1)(q-1)$, and then all we need to do is find the number d such that $ed = 1 \bmod \phi(n)$. This we can do with Euclid's algorithm.

There are two strategies one can use to ensure that e and $(p-1)(q-1)$ are relatively prime.

1. After p and q are selected, choose e at random. Test to see if e is relatively prime to $(p-1)(q-1)$. If not, select another e.

2. Don't pick p and q first. Instead, first choose e, then select p and q carefully so that $(p-1)$ and $(q-1)$ are guaranteed to be relatively prime to e. The next section will explain why you'd want to do this.

5.3.4.3 Having a Small Constant e

A rather astonishing discovery is that RSA is no less secure (as far as anyone knows) if e is always chosen to be the same number. And if e is chosen to be small, or easy to compute, then the operations of encryption and signature verification become much more efficient. Given that the procedure for finding a d and e pair is to pick one and then derive the other, it is straightforward to make e be a small constant. This makes public key operations faster while leaving private key operations unchanged. You might wonder whether it would be possible to select small values for d to make private key operations fast at the expense of public key operations. The answer is that you can't. If d were a constant, the scheme would not be secure because d is the secret. If d were small, an attacker could search small values to find d.

Two popular values of e are 3 and 65537.

Why 3? 2 doesn't work because it is not relatively prime to $(p-1)(q-1)$ (which must be even because p and q are both odd). 3 can work, and with 3, public key operations require only two multiplies. Using 3 as the public exponent maximizes performance.

As far as anyone knows, using 3 as a public exponent does not weaken the security of RSA if some practical constraints on its use are followed. Most dramatically, if a message m to be encrypted is small—in particular, smaller than $\sqrt[3]{n}$—then raising m to the power of three and reducing mod n will simply produce the value m^3. Anyone seeing such an encrypted message could decrypt it simply by taking a cube root. This problem can be avoided by padding each message with a random number before encryption, so that m^3 is always large enough to be guaranteed to need to be reduced mod n.

A second problem with using 3 as an exponent is that if the same message is sent encrypted to three or more recipients each of whom has a public exponent of 3, the message can be derived from the three encrypted values and the three public keys $\langle 3, n_1 \rangle$, $\langle 3, n_2 \rangle$, $\langle 3, n_3 \rangle$.

Suppose a bad guy sees $m^3 \bmod n_1$, $m^3 \bmod n_2$, and $m^3 \bmod n_3$ and knows $\langle 3, n_1 \rangle$, $\langle 3, n_2 \rangle$, $\langle 3, n_3 \rangle$. Then by the Chinese Remainder computation (see §6.5 *Chinese Remainder Theorem*), the bad guy can compute $m^3 \bmod n_1 n_2 n_3$. Since m is smaller than each of the n_is (because RSA can only encrypt messages smaller than the modulus), m^3 will be smaller than $n_1 n_2 n_3$, so $m^3 \bmod n_1 n_2 n_3$ will just be m^3. Therefore, the bad guy can compute the ordinary cube root of m^3 (which again is easy if you are a computer), giving m.

Now this isn't anything to get terribly upset about. In practical uses of RSA, the message to be encrypted is usually a key for a secret key encryption algorithm and in any case is much smaller than n. As a result, the message must be padded before it is encrypted. If the padding is randomly chosen (and it should be for a number of reasons), and if it is rechosen for each recipient, then there is no threat from an exponent of 3 no matter how many recipients there are. The padding doesn't really have to be random—for example, the recipient's ID would work fine.

Finally, an exponent of 3 works only if 3 is relatively prime to $\phi(n)$ (in order for it to have an inverse d). How do we choose p and q so that 3 will be relatively prime to $\phi(n) = (p-1)(q-1)$? Clearly, $(p-1)$ and $(q-1)$ must each be relatively prime to 3. To ensure that $p-1$ is relatively prime to 3, we want p to be 2 mod 3. That will ensure $p-1$ is 1 mod 3. Similarly we want q to be 2 mod 3. We can make sure that the only primes we select are congruent to 2 mod 3 by choosing a random number, multiplying by 3 and adding 2, and using that as the number we will test for primality. Indeed, we want to make sure the number we test is odd (since if it's even it is unlikely to be prime), so we should start with an odd number, multiply by 3 and add 2. This is equivalent to start-ing with any random number, multiplying by 6 and then adding 5.

Another popular value of e is 65537. Why 65537? The appeal of 65537 (as opposed to others of the same approximate size) is that $65537 = 2^{16}+1$ and it is prime. Because its binary representa-tion contains only two 1s, it takes only 17 multiplies to exponentiate. While this is much slower than the two multiplies required with an exponent of 3, it is much faster than the 768 (on average) required with a randomly chosen 512-bit value (the typical size of an RSA modulus in practical use today). Also, using the number 65537 as a public exponent largely avoids the problems with the exponent 3.

The first problem with 3 occurs if $m^3 < n$. Unless n is much longer than the 512 bits in typical use today, there aren't too many values of m for which $m^{65537} < n$, so being able to take a normal 65537th root is not a threat.

The second problem with 3 occurs when the same message is sent to at least 3 recipients. In theory, with 65537 there is a threat if the same message is sent encrypted to at least 65537 recipi-ents. A cynic would argue that under such circumstances, the message couldn't be very secret.

The third problem with 3 is that we have to choose n so that $\phi(n)$ is relatively prime to 3. For 65537, the easiest thing to do is just reject any p or q which is equal to 1 mod 65537. The probabil-ity of rejection is very small (2^{-16}), so this doesn't make finding n significantly harder.

5.3.4.4 Optimizing RSA Private Key Operations

There is a way to speed up RSA exponentiations in generating signatures and decrypting (the operations using the private key) by taking advantage of knowledge of p and q. Feel free to skip this section—it isn't a prerequisite for anything else in the book. And it requires more than the usual level of concentration.

In RSA, d and n are on the order of 512-bit numbers, or 150 digits. p and q are on the order of 256 bits, or 75 digits. RSA private key operations involve taking some c (usually a 512-bit number) and computing $c^d \bmod n$. It's easy to say "raise a 512-bit number to a 512-bit exponent mod a 512-bit number," but it's certainly processor-intensive, even if you happen to be a silicon-based computer. A way to speed up RSA operations is to do all the computation mod p and mod q, then use the Chinese Remainder Theorem to compute what the answer is mod pq.

So suppose you want to compute $m = c^d \bmod n$.

Instead, you could take $c_p = c \bmod p$ and $c_q = c \bmod q$ and compute $m_p = c_p^{\,d} \bmod p$ and $m_q = c_q^{\,d} \bmod q$, then use the Chinese Remainder Theorem to convert back to what m would equal mod n, which would give you $c^d \bmod n$. Also, it is not necessary to raise to the dth power mod p, given that d is going to be bigger than p (by a factor of about q). Since (by Euler's Theorem) any $a^{p-1} = 1 \bmod p$, we can take d's value mod $p-1$ and use that as the exponent instead. In other words, if $d = k(p-1) + r$, then $c^d \bmod p = c^r \bmod p$.

So, let us compute $d_p = d$ mod $(p-1)$ and $d_q = d$ mod $(q-1)$. Then, instead of doing the expected RSA operation of $m = c^d$ mod n which involves 512-bit numbers, we'll compute both $m_p = c_p^{d_p}$ mod p and $m_q = c_q^{d_q}$ mod q and then compute m from the Chinese Remainder Theorem. To save ourselves work, since we'll be using d_p and d_q a lot (every time we do an RSA private key computation), we'll compute them once and remember them. Similarly, to use the Chinese Remainder Theorem at the end, we need to know p^{-1} mod q and q^{-1} mod p, so we'll precompute and remember them as well.

All told, instead of one 512-bit exponentiation, this modified calculation does two 256-bit exponentiations, followed by two 256-bit multiplies and a 512-bit add. This might not seem like a net gain, but because the exponents are half as long, using this variant makes RSA about twice as fast.

Note that to do these optimizations for RSA operations, we need to know p and q. Someone who is only supposed to know the public key will not know p and q (or else they can easily compute d). Therefore, these optimizations are only useful for the private key operations (decryption and generating signatures). However, that's okay because we can choose e to be a convenient value (like 3 or 65537) so that raising a 512-bit number to e will be easy enough without the Chinese Remainder optimizations.

5.3.5 Arcane RSA Threats

Any number $x < n$ is a signature of x^e mod n. So it's trivial to forge someone's signature if you don't care what you're signing. The trick is to find a way to sign a specific number. Typically what is being signed is sufficiently constrained so that a random number has negligible probability of being a valid message. For example, often what is being signed is a message digest padded in a specific manner. If the pad is hundreds of zero bits, it is extremely unlikely that a random number will look like a padded message digest.

If you're not careful about how you pad your message data, you may allow an attacker without knowledge of your private key to forge your signature on valid messages.

Note: RSA deals with large numbers, and there is unfortunately more than one way to represent such numbers. In what follows, we have chosen to order the bytes left to right from most significant to least significant.

5.3.5.1 Smooth Numbers

A **smooth number** is defined as one that is the product of reasonably small primes. There's no absolute definition of a smooth number, since there's no real definition of *reasonably small*. The more compute power the attacker has at her disposal, and the more signatures she has access to, the larger the primes can be.

The threat we are about to describe is known as the **smooth number threat**. It is really only of theoretical interest, because of the immense amount of computation, gathering of immense numbers of signed messages, and luck involved. However, it costs very little to have an encoding that avoids this threat. The smooth number threat was discovered by Desmedt and Odlyzko [DESM86].

The first observation is that if you have signed m_1 and m_2, and a bad guy Carol can see your signature on m_1 and m_2, she can compute your signature on $m_1 \cdot m_2$, and on m_1/m_2, and m_1^j, and on $m_1^j \cdot m_2^k$. For instance, if Carol sees $m_1^d \mod n$ (which is your signature on m_1), then she can compute your signature on m_1^2 by computing $(m_1^d \mod n)^2 \mod n$ (see Homework Problem 7).

If Carol collects a lot of your signed messages, she will be able to compute your signature on any message that can be computed from her collection by multiplication and division. If the messages you sign are mostly smooth, there will be a lot of other smooth messages on which she will be able to forge your signature.

Suppose she collects your signatures on two messages whose ratio is a prime. Then she can compute your signature on that prime. If she's lucky enough to get many such message pairs, she can compute your signature on lots of primes, and then she can forge your signature on any message that is the product of any subset of those primes, each raised to any power. With enough pairs, she will be able to forge your signature on any message that is a smooth number.

Actually, Carol does not have to be nearly that lucky. With as few as k signatures on messages which are products of different subsets of k distinct primes, she will be able to isolate the signatures on the individual primes through a carefully chosen set of multiplications and divisions.

The typical thing being signed with RSA is a padded message digest. If it is padded with zeroes, it is much more likely to be smooth than is a random mod n number. A random mod n quantity is extremely unlikely to be smooth (low enough probability so that if you are signing random mod n numbers, we can assume Carol would have to have a lot of resources and a lot of luck to find even one smooth number you've signed, and she might need millions of them in order to mount the attack).

Padding on the left with zeroes keeps the padded message digest small and therefore likely to be smooth. Padding on the right with zeroes is merely multiplying the message digest by some power of 2, and so isn't any better.

Another tempting padding scheme is to pad on the right with random data. That way, since you are signing fairly random mod n numbers, it is very unlikely that any of the messages you sign will be smooth, so Carol won't have enough signed smooth messages to mount the threat. However, this leaves us open to the next obscure threat.

5.3.5.2 The Cube Root Problem

Let's say you pad on the right with random data. You chose that scheme so that there is a negligible probability that anything you sign will be smooth. However, if the public exponent is 3, this enables Carol to forge your signature on virtually any message she chooses!

Let's say Carol wants your signature on some message. The message digest of that message is h. Carol pads h on the right with zeroes. She then computes its ordinary cube root and rounds up to an integer r. Now she has forged your signature, because $r^e = r^3 = (h$ padded on the right with a seemingly random number).

5.3.6 Public-Key Cryptography Standard (PKCS)

It is useful to have some standard for the encoding of information that will be signed or encrypted through RSA, so that different implementations can interwork, and so that the various pitfalls with RSA can be avoided. Rather than expecting every user of RSA to be sophisticated enough to know about all the attacks and develop appropriate safety measures through careful encoding, RSADSI has developed a standard known as **PKCS** which recommends encodings. PKCS is actually a set of standards, called PKCS #1 through PKCS #9. There are also two companion documents, *An overview of the PKCS standards*, and *A layman's guide to a subset of ASN.1, BER, and DER*. (**ASN.1** = *Abstract Syntax Notation 1*, **BER** = *Basic Encoding Rules*, and **DER** = *Distinguished Encoding Rules*—aren't you glad you asked?).

The PKCS standards define the encodings for things such as an RSA public key, an RSA private key, an RSA signature, a short RSA-encrypted message (typically a secret key), a short RSA-signed message (typically a message digest), and password-based encryption.

The threats that PKCS has been designed to deal with are:

- encrypting guessable messages

- signing smooth numbers

- multiple recipients of a message when $e = 3$

- encrypting messages that are less than a third the length of n when $e = 3$

- signing messages where the information is in the high-order part and $e = 3$

5.3.6.1 Encryption

PKCS #1 defines a standard for formatting a message to be encrypted with RSA. RSA is not generally used to encrypt ordinary data. The most common quantity that would be encrypted with RSA is a secret key, and for performance reasons the ordinary data would be encrypted with the secret key.

The recommended standard is

0	2	at least eight random nonzero bytes	0	data

The actual data to be encrypted, usually a secret key, is much smaller than the modulus. If it's a DES key, it's 64 bits. If multiple DES encryption is used, then there might be two DES keys there, or 128 bits.

The top byte is 0, which is a good choice because this guarantees that the message m being encrypted is smaller than the modulus n. (If m were larger than n, decryption would produce m mod n instead of m.) Note that PKCS specifies that the high-order byte (not bit!) of the modulus must be non-zero.

The next byte is 2, which is the format type. The value 2 is used for a block to be encrypted. The value 1 is used for a value to be signed (see next section).

Each byte of padding is chosen independently to be a random nonzero value. The reason 0 cannot be used as a padding byte is that 0 is used to delimit the padding from the data.

Let's review the RSA threats and see how this encoding addresses them:

- encrypting guessable messages—Since there are at least eight bytes of randomly chosen padding, knowing what might appear in the data does not help the attacker who would like to guess the data, encrypt it, and compare it with the ciphertext. The attacker would have to guess the padding as well, and this is infeasible.

- sending the same encrypted message to more than three recipients (assuming 3 is chosen for e)—As long as the padding is chosen independently for each recipient, the quantities being encrypted will not be the same.

- encrypting messages that are less than a third the length of n when $e = 3$—Because the second byte is nonzero, the message will be guaranteed to be more than a third the length of n.

5.3.6.2 Signing

PKCS #1 also defines a standard for formatting a message to be signed with RSA. Usually the data being signed is a message digest, typically 128 bits. As with encryption, padding is required.

0	1	at least eight bytes of ff_{16}	0	ASN.1-encoded digest type and digest

As with encryption, the top byte of 0 ensures that the quantity to be signed will be less than n. The next byte is the PKCS type, in this case, a quantity to be signed. The padding ensures that the quantity to be signed is very large and therefore unlikely to be a smooth number.

Inclusion of the digest type instead of merely the digest serves two purposes. It standardizes how to tell the other party which digest function you used, and it prevents an obscure threat. The threat is that one of the message digest functions, say MD4, might be weak, so that bad guys with big budgets can generate a message with a particular MD4 message digest. Now suppose you were suspicious of MD4 and therefore used MD5. You signed the MD5 message digest of your message m. If the digest type were not included in the quantity that you RSA signed, then a bad guy could generate some message m' such that MD4(m') = MD5(m), and use the same signature you'd generated for m as the signature for m'. Including the digest type in the signature means you're at risk only for the cryptographic strength of the message digest functions you choose to use. Note that we're not implying that MD4 is actually weak—we're just using it as an example.

5.4 DIFFIE-HELLMAN

The Diffie-Hellman public key cryptosystem predates RSA and is in fact the oldest public key system still in use. It is less general than RSA (it does neither encryption nor signatures), but it offers better performance for what it does. If Diffie-Hellman neither encrypts nor signs, how can it be called a cryptosystem? What does it do?

Diffie-Hellman allows two individuals to agree on a shared key, even though they can only exchange messages in public. In other words, assume our famous two people, Alice and Bob, want to have a secret number that they share so that they can start encrypting messages to each other. But the only way they can talk is by some means of communication that lots of people can overhear. For instance, they might be sending messages across a network, or on a telephone that might be tapped, or they might be shouting at each other across a crowded room, or they might for some reason have to resort to communication by placing ads in the personals section of the local newspaper.

> Dear Bob, the magic number is
> 1890289304789234789279189028902.
> Wish you were here. Love, Alice.

In its original conception, the Diffie-Hellman algorithm has limited functionality, since the only thing it really accomplishes is having a secret number that both Alice and Bob know, and nobody else can figure out based on the messages they overhear between Alice and Bob. Neither Alice nor Bob start out with any secrets, yet after the exchange of two messages that the world can overhear, Alice and Bob will know a secret number. Once they know a secret number, they can use conventional cryptography (secret key cryptography like DES, for instance) for encryption. Diffie-Hellman is actually used for key establishment (getting two things to agree on a common secret key) in some applications, for instance data link encryption on a LAN.

A weakness of Diffie-Hellman is that although two individuals can agree on a shared secret key, there is no authentication, which means that Alice might be establishing a secret key with a bad guy. We will talk about this more after we force you to read through how Diffie-Hellman works.

To start out, there are numbers p, a prime which is about 512 bits, and g, which is a number less than p with some restrictions that aren't too important for a basic understanding of the algorithm. p and g are known beforehand and can be publicly known. For instance, Alice could choose a p and g and send them (publicly) to Bob, for instance by publishing them in *The New York Times*.

> Dear Alice, I'd like our prime
> to be 128903289023 and our
> g to be 23489. Love, Bob.

Once Alice and Bob agree on a p and g, each chooses a 512-bit number at random and keeps it secret. Let's call Alice's secret number S_A and Bob's secret number S_B. Each raises g to their secret number, mod p. The result is that Alice computes some number T_A and Bob computes some number T_B. They exchange their Ts. Finally, each raises the received T to their secret number.

> Alice picks S_A at random. Bob picks S_B at random.
>
> Alice computes $T_A = g^{S_A} \bmod p$. Bob computes $T_B = g^{S_B} \bmod p$.
>
> They exchange Ts (in either order or simultaneously): $T_A \leftrightarrow T_B$
>
> Now each raises the number they receive to their private secret number:
>
> Alice computes $T_B{}^{S_A} \bmod p$. Bob computes $T_A{}^{S_B} \bmod p$.
>
> They will both come up with the same number. That is because
>
> $$T_B{}^{S_A} = (g^{S_B})^{S_A} = g^{S_B S_A} = g^{S_A S_B} = (g^{S_A})^{S_B} = T_A{}^{S_B} \bmod p.$$

Nobody else can calculate $g^{S_A S_B}$ in a reasonable amount of time even though they know g^{S_A} and g^{S_B}. If they could compute discrete logarithms, i.e. figure out S_A based on seeing g^{S_A}, then they could figure out the Alice/Bob shared key. But we assume they can't compute discrete logarithms, because of the Fundamental Tenet of Cryptography (mathematicians haven't figured out how to do that easily in spite of considerable effort, or at least they haven't told us they have).

5.4.1 The Bucket Brigade Attack

If Alice receives T_B indirectly, there is no way for her to know for sure whether the number came from Bob. She will establish a secret key with whoever transmitted T_B, but it certainly might not be Bob. Let's assume Alice is talking to X, who may or may not be Bob. Once Alice and X establish a secret key, they can encrypt all their messages so that only Alice and X can read them. Let's say the first thing Alice and X exchange in their encrypted communication is a password that Alice and Bob have previously agreed upon, one password that Bob is to say to Alice, perhaps **The fish are green**, and one that Alice is to say to Bob, for instance **The moon sets at midnight**. If Alice receives the expected password from X, can she assume she is talking to Bob? (Think about this a bit before reading the next paragraph—it's fun. Hint: Obviously, there must be some subtle attack or we wouldn't claim it was an interesting question.)

Assume p and g are publicly known (if not, Alice can put them into her message). Alice places the ad **Dear Bob. I'd like to talk to you. 8389. Love, Alice.** Suppose there's a bad guy, Mr. X, who works for the newspaper. He makes one copy of the newspaper with Alice's ad printed as Alice wished, and bribes the newspaper deliverer to give that copy to Alice. Meanwhile, Mr. X picks his own S_X and computes $g^{S_X} \bmod p$. He edits the ad slightly by substituting this number instead of 8389, and has that version printed in the rest of the newspapers. Later, Bob replies, by ordering the ad **So pleased to talk to you. My magic number is 9267. Love, Bob.** Mr. X makes one copy of the newspaper with Bob's ad printed as Bob wished, and arranges for Bob to receive that copy. Mr. X edits Bob's ad slightly to substitute his own number for Bob's, and arranges for the newspaper with that version of the ad to get to Alice. Mr. X computes $K_{AX} = 8389^{S_X}$ and uses that for talking to Alice, and computes $K_{BX} = 9267^{S_X}$ and uses that for talking to Bob.

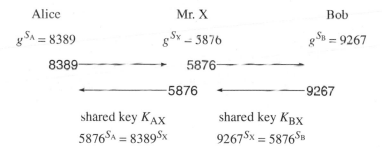

Figure 5-4. Bucket Brigade Attack

Now suppose Alice sends an encrypted message (to Mr. X) which includes the password **The fish are green**. Mr. X can decrypt the message because it is encrypted using the key he shares with Alice. Mr. X reencrypts and transmits Alice's password to Bob, which reassures Bob that he is indeed talking to Alice, and Bob then transmits (encrypted, to Mr. X) **The moon sets at midnight**.

Mr. X decrypts Bob's message, extracts the password, and reencrypts and transmits the password to Alice. Now both Alice and Bob think they are talking to each other.

To guard against this threat, perhaps Alice and Bob should transmit the actual secret number they think they are using, over the encrypted channel they have established? That won't work either. Alice sends the message I think we are using K_{AX}; however, Mr. X decrypts the message and edits it to be I think we are using K_{BX} before encrypting and forwarding it on to Bob.

Suppose instead Alice and Bob attempt to reassure themselves that they are indeed talking to each other by asking each other personal questions. If Bob asks What movie did we see the first night we met in Paris?, Mr. X merely decrypts the message with K_{BX}, encrypts it with K_{AX}, and forwards the message on to Alice. When Alice replies, Mr. X merely forwards the message on to Bob. (We're assuming Alices's memory of past evenings makes it worthwhile for Mr. X to actually wait for her answer rather than making one up himself.)

There is a name for what Mr. X is doing it this case—it's called a **bucket brigade attack**, named after they way firefighters of old formed a line of people between a water source and a fire and passed full buckets toward the fire and empty buckets back. After establishing the shared keys, Mr. X passes messages back and forth and can examine them and/or modify them as they go. Using Diffie-Hellman alone, there's really nothing Alice and Bob can do to detect the intruder through whom they are communicating. As a result, this form of Diffie-Hellman is only secure against passive attack where the intruder just watches the messages. Coupled with additional cryptographic mechanisms, Diffie-Hellman can be made secure against active attacks as well.

5.4.2 Diffie-Hellman with Published Public Numbers

One technique by which Diffie-Hellman can be secure against active attacks is for each person to have a somewhat permanent public and secret number instead of inventing one for each exchange. For this to work, everyone (in the communicating set) has to agree on a common p and g. The public numbers are then all published by some means that is assumed reliable.

To the extent an intruder can't get in and modify the published public numbers, this makes Diffie-Hellman immune to active attacks. It has the additional advantage of eliminating the first two messages of the protocol. Knowing my own secret and looking up the public number of the person with whom I want to communicate, I can compute a key that the two of us will share for all messages we send to one another.

5.4.3 Encryption with Diffie-Hellman

We've described the lack of authentication with Diffie-Hellman. There's another disadvantage with classic Diffie-Hellman: in order for two individuals to communicate, they have to first have an active exchange. This is easy to remedy. Suppose Alice is working late and wants to send an encrypted message to Bob, that Bob will be able to read when he shows up at work the next morning at 7 AM (and Alice has no intention of being around at 7 AM).

First everyone computes a public key, which consists of the three numbers $\langle p, g, T \rangle$, where $T = g^S \bmod p$, for the private key S. These public keys are displayed in a reliable and public place (like being published in *The New York Times*).

So Bob has published a $\langle p_B, g_B, T_B \rangle$.

If Alice wants to send Bob an encrypted message, she picks a random number S_A, computes $g_B{}^{S_A} \bmod p_B$ and computes $K_{AB} = T_B{}^{S_A} \bmod p_B$, and uses that as the encryption key to share with Bob. She uses K_{AB} to encrypt the message according to any secret key cryptographic technique, and sends the encrypted message, along with $g_B{}^{S_A} \bmod p_B$ to Bob. Bob raises $g_B{}^{S_A} \bmod p_B$ to his own secret S_B, and thereby calculates K_{AB} which enables him to decrypt the message.

5.4.4 El Gamal Signatures

Using the same sort of keys as Diffie-Hellman, El Gamal came up with a signature scheme [ELGA85]. It is much harder to understand than signing with RSA. While it's important to know that it's possible and to understand the political and performance implications, the mathematics is tedious and unintuitive. We reluctantly recommend that all but true die-hards skip this section.

El Gamal signatures require each individual to have a long-term public/private key pair (the public key being $\langle g, p, T \rangle$ and the secret key being S, where $g^S \bmod p = T$, as described for Diffie-Hellman), and (surprisingly) require an individual to generate a new and different public/private key pair for each item that needs to be signed. Luckily the per-message public/private key pair is easy to compute. For a particular message m, choose a random number S_m and (using the same g and p as in the long-term key) compute $g^{S_m} \bmod p = T_m$. To use El Gamal, there has to be a message digest function that is well-known. Given a message m, to compute a signature, you first compute the message digest of (m concatenated with T_m). Call that message digest d_m. Then you calculate $S_m + d_m S \bmod (p-1)$, which is the signature. Let's call that X (since we've already used S for the Secret number, and some people sign documents with an X).

m is transmitted, along with X and T_m. To verify this signature, you compute d_m and check that $g^X = T_m T^{d_m} \bmod p$. This will be true, assuming the signature is valid, because

$$g^X = g^{S_m + d_m S} = g^{S_m} g^{d_m S} = T_m T^{d_m} \bmod p.$$

This is not terrifically intuitive. The important things to try to convince oneself of are:

- If the signature is done correctly, the verification will succeed.

- If the message is modified after being signed, the inputs to the signature function will have changed and with overwhelming probability the signature will not match the modified message.

- Knowledge of the signature will not help divulge the signer's private key, S.

- Someone without knowledge of S will not be able to produce a valid signature.

5.4.5 Diffie-Hellman Details—Strong Primes

While Diffie-Hellman works with any prime p and any number g, it is less secure if p and g don't have additional mathematical properties.

It turns out that for obscure mathematical reasons it is particularly nice if $(p-1)/2$ is also prime. A prime p that satisfies this additional constraint is called a **strong prime**. It is also particularly nice if $g^x \neq 1 \bmod p$ unless $x = 0 \bmod p-1$. If p is a strong prime, this is satisfied by any $g \neq -1 \bmod p$ for which $g^{(p-1)/2} = -1 \bmod p$, which is true for almost half of all mod p numbers.

It is computationally expensive to choose p and g. Theoretically, one only needs to do it once. You could keep using the same p and g. It could even be a standard, and everyone could use the same p and g. However, that is not advisable. It turns out to be possible, though incredibly space- and computation-intensive, to calculate a large table based on a single p, which would allow you to compute discrete logarithms *for that p*. A similar scheme would allow you to break RSA, in the sense of being able to calculate someone's private key based on their public key, but there is not that much incentive to do so because that would only allow you to break one person's key. If the p for Diffie-Hellman were broken, then every key exchange based on Diffie-Hellman could be broken. Simply changing p occasionally will eliminate this threat.

5.5 DIGITAL SIGNATURE STANDARD (DSS)

NIST, the (U.S.) National Institute of Standards and Technology, has proposed an algorithm for digital signatures based on El Gamal. The algorithm is known as **DSA**, for **Digital Signature Algorithm**. As a proposed standard it is known as **DSS**.

The differences between it and El Gamal mainly have to do with performance. Instead of all calculations being done mod p (where p is a 512-bit prime), some are done mod q (where q is a 160-bit prime which divides $p-1$). This makes the exponents 160 bits rather than 512 bits, which makes signing three times faster. However, there are other differences that make DSS slower than it might have been. In particular, an inverse calculation is required by both the signer and the verifier.

DSS could easily have been defined to require only the signer to calculate an inverse. Instead, DSS allows the signer to precalculate its inverse before it even has a message, at the expense of requiring the verifier to also calculate an inverse.

But why should we make it more convenient for the signer, given that it's less convenient for the verifier? Presumably there is at least one verification for each signature—otherwise why would one bother signing anything?

There is one important application in which DSS's approach might be an important optimization: smart cards (see §8.8 *Authentication Tokens*). A smart card is likely to have a very low-performance processor. It will have to do a signature in order for a user to successfully log in. If the operation of signing takes a long time, say two minutes or more, it will annoy the human who is trying to use the network.

Taking inverses is one of the most computationally expensive parts of generating a DSS signature. If it had to be done on a smart card at the time the user logged in, the user would be forced to wait many seconds. However, if the smart card generated some $\langle S_m, S_m^{-1} \rangle$ pairs while the user was logged in, then when the user next wants to log in, the smart card will have already done the requisite inverse operation.

The machines doing verifications, the DSS designers believe, will be fast machines, so doing an extra inverse operation will not be annoying.

5.5.1 The DSS Algorithm

- Generate p and q (which will be public).

  Find 160-bit prime q. Find a 512-bit prime p of the form $kq+1$. This is a very expensive operation, but it need not be done often. As a matter of fact it can be done once and the p can be published in the standard. Everyone can use the same p, with some caveats. It is rumored to be possible for someone to generate a p in such a way that someone can break cryptographic operations based on that p, but no other someone would be able to tell that there was anything wrong with using that p. So having a particular p published in the standard as the one everyone should use is controversial. In addition, if there is a p that everyone uses, there is an efficiency gain (because you don't have to generate new ps and qs), but the chosen p presents a target for attacking the algorithm.

- Generate g (which will be public).

  Find a number g such that $g^q = 1 \bmod p$.
  This is done by taking any random number $h > 1$ and raising it to $(p-1)/q$ to get g. Then, since $g = h^{(p-1)/q}$, $g^q = h^{p-1} = 1$ by Fermat's theorem.

(Actually, h can't be just *any* old random number. It is important that g not be 1, or else things will not be secure at all. So a new h is tried if $g = h^{(p-1)/q}$ turns out to be 1.)

- Choose a long-term public/private key pair $\langle T, S \rangle$.

  This is done by choosing a random $S < q$ and setting $T = g^S \bmod p$.

- Choose a per message public/private key pair $\langle T_m, S_m \rangle$.

  This is done by choosing a random S_m and setting $T_m = ((g^{S_m} \bmod p) \bmod q)$. While you're at it, calculate $S_m^{-1} \bmod q$ so it won't need to be done in real time when signing the message.

- Calculate a message digest d_m of the message.

  The DSS has a sister function, **SHS**, that is a hashing algorithm recommended by NIST for use with DSS. SHS happens to hash to 160 bits, but it is only coincidence that the size of the hash matches the size of q. 160 bits seemed a logical number for both because it's about the right size and it's a multiple of 32, so it's conveniently stored on machines with 32-bit words. DSS could be used with any hash function, though no security would be gained by using one longer than 160 bits.

- Compute the signature $X = S_m^{-1}(d_m + ST_m) \bmod q$.

- Transmit all relevant information:

  > the message m;
  > the per-message public number T_m;
  > the signature X.

  The public key information, consisting of T, p, q, and g, is known beforehand and doesn't need to be transmitted with the message.

- Verify the signature:

  Calculate the mod q inverse of the signature, X^{-1}.
  Calculate d_m.
  Calculate $x = d_m \cdot X^{-1} \bmod q$.
  Calculate $y = T_m \cdot X^{-1} \bmod q$.
  Calculate $z = (g^x \cdot T^y \bmod p) \bmod q$.
  If $z = T_m$, then the signature is verified.

5.5.2 Why Does the Verification Procedure Work?

Let $v = (d_m + ST_m)^{-1} \bmod q$. Then,

$X^{-1} = (S_m^{-1}(d_m + ST_m))^{-1} = S_m(d_m + ST_m)^{-1} = S_m v \bmod q,$

$x = d_m \cdot X^{-1} = d_m S_m v \bmod q,$

$y = T_m \cdot X^{-1} = T_m S_m v \bmod q,$

$z = g^x \cdot T^y = g^{d_m S_m v} g^{ST_m S_m v} = g^{(d_m + ST_m)S_m v} = g^{S_m} = T_m \bmod p \bmod q.$

(We're not worried about the mod q in the exponents of g since $g^q = 1 \bmod p$.)

5.5.3 Why Is This Secure?

What does it mean to be secure? It means several things.

- Signing something does not divulge the private key S.

- Nobody should be able to generate a signature for a given message without knowing S.

- Nobody should be able to generate a message that matches a given signature.

- Nobody should be able to modify a signed message in a way that keeps the same signature valid.

Why does DSS have all these properties? The Fundamental Tenet of Cryptography (nobody knows how to break it). DSS also has the blessing of the NSA, arguably the best cryptographers in the world. Unfortunately it's a mixed blessing, since some cynics believe NSA would never propose an algorithm it couldn't break.

5.5.4 The DSS Controversy

DSS was published by NIST on August 30, 1991 as a proposed standard for digital signatures. NIST announced a 90-day comment period, which sparked a flurry of debate and an extension of the comment period. At the time of this writing the debate continues with no end in sight.

The hidden (or sometimes not hidden) question in the debate over DSS is why NIST chose a variant of El Gamal rather than standardizing on RSA, which had become the de facto industry standard. The arguments about standardizing on DSS are:

- Test of time—DSS may have undetected flaws, since it has not be subjected to the intense scrutiny of RSA.

- Mandated 512-bit/160-bit moduli—DSS fixes the key length at 512 bits for p and 160 bits for q. It is true that a DSS key of 512 bits might be a little more secure than a 512-bit RSA key, because the RSA key is a composite number and the DSS key is a prime, but it certainly won't be as secure as a 600-bit RSA key. According to calculations made by Ron Rivest [RIVE91b], a determined and well-financed attacker, say with a budget of $25 million, could break DSS with a 512-bit modulus in a year.

- Since choosing a DSS $\langle p, q, g \rangle$ triple is computationally expensive, it is likely that many people will base their own key on parameters that have been published. With RSA, an attacker that breaks a key breaks only a single key. With DSS, an attacker that breaks a $\langle p, q, g \rangle$ triple breaks all keys upon which it is based.

- Trapdoor primes—Another problem with using a published $\langle p, q, g \rangle$ triple is that you have to trust the source. It is possible for the source to generate a triple that is "pre-broken" in the sense that the source knows how to forge signatures for any key based on that triple. It's been claimed that the sample $\langle p, q, g \rangle$ published in the DSS document is suspicious, in that it has interesting mathematical properties which make it unlikely that it was chosen at random. This does not by any means prove that it is pre-broken, but it does make people nervous.

- Performance—DSS is about a hundred times slower for signature verification than RSA with $e = 3$, and in many applications, signature verification happens frequently and is performance-sensitive. In terms of the other operations, DSS is much faster for key generation, though for most applications the performance of key generation is not an issue since it is not done frequently. RSA and DSS are similar in performance for generating signatures, though DSS has the advantage that some of the signature computation can be precomputed before seeing the message. The NIST reasoning is that for the application of smart cards, this ability to precompute for signatures makes DSS superior, since a human will not need to wait as long when logging into a system.

- DSS requires choosing a unique secret number for each message. There are several ways of doing this, but they all have problems (see next section).

- Patents—One of the advantages of DSS was that it was not owned by RSADSI or PKP (which own exclusive rights to most other public key techniques) and could be used royalty-free. PKP subsequently acquired a patent by Schnorr, which it claims covers DSS. NIST has never conceded that Schnorr covers DSS, and at this time the issue remains unresolved.

5.5.5 Per-Message Secret Number

Anyone who considers arithmetical methods of producing random digits is,
of course, in a state of sin.   —John Von Neumann (1951)

Both DSS and El Gamal require that the signer generate a unique secret number for each message. If the same secret number were used for two different messages, it would expose the signer's private key. Likewise, if a secret number were predictable or guessable, the signer's private key would be exposed.

How is the private key exposed if the secret number for a message is known? In DSS, the signature is $X_m = S_m^{-1}(d_m + ST_m) \bmod q$. Remember that S_m is the secret number, d_m is the message digest, T_m is $g^{S_m} \bmod p \bmod q$, and S is the signer's private key. So if S_m is known, then we can compute

$$(X_m S_m - d_m)T_m^{-1} \bmod q = S \bmod q$$

This is all we need to forge DSS signatures.

How is the private key exposed when two messages share the same secret number? In DSS, if m and m' are signed using the same secret number S_m, then we can compute

$$(X_m - X_{m'})^{-1}(d_m - d_{m'}) \bmod q = S_m \bmod q$$

This is enough to compute $S \bmod q$ as we did above, allowing us to forge signatures.

Similar arguments exist for El Gamal signatures. See Homework Problem 9.

There are several ways of generating a unique secret number for each message. Keep in mind that signatures might be done with a device with minimal computational ability.

- Use truly random numbers. The problem with this is that it requires special hardware. It's difficult enough to make hardware predictable, but it's even harder to make it predictably unpredictable.

- Use a cryptographic pseudo-random number generator. The problem with this is that it requires nonvolatile storage in order to store its state.

- Use a cryptographic hash of a combination of the message and the signer's private key. The problem with this is that it can't be computed until the message is known, eliminating a claimed advantage of DSS and El Gamal over RSA.

5.6 ZERO KNOWLEDGE PROOF SYSTEMS

A zero knowledge proof system only does authentication. It allows you to prove that you know a secret (something associated with your public key) without actually revealing the secret. RSA is a zero knowledge proof system, in the sense that you can prove you know the secret associated with your public key without revealing your private key. However, there are zero knowledge proof systems with much higher performance than RSA, although they do not have the ability to do signatures or encryption.

The classic example of a zero knowledge authentication scheme is based on graphs. A graph is a bunch of vertices connected by a bunch of edges. Typically, we name the vertices and specify the edges as pairs of vertices. We consider two graphs **isomorphic** if we can rename the vertices of one to get a graph identical to the other. Nobody knows how to efficiently determine whether two arbitrary graphs are isomorphic. The assumption that this is hard forms the basis of the authentication scheme.

Alice specifies a large graph (say 500 vertices). She renames the vertices to produce an isomorphic graph. Call the two graphs Graph A and Graph B. Alice knows the mapping that will transform Graph A into Graph B. Nobody else can compute it (in reasonable time). Her public key is the specification of the two graphs. Her private key is the mapping between the two graphs.

To prove to Bob that she is Alice, she renames the vertices to find a new set of graphs, say $G_1, G_2, \ldots G_k$, which she sends to Bob. Then Bob asks, for each i, for Alice to show him the mapping between G_i and one of Graph A or Graph B. Bob can choose which one, but he can't ask Alice to show both mappings for any i (or else Bob could piece the two mappings together to get a mapping from Graph A to Graph B). If Fred tries to impersonate Alice, he can make some graphs that are mapped from Graph A and some graphs that are mapped from Graph B, but he won't be able to find any graph for which he could show a map for both. So for each graph he sends to Bob, he will have only a 50% chance of successfully showing the requested mapping. For 30 graphs, the odds of Fred successfully impersonating Alice are only 1 in 2^{30}, or one in ten billion.

Why is this zero knowledge? After Alice proves herself to Bob, Bob knows some graphs with mappings to Graph A, and some with mappings to Graph B. He could have generated these himself, so Alice can't have given him any actual information.

The graph-based authentication scheme is unfortunately too inefficient for practical use. The following authentication protocol, while not quite zero knowledge, is extremely efficient. It is a variant of Fiat-Shamir [FEIG87].

Alice establishes a public key consisting of $\langle n, v \rangle$, where n is the product of two large primes (just like the n in RSA), and v is a number for which only Alice knows the square root mod n. Finding such an n is done just like in RSA. Finding v is really easy. Alice merely selects any random number s and squares it mod n to obtain v. After doing so, Alice can forget n's factors and only remember s as her secret, and divulge $\langle n, v \rangle$ as her public key.

To prove to Bob that she is Alice, she does the following:

1. Alice chooses k random numbers, $r_1, r_2, \ldots r_k$. For each r_i, she sends $r_i^2 \bmod n$ to Bob.

2. Bob chooses a random subset of the r_i^2 and tells Alice which subset he has selected to be known as subset 1. The others will be known as subset 2.

3. Alice sends $sr_i \bmod n$ for each r_i^2 of subset 1, and sends $r_i \bmod n$ for each r_i^2 of subset 2.

4. Bob squares Alice's replies mod n. For those r_i^2 in subset 1 he checks that the square of the reply is $vr_i^2 \bmod n$. For those r_i^2 in subset 2 he checks that the square of the reply is $r_i^2 \bmod n$.

Why does this work?

- Finding square roots mod n is at least as hard as factoring n. This means that if you knew an easy way to find square roots mod n, you'd be able to factor n. And we all hope that factoring is difficult.

How to factor n if you can compute square roots mod n

We'll assume n is odd and not the power of a prime. (If n is even, you can factor out all the factors of 2. If n is a power of a prime, you can try computing its kth root using ordinary arithmetic, and you'll only need to try for $k \le \log_p n$ where p is the smallest prime you're not willing to try dividing into n directly.)

Assume you have a method to compute square roots mod n. You choose a random x and compute $s = x^2 \bmod n$. Then you use your method of computing square roots mod n to compute the square root of s mod n, say y. This gives you two numbers, x and y, with the same square mod n. So $(x + y)(x - y) = x^2 - y^2 = 0 \bmod n$. If n has k distinct prime factors, then x^2 has 2^k square roots mod n (see §6.5 *Chinese Remainder Theorem*). So if n has at least 2 distinct prime factors, there is at least a 50% chance that y isn't x or $-x$ mod n. In that case, neither $x + y$ mod n nor $x - y$ mod n is 0 mod n. And so the gcd of either of them with n must be a nontrivial factor of n.

- Suppose Fred wants to impersonate Alice. Anyone (including Fred) can compute squares mod n. Fred cannot take square roots mod n, but if he starts with a random r, he can compute r^2. Fred can give the correct answers for subset 2. But he cannot give the correct answers for subset 1, since he does not know s. So, what is the purpose of subset 2? Why isn't the protocol simply that Alice sends pairs $\langle r_i^2, sr_i \rangle$?

The problem with the simpler protocol is that once Alice sends a list of values to Bob, Bob can send the same values to Carol and successfully impersonate Alice. With the protocol as specified, the only information Bob can get is some numbers z_i for which Alice tells him the square root of z_i (those in subset 2), and some numbers z_i for which Alice tells him the square root of vz_i. He doesn't need Alice in order to find numbers for which he knows the square root—he can get such numbers himself by taking random numbers and squaring them. But he does need Alice for finding pairs $\langle r_i^2, sr_i \rangle$. However, for any $\langle r_i^2, sr_i \rangle$ he obtains from Alice rather than starting with r_i and squaring it himself, he will not know r_i—he will only know sr_i.

So, assuming Fred has overheard Alice proving her identity to some people (maybe even Fred), Fred may have collected some values of $\langle r_i^2, sr_i \rangle$. When Fred attempts to impersonate Alice he has a choice for each number of taking one of the values he has overheard from Alice, and for those he will be able to know the answer if they are selected to be in subset 1, or he can choose a random r and square it, and for those he will know the answer if they are selected to be in subset 2. But there will be no number for which he'll know both answers. That means there is a 50% probability, for each i, that Fred will be unlucky, and Carol will ask for the answer Fred does not know. If the protocol demands that Fred sends enough values (say 30), then the probability is overwhelming that his impersonation will be discovered.

This scheme is much less work than RSA. Work for Alice is 45 modular multiplies (30 squarings plus an average 15 multiplies by s). Work for Bob is the same. By contrast, using RSA Alice must do a modular exponentiation with an average 768 modular multiplies, while Bob would get off easier with three (assuming a public exponent of 3).

5.6.1 Zero Knowledge Signatures

Any zero knowledge system can be transformed into a public key signature scheme, though the performance in terms of bandwidth and CPU power usually makes the resulting scheme unattractive. Let's assume a typical sort of zero knowledge system. Alice has some sort of secret that enables her to transmit something and compute any answer to a question Bob might pose about that something, whereas an impostor can answer only one specific question Bob might pose. For example, in the case of the graph isomorphism scheme, Alice's secret is the mapping between graphs G_1 and G_2. The "something" that Alice transmits is a new graph, G_i. Bob's challenges are binary values. Only Alice can answer both 0 (show me the mapping from G_i to G_1) and 1 (show me the mapping from G_i to G_2). An impostor, say Trudy, can only answer one of the values (if she derived G_i from G_1, she'll be lucky if Bob asks 0 but be unable to respond if Bob asks 1).

In some other zero knowledge proof schemes Bob's challenge is a larger number (say 16 bits). Alice can answer any value Bob supplies, whereas impostor Trudy can only know a single value. So Trudy in that case would have only a 1 in 2^{16} chance (per challenge) of being lucky enough for Bob to supply the question she can answer.

A signature scheme is not interactive. Bob cannot supply a challenge, or set of challenges. Instead, Alice has a message m that she wishes to sign. We're going to use a message digest function as a Bob surrogate. The message digest function will create a set of challenges that Alice cannot predict, and the fact that she can answer all the queries will reassure someone that Alice did produce the signature.

Let's use Fiat-Shamir as an example. If Alice were proving her identity to Bob using Fiat-Shamir, her public key would be $\langle n, v \rangle$ and she'd transmit r_i^2 mod n (for randomly chosen $r_1, \ldots r_k$). Then Bob would send her k binary challenges. Now let's transform it into a signature scheme. Alice (and someone verifying Alice's signature) will take the message m, concatenated with the k values r_i^2 mod n. The result is message digested, and the resulting message digest is used as the surrogate Bob. For a 128-bit message digest, if k is 128, then each bit in the message digest corresponds to the challenge for the corresponding r_i. The signature on m consists of the k values r_i^2 mod n and the k responses to the calculated challenges.

Why can't impostor Trudy forge a signature? She can choose any k values of r_i, but until she chooses them, she cannot predict the generated challenge for each one. She can spend a lot of off-line searching for a set of r_i that will happen to generate the challenges she can answer, so k probably needs to be a bit larger than it would be in an interactive zero knowledge proof. For instance, it might be acceptable for an impostor to have only a one in a billion chance of fooling an interactive Bob, but an impostor that was constructing a signature might be able to test a billion signatures for one that wound up asking the right questions. If there's a 1 in 2^{64} chance, then a signature verifier can be reasonably certain that an impostor could not have been lucky enough, even with an off-line search, to find an appropriate set of r_i.

5.7 HOMEWORK PROBLEMS

1. In mod n arithmetic why does x have a multiplicative inverse if and only if x is relatively prime to n?

2. In RSA, is it possible for more than one d to work with a given e, p, and q?

3. In RSA, given that the primes p and q are approximately the same size, approximately how big is $\phi(n)$ compared to n?

4. In DSS, other than saving users the trouble of calculating their own p, q, and g, why is there an efficiency gain if the value of p, q, and g are constant, determined in the specification?

5. What is the probability that a randomly chosen number would not be relatively prime to some particular RSA modulus n? What threat would finding such a number pose?

6. How would you modify El Gamal to operate with a smaller exponent like DSS?

7. Suppose Fred sees your RSA signature on m_1 and on m_2 (i.e. he sees $m_1{}^d \bmod n$ and $m_2{}^d \bmod n$). How does he compute the signature on each of $m_1{}^j \bmod n$ (for positive integer j), $m_1{}^{-1} \bmod n$, $m_1 \cdot m_2 \bmod n$, and in general $m_1{}^j \cdot m_2{}^k \bmod n$ (for arbitrary integers j and k)?

8. Suppose we have the encoding that enables Carol to mount the cube root attack (see §5.3.5.2 *The Cube Root Problem*). If Carol sends a message to Bob, supposedly signed by you, will there be anything suspicious and noticeable about the signed message, so that with very little additional computation Bob can detect the forgery? Is there anything Carol can do to make her messages less suspicious?

9. In El Gamal, how does knowing the secret number used for a signature reveal the signer's private key? How do two signatures using the same secret number reveal the signer's private key? [Hint: $p-1$ is twice a prime. Even though not all numbers have inverses mod $p-1$, division can still be performed if one is willing to accept two possible answers. (We're neglecting the case where the divisor is $(p-1)/2$, since it is extremely unlikely.)]

10. Transform the graph isomorphism scheme described in §5.6 *Zero Knowledge Proof Systems* into a signature scheme. Make an estimate of how large a signature would need to be.

NUMBER THEORY

6.1 INTRODUCTION

This chapter describes enough of number theory to understand not only the mathematical operations necessary to perform cryptographic algorithms such as RSA, but to understand why they work. The chapter requires no background other than intellectual curiosity, a vague remembrance of high school algebra, a certain amount of trust that it will all be understandable with just a little bit of thought, and a reasonable night's sleep in the recent past.

Some of this material has been covered in previous chapters with a large waving of hands. Other material in here has merely been referenced. If you're happy to take the results on faith, don't bother reading this chapter.

6.2 MODULAR ARITHMETIC

We were rather imprecise when we discussed modular arithmetic in previous chapters. While we didn't lie, we didn't tell the whole truth either. What we did was good enough for a vague intuitive grasp, but not really good enough for a deep understanding. Armed with a vague intuitive grasp, this should be fairly painless.

First we need to define *remainder*. (You may think you know what a remainder is, but if you've been using computers for too long you may have assimilated their strange ideas associated with negative numbers.) If m and n are two integers and $n > 0$, the **remainder** of m divided by n is the smallest non-negative integer that differs from m by a multiple of n. For example, 3, 13, and −7 each have remainder 3 when divided by 10.

In arithmetic modulo n, two integers are **equivalent** if their difference is a multiple of n. Another way of saying this is that two integers are equivalent if they have the same remainder when divided by n. Among other things, this means that there are only n different integers mod n. Normally we represent a mod n number by its remainder when divided by n, but any equivalent number would do. For example, 3, 13, and -7 all represent the same mod 10 number.

While it is fairly conventional to use the symbol "$\equiv$" for equivalence, we have chosen to use the symbol "$=$" to emphasize that in modular arithmetic two equivalent numbers are really just two different names for the same mod n number.

It turns out that we can define mod n addition using ordinary addition—if a and b are names for two mod n numbers, then $a+b$ (ordinary addition) is a name for the mod n sum. This wouldn't make any sense if, by choosing different names for the two mod n numbers, we could get a sum (by ordinary addition) which was a name for a different mod n sum. But we can't:

Suppose we chose different names for a and b, say $a+kn$ and $b+ln$. Then the new sum would be $(a+kn)+(b+ln) = (a+b)+(k+l)n$, which is just another name for $a+b$.

Similarly, we can define mod n multiplication using ordinary multiplication—if a and b are names of two mod n numbers, then ab (ordinary multiplication) is a name for the mod n product. Again if we chose different names we'd just get a different name for the same mod n result: $(a+kn)(b+ln) = ab+(al+kb+kln)n$.

We have to be careful about exponentiation. Exponentiation is repeated multiplication, with the repeat count being the exponent. So when we do mod n exponentiation, the exponent is not a mod n number, it is a real positive integer. It turns out that in certain cases we will be able to treat the exponent as a mod $\phi(n)$ number, but we'll discuss that later in the chapter.

6.3 PRIMES

(Yeah, I know you already know this…) A positive integer p is prime iff it is evenly divisible by exactly two positive integers (itself and 1). [Remember—**iff** means *if and only if*.] The smallest primes are

$$2, 3, 5, 7, 11, 13, 17, 19, 23, 29, 31, 37, 41, 43, 47,\ldots$$

There are infinitely many primes. The proof of this is very interesting: Suppose you have a finite set of primes. Multiply them together and add one. The result will not be divisible by any of the primes in your set (the remainder would be one when you divided by any one of them). So the result has a prime factor not in your set—you've found another prime. In other words, you can always find another prime, so the set of all primes is infinite.

While there are infinitely many of them, primes do thin out as numbers get bigger. There are 25 primes less than 100, so the density of the primes is 1 in 4 for the first hundred integers. By the time you get up to ten-digit numbers, the density of primes is only 1 in 23. For hundred-digit numbers, the density is 1 in 230. While there is a lot of variation in small ranges, in general the density of primes is inversely proportional to their length in digits.

Why do we care how many primes there are? Well, many of the cryptographic algorithms (including RSA) require finding large primes. This is done by choosing numbers at random and testing whether they are prime (we discussed how this is done in §5.3.4.2.1 *Finding Big Primes p and q*). If only one in a zillion numbers of the appropriate size were prime, then it would take too long to find an appropriate prime for such cryptographic algorithms to be practical. Luckily, a common-sized prime to look for is about a hundred digits, and a random hundred-digit number has a 1 in 230 chance of being prime. With such slim odds, it may sound unlikely that one would be lucky enough to select a prime, but a computer doesn't mind checking a few hundred numbers before finding one that is prime. On the average, it will be necessary to select 230 hundred-digit numbers before a prime is found. If you do select 230 random hundred-digit numbers, the probability that none of them is prime is about $1/e$ (≈ 0.37).

6.4 EUCLID'S ALGORITHM

One of the earliest algorithms was Euclid's Algorithm, invented by Euclid (yeah, I bet you guessed). It finds the greatest common divisor of two integers. It can also be used to efficiently find multiplicative inverses mod n. (The **multiplicative inverse** of x is the number by which you need to multiply x to get 1.) In RSA the numbers d and e are inverses. We choose one and then calculate the other using Euclid's algorithm.

The **greatest common divisor (gcd)** of two integers is the largest integer that evenly divides both of them. Two integers are **relatively prime** iff their gcd is 1. For example, $\gcd(12,8) = 4$, $\gcd(12,25) = 1$, $\gcd(12,24) = 12$, so 12 and 25 are relatively prime but the other pairs are not.

Note that by the above definitions, for any positive integer x, 1 is relatively prime to x and $\gcd(0,x) = x$.

Euclid's algorithm is a method of finding the gcd of two numbers x and y. The idea is to repeatedly replace the original numbers with smaller numbers that have the same gcd until one of the numbers is zero. Then the remaining number is the gcd.

We first note that $\langle x,y \rangle$ and $\langle x-y, y \rangle$ have the same common divisors (and so the same greatest common divisor), because if d is a divisor of both x and y, then $y = kd$ and $x = jd$, so $x - y = jd - kd = (j - k)d$; while if d is a divisor of both y and $x - y$, then $y = kd$ and $x - y = ld$, so $x = (k + l)d$.

So we can subtract y from x and still have the same gcd. But since we would like to get our new numbers as small as possible, we may as well subtract as many ys as we can from x, so we replace x with its remainder when divided by y. Since this won't get us anywhere once x is smaller than y, we now switch our new x and y, then repeat the process. Each step now looks like

$$\langle x,y \rangle \rightarrow \langle y, \text{remainder}(x/y) \rangle$$

Since at each step one of the numbers gets smaller, eventually one of the numbers will be zero, and so the other will be the gcd.

For example, to find the gcd of 408 and 595:

$$595/408 = 1 \text{ remainder } 187$$
$$408/187 = 2 \text{ remainder } 34$$
$$187/34 = 5 \text{ remainder } 17$$
$$34/17 = 2 \text{ remainder } 0$$

Therefore, $\gcd(408, 595) = 17$.

We describe Euclid's algorithm elegantly as follows. (Mathematicians are very big on elegance!)

- Initial setup:
  Let $r_{-2} = x$ and $r_{-1} = y$.
  [We're using the subscripts -2 and -1 just to show you that these two rs aren't really remainders—they just get us started.]
  Set $n = 0$.

- Step n:
  [This is where we replace the larger number (r_{n-2}) by its remainder when divided by the smaller number (r_{n-1}).]
  If $r_{n-1} = 0$, $\gcd(x,y) = r_{n-2}$.
  Otherwise, divide r_{n-2} by r_{n-1} to get quotient q_n and remainder r_n.
  Set $n = n + 1$.
  Repeat.

If we do a little extra bookkeeping, we can keep track of numbers u_n and v_n such that $r_n = u_n x + v_n y$:

- In the initial setup, set $u_{-2} = 1$, $v_{-2} = 0$ and $u_{-1} = 0$, $v_{-1} = 1$.
  [Notice that this makes $r_n = u_n x + v_n y$ for $n = -2$ and $n = -1$.]

- At step n, set $u_n = u_{n-2} - q_n u_{n-1}$ and $v_n = v_{n-2} - q_n v_{n-1}$.
  [Since $r_n = r_{n-2} - q_n r_{n-1}$, $r_{n-2} = u_{n-2} x + v_{n-2} y$, and $r_{n-1} = u_{n-1} x + v_{n-1} y$, this ensures $r_n = u_n x + v_n y$.]

For example, if $x = 408$ and $y = 595$

n	q_n	r_n	u_n	v_n
-2		408	1	0
-1		595	0	1
0	0	408	1	0
1	1	187	-1	1
2	2	34	3	-2
3	5	17	-16	11
4	2	0	35	-24

Since $r_4 = 0$, we can read the $n = 3$ line to see that

$$\gcd(408,595) = r_3 = 17 = -16 \cdot 408 + 11 \cdot 595$$

So when we are done we have found u and v such that $\gcd(x,y) = ux + vy$. This is a remarkable fact—the gcd of two numbers can be expressed as the sum of some multiple of each. And of course any such sum must be a multiple of the gcd since each of the numbers is. In particular, two numbers x and y are relatively prime iff there are integers u and v such that $ux + vy = 1$.

6.4.1 Finding Multiplicative Inverses in Modular Arithmetic

How does Euclid's Algorithm find multiplicative inverses? Suppose we want to find a multiplicative inverse of m mod n. This means we want to find a number u such that $um = 1$ mod n. Another way of saying this is that um differs from 1 by a multiple of n, so there is an integer v such that $um + vn = 1$. From the previous paragraph, we see that using Euclid's Algorithm to calculate $\gcd(m,n)$ finds u and v provided $\gcd(m,n) = 1$, i.e. provided m and n are relatively prime. Furthermore, if m and n are not relatively prime, we can't find such u and v, so in that case m doesn't have a multiplicative inverse mod n.

Could there be more than one u mod n for which $um = 1$ mod n? Well, suppose $xm = 1$ mod n. Multiplying both sides by u gives $xmu = u$ mod n, and noticing that $mu = um = 1$ mod n, we get $x = u$ mod n. So there is at most one multiplicative inverse of m mod n.

Summarizing, if m and n are relatively prime, we can use Euclid's algorithm to find u (and v) such that $um + vn = 1$. Mod n, the number u behaves just like $1/m$, so we will call it the mod n

inverse of m, and represent it by m^{-1}. (The conclusion of the previous paragraph allows us to say *the* mod n inverse.) If m and n are not relatively prime, m^{-1} mod n doesn't exist.

For example, say we wanted to find the inverse of 797 mod 1047.

n	q_n	r_n	u_n	v_n
−2		797	1	0
−1		1047	0	1
0	0	797	1	0
1	1	250	−1	1
2	3	47	4	−3
3	5	15	−21	16
4	3	2	67	−51
5	7	1	−490	373

From the last line we see that $1 = -490 \cdot 797 + 373 \cdot 1047$. This gives $797^{-1} = -490$ mod $1047 = 557$ mod 1047.

6.5 CHINESE REMAINDER THEOREM

The Chinese Remainder Theorem states that if $z_1, z_2, z_3, \ldots, z_k$ are relatively prime, and you know that some number is x_1 mod z_1, and is x_2 mod z_2, and in general is x_k mod z_k, then you can calculate what the number is mod $z_1 z_2 z_3 \cdots z_k$. Likewise, if something equals x mod $z_1 z_2 z_3 \cdots z_k$, then you can calculate what the number is mod z_1, mod $z_2, \ldots$. In other words, there are two representations of a number. These representations are equivalent in the sense that they define the same number, and it is easy to convert from one representation to the other.

Standard Representation: x mod $z_1 z_2 z_3 \cdots z_k$ (all the zs relatively prime)

Decomposed Representation: $\langle x_1 \bmod z_1, x_2 \bmod z_2, \ldots, x_k \bmod z_k \rangle$

Why is it true? Well, it's pretty easy to see that if you have a number x, you can calculate what it is mod z_i simply by dividing by z_i and taking the remainder. Therefore going from the standard representation to the decomposed representation is very easy.

To go from the decomposed representation to the standard representation is not as obvious, but it is still fairly easy. We'll do the special case where $k = 2$. You can do the general case (Homework Problem 5).

We know that the number is $x_1 \bmod z_1$ and $x_2 \bmod z_2$. We want to find out what it is mod $z_1 z_2$. We also know that z_1 and z_2 are relatively prime. And to get rid of subscripts, and to match the notation used for RSA, we'll call the two zs p and q. So we know that something equals $x_1 \bmod p$ and $x_2 \bmod q$, and we want to know what it equals mod pq. Call this mod pq value x.

Given that p and q are relatively prime, we can use Euclid's algorithm to find a and b such that $ap + bq = 1$. (Note that $a = p^{-1} \bmod q$ and $b = q^{-1} \bmod p$.) If we multiply this equation by x, we get $x = xap + xbq$. Since x differs from x_1 by a multiple of p and x differs from x_2 by a multiple of q, taking both sides mod pq gives $x = x_2 ap + x_1 bq \bmod pq$.

The Chinese Remainder Theorem will help us compute Euler's totient function and generalize Euler's theorem. It also gives us some other interesting results that we used in Chapter 5 *Public Key Algorithms*:

- an explanation of why 1 has more than two square roots mod n if n has two relatively prime factors > 2

- a way to speed up RSA exponentiations in generating signatures and decrypting (the operations using the private key)

- an amusing reason not to use 3 as the public exponent, since seeing a message m encrypted according to three different public keys will enable you to figure out what m is

Why does 1 have more than two square roots mod n if n has two relatively prime factors > 2? Suppose $n = pq$ where p and q are relatively prime and > 2.

1 mod n will equal 1 mod p and 1 mod q. Also, $-1 \bmod n$ will equal $-1 \bmod p$ and $-1 \bmod q$. Both -1 and 1 are square roots of n.

However, look at the number z which is $-1 \bmod p$ and 1 mod q. It won't be 1 or -1 mod n (since by the Chinese Remainder Theorem, there can't be two different values of the form $\langle x_1 \bmod p, x_2 \bmod q \rangle$ that equal the same value mod pq.) However, if you square z mod p you'll get 1 (since $-1 \cdot -1 = 1 \bmod p$). And if you square z mod q you'll also get 1. So $z^2 = 1 \bmod n$, which means z is a square root of n different from 1 or -1. And the number (1 mod p, -1 mod q) also is a square root of 1. So 1 will have at least four square roots. If n has k relatively prime factors > 2, 1 will have at least 2^k square roots! (every combination of 1's and -1's mod each of the factors).

In general, if $n = 2^{\alpha_0} p_1^{\alpha_1} p_2^{\alpha_2} p_3^{\alpha_3} \cdots p_k^{\alpha_k}$ where p_i are distinct odd primes and $\alpha_i > 0$ for $i > 0$, then, mod n, 1 will have 2^k square roots if $\alpha_0 \leq 1$, 2^{k+1} square roots if $\alpha_0 = 2$, and 2^{k+2} square roots if $\alpha_0 \geq 3$. The number of square roots of 1 mod n is important, as we saw in §5.3.4.2.1 *Finding Big Primes p and q*, because of the Miller-Rabin primality test.

6.6 Z_n*

First we'll define some notation. $\mathbf{Z}$ is used as the symbol for the set of all integers. $\mathbf{Z}_n$ is the symbol for the set of integers mod n. So, for instance, $\mathbf{Z}_{10} = \{0,1,2,3,4,5,6,7,8,9\}$.

$\mathbf{Z}_n*$ is defined as the set of mod n integers that are relatively prime to n. So $\mathbf{Z}_{10}*$ is $\{1,3,7,9\}$. Notice that 0 is missing from $\mathbf{Z}_{10}*$. That is because $\gcd(0,10) = 10$, so 0 is not relatively prime to 10. It turns out that the multiplication table for $\mathbf{Z}_{10}*$ has some surprising properties.

	1	3	7	9
1	1	3	7	9
3	3	9	1	7
7	7	1	9	3
9	9	7	3	1

Figure 6-1. $\mathbf{Z}_{10}*$ Multiplication

One interesting observation about the above table is that all the answers are either 1, 3, 7, or 9. If you multiply any two numbers in $\mathbf{Z}_{10}*$, you get another number in $\mathbf{Z}_{10}*$. Even more surprising, each row and column contains all the elements of $\mathbf{Z}_{10}*$, with no repeats. You might wonder whether this is a coincidence having to do with the number 10, particularly if you weren't paying attention earlier in this chapter. Let's try the same thing with 15. The integers smaller than 15 that are relatively prime to 15 are $\{1,2,4,7,8,11,13,14\}$.

	1	2	4	7	8	11	13	14
1	1	2	4	7	8	11	13	14
2	2	4	8	14	1	7	11	13
4	4	8	1	13	2	14	7	11
7	7	14	13	4	11	2	1	8
8	8	1	2	11	4	13	14	7
11	11	7	14	2	13	1	8	4
13	13	11	7	1	14	8	4	2
14	14	13	11	8	7	4	2	1

Figure 6-2. $\mathbf{Z}_{15}*$ Multiplication

It turns out to be true in all cases that if you construct the multiplication table for $Z_n{}^*$, each row and column contains the elements of $Z_n{}^*$ rearranged. (Homework Problem 6.)

Theorem: $Z_n{}^*$ is closed under multiplication mod n.

Proof. $Z_n{}^*$ is closed under multiplication mod n means that if a and b are in $Z_n{}^*$, then so is their product ab mod n. We know that m is relatively prime to n iff there are integers u and v such that $um + vn = 1$. So if a and b are in $Z_n{}^*$, there are integers u_a, v_a, u_b, and v_b such that

$$u_a a + v_a n = 1 \quad \text{and} \quad u_b b + v_b n = 1.$$

Multiplying these two equations together gives

$$(u_a u_b) ab + (u_a v_b a + v_a u_b b + v_a v_b n)n = 1,$$

so ab is in $Z_n{}^*$.

6.7 EULER'S TOTIENT FUNCTION

The symbol $\phi(n)$ is known as Euler's totient function and is defined as the number of elements in $Z_n{}^*$. For instance, $\phi(10)$ is 4, since $Z_{10}{}^*$ is $\{1,3,7,9\}$. You may remember how pervasive the totient function was in Chapter 5 *Public Key Algorithms*.

Given n, can we calculate $\phi(n)$? Suppose n is prime. What is $\phi(n)$? That's fairly easy $-Z_n{}^*$ is $\{1,2,...,n-1\}$. So $\phi(n)$ is $n-1$.

What is $\phi(n)$ when $n = p^\alpha$, where p is prime and $\alpha > 0$? Only multiples of p are not relatively prime to p^α, and every pth number is a multiple of p, so there are $p^{\alpha-1}$ of them less than p^α. So $\phi(p^\alpha) = p^\alpha - p^{\alpha-1} = (p-1) \cdot p^{\alpha-1}$.

What is $\phi(n)$ when $n = pq$ and p and q are relatively prime? Here's where we get to use the Chinese Remainder Theorem. The Chinese Remainder Theorem says there is a one-to-one correspondence between numbers m in Z_{pq} and pairs of numbers m_p in Z_p and m_q in Z_q for which $m_p = m \bmod p$ and $m_q = m \bmod q$. We'll show that m is relatively prime to pq iff m_p is relatively prime to p and m_q is relatively prime to q.

If m in Z_{pq} is relatively prime to pq, then there are integers u and v such that $um + vpq = 1$. Substituting $m = m_p + kp$, we get $um_p + (uk + vq)p = 1$, so m_p is relatively prime to p. Similarly, m_q is relatively prime to q.

Conversely, if m_p in Z_p is relatively prime to p and m_q in Z_q is relatively prime to q, then there are integers u_p, v_p, u_q, v_q such that $u_p m_p + v_p p = 1$ and $u_q m_q + v_q q = 1$. Since $m_p = m - kp$ for some k, and $m_q = m - lq$ for some l, we have $u_p m + (v_p - u_p k)p = 1$ and $u_q m + (v_q - u_q l)q = 1$. Multiplying these together gives $(u_p u_q m + u_p (v_q - u_q l)q + u_q (v_p - u_p k))m + (v_p - u_p k)(v_q - u_q l)pq = 1$, so m is relatively prime to pq.

So there is a one-to-one correspondence between numbers m in $\mathbf{Z}_{pq}*$ and pairs of numbers m_p in $\mathbf{Z}_p*$ and m_q in $\mathbf{Z}_q*$. So $\phi(pq) = \phi(p)\phi(q)$.

6.8 EULER'S THEOREM

For all a in $\mathbf{Z}_n*$, $a^{\phi(n)} = 1 \bmod n$.

Proof. Multiply all $\phi(n)$ elements of $\mathbf{Z}_n*$ together, and call the product x. Notice that since $\mathbf{Z}_n*$ is closed under multiplication, x is in $\mathbf{Z}_n*$ and so has an inverse x^{-1}. Now multiply each element of $\mathbf{Z}_n*$ by a, and multiply all those together. The result will be $a^{\phi(n)}x$. But remember that multiplying the elements of $\mathbf{Z}_n*$ by a merely rearranges them (see Homework Problem 6), so the product must also be x. In other words, $a^{\phi(n)}x = x$. Multiplying both sides by x^{-1} gives the desired result.

Euler's Theorem variant: For all a in $\mathbf{Z}_n*$, and any integer k, $a^{k\phi(n)+1} = a \bmod n$.

Proof. $a^{k\phi(n)+1} = a^{k\phi(n)}a = a^{\phi(n)k}a = 1^k a = a$.

The variant doesn't tell us that raising any number m to the power $k\phi(n) + 1$ gets m back mod n. It only works for m in $\mathbf{Z}_n*$, which means m must be relatively prime to n. It turns out that for numbers n of the form we are interested in for RSA (the product of two primes), it is still the case that $m^{k\phi(n)+1} = m \bmod n$, even if m was not relatively prime to n, as long as k is non-negative (negative exponents don't make sense if m is not relatively prime to n).

Do we really care? What is the probability that we'll ever find a number to encrypt that isn't relatively prime to n? (See Homework Problem 11.) Well, in case we care, RSA will still work even if the message is not relatively prime to n. And the proof isn't very hard.

6.8.1 A Generalization of Euler's Theorem

We will show that for numbers n of the form used in RSA, namely $n = pq$, where p and q are distinct primes, $a^{k\phi(n)+1} = a \bmod n$ for all a in $\mathbf{Z}_n$ (not just for a in $\mathbf{Z}_n*$) as long as k is a non-negative integer. We will use the Chinese Remainder Theorem.

If a is relatively prime to n, the result is true by Euler's Theorem variant. So our only problem is if a is not relatively prime to n, which means a is a multiple of p or q. Let's say a is a multiple of q. Let's compute the decomposed representation for $a^{k\phi(n)+1} \bmod n$. In other words, we want to find out what $a^{k\phi(n)+1}$ is mod p and mod q. Then, by the Chinese remainder theorem, we'll know what it is mod n.

Since a is a multiple of q, it must be relatively prime to p (or else a is a multiple of n, in which case it is 0 and the result is trivially true). Since a is relatively prime to p, by Euler's theorem $a^{\phi(p)} = 1$ mod p. Since $\phi(n) = \phi(p)\phi(q)$, we find that, mod p, $a^{k\phi(n)+1} = a^{k\phi(n)} \cdot a = a^{k\phi(p)\phi(q)} \cdot a = 1^{k\phi(q)} \cdot a = a$. And mod q, $a = 0$, so $a^{k\phi(n)+1} = 0^{k\phi(n)+1} = 0 = a$.

So $a^{k\phi(n)+1} = a$ mod p and $a^{k\phi(n)+1} = a$ mod q, so by the Chinese remainder theorem, $a^{k\phi(n)+1} = a$ mod n.

6.9 HOMEWORK PROBLEMS

1. If m and n are any two positive integers, show that $m/\gcd(m,n)$ and $n/\gcd(m,n)$ are relatively prime. [Hint: use the result of Euclid's algorithm.]

2. If a and b are relatively prime, and bc is a multiple of a, show that c is a multiple of a. [Hint: use the result of Euclid's algorithm.]

3. In mod n arithmetic, the quotient of two numbers r and m is a number q such that $mq = r$ mod n. Given r, m, and n, how can you find q? How many qs are there? Under what conditions is q unique? [Hint: $mq = r$ mod n iff there is an integer k such that $qm + kn = r$. Divide by $\gcd(m,n)$.]

4. In the final step of Euclid's algorithm for finding $\gcd(m,n)$, we get u and v such that $um + vn = 0$. Is $|um|$ (which $= |vn|$) the least common multiple of m and n?

5. Prove the general case of the Chinese Remainder Theorem. [Hint: z_1 is relatively prime to $z_2 z_3 \cdots z_k$.]

6. Show that each row of the Z_n^* multiplication table is a rearrangement of the 1 row. [Hint: multiply the row by the inverse of its first element.]

7. For what type of number n is $\phi(n)$ largest (relative to n)?

8. For what type of number n is $\phi(n)$ smallest (relative to n)?

9. Is it possible for $\phi(n)$ to be bigger than n?

10. If $n = p_1^{\alpha_1} p_2^{\alpha_2} p_3^{\alpha_3} \cdots p_k^{\alpha_k}$ where p_i is prime, what is $\phi(n)$?

11. In RSA, what is the probability that something to be encrypted will not be in Z_n^*?

12. Euler's Theorem variant states that for all a in $\mathbf{Z}_n^*$, $a^{k\phi(n)+1} = a \bmod n$. As stated in §6.8.1 *A Generalization of Euler's Theorem*, if n is the product of two distinct primes, $a^{k\phi(n)+1} = a \bmod n$ for all a in $\mathbf{Z}_n$. For what other forms of n will this be true? For what forms of n does it fail?

13. Prove that if $n = 2^{\alpha_0}p_1^{\alpha_1}p_2^{\alpha_2}p_3^{\alpha_3}\cdots p_k^{\alpha_k}$ where p_i are distinct odd primes and $\alpha_i > 0$ for $i > 0$, then, mod n, 1 will have 2^k square roots if $\alpha_0 \le 1$, 2^{k+1} square roots if $\alpha_0 = 2$, and 2^{k+2} square roots if $\alpha_0 \ge 3$. [Hints: use the Chinese Remainder Theorem to show that a number is a square root of 1 mod n iff it is a square root of 1 mod each of the prime power factors; show that 1 and -1 are the only square roots of 1 mod a power of an odd prime; finally, find the square roots of 1 mod a power of 2.]

PART 2

AUTHENTICATION

7 AUTHENTICATION SYSTEMS

Authentication is the process of reliably verifying the identity of someone (or something). There are lots of examples of authentication in human interaction. People who know you can recognize you based on your appearance or voice. A guard might authenticate you by comparing you with the picture on your badge. A mail order company might accept as authentication the fact that you know the expiration date on your credit card.

This chapter deals with authenticating a device across a network. There are two interesting cases. One case is when a computer is authenticating another computer, such as when a print spooler wants to authenticate a printer. The other case occurs when a person is using a public workstation, for instance a workstation installed in a public area (like a roomful of workstations set up for the convenience of attendees at a convention). Such a workstation can perform sophisticated operations, but it will not store secrets for every possible user. Instead, the user's secret must be remembered by the user. A person is most likely to remember a secret if it is a text string (a password) and the user is allowed to choose it. Many users will not choose passwords wisely, and therefore the secret is a low-quality secret (one vulnerable to guessing). In this chapter we'll discuss various forms of authentication: password-based, address based, and cryptographic. In Chapter 8 *Authentication of People* we'll discuss special issues to be considered when authenticating people. In Chapter 9 *Security Handshake Pitfalls* we'll discuss cryptographic handshakes. In Chapter 10 *Kerberos V4* and Chapter 11 *Kerberos V5* we'll discuss Kerberos, a specific security system. In Chapter 17 *More Security Systems* we'll discuss other authentication systems developed by Digital, Novell, HP, Lotus, and IBM.

7.1 PASSWORD-BASED AUTHENTICATION

It's not who you know. It's what you know.

Everyone knows what a password is, right? We thought so, too, until we tried to define it. When we use the phrase **password-based authentication** we are referring to a secret quantity (the

password) that you state to prove you know it. The big problem with password-based authentication is eavesdropping.

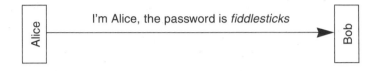

There are certain types of systems that might be thought of as password-based that we are excluding from our definition. For instance, in some systems a user has a secret word or phrase that the user thinks of as a password, but the string known by the user is converted into a cryptographic key. We consider such a system a cryptographic rather than a password-based authentication system.

Why does anyone use password-based authentication when cryptographic authentication is more secure? When dealing with people unaided by a workstation (e.g. the declining fraction of people at "dumb terminals"), it's difficult to avoid basing protocols on passwords, though as we will see, there are some clever devices being manufactured today that make cryptographic solutions compatible with human beings.

Unfortunately, even computer-computer authentication is often based on passwords. Sometimes cryptography is not used because the protocol started out as a human-computer protocol and was not redesigned when its use got expanded to computer-computer communication. Sometimes it isn't used because the protocol designers assumed (perhaps correctly) that cryptography would be overly expensive in implementation time or processing resources. And sometimes cryptography is avoided because of legal issues.

There are some cases in which it is really annoying that the designers opted for a simple password-based scheme. For instance, cellular phones transmit the telephone number of the phone and a password when making a call, and if the password corresponds to the telephone number, the phone company lets the call go through and bills that telephone number. The problem is, anyone can eavesdrop on cellular phone transmissions and **clone** a phone, meaning they can make a phone that uses the overheard ⟨telephone number, password⟩ pair. Indeed, this *is* a problem—criminals do clone phones for stealing phone service and/or making untraceable calls. It would have been technologically easy to implement a simple cryptographic challenge-response protocol in the phone.

There are other issues involved in using passwords. If you are using a workstation, accessing lots of resources across the network, it would be inconvenient for you to have to do a remote login, typing a name and password, every time you accessed a resource such as a file server. For a distributed system to be as convenient to use as a centralized one, you should only need a single password and should only need to enter it once per session. Your workstation could remember your name and password and transmit them on your behalf every time you accessed a remote resource, but this assumes you have the same password on every remote system. How could it be possible to have the same password on many systems? You could individually set your password to the same value on all the systems, but how would you manage to change your password and have the stored password information change simultaneously on all the systems?

7.1.1 Off- vs On-Line Password Guessing

One way of guessing passwords is simply to type passwords at the system that is going to verify the password. To thwart such an **on-line attack**, the system can make it impossible to guess too many passwords in this manner. For instance, ATM machines eat your card if you type three incorrect passwords. Alternatively, the system can be designed to be slow, so as not to allow very many guesses per unit time. Also, with an on-line attack, the system can become suspicious that someone might be attempting to break in, based on noticing an unusually large number of incorrect passwords. The system might then dispatch a human to investigate.

In contrast, in an **off-line attack**, an intruder can capture a quantity X that is derived from a password in a known way. Then the intruder can, in complete privacy, use an arbitrary amount of compute power to guess passwords, convert them in the known way, and see if X is produced. Because a source of good password guesses is a dictionary, an off-line password guessing attack is sometimes referred to as a **dictionary attack**.

If it is possible for an intruder to do off-line guessing, the secret must be chosen from a much larger space (sec §8.3 *Off-Line Password Guessing*).

7.1.2 Storing User Passwords

How does a server know Alice's password? There are several possibilities.

1. Alice's authentication information is individually configured into every server Alice will use.

2. One location, which we'll call an **authentication storage node,** stores Alice's information, and servers retrieve that information when they want to authenticate Alice.

3. One location, which we'll call an **authentication facilitator node**, stores Alice's information, and a server that wants to authenticate Alice sends the information received from Alice to the authentication facilitator node, which does the authentication and tells the server yes or no.

In cases 2 and 3, it's important for the server to authenticate the authentication storage or facilitator node, since if the server were fooled into thinking a bad guy's node was the authentication storage or facilitator node, the server could be tricked into believing the wrong authentication information, and therefore let bad guys impersonate valid users.

Regardless of where authentication information is stored, it is undesirable to have the database consist of unencrypted passwords because anyone who captured the database could impersonate all the users. Someone could capture the database by breaking into the node with the database, or by stealing a backup tape. In the first case above (authentication information individually configured into every server), capturing a server's database (of unencrypted passwords) would enable someone to impersonate all the users of that server. Also, if a user had the same password on multiple servers, that user could then be impersonated at the other servers as well. In the second and third cases, many servers would use the one location, and capturing its database would enable someone to impersonate the users of all those servers. There's a tradeoff, though. It might be difficult to physically protect every server, whereas if all the security information is in one location, it is only necessary to protect that one location.

> *Put all your eggs in one basket, and then watch that basket very carefully.*
> —Anonymous

An alternative to storing unencrypted passwords is to store hashes of passwords, as is done in UNIX and VMS (see §8.3 *Off-Line Password Guessing*). Then if anyone were to read the password database they could do off-line password-guessing attacks, but would not be able to obtain passwords of users who chose passwords carefully.

Alternatively, we could have the node that stores the password information encrypt the stored passwords (so that the server could decrypt a given password when needed). With hashed passwords an intruder who can read the hashed password database can do a password-guessing attack because the intruder will likely know the hash function (the function itself would not be secret). But with encrypted passwords the intruder can't get the passwords without knowledge of the node's key. Since the node would be a computer, the node's key would be a high-quality key, not derived from a password a human might be able to remember, and therefore invulnerable to guessing. Seemingly, then, encrypting (rather than hashing) the password database would be more secure, since an intruder would not only have to be able to read the node's database of encrypted passwords, but also acquire the node's key.

Encryption of the password database is indeed fairly secure for storage of the database on backup media, but it really isn't much protection against an intruder compromising the node itself, since the node's key is probably easily obtainable once inside the system. Most likely the node's key would be stored in some easily accessible place, readable by anyone with privileges (intruders always seem to obtain privileges). Worse yet, if the key isn't stored in nonvolatile memory somewhere, it likely would have to be typed in by the system manager every time the node was rebooted, in which case the key would most likely be handwritten and pasted to the keyboard.

It is possible to combine both techniques by encrypting the database of hashed passwords. Then you get the security benefits of both.

Sun Microsystems' NIS (Network Information Service), formerly known as YP (Yellow Pages), uses the directory service as an authentication storage node and stores the user's hashed password there. Like the original UNIX password file, the directory service information is world-readable, which means that anything can claim to be a server needing to see some user's authentication information. As generally deployed, the NIS directory service does not prove its identity to the server requesting the user's authentication information, so impersonation of the directory service is somewhat of a security hole. NIS does make authentication across a network more convenient, but we suspect its availability will not convince NSA that it is safe to hook all its computers to the Internet.

7.2 ADDRESS-BASED AUTHENTICATION

It's not what you know. It's where you are.

Address-based authentication does not rely on sending passwords around the network, but rather assumes that the identity of the source can be inferred based on the network address from which packets arrive. It was adopted early in the evolution of computer networks by both UNIX and VMS. The basic idea is that each computer stores information which specifies accounts on other computers that should have access to its resources. For instance, suppose account name Smith on the machine residing at network address N is allowed access to computer C. Requests for resources are commands like copy a specified file, log in, or execute the following command at the specified remote machine. If a request arrives from address N claiming to be sent on behalf of user Smith, then C will honor the request.

On UNIX, the *Berkeley rtools* support such access; on VMS, similar functionality is called *PROXY.* The general idea can be implemented in various ways.

- Machine B might have a list of network addresses of "equivalent" machines. If machine A is listed, then any account name on A is equivalent to the same account name on B. If a request from A arrives with the name JohnSmith, then the request will be honored if it is for anything that the account JohnSmith on B was allowed to do. This has the problem that the user has to have the identical account name on all systems.

- Machine B might instead have a list of ⟨address, remote account name, local account name⟩. If a request arrives from address A with the name Jekyll, then the database is scanned for the matching entry, say ⟨A, Jekyll, Hyde⟩. Then the request is honored provided the local account Hyde is authorized to do the request.

UNIX implements two account mapping schemes:

- /etc/hosts.equiv file. There is a global file (named /etc/hosts.equiv) which implements the first scheme above. The file /etc/hosts.equiv on machine A contains a list of computers that have identical user account assignments. Suppose a computer B is listed in /etc/hosts.equiv. Suppose A receives a request with account name Smith, and B's address in the source address field of the network header. If an account with the name Smith exists on machine A, the request will be given the same privileges as the local user Smith. (Actually, an exception is made for the privileged account root; it will not be given access by virtue of an entry in /etc/hosts.equiv). The /etc/hosts.equiv file is useful for managing corresponding accounts in bulk on machines with common accounts and common management.

- Per-user .rhosts files. In each UNIX user's home directory, there can be a file named .rhosts, which contains a list of ⟨computer, account⟩ pairs that are allowed access to the user's account. Any user Bob can permit remote access to his account by creating a .rhosts file in his home directory. The account names need not be the same on the remote machine as they are on this one, so Bob can handle the case where he has different account names on different systems. Because of the way the information is organized, any request that is *not* for an account named the same as the source account must include the name of the account that should process the request. For instance, if the local account name on system A is Bob and the request is from computer B, account name Smith, the request has to specify that it would like to be treated with the privileges given account name Bob. (See Homework Problem 1.)

On VMS, individual users are not permitted to establish their own proxy access files. (This is considered a security feature to prevent users from giving access to their friends). Instead, there is a centrally managed **proxy database** that says for each remote ⟨computer, account⟩ pair what account(s) that pair may access, usually with one of them marked as the default. For example, there might be an entry specifying that account Smith from address B should have access to local accounts Bob and Alice, where the account Bob might be marked as the default.

The VMS scheme makes access somewhat more user-friendly than the UNIX scheme in the case where a user has different account names on different systems. Generally (in VMS) the user need not specify the target account in that case. In the rare case where a user is authorized to access multiple accounts on the remote computer, a target account can be specified in the request to access an account other than the default. (In UNIX, it is always necessary to specify the target account in the request if the account name is different.)

Address-based authentication is safe from eavesdropping, but is subject to two other threats:

- If someone, say Trudy, gains privilege on a node FOO, she can access all users' resources of FOO—there's nothing authentication can do about that. But in addition, she can access the network resources of any user with an account on FOO by getting FOO to claim the request comes from that user. Theoretically, it is not obvious how Trudy, once she gains access to

FOO, would know which other machines she could invade, since the ⟨machine, account⟩ pairs reachable from ⟨FOO, Smith⟩ are not listed at FOO, but are instead listed at the remote machine. However, in a lot of cases, if ⟨FOO, Smith⟩ allows proxy access from ⟨BAR, JohnS⟩, then it is likely that node BAR specifically allows account Smith at node FOO access to account JohnS at BAR. So Trudy, once she has privileges on FOO, can scan the proxy database (in the case of VMS) or the /etc/hosts.equiv file and the .rhosts files of each of the users (in the case of UNIX), and make a guess that any ⟨node, account name⟩ pairs she finds are likely to let her in from node FOO with the specified account name.

- If someone on the network, say Trudy, can impersonate network addresses of nodes, she can access all the network resources of all users who have accounts on any of those nodes. It is often relatively easy to impersonate a network address. For instance, on broadcast LANs (like Ethernet and Token Ring), it is easy not only to send traffic with the address of a different node on that LAN, but also to receive traffic destined for that node. In many other cases, although it is easy to transmit a packet that has a false source address, the returning traffic would be delivered to the real node rather than the impersonating node.

Depending on the environment, therefore, address-based authentication may be more or less secure than sending passwords in the clear. It is unquestionably more convenient and is the authentication mechanism of choice in most distributed systems deployed today.

7.2.1 Network Address Impersonation

How can Trudy impersonate Alice's network address? Generally it is easy to transmit a packet claiming any address as the source address, either at the network layer or the data link layer. Sometimes it is more difficult. For instance, due to the design of token rings, if Trudy and Alice were on the same ring and Trudy were to transmit a packet using Alice's data link address, then Alice might remove Trudy's packet from the ring or raise a duplicate address error. Another example is star-topology LANs, where each node is connected via a point-to-point link to a central hub. The hub in many cases will refuse to forward a packet if the data link source address is not correct for that line, though these hubs do not generally check the network layer source address.

A router could also have features to make it difficult for someone to claim to be a different network address, but this is not generally done. If a router has a point-to-point link to an endnode, it could (like the hub) refuse to accept a packet if the network layer source address is not correct according to the router's configuration. A router could also be configured, on a per-link basis, with a set of addresses that it should expect to appear on each link, and refuse packets with unexpected source addresses. Perhaps if the routers were all trusted, and authentication were added to routing messages to prevent someone from injecting bad routing messages, then a router would not need to be configured on a per-link basis with a set of expected source addresses, but instead could derive the per-link expected source addresses from the routing database.

It is often more difficult for Trudy to receive messages addressed to Alice's network address than for Trudy to claim Alice's address as the source address. If Trudy is on the same LAN as Alice, it is trivial—Trudy just needs to listen to packets addressed to Alice's data link address. If Trudy is not on the same LAN as Alice, but is on one of the LANs in the path between the source and Alice, it's a little harder but still easy. The reason it's a little harder is that Trudy would need to listen to the data link address of the router that forwards packets towards Alice from the LAN on which Trudy resides. This is harder than listening to Alice's data link address because a router will probably be receiving many more packets, and Trudy will have to be fast enough to ignore the messages that aren't specifically for Alice.

If Trudy is not on the same LAN as Alice, and not on the path between the source and Alice, then it is more difficult. Trudy could potentially inject routing messages that would trick the routers into sending traffic for Alice's address to Trudy. It is possible to add a cryptographic authentication mechanism to router messages which would prevent Trudy from injecting routing information.

Even with cryptographic authentication of routers, it may be possible for Trudy to be able to both transmit from and receive packets for Alice's network address. For instance, in IP, there is a feature known as *source routing*, in which Trudy can inject an IP packet containing not just a source address (Alice's network address) and destination address D, but also a *source route* that gives intermediate destinations. IP will route to each intermediate destination in turn. Assume Trudy uses the source route ⟨Alice, Trudy, D⟩. The applications that run on IP that do address-based authentication will use the field Alice for the address check. When D receives a packet from Alice via source route ⟨Alice, Trudy, D⟩, then D, following the IP host requirements document (RFC 1122), will reply with source route ⟨D, Trudy, Alice⟩. The return traffic will go to Trudy.

7.3 CRYPTOGRAPHIC AUTHENTICATION PROTOCOLS

> *It's not what you know or where you are, it's*
> *%zPy#bRw Lq(ePAoa&N5nPk9W7Q2EfjaP!yDB$S*

Cryptographic authentication protocols can be much more secure than either password-based or address-based authentication. The basic idea is that Alice proves her identity to Bob by performing a cryptographic operation on a quantity Bob supplies. The cryptographic operation performed by Alice is based on Alice's secret. We talked in Chapter 2 *Introduction to Cryptography* about how hashes, secret key cryptography, and public key cryptography could all be used for authentication.

The remainder of this chapter discusses some of the more subtle aspects of making these protocols work.

7.4 WHO IS BEING AUTHENTICATED?

Suppose user Bob is at a workstation and wants to access his files at a file server. The purpose of the authentication exchange between the workstation and the file server is to prove Bob's identity. The file server generally does not care which workstation Bob is using.

There are other times when a machine is acting autonomously. For instance, directory service replicas might coordinate updates among themselves and need to prove their identity to each other.

Sometimes it might be important to authenticate both the user and the machine from which the user is communicating. For example, a bank teller might be authorized to do some transactions, but only from the terminal at the bank where that teller is employed.

What's the difference between authenticating a human and authenticating a computer? A computer can store a high-quality secret, such as a long random-looking number, and it can do cryptographic operations. A workstation can do cryptographic operations on behalf of the user, but the system has to be designed so that all the person has to remember is a password. The password can be used to acquire a cryptographic key in various ways:

*   directly, as in doing a hash of the password

*   using the password to decrypt a higher-quality key, such as an RSA private key, that is stored in some place like a directory service

7.5 PASSWORDS AS CRYPTOGRAPHIC KEYS

Cryptographic keys, especially public key based cryptographic keys, are specially chosen very large numbers. A normal person would not be able to remember such a quantity. But a person can remember a password. It is possible to convert a text string memorizable by a human into a cryptographic key. For instance, to form a DES secret key, a possible transformation of the user's password is to do a cryptographic hash of the password and take 56 bits of the result. It is much more tricky (and computationally expensive) to convert a password into something like an RSA private key, since an RSA key has to be a carefully constructed number.

Jeff Schiller proposed a method of converting a password into an RSA key pair that has plausible efficiency. The basic idea is to convert the user's password into a seed for a random number generator. Choosing an RSA key pair involves testing a lot of randomly chosen numbers for primality to obtain two primes. And the primality tests involve choosing random numbers with which to test the randomly chosen primes. If the RSA key pair generator is run twice, and if for each run the sequence of the random numbers selected by the random number generator is the same, the RSA key pair generator will find the same RSA key pair. So if the user's password is the seed for the random number generator, the RSA key pair generator will always generate the same RSA key pair for the user.

Running the RSA key pair generator from the beginning, seeded with the user's password, is likely to take an unacceptable amount of computation, since typically the RSA key generator will find many non-primes before it finally finds two primes. If it had to be done every time the user logged in, it would be prohibitively expensive. But after the workstation successfully finds the RSA key pair derived from the user's password, it can give the user something to remember that would enable it to complete its work more quickly. For example, if (starting with the user's password as seed) the first prime was found after 857 guesses and the second after 533 guesses, then the user might be told to remember $\langle 857, 533 \rangle$. It is an interesting problem to come up with a scheme that minimizes the amount of information the user needs to remember while still significantly lowering the work necessary for the computer. Note that since the $\langle 857, 533 \rangle$ quantity is not particularly security-sensitive, it could be posted on the user's workstation without significant loss of security.

Schemes based on this idea (direct conversion of the user's password to a public key pair) are not used because they perform poorly and because knowledge of the public key alone gives enough information for an off-line password-guessing attack. So the usual practice when using public keys with humans is to encrypt the user's private key with the user's password and store it somewhere (e.g., the directory service) from which it can be retrieved by the user's workstation and decrypted. In order for Alice's workstation, on behalf of Alice, to prove Alice's identity, it must first retrieve her encrypted private key from the directory service. Then it takes the password as typed by Alice, converts it into a secret key, and uses that secret key to decrypt the encrypted private key.

7.6 EAVESDROPPING AND SERVER DATABASE READING

Public key technology makes it easy to do authentication in a way that is both secure from eavesdropping and from an intruder reading the server database. Alice knows her own private key. Bob stores Alice's public key. An intruder who reads Bob's database (and therefore obtains Alice's public key) will not be able to use the information to impersonate Alice. Authentication is done by

Alice using her private key to perform a cryptographic operation on a value Bob supplies, and then transmitting the result to Bob. Bob checks the result using Alice's public key.

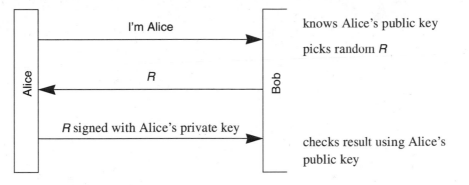

Without public key cryptography, it's difficult to protect against both eavesdropping and server database reading with a single protocol, although it is easy to do one or the other. For instance, let's try a protocol such as is used when a person logs into a system such as UNIX. Bob (the computer authenticating the user Alice) stores a hash of Alice's password. Let's say Alice's password is fiddlesticks. The protocol is as follows:

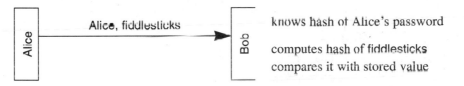

In this protocol someone, say Trudy, who accessed Bob's database would not be able to impersonate Alice. She could do an off-line password-guessing attack if she were to obtain Alice's hashed password from Bob's database, but that would not help her if Alice had chosen a good password. But if Trudy were to eavesdrop when Alice was proving her identity to Bob, Trudy would obtain Alice's password. So this protocol is secure against server database disclosure but not against eavesdropping.

Now consider another protocol. Let's assume that Bob stores Alice's actual secret.

```
                            I'm Alice              knows Alice's secret
                        ─────────────────▶
                                                  picks random R

              Alice            R             Bob
                        ◀─────────────────

computes X = cryptographic
function of her secret and R        X
                        ─────────────────▶

                                                  computes same function
                                                  and compares it to X
```

In this case Trudy, if she were to eavesdrop, would not be able to obtain information to allow her to impersonate Alice (except by an off-line password-guessing attack). But if she were to read Bob's database, she'd obtain Alice's secret. We'd almost claim it was impossible to simultaneously protect against eavesdropping and server database disclosure without using public key cryptography. However, an elegant protocol invented by Leslie Lamport can claim to accomplish this feat. Lamport's scheme does have a serious drawback, though. A user can only be authenticated a small finite number of times (such as 1000) before it is necessary to reinstall the user's information at the server; that is, someone with privileges at the server and knowledge of the user's password must reconfigure the server with the user's security information. Phil Karn has implemented Lamport's scheme in his S/Key software, and it is being used in the Internet. Lamport's scheme is described in §9.1.3 *Lamport's Hash*.

7.7 TRUSTED INTERMEDIARIES

Assume that network security is based on secret key technology. If the network is fairly large, say n nodes, and each computer might need to authenticate each other computer, then each computer would need to know $n-1$ keys, one for each other system on the network. If a new node were added to the network, then n keys would need to be generated, enough for that new node to have a shared secret with each of the other nodes. Somehow the keys would have to be securely distributed to all the other nodes in the network. This is clearly unworkable in any but very small networks.

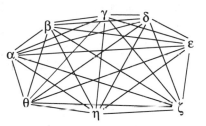

7.7.1 KDCs

One way to make things manageable is to use a trusted node known as a **Key Distribution Center (KDC)**. The KDC knows keys for all the nodes. If a new node is installed in the network,

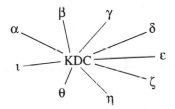

only that new node and the KDC need to be configured with a key for that node. If node α wants to talk to node β, α talks to the KDC (securely, since α and the KDC share a key), and asks for a key with which to talk to β. The KDC authenticates α, chooses a random number $R_{\alpha\beta}$ to be used as a key to be shared by α and β for their conversation, encrypts $R_{\alpha\beta}$ with the key the KDC shares with α and gives that to α. The KDC also encrypts $R_{\alpha\beta}$ with the key the KDC shares with β and gives that to β, with the instruction that it is to be used for conversing with α. (Usually, the KDC will not bother to actually transmit the encrypted $R_{\alpha\beta}$ to β but rather will give it to α to forward to β.) The encrypted message to β that the KDC gives to α to forward is often referred to as a **ticket**. Besides containing $R_{\alpha\beta}$, the ticket generally contains other information such as an expiration time and α's name. We'll discuss protocols involving KDCs in §9.4 *Mediated Authentication (with KDC)*.

KDCs make key distribution much more convenient. When a new user is being installed into the network, or when a user's key is suspected of having been compromised, there's a single location (the KDC) that needs to be configured. The alternative to using a KDC is installing the user's information at every server to which the user might need access. There are some disadvantages to KDCs, though:

- The KDC has enough information to impersonate anyone to anyone. If it is compromised, all the network resources are vulnerable.

- The KDC is a single point of failure. If it goes down, nobody can use anything on the network (or rather, nobody can start using something on the network—keys previously distributed can continue to be used). It is possible to have multiple KDCs which share the same database of keys, but that means added complexity and cost for extra machines and replication protocols, and added vulnerability, since there are now more targets that need to be protected.

- The KDC might be a performance bottleneck, since everyone will need to frequently communicate with it. Having multiple KDCs can alleviate this problem.

7.7.2 Certification Authorities (CAs)

Key distribution is easier with public key cryptography. Each node is responsible for knowing its own private key, and all the public keys can be accessible in one place. But there are problems with public keys as well. If, for instance, all the public keys are published in the New York Times, or stored in the directory service, how can you be sure that the information is correct? An intruder, Trudy, might have overwritten the information in the directory service or taken out her own ad in *The New York Times*. If Trudy can trick you into mistaking her public key for Alice's, she can impersonate Alice to you.

The typical solution for this is to have a trusted node known as a **Certification Authority** (**CA**) that generates **certificates**, which are signed messages specifying a name (Alice) and the corresponding public key. All nodes will need to be preconfigured with the CA's public key so that they can verify its signature on certificates, but that is the only public key they'll need to know *a priori*. Certificates can be stored in any convenient location, such as the directory service, or each node can store its own certificate and furnish it as part of the authentication exchange. CAs are the public key equivalent of KDCs. A CA or a KDC is the single trusted entity whose compromise can destroy the integrity of the entire network. The advantages of CAs over KDCs are:

- The CA does not need to be on-line. It might be in a locked room protected by a scary-looking guard. Perhaps only a single very trusted individual has access to the CA. That person types the relevant information at the CA, and the CA writes a floppy disk with the new user's certificate, and the floppy disk can be hand-carried to a machine which is on the network. If the CA is not on-line it cannot be probed by curious intruders.

- Since the CA does not have to be on-line or perform network protocols, it can be a vastly simpler device, and therefore it might be more secure.

- If the CA were to crash, the network would not be disabled (as would be the case with a KDC). The only operation that would be impacted is installing new users (until things start expiring, such as certificates or Certificate Revocation Lists—see §7.7.3 *Certificate Revocation*). So it's not as essential to have multiple CAs.

- Certificates are not security-sensitive. If they are stored in a convenient, but potentially insecure, location like the directory service, a saboteur might delete certificates, which might prevent network access by the owners of those certificates, but the saboteur cannot write bogus certificates or modify certificates in any way, since only the CA can generate signatures.

- A compromised CA cannot decrypt conversations, whereas a compromised KDC that sees a conversation between any two parties it serves can decrypt the conversation. A compromised CA can fool Alice into accepting an incorrect public key for Bob, and then the CA can impersonate Bob to Alice, but it will not be able to decrypt a conversation between the real Alice and the real Bob. (It's still really bad for a CA to be compromised, but we're just saying it's not quite as bad as compromise of a KDC.)

> *Why do you security people always speak of compromise as if it's a bad thing? Good engineering is all about compromise.*
> —overheard at a project review

7.7.3 Certificate Revocation

There is a potential disadvantage with CAs. Suppose Fred is given a certificate with an expiration time a year in the future, and then Fred is fired. Since Fred is now a disgruntled ex-employee, it would be nice to alert the network not to allow him access. With KDCs it's easy—merely delete his key from the KDC. With CAs, though, it's not as straightforward to deny access to someone once he is given a certificate. It is common practice to put an expiration date in a certificate. The certificate becomes invalid after that date. The typical validity interval is about a year. A disgruntled ex-employee can do a lot of damage in a year, even without a machine gun. But you wouldn't want validity intervals much smaller than that, because then you'd have to reissue certificates more often.

The solution is similar to what was done for credit cards. When the bank issues a credit card, it prints an expiration date, perhaps a year in the future. But sometimes a card is reported stolen, or the bank might for some other reason like to revoke it. The credit card company publishes a book of credit card numbers that stores should refuse to honor. These days, most stores are hooked to computer networks where they check the validity of the card, but in ancient times merchants needed to rely on the book of bad credit card numbers, which was presumably published frequently.

X.509 [ISO88] has a defined format for a certificate, as well as of a **Certificate Revocation List (CRL)**. We document the formats in §13.6 *X.509 Certificates and CRLs*. A CRL lists serial numbers of certificates that should not be honored. A new CRL is posted periodically, and lists all revoked and unexpired certificates. A certificate is valid if it has a valid CA signature, has not expired, and is not listed in the CA's most recent CRL. The CRL has an issue time. If an application wants to ensure that none of the certificates it honors has been revoked in the last hour, say, then the application will need to see a CRL issued within the last hour before it will honor any certificates. This means, in this case, that a new CRL must be posted at least once an hour. An intruder might delete the latest CRL, in which case applications that want to see a CRL posted within the last hour will refuse to honor any certificates, but the intruder cannot impersonate a valid user by destroying the CRL or overwriting it with a CRL issued longer ago than the application's tolerance.

A certificate includes the user's name, the user's public key, an expiration time, a serial number, and the issuing CA's signature on the entire contents of the certificate. A CRL includes a list of serial numbers of unexpired revoked certificates and an issue time for the CRL.

Suppose Bob is an application that needs to authenticate the user Alice. Bob needs Alice's certificate and a recent CRL. Bob can obtain them from the directory service, or perhaps Alice transmits them to Bob. Armed with the certificate and CRL, Bob decides what public key is associated with the name Alice. If the certificate is validly signed by the CA and has not expired, and the CRL is validly signed by the CA and is sufficiently recent and does not list Alice's certificate, then Bob will assume that Alice's public key is as stated in the certificate. Then Bob will go through an authentication handshake whereby Alice proves she knows the private key that corresponds to the public key listed in her certificate.

We suggest a small modification to the X.509 CRL scheme with potentially significant performance gains. With the X.509 scheme, you have to guess what a reasonable validity period for certificates should be. If you guess too short a value, then you waste resources reissuing certificates. If you guess too long a value, then the CRL might get unmanageably long. If you have a reasonable value, and then suddenly your company has a layoff of 30000 employees, you'll have a very large CRL for a long time.

In our scheme, certificates do not have a predetermined expiration time when they are issued. Instead, they are only marked with a serial number, which increases every time a certificate is issued (or the issue time could be used instead of a serial number). Our version of a CRL would have one additional field that is not included in X.509. The CRL would contain a FIRST VALID CERTIFICATE field. Any certificates with lower serial numbers (or issue times) are invalid.

Certificates in our scheme would have no predetermined expiration time. As long as the CRL is of manageable size there is no reason to reissue any certificates. If it looks like the CRL is getting too large, the company issues a memo warning everyone with certificate serial numbers less than some number n that they'll need new certificates by, say, a week from the date of the memo. The number n might be the next-to-be-issued certificate serial number, or it could be some earlier one. The number n is chosen so that few of the serial numbers in the current CRL are less than n.

Revoked certificates with serial numbers greater than n must continue to appear in the new CRL, while valid certificates with numbers greater than n do not have to be reissued. Some time, say two weeks, after the memo is sent, the CA issues a new CRL with n in the FIRST VALID CERTIFICATE field. Affected users (those with serial numbers less than n) who ignored the memo will thenceforth not be able to access the network until they get new certificates.

There are cases when it is still reasonable to have expiration times in certificates. For example, at a university, students might be given certificates for use of the system on a per-semester basis, with a certificate that expires after the semester. Upon paying tuition for the next semester, the student is given a new certificate. But even in those cases, it may still be reasonable to combine expiration times in some certificates with our scheme, since our scheme would allow an emergency mass-revocation of certificates.

7.7.4 Multiple Trusted Intermediaries

A problem with both KDCs and CAs as described so far is that they require that there be a single administration trusted by all principals in the system. Anyone who compromises the KDC or the CA can impersonate anyone to anyone. As you try to scale authentication schemes up to international or intercorporate scale, you discover that there is no one who everyone trusts (and if there were, they would be too busy with more important tasks to operate and manage a KDC or CA).

The solution is to break the world into **domains**. Each domain has one trusted administration (one logical KDC or one CA—there might be replicas for availability, but they are all are functionally equivalent) If Alice and Boris are in the same domain, they authenticate as described above. If they are in different domains, then authentication is still possible, but a little more complicated.

7.7.4.1 Multiple KDC Domains

How does key distribution work with multiple KDC domains? Let's say Alice is in the CIA and Boris is in the KGB. The CIA will manage a KDC, and the CIA's KDC will know Alice's key. Boris's key is known to the KGB's KDC. Given that the two organizations want to be able to exchange secure electronic mail (perhaps so they can express outrage that the other organization is engaged in, gasp, *spying*), they can make this possible by having a key that the two KDCs share. So the CIA's KDC, in addition to having keys for all its users, will also have configured a key which it shares with the KGB's KDC. Let's call that shared key $K_{\text{KGB-CIA}}$.

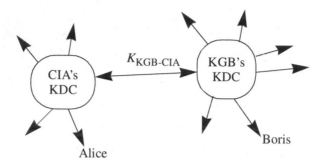

$K_{\text{KGB-CIA}}$ is used when a user in the CIA wants to have a secure communication with a user in the KGB. Alice, knowing Boris is in the KGB, tells her KDC that she wants to talk to the KGB's KDC. Her KDC facilitates this the same way it would facilitate communication between two CIA users. It generates a new random key, K_{new}, and encrypts a message containing K_{new} using Alice's key. This message is to inform Alice of K_{new}. It separately encrypts a message containing K_{new} using the key $K_{\text{KGB-CIA}}$. That message, which also contains Alice's name, will be sent to the KGB's KDC. The fact that the message is encrypted with $K_{\text{KGB-CIA}}$ lets the KGB's KDC know that Alice is from the CIA's domain. (Note that the KGB's KDC will probably have many KDCs with which it shares keys. For performance reasons, a cleartext clue that the message is coming from the CIA's KDC will have to be sent along with the encrypted message so that the KGB's KDC will know to try the key $K_{\text{KGB-CIA}}$.) After verifying that the message is encrypted with $K_{\text{KGB-CIA}}$, the KGB's KDC will generate a key $K_{\text{Alice-Boris}}$ and send that to Alice, encrypted with K_{new}. It will also generate a message for Boris (which it gives to Alice to deliver) that will be encrypted with Boris's key. The message will contain $K_{\text{Alice-Boris}}$ and the information that Alice is from the CIA domain.

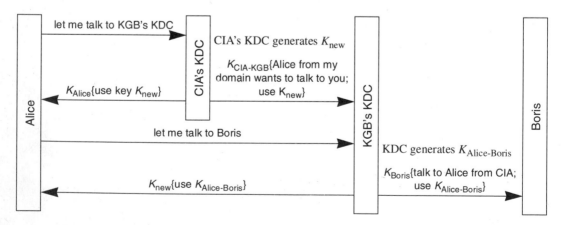

There would likely be thousands of domains in an international/intercorporate/interdenominational internetwork. The conceptually simplest method of allowing users from one domain to talk to users in another domain securely is to have every pair of KDCs configured with a shared key. So the CIA KDC would have a shared key, not only with the KGB's KDC, but with Greenpeace's KDC, and MIT's KDC, and IBM's KDC. Perhaps someone (either in Greenpeace or the CIA) might decide that there was no reason for traffic between the two domains, in which case those KDCs would not need to share a key. But most likely there would be so many domains that it would be unworkable to have every pair of domains configured with a shared key. So there would likely be either a tree of KDCs, or some perhaps less structured logical interconnection of KDCs.

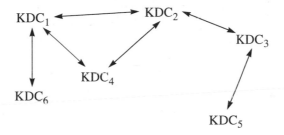

Users can securely authenticate even if their KDCs are not directly linked, if a chain of KDCs can be found. It isn't obvious how one would find an appropriate chain of KDCs. For instance, as we will discuss in the Kerberos chapters, Kerberos V4 does not allow chains of KDCs; to have interdomain communication between two KDCs, they have to have a shared key. Kerberos V5 allows arbitrary connectivity, but assumes there is a default hierarchy, with perhaps additional links (shared keys) between pairs of KDCs that are not directly connected in the default hierarchy.

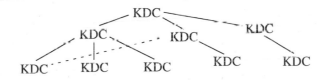

After Alice has negotiated a chain of KDCs to get to Boris's KDC, the encrypted message Boris receives should list the chain of KDCs that helped establish the path. The reason for this is that Boris might trust some chains more than others. For instance, the KGB's KDC might have a shared key with MIT's KDC. That KDC, if overtaken by playful undergraduates, could send a message to the KGB's KDC that Alice, from the CIA, wants to talk to the KGB's KDC, through the path CIA–MIT. It is likely that the KGB's KDC would not trust anything more than one hop through MIT; that is, it will believe MIT's KDC when it tells it there are users from MIT who wish to communicate, but it won't believe it if MIT claims a different organization is attempting communication with the KGB through MIT's KDC.

7.7.4.2 Multiple CA Domains

The situation is similar with CAs. Each CA services a set of users, and issues certificates for those users. This is functionally similar to a KDC having a shared key with a user. The users of a particular CA can verify each other's certificates, since all users of a particular CA know its public key.

How can Alice be sure she knows Boris's public key if Alice's CA is different from Boris's CA? This is accomplished by having the two CAs issue certificates for each other. Alice obtains a certificate, signed by her own CA, stating the public key of Boris's CA. Then, using that certificate plus Boris's certificate (which has been signed by Boris's CA), she can verify Boris's public key.

- Alice obtains Boris's CA's certificate stating that its public key is P_1, signed by her own CA.

- Alice obtains Boris's certificate stating that his public key is P_2, signed with key P_1.

Because she has both of those certificates, she now can verify Boris's public key.

As with chains of KDCs, it is possible that some CAs will not have certificates for each other, but there will be a chain of CAs which works. In Chapter 12 *Electronic Mail Security* and those following, we discuss various strategies for finding appropriate chains of certificates. It is really no different from the problem of navigating through logically interconnected KDCs, and there is really no universally accepted wonderful answer, though there are several workable schemes.

7.8 SESSION KEY ESTABLISHMENT

If all that was done about computer network security was to replace all the cleartext password exchanges with cryptographic authentication, computer networks would be a lot more secure than they are today. But there are security vulnerabilities that occur after authentication. An eavesdropper might steal information by seeing your conversation. Something along the path (e.g., a router) might intercept messages in transit and modify them or replay them. Or someone on the path might "hijack" the entire session by impersonating the network address of one of the parties after the initial authentication is complete. We can protect against eavesdroppers, session hijackers, and message manglers by using cryptography throughout the conversation. But cryptography, of course, involves keys. What should we use for a key?

One possibility is that our authentication exchange is based on public keys. In theory, in a conversation between Alice and Bob, Alice could encrypt all of the data she sends to Bob with

Bob's public key (for privacy), and sign each message with her own private key (for integrity). Bob could similarly encrypt all the data he sends to Alice with Alice's public key, and sign the data with his private key. This isn't generally done because public key operations are computationally expensive. It is far more practical to have Alice and Bob somehow agree on a secret key, and protect the remainder of the conversation with the secret key. It would be nice if the authentication protocol helped them agree on a secret key, in addition to having Alice and Bob authenticate each other.

When Alice and Bob are using a shared secret key to authenticate each other they could continue to use that key to protect their conversation. However, it is a good idea to generate a separate session key:

- Keys sort of "wear out" if used a lot. If you're an intruder trying to find a key, the more encrypted data you have the more likely you'll succeed. Since establishing a shared authentication key is usually an expensive operation involving out-of-band mechanisms, it is desirable that the authentication key be used only for the initial exchange. A secret per-session key can be generated at the time of authentication and used for integrity protection and encryption for the remainder of the session.

- If Alice and Bob were to use the same secret key for authentication as for integrity-protecting their data, it might be possible for an intruder to record messages from a previous Alice-Bob conversation and inject those packets into a current Alice-Bob conversation, tricking them into thinking the messages were part of the current session. Within a session there is generally a sequence number to prevent an intruder from adding, deleting, or reordering messages. But there might be nothing in the packet to distinguish packets transmitted a month ago from packets transmitted today. For instance, the transport protocol might always start with sequence number 1. If the authentication protocol agreed upon a new session key for each conversation, then replayed messages from previous conversations would not be accepted as valid.

- If the long-term shared secret key is compromised, it would be nice to prevent an old recorded conversation from being decryptable. If every conversation is encrypted with a different per-session key, then a suitable authentication protocol can prevent old conversations from being decrypted.

- You may want to establish a session and give a relatively untrusted piece of software the session key, which is good only for that conversation, rather than giving it your long-term secret key, which the untrusted software could store away for future use.

For these reasons, authentication protocols usually establish a session key, in addition to providing authentication. We'll describe the subtleties of authentication protocols in Chapter 9 *Security Handshake Pitfalls*.

7.9 AUTHORIZATION

Authentication establishes who you are. Authorization establishes what you're allowed to do. Sometimes you can prove authorization without divulging your identity. For instance, back in King Arthur's day, anyone who could pull the sword Excaliber from the stone was authorized to be King of England. A more contemporary example is that all members of a family might have copies of the same physical door key, and possession of a key is proof enough to the door that it should let you in. And possession of a gun in a bank grants you many privileges (at the time). The bank employees are instructed not even to ask you your name in such a situation. PCs are usually configured with the assumption that just because you are within reach of the keyboard, you are authorized to use it. The reasoning is that the PC is located in a place with physical security (your house), and that anyone who can reach it is allowed to do anything with it. If a bad guy gets into your home, you are probably more worried about your jewelry collection than whether the bad guy can play *Minesweeper* or read your resume.

In most situations, especially those involving resource access across a network, security does involve the two steps of authentication (establishing who you are) and then determining your authorization. An **ACL** (**access control list**) associated with each resource, which lists every individual allowed to use that resource, could be used for authorization. Let's assume a computer has authenticated user Donald. Now it needs to decide whether to let Donald do something, for instance read a particular file stored on that computer. The ACL for that file specifies who is allowed to use the file and in what way (e.g., read, write, execute, delete). Once you prove (via authentication) that you are Donald, you are allowed access to any resource that lists Donald in its ACL.

Maintaining ACLs on every file can quickly become prohibitively expensive. Imagine a file that all Disney employees are allowed to see. That would be a large ACL. And furthermore, there might be many files that should be accessible to all Disney employees. The person maintaining the ACLs for the files would get pretty annoyed at typing in all those names for the second such file, and would be downright unpleasant to live with after the seventeenth such file. And when a new creature was hired into the Disney organization, the person maintaining all the ACLs would have to remember every file intended for Disney employees and edit all those ACLs. This would make him even more grumpy.

7.9.1 Groups

A common solution is to introduce the concept of **groups**. Instead of specifying all the individuals on every file, have a separate file called something like DisneyEmployees, and have the ACL for each file (intended for that group) have an entry DisneyEmployees.

> *Every problem in computer science can be solved with one more level of*
> *indirection.*   —David Wheeler

However, there is still some inefficiency. There might be files on several different systems all intended to be accessed by all the employees at Disney. If the system managers of the various systems talked to each other, they'd realize they were duplicating effort, since every one of them had to maintain a file listing all the individuals in the Disney organization. There are two possible methods of eliminating this duplication of effort. The first one involves storing the file DisneyEmployees at some central location, and having every system query the central location when deciding whether to grant a given user access to a resource whose ACL lists DisneyEmployees. The second method is to include information about what groups an individual belongs to inside that individual's certificate (in the case of public key based schemes) or ticket (in the case of a secret key KDC based scheme). So Donald's certificate (or ticket) would specify that he was a member of DisneyEmployees, and any other groups that he was a member of (such as Engineers or Quacks).

What are the tradeoffs between these two approaches? In the first approach (maintaining the file DisneyEmployees at some central location), it is inefficient to evaluate an ACL (i.e., find out if a particular individual should be granted access to a resource that lists DisneyEmployees in its ACL). Every access requires a message to the central location.

The second approach (listing group names inside the ticket or certificate) has problems as well. People might invent hundreds or thousands of groups (employees who have been hired less than a year ago, employees who are left-handed Lithuanians, employees who were hired through headhunters, employees who are working on a specific project, etc.). Then an individual's certificate/ticket can get to be very large.

Another issue involves who is trusted to assert that someone belongs in a certain group. With the first scheme, there is one individual entrusted with keeping the file listing the group members. With the second scheme, the certificates (or tickets) of the members of the group might have been issued by different CAs (or KDCs). Suppose there's a group CIA_EMPLOYEES. Suppose Boris's certificate, issued by the KGB's CA, specifies that Boris belongs in CIA_EMPLOYEES. Should Boris then be allowed access to all files accessible to CIA employees? The KGB probably controls its own CA and therefore can have it specify any information in any certificates. Whoever would be maintaining the CIA_EMPLOYEES list might be suspicious that a different CA might claim someone was a member of that list who really wasn't. A logical restriction, then, is to force all members of a group to be certified by a single CA (or KDC). But Boris might actually belong in the group CIA_EMPLOYEES. So this scheme places a restriction on groups that does not exist with the first approach.

Yet another issue involves revoking group membership. If an individual gets kicked out of a group, then that individual needs a new certificate, and worse yet, if we don't trust the individual not to keep using the old certificate, the old certificate will need to be listed in the CRL. Since group membership is likely to change a lot more frequently than certificates are otherwise revoked, this will make the CRLs get large too quickly.

And still another issue is that it's desirable to be able to update group membership on-line. A significant advantage of CAs over KDCs is that the CA does not have to be on-line. If group membership is listed in someone's certificate, then any change to a group must involve accessing the CA, which would be so inconvenient that people would probably resort to having the CA on-line, thus making it less secure.

What is actually used in practice? DCE security (which we'll discuss further in §17.7 *DCE Security*) lists in Alice's ticket the groups to which she belongs. Most systems don't explicitly deal with groups at all, so the assumption is that group names and memberships are handled locally at each computer Alice might access.

7.9.2 Hierarchical Groups

The concept of groups becomes even more flexible, convenient, and scalable if groups can have other groups as members. For instance, rather than having a single file **DisneyEmployees**, it might be more convenient to have someone at each site keep track of the employees from that site. Let's say Disney had various sites called ANHM, ORL, EURO, and so on. There might be a group called **ANHM-EMPL** and a group called **ORL-EMPLOYEES**. The group **DisneyEmployees** might list as members only **ANHM-EMPL**, **ORL-EMPL**, and **EURO-EMPL**. There might be even more levels of hierarchy.

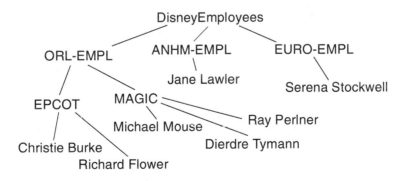

Now it becomes easy to manage the group membership, since the lists of individuals can be of reasonable size. But it becomes potentially inefficient to decide whether some user, say Dawn Perlner, is authorized to use a resource with an ACL that lists the group **DisneyEmployees**. The authorization decision has to be made after retrieving the **DisneyEmployees** group membership: **ANHM-EMPL**, **ORL-EMPL**, **EURO-EMPL**. But you still don't know whether Dawn Perlner is an authorized Disney employee. So you have to retrieve the expansion of each of the groups listed. In our diagram there were only three groups listed. In the real world there could be hundreds of group names, all stored on different nodes in the network, some of which might currently be down or inaccessible.

The world hasn't figured out how to make large groups practical. One possibility is to list all the groups you're a member of in your certificate. So for instance, Michael Mouse's certificate would list DisneyEmployees, ORL-EMPL, MAGIC and any other groups he might be a member of, such as FELINE-PHOBES, HOUSEPESTS, and so on. If the groups are listed in the user's certificate there is no need to actually expand the membership list to check if the user is indeed listed, since the certificate has been signed by the CA. An alternative solution is to list the user's group memberships in the user's entry in the directory service. In that case the list would only be a performance enhancement, a hint to help the authorization decision maker find the right groups to expand. That is because the directory service information (if not signed by the CA) cannot be considered completely trustworthy. Someone could modify the user's entry to include groups to which the user does not belong, so it is necessary to actually check the membership of the group. Someone could also modify the user's entry to delete a group to which the user does belong. In this case, the effect would be that the user might be incorrectly denied rights.

7.10 DELEGATION

It's not who you are. It's who you're working for.

Sometimes it is necessary to have things act on your behalf. For instance, you might be logged into system Bob, and then need to access remote files from Bob. In that case, Bob will need to retrieve the files on your behalf, and will need to have the same privileges for those files as you have. Similarly you might tell a printserver to print a remote file that you are authorized to read. You could allow the required access by explicitly being available to log in to each resource that is ever needed on your behalf. That would be inconvenient at best, and sometimes impossible, for instance when you run a batch job when you aren't around.

One possible means of allowing access is to give your password to everything that might need to act on your behalf (printservers, foreign systems). This might be reasonable if you changed your password immediately after the work was completed. But most users would not change their password that frequently. Another possibility is that you could explicitly add every system to every ACL for every resource that they need to access on your behalf, and then, if you are conscientious, delete them from the ACL when the operation completes. These mechanisms are far too inconvenient, and most users would opt for no security at all if that was the alternative. Therefore it is advisable to have some more convenient mechanism for giving something permission to act on your behalf. This permission is known as **delegation** or **authentication forwarding**. The best mechanism for delegation in a computer network is to generate a special message, signed by you, specifying to whom you are delegating rights, which rights are being delegated, and for how long. Once the duration specified in the message has expired, the message no longer grants any permissions.

Using public key cryptography, the usual approach is for you to sign the delegation message with your own private key. Using KDCs, the usual approach is for you to ask the KDC to give Fred certain permissions. The KDC constructs a message listing the permissions you'd like to grant Fred, encrypts the message with a key known only to the KDC, and Fred is given the encrypted message. Fred cannot decrypt the message, but he can present it to the KDC when asking for access; the KDC can decrypt it and then see the rights that have been delegated to Fred.

Why is it necessary for the delegation message to expire? If you are delegating rights to a printserver and it can be trusted for the hour it takes to finish printing all the documents ahead of yours, and then print your document, can't it always be trusted? If it were untrustworthy, surely it could have retrieved all your documents during the one hour in which you gave it access rights to your files. In theory this argument is true. You can't necessarily know that the printserver hasn't had some Trojan horse software installed which will steal all your files during the limited time you give it access, but limiting the delegation in time limits the window of vulnerability. You can further limit the vulnerability by limiting the scope of the delegation. Instead of specifying that the printserver has rights to see all your files, you might specify only the single file that you'd like printed.

7.11 HOMEWORK

1. As stated in §7.2 *Address-Based Authentication*, UNIX requires a request from system A for a resource at B to explicitly state the desired account name at B if it is not identical to the account name at A. Why do you suppose it makes that requirement? How would one implement this feature without the requirement?

2. In §7.6 *Eavesdropping and Server Database Reading* we asserted that it is extremely difficult, without public key cryptography, to have an authentication scheme which protects against both eavesdropping and server database disclosure. Consider the following authentication protocol (which is based on Novell version 3 security). Alice knows a password. Bob, a server that will authenticate Alice, stores a hash of Alice's password. Alice types her pass-

word (say **fiddlesticks**) to her workstation. The following exchange takes place:

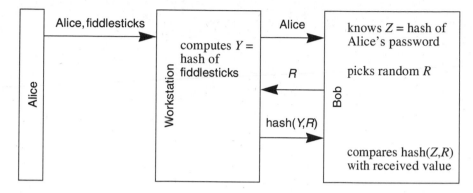

Is this an example of an authentication scheme that isn't based on public key cryptography and yet guards against both eavesdropping and server database disclosure?

3. Extend the scenario in §7.7.4.1 *Multiple KDC Domains* to a chain of three KDCs. In other words, assume that Alice wants to talk to Boris through a chain of three KDCs (Alice's KDC, a KDC that has shared keys with both Alice's KDC and Boris's KDC, and finally, Boris's KDC). Give the sequence of events necessary to establish communication.

# AUTHENTICATION OF PEOPLE

In the previous chapter we discussed in general how a computer authenticates a computer across a network. This chapter deals with the special issues involved when a computer is authenticating a human. We use the terms *user* and *human* interchangeably. This chapter deals with password-related issues like how to force users to choose unguessable passwords, how to store password information securely at the system being logged into, and how to avoid divulging information to eavesdroppers.

Authentication is done somewhat differently depending on the capabilities of the thing being authenticated. The two most important capabilities are the ability to store a high-quality cryptographic key and the ability to perform cryptographic operations. (A **high-quality key** is a secret chosen from a very large space so that it is computationally infeasible to guess the secret by exhaustive search.)

A computer has both of these capabilities; a person has neither of them. Humans are incapable of securely storing high-quality cryptographic keys, and they have unacceptable speed and accuracy when performing cryptographic operations. (They are also large, expensive to maintain, difficult to manage, and they pollute the environment. It is astonishing that these devices continue to be manufactured and deployed. But they are sufficiently pervasive that we must design our protocols around their limitations.)

User authentication consists of a computer verifying that you are who you claim to be. There are three main techniques:

- *what you know*

- *what you have*

- *what you are*

Passwords are one method of reassuring someone that you are who you claim to be, and fit into the *what you know* category. Physical keys or ATM cards fit into the *what you have* category. Biometric devices, such as voice recognition systems or fingerprint analyzers, fit into the *what you are* category.

8.1 PASSWORDS

Passwords predate computers. The concept is simple: if Alice needs to prove to Bob that she is Alice, and Bob does not know Alice by sight, they can prearrange a special greeting (a password), and Bob can assume that someone who says the magic word is Alice. As with many aspects of security, the classic uses of passwords are in the military. All members of a group are given the password of the day, and when they return to the fort after dark they state the password to prove they are not the enemy.

Most readers have undoubtedly logged into a timesharing system by typing their user name and password so often that they no longer think about it. Actually, there are a lot of real problems with using passwords for authentication:

- An eavesdropper might see the password when Alice is using it to log in.

- An intruder might read the file where the computer stores password information.

- Alice's password might be easy to guess by someone making direct login attempts to the computer.

- Alice's password may be crackable by an off-line computer search, given information such as a recognizable quantity encrypted with the password. (The difference between this off-line attack and the on-line attack above is in the number of password guesses that can be practically tried.)

- In attempting to force users to choose unguessable passwords, the system might become so inconvenient that it becomes unusable, or users might resort to writing passwords down.

This chapter describes the mechanisms in use to prevent unauthorized people from gaining access to passwords. The main lines of defense are keeping transmission of the password from being overheard, limiting the number of incorrect guesses, and making passwords difficult to guess. However, the intruder isn't the only bad guy. The authorized users will become the enemy, too, if the security mechanism becomes too inconvenient to deal with.

8.2 ON-LINE PASSWORD GUESSING

I can impersonate you if I can guess your password. And that might not be hard. I_2 once heard someone remark, about a faculty member at a major university, that "although in all other respects she appears to be a sentient human being, she insists on using her first name as her password." On some systems, passwords are administratively set to a fixed attribute of a person, such as their birthday or their badge number. This makes passwords easy to remember and distribute, but it also makes them easy to guess. I_1 once worked on a system where students' passwords were administratively set to their initials. Faculty accounts were considered more sensitive, so they were protected with *three* initials.

Even if passwords are chosen so they are not obvious, they may be guessable if the impostor gets enough guesses. In fact, given enough guesses, any password, no matter how carefully chosen, can be guessed (by enumerating all finite character sequences until you hit on the correct password). Whether this is feasible depends on how many guesses it takes and how rapidly passwords can be guessed.

In the military use of passwords, guessing is not a problem. You show up at the door. You utter a word. If it's the right word, they let you in; if it's the wrong word, they shoot you. Even if you know the password is the month in which the general was born, guessing is not an attractive pursuit.

Most terminals do not have an "execute user" function controllable from the remote end (as useful as that might be), so this mechanism for limiting password guessing is not available. Given that people's fingers slip or they forget that they changed their password, it's important that they get more than one chance anyway. There are ways to limit the number or rate of guesses. The first is to design the system so that guesses have to actually be typed by a human. Computers are much faster and more patient than people at making guesses, so the threat is much greater if the impostor can get a computer to do the dirty work. Before the days of networks and PCs, this just meant that operating systems needed to ensure that they got passwords from terminals rather than programs. But now that login requests can come in over networks and lots of terminals are really PCs emulating terminals, there's really no way to prevent this.

One seemingly attractive mechanism for preventing password guessing is to keep track of the number of consecutive incorrect passwords for an account and when the number exceeds a threshold, say five, "lock" the account and refuse access, even with a correct password, until the system is administratively reset. This technique is used with PINs on ATM cards—three wrong guesses and the machine eats your card. You have to show up at the bank with ID to get it back. An important downside of this approach is that a computer vandal (someone who simply wants to annoy people and disrupt operations) can, possibly with the aid of a computer, guess five bad passwords against all the accounts on a system and lock them all up, effectively shutting the system down until it is administratively reset (assuming it can be administratively reset when all of the administrators' accounts are locked!). This represents little work for the vandal and can cause serious disruption. So this approach is unacceptable in most environments.

Another approach to slow down a guesser is to only allow a limited number of account/password guesses per connect attempt. If the system is based on dialing in via modem, the overhead of having to redial for each five attempts can slow down the guessing rate considerably (even with an auto-dial modem). A variant on this theme is simply to have incorrect passwords (or even all passwords) be processed   s l o w l y .

If you can't prevent guessing, maybe you can catch the guesser. By auditing invalid password attempts, a system manager can be alerted to the fact that an attempt is being made to penetrate the system. It might then be possible to try to trace the phone call or take other corrective action. False alarms in audit logs can be prevented by filtering out the common case where a user mistypes a password and then immediately thereafter types it correctly. Events where a password fails and the connection then switches to a different account or disconnects are substantially more suspicious. A method for distributing the detective work is for systems to report to users when they log in the time of their previous login and the number of unsuccessful password attempts since the last successful login. In practice, few users will check the time of last successful login to see whether it looks right, but most will notice reports of failed login attempts if they did not mistype the password themselves. This doesn't work for "stale" accounts that the user never logs into. Such accounts are subject to other threats as well; it's good security policy to eliminate accounts not in regular use.

The expected time to guess a password is the expected number an impostor has to guess before getting it right divided by the guess rate. So far, we've concentrated on limiting the rate of password guesses. Another promising approach is to ensure that the number of passwords an attacker would need to search is large enough to be secure against an off-line, unaudited search with a lot of CPU power. If passwords are randomly chosen eight-character strings made from the characters a–z, then even if an attacker could guess a password every millisecond, it would take (on average) over three years to guess it. This would make all the more obtrusive and expensive preventive mechanisms unnecessary. Some administrations assign such passwords (randomly chosen 8-character strings). These systems have another problem:

Users hate them...and forget them...and write them down. As discussed later, when users write down passwords rather than memorizing them, a whole new class of threats open up. Many otherwise fine minds are genetically incapable of memorizing randomly chosen eight-character passwords. Sometimes the random password generator is clever enough to generate pronounceable strings, which makes it a little easier for the human to remember the password. Constraining the generated passwords to pronounceable strings of the same length limits the number of possible passwords by at least an order of magnitude, but since a 10-character pronounceable string is probably easier to remember than an 8-character completely random string, and is about as secure, generating pronounceable strings is a good idea if the administrator wants to impose passwords.

A better approach is to let users choose their own passwords but to warn them to choose "good" ones and enforce that choice where possible. Usually the best combination of memorability and difficulty of guessing is a "pass-phrase" with intentional misspelling or punctuation and odd capitalization, like GoneFi$hing or MyPassworDisTuff!, or the first letter of each word of a phrase, like Mhall;Ifwwas (Mary had a little lamb; Its fleece was white as snow).

The program that lets users set passwords should check for easy-to-guess passwords and disallow them. It might, for example, run them through a spell-checking dictionary and reject them if they are spelled correctly! (A favorite attack is to guess all the words in a dictionary as passwords; a large dictionary might contain 500 000 words, and it is not difficult to check that many.) If possible, the dictionary should be extended with common first and last names. The program could also require mixed cases, non-alphabetic characters, a minimum length, and a minimum number of different characters.

Surprisingly, most variants of UNIX limit password length to eight characters (or more precisely, they only check the first eight). VMS allows long passwords, and allows the administrator to set policies such as how long they must be, how often they must be changed, and how many old passwords the system remembers in order to prevent a user from reusing an old password.

8.3 OFF-LINE PASSWORD GUESSING

In the previous section, we discussed on-line password guessing, where guessing can be slowed down and audited. Passwords do not have to be very strong if the only threat is on-line password guessing. But sometimes it is possible for an attacker, through either eavesdropping or reading a database, to obtain a cryptographic hash of the password or a quantity encrypted with the password. In such a case, even though the attacker cannot reverse the hash of the password, the attacker can guess a password, perform the same hash, and compare it with the stolen quantity. Once the attacker has obtained the hash of the password, the attacker can perform password guessing without anyone knowing it, and at a speed limited only by procurable compute power.

We've talked a lot about how users should protect their passwords. Remember that passwords must be stored in two places—users must know their own, and systems must be able to verify passwords. If the system simply directly stores passwords, the password list on a system must be protected at least as well as anything else on the system. Even that is not sufficient. Most systems keep backup tapes for use in the case where a disk fails or a user accidentally destroys a file. If those tapes contain password lists, they must be protected as carefully as the system; anyone who can read them will subsequently be able to impersonate all users.

Several techniques can lessen this threat. Some operating systems, for instance UNIX and VMS, do not store actual user passwords. They take passwords as typed, run them through a one-way algorithm such as a cryptographic hash, and store the results. With such a system, the password file needs to be carefully protected from modification, but disclosure of the file is not immediately of use to an attacker. Standard UNIX systems, in fact, place such confidence in this technique that they make the password file publicly readable. This turns out to be a bad idea. Even though it is impossible to compute the password from the hash, it is possible to guess a password and verify whether you got it right by hashing it and comparing it to the stored value. This gives attackers an unaudited and fairly high-performance way of guessing passwords. Many systems have now been modified to prevent unprivileged programs from reading the password file. Another interesting downside of this technique is that if a user forgets a password, the system administrator can't look it up. Instead, the user must choose a new password and the system administrator must install it. The only time this is a problem is when an attacker has changed the user's password but the user isn't sure whether it was changed nefariously or merely forgotten. Being able to read the old value might make it easier to tell the difference.

Password Hash Quirk

There was an operating system (which we'll allow to remain nameless) that stored hashes of passwords, and the password hash used by that operating system had an interesting property. We are purposely not giving the exact details, but the general idea is that there was a magic character sequence X such that the hash of any string S was the same as the hash of X concatenated with S. This is not exactly a security flaw, but instead is a wonderfully user-friendly feature. How can this odd feature be useful?

Suppose the system administrator made the common policy decision that user passwords had to be some minimum length. This particular operating system enforced the policy only when you set your password (as opposed to when you logged in). Now suppose you wanted a password you could type quickly, like FOO. The operating system would not let you set your password to FOO because it's not long enough. But it would let you set it to X concatenated with FOO. Let's say the magic string was %#v27dR678riwueyru3ir3. You'd set your password to %#v27dR678riwueyru3ir3FOO. That would be the last time you'd have to type %#v27dR678riwueyru3ir3FOO. From then on, FOO would work just fine, since the hash of FOO is the same as the hash of %#v27dR678riwueyru3ir3FOO.

When disclosure of whole files full of hashed passwords is a concern, another useful technique is to apply *salt*. Rather than guessing passwords against a single user account, an attacker with a file full of hashed passwords might hash all the words in a dictionary and check to see whether any of the passwords match any of the stored hashed values. This would be a much more efficient means of attack, particularly when the attacker just wanted any account on the system or, more likely, as many accounts as possible on the system. Tests at universities have shown 30% hit rates with fairly small dictionaries. A way to slow down such an attacker is as follows:

When a user chooses a password, the system chooses a random number (the **salt**). It then stores both the salt and a hash of the combination of the salt and the password. When the user supplies a password during authentication, the system computes the hash of the combination of the stored salt and the supplied password, and checks the computed hash against the stored hash. The presence of the salt does not make it any harder to guess any one user's password, but it makes it impossible to perform a single cryptographic hash operation and see whether a password is valid for any of a group of users.

user ID	salt value	password hash
Mary	2758	hash(2758|password$_{Mary}$)
John	886d	hash(886d|password$_{John}$)
Ed	5182	hash(5182|password$_{Ed}$)
Jane	1763	hash(1763|password$_{Jane}$)

Another technique is to encrypt the password file. This doesn't eliminate the problem of keeping passwords secret; it just reduces it to the problem of protecting the key that decrypts the password file. This might be done by having the key held in operating system memory, not backed up to disk or tape, and having it either stored in special nonvolatile memory in the machine or reentered by the operator on boot-up.

8.4 HOW BIG SHOULD A SECRET BE?

From how big a space must a secret be chosen in order to be secure? To thwart an on-line attack the secret does not have to be chosen from a large space, because the intruder is detected after a small number of guesses or because the amount of time the intruder needs to guess correctly is worth much more than the payoff. For instance, many ATM systems have only four decimal digits worth of secret, which means there are only 10000 different secrets, and this is really sufficiently secure because you only get three guesses.

If there's the opportunity to do off-line password guessing, the secret must be chosen from a much larger space. The general rule of thumb is that a secret needs about 64 bits of randomness, since it is considered computationally infeasible to search 2^{64} possibilities. Therefore a 64-bit secret cryptographic key is reasonably secure.

Humans aren't usually willing to remember or type 64-bit (about 20-digit) random numbers (though one of our children is perfectly happy to remember dozens of digits of $\sqrt{2}$, and another of our children seems to know innumerable 7-digit phone numbers). How big does a password have to be in order to have the equivalent security of a 64-bit random number? If the text string is truly randomly chosen from upper- and lower-case letters, the 10 digits, plus a couple of punctuation marks, there are 64 possibilities per keystroke (6 bits), so an 11-character password would be necessary. A human will not remember a randomly chosen 11-character string.

What about a randomly chosen pronounceable password? If a computer were to generate such strings (as opposed to allowing a human to choose), the pronounceability constraint means that about every third character must be a vowel. To be memorizable, the password should be a case-insensitive string of letters, giving only about 4½ bits per character, and only about 2½ bits per vowel (since there are 6 vowels in English). The combination of limiting characters to case-insensitive letters and having a reasonable percentage of vowels yields randomness of about 4 bits per character. This would require a 16-character computer-generated pronounceable string, which is also too long for a person to willingly memorize or type.

What about if people are allowed to choose their own passwords? The general wisdom is that the randomness achievable in human-generated passwords is about 2 bits per character, which would result in a 32-character password, which is also too long.

The conclusion is that a secret a person would be willing to memorize and type will not be as good as a 64-bit random number, and therefore passwords will be open to off-line password-guessing attacks.

8.5 EAVESDROPPING

A second important weakness in using passwords is that they must be "uttered" to be used, and there is always a chance of eavesdropping when they are uttered. The lowest-tech form of eavesdropping is to watch as someone types a password. There is an etiquette around the operation of ATMs. Even when there is a substantial line, the second person stands a discreet distance behind the person operating the machine and looks away. The etiquette is not so highly evolved in an office environment, and it often isn't difficult to pick up passwords this way. The only prevention beyond training people to be more paranoid is to pick passwords involving shift and control characters so more fingers are involved.

Of course, it's easier to watch the screen than fingers. Most systems have the sophistication to not display passwords as they are being typed.

A more high-tech method of eavesdropping is to place a wiretap on the communications line between the terminal and the computer and watch all the passwords (and everything else, for that matter) go by. Whether this is easy or hard depends on the environment.

If you're going to give up on memorization and accept the risks of written-down passwords, an effective mechanism is **one-time passwords**. Here, the user and the system have a list of valid passwords, but each one is only valid once. After it's used, it is crossed off the list (at both ends). Periodically, the user must get a new list from the system administrator. This mechanism is impervious to eavesdropping.

A variant is to have a numbered list of passwords and have the system ask for specific ones on each authentication. An attacker would have to eavesdrop on many authentications before obtaining enough information to impersonate the user. With this technique, the list can be somewhat shorter and can be used for longer than the one-time password list, but at some loss of security and convenience. (See Homework Problem 2.)

8.6 PASSWORDS AND CARELESS USERS

At a lecture on computer security, a professor asked, "Are there any advantages of passwords over biometric devices?" A helpful student replied "When you want to let someone use your account, with a password you just give it to them, while with a biometric device you have to go with them until they are logged in." This is the sort of remark that sends chills down the back of security administrators and makes them think of their users as adversaries rather than the customers they are trying to protect. Security people need to remember that most people regard security as a nuisance rather than as needed protection, and left to their own devices they often carelessly give up the security that someone worked so hard to provide. The solution is to educate users on the importance of security, helping them to understand the reasons for the procedures they are asked to follow, and making those procedures sufficiently tolerable that they don't develop contempt for the process.

Passwords are particularly easy to abuse. The classic tale is one where the system manager's password is posted on the console because it is too long and complex to remember.

One particular danger is users' including passwords on-line in accessible places. In addition to doing this as a substitute for little black books, users might find it convenient to include passwords in scripts used to automate access to other systems, or they might include passwords in messages sent via electronic mail. Electronic mail messages are frequently archived. Both schemes allow an attacker who has gotten into one account to cascade those rights into other accounts on other systems.

8.6.1 Using a Password in Multiple Places

One of the tough trade-offs is whether to recommend that users use the same password in multiple places or keep their passwords different for different systems. All things being equal, use of different passwords is more secure because if one password is compromised it only gives away the user's rights on a single system. Things are rarely equal, however. When weighed against the likelihood that users will resort to writing passwords down if they need to remember more than one, the trade-off is less clear.

An issue that weighs in favor of different passwords is that of a cascaded break-in. An attacker that breaks in to one system may succeed in reading the password database. If users have different passwords on different systems, this information will be of no use. But if passwords are common, a break-in to a system that was not well protected because it contained no "important" information might in fact leak passwords that are useful on critical systems.

8.6.2 Requiring Frequent Password Changes

> *Security is a wet blanket.*   —apologies to Charles Schulz

A technique that offers some security but is probably overused, is requiring frequent password changes. The idea behind frequent password changes is that if someone does learn your password, it will only be useful until it next changes. This protection may not be worth much if a lot of damage can be done in a short time.

The problem with requiring frequent password changes is that users are more likely to write passwords down and less likely to give much thought or creativity to choosing them. The result is observable and guessable passwords. It's also true that users tend to circumvent password change policy unless enforcement is clever. In a spy-vs.-spy escalation, the following is a common scenario:

1. The system administrator decides that passwords must be changed every 90 days, and the system enforces this.

2. The user types the change password command, resetting the password to the same thing as before.

3. The system administrator discovers users are doing this and modifies the system so that it makes sure the password, when changed, is set to a different value.

4. The user then does a change password procedure that sets the password to something new, and then immediately sets it back to the old, familiar value.

5. The system administrator then has the system keep track of the previous n password values and does not allow the password to be set to any of them.

6. The user then does a change password procedure that goes through n different password values and finally, on the $n+1^{st}$ password change, returns the password to its old familiar value.

7. The system is modified to keep track of the last time the password was changed and does not allow another password change for some number of days.

8. The user, when forced to change passwords, constructs a new password by appending '1' to the end of the previous password. Next time the user replaces the '1' with a '2', ...

9. The system, in looking for guessable passwords, looks for passwords that look "too much like" one of the previous *n* passwords.

10. The users throw up their hands in disgust, accept impossible-to-remember passwords, and post them on their terminals.

All of these techniques have been tried on some system or another. In general, it's impossible to make systems secure without the cooperation of the legitimate users. If frequent password changes address a real threat, users must be educated to fear that threat so they will strive for good passwords. If the threat cannot be made real to the users, the inconvenience won't be worth the trouble.

8.6.3 A Login Trojan Horse to Capture Passwords

A threat as old as timesharing is to leave a program running on a public terminal that displays a login prompt. An unsuspecting user then enters a user name and password. The Trojan horse program logs the name and password to a file before the program terminates in some way designed to minimize suspicion. There is no protection from this threat given a sufficiently naive user. Approaches toward minimizing it are based on making it difficult for a program to "look like" a normal login prompt. For example:

- On some systems, any program request for input is preceded by an automatically inserted '?'. If the real login prompt is made to have no '?', a program can't produce a believable counterfeit.

- On the bit-mapped screens associated with workstations and X-windows terminals, the login screen takes up the entire screen and has no border. If the protocol prevents ordinary programs from displaying such a screen, they can't counterfeit a login prompt very reasonably.

- On most systems, there is some way to interrupt running programs. Training users to enter the interrupt key sequence before logging in would then thwart such Trojan horses. Unfortunately, many systems allow programs to disable interrupts; for those systems, this technique would not be useful.

Even if the Trojan horse program can do the login prompt exactly, it might not be able to exactly duplicate the way the system behaves after a user logs in. This will make an alert user suspicious. For example:

- A reasonable action following the capture of a password is to log it, put out the message the user would get if the password were mistyped, and then terminate and return to a regular login prompt. The user will assume the password was mistyped the first time and try again. This can be prevented if a program can't end its session without a logout banner. Such a banner before the second login message is a dead giveaway. Mentioned earlier was having a message displayed at login telling users the number of unsuccessful login attempts to the account since the last successful attempt. This doubles as Trojan horse protection because the successful login would not report that there had just been a failed login attempt.

- Another thing the Trojan horse program can do is hang after accepting the user's name and password, as if the system got into a wedged state. If it can prevent the user from using any escape characters, the user will just get frustrated and redial. Very few users would find this behavior suspicious.

- An optimally designed Trojan horse would actually use the username and password to log the user in and run a session. Some operating systems offer sufficient modularity and generality to make this possible. It would be a security feature to make this evident to processes started in non-standard ways so that some sort of warning banner could be displayed.

8.6.4 Non-Login Use of Passwords

Entering a single password to log into a system and subsequently having access to all the user's resources is, in most environments, a reasonable mix of security and convenience. It's not the only way to do it. Some systems permit password protection on individual files. A user could specially protect certain files so that someone learning the user's login password still couldn't get at those files.

Similarly, applications could require their own authentication of a user before permitting access to certain databases (even after the user has logged in).

8.7 INITIAL PASSWORD DISTRIBUTION

Everything we've discussed so far describes how systems work once users have passwords and the systems know them. Another opportunity to get it wrong exists in the administrative procedures involved in getting to that state. After all, if you can impersonate the user to the system administrator, you can get the password by whatever mechanism the user could.

A secure method for the initial distribution of passwords is for the user to appear at the terminal of the system administrator and authenticate by whatever means humans use to authenticate (driver's license, student ID, birth certificate and two major credit cards, whatever). The system administrator then sets up all the particulars of the account for the user except the password (name, rights, quotas, choice of shell, ...) and then lets the user choose a password. This method has two drawbacks: it may be inconvenient for the user to meet the system administrator; and it's a little scary to let this new user type to this highly privileged terminal session while the system administrator discreetly looks away. A skilled user could probably do substantial damage in a short time. Even this problem could be circumvented by giving the user access to a special keyboard that only accepts passwords. This mechanism is sometimes used in special-case environments like establishing the PIN for an ATM. For a bank this is a sufficiently high-volume and security-sensitive application to justify special hardware.

Another variant on this theme is for the system administrator to create the account and an initial **strong** (randomly chosen from a large space) password, give it to the user, and instruct the user to use the password only for an initial login and then change it to something more easily remembered. Some systems support the notion of **pre-expired** passwords that require the user to change them as part of the login process. Even if the initial strong password is written down and the paper handed to a user, little security is lost because the password is no good after it is used and the user is likely to keep it safe that long.

In the name of convenience, there are weaker versions of this protocol. The administrator could set up the account and distribute the password by (paper) mail, in which case the security is as good as the security of mail. A common but insecure practice is to have the initial password be either a constant or an easily determined property of the user. A school might, for example, set all student passwords initially to their student IDs. Then they could communicate passwords to students with a broadcast (published) message rather than sending individualized notes. The security of this might be vaguely acceptable if the only thing a student account password protects is the work of the student, which is presumably nothing until the student uses the account for the first time. Even so, an attacker could log into the student's account ahead of time and plant Trojan horses.

The following story is true (or rather was told to me[1] as true by a person supposedly involved). Names are omitted to protect the guilty. See how many things you can find wrong with the way security was administered.

At a large commercial timesharing service bureau, security of privileged accounts (those that could access other users' data) was considered paramount. One of the security measures used to protect these accounts was that the passwords were randomly chosen and changed weekly. Every Sunday afternoon a batch job was run, selecting new random passwords and changing all the privileged accounts. Part of the batch job was to print a list of all the accounts and their passwords. This list was posted on a bulletin board so that as people came in Monday morning they could get their new passwords.

This worked fine until one Sunday the printer was broken. All the passwords were changed, but they weren't printed. Monday morning the printer was fixed, but no one could log in to request that the list be printed. In fact, no one could log in at all (except the commercial users, who saw no disruption). Some systems have a way to perform a privileged login given physical access to the machine, but this operating system didn't—it would support such an override only upon also erasing the disks, which by that time included unbacked-up commercial data. Many systems that do have such an override require that the system be rebooted in single-user mode, which would have been an unacceptable interruption of commercial service.

After thinking hard, some bright fellow noticed that the space from which the passwords were randomly selected was not unmanageably large, so they got all the people who couldn't do any work anyway (about 50) to repeatedly attempt logins to a single account with each of them assigned a range of passwords. By the end of the day Monday, one of them had succeeded and they were able to return to business as usual.

8.8 AUTHENTICATION TOKENS

An authentication token is a physical device that a person carries around and uses in authenticating. In the breakdown of security according to *what you know*, *what you have*, and *what you are*, authentication tokens fall in the middle category (passwords are in the first, and biometric devices the third). Generally, authentication tokens offer security advantages and disadvantages over other mechanisms. Unless they are physically attached to users (which is unacceptable in our culture), they are subject to theft. Generally they must be coupled with one of the other two mechanisms to be secure.

There are several forms of authentication token in use today. The most ubiquitous is the key that people use to unlock their home or car. Another common form of authentication token is the credit card. If a credit card includes a picture or a signature, it combines an authentication token with a primitive biometric device (the person who compares signatures or sees whether you look like the picture).

Credit cards these days contain a magnetic strip that contains information. The advantage that magnetic strip cards offer over simple passwords is that they are not trivial to reproduce and they can conveniently hold a secret larger than most people are willing to memorize. Perhaps the biggest advantage is psychological —people tend to be less willing to "loan" a token to a friend than to share a password. There are a number of disadvantages:

- Use of these tokens requires custom hardware (a key slot or card reader) on every access device. This may be expensive and it requires standardization.

- Tokens can be lost or stolen. For reasonable security, tokens must be supplemented with a PIN or password. In most environments, a convenient override must be available for when "I forgot my card at home." That override should not be substantially less convenient than the one for "I forgot my password."

These devices offer little or no protection against communications eavesdropping. Whatever information is sent "over the wire" can be collected just like a password and replayed later. To make use of the information using a "standard terminal" requires that a card be manufactured to regurgitate the stolen information, but someone who can eavesdrop can likely connect a nonstandard terminal to the network and replay the information without making a card. There is nothing conceptually difficult about copying a key or mag-stripe card; devices for doing so are readily available.

A better form of authentication token is the **smart card**. This is a device about the size of a credit card but with an embedded CPU and memory. When inserted in a (misleadingly named) **smart card reader**, the card carries on a conversation with the device (as opposed to a magnetic strip, which simply dumps its contents). There are various forms of smart cards:

- **PIN protected memory card**. With this card, there is information in the memory of the card that can only be read after a PIN is input to the card. Usually, after some number of wrong PIN guesses, the card "locks" itself and will not give the information to anyone. Information stored on such a smart card is safer than that stored on a magnetic strip card because a stolen card is useless without the PIN. These cards are more difficult to duplicate than magnetic strip cards, but it's still possible given the PIN.

- **Cryptographic challenge/response cards**. With this card, there is a cryptographic key in memory, and the card is willing to encrypt or decrypt using the key but will not reveal the key even after the PIN is entered. A computer that knows the key in the card can authenticate the user by creating a random challenge and "challenging" the card to encrypt or decrypt it. If the correct answer is returned, the computer can have confidence that the smart card is present and the correct PIN was entered. These cards can be constructed so as to be nearly impossible to duplicate or to extract the key from. Since there is no way to directly extract the key, it can only be done by disassembling or inserting probes into the card. There is a reciprocating escalation in the technologies for probing the card and for packaging it to be unreadable. For most practical purposes, the cards are unreadable. Like keys and magnetic strip cards, the serious practical problems with smart cards are the need for readers at every access point and the need for recovery when a card is lost or forgotten. The cryptographic card offers substantial protection against eavesdropping.

- **Cryptographic calculator** (sometimes called a **readerless smart card**). A cryptographic calculator is like a smart card in that it performs cryptographic calculations using a key that it will not disclose. It is unlike a smart card in that it requires no electrical connection to the terminal. It has a display and usually a keyboard, and all interaction is through the user. One way it could work is by simulating a smart card: The user enters a PIN to unlock the device; the computer wishing to authenticate the user generates a random challenge and displays it to the user; the user types it into the calculator; the calculator encrypts the value and displays the result; the user enters the result on the terminal; the computer does the same calculation and compares the results.

An alternative protocol that cuts the typing in half is for the calculator to encrypt the current time and display the result. The user types in this number in place of a password. There's a little more work for the computer since it will not be sure of the exact time that the calculator thinks it is (clocks drift); it will have to do the calculation on several candidate time values to verify what the device said. It might then record the accumulated clock skew to make the next such calculation easier. It's possible to eliminate the keyboard (needed for entering the PIN) from the calculator by having a PIN or password sent to the computer instead. It is important to have some form of PIN to prevent someone who steals the calculator from impersonating its owner. In addition to saving typing, another advantage of the time encryption protocol is that it fits the "form factor" of protocols designed for passwords. If a protocol has a "password" field and no way for the authenticating application to send a challenge, the encrypted time variant can still be made to work.

The biggest advantage of these readerless smart cards is that they can be used from ordinary terminals with no special hardware. Their popularity is growing among companies that want to let their employees log in from home using terminals and modems but are afraid of opening their networks up to intruders.

8.9 PHYSICAL ACCESS

A low-tech way of performing user authentication is to have human guards do it "at the door". If a system is only accessible from protected areas, and it requires some form of person-to-person authentication to enter those areas, then any authentication the system does is for purposes of differentiating legitimate users from each other as opposed to differentiating legitimate users from illegitimate users. For high-security applications, this may be perfectly reasonable. Many bank transactions, for example, can only be initiated at tellers' terminals inside the bank.

Alternatively, the location from which access is requested can be part of the authentication process, where fewer rights are granted from less secure access points. For instance, ATMs and the tellers' terminals connect to the same computer, but support different transaction types.

8.10 BIOMETRICS

> *Biometric devices sell best in places where users aren't afraid of technology or don't have a choice.*
> —*Wall Street Journal*, Oct 13, 1992, William M. Bulkeley

In dividing authentication mechanisms into *what you know*, *what you have*, and *what you are*, biometric devices authenticate you according to *what you are*. They measure your physical characteristics and match them against a profile. You can't "loan out" anything that would help someone fool a biometric authentication device, nor can anything be stolen.

There are a variety of biometric devices available. All are too expensive to be in everyday use, but in some cases the costs are coming down to where we may see these. Technology available today includes:

- **Retinal scanner**. This is a device that examines the tiny blood vessels in the back of your eye. The layout is as distinctive as a fingerprint and apparently easier to read. These devices are quite expensive and have a "psychologically threatening" user interface.

- **Fingerprint readers**. This would seem an obvious technology since fingerprints have been used as a method of identification for many years. For some reason, automating this technology has never been very successful, though there are devices available.

- **Handprint readers**. These are more widely used than fingerprint readers. They measure the dimensions of the hand: finger length, width, and so on. They are not as accurate as fingerprints (more false positives), but they are less expensive and less problem-prone.

- **Voiceprints**. It turns out that it's possible to do a frequency spectrum analysis of someone's voice and get identification nearly as accurate as a fingerprint. This technology is in use, but has not caught on in spite of the fact that it should be fairly cheap. It can be defeated with a tape recording, and it may refuse to authenticate someone whose voice has shifted due to illness.

- **Keystroke timing**. The exact way in which people type is quite distinctive, and experiments have been done with identification based on the way people type. There is a problem that various injuries can throw off timing, and the networks that connect terminals and computers tend to lose the keystroke timing information before it reaches a processor that can use it.

- **Signatures**. These are a classic human form of authentication, and there are human experts quite adept at determining whether two signatures were produced by the same person. Machines thus far have not been able to duplicate that ability. However, when not just the signature is recorded, but the actual timing of the movements that go into scribing the signature, there is sufficient information for authentication, and some systems use this method, with the user signing on an electronic tablet.

It might seem tempting to build a portable fingerprint reader as a peripheral to a laptop or PC that lets you stick your finger in and turns it into bits. (I_1 have some experience with such a device—a meat grinder. Table saws are also quite effective.) It then sends the bits to a remote computer as a form of authentication. The problem with this approach is that the biometric properties cannot reasonably be kept secret. Anyone who knows your fingerprint can transmit the relevant fingerprint data. The only way in which a remote biometric device can be secure is if the device possesses a tamper-resistant secret and communicates with the remote computer via a cryptographically protected exchange.

8.11 HOMEWORK

1. Design a password hash algorithm with the property stated in *Password Hash Quirk* on page 210. It should be impossible to reverse, but for any string *S* it should be easy to find a longer string with the same hash.

2. In §8.5 *Eavesdropping* we described a scheme in which a user has a numbered list of passwords and the system asks for some small subset on each login. Is there any advantage in asking for more than one password per login? Note that the more passwords requested, the more information an eavesdropper will get. On the other hand, when the eavesdropper attempts to impersonate the user, the more passwords requested, the less likely the eavesdropper will know all of them.

9 SECURITY HANDSHAKE PITFALLS

Knock Knock!
Who's there?
Alice.
Alice who?

and you'll have to read on to find secure ways of continuing...

Security in communications almost always includes an initial authentication handshake, and sometimes, in addition, integrity protection and/or encryption of the data. Let's assume Alice and Bob wish to communicate. In order to communicate, they need to know some information about themselves and about the other party. Some of this information is secret. Some isn't, such as the names **Alice** and **Bob**.

In §7.3 *Cryptographic Authentication Protocols* we described some example security handshakes. Although they may seem straightforward, minor variants of secure protocols can have security holes. As a matter of fact, many deployed protocols have been designed with security flaws.

This stuff just isn't that hard. How come nobody gets it right?
—Al Eldridge

This book does not tell you the one "best" protocol. Different protocols have different trade-offs. Some threats are more likely in some situations, and different resources are available in terms of computational power, specialized hardware, money to pay off patent holders, humans willing and able to be careful, and so forth. We mortals should never need to design our own cryptographic algorithms (like DES, RSA, or MD5)—we can leave that in the able hands of Ron Rivest and a handful of other specialists. But it is often the case that people outside the security community, such as implementers or protocol designers, have to design security features into protocols—including authentication handshakes. It is crucial that potential flaws be well understood. Even when a protocol is patterned after known protocols, the slightest alteration, even in something that "couldn't conceivably matter", can introduce subtle security flaws. Or even if a new flaw is not introduced, a weakness that was not important in the original protocol might be serious in a different environment.

In practice, the way that security protocols are designed is by starting with some design, which is almost certainly flawed, and then checking for all the weaknesses one can imagine, and fixing them. So the more educated we can become about the types of flaws likely to be in a protocol, the more likely it is that we'll understand all the properties of a protocol we deploy.

In this chapter we describe some typical protocols and evaluate them according to performance (number of messages, processing power required, compactness of messages) and security.

9.1 LOGIN ONLY

A lot of existing protocols were designed in an environment where eavesdropping was not a concern (rightly or wrongly), and bad guys were (rightly or wrongly) not expected to be very sophisticated. The authentication in such protocols generally consists of:

- Alice (the initiator) sends her name and password (in the clear) across the network to Bob.

- Bob verifies the name and password, and then communication occurs, with no further attention to security—no encryption, no cryptographic integrity protection.

A very common enhancement to such a protocol is to replace the transmission of the cleartext password with a cryptographic challenge/response. First we'll discuss protocols based on shared secrets, using either secret key cryptographic algorithms or message digest algorithms. Then we'll discuss similar protocols using public key technology.

9.1.1 Shared Secret

Consider Protocol 9-1. The notation $K_{\text{Alice-Bob}}\{R\}$ means that R is cryptographically transformed, somehow, with Alice and Bob's shared secret $K_{\text{Alice-Bob}}$. This could be done by using $K_{\text{Alice-Bob}}$ as a secret key in some algorithm such as DES or IDEA, and using $K_{\text{Alice-Bob}}$ to encrypt R. Or it could be done by hashing R and $K_{\text{Alice-Bob}}$, for instance by concatenating R and $K_{\text{Alice-Bob}}$ and computing a message digest on the result. The only important thing is that we must assume an eavesdropper will see both R and the transformed R. It is essential that seeing the pair does not enable the eavesdropper to derive $K_{\text{Alice-Bob}}$.

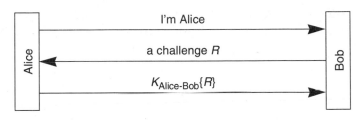

Protocol 9-1. Bob authenticates Alice based on a shared secret $K_{\text{Alice-Bob}}$

This protocol is a big improvement over passwords in the clear. An eavesdropper cannot impersonate Alice based on overhearing the exchange, since next time there will be a different challenge. However, there are some weaknesses to this protocol:

- Authentication is not mutual. Bob authenticates Alice, but Alice does not authenticate Bob. If Trudy can receive packets transmitted to Bob's network address, and respond with Bob's network address (or through other means convince Alice that Trudy's address is Bob's), then Alice will be fooled into assuming Trudy is Bob. Trudy doesn't need to know Alice's secret in order to impersonate Bob—she just needs to send any old number R to Alice and ignore Alice's response.

- If this is the entire protocol (i.e., the remainder of the conversation is transmitted without cryptographic protection), then Trudy can hijack the conversation after the initial exchange, assuming she can generate packets with Alice's source address. It's also useful to Trudy, but not absolutely essential, that she be able to receive packets transmitted to Alice's network layer address. (See Homework Problem 1.)

- An eavesdropper could mount an off-line password-guessing attack (assuming $K_{\text{Alice-Bob}}$ is derived from a password), knowing R and $K_{\text{Alice-Bob}}\{R\}$. (Recall that an off-line password-guessing attack is one in which an intruder captures information against which passwords can be tested in private, so in this context it means guessing a password, turning that password into a key, and then seeing whether encrypting R with that key results in $K_{\text{Alice-Bob}}\{R\}$.)

- Someone who reads the database at Bob can later impersonate Alice. In many cases it is difficult to protect the database at Bob. There might be many servers where Alice uses the same password, and although the administrators of most of the servers might be very conscientious about security (not letting unauthorized people get near their machines, and enforcing unguessable passwords), it only takes one unprotected server for an intruder to read the relevant information. Furthermore, protecting the database implies protecting all the backup media as well, by either preventing access to it (locking it in a safe) or encrypting the contents and somehow protecting the key with which it was encrypted.

Despite these drawbacks, if there are limited resources available for adding security, replacing the cleartext password transmission is the single most important security enhancement that can be done.

A minor variant on Protocol 9-1 is the following:

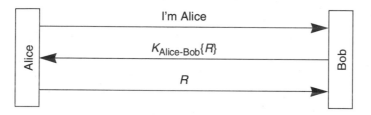

Protocol 9-2. Bob authenticates Alice based on a shared secret key $K_{\text{Alice-Bob}}$

In this protocol Bob chooses a random challenge R, encrypts it, and transmits the result. Alice then decrypts the received quantity, using the secret key $K_{\text{Alice-Bob}}$ to get R, and sends R to Bob. This protocol has only minor security differences from Protocol 9-1:

- This protocol requires reversible cryptography, for example a secret key cryptographic algorithm. Protocol 9-1 can be done using a hash function. For example, $K_{\text{Alice-Bob}}\{R\}$ could be the message digest of $K_{\text{Alice-Bob}}$ concatenated with R. But in Protocol 9-2, Alice has to be able to reverse what Bob has done to R in order to retrieve R. Sometimes there is a performance advantage to being able to use one of the message digest functions rather than having to use, say, DES. Sometimes there are export issues involved in having code for encryption available, even if it's only used for authentication, whereas using a message digest function would be less likely to create export problems.

- If R is a recognizable quantity, for instance a 32-bit random number padded with 32 zero bits to fill out an encryption block, then Trudy can, without eavesdropping, mount a password-guessing attack by merely sending the message I am Alice and obtaining $K_{\text{Alice-Bob}}\{R\}$. If Trudy is eavesdropping, however, and sees both R and $K_{\text{Alice-Bob}}\{R\}$, she can mount a password-guessing attack with either protocol. It is often the case that eavesdropping is more difficult than merely sending a message claiming to be Alice. Kerberos V4 (see Chapter 10 *Kerberos V4*) is an example of a protocol that has this security weakness.

- If R is a recognizable quantity with limited lifetime, such as a random number concatenated with a timestamp, Alice authenticates Bob on the grounds that only someone knowing $K_{\text{Alice-Bob}}$ could generate $K_{\text{Alice-Bob}}\{R\}$.

Another variant on Protocol 9-1 is to shorten the handshake to a single message by having Alice use a timestamp instead of an *R* that Bob supplies:

Protocol 9-3. Bob authenticates Alice based on synchronized clocks and a shared secret $K_{Alice-Bob}$

This modification requires that Bob and Alice have reasonably synchronized clocks. Alice encrypts the current time. Bob decrypts the result and makes sure the result is acceptable (i.e., within an acceptable clock skew). The implications of this modification are:

- This modification can be added very easily to a protocol designed for sending cleartext passwords, since it does not add any additional messages—it merely replaces the cleartext password field with the encrypted timestamp in the first message transmitted by Alice to Bob.

- The protocol is now more efficient. It goes beyond saving two messages. It means that a server, Bob, does not need to keep any volatile state (such as *R* in Protocol 9-1) regarding Alice (but see next bullet). This protocol can be added to a request/response protocol (such as RPC) by having Alice merely add the encrypted timestamp into her request. Bob can authenticate the request, generate a reply, and forget the whole thing ever happened.

- Someone eavesdropping can use Alice's transmitted $K_{Alice-Bob}\{timestamp\}$ to impersonate Alice, if done within the acceptable clock skew. This threat can be foiled if Bob remembers all timestamps sent by Alice until they "expire" (i.e., they are old enough that the clock skew check would consider them invalid).

- Another potential security pitfall occurs if there are multiple servers for which Alice uses the same secret $K_{Alice-Bob}$. Then an eavesdropper who acts quickly can use the encrypted timestamp field Alice transmitted, and (if still within the acceptable time skew) impersonate Alice to a different server. This can be foiled by concatenating the server name in with the timestamp. Instead of sending $K_{Alice-Bob}\{timestamp\}$, Alice sends $K_{Alice-Bob}\{"Bob"|timestamp\}$. That quantity would not be accepted by a different server.

- If our bad guy Trudy can convince Bob to set his clock back, she can reuse encrypted timestamps she had overheard in what is now Bob's future. In practice there are systems that are vulnerable to an intruder resetting the clock. Although it might be obvious that a password file would be something that needed to be protected, if the security protocols are not completely understood, it might not be obvious that clock-setting could be a serious security vulnerability.

- If security relies on time, then setting the time will be an operation that requires a security handshake. A handshake based on time will fail if the clocks are far apart. If there's a system with an incorrect time, then it will be impossible to log into the system in order to manage it (in order to correct its clock). A plausible solution to this is to have a different authentication handshake based on challenge/response (i.e., not dependent on time) for managing clock setting.

In Protocol 9-1, computing $K_{\text{Alice-Bob}}\{R\}$ may be done with a secret key encryption scheme using $K_{\text{Alice-Bob}}$ as a key, or by concatenating $K_{\text{Alice-Bob}}$ with R and doing a hash as in $\text{MD}(K_{\text{Alice-Bob}}|R)$. When we're using timestamps the same is true (a message digest works), except for a minor complication. How does Bob verify that $\text{MD}(K_{\text{Alice-Bob}}|R)$ is reasonable? Suppose the timestamp is in units of minutes, and the believable clock skew is 10 minutes. Then Bob would have to compute $\text{MD}(K_{\text{Alice-Bob}}|timestamp)$ for each of the twenty possible valid timestamps to verify the value Alice sends (though he could stop as soon as he found a match). With a reversible encryption function, all he had to do was decrypt the quantity received and see if the result was acceptable. While checking 20 values might have acceptable performance, this approach would become intolerably inefficient if the clock granularity allows a lot more legal values within the clock skew. For instance, the timestamp might be in units of microseconds. There are 600 million valid timestamps within a five-minute clock skew. This would be unacceptably inefficient for Bob to verify. The solution (assuming you wanted to use a microsecond clock and a hash function rather than a reversible encryption scheme) is to have Alice transmit the actual timestamp unencrypted, in addition to transmitting the hashed value. So the protocol would be:

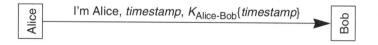

Protocol 9-4. Bob authenticates Alice based on high-resolution time and a shared secret $K_{\text{Alice-Bob}}$

9.1.2 One-Way Public Key

With protocols in the previous section, which are based on shared secrets, Trudy can impersonate Alice if she can read Bob's database. If the protocols are based on public key technology instead, this can be avoided, as in Protocol 9-5.

In this case $[R]_{\text{Alice}}$ means that Alice signs R (i.e. transforms R using her private key). Bob will verify Alice's signature $[R]_{\text{Alice}}$ using Alice's public key, and accept the login if the result matches R. This is very similar to Protocol 9-1. The advantage of this protocol is that the database at Bob is no longer security-sensitive to an attacker reading it. Bob's database must be protected from unauthorized modification, but not from unauthorized disclosure.

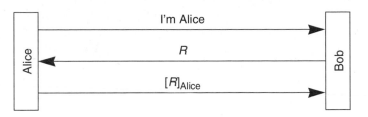

Protocol 9-5. Bob authenticates Alice based on her public key signature

And as before, the same minor variant works:

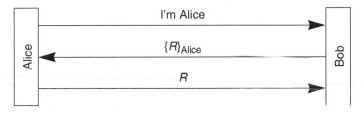

Protocol 9-6. Bob authenticates Alice if she can decrypt a message encrypted with her public key

In this variant, Bob chooses R, encrypts it using Alice's public key, and Alice proves she knows her private key by decrypting the received quantity to retrieve R. A problem with this variant is that some public key schemes (such as DSS) can only do signatures, not reversible encryption. So in those cases this variant cannot be used.

In both Protocol 9-5 and Protocol 9-6 there is a potential serious problem. In Protocol 9-5 you can trick someone into signing something. That means, if you have a quantity on which you'd like to forge Alice's signature, you might be able to impersonate Bob's network address, wait for Alice to try to log in, and then give her the quantity as the challenge. She'll sign it, and now you know her signature on that quantity. Protocol 9-6 has Alice decrypting something. So, if there's some encrypted message someone sent to Alice and you're wondering what's in it, you might again impersonate Bob's address, wait for Alice to log in, and then have Alice decrypt it for you.

How can we avoid getting in trouble? The general rule is that you should not use the same key for two different purposes unless the designs for all uses of the key are coordinated so that an attacker can't use one protocol to help break another. An example method of coordination is to ensure that R has some structure. For instance, if you sign different types of things (say an R in a challenge/response protocol versus an electronic mail message), each type of thing should have a structure so that it cannot be mistaken for another type of thing. For example, there might be a type field concatenated to the front of the quantity before signing, with different values for *authentication challenge* and *mail message*. Part of the purpose of the PKCS standards (see §5.3.6 *Public-Key Cryptography Standard (PKCS)*) is to impose enough structure to prevent this sort of problem when the same RSA key is used for different purposes.

Note the chilling implication—you can design several schemes where each is independently secure, but when you use more than one, you can have a problem. Perhaps even more chilling, you could design a new protocol whose deployment would compromise the security of existing schemes (if the new protocol used the same keys).

9.1.3 Lamport's Hash

It's a poor sort of memory that only works backwards.
                            —The White Queen (in *Through the Looking Glass*)

Leslie Lamport invented an interesting one-time password scheme [LAMP81]. This scheme allows Bob to authenticate Alice in a way that neither eavesdropping on an authentication exchange nor reading Bob's database enables someone to impersonate Alice, and it does it without using public key cryptography. Alice (a human) remembers a password. Bob (the server that will authenticate Alice) has a database where it stores, for each user:

* username

* n, an integer which decrements each time Bob authenticates the user

* hash^n(*password*), i.e., hash(hash(…(hash(*password*))…))

First, how does user Alice set a password? Alice chooses a password, and the workstation chooses the number n to be something reasonably large (like 1000). The workstation computes x_1=hash(*password*). Then it computes x_2=hash(x_1). It continues this process n times, resulting in x_n=hash^n(*password*), which it sends to Bob, along with n.

When Alice wishes to prove her identity to Bob, she types her name and password to her workstation. The workstation then sends Alice's name to Bob, which sends back n. Then the workstation computes hash^{n-1}(*password*) and sends the result to Bob. Bob takes the received quantity, hashes it once, and compares it with its database. If it matches, Bob considers the response valid, replaces the stored quantity with the received quantity, and replaces n by $n-1$.

If n ever gets to 1, then Alice needs to set her password again with Bob. There is no completely secure way of doing this over an insecure network, since this scheme does not allow encryption or integrity protection of messages between Alice and Bob. But in practice, in many situations, it suffices for Alice to choose a new password, compute hash^n(*new password*), and transmit hash^n(*new password*) and n to the server unencrypted across the network.

An enhancement we might suggest is to add **salt**, a large random number chosen at password installation time and stored at Bob. The salt is concatenated to the password before hashing. So rather than computing hash^n(*password*), the enhanced Lamport hash computes hash^n(*password*|*salt*). To set the password, the workstation chooses a value for salt, and it com-

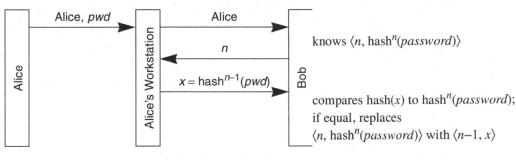

Protocol 9-7. Lamport's Hash

putes x_1=hash($password|salt$). Then it computes x_2=hash(x_1). It continues this process n times, resulting in x_n=hash^n($password$), which it sends to Bob, along with n and *salt*. What do we gain by adding salt? It allows Alice to securely use the same password on multiple servers as long as a different salt value is used when installing the password on each of the other servers. When she logs into Bob, she'll wind up decrementing the n stored at Bob, but this will not affect the n stored at other servers. In other words, when she logs into Bob, if Bob sends her workstation $\langle n$=87, $salt$=69$\rangle$, her workstation will compute hash^{86}($password|$69). If when Bob hashes the received quantity the result matches hash^{87}($password|$69) in his database, then Bob will decrement n and replace the stored hash with the received hash. When she logs into Fred, Fred might send her work station $\langle n$=127, $salt$=105$\rangle$, in which case her workstation will compute hash^{126}($password|$105) to send to Fred.

Another advantage of salt is that Alice does not need to change her password when n decrements to 1 at Bob. Instead the same password can be reinstalled with a different salt value.

There's an additional value to salt, which is the same as the original UNIX reason for adding salt to the password database (see §4.2.4.1 *UNIX Password Hash*). Adding salt prevents an intruder from precomputing hash^k for all passwords in a dictionary and all values of k from 1 through 1000, stealing the database at Bob, and then comparing the precomputed hashes with the stolen password hashes of all the users.

Lamport's hash has interesting properties. It is similar to public key schemes in that the database at Bob is not security sensitive (for reading). It has the disadvantage relative to public key schemes that you can only log in a finite number of times before having to reinstall password information at the server.

There are some potential problems with the Lamport scheme. There is no mutual authentication, i.e., Alice does not know she is definitely talking to Bob. But there's a security weakness that is worse than that, which we'll call the **small n attack**. Suppose an intruder, Trudy, were to impersonate Bob's network address and wait for Alice to attempt to log in. When Alice attempts to log into Bob, Trudy sends back a small value for n, say 50. When Alice responds with hash^{50}($password$), Trudy will have enough information to impersonate Alice for some time, assuming that the actual n at Bob is greater than 50. What can be done to protect against this? Alice's workstation could display n to the human Alice. If Alice remembers approximately what n should be, then Alice can do a rough sanity check on n.

Lamport's hash can be used in the environment where Alice is logging in from a "dumb terminal" or from a workstation that does not have Lamport hash code. We'll call this the *human and paper* environment, and call the other environment the *workstation* environment. The way Lamport's hash works in the human and paper environment is that when the information $\langle n, \text{hash}^n(password) \rangle$ is installed at the server, all the values of $\text{hash}^i(password)$ for $i<n$ are computed, encoded into a typeable string, printed on a paper, and given to Alice. When she logs in, she uses the string at the top of the page, and then crosses that value out, using the next value the next time. Of course, losing the piece of paper, especially if it falls into the wrong hands, is a problem.

How big a string does Alice have to type? Ordinarily, a hash function is 128 bits, which would mean a string of about 20 characters. This would be fairly annoying to type. But the scheme is really sufficiently secure if a 64-bit hash is used, and then Alice only has to type about 10 characters. It's not necessary to invent a 64-bit hash function. Any hash function (such as MD5) can be used, and have all but 64 bits of the output discarded.

It is interesting that the human and paper environment is not vulnerable to the small n attack, since the human just always uses the next value on the list and can't be tricked into sending an item further down on the list.

There is a deployed version of Lamport's hash, known as S/KEY, implemented by Phil Karn when he was at Bellcore. It operates in both the workstation and human and paper environments. It makes no effort to address the small n attack, but it certainly is a vast improvement over cleartext passwords and is gaining popularity.

9.2 MUTUAL AUTHENTICATION

Suppose we want to do mutual authentication, i.e. Alice will know for sure she is communicating with Bob. We could just do an authentication exchange in each direction:

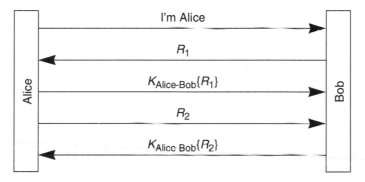

Protocol 9-8. Mutual authentication based on a shared secret $K_{\text{Alice-Bob}}$

9.2.1 Reflection Attack

The first thing we might notice is that the protocol is inefficient. We can reduce the protocol down to three messages (instead of five used above) by putting more than one item of information into each message:

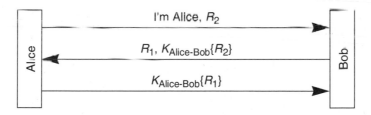

Protocol 9-9. Optimized mutual authentication based on a shared secret $K_{\text{Alice-Bob}}$

This version of the protocol has a security pitfall known as the **reflection attack**. Suppose Trudy wants to impersonate Alice to Bob. First Trudy starts Protocol 9-9, but when she receives the challenge from Bob, she cannot proceed further, because she can't encrypt R_1.

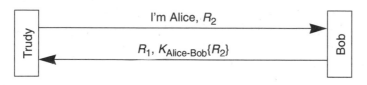

Protocol 9-10. Beginning of reflection attack

"I can't explain myself, I'm afraid sir," said Alice, *"because I'm not myself, you see."*

Alice in Wonderland

However, note that Trudy has managed to get Bob to encrypt R_2. So at this point Trudy opens a second session to Bob. This time she uses R_1 as the challenge to Bob:

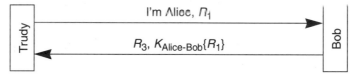

Protocol 9-11. Second session in reflection attack

Trudy can't go any further with this session, because she can't encrypt R_3. But now she knows $K_{\text{Alice-Bob}}\{R_1\}$, so she can complete the first session.

This is a serious security flaw, and there are deployed protocols that contain this flaw. In many environments it is easy to exploit this, since it might be possible to open multiple simultaneous connections to the same server, or there might be multiple servers with the same secret for Alice (so Trudy can get a different server to encrypt Bob's challenge R_1 with $K_{\text{Alice-Bob}}$ so that she can impersonate Alice to Bob).

We can foil the reflection attack if we are careful and understand the pitfalls. Here are two methods of fixing the protocol, both of which are derived from the general principle *don't have Alice and Bob do exactly the same thing*:

* different keys—Have the key used to authenticate Alice be different from the key used to authenticate Bob. We could use two totally different keys shared by Alice and Bob at the cost of additional configuration and storage. Alternatively we could derive the key used for authenticating Bob from the key used to authenticate Alice. For instance, Bob's key might be $-K_{\text{Alice-Bob}}$, or $K_{\text{Alice-Bob}}+1$, or $K_{\text{Alice-Bob}} \oplus \text{F0F0F0F0F0F0F0F0}_{16}$. Any of these would foil Trudy in her attempt to impersonate Alice to Bob since she would not be able to get Bob to encrypt anything using Alice's key.

- different challenges—Insist that the challenge from the initiator (Alice) look different from the challenge from the responder. For instance, we might require that the initiator challenge be an odd number and the responder challenge be an even number. Or the name of the party that created the challenge might be concatenated with the challenge before encryption, so that if the challenge from Alice to Bob was R, Bob would encrypt $Bob|R$ (the string Bob concatenated with R). This would foil Trudy, since in order to impersonate Alice to Bob, Trudy would need to get Bob to encrypt the string Alice concatenated with some number.

Notice that Protocol 9-8 did not suffer from the reflection attack. The reason is that it follows another good general principle of security protocol design: *the initiator should be the first to prove its identity*. Ideally, you shouldn't prove your identity until the other side does, but since that wouldn't work, the assumption is that the initiator is more likely to be the bad guy.

> *...if you only spoke when you were spoken to, and the other person always waited for you to begin, you see nobody would ever say anything...*
> —Alice (in *Through the Looking Glass*)

9.2.2 Password Guessing

Another security weakness of Protocol 9-9 (which doesn't exist in Protocol 9-8) is that Trudy can mount an off-line password-guessing attack without needing to eavesdrop. All she needs to do is send a message to Bob claiming to be Alice and enclosing a number to be encrypted, and Bob will obligingly return the encrypted value. Then Trudy has the pair $\langle R, K_{\text{Alice-Bob}}\{R\}\rangle$ which she can use to check password guesses. We could fix that by making the protocol one message longer (Protocol 9-12).

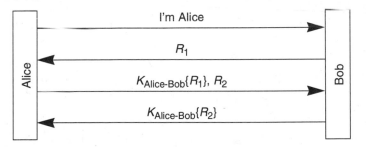

Protocol 9-12. Less optimized mutual authentication based on a shared secret $K_{\text{Alice-Bob}}$

Now Trudy can't obtain a quantity with which to do off-line password guessing by claiming to be Alice, but she can by impersonating Bob's address and tricking Alice into attempting a connection to her. The threat of having Trudy impersonate Bob should not be ignored, but it is much more difficult than impersonating Alice.

9.2.3 Public Keys

Mutual authentication can also be done with public key technology, assuming that Bob and Alice know each other's public keys. It can be done with three messages:

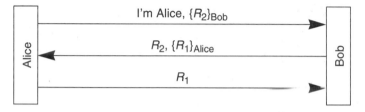

Protocol 9-13. Mutual authentication with public keys

A variant is for Alice to send R_2 and for Bob to return it signed (and similarly for Alice to sign R_1).

Public key mutual authentication presents some special challenges. How does Alice (or Alice's workstation) know Bob's public key? Often the situation is that Alice is a human, working on a generic workstation. In such cases Alice isn't going to remember Bob's public key, nor is Alice's workstation likely to have it stored. It could be done by having Alice attach to something, hoping it's Bob, and having the thing she's talking to send its public key. But that would not be secure if Trudy is impersonating Bob.

We also have the problem of having Alice's workstation obtain Alice's private key when all Alice knows is a password. It is generally straightforward to convert a password into a secret key, because most secret key algorithms will accept any value of the right size as a key. Some public key algorithms—notably RSA—have private keys that take special forms and cannot easily be derived from passwords. The usual method of dealing with this is to have Alice's workstation retrieve Alice's private key, encrypted with her password, from a directory service, or perhaps from Bob. It is not much more trouble to store, in the same place, information that would allow Alice to reliably learn Bob's public key. Two possible techniques:

- Store Bob's public key encrypted with Alice's password. If anyone is impersonating Bob, they will not be able to give Alice a quantity encrypted with her password for which they'd know a corresponding private key.

- Store a certificate for Bob's public key, signed with Alice's private key. Once her workstation obtains her private key, it can validate the certificate for Bob's public key.

9.2.4 Timestamps

We can reduce the mutual authentication down to two messages by using timestamps instead of random numbers for challenges:

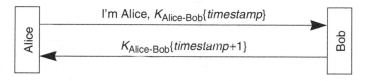

Protocol 9-14. Mutual authentication based on syncrhonized clocks and a shared secret $K_{Alice\text{-}Bob}$

This two message variant is very useful because it is easy to add onto existing protocols (such as request/response protocols), since it does not add any additional messages. But it has to be done carefully. In the diagram we have Bob encrypt a timestamp later than Alice's timestamp. Obviously Bob can't send the same timestamp back to Alice, since that would hardly be mutual authentication. (Alice would be assured that she was either talking to Bob or someone smart enough to copy a field out of her request!) So in the exchange, Alice and Bob have to encrypt different timestamps, use different keys for encrypting the timestamp, concatenate their name to the timestamp before encrypting it, or use any other scheme that will cause them to be sending different things. And the issues involved with the one-way authentication done with timestamps apply here as well (time must not go backwards, they must remember values used within the clock skew, etc.).

Note that any modification to the timestamp would do. The idea of *timestamp*+1 comes from Needham-Schroeder, where they have one side use the incremented challenge of the other. We use *timestamp*+1 in our example because that's what Kerberos V4 uses, but *timestamp*+1 is probably not the best choice. *timestamp*+1 has the potential problem that Trudy eavesdropping could use $K_{Alice\text{-}Bob}\{timestamp+1\}$ to impersonate Alice. A better choice would be a flag concatenated with the timestamp indicating whether the initiator or responder is transmitting. Although the threat of Trudy using $K_{Alice\text{-}Bob}\{timestamp+1\}$ can be avoided if Bob keeps both *timestamp* and *timestamp*+1 in his replay cache, in general it is poor security practice to use something like +1, where there isn't anything intrinsically different between what Bob does and what Alice does.

9.3 INTEGRITY/ENCRYPTION FOR DATA

In order to provide integrity protection and/or encryption of the data following the authentication exchange it is necessary for Alice and Bob to use cryptography to encrypt and/or add integrity checks to the data messages. We described several bases for the authentication exchange:

- §9.1.1 *Shared Secret*—Alice and Bob share a secret key $K_{\text{Alice-Bob}}$.

- §9.2.3 *Public Keys*—Alice and Bob know each other's public keys, as well as their own private keys.

- §9.1.2 *One-Way Public Key*—Bob knows Alice's public key, and Alice knows her own private key.

- §9.1.3 *Lamport's Hash*—Alice knows her own password, Bob knows n and $\text{hash}^n(password)$.

As we discussed in §7.8 *Session Key Establishment*, it is desirable for Alice and Bob to establish a shared secret per-conversation key (known as the **session key**) to be used for integrity protection and encryption, even if they already know enough long-term secrets to be able to encrypt and add integrity checks to messages. So we'll want to enhance the authentication exchange so that after the initial handshake both Alice and Bob will share a session key. It is important that an eavesdropper not be able to figure out what the session key is. Once a session key is established, the workstation can forget the user's password, or at least a piece of untrusted software can proceed with a cryptographically protected conversation without being told any long-term secrets. First we'll discuss how to establish a session key in each of the four cases above. Then we'll discuss how to use the session key for encryption and/or integrity protection.

9.3.1 Shared Secret

Alice and Bob have a shared secret key $K_{\text{Alice-Bob}}$. The authentication exchange is something like Protocol 9-1. Perhaps mutual authentication was done, in which case there are two Rs, R_1 and

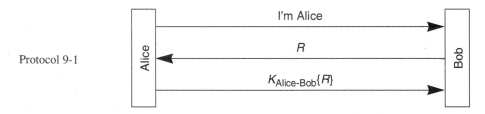

Protocol 9-1

R_2. Perhaps authentication was done using timestamps instead of random Rs. At any rate, there is sufficient information in this protocol so that Alice and Bob can establish a shared session key at this point in the conversation. They can, for example, use $(K_{\text{Alice-Bob}}+1)\{R\}$ as the session key. More generally, they can take the shared secret $K_{\text{Alice-Bob}}$ and modify it in some way, then encrypt the challenge R using the modified $K_{\text{Alice-Bob}}$ as the key, and use the result as the session key.

Why do they need to modify $K_{\text{Alice-Bob}}$? Why can't they use $K_{\text{Alice-Bob}}\{R\}$ as the key? The reason they can't use $K_{\text{Alice-Bob}}\{R\}$ is that $K_{\text{Alice-Bob}}\{R\}$ is transmitted by Alice as the third message in the authentication handshake, so an eavesdropper would see that value, and it certainly would not be secure as a session key.

How about using $K_{\text{Alice-Bob}}\{R+1\}$ as the session key? There's a more subtle reason why that isn't secure. Suppose Alice and Bob have started a conversation in which Bob used R as the challenge. Perhaps Trudy recorded the entire subsequent conversation, encrypted using $K_{\text{Alice-Bob}}\{R+1\}$. Later, Trudy can impersonate Bob's network layer address to Alice, thereby tricking Alice into attempting to communicate with Trudy instead of Bob, and Trudy (pretending to be Bob) can send $R+1$ as a challenge, to which Alice will respond with $K_{\text{Alice-Bob}}\{R+1\}$:

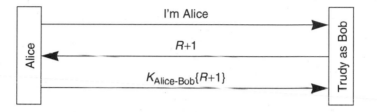

Then Trudy will be able to decrypt the previous Alice-Bob conversation.

So, Alice and Bob, after the authentication exchange, know $K_{\text{Alice-Bob}}$ and R, and there are many combinations of the two quantities that would be perfectly acceptable as a session key, but there are also some that are not acceptable as a session key. What makes a good session key? It must be different for each session, unguessable by an eavesdropper, and should not consist of a quantity X encrypted with $K_{\text{Alice-Bob}}$, where X is a value that can be predicted or extracted by an intruder (as just discussed for $X = R+1$). See Homework Problem 3.

9.3.2 Two-Way Public Key Based Authentication

Suppose we are doing two-way authentication using public key technology, so that Alice and Bob know their own private keys and know each other's public keys. How can they establish a session key? We'll discuss various possibilities, with their relative security and performance strengths and weaknesses.

1. One side, say Alice, could choose a random number R, encrypt it with Bob's public key, and send $\{R\}_{\text{Bob}}$ to Bob attached to one of the messages in the authentication exchange. This scheme has a security flaw. Our intruder, Trudy, could hijack the conversation by picking her own R, encrypting it with Bob's public key, and send that to Bob (while impersonating Alice's network layer address) in place of the encrypted key supplied by Alice.

2. Alice could, in addition to encrypting R with Bob's public key, sign the result. So she'd send $[\{R\}_{\text{Bob}}]_{\text{Alice}}$ to Bob. Bob would take the received quantity, first verify Alice's signature

using Alice's public key, and then use his private key on the result to obtain R. If Trudy were to attempt the same trick as in scheme 1, namely choosing her own R and sending it to Bob, she wouldn't be able to forge Alice's signature on the encrypted R.

This scheme is reasonable. It has a minor security weakness that can be fixed partially (in 3, below) or completely (in 4, below). The flaw is that if Trudy records the entire Alice-Bob conversation, and then later **overruns** Bob (i.e., manages to take over node Bob and learn all Bob's secrets), she will be able to decrypt the conversation she'd recorded. It seems like the kind of threat that only a very energetic paranoid would bother worrying about, but we'll show how to fix it. First note that if Alice is careful to forget R after terminating the conversation with Bob, then overrunning Alice will not enable Trudy to decrypt the recorded conversation, since Trudy needs Alice's public key and Bob's private key to retrieve the session key R. She can only get that by overrunning Bob.

3. This is like 2, above, but Alice picks R_1 and Bob picks R_2. Alice sends $\{R_1\}_{\text{Bob}}$ to Bob. Bob sends $\{R_2\}_{\text{Alice}}$ to Alice. The session key will be $R_1 \oplus R_2$. Overrunning Alice will enable Trudy to retrieve R_2. Overrunning Bob will enable Trudy to retrieve R_1. But in order to retrieve $R_1 \oplus R_2$, she'll need to overrun them both.

In 2 we had Alice sign her quantity (i.e., she sent $[\{R\}_{\text{Bob}}]_{\text{Alice}}$ instead of merely $\{R\}_{\text{Bob}}$). Why isn't it necessary for Bob and Alice to sign their quantities here? Alice and Bob don't need to sign their quantities because although Trudy is perfectly capable of inserting her own $\{R_1\}_{\text{Bob}}$, she cannot decrypt $\{R_2\}_{\text{Alice}}$. Trudy might therefore be able to inject confusion into the system by having Bob think $R_1 \oplus R_2$ is a key he shares with Alice, but since Trudy only knows R_1, she can't actually see any data intended for Alice.

4. Alice and Bob can do a Diffie-Hellman key establishment exchange (see §5.4 *Diffie-Hellman*), where each signs the quantity they are sending. In Diffie-Hellman, Alice chooses a random R_A. Bob chooses a random R_B. They have already agreed on public numbers g and p. Alice transmits $g^{R_A} \bmod p$. Bob transmits $g^{R_B} \bmod p$. They will use $g^{R_A R_B} \bmod p$ as their session key. When we say they each sign the quantity they send, we mean that Alice doesn't simply transmit $g^{R_A} \bmod p$. She actually transmits $[g^{R_A} \bmod p]_{\text{Alice}}$. And Bob actually transmits $[g^{R_B} \bmod p]_{\text{Bob}}$. In this scheme, even if Trudy overruns both Alice and Bob, she won't be able to decrypt recorded conversations because she won't be able to deduce either R_A or R_B.

9.3.3 One-Way Public Key Based Authentication

In some cases only one of the parties in the conversation has a public/private key pair. For instance it might only be Alice who needs to prove her identity to a server Bob, and it is not considered vital for Bob to have his own keys. Here are some ways of establishing a shared session key in this case.

1. Bob could choose a random number R, encrypt it with Alice's public key, send $\{R\}_{Alice}$ to Alice, and R could be the session key. A weakness in this scheme is that if Trudy records the conversation and later overruns Alice, she can decrypt the conversation (since she can retrieve R once she steals Alice's private key).

2. Bob and Alice could do a Diffie-Hellman exchange, where Alice signs her Diffie-Hellman quantity. Bob can't sign his because he doesn't have a public key. This is slightly more secure than scheme 1 because Trudy can't later overrun Alice and retrieve the session key (assuming Alice has diligently forgotten the session key after terminating the conversation with Bob).

Note that neither of these schemes assure Alice she's really talking to Bob, but in either scheme Bob is assured throughout the connection that he is talking to Alice. Again, if Alice wanted to be assured she was talking to Bob, she'd need some means of authenticating Bob. Although the protocol doesn't prove she's talking to Bob, it does ensure that the entire conversation is with a single party.

9.3.4 Lamport Hash

With the Lamport hash neither side has a public key, and they don't have a shared secret key. One possibility for establishing a shared session key is to first do the authentication handshake, and then have Alice and Bob do Diffie-Hellman to establish a session key. This has the problem that Trudy could hijack the conversation after the initial authentication (and before the Diffie-Hellman exchange).

Another idea is for Alice and Bob to first do a Diffie-Hellman exchange, and then do the authentication handshake as part of a conversation protected with the Diffie-Hellman key. That has a security weakness as well. Trudy could do a bucket brigade attack (see §5.4.1 *The Bucket Brigade Attack*), establishing a separate Diffie-Hellman key with each of Alice and Bob, and then simply relay the authentication handshake. Once Alice sends the authentication information, Trudy can break her connection with Alice and continue conversing with Bob, impersonating Alice to Bob. In contrast, schemes that establish a shared session key based on a shared secret between Alice and Bob are not vulnerable to a bucket brigade attack. With a stored Alice-Bob secret (as opposed to a dynamically generated one using Diffie-Hellman), Trudy can get in between Alice and Bob and relay the messages back and forth, but Trudy cannot figure out the session key since she doesn't know the stored Alice-Bob secret. So all she can do is act like a router, relaying encrypted messages unmodified between Alice and Bob. If she wants to perform that service, there's no reason to stop her from doing so.

9.3.5 Privacy and Integrity

In §3.7 *Generating MICs* we discuss various methods of computing a message integrity code (MIC) with secret key cryptography. In §4.2.2 *Computing a MIC with a Hash* we discuss how to do it with a message digest function. As noted in §3.7.1 *Ensuring Privacy and Integrity Together*, there is no standard algorithm for providing both privacy and integrity with a single key and a single cryptographic pass over the data. Yet that is what is wanted. Plausible solutions are: develop two keys in the authentication exchange and do the two operations independently; make a second key by modifying the first (by changing a few bits in a predictable way); use different cryptographic algorithms so a common key is (presumably) irrelevant; or use a weak checksum for integrity inside a strong algorithm for privacy.

The messages exchanged on a connection once the keys are known are likely to be in the form of discrete messages, where the authenticity of each must be determined before the conversation can proceed. Even if a message is authentic, it could be misinterpreted if played out of order. An attacker might, for example, record a message and then replay it later on in the exchange. This can be prevented by having all of the messages contain sequence numbers so that an out-of-order message is detected. Sequence numbers are used in both versions of Kerberos. Alternatively, the integrity code can be computed using not just the current message, but information about all previous messages, so that a replayed message will not be valid. This technique is used by Novell (see §17.1 *NetWare V3*).

An implausible attack, but one that should nevertheless be prevented, is reflection. Here the attacker records a message going in one direction and replays it in the other. If the same sequence number could be valid in both directions, such a message could be misinterpreted. This can be avoided by using sequence numbers in different ranges for the two directions, by having a DIRECTION BIT somewhere in the message, or by having the integrity code computed by some subtly different algorithm in the two directions.

Sequence numbers have to be very large or you face the possibility of running out during a conversation. If you reuse sequence numbers during a conversation (i.e. while using the same session key), an attacker can replay an old recorded message when its sequence number recurs. This is an unlikely threat, but it is good form to prevent it. The best method is to change keys periodically during the conversation. (This also limits the amount of material a cryptanalyst can gather all encrypted under one key.) Changing keys in the middle of a conversation is known as **key rollover**. The simplest method of rolling over a key is to have one end choose a random key, encrypt it under the existing key, and send it to the other end. Because an attacker might cryptanalyze one key and use it to decrypt the subsequent keys, a stronger design would periodically repeat the authentication protocol or roll over keys by doing a Diffie-Hellman exchange to get the new key and integrity-protecting the public numbers with the old key.

Sequence number maintenance and key rollover can be significantly complicated if encryption is done using a communications protocol that does not automatically retry transmissions after errors and put messages back in order before decrypting them.

9.4 MEDIATED AUTHENTICATION (WITH KDC)

In Chapter 7 *Authentication Systems*, we discussed the concept of a KDC, which has a database consisting of keys for all users. Any user Alice registered with the KDC can securely communicate with the KDC. Alice and the KDC can authenticate each other and encrypt their communication to one another because they each know Alice's key:

Protocol 9-15. KDC operation (in principle)

In the above exchange, the KDC does not know whether it was really Alice that asked to talk to Bob. Some bad guy, Trudy, could send the message to the KDC saying I am Alice, I'd like to talk to Bob. But that won't do Trudy any good because she cannot decrypt the encrypted K_{AB}. Trudy is causing Bob to get a spurious message that Alice wants to talk to him using key K_{AB}, but it doesn't do any harm. The only parties that can know K_{AB} after this exchange are the KDC, Bob, and Alice, so after this exchange Alice and Bob can mutually authenticate using key K_{AB} (using a protocol such as discussed in §9.2 *Mutual Authentication*).

Protocol 9-15 is not the way it is done in practice. That protocol has some practical problems, the most important of which is that if Alice immediately sends a message to Bob based on the new shared key, it's possible, given the vagaries of networks, for Alice's message to arrive first, in which case Bob would not know how to decrypt it. It also is a lot of trouble for the KDC to initiate a connection to Bob. Instead, since Alice is going to communicate with Bob anyway, the KDC gives Alice the information the KDC would have sent to Bob. The Kerberos protocol, which we'll describe in Chapter 10 *Kerberos V4* and Chapter 11 *Kerberos V5*, refers to the encrypted piece of information that the KDC gives to Alice to pass along to Bob as a **ticket** to Bob. The ticket is information that will allow Alice to access Bob:

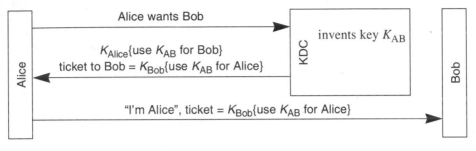

Protocol 9-16. KDC operation (in practice)

Protocol 9-16 is incomplete. It has to be followed by a mutual authentication exchange between Bob and Alice in which they prove to each other that they know key K_{AB}. But in §9.2 *Mutual Authentication* we've described how they can do that.

9.4.1 Needham-Schroeder

A classic protocol for authentication using KDCs was designed by Needham and Schroeder. It is very similar to the protocol we just described, and it completes the exchange by doing the mutual authentication between Alice and Bob. [NEED78]. The Needham Schroeder protocol is important because it is a classic KDC-arbitrated authentication protocol and many others have been modeled after it. The Kerberos protocol is based on it, and it is instructive to understand its strengths and weaknesses.

The paper gives a few variants, but the basic Needham-Schroeder protocol is shown as Protocol 9-17. Let's analyze this protocol. First we must apologize for the arcaneness of the analysis. It's unfortunately necessary to go into this depth in order to really understand a protocol. Without a thorough understanding, there might be subtle security flaws.

The terminology **nonce** refers to a number that is used only once. A nonce could be a sequence number (provided that state is not lost during crashes), or a large random number. It also could be a timestamp, if you believe that your clock never goes backwards, but Needham and Schroeder specifically wanted to avoid dependence on timestamps (see §9.7 *Nonce Types* for more detail on nonces).

Message 1 tells the KDC that Alice wants to talk to Bob. The purpose of the nonce N_1 is to assure Alice that she is really talking to the KDC. The (admittedly far-fetched) threat the protocol is trying to avoid is where Trudy has stolen an old key of Bob's, and stolen the message where Alice had previously requested a key for Bob. Bob, realizing Trudy has stolen his key, has changed his

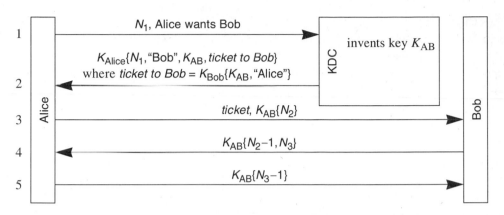

Protocol 9-17. Needham-Schroeder

key. Trudy waits around until Alice makes a request to the KDC to talk to Bob. Trudy then replays the stolen message, which looks like an ordinary reply from the KDC. Then Trudy pretends to be Bob, and will fool Alice because Trudy will know the shared key that Alice thinks the KDC just invented for them. As we've already said, it is hard to imagine a circumstance where this would be a practical threat, but adding the nonce costs virtually nothing, and it removes the need to think about whether the threat might be practical in any particular circumstance.

In message 2, the KDC securely (i.e. encrypted and integrity-protected) gives Alice the key K_{AB} it has generated for Alice and Bob to share. It puts in the string "Bob" to make it impossible for Trudy to tamper with Alice's request, substituting the string "Trudy" for "Bob" and then being able to trick Alice into talking to Trudy and thinking that Trudy is Bob. If Trudy were to tamper with message 1 by substituting her name for Bob's, then Alice will discover, in message 2, that the KDC has just given her a key to communicate with Trudy, not Bob. In message 2, along with the encrypted key K_{AB} and Bob's name, the KDC also gives Alice a ticket to Bob. The ticket to Bob consists of the key K_{AB} and Alice's name, encrypted with Bob's key. To Alice, the ticket will just be a pile of unintelligible bits. The Needham-Schroeder protocol has been criticized for doubly encrypting the ticket. The ticket is sent encrypted with Alice's key, though it would have been just as secure to send it in the clear.

In message 3, Alice sends a challenge (N_2) to Bob, encrypted with K_{AB}, along with the ticket. Bob decrypts the ticket to find the shared key K_{AB}. He uses K_{AB} to extract N_2. Alice knows that only someone who knows Bob's key can decrypt the ticket and thereby discover the shared key K_{AB}. In message 4, Bob proves he knows K_{AB}, since he was able to find N_2. Likewise, Bob assumes that it must be Alice if she knows K_{AB} because the KDC puts Alice's name in the ticket with K_{AB}. In message 4, in addition to sending back N_2 (actually a decremented version of N_2), he includes a challenge N_3 encrypted with K_{AB}, and Alice sends back (in message 5) a message proving she knows K_{AB}.

There is an interesting reflection attack to which the protocol would be vulnerable if the encryption in message 4 were done using, say, DES in ECB mode. Suppose each of the nonces were 64 bits long. Because of the nature of ECB, N_2-1 and N_3 would each be separately encrypted. Suppose Trudy wants to impersonate Alice to Bob. First she eavesdrops on an authentication handshake where Alice talks to Bob. So Trudy sees messages 3 and 4. Later, she replays message 3 to Bob. Bob will respond with $K_{AB}\{N_2-1,N_4\}$ (where N_4 is a nonce different from the one Bob chose last time he talked to Alice). Trudy can't return $K_{AB}\{N_4-1\}$, but she can open a new connection to Bob, this time splicing in $K_{AB}\{N_4\}$ instead of $K_{AB}\{N_2\}$. Bob will return $K_{AB}\{N_4-1,N_5\}$. Then Trudy can take the first encrypted block, which will be $K_{AB}\{N_4-1\}$ and return that as message 5 of her first connection. In fact she will never have found out what N_4 was, but she didn't need to know N_4. She just needed to know $K_{AB}\{N_4-1\}$.

If encryption were done in CBC mode instead of ECB mode, Trudy would not be able to accomplish this, because she couldn't splice pieces of messages. But if encryption were done in CBC mode, there would be no reason to have Bob and Alice decrement each other's nonces. Message 4 could just as securely be $K_{AB}\{N_2,N_3\}$, and message 5 could just as securely be $K_{AB}\{N_3\}$.

The lesson to be learned is that if pieces of a message must, for security reasons, be sent together, then the entire message must be integrity-protected so that parts of it cannot be modified by an attacker.

9.4.2 Expanded Needham-Schroeder

There is a remaining security vulnerability with Protocol 9-17. Suppose Trudy finds out Alice's key. Trudy can of course, at that point, claim to be Alice and get the KDC to give Trudy (which the KDC thinks is Alice), a shared key to Bob and a ticket to Bob. There's really nothing we can do about Trudy impersonating Alice if Trudy steals Alice's key. But we'd like it to be possible to prevent Trudy from doing any more damage once Alice changes her key. The problem is, with the protocol we've just described, the ticket to Bob stays valid even if Alice changes her key.

The vulnerability can occur even if Trudy only manages to capture a previous key used by Alice, say J_{Alice}, and not the key Alice is using now. Suppose that when Alice was using J_{Alice}, Trudy had overheard (and recorded) Alice asking the KDC for a ticket for Bob. At that time, the KDC would have generated a shared key J_{AB}, and Trudy would have seen $J_{Alice}\{N_1,\text{"Bob"},J_{AB},K_{Bob}\{J_{AB},\text{"Alice"}\}\}$. At the time, Trudy could not decrypt the message, but we'll assume she's stored it away, hoping to capture an old key of Alice's. Once Trudy does discover J_{Alice}, she can interpret the messages she's recorded, discover J_{AB}, and, using the ticket $K_{Bob}\{J_{AB},\text{"Alice"}\}$, she can convince Bob that Alice will be talking to him using J_{AB}. The fact that the KDC knew Alice's key changed is irrelevant; the KDC doesn't participate in this new authentication.

A paper [DENN81] pointed out this weakness, and in [NEED87], a suggested fix was proposed by adding two additional messages. Alice requests a nonce N_B from Bob, which Alice will send to the KDC, and the KDC will package N_B in the ticket to Bob. This will reassure Bob that whoever is talking to him has talked to the KDC since Bob generated N_B. Once Alice changes her key, Trudy will not be able to talk to the KDC using Alice's old key, and any recorded messages from the KDC using an old key of Alice's will also not be useful. The proposed protocol added 2 messages, and therefore uses 7 messages. The protocol can, however, be reduced to 6 messages (see Homework Problem 9).

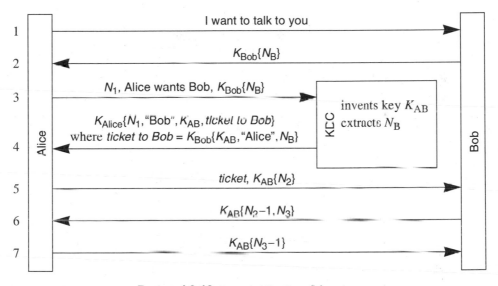

Protocol 9-18. Expanded Needham-Schroeder

9.4.3 Otway-Rees

In [OTWA87], an improved authentication protocol is given. It also solves the ticket invalidation problem, and it does mutual authentication in 5 messages.

Otway and Rees mention that they were inspired by a remark from Needham that *the suspicious party should always generate a challenge*. Let's look at their protocol (Protocol 9-19). Alice generates two nonces. One, N_C, is sent in the clear to Bob. In addition N_C is included (along with the other nonce, N_A) in a message encrypted by Alice that Bob cannot interpret. It just looks like a pile of bits, and he will simply forward $K_{Alice}\{N_A, N_C, \text{"Alice"}, \text{"Bob"}\}$ to the KDC.

In message 2, Bob forwards the encrypted message Alice sent, along with a message Bob encrypts which includes his own nonce N_B, the nonce N_C that Alice sent in the clear, "Alice", and

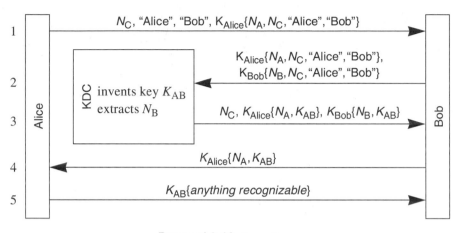

Protocol 9-19. Otway-Rees

"Bob", to the KDC. The KDC checks to make sure that the common nonce N_C is the same in both encrypted messages. If not, the KDC will reject the message. The fact that they are the same proves that Bob is really Bob, since only someone knowing K_{Bob} can encrypt N_C inside a message.

In message 3, the KDC gives Bob a message to forward to Alice. That message, when forwarded to Alice, reassures Alice that both the KDC and Bob are legitimate. (Alice knows the KDC is legitimate because it encrypts N_A with key K_{Alice}. Alice knows Bob is legitimate because the KDC would not have continued the protocol if it hadn't already verified that Bob was legit.) The KDC also tells Bob the common key, and reassures Bob that it is really the KDC by putting Bob's nonce N_B inside the message to Bob.

Message 4 is merely having Bob forward $K_{Alice}\{N_A, K_{AB}\}$ to Alice. In message 5, Alice proves her identity to Bob by showing that she knows K_{AB}. Bob does not need to prove his identity explicitly to Alice because Alice will assume that the KDC authenticated Bob.

In fact, this protocol could be simplified by getting rid of one of Alice's nonces (see Homework Problem 4).

If we want to be really paranoid, then for subtle reasons it is necessary in the Otway-Rees protocol that N_C be not just a nonce but also unpredictable. Otherwise Trudy, in a rather involved scenario, could impersonate Bob to Alice. This is the way it would work: Suppose Alice is using a sequence number for N_C. Trudy watches and sees that Alice is currently using, say, 007 for N_C. So Trudy sends a message to Bob claiming to be Alice. She sends 008, "Alice", "Bob", *garbage*. Bob can't tell that the fourth element in the message is garbage. He forwards *garbage* on, along with his own message $K_{Bob}\{N_B, 008, "Alice", "Bob"\}$. Trudy records that message. The KDC will reject Bob's message, since the garbage won't decrypt properly. Then Trudy waits until Alice generates her next request to talk to Bob. That will be 008, "Alice", "Bob", $K_{Alice}\{N_A, 008, "Alice", "Bob"\}$. Trudy forwards that, along with the message $K_{Bob}\{N_B, 008, "Alice", "Bob"\}$ she recorded from

Bob, to the KDC. The KDC will accept the messages now since both will contain 008. The only authentication of Bob in the Otway-Rees protocol is done by the KDC verifying that the nonce N_C is the same in the message encrypted with K_{Bob} and the message encrypted with K_{Alice}. Trudy can complete the exchange by forwarding to Alice the message the KDC sends her for Alice. Alice will wrongly assume the party to whom she is talking is Bob. If Alice and Bob are planning on using the shared key, say for encrypting the messages to one another, then Trudy won't have succeeded. But if all Alice and Bob want to do is authenticate, then Trudy will have successfully impersonated Bob to Alice.

The Kerberos authentication service (see Chapter 10 *Kerberos V4*) is roughly based on the Needham-Schroeder protocol. It looks a lot simpler than these protocols because it assumes a universal idea of time, and includes expiration dates in messages. The basic Kerberos protocol is:

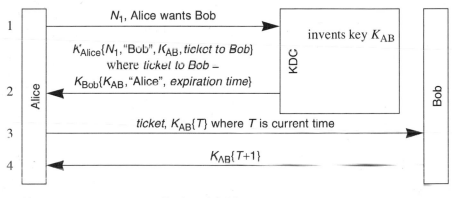

Protocol 9-20. Kerberos

9.5 BELLOVIN-MERRITT

In most of the protocols we've discussed, the user's key could be derived from a password—a text string memorizable by a mere human. Whenever a key is derived from a password, there's the potential for having our bad guy Trudy capture some quantity with which she can do an off-line password-guessing attack. In some of our protocols, Trudy can eavesdrop and obtain such a quantity. In others, Trudy can obtain such a quantity by impersonating Bob or Alice.

For example, in Protocol 9-1, Trudy can eavesdrop to obtain R and $K_{Alice-Bob}\{R\}$, and assuming $K_{Alice-Bob}$ is derived from a password, Trudy can perform an off-line password-guessing attack.

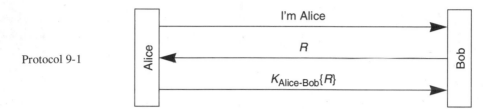

Protocol 9-1

She can do the same thing in Protocol 9-3, providing she knows the approximate time of transmission.

Protocol 9-3

In most of the protocols we've been careful not to allow Trudy to mount a password-guessing attack by initiating a connection with Bob, claiming to be Alice. But if she can impersonate Bob's address and deceive Alice into starting up a connection to Trudy thinking it is to Bob, then Trudy can capture a quantity with which to do password guessing.

In this section we discuss two protocols by Bellovin and Merritt designed to prevent off-line password guessing. We are not aware of any deployed protocols based on these, perhaps because they have only recently been published. But these Bellovin-Merritt protocols are really incredibly elegant, and we just think the book would be incomplete if we didn't get to share them with you. They are the ultimate in security when authentication must be based on a user-chosen password.

Bellovin and Merritt's [BELL92a] first scheme prevents password guessing whether Trudy eavesdrops, pretends to be Alice, or pretends to be Bob. The basic idea is that Alice and Bob do a Diffie-Hellman exchange, but encrypt the values they send to one another with the user's password. Assuming they are both using the same password (or a secret key derived from the password), then following the Diffie-Hellman exchange Alice and Bob will agree on a Diffie-Hellman key $K=g^{R_A R_B} \bmod p$. Then they do a standard mutual authentication exchange proving to each other that they both know K.

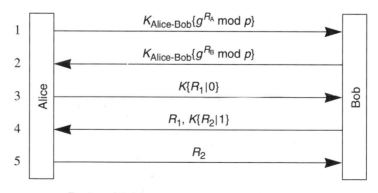

Protocol 9-21. Bellovin and Merritt's First Scheme

Messages 1 and 2 are the Diffie-Hellman exchange encrypted with the user's password. After those two messages, assuming Alice and Bob both know the same password, they'll have agreed upon a secret key K. Messages 3, 4, and 5 are a standard mutual authentication three-way handshake. We've concatenated 0 to R_1 and 1 to R_2 to prevent a reflection attack.

Why can't an eavesdropper gain any information? There is no way to do a password-guessing attack based on $K_{\text{Alice-Bob}}\{g^R \bmod p\}$ because if Trudy (our eavesdropper) were to guess a password, convert it into a key, qnd then use that key to decrypt the transmissions, there is no way for her to verify that what she's got after decrypting is indeed $g^{R_A} \bmod p$ and $g^{R_B} \bmod p$, since those would be indistinguishable from random numbers. And there's no way to do a password guessing attack based on messages 3–5 because they are based on a key that has nothing to do with the user's password (unless she can break Diffie-Hellman).

Actually there's a subtle point, which is that the encryption algorithm will operate on some block size, typically 64 bits. The Diffie-Hellman prime p will be a number, perhaps of size 500 bits. If Alice and Bob perform $g^R \bmod p$ the usual way, the result will fill some number of blocks but only partially fill a final one. Trudy can gain some information from guessing a password and decrypting $K_{\text{Alice-Bob}}\{g^R \bmod p\}$, since if the result is greater than p, she'll know that the guessed password is not correct. To prevent this, Alice and Bob choose a random multiple of p (of all the multiples of p that will result in a number in the correct range) to add to $g^R \bmod p$. The result is that all numbers in the range of the field size are about equally likely, and Trudy will gain no information from attempting to decrypt $K_{\text{Alice-Bob}}\{g^R \bmod p\}$ with a guessed password.

Why do we need to encrypt the Diffie-Hellman exchange? An eavesdropper won't be able to find the user's password or the Diffie-Hellman key based on seeing unencrypted versions of messages 1 and 2. Of course if we don't use the user's password in messages 1 and 2 then we'll just have established a secret key at that point, and not authenticated the other side. But suppose we do standard (unencrypted) Diffie-Hellman in messages 1 and 2, and then use the established Diffie-Hellman key to encrypt a three-way authentication handshake using $K_{\text{Alice-Bob}}$? If we were to do that, then Trudy could gain information for doing a password-guessing attack by either impersonating Alice (i.e., initiating a connection to Bob claiming to be Alice) or impersonating Bob (i.e., tricking Alice into connecting to her). Under certain circumstances, it may be acceptable to encrypt only one of the two Diffie-Hellman public numbers.

Bellovin and Merritt, in a subsequent paper [BELL93], noted that their first protocol required Bob to know the user's password (or a quantity that could be directly used in order to impersonate Alice). They devised a second protocol which only has Bob store a hash of the user's password, a quantity that Bob can use to verify that Alice knows the password but cannot be used directly by anyone who captured the quantity from Bob's database to impersonate Alice to Bob. Someone that captures Bob's database can still do a password-guessing attack, however.

Their paper had several variants. We've done our own variant, for ease of explanation, but it captures the essence of the Bellovin-Merritt protocol. In this variant, Alice has a private key which Bob stores encrypted under Alice's password and which he gives to Alice after she proves she knows a hash of her password. She then authenticates again using her private key, proving that she knows the password itself.

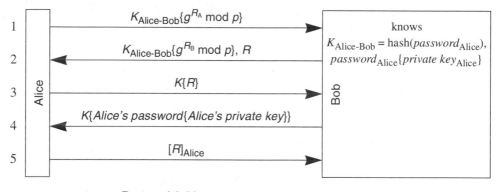

Protocol 9-22. Bellovin and Merritt's Second Scheme

What's going on in this protocol? In the first two messages, Alice and Bob do a Diffie-Hellman exchange encrypted with a hash of Alice's password. In this stage of the protocol, they have established a shared key provided they both use the same value for the hashed password. Since Alice's private key is encrypted with her password (or at least a different function of the password than the hash stored at Bob), the information in Bob's database will not be sufficient for someone to learn Alice's private key and impersonate Alice to Bob.

Piggybacked onto the second message of the Diffie-Hellman exchange is a challenge, R, picked by Bob. After the second message Alice and Bob have agreed on a Diffie-Hellman key $K=g^{R_A R_B} \bmod p$, and Alice knows Bob's challenge R.

In the third message Alice proves to Bob that she knows K by encrypting R. That means she knew $K_{\text{Alice-Bob}}$, because the Diffie-Hellman exchange was encrypted using $K_{\text{Alice-Bob}}$. This doesn't quite prove she's Alice. It proves she knows a hash of the password, which perhaps she got by stealing Bob's database. So the protocol continues. In message 4, Bob transmits the encrypted private key, encrypted again with K. The purpose of encrypting with K is so that an eavesdropper will not be able to see Alice's encrypted private key, which would be a quantity against which an eavesdropper could guess passwords. Only someone who actually knows Alice's password, as opposed to someone who has peeked at Bob's database, can decrypt Alice's private key, so the fact that Alice signs R with her private key in message 5 proves to Bob that it's really Alice. Bob verifies her signature on R using her public key.

Where in this protocol has Alice authenticated Bob? She knows it's Bob because he sends her $password_{\text{Alice}}\{private\ key_{\text{Alice}}\}$ in message 4. Only Bob should know that quantity. But how does Alice know, when she decrypts the pile of bits from Bob, that she's actually extracted her private key? To be really careful, we have to make sure that the quantity is recognizable once decrypted. So, for instance, $private\ key_{\text{Alice}}$ could be a concatenation of her name and the actual number.

This protocol illustrates a concept sometimes used in protocols, which is that someone needs to prove they know a low-quality secret before being given the high-quality secret. For example, in Novell's security protocol (see §17.2 *NetWare V4*), a server stores the user's encrypted private RSA key as well as a hash of the user's password. The user's workstation has to first prove it knows the hash of the user's password before the server will transmit the encrypted private RSA key. In contrast, the Kerberos V4 protocol will give anyone who claims to be Alice an encrypted message that would enable password guessing.

9.6 NETWORK LOGIN AND PASSWORD GUESSING

Let's look at some techniques for turning a user's low-quality secret, one derived from a password and therefore vulnerable to off-line password-guessing attacks, into a high-quality secret (either a private key or an unguessable secret key). We'll assume Alice's high-quality secret is stored at some location, say B, encrypted with Alice's password. Alice's workstation needs to retrieve this information somehow from B, and then decrypt it using the password Alice supplies. Let's call Alice's workstation, or whatever is requesting Alice's encrypted high-quality secret, A. These techniques are arranged from least secure to most.

1. Alice's information is available to anyone who requests it. A sends "Give me Alice's encrypted secret" to B, and B transmits the secret to A. This is commonly done when Alice's private key, encrypted with Alice's password, is stored in the directory service. And it is what is done for obtaining the original ticket in Kerberos V4. This technique allows both an eavesdropper and an active attacker (one who sends a message asking for Alice's information) to obtain a quantity with which to verify password guesses.

2. Before B is willing to transmit Alice's encrypted high-quality secret, B requires that A prove knowledge of Alice's password by sending something like a hash of the password. This technique still allows an eavesdropper to obtain a quantity with which to verify password guesses, but it no longer allows an active attacker (one who has never eavesdropped) to send a message and get such a quantity in the reply. This technique is used for Kerberos V5.

3. As in 2, but encrypt the exchange between B and A by using a key established "on the fly", for instance by having A or B transmit to the other side a public key with which to encrypt the exchange, or by having A and B do a Diffie-Hellman exchange. This prevents an eavesdropper or an active attacker impersonating A from obtaining a password-guessing quantity, but it allows someone impersonating B's network address to obtain such a quantity. This technique is similar to NetWare V4.0 authentication (see §17.2 *NetWare V4*).

4. As in 2, but encrypt the exchange by having **A** configured with a secret or public key for **B**. This is secure, but administratively difficult.

5. Use the first two messages of Bellovin-Merritt (Protocol 9-21) to establish a secret session key between **A** and **B**, and then do 1 or 2. Note that 1 is as secure as 2 in this case because in order to successfully do Bellovin-Merritt, **A** has to know Alice's password. So this technique (first two messages of Bellovin-Merritt combined with 1 or 2) is as secure as 4, but administratively much easier. No currently deployed authentication schemes use this technique, to our knowledge, but we would recommend it.

9.7 NONCE TYPES

A **nonce** is a quantity which any given user of a protocol uses only once. Many protocols use nonces, and there are different types of nonces with different sorts of properties. It is possible to introduce security weaknesses by using a nonce with the wrong properties. Various forms of nonce are a timestamp, a large random number, or a sequence number. What's different about these quantities? A large random number tends to make the best nonce, because it cannot be guessed or predicted (as can sequence numbers and timestamps). This is somewhat unintuitive, since non-reuse is only probabilistic. But a random number of 128 bits or more has a negligible chance of being reused. A timestamp requires reasonably synchronized clocks. A sequence number requires non-volatile state (so that a node can be sure it doesn't use the same number twice even if it crashes and restarts between attempts). When are these properties important?

Protocol 9-2 is a protocol in which the unpredictability of the challenge is important. Let's

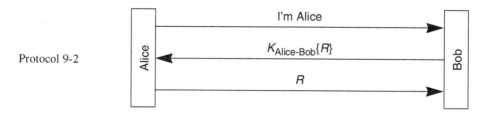

Protocol 9-2

say Bob is using a sequence number, and when Alice attempts to log in, Bob encrypts the next sequence number and transmits it to Alice, Alice decrypts the challenge and transmits it to Bob. Let's say our eavesdropper Eve watches Alice's authentication exchange, and sees Alice return an R of 7482. If Eve knows Bob is using sequence numbers for the challenge, she can then claim to be Alice, get an undecipherable pile of bits from Bob (the encrypted challenge), and return 7483. Bob will be suitably impressed and assume he's talking to Alice. So it is obvious in this protocol that Bob's challenge has to be unpredictable.

How about if we do it the other way, i.e., make Alice do the encryption as in Protocol 9-1?

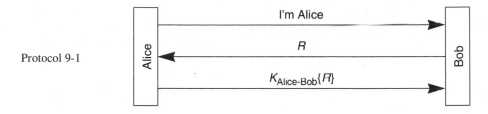

Protocol 9-1

Must the challenge then be unpredictable? Let's say again that Bob is using sequence numbers. Eve watches Alice's authentication exchange and sees that R is 7482. Then Eve lies in wait, impersonating Bob's network address, hoping to entrap Alice into authenticating to Eve. When she does, Eve sends her the challenge 7483, and Alice will return the encrypted 7483. Now Eve can impersonate Alice to Bob, since Bob's challenge will be 7483, and Eve will know how to encrypt that. This is a lot like a bucket brigade attack (see §5.4.1 *The Bucket Brigade Attack*), to which any authentication-only protocol is vulnerable, but this is somewhat worse. In the bucket brigade attack, Eve has to impersonate Bob's address to Alice and Alice's address to Bob while both Alice and Bob are available on the network. In contrast this attack allows Eve to impersonate Bob's address to Alice when Bob is down (and likewise Alice's address when Alice is down). In many cases it is easier to impersonate someone's address if that someone is not available on the network.

These protocols are also insecure if timestamps are used. Eve has to guess the timestamp Bob will use, and she might be off by a minute or two. If the timestamp has coarse granularity, say seconds, Eve has a good chance of being able to impersonate Alice. If the timestamp has, say, nanosecond granularity, then it really does become just like a random number and the protocol is secure.

Here's a protocol in which it would be perfectly secure to use a predictable nonce for R. Even

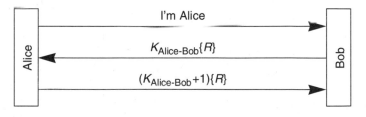

if Eve could predict what R would be, she can't predict either the value sent by Bob or the appropriate response from Alice.

Getting truly random numbers can be expensive. A standard method of obtaining pseudorandom numbers is by using a key known only to the node generating the numbers, and encrypting any sort of nonce, say a sequence number or timestamp.

9.8 PICKING RANDOM NUMBERS

The use of pseudo-random processes to generate secret quantities can result in pseudo-security. —Richard Pitkin

You can have perfect cryptographic algorithms, and perfectly designed protocols, but if you can't select good random numbers, your system can be remarkably insecure. Random numbers may be required in choosing cryptographic keys, challenges, IVs, or per-message secrets for El Gamal/ DSS signatures (see §5.5.5 *Per-Message Secret Number*).

Although I_3'd love to rigorously define "random", I_2 won't let me$_3$ because a really rigorous definition is beyond the scope and spirit of the book. For instance, in [KNUT69], fifteen pages are devoted to coming up with a definition of a random sequence. For those readers who are not intimidated by notions such as (m,k)-distributed, serial correlation coefficients, and Riemann-integrability (don't try to find those terms in our glossary), the discussion of randomness in [KNUT69] is actually very interesting.

The distinction is often made between *random* and *pseudorandom*. A *pseudorandom* number generator is a deterministic algorithm. The entire sequence it will generate is determined by its initial state. A *random* number generator is one that truly picks numbers unpredictably. It is difficult to have a source of true randomness. It can be done with special hardware that does something like measure the low order bits of a counter that counts radioactive particles per unit time. Although such hardware would not be difficult or expensive to provide [DAVI84b], most computers do not have it, so the typical technique is to use a pseudorandom number generator. Sometimes computers use the people they interact with as a source of randomness, for instance, by timing their keystrokes. Such a technique is useful to obtain a few bits of randomness, perhaps to seed a pseudorandom number generator.

Applications that use random numbers have different requirements. For most applications, for instance one that generates test cases for debugging a computer program, all that might be required is that the numbers are spread around with no obvious pattern. For such applications it might be perfectly reasonable to use something like the digits of π. However, for cryptographic applications such as choosing a key, it is essential that the numbers be unguessable.

Consider the following pseudorandom number generator. It starts with a truly random seed, say by timing a human's keystrokes. Then it computes a hash of the seed, then at each step it computes a hash of the output of the previous step. Assuming a good hash function, the output will pass any sort of statistical tests for randomness, but an intruder that captures one of the intermediate quantities will be able to compute the rest.

It is possible to make a pseudorandom number generator that is as good as a source of true random numbers provided that it can be provided with an adequately unguessable seed. For example, a generator that outputs the hash of the seed, and thereafter outputs the hash of the previous output concatenated with the seed would be adequate provided, of course, that the seed was sufficiently unguessable.

Implementations have made some amusing mistakes. Typical mistakes are:

- seeding the generator with a seed that is from too small a space, say 16 bits. Suppose each time a cryptographic key needed to be chosen the application obtained 16 bits worth of true randomness from special purpose hardware and used those 16 bits to seed a pseudorandom number generator. The problem is, there would be only 65536 possible keys it would ever choose, and that is a very small space for an adversary (equipped with a computer) to search. Jeff Schiller found an application that used this technique with a seed that was only 8 bits! (The application has since been fixed.)

- using a hash of the current time when an application needs a random value. The problem is, some clocks do not have fine granularity, so an intruder that knew approximately when the program was run would not need to search a very large space to find the exact clock value for the seed. For instance, if a clock has 1/60 second granularity and the intruder knew the program chose the user's key somewhere within a particular hour, there would only be $60{\times}60{\times}60 = 216000$ possible values.

- divulging the seed value. An implementation, again discovered by Jeff Schiller (who warned the implementers so that the implementation has been fixed), used the time of day to choose a per-message encryption key. The time of day in this case may have had sufficient granularity, but the problem was that the application included the time of day in the unencrypted header of the message!

In general the subroutines provided in programming languages for "random numbers" are not designed to be unguessable. Instead they are designed merely to pass statistical tests.

A good strategy for finding a suitable seed for a pseudorandom number generator is to hash together all the sources of randomness you can find, e.g., timing of keystrokes, disk seek times, count of packet arrivals, etc. If any of the sources are unguessable the result will be. Even better, if there is any access to a good quality secret, hashing in the secret will make the seed unguessable. Note that if the secret is not of good quality, this strategy can backfire and give the attacker who learns one of your random numbers (say for an IV) enough information to do off-line password guessing.

For more reading on the subject of randomness, see RFC 1750.

9.9 X.509 PROBLEM

Here's an example of something with a security flaw. In the course of researching this book, we found a fair number of security flaws in deployed systems, but decided it was better not to describe them even though they made good illustrations. This one is fair game since there's no way to exploit it in any deployed system, but it's an accident waiting to happen. X.509 is a standard format for certificates and CRLs (see §13.6 *X.509 Certificates and CRLs*).

X.509 defines two kinds of CRLs. (See §7.7.3 *Certificate Revocation*.) One kind lists revoked certificates of individuals. We'll call that an **ICRL** (Individuals CRL). The other kind lists revoked certificates of CAs. We'll call that a **CACRL** (CAs CRL). The theory behind having two CRLs rather than one is that the revoked CA certificate list will be very short, and perhaps more security-sensitive, so it might want to be checked very often. If the revoked individual certificates were included, then it would be a long message that would need to be accessed frequently by many processes.

The problem is that the two kinds of CRL share a common syntax. The only way to tell which kind a particular CRL is is by where it is found in the X.500 directory service. Suppose a CA has issued both an ICRL and a CACRL. Suppose Trudy, an individual, has had her certificate revoked. Her certificate will then be listed in the most recent ICRL (and will continue to be in all the ICRLs until her certificate expires). But her certificate will certainly not be listed in the CACRL. Most likely the CACRL will be empty, indicating there are no revoked certificates, since a revoked CA certificate is probably a very rare event. If Trudy has control of a directory service replica (or can impersonate one), she can take the CACRL and return it in response to requests for the ICRL. Her certificate will then be honored.

An easy fix is to have a flag indicating CRL type in the CRL's cryptographically protected information. This appears to be headed for standardization as an amendment to the 1993 standard.

X.509 syntax is used in several systems, including PEM (see Chapter 13 *Privacy Enhanced Mail (PEM)*). PEM today only uses the ICRL. But if it were deployed in an environment where some CA issued both types of CRL and didn't implement the amendment, then someone could exploit this flaw.

9.10 PERFORMANCE CONSIDERATIONS

In addition to the security issues in the design of authentication protocols, there are also performance considerations. As CPUs get faster, performance becomes less important, but we haven't yet reached the point where it can be ignored. Metrics to be considered in evaluating the performance of an authentication protocol include:

- number of cryptographic operations using a private key

- number of cryptographic operations using a public key

- number of bytes encrypted or decrypted using a secret key

- number of bytes to be cryptographically hashed

- number of messages transmitted

Note that public key operations are typically counted in blocks, while secret key and message digest operations are counted in bytes. The reason for this is that public key operations are so expensive that large amounts of data are not processed with public key operations. Public key operations are typically done on something that fits within a block, such as a secret key or a message digest of a message.

For RSA, the de facto standard public key cryptographic algorithm, private key operations are much more expensive than public key operations. Other public key algorithms have different rules. Most secret key algorithms have similar performance for encrypting and decrypting. As a general rule, computing a message digest has somewhat better performance (per byte) than secret key encryption, but there is not a dramatic difference.

Besides the processing power cost of cryptographic operations, there is also the real time cost of performing an authentication. If an authentication protocol is running over a link to Mars, the number of round-trip message exchanges will certainly be the dominant factor in authentication time (as opposed to the processing time required to do the cryptographic operations). As processors get faster and the speed of light stays the same, the number of round-trip exchanges grows in relative importance as a factor in authentication time. Another consideration in real-time calculations is that if cryptographic operations can go on in parallel at the two ends of a connection, they will take less real time to complete. Some protocols are designed with this in mind (see §17.6.5 *Lotus Notes Authentication*, for example).

Perhaps the most important optimization that can be added to a protocol is the ability to cache state from a previous authentication to make it easier for the same two parties to authenticate a second time. If a public key based authentication establishes a shared secret key as a side effect, that shared secret key can be used to do a more efficient authentication protocol on a second round if both ends remember it (see §17.5.4 *DASS Authentication Handshake*, for example). In a KDC-based scheme, it may be possible for one of the parties to remember a ticket from a previous authentication and thus avoid having to interact with the KDC on a second authentication (see §10.2 *Tickets and Ticket-Granting Tickets*).

9.11 AUTHENTICATION PROTOCOL CHECKLIST

By way of review, the following is a checklist of things to consider when designing or evaluating an authentication protocol. Assume that Alice initiates conversations with Bob, and that Alice and Bob each have a database of information (some secret, some not) used in running the protocol. The list is organized around what intruder Trudy might attempt to do and what the protocol being designed should protect against.

- *Eavesdrop*. Even if Trudy can watch the messages between Alice and Bob pass over the network, she shouldn't be able to

  - learn the contents of the messages between Alice and Bob

  - learn information that would enable her to impersonate either Alice or Bob in a subsequent exchange

  - learn information that would enable her to impersonate Alice to another replica of Bob

  - learn information that would permit her to do an off-line password-guessing attack against either Alice's or Bob's secret information

- *Initiate a conversation pretending to be Alice*. Trudy can send a message to Bob and claim to be Alice and proceed at least partway through an authentication exchange. In doing so, she shouldn't be able to

  - convince Bob she is Alice

  - learn information that would enable her to do an off-line password-guessing attack against either Alice's or Bob's secret information

  - learn information that would enable her to impersonate Alice on a subsequent (or interleaved) attempt

  - learn information that would enable her to impersonate Bob to Alice

  - trick Bob into signing or decrypting something (for instance an electronic mail message)

- *Lie in wait at Bob's network address and accept a connection from Alice*. Trudy can get at least partway through an authentication exchange. In doing so, she shouldn't be able to

  - convince Alice that Trudy is Bob

  - learn information that would enable her to do an off-line password-guessing attack against either Alice's or Bob's secret information

  - learn information that would enable her to impersonate Bob on a subsequent attempt

- learn information that would enable her to impersonate Alice to Bob
- trick Alice into signing or decrypting something

- *Read Alice's database.* If Trudy can get all of Alice's secrets, she can convince Bob she is Alice; she can also conduct an off-line password-guessing attack against Bob's secret information (assuming Bob's secret is derived from a password), since Alice must have enough information to know if someone is really Bob. She should not, however, be able to

  - impersonate Bob to Alice
  - decrypt old recorded conversations between Alice and Bob

- *Read Bob's database.* If Trudy can get all of Bob's secrets, she can convince Alice she is Bob; she can also conduct an off-line password-guessing attack against Alice's secret information since Bob must have enough information to know if someone is really Alice. She should not, however, be able to

  - impersonate Alice to Bob
  - decrypt old recorded conversations between Alice and Bob

- *Sit on the net between Alice and Bob (e.g. as a router) and examine and/or modify messages in transit between them.* Trudy can clearly prevent Alice and Bob from communicating, but she shouldn't be able to

  - learn information that would permit her to do an off-line password-guessing attack against either Alice's or Bob's secret information
  - learn the contents of Alice's and Bob's messages
  - hijack a conversation (continue a conversation started up by a legitimate party without the other side noticing the change)
  - modify messages or rearrange/replay/reverse the direction of messages, causing Alice and/or Bob to misinterpret their messages to one another

- *Some combination of the above.* There are clearly too many possibilities to enumerate, but some examples would be

  - Even after reading both Alice's and Bob's databases, it should not be possible to decrypt old recorded conversations between them.
  - Even after reading Bob's database and eavesdropping on an authentication exchange, it should not be possible to impersonate Alice to Bob.

It isn't necessarily the right engineering trade-off to devise a protocol that passes all the criteria we mention above. For instance, in some cases eavesdropping or address impersonation might be a sufficiently unlikely threat that a much simpler protocol will suffice. Also, sometimes secrets are chosen from a large enough space that password guessing is not feasible.

9.12 HOMEWORK

1. Suppose Trudy hijacks a conversation between Alice and Bob. This means that after the initial handshake, Trudy sends messages with source address equal to Alice's source address. Suppose the network allows Trudy to insert a fake source address (Alice's source address), but does not deliver packets destined for Alice's address to Trudy. What are the problems involved in having Trudy transmit a file to Bob as if she were Alice? Consider potential problems with flow control and file transfer protocols when Trudy cannot see return traffic from Bob.

2. In §9.2 *Mutual Authentication*, we discuss the reflection attack and note that Protocol 9-9 is susceptible, but Protocol 9-8 is not. How about Protocol 9-12?

3. In §9.3.1 *Shared Secret* we discuss various possibilities for forming a session key. Remember that R is the challenge sent by Bob to Alice, and A is Alice's secret, which Bob also knows. Which of the following are secure for a session key?

    $$A \oplus R \qquad \{R+A\}_A \qquad \{A\}_A \qquad \{R\}_{R+A}$$

4. Design a variant of Otway-Rees (page 248) that only has one nonce generated by Alice and one nonce generated by Bob. Explain why it is still as secure.

5. Suppose we are using a three-message mutual authentication protocol, and Alice initiates contact with Bob. Suppose we wish Bob to be a stateless server, and therefore it is inconvenient to require him to remember the challenge he sent to Alice. Let's modify the exchange so that Alice sends the challenge back to Bob, along with the encrypted challenge. So the protocol is:

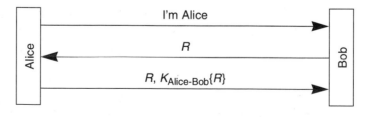

Is this protocol secure?

6.   Let's modify the protocol from the previous problem so that Bob sends both a challenge, and a challenge encrypted with a key that only he knows, to Alice:

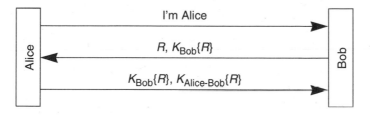

Is this protocol secure?

7.   In the discussion of Protocol 9-3 on page 227, Bob remembers all the timestamps he's seen within the last 10 minutes. Why is it sufficient for him to remember only 10 minutes worth of timestamps?

8.   Design a two-message authentication protocol, assuming that Alice and Bob know each other's public keys, which accomplishes both mutual authentication and establishment of a session key.

9.   The Expanded Needham-Schroeder Protocol (page 247) can be shortened to a 6-message protocol without loss of security by merely removing the 7th message. Why is this true? (Hint: the purpose of the 7th message is to prove to Bob that he is talking to Alice, but he already knows that. Why?)

10. §9.4 *Mediated Authentication (with KDC)* describes several protocols. For each of those protocols, describe which nonces have to be unpredictable (i.e., sequence numbers would not be good).

11. As we pointed out in §7.1 *Password-Based Authentication*, cellular phones are vulnerable to a fraud known as "cloning". The protocol cellular phones use is that a phone transmits its telephone number followed by a cleartext password. The phone company checks its database of phone number/password to make sure the phone is legitimate before allowing the call to go through. The phone number is the one billed. Suggest a design based on public key, and one based on secret key, technology. Can you guard against the phone company database being stolen?

12. There is a product which consists of a fancy telephone that, when talking to a compatible fancy telephone, does a Diffie-Hellman key exchange in order to establish a secret key, and the remainder of the conversation is encrypted. Suppose you are a wiretapper. How can you listen to a conversation between two such telephones?

13. In §9.1.1 *Shared Secret*, we discussed using $MD5(K_{\text{Alice-Bob}}|R)$ as the method of encrypting R with $K_{\text{Alice-Bob}}$. (When we say $K_{\text{Alice-Bob}}|R$ we mean $K_{\text{Alice-Bob}}$ concatenated with R.) Suppose instead we used $MD5(K_{\text{Alice-Bob}} \vee R)$. Would that be secure? How about $MD5(K_{\text{Alice-Bob}} \oplus R)$?

14. In §9.1.3 *Lamport's Hash* we mentioned the notion of using only 64 bits of the hash. At each stage, 128 bits are computed, 64 bits are thrown away, and the hash of the retained 64 bits is used in the next stage. The purpose of only using 64 bits is so that a human does not need to type as long a string. Assuming the person will still only type 64 bits, does it work if hash^n does a hash of all 128 bits of hash^{n-1}, but what the person actually transmits is 64 bits of the result?

15. Design a variant of Lamport's hash using k times more storage at the server but needing only $1/k$ as much processing, on average, at the client.

16. Suppose we are using Lamport's hash, and Bob crashes before receiving Alice's reply. Suppose an intruder, Trudy, can eavesdrop and detect that Bob crashed (maybe Trudy can even cause Bob to crash). Then Trudy has a quantity (whatever Alice replied that Bob did not receive) which Trudy can use to impersonate Alice, if Trudy logs in before Alice attempts to log into Bob again. How can we modify Bob's behavior to prevent this threat? (Exactly when do we overwrite Bob's database, and with what)?

17. We claim both §9.5 *Bellovin-Merritt* protocols can be shortened to 3 messages without loss of security. Design a 3-message version of each, and explain why it is just as secure.

18. Bellovin-Merritt would be equally secure if the initiator (Alice, in Protocol 9-21 and Protocol 9-22), in message 1, sent $g^{R_A} \bmod p$ instead of $K_{\text{Alice-Bob}}\{g^{R_A} \bmod p\}$. Why is this true? Would it be secure if Alice sent $K_{\text{Alice-Bob}}\{g^{R_A} \bmod p\}$ but Bob sent $g^{R_B} \bmod p$ instead of $K_{\text{Alice-Bob}}\{g^{R_B} \bmod p\}$? What about the three-message variant in Homework Problem 17? Which side can, without loss of security, send their Diffie-Hellman number unencrypted?

10 KERBEROS V4

10.1 INTRODUCTION

Kerberos is a secret key based service for providing authentication in a network. When a user Alice first logs into a workstation, she'll type her account name and password. We'll call the period from when she logs in to when she logs out her **login session**. During her login session Alice will probably need to access remote resources (such as hosts on which Alice has accounts, or file servers on which Alice has files). These remote resources will need to authenticate her, but Alice's workstation performs the authentication protocol on Alice's behalf, and Alice need not be aware that it is happening. The network itself is assumed to be insecure. Bad guys might eavesdrop or modify messages.

Kerberos was originally designed at MIT. It is based on work by Needham and Schroeder (see §9.4 *Mediated Authentication (with KDC)*). The first three versions of Kerberos are no longer in use and hence are not of much interest. Version 4 and Version 5, although conceptually similar, are substantially different from one another and are competing for dominance in the marketplace. Version 4 has a greater installed base, is simpler, and has better performance, but works only with TCP/IP networks, while Version 5 has greater functionality. We'll describe Version 4 in detail in this chapter, and the differences between Version 4 and Version 5 in the next. For any inquiring minds out there, the name Kerberos is the name of the three-headed dog that guards the entrance to Hades. (Wouldn't it be more useful to guard the exit?)

An implementation of Kerberos consists of a Key Distribution Center (KDC) that runs on a physically secure node somewhere on the network, and a library of subroutines that are used by distributed applications which want to authenticate their users. While there are many possible modes of operation, Kerberos was designed for an environment where a user logs into a workstation by providing a user name and a password. These are used by the workstation to obtain information from the KDC that can be used by any process to access remote resources on behalf of the user. The basic ideas behind Kerberos should be familiar by now, since we've already discussed the concept of KDCs in §7.7 *Trusted Intermediaries* and §9.4 *Mediated Authentication (with KDC)*.

Some applications that have been modified to call subroutines in the Kerberos library as part of their startup include

- telnet (RFC 854)—a protocol for acting as a terminal on a remote system

- BSD rtools—a group of utilities included with BSD UNIX that support remote login (rlogin), remote file copying (rcp), and remote command execution (rsh)

- NFS (Network File System, RFC 1094)—a utility that permits files on a remote node on the network to be accessed as though they were local files

10.2 TICKETS AND TICKET-GRANTING TICKETS

The KDC shares a secret key, known as a **master key**, with each **principal** (each user and each resource that will be using Kerberos). When Alice informs the KDC that she wants to talk to Bob, the KDC invents a session key K_{AB} for Alice and Bob to share, encrypts K_{AB} with Alice's master key for Alice, encrypts K_{AB} with Bob's master key for Bob, and returns all this information to Alice. The message consisting of the session key K_{AB} (and other information such as Alice's name) encrypted with Bob's master key is known as a **ticket** to Bob. Alice can't read what's inside the ticket, because it's encrypted with Bob's master key. Bob can decrypt the ticket and discover K_{AB} and Alice's name. Bob knows, based on the ticket, that anyone else who knows K_{AB} is acting on Alice's behalf. So Alice and Bob can authenticate each other, and optionally encrypt or integrity-protect their entire conversation, based on the shared key K_{AB}. The session key K_{AB} together with the ticket to Bob are known as Alice's **credentials** to Bob.

Alice logs into a workstation by supplying her name and password. Alice's master key is derived from her password. The workstation, which performs the authentication protocol on behalf of Alice, could remember her password during the whole login session and use that when proof of her identity was required. But that is not good security practice for various reasons. One worry is that Alice might, during the login session, run untrustworthy software that might steal her password. To minimize harm, the first thing that happens is that the workstation asks the KDC for a session key S_A for Alice to use for just this one session. The session key S_A is then used on Alice's behalf when asking for tickets to resources on the network. The key S_A is only valid for some small amount of time, generally a few hours. If anyone steals S_A, then they can impersonate Alice, but only until S_A expires.

During the initial login, the workstation, on Alice's behalf, asks the KDC for a session key for Alice. The KDC generates a session key S_A, and transmits S_A (encrypted with Alice's master key) to the workstation. The KDC also sends a **ticket-granting ticket** (**TGT**), which is S_A (and other information such as Alice's name and the TGT's expiration time) encrypted with the KDC's master key.

The workstation uses Alice's master key (derived from her password) to decrypt the encrypted S_A. Then the workstation forgets Alice's password and only remembers S_A and the TGT. When Alice later needs to access a remote resource, her workstation transmits the TGT to the KDC, along with the name of the resource to which Alice needs a ticket (say Bob). The KDC decrypts the TGT to discover S_A, and uses S_A to encrypt the Alice-Bob session key for Alice. Essentially, the TGT informs the KDC to use S_A instead of Alice's master key.

Earlier versions of Kerberos did not have the notion of a TGT. The user's master key was always used when communicating with the KDC. Later, for enhanced security, the notion of obtaining a limited-lifetime session key at login time was added. The idea was that only TGTs were gotten from the KDC, and that other tickets were obtained from what was theoretically a different entity, which Kerberos calls a **Ticket-Granting Server** or **TGS**. However, the Ticket-Granting Server has to have the same database as the KDC (it needs to know Bob's secret key in order to give Alice a ticket for Bob). So in Kerberos, the Ticket-Granting Server and the KDC are really the same thing. It would be easier to understand Kerberos if the documentation didn't refer to two different entities (KDC and TGS), and two sets of protocol messages that basically do the same thing. The reason it is described that way in Kerberos documentation is solely due to how the protocol evolved.

The Kerberos documentation refers to an Authentication Server (AS), and a Ticket-Granting Server (TGS), which are collocated at the KDC, meaning they are really the same thing. We will use the terms KDC, AS, and TGS interchangeably, since we do not find the distinction to be useful for understanding Kerberos, and in reality there is no distinction.

10.3 CONFIGURATION

As we said before, each principal has its own secret key, known as the master key for that principal. The Kerberos server is called a KDC (Key Distribution Center). Sometimes the Kerberos documentation calls the KDC an Authentication Server, or a KDC/AS. The KDC has a database of names of principals and their corresponding master keys. To keep the KDC database reasonably secure, the stored master keys are stored encrypted by a key that is the personal secret of the KDC, known as the **KDC master key**. The master key for a human user is derived from the user's password. Resources other than human beings are configured with their own master keys.

Kerberos is based on secret key technology, and all current implementations use DES. Kerberos V5 has fields in packets for identifying the cryptographic algorithm, so theoretically an algorithm other than DES can be used in V5, but in reality we can assume the algorithm is DES because there are no implementations of Kerberos with the ability to use a different algorithm.

To summarize, human users need to remember a password. Other network devices need to remember a secret key. The KDC needs to have a database of names of all the principals for which it is responsible, together with a secret key for each of them. It also needs a secret key K_{KDC} for itself (in order to encrypt the database of user keys and in order to generate ticket-granting tickets).

10.4 LOGGING INTO THE NETWORK

By way of introduction, let's look at the steps that take place as Alice uses the network. She'll expect the login procedure to be pretty much the same as for logging into an operating system. First, the workstation prompts Alice for a name and a password.

10.4.1 Obtaining a Session Key and TGT

Alice types her account name and password at the workstation. The workstation sends a message to the KDC, in the clear (unencrypted), which gives Alice's account name. On receipt of the request, the KDC returns credentials to the KDC, encrypted with Alice's master key. The credentials consist of:

- a session key S_A (a secret key to be used during the login session).

- a ticket-granting ticket (TGT). The TGT contains the session key, the user's name, and an expiration time, encrypted with K_{KDC}. Because it is encrypted with the KDC's master key, the TGT is an unintelligible bunch of bits to anyone other than the KDC.

These credentials are sent back to the workstation encrypted with Alice's master key, K_A. Note that the information in the TGT is therefore doubly encrypted when transmitted by the KDC—first with K_{KDC} and then with K_A. Kerberos V4 is sometimes criticized for this minor performance suboptimality, since encrypting the already-encrypted TGT offers no security benefit.

The workstation converts the password Alice types into a DES key. When the workstation receives the credentials, it attempts to decrypt them using this DES key. If this decryption succeeds (which it will if Alice typed her password correctly), then the workstation discards Alice's master key (the key derived from her password), retaining instead the TGT and the session key.

Kerberos documentation refers to the request sent by the workstation to the KDC as a **KRB_AS_REQ**, for **Kerberos Authentication Server Request**. We'll call it **AS_REQ**. The message in which the KDC returns the session key and TGT is known in the Kerberos documentation as a **KRB_AS_REP**, for **Kerberos Authentication Service Reply**. We'll call it **AS_REP**.

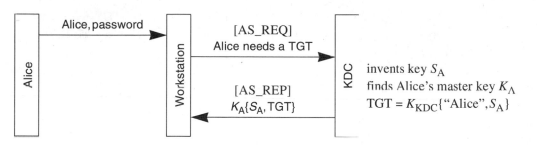

Figure 10-1. Obtaining a TGT

Actually, Kerberos V4 does not prompt the user for her password until after the workstation has received the credentials from the KDC. This is because Kerberos V4 was very serious in following the generally good security rule of having the workstation know the user's password for the minimum time possible. Waiting the few seconds to get the credentials before asking the user for the password really doesn't enhance security significantly, and in fact V5 has the user type the password before the workstation sends the AS_REQ. The reason V5 changed the order was that V5 requires the workstation to prove it knows the user's password before it sends the credentials, which makes it less easy to obtain a quantity with which to do off-line password guessing. An eavesdropper will still be able to do off-line password guessing with V5, but in V4 all you have to do is send the name Alice to the KDC and it will return a quantity with which you can do password guessing. This is likely to be easier than eavesdropping.

What is the purpose of the TGT? When Alice needs to access a remote resource, her workstation sends the TGT to the KDC along with a request for a ticket to the resource's node. The TGT contains the information the KDC needs about Alice's login session (session key, Alice's name, expiration time,…). This allows the KDC to operate without having any volatile data; it has a largely static database, and for each request it sends a response and then forgets that it happened. This offers a number of operational advantages, like making it easy to replicate the KDC and not having to maintain state across crashes.

An interesting variant might be to have the workstation generate the TGT (see Homework Problem 1).

10.4.2 Alice Asks to Talk to a Remote Node

Suppose that after logging in as described above, Alice types a command that requires access to a remote node (like rlogin Bob, which logs Alice into Bob). The workstation sends to the KDC the TGT, the name Bob, and an **authenticator** which proves that the workstation knows the session key. The authenticator consists of the time of day encrypted with the session key (in this case S_A). This request is known in the Kerberos documentation as a **KRB_TGS_REQ**, and the reply is known as **KRB_TGS_REP**; we'll call them **TGS_REQ** and **TGS_REP**. The TGS_REP contains a ticket to Bob and K_{AB} (the session key to be shared by Alice and Bob), encrypted with S_A (the session key to the KDC).

Because of the use of authenticators it is necessary for resources on the network to keep reasonably synchronized time. The times can be off by some amount. The allowable time skew is independently set at each server, and therefore some servers may be configured to be fussier than others about times being close. The allowed time skew is usually set to be on the order of five minutes on the assumption that it is possible to get computers' clocks to be accurate within five minutes without undue administrative burden. In practice, that assumption has turned out to be more problematic than expected. Distributed time services, once deployed, make much tighter synchronization straightforward.

It turns out that there is no security or functionality gained by having Kerberos require an authenticator when Alice's workstation requests a ticket to Bob. If someone who didn't know the session key transmitted the TGT and the name Bob to the KDC, the KDC would return information encrypted with S_A, which would be of no use to someone who didn't know Alice's session key. The reason the designers of Kerberos did it this way is to make the protocol for talking to the Ticket-Granting Service of the KDC be the same as for talking to other resources. When talking to most resources other than the KDC, the authenticator does provide security, because it prevents the replay of old requests and authenticates the sender (which is important if the reply is unencrypted).

The KDC decrypts the TGT (with K_{KDC}) and discovers the session key S_A. It also checks the expiration time in the TGT. If the TGT is valid, the KDC constructs a new key K_{AB}, for use in talking between Alice and Bob, and constructs a **ticket**, which consists of the newly generated key K_{AB}, the name Alice, and an expiration time, all encrypted with Bob's master key, K_B. The KDC sends the ticket, along with the name Bob and K_{AB}, to the workstation. Again this information must be encrypted, and it is encrypted with S_A. On receipt, the workstation decrypts the information using S_A.

Now the workstation sends a request to Bob. In the Kerberos documentation this request is called a **KRB_AP_REQ**, for *application request*, which we'll call **AP_REQ**. It consists of the ticket and an authenticator (in this case the time encrypted with the session key K_{AB}). The reply from Bob is known in Kerberos as **KRB_AP_REP**, and we'll call it **AP_REP**. Bob decrypts the ticket and discovers the key K_{AB} and the name Alice. Bob now assumes that anyone with knowledge of K_{AB} is acting on Alice's behalf. Then Bob decrypts the authenticator to know that the party to which he is speaking does indeed know the session key K_{AB}. He checks that the time in the decrypted authenticator is close to current (within five minutes) to ensure that this is not a replay of some earlier request.

To make sure it is not a replay of a request recent enough to look current given the time skew, Bob should keep all timestamps he has received recently, say in the last five minutes (a parameter set appropriately for the maximum allowable time skew) and check that each received timestamp from a given source is different from any of the stored values. Any authenticator older than five

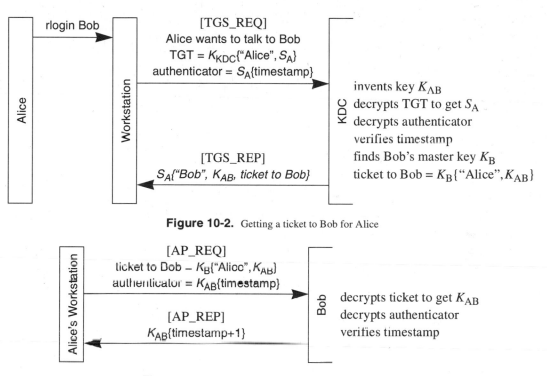

Figure 10-2. Getting a ticket to Bob for Alice

Figure 10-3. Logging into Bob from Alice's workstation

minutes (or whatever the value of the maximum allowable time skew) would be rejected anyway, so Bob need not remember values older than 5 minutes. Kerberos V4 doesn't bother saving timestamps. Saving timestamps doesn't help anyway if Bob is a replicated service in which all the instances of Bob use the same master key. The threat of an eavesdropper replaying the authenticator Alice sent to one instance of Bob to a different instance of Bob could have been avoided if Kerberos had done something like put the network layer address of the instance of Bob in the authenticator.

To provide mutual authentication, Bob adds one to the time he decrypted from the authenticator, reencrypts that with K_{AB} and sends it back. Alice's workstation is now reassured that it is talking to Bob, since the party at the other side was able to decrypt the ticket, which meant he knew K_{AB}, which was encrypted with K_B.

Thereafter, depending on the application, messages between Alice and Bob may be unprotected, integrity-protected, or encrypted and integrity-protected. Some applications always use the same Kerberos protection (authentication only, data integrity protection, or data encryption plus integrity protection). Others make it optional (a switch setting when calling the application). The decision is a security vs. performance tradeoff when using Kerberos.

10.5 REPLICATED KDCs

A serious problem with having all authentication rely on a single KDC is that it is a single point of failure. If the KDC is unavailable, either because it is down or because the path through the network to the KDC is broken, it is impossible to access remote resources, making the network unusable to everyone. In addition, a single KDC might be a performance bottleneck, since all logins and all attempts to start conversations to anything must involve communication with the KDC.

For these reasons it is desirable to have multiple KDCs, where each KDC is interchangeable with every other KDC. They share the same master KDC key and have identical databases of principal names and master keys.

Keeping the databases at all the KDCs the same is done by having one site hold the **master copy** to which any updates must be made. An update consists of adding an entry for ⟨principal name, key⟩, modifying an entry (for instance to change a key), or deleting an entry. Other sites download the database periodically, either on a timer or as a result of a human issuing a command. Having a single master copy avoids problems such as combining updates made at different replicas and resolving conflicting updates.

Of course, by having a single master copy to which updates must be made, Kerberos still has a single point of failure. Fortunately, Kerberos is designed so that most operations—and all critical operations—are read-only operations of the KDC database. It's true that if the master is down, administrators can't add and delete users (but when the KDC is down the administrators are probably too busy to bother with adding and deleting users since they're trying to fix the KDC), and users can't change their passwords (which may be inconvenient but is not life-threatening). These operations can wait for a few hours until the master copy is repaired. In contrast, the read-only KDC operations are required for any use of the network. If there were only a single KDC, and it was unavailable, none of the network users would be able to get any (computer-related) work done.

Another reason for replication is to avoid a performance bottleneck at the KDC. Updates are sufficiently rare that the master copy will be easily capable of keeping up with all updates. Most of the operations will be read-only, and these operations will be spread among the read-only replicas. Another reason that replication may improve performance is so that a KDC replica is usually nearby.

When downloading the KDC database from the master replica to a read-only slave, it is important to protect the data from disclosure and modification. Disclosure would permit an attacker to learn the master keys of all principals; modification would permit an attacker to create new accounts or change the properties of existing ones. This protection could have been provided by encrypting the KDC database as a unit when it was being transferred. The Kerberos designers chose not to do that.

Because the principals' master keys are stored in the database encrypted under the KDC master key, there is no serious disclosure threat. An attacker could learn the names of all principals and their properties, but not their master keys. The threat remains that an attacker could rearrange data in transit so that, for example, some privileged user was given the attacker's master key (by simply copying the encrypted key field). This second threat is avoided by transferring the KDC database as a file in the clear but then sending a cryptographic hash of the file in a Kerberos protected exchange. By using the integrity protection of Kerberos, which includes a timestamp, the protocol prevents the attacker from substituting an old version of the KDC database, for instance one from before the attacker was fired.

10.6 REALMS

Having a single KDC for an entire network is a problem for many reasons. With replicated KDCs, you can alleviate bottleneck problems and eliminate the single-point-of-failure problem. However, there is a serious problem which creation of redundant KDCs does not solve.

Imagine a big network consisting of several organizations such as companies in competition with each other, various universities, banks, and government agencies. It would be hard to find an organization that everyone would trust to manage the KDC. Whoever manages the KDC can access every user's master key, and therefore access everything that every user can access. Furthermore, that highly trusted entity would also be a busy one, having to process all instances of users and services joining and leaving the network.

Even if there were an organization everyone was willing to trust, this is not enough. Everyone must also trust the physical controls around every replica of the KDC, and there would have to be widely dispersed replicas to ensure availability and convenience. Compromise of any replica, no matter how obscurely placed it was, would yield everyone's keys.

For this reason the principals in the network are divided into **realms** Each realm has its own KDC database. There can be multiple KDCs in a realm, but they would be equivalent, have the same KDC master key, and have the same database of principals' master keys. Two KDCs in different realms, however, would have different KDC master keys and totally different principals' master key databases, since they would be responsible for a different set of principals.

In V4, a name of a principal has three components, each of which is a null-terminated case-sensitive text string of up to 40 characters: NAME, INSTANCE, and REALM. The Kerberos protocol does not particularly care how the NAME and INSTANCE fields are used. They are merely text strings. However, in practice, services have a name, and the INSTANCE field is used to indicate the particular machine on which the service is running. For example the file service might be called fileserv and a particular instance might be jailbreak, for the name of one of the fileserver machines.

The INSTANCE field is not as useful for human principals, and usually the null string would be used for the instance part of the name. But as long as there is that component to a name, the convention for humans is that it is used to denote something about the role of the human for that particular login session. For example, someone can have the name Alice and the instance systemmanager, or the name Alice and the instance gameplayer. Presumably Alice.systemmanager would have access to many more network resources than Alice.gameplayer. In effect, a name is really a concatenation of the two strings NAME and INSTANCE. Kerberos could certainly have done without the concept of instance, and by convention principals could just use different names in their various roles. As a matter of fact, if "." were a legal character in the text string for a name, the names could be identical to what they are currently, without having to separate them officially into two fields (NAME and INSTANCE).

10.7 INTERREALM AUTHENTICATION

Suppose the world is partitioned into n different Kerberos realms. It might be the case that principals in one realm need to authenticate principals in another realm. This is supported by Kerberos. The way it works is that the KDC in realm B can be registered as a principal in realm A. This allows users in realm A to access realm B's KDC as if it were any other resource in realm A.

Suppose Alice, in realm Wonderland, wishes to communicate securely to Dorothy in realm Oz. Alice (or rather her workstation, on her behalf) notices that Dorothy is in a different realm. She asks her KDC for a ticket to the KDC in realm Oz (see Figure 10-4). If the managers of Wonderland and Oz have decided to allow this, the KDC in Oz will be registered as a principal in Wonderland, and the Wonderland KDC will have assigned a master key to Oz's KDC. Wonderland's KDC will give Alice a ticket (encrypted with that master key) to the KDC in Oz. Then Alice sends a TGS_REQ to Oz's KDC. The message lists Wonderland as the source realm, which tells Oz's KDC what key to use to decrypt the ticket. The Oz KDC then issues a ticket for Alice to talk to Dorothy.

After Alice sends this ticket to Dorothy, Alice and Dorothy will know they are talking to each other, and they will have a key K_{A-D} they can use to protect data they send back and forth, exactly as if they were in the same realm.

It doesn't work in Kerberos V4 to start in realm A, get a ticket to realm B, and from there get a ticket to realm C. In order for a principal in realm A to talk to a principal in realm C, C's KDC has to be registered as a principal in realm A. What prevents going from realm A to C through B? Suppose realms A and B share a key, and realms B and C share a key, but A and C do not share a key. Suppose Alice@A would like to talk to Carol@C. Alice can indeed get a ticket to B, since B is registered as a principal in realm A. Then, with a ticket to B, Alice can request, from B, a ticket to C. B

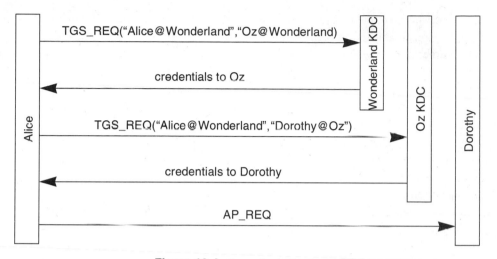

Figure 10-4. Interrealm Authentication

will comply, since *B* thinks of *C* as just another principal in realm *B*. But then when *A* attempts to ask *C* for a ticket to Carol, the TGS_REQ she sends *C* will have the REALM field as *B* (so that *C* will know what key to use to decrypt the ticket), and in the ticket, Alice's realm will be *A*. *C* will refuse to issue a ticket for Carol since the two realms don't match. (See §10.12.5 *TGS_REQ* for a description of the fields in the TGS_REQ.)

Kerberos V4 deliberately prevents access through a chain of KDCs. If it didn't, then a rogue KDC could impersonate not only its own users, but those of any other realm, by claiming to be the penultimate KDC in a chain.

10.8 KEY VERSION NUMBERS

In most operating systems, Alice can change her password without inconveniencing anyone else. The Kerberos designers wanted the same to be true when using Kerberos. However, with Kerberos, a change in a principal's master DES key or a change in the KDC's master DES key would affect tickets held by other users. For instance, if Alice has a ticket to Bob, and Bob changes his master DES key, Alice's ticket will still be encrypted with Bob's old master DES key. Similarly, if Alice has a TGT with a session key for her login session, and the KDC's master key is changed, then Alice's TGT will still be encrypted with the old KDC master key.

The Kerberos designers could simply have ignored the problem, and then communication would fail. Presumably principals would at that point ask for a new ticket and things would proceed. But that would be quite inconvenient, especially in cases like batch jobs where the human user is no longer available to type her password.

The Kerberos designers did not simply ignore the problem. Instead, each key has a **version number**. Network resources (including the KDC) should remember several versions of their own key. Since tickets expire in about 21 hours, there is no reason to remember a superseded key any longer than that. In tickets and other protocol messages, the key version number is sent, so that it can be known which key to use.

Key version numbers are a little more problematic for humans. If Alice changes her password, the new value will be immediately reflected at the master replica of the KDC. If she subsequently attempts to log in before the change has been propagated to the slaves and her workstation contacts one of those slaves, the slave will return credentials encrypted with her old password. Her workstation will then fail to decrypt the credentials and so refuse to log her in. If Alice were as robust as the other processors supporting Kerberos, there would be no problem. The message would contain the key version number, and Alice would then know which password to supply. The Kerberos designers decided wisely not to introduce this piece of complexity into the user interface, but it does have the downside that for some period after a password change, the new password may fail. If the user tries the old password in such a situation, it may work, and the user may be a little confused.

10.9 ENCRYPTION FOR PRIVACY AND INTEGRITY

Many of the data structures that Kerberos encrypts need to be protected from both disclosure and modification. In a ticket, for example, the KEY field needs to be protected from both disclosure and modification, and the NAME and EXPIRATION fields need to be protected from modification.

Unfortunately, there is no standard mechanism for protecting both the confidentiality and integrity of a message with a single cryptographic pass. Generally the most useful way to protect the confidentiality of a message is to encrypt it in CBC mode (see §3.6.2 *Cipher Block Chaining (CBC)*). The most standard way to protect its integrity is with a CBC residue. But securely applying both of these techniques would require double the encryption effort and two separate keys (see §3.7.1 *Ensuring Privacy and Integrity Together*).

Intuitively, it seems like it should be possible to make do with a single cryptographic pass by including some redundant information in the message to be encrypted and then to have the integrity of the message protected by having the recipient check that the redundancy is correctly done. A number of schemes have been proposed for doing this. Many have been found to have cryptographic weaknesses. None has gained general acceptance. The designers of Kerberos came up with their own variation on this theme, and subsequently cryptographic flaws were found with it. The flaws were not so egregious as to justify recalling Kerberos V4; however, a different approach is followed in Kerberos V5.

One method for using DES on a long message is CBC. CBC does a good job on privacy. An intruder will not gain any information from analysis of the encrypted blocks. However, there is no integrity check that Kerberos can do to assure an application that the data was not tampered with. If an intruder were to modify block c_n, then m_n would be garbage, as would m_{n+1}, but starting from m_{n+2} everything would decrypt properly. Kerberos would not be able to detect that m_n and m_{n+1} had been garbled. Some applications might be able to tell, but Kerberos would like to provide the integrity assurance without depending on the application.

Therefore, Kerberos did a modified version of CBC which they called **Plaintext Cipher Block Chaining (PCBC)**. It is similar to CBC except that in addition to $\oplus$ing c_n with m_{n+1}, m_n is also $\oplus$'d. In other words, in CBC, $m_{n+1} \oplus c_n$ is encrypted to yield c_{n+1}. In PCBC, $m_{n+1} \oplus c_n \oplus m_n$ is encrypted to yield c_{n+1}.

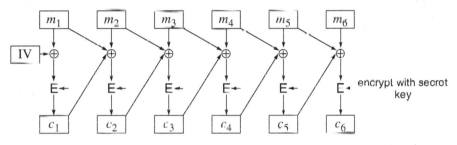

Figure 10-5. Plaintext Cipher Block Chaining (PCBC)

PCBC has the property that modifying any c_i will result in garbling of all decrypted plaintext blocks starting with m_i all the way to the end. Kerberos puts some recognizable data at the end of a message that it will encrypt so that it can recognize whether the final block decrypts properly. It makes the assumption that if the final block decrypts properly, then the data has not been tampered with between the time it was transmitted by the source and received by the destination.

However, using PCBC and checking the contents of the final decrypted block does not guarantee that Kerberos will be able to detect message corruption. For instance, if an intruder were to swap two adjacent blocks, PCBC will "get back in sync" after those two blocks, and the final block will decrypt properly (see Homework Problem 5).

10.10 ENCRYPTION FOR INTEGRITY ONLY

Kerberos is often used by applications just for authentication. Kerberos also provides integrity protection and combined privacy and integrity protection for those applications that desire this facility. Combined privacy and integrity protection is provided by PCBC as described above. Integrity protection without privacy is described in this section.

Kerberos V4 was designed with the expectation that DES encryption would be done in software, and that the processing cost of doing so would be a limiting factor in its acceptance. The designers were willing to use new or even cryptographically weak techniques in order to improve the performance. When integrity-protecting messages, the most straightforward and standard technique would have been to compute a DES CBC residue. Instead, they invented their own. It was based on a checksum algorithm designed by Jueneman [JUEN85]. Jueneman intended for his checksum to be used as a piece of redundant information inside an encrypted message, where it was less subject to cryptographic attack. Furthermore, the version implemented by Kerberos is substantially different (for instance, Jueneman did arithmetic based on mod $2^{31}-1$, which Jueneman chose because it was prime, and Kerberos chose $2^{63}-1$, which is not prime). The actual algorithm used by Kerberos V4 was never documented. In order to break it, or implement a compatible implementation, one would have to read the publicly available source code. No one has demonstrated the ability to break the Kerberos integrity checksum, perhaps because it has not been widely deployed for applications in which the payoff for breaking the scheme was worth the effort. So the fact that it never was broken is not strong evidence of its security. As with PCBC, it's a design upon which cryptographers would frown, but in practice it appears to have been good enough.

The V4 checksum is computed on the session key concatenated with the message. Only the message and the checksum are transmitted—the session key is not sent. An intruder would not be able to compute a valid checksum on a modified message, since that would require knowledge of the session key.

There are two possible problems with the use of the V4 checksum as a message digest function. One is that it might not be as cryptographically strong as a real message digest, and therefore it might be relatively easy to find a different message that yielded the same checksum, even without knowing the session key, since it might be possible to know how to modify a message in a way that would not change the value of the checksum. The second, and potentially more serious, problem is that it might be reversible. An intruder can see the entire plaintext message and the checksum. If it's possible to calculate the previous block, then perhaps it's possible to work backwards from the end and calculate the session key.

Because of these possible weaknesses, this approach was abandoned in Kerberos V5. Instead, a choice of checksum algorithms is given, and in cases such as integrity only, one of the standard message digest functions is used (see §11.8.1 *Integrity-Only Algorithms*).

10.11 NETWORK LAYER ADDRESSES IN TICKETS

When Alice requests a TGT or a ticket to Bob, the KDC puts her network layer address inside the ticket. Bob, when presented with a ticket, will check to make sure that the network layer source address on the connect request is the same as the one specified inside the ticket. Likewise, when the KDC receives a ticket request, it checks that the request is coming from the network layer address specified in the TGT. There are two reasons for putting Alice's network layer address in the ticket. The first reason is to prevent Alice from giving the ticket and session key to some third party, Ted, so that he can impersonate Alice. This restriction makes it more difficult for an intruder to walk up to the workstation Alice is using (when Alice steps out of her office), steal her session key and TGT, and use them from a safe location. But the restriction also prevents delegation, where Alice legitimately wants to allow something to act on her behalf. Indeed in Kerberos V5 delegation is specifically allowed (see §11.3 *Delegation of Rights*). The second reason is to prevent some third party Trudy from intercepting the ticket and authenticator on the wire and using it from Trudy's network layer address. Without Alice's network layer in the ticket, Trudy merely has to eavesdrop to obtain the ticket and an authenticator, use them within five minutes (or whatever the allowable clock skew is), and arrange for the authenticator as transmitted by Alice not to arrive. With Alice's network layer address in the ticket, Trudy has to additionally impersonate Alice's network layer address. This isn't necessarily difficult, but it adds one more hurdle for the attacker.

It might be better to have Alice's network layer address be in the authenticator rather than the ticket. This allows the person using the ticket to pick the network layer address, which makes it easier to support a principal with multiple network layer addresses (Alice can choose which one to put into the authenticator), and it allows delegation. If Alice is willing for Ted to act on her behalf, and has therefore given him the session key and ticket, he can put his own network layer address into the authenticator. But Fred, who has not been given permission by Alice to act on her behalf, cannot generate an authenticator with his network layer address, so any security against eavesdroppers gained by having the network address in the ticket is equally applicable to having the network layer address in the authenticator.

Putting the network layer address in the ticket instead of the authenticator is done to specifically disallow delegation. Kerberos V5 does allow delegation, but only with the mediation of the KDC and only if the originally acquired ticket explicitly permits it.

We feel that since it is usually easy to forge a network layer source address, all the effort Kerberos has put into checking network layer source addresses is more trouble than it's worth.

10.12 MESSAGE FORMATS

In this section we'll go through the Kerberos V4 message formats. In all of the messages, we assume that Alice wants to talk to Bob. In Kerberos documentation Alice is sometimes referred to as the *client* and Bob as the *server*. We find that terminology confusing since both Alice and Bob are clients of the Kerberos system, and principals like file servers can indeed act in the role of client in terms of a Kerberos authentication. Therefore we will not use that terminology and will instead use *Alice* for the initiator of an authentication and *Bob* for the entity with which Alice would like to communicate, and the pronouns *she* for *Alice* and *he* for *Bob*.

Fields that appear in packets:

- NAME/INSTANCE/REALM of Alice or Bob—variable-length null-terminated character strings.

- TIMESTAMP—a four-octet value representing the number of seconds since 00:00:00 GMT, Jan 1, 1970. This is a common representation of time in UNIX-based systems. If treated as a signed integer, it can represent times between 1902 and 2038. If treated as an unsigned integer, it can represent times between 1970 and 2106. In Kerberos, some of the messages in which timestamps appear use the most significant bit as the D BIT (see below); in other messages, the most significant bit is set to zero. Therefore, Kerberos V4 effectively expires in 2038. (It's hoped that most people will have converted to V5 by then—or is that V19?). Kerberos V5 will not expire until December 31, 9999 (at least the timestamps will last till then).

- D BIT, DIRECTION BIT—The purpose of this flag is to prevent an intruder from mirroring a message back to the sender (called a reflection attack) and having the sender accept it as a response. An asymmetry is created between the two ends of a conversation based on IP address. When the packet is traveling from the higher IP address to the lower IP address, the D BIT is set to 1. When the packet is traveling between two processes in a single node (so that both ends of the conversation have the same IP address), the TCP port number is used as a tie-breaker. By checking the D BIT, the receiver of a message can be assured that the message was generated by the other end of the connection. In the actual layout of the data, the D BIT is stolen from the high-order bit of the TIMESTAMP. Note that this is a dependency on IP, though one that could be adapted to most communication protocols.

- LIFETIME—a one octet field, specified in units of 5 minutes. Therefore the maximum lifetime that can be expressed is a little over 21 hours. This limit has been seen as a major shortcoming of Kerberos V4, since it prevents giving tickets to long-running batch jobs.

- 5-MILLISECOND TIMESTAMP—this field extends the TIMESTAMP field to give time granularity down to 5 milliseconds instead of 1 second. Its purpose is to allow more than one authenticator to the same service to be generated in a single second without having it rejected as a duplicate. Actual time accuracy at that granularity is never needed. An acceptable implementation of this field would be a sequence number within the second.

- PADDING—a field containing between zero and seven octets added to the end of any message that will be encrypted to ensure that the value to be encrypted is a multiple of eight octets.

- NETWORK LAYER ADDRESS—a four-octet quantity which is an IP address

- SESSION KEY—an eight-octet quantity which is used as a DES key.

- KEY VERSION NUMBER—a one-octet quantity (see §10.8 *Key Version Numbers*)

- KERBEROS VERSION NUMBER—a one-octet quantity equal to the constant 4.

- MESSAGE TYPE—a one-octet quantity, with the low-order bit stolen for the B BIT (see next item). The high-order seven bits indicate one of the following message types:

    - AS_REQ—Used when asking for the initial TGT.

    - AS REPLY (also TGS_REP)—Used to return a ticket, either a TGT or a ticket to some other principal.

    - AP_REQ (also TGS_REQ)—Used to talk to another principal (or the TGS) using a ticket (or a TGT).

    - AP_REQ_MUTUAL—This was intended to be used to talk to another principal and request mutual authentication. In fact, it is never used; instead, applications know whether mutual authentication is expected.

    - AS_ERR—Used for the KDC to report why it can't return a ticket or TGT in response to AS_REQ or TGS_REQ.

    - PRIV—This is a message that carries encrypted integrity-protected application data.

    - SAFE—This is a message that carries integrity protected application data.

    - AP_ERR—Used by an application to report why authentication failed.

Note: the names of the message types above do not match the names used in either the Kerberos V4 documentation or code. Because there was no consistent pattern, we used the names for the equivalent functions from Kerberos V5.

- B BIT, BYTE-ORDER FLAG—This bit indicates whether fields holding 4-byte integers have them in **big-endian** (most significant byte first) or **little-endian** (least significant byte first) order. Different machines have different native internal formats. Most protocols define a **network byte order** and force machines with a different native format to byte-swap whenever they send or receive integers. Kerberos allows either order in transmitted packets—with this flag—so that in the common case where the native formats on the sending machines are the same, no byte-swapping is necessary. This approach trades complexity for performance. If B BIT is 1, it means the least significant byte is in the lowest address in a multibyte field. This is convenient for some machines, like the Intel 80x86. Other machines like to put the most significant byte in the lowest address, like the Motorola 680x0.

The following three data structures are never actually free-standing messages, but are instead pieces of information included in other messages. They are tickets, authenticators, and credentials.

10.12.1 Tickets

A ticket for Bob is an encrypted piece of information that is given to principal Alice by the KDC and stored by Alice. It is encrypted by the KDC with Bob's master key. Alice cannot read what is inside, but she sends it to Bob who can decrypt it and thereby authenticate her.

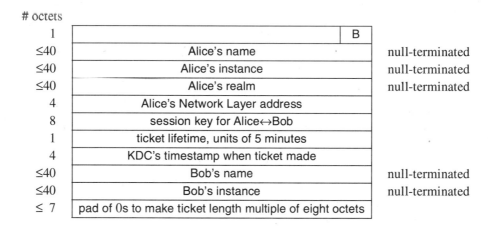

# octets		
1	B	
≤40	Alice's name	null-terminated
≤40	Alice's instance	null-terminated
≤40	Alice's realm	null-terminated
4	Alice's Network Layer address	
8	session key for Alice↔Bob	
1	ticket lifetime, units of 5 minutes	
4	KDC's timestamp when ticket made	
≤40	Bob's name	null-terminated
≤40	Bob's instance	null-terminated
≤ 7	pad of 0s to make ticket length multiple of eight octets	

Now some comments about the fields which are not self-explanatory.

- B BIT, BYTE-ORDER FLAG—LSB in a one-octet field, with the other bits unused.

- ALICE'S NETWORK LAYER ADDRESS—four octets. Note that the field is fixed-length and four octets. Kerberos was designed to run in the network using the TCP/IP protocol suite. This fixed-length field means that this version of Kerberos cannot be used in a network with longer addresses.

- TICKET LIFETIME. The units are 5 minutes, so the maximum ticket lifetime is a little over 21 hours.

- TIMESTAMP—four octets. Time when ticket was created (the number of seconds since 00:00:00 GMT, Jan 1, 1970).

- BOB'S NAME and INSTANCE. Including Bob's name and instance is of dubious value. There are two possible reasons for inclusion of this field in the ticket. One reason is that the field supports a node where several services share a key. If someone were to get a ticket to the gameplaying service on node DoD, and that service used the same key as the nuclear-missile-launching service on the same node (it happened in *War Games*, right?), then having the name of the service in the ticket makes it impossible to use the ticket for the wrong service. For instance, suppose only once in a while (hopefully) does anyone ever use the nuclear-missile-launching service, but people often use the gameplaying service. Good guy *A* has rights to both services, and often uses the gameplaying service. One day bad guy *C* intercepts the ticket and authenticator that *A* was attempting to use to get to the gameplaying service, and then *C* quickly (within the clock skew) impersonates *A*'s network layer address, substitutes as the destination socket number the nuclear-missile-launching service, and starts World War III. You wouldn't want *that* to happen now, would you?

The other dubious purpose for this field is so that Kerberos can tell that the ticket decrypts properly. Kerberos V4 uses PCBC (see §10.9 *Encryption for Privacy and Integrity*), and therefore assumes that any tampering with the data woul result in the final block not decrypting properly. Since the final blocks include Bob's name and instance, Bob will be able to recognize if they are correct. (This is not a strong reason for the field because, even if PCBC worked as hoped, there is no value to be gained from tampering with a ticket and turning the information inside to garbage. User data is a different matter, however, and the PCBC check is more valuable there.)

10.12.2 Authenticators

The authenticator is a piece of information included in a message at the start of a communication attempt between Alice and Bob which enables Alice and Bob to prove to each other that they are who they claim to be. It is encrypted with the session key Alice requested from the KDC for conversing with Bob. We will assume in the following that Alice is sending the authenticator to Bob.

- ALICE'S NAME/INSTANCE/REALM. The presence of these fields avoids an extremely obscure threat. Without these fields, if two principals have the same master key, then an attacker who could intercept messages between one of them and the KDC could change the AS_REQ to have the other principal's name. The returned ticket would then be for the other principal, so that when this principal used the ticket to Bob, Bob would believe it to be the other principal. Now you know.

octets

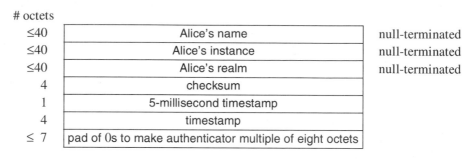

# octets		
≤40	Alice's name	null-terminated
≤40	Alice's instance	null-terminated
≤40	Alice's realm	null-terminated
4	checksum	
1	5-millisecond timestamp	
4	timestamp	
≤ 7	pad of 0s to make authenticator multiple of eight octets	

- CHECKSUM—four octets. This field can be used in an application-specific way. None of the applications that have been Kerberized use this field in a way in which the name *checksum* makes sense. Many applications set this field to Alice's process id. The application that copies the KDC database to KDC replicas sets this field to the size of the KDC database. The sample application provided to help implementers build a Kerberized application suggests having the user type in a value for that field.

- 5-MILLISECOND TIMESTAMP. This field extends the timestamp field to give time granularity down to 5 milliseconds instead of 1 second. Its purpose is to allow more than one authenticator to the same service to be generated in a single second without having it rejected as a duplicate. The simplest implementation of this field would actually be a sequence number within the second (in which case the name is misleading, since it has nothing to do with the unit of time of 5 milliseconds).

- TIMESTAMP—four octets, time in seconds. This is really the main information in the authenticator. Bob decrypts the authenticator, verifies that the time is acceptably close to current, and, if mutual authentication is used, increments this field, encrypts the result, and sends it back to Alice. Because only Bob (or Alice) is able to encrypt the incremented value, when Alice verifies the response she knows that the authenticator arrived at Bob.

10.12.3 Credentials

The CREDENTIALS field in a message is encrypted. When returned in an **AS_REP** (the message that returns a ticket-granting ticket), it is encrypted in Alice's master key. When returned in a **TGS_REP** (the message which requests a ticket to another principal, from the Ticket-Granting Server), it is encrypted with Alice's session key.

Again, we're assuming Alice has requested to talk to Bob.

# octets	
8	session key for Alice↔Bob
≤40	Bob's name
≤40	Bob's instance
≤40	Bob's realm
1	ticket lifetime
1	Bob's key version number
1	length of ticket
variable	ticket
4	timestamp
≤ 7	pad of 0s

(Bob's name, instance, and realm are null-terminated)

- SESSION KEY—eight octets. In an **AS_REP**, this gives the login session key for Alice. In a **TGS_REP**, this gives the key to be used when Alice communicates with Bob.

- BOB'S NAME/INSTANCE/REALM. These fields identify the ticket target. Since Alice sends the ticket request unprotected, the presence of these fields assures Alice that the ticket is for who she thinks it is for.

- TICKET LIFETIME—one octet. Number of 5 minute intervals from the time in TIMESTAMP during which the ticket should be valid.

- KEY VERSION NUMBER. This field allows Bob to change his key in a way that won't disrupt principals that are currently talking to Bob or holding tickets for Bob. Bob must keep track of his old keys for 21 hours after he reports the new key to the KDC (or somewhat longer to allow for propagation to slave KDCs). All such **active** keys for Bob should have unique key version numbers. When a ticket arrives, Bob can use the key version number in the unencrypted header to decide which key to use to decrypt it. 21 hours after Bob reports a new key, any issued tickets encrypted under older keys will have expired and Bob can safely forget the older keys.

- TIMESTAMP—four octets. Time when ticket generated.

10.12.4 AS_REQ

This message is used to ask for a ticket (when one doesn't already have a TGT). It is almost always used to ask for a TGT, which is a ticket to the Ticket-Granting Service. Theoretically it could be used to ask for a ticket to any service, using the requester's master key.

# octets		
1	version of Kerberos (4)	
1	message type (1)	B
≤40	Alice's name	null-terminated
≤40	Alice's instance	null-terminated
≤40	Alice's realm	null-terminated
4	Alice's timestamp	
1	desired ticket lifetime	
≤40	service's name	null-terminated
≤40	service's instance	null-terminated

- MESSAGE TYPE. AS_REQ (1).

- B BIT, BYTE-ORDER FLAG.

- ALICE'S TIMESTAMP. This field is here in order to help Alice match up requests with replies.

- DESIRED TICKET LIFETIME—one octet. In units of 5 minutes, how long the requester would like the issued ticket to be good for. This was a mistake in the design—the upper bound (about 21 hours) is not long enough for some applications.

- SERVICE'S NAME. For the normal case of a request for a ticket to the Ticket-Granting Service, the name will be the constant krbtgt.

- SERVICE'S INSTANCE. For the normal case of a request for a ticket to the Ticket-Granting Service, the instance will be the realm name.

10.12.5 TGS_REQ

The TGS_REQ is used by Alice to request a ticket to Bob from the TGS. In order to do this, Alice needs to send the TGS the TGT (so that the TGS can know the proper session key for Alice), and an authenticator. It turns out sending an authenticator in a TGS_REQ has no security value, but it is necessary in an AP_REQ, and therefore it is in the TGS_REQ to make the two protocols similar.

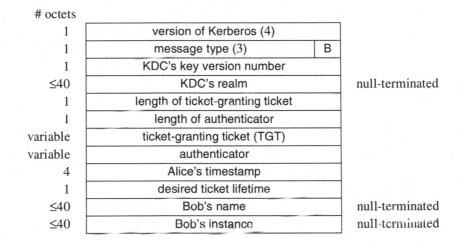

# octets		
1	version of Kerberos (4)	
1	message type (3)	B
1	KDC's key version number	
≤40	KDC's realm	null-terminated
1	length of ticket-granting ticket	
1	length of authenticator	
variable	ticket-granting ticket (TGT)	
variable	authenticator	
4	Alice's timestamp	
1	desired ticket lifetime	
≤40	Bob's name	null-terminated
≤40	Bob's instance	null-terminated

- MESSAGE TYPE—AP_REQ (3)

- KDC'S KEY VERSION NUMBER. Copied from BOB'S KEY VERSION NUMBER in the credentials which Alice obtained in the **KRB_TGS_REP** she received when she asked for a TGT.

- KDC'S REALM. This field is here so that the KDC, in interrealm authentication, will know which key to use to decrypt the ticket. Suppose the KDC in realm *B* is registered in many different realms. The KDC in *B* will have a different key for each realm in which it is registered. For example, if realm *B* can talk to realm *A*, then *B* will have a master key stored at realm *A*'s KDC. If *B* can also talk to realm *C*, then *B* will have a different master key stored at realm *C*'s KDC. When Alice, in realm *A*, gets a ticket to the KDC in *B*, and then asks *B* for a ticket to a principal in *B*'s realm, it is necessary to inform *B* which key it should use to decrypt the ticket (in this case, the one it shares with the KDC in realm *A*).

10.12.6 AS_REP and TGS_REP

This message is the reply to an **AS_REQ** or a **TGS_REQ**. It's really a single message type (2), but it can occur in response to two different sorts of request.

In the following fields, we'll assume the reply is in response to a request from Alice to get a ticket for Bob.

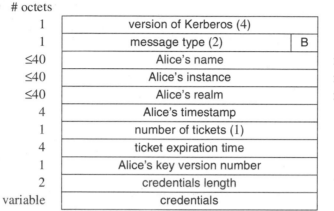

# octets	
1	version of Kerberos (4)
1	message type (2) B
≤40	Alice's name null-terminated
≤40	Alice's instance null-terminated
≤40	Alice's realm null-terminated
4	Alice's timestamp
1	number of tickets (1)
4	ticket expiration time
1	Alice's key version number
2	credentials length
variable	credentials

- MESSAGE TYPE. AS_REP (2).

- ALICE'S NAME/INSTANCE/REALM. Useful in case there are multiple principals on the same node. If a response comes back, the service might not be able to know to which principal the credentials belongs without that field there. Given that the field is not encrypted, it has no security value. It is just there to prevent nonmalicious confusion. The MIT implementation ignores these fields.

- ALICE'S TIMESTAMP. As sent in request (this is to match requests and replies).

- NUMBER OF TICKETS—one octet. Ignored by Kerberos Version 4. In earlier versions of Kerberos, it was possible to request multiple tickets in a single request. Because this feature was never used and complicated the message formats, it was simplified out of V4. This field remains for backwards compatibility.

- TICKET EXPIRATION TIME—four octets.

- ALICE'S KEY VERSION—one octet. Unused if this message is in response to a TGS_REQ.

- CREDENTIALS LENGTH—two octets.

- CREDENTIALS.

10.12.7 Error Reply from KDC

This message is in response to an **AS_REQ** or a **TGS_REQ**, if the KDC fails to reply with a ticket. Again, assume this is in response to principal Alice requesting a ticket for principal Bob.

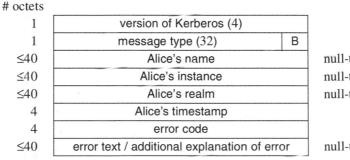

# octets		
1	version of Kerberos (4)	
1	message type (32) B	
≤40	Alice's name	null-terminated
≤40	Alice's instance	null-terminated
≤40	Alice's realm	null-terminated
4	Alice's timestamp	
4	error code	
≤40	error text / additional explanation of error	null-terminated

The defined values for error code are:

1—Alice's database entry at the KDC expired. (Note: Kerberos allows database entries to expire. There is an expiration date on each entry.)

2—Bob's database entry expired.

3—authenticator on the request expired.

4—wrong protocol version number.

7—byte order unknown. (C'mon—it's a bit! How can you not know the two values of a bit?!—and we left out errors 5 and 6 because they were even sillier, and they also were never invoked in the code, so they are irrelevant.)

8—Alice or Bob not found in database.

9—Alice or Bob found in multiple places in the database (though it seems like it would be more sensible to generate an error when adding a duplicate rather than checking for it on every read)

10—Alice or Bob found, but no key is in the database.

20—Generic error from KDC.

10.12.8 AP_REQ

This message is sent from Alice to Bob early in their conversation in order to authenticate. Exactly how this message is passed within the application protocol is not defined by Kerberos. The receiving end must be able to figure out that this is a Kerberos message and pass it to its own Kerberos subroutines.

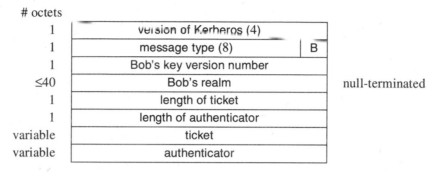

# octets		
1	version of Kerberos (4)	
1	message type (8)	B
1	Bob's key version number	
≤40	Bob's realm	null-terminated
1	length of ticket	
1	length of authenticator	
variable	ticket	
variable	authenticator	

• BOB'S REALM. This is in case Bob is registered in different realms, with different keys in each one. This field enables Bob to choose the proper key to use to decrypt the ticket.

10.12.9 AP_REP

The Kerberos documentation does not define an explicit reply from Bob when Alice sends an AP_REQ. However, the library routines include subroutine krb_sendauth, used by Alice, and krb_recvauth, used by Bob, which most applications use. If all that is necessary is for Bob to authenticate Alice, then there is no necessity for a Kerberos reply from Bob. The application just starts conversing.

If mutual authentication is desired, then Bob needs to send information to Alice that will prove that Bob has decrypted the ticket and therefore knows the session key. The Kerberos routine krb_recvauth accomplishes this by having Bob extract the value of the CHECKSUM field and increment it.

The message format of the message sent by krb_recvauth is the same as KRB_PRV (described in following section), but the data part of the ENCRYPTED STUFF field is the four-byte incremented checksum.

10.12.10 Encrypted Data (KRB_PRV)

Some applications want privacy as well as authentication, i.e. they want their data encrypted. They call a Kerberos subroutine that encrypts the application-supplied data and packages it into a message of the following form:

# octets		
1	version of Kerberos (4)	
1	message type (6)	B
4	length of encrypted stuff	
variable	encrypted stuff	

The ENCRYPTED STUFF is encrypted using DES in the PCBC mode using the session key. Once decrypted, its format is:

# octets		
4	length of data	
variable	data	
1	5 millisecond timestamp	
4	sender's IP address	
4	D	timestamp
variable	padding	

By the nature of PCBC, the sender's IP address and the timestamp serve as an integrity check on the data. The timestamp serves a second function of providing some protection against replay.

Because encryption for privacy is an export-controlled technology, certain versions of Kerberos exclude the capacity to encrypt application supplied data. This message type will still occur, however, in the context of a mutual authentication message.

10.12.11 Integrity-Checked Data (SAFE)

For some applications, privacy of the data is not a concern, but protection of the integrity of the data in transit is. Others may be willing to give up privacy in order to get better performance or in order to satisfy government regulations, but are still willing to pay a price for integrity protection.

The SAFE message is basically application data to which Kerberos appends a checksum and timestamp. The format for integrity-protected data is

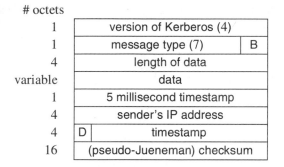

# octets	
1	version of Kerberos (4)
1	message type (7) · B
4	length of data
variable	data
1	5 millisecond timestamp
4	sender's IP address
4	D · timestamp
16	(pseudo-Jueneman) checksum

- SENDER'S IP ADDRESS. It does not appear that having this field in every message adds anything to security, but the Kerberos code checks that it matches the address from which the packet came.

- TIMESTAMP. The purpose of this field is to prevent delayed and replayed messages. An application could save all timestamps that were used within the allowable clock skew and refuse additional messages with the same timestamp. It could also require that messages encrypted under a given key be processed in strictly ascending order by timestamp (if using a connection type that prevents reordering). All the Kerberos-V4-provided subroutine does is make sure the timestamp is within the allowable clock skew.

- 5 MILLISECOND TIMESTAMP. This field allows more than one message within a second. Theoretically it is in units of 5 milliseconds, but in practice can be a sequence number of messages sent within a particular value of the four-octet TIMESTAMP field. If this format survives long enough, a limit of one message every 5 milliseconds may someday be a problem.

- CHECKSUM. The modified Jueneman checksum is seeded with the session key as described in §10.10 *Encryption for Integrity Only* so that only someone with knowledge of the session key can compute a new valid checksum for a modified message.

10.12.12 AP_ERR

This is returned if the authentication failed.

octets

1	version of Kerberos (4)
1	message type (8) B
4	error code
≤40	error text / additional explanation of error null-terminated

The possible errors are

31—can't decode authenticator.

32—ticket expired.

33—ticket not yet valid.

34— repeated request. Receiver of message remembers receiving the same timestamp and 5 milli-second timestamp before.

35—ticket isn't for us. Well, we're not sure what they intended by this error message, but it's never used anywhere. The intention was most likely for Bob to check Bob's name and instance inside the ticket, but none of the applications implemented actually check this.

36—request is inconsistent. The name, instance, and realm of Bob as listed in the ticket does not match the name, instance, and realm in the authenticator.

37—delta_t too big. There is too much skew in the clocks. This is determined based on comparison of the timestamp in the authenticator and the local time at Bob. This skew can be set independently at each node, but a common time is five minutes.

38—incorrect net address. The address in the ticket does not match the source address in the Network Layer header of the received message.

39—protocol version number mismatch.

40—invalid message type.

41—message stream modified. Either the checksum failed or some other piece of bad formatting was detected in an encrypted or integrity-protected message.

42—message out of order. Timestamps are not in ascending order. This assumes the application is running over a reliable Transport protocol (in this case, TCP), so that reordering is not due to the network.

43—unauthorized request. This is an application-specific complaint, i.e. it is not generated by Kerberos. It might be used by Bob to tell Alice that Alice is not authorized to use Bob.

10.13 HOMEWORK

1. Design a variant of Kerberos in which the workstation generates a TGT. The TGT will be encrypted with the user's master key rather than the KDC's master key. How does this compare with standard Kerberos in terms of efficiency, security, etc.? What happens in each scheme if the user changes her password during a login session?

2. §10.5 *Replicated KDCs* explains that the KDC database isn't encrypted as a unit. Rather each user's master key is independently encrypted with the KDC master key. Suppose replication were done with a simple download (i.e., no cryptographic integrity check is performed). How could a bad guy who is a principal registered with a KDC impersonate Alice, another principal registered with that KDC? Assume he can see and modify the KDC database in transit, but that he does not know the KDC master key.

3. Why is the authenticator field not of security benefit when asking the KDC for a ticket for Bob, but useful when logging into Bob?

4. Specify the Kerberos messages involved from the time a user first walks up to a workstation to the time the user is successfully talking to something in another realm.

5. With CBC, if one ciphertext block is lost, how many plaintext blocks are lost? With PCBC, why do things get back in sync if c_n and c_{n+1} are switched? How about if a cyphertext block is lost? How about if cyphertext block n is switched with cyphertext block $n+2$? How about any permutation of the first n blocks?

11 KERBEROS V5

This chapter describes Kerberos Version 5, but it assumes you already understand Kerberos V4. So even if you think you're only interested in V5, it's a good idea to read the previous chapter first.

Kerberos V5 represents a major overhaul of Version 4. While the basic philosophy remains the same, there are major changes to the encodings and major extensions to the functionality. The motivation behind the changes in Kerberos V5 is to allow greater flexibility in the environments in which Kerberos can be used.

11.1 ASN.1

ASN.1 [ISO87, PISC93] is a data representation language standardized by ISO. It looks very similar to data structure definitions in programming languages. ASN.1 is popular among spec writers and standards bodies because it gives people a way to precisely define data structures without worrying about different data representations, such as bit and byte order, on different machines.

Where Kerberos V4 messages had a largely fixed layout with variable-length fields marked in an ad hoc way, Kerberos V5 uses ASN.1 syntax with the Basic Encoding Rules (BER), which makes it easy for fields to be optional, of varying length, and tagged with type information to allow future versions to include additional encodings.

This flexibility comes with a price. ASN.1 has a lot of overhead. It adds bytes of overhead in databases and bytes on the wire, and increases the complexity of the code. Often when people define things in ASN.1, they don't realize what the actual format will be. It is possible to use ASN.1 in a way that would create less overhead, but that takes expertise in ASN.1, and there are very few security protocol designers who have any interest in the specifics of ASN.1.

To illustrate the point, in Kerberos V4 an address is four octets. Admittedly this is not sufficiently flexible, since it assumes IP addresses. Had the Kerberos designers custom-designed a more flexible address format, they'd probably have designed something like

- a one-byte address type (defining type codes for IP and perhaps DECnet, CLNP, IPX, and Appletalk)

- a one-byte length, specifying the length in bytes of the address (this is needed because some address types, for instance CLNP, are variable-length)

- and then the address.

With this format it would have taken six bytes to encode an IP address, rather than four in Kerberos V4. However, Kerberos V5 defines an address using the ASN.1 definition:

```
HostAddress ::= SEQUENCE {
        addr-type[0]      INTEGER,
        address[1]        OCTET STRING }
```

What does this mean? It means that an address has two components: **addr-type** and **address**. That sounds reasonable. But what does the Kerberos V5 definition of an address actually expand into? Somehow it adds 11 octets of overhead to each address, meaning that encoding an IP address in V5 requires 15 octets instead of V4's four octets.

Where does this 11 octet overhead come from? The construct **SEQUENCE** requires an octet to specify that it's a sequence, and an octet to specify the length of the entire sequence. The first component, **addr-type[0] INTEGER**, requires four octets of overhead in addition to the single-octet integer that specifies the type of address:

- **addr-type[0]** requires an octet to specify that it's type 0, then an octet to specify the length of what follows.

- **INTEGER** requires a minimum of three octets: an octet to specify that it's an integer (TYPE), an octet to specify how many octets (LENGTH) of integer, and at least one octet giving the value of the integer.

Similarly, the next component, **address[1] OCTET STRING**, requires four octets of overhead in addition to the actual address.

With clever use of ASN.1, it would have been possible to reduce the overhead substantially. For instance, by defining things with **IMPLICIT**, the representations are more compact, because then the TYPE and LENGTH fields do not appear. For example, four bytes of overhead are avoided by defining an address as follows:

```
HostAddress ::= SEQUENCE {
        addr-type[0]      IMPLICIT INTEGER,
        address[1]        IMPLICIT OCTET STRING }
```

The above definition would reduce the overhead from 11 octets to 7 octets. An ASN.1 guru might define an address as follows:

```
HostAddress ::= CHOICE {
    ip_address[0]    IMPLICIT OCTET STRING,
    clnp_address[1]  IMPLICIT OCTET STRING,
    ipx_address[2]   IMPLICIT OCTET STRING,
    ...}
```

That definition produces only two bytes of overhead for an address (provided that the world doesn't invent more than 64 types of address), since it expands into a type (the number in square brackets), followed by a length, followed by the address.

Because ASN.1 is ugly to look at, and since the actual byte-expansion is pretty much irrelevant to any reader of this book, when we describe message formats and data structures in Kerberos V5 we'll just list the contents without being specific about the exact encoding.

In Kerberos V4, the B BIT in all the messages specifies the byte order of multibyte fields. In V5, fields are described using ASN.1 syntax, which defines a canonical format for integers. This is an example where use of ASN.1 hides the complexity of the protocol, since ASN.1 ensures a canonical format.

11.2 NAMES

In Kerberos V4, a principal is named by the three fields NAME, INSTANCE, and REALM, which must each be a null-terminated text string up to 40 characters long (including the null). The size of these fields is too short for some environments, and certain characters (like ".") are illegal inside Kerberos strings but required for account names on some systems. In V5, there are two components: the REALM and the NAME. The NAME component contains a type and a varying number of arbitrary strings, so the purpose served by the V4 INSTANCE field is accomplished by using an extra string in the NAME component. In V4, REALMs are DNS standard names, whereas in V5 they can be DNS standard names or X.500 names, and the syntax allows for other name types as well.

11.3 DELEGATION OF RIGHTS

Delegation of rights is the ability to give someone else access to things you are authorized to access. Usually delegation is limited in time (Alice allows Bob to access her resources only for a specified amount of time), or limited in scope (Alice only allows Bob to access a specified subset of her resources). Why would Alice want to let Bob use her resources? Alice might want to start up a batch job on some remote node Bob that will run in the middle of the night and need to access many of her files located around the network. Or Alice might be logged into host Bob but then want to log into host Farnest from Bob.

One way delegation could be provided is for Alice to send Bob her master key (in an encrypted message to Bob), allowing him to obtain tickets to whatever resources he might need on Alice's behalf. That is clearly not desirable, since it would allow Bob to forever be able to impersonate Alice. If she knew what resources Bob would need to access on her behalf, she could obtain tickets for those resources in advance and send Bob the tickets and keys (in an encrypted message to Bob). Or if she didn't know all the resources in advance, she could give Bob her TGT and session key, which he could use to obtain specific tickets on Alice's behalf as necessary. Not only are these mechanisms inconvenient and/or insecure and therefore undesirable, but they wouldn't work with Kerberos (either V4 or V5) because the ticket contains a network layer address, and Kerberos insists that a ticket must be used from the specified network layer address. In V4, the network layer address in the ticket is the address from which the ticket was requested.

Kerberos V5 explicitly allows delegation by allowing Alice to ask for a TGT with a network layer address different from hers. As a matter of fact it allows Alice to specify multiple addresses to include (in which case the ticket can be used from any of the specified addresses), or allows Alice to request that no address be included (in which case the ticket can be used from any address). Alice logs in as in Kerberos V4, getting a session key and a TGT with her own network layer address. When she later decides that she needs to allow Bob to act on her behalf, she requests a new TGT from the KDC, but this time specifically says that she'd like the network layer address in the TGT to be Bob's address. The new TGT so obtained is not useable by Alice directly, but can be passed to node Bob (along with the corresponding session key). It is a policy decision by the KDC as to whether to issue tickets with no specified address. It's also a policy decision by services on the network as to whether to accept such tickets.

Kerberos could have provided delegation by removing the network layer address from tickets and TGTs and instead having the network layer address in the authenticator. The Kerberos method has the disadvantage and advantage that Alice has to do an extra interaction with the KDC. It's a disadvantage for performance reasons. But it's an advantage because requiring Alice to do something that lets the KDC know she's delegating to Bob enables the KDC to audit delegation events. In the event of a security compromise, the audit trail will tell which nodes had access to which resources.

Sometimes Alice might know enough and be sufficiently security-conscious to specify the range of rights she wishes to delegate to Bob. Kerberos V5 supports two forms of limited delegation:

- Alice can give Bob tickets to the specific services he will need to access on her behalf (rather than giving him a TGT, which would allow him to request tickets to any services).

- When requesting a ticket or TGT that she intends to give to Bob, Alice can request that a field AUTHORIZATION-DATA be added to the ticket or TGT. The field is not interpreted by Kerberos, but is instead application-specific, which means it is left up to the application to define and use the field. The intention is that the field specifies to the application restrictions on what Bob is allowed to do with the ticket. If the field is in a TGT Alice gives to Bob, the field will be copied by the KDC into any ticket Bob gets using that TGT. OSF/DCE security (see §17.7 *DCE Security*) makes extensive use of this field.

Because there is not universal agreement that allowing delegation is always a good idea, Kerberos V5 makes it optional. A flag inside a TGT indicates whether a request for a TGT or ticket with a different network layer address should be allowed. The Kerberos protocol itself does not specify how the KDC should know how to set the various permission flags when creating an initial TGT. One method is the method the MIT implementation chose, which is to configure instructions for setting the permissions into the user's entry in the KDC database. Another possible way of deciding how to set various flags inside the TGT would be to ask the user Alice when she logs in, but that leaves the potential for a horrible user interface: Name_____   Password_____ Proxiable? (Y/N)__   Allow postdated? (Y/N)__   Forwardable? (Y/N)__   Renewable? (Y/N)__ Aisle/Window__   Smoking/Nonsmoking__   ....

There are two flags in a TGT involving delegation permission. One indicates that the TGT is **forwardable**, which means that it can be exchanged for a TGT with a different network layer address. This gives Alice permission to give Bob a TGT, with which Bob can request tickets to any resources on Alice's behalf. When Alice uses a forwardable TGT to request a TGT to be used from Bob's network layer address, she also specifies how the FORWARDABLE flag should be set in the requested TGT. If she requests that the TGT have the FORWARDABLE flag set, then Bob will be able to use that TGT to obtain a TGT for some other entity Carol, allowing Carol to act on Alice's behalf.

The other flag indicates that the TGT is **proxiable**, meaning that it can be used to request tickets for use with a different network layer address than the one in the TGT. This gives Alice permission to get tickets that she can give to Bob, but not a TGT for use by Bob. The Kerberos documentation refers to tickets Alice gives to Bob for use on her behalf as **proxy tickets**.

TGTs have a FORWARDED flag. Tickets have a FORWARDED flag and a PROXY flag. A TGT given to Bob by Alice is marked forwarded. The FORWARDED flag will also be set in any ticket Bob obtains using a TGT marked forwarded. A ticket given to Bob by Alice is marked proxy. The reason for marking tickets in this way is that some applications may want to refuse to honor delegated tickets, and need to recognize them as such. Note that allowing both the KDC and applications to make decisions on whether delegation is allowed makes for a flexible but confusing access control model.

11.4 TICKET LIFETIMES

In V4, the maximum lifetime of a ticket was about 21 hours, since the time in a ticket was encoded as a four-octet start time and a one-octet lifetime (in units of 5 minutes). This was too short for some applications. In Kerberos V5, tickets can be issued with virtually unlimited lifetimes (the farthest in the future that can be specified with a V5 timestamp is Dec 31, 9999). The timestamp format is an ASN.1-defined quantity that is 17 bytes long. Although it has a virtually unlimited lifetime (unlike the V4 timestamp), it is only in seconds, and Kerberos V5, in some cases, would have preferred time expressed down to microseconds. As a result, much of the time when Kerberos V5 passes around a timestamp it also passes around a microsecond time, which is an ASN.1 integer whose representation requires sufficiently many bytes to express the value (in this case one to three bytes, since 999999 is the biggest value), plus a type and length.

Long-lived tickets pose serious security risks, because once created they cannot be revoked (except perhaps by invalidating the master key of the service to which the ticket was granted). So V5 has a number of mechanisms for implementing revocable long-lived tickets.

These mechanisms involve use of several timestamp fields in tickets (and TGTs). Each timestamp is encoded, using glorious ASN.1 format, in 17 octets of information. First we'll give the names of the timestamps, and then we'll explain how they're used:

- START-TIME—time the ticket becomes valid.

- END-TIME—time the ticket expires.

- AUTHTIME—time at which Alice first logged in, i.e. when she was granted an initial TGT (one based on her password). AUTHTIME is copied from her initial TGT into each ticket she requests based on that TGT.

- RENEW-TILL—latest legal end-time (relevant for renewable tickets, see below).

11.4.1 Renewable Tickets

Rather than creating a ticket valid for say, 100 years, the KDC can give Alice a ticket that will be valid for 100 years, but only if she keeps renewing it, say once a day. Renewing a ticket involves giving the ticket to the KDC and having the KDC reissue it. If there is some reason to want to revoke Alice's privileges, this can be done by telling the KDC not to renew any of Alice's tickets.

The KDC is configured with a maximum validity time for a ticket, say a day. If there is a reason for Alice's ticket to be valid for longer than that time, then when Alice requests the ticket, the KDC sets the RENEWABLE flag inside the ticket. The RENEW-TILL time specifies the time beyond which the ticket cannot be renewed.

In order to keep using the ticket, Alice will have to keep renewing it before it expires. If she is ever late renewing it, the KDC will refuse to renew it. Why did Kerberos choose to do it that way? It seems somewhat inconvenient. Node Alice has to keep a demon running checking for tickets that will expire soon, and renew them. If Kerberos allowed renewal of expired tickets, then Alice could wait until she attempts to use a ticket and gets an error message indicating the ticket expired, and then renew it. This would be more convenient. The reasoning in Kerberos is that if Alice could present a ticket a long time after it expired, then if the KDC has been told to revoke the ticket it would have to remember the revoked ticket until that ticket's RENEW-TILL time. As it is, it just has to remember the revoked ticket for a maximum validity time.

The END-TIME specifies the time at which the ticket will expire (unless renewed). When Alice gives the KDC a renewable ticket and requests that it be renewed, the KDC does this by changing END-TIME to be the maximum ticket lifetime as configured into the user's entry in the KDC database, added to the current time (but not greater than RENEW-TILL).

11.4.2 Postdated Tickets

Postdated tickets are used to run a batch job at some time in the future. Suppose you want to issue a ticket starting a week from now and good for two hours. One possible method is to issue a ticket with an expiration time of one week plus two hours from the present time, but that would mean the ticket would be valid from the time it was issued until it expired. Kerberos instead allows a ticket to become valid at some point in the future. Kerberos does this by using the START-TIME timestamp, indicating when the ticket should first become valid. Such a ticket is known as a **postdated ticket**.

In order to allow revocation of the postdated ticket between the time it was issued and the time it becomes valid, there's an INVALID flag inside the ticket that Kerberos sets in the initially issued postdated ticket. When the time specified in START-TIME occurs, Alice can present the ticket to the KDC and the KDC will clear the INVALID flag. This additional step gives the opportunity to revoke the postdated ticket by warning the KDC. If the KDC is configured to revoke the postdated ticket, the validation request will fail.

There's an additional flag inside the ticket, the POSTDATED flag, which indicates that the ticket was originally issued as a postdated ticket. An application could in theory refuse to accept such a ticket, but none currently do and we can't imagine why any applications would care.

A flag, MAY-POSTDATE, which appears in a TGT, indicates whether the KDC is allowed to issue postdated tickets using this TGT.

11.5 KEY VERSIONS

If Alice holds a ticket to Bob and then Bob changes his key, Kerberos enables Alice's ticket to work until it expires by maintaining multiple versions of Bob's key, and tagging Bob's key with a version number where necessary for the KDC or for Bob to know which key to use.

In the KDC database, each version of Bob's key is stored as a triple: ⟨*key*, *p_kvno*, *k_kvno*⟩. *key* is Bob's key encrypted according to the KDC's key. *p_kvno* is the version number of this key of Bob's (*p_* stands for *principal*). *k_kvno* is the version number of the KDC's key that was used to encrypt *key*, since the KDC might also have changed its key recently (*k_* stands for *KDC*).

If Alice asks for a ticket to Bob, the KDC encrypts the ticket with the key for Bob with the highest *p_kvno*. In V4, the KDC did not keep track of more than one key for Bob. It was up to Bob to keep track of all his keys for a ticket expiration interval, in order for Bob to honor unexpired tickets issued with his old key. So why does the KDC need to keep track of multiple keys for Bob in V5? It is because of renewable tickets and postdated tickets. If Alice has a renewable ticket to Bob, and Bob changed his key since the ticket was originally issued, the KDC needs to be able to decrypt the ticket, so it needs to have stored the key with which that ticket was encrypted. When the KDC renews the ticket, it will issue the renewed ticket with the most recent key for Bob. That way the KDC and Bob can forget old key version numbers after a predictable, reasonably small time (like a day) (except for postdated tickets, which is somewhat of a design flaw in Kerberos).

11.6 MAKING MASTER KEYS IN DIFFERENT REALMS DIFFERENT

Suppose Alice is registered in different realms, and suppose Alice is human. Given that humans have a limited capacity for remembering passwords, Alice might wish to have a single password in all the realms in which she is registered. This means that if an intruder discovers her master key in one realm, he can impersonate her in the other realms as well.

In Kerberos V5, the password-to-key conversion hash function uses the realm name. This means that the function, given the same password, will come up with a different master key if the name of the realm is different. The function is such that it is not possible to derive the master key in realm FOO even if the master key derived from the same password in realm BAR is known.

This does not protect against an intruder who manages to obtain Alice's password. This just helps in the case where Alice has chosen a good password and an intruder manages to steal a KDC database from some realm. Stealing that database will allow the intruder to impersonate Alice in that realm, but not to impersonate Alice in any other realms for which she is using the same password. Note that stealing the database will also allow an intruder to mount an off-line password-guessing attack, and if the password-guessing attack succeeds, then the intruder *can* impersonate Alice in other realms for which she is using the same password.

11.7 OPTIMIZATIONS

There were certain fields in Kerberos V4 that were not necessary and were taken out in V5. In particular, encryption is expensive (especially when done in software), so it is undesirable to unnecessarily encrypt information. In Kerberos V4, a ticket is included in the CREDENTIALS portion of an AS_REP, and the entire CREDENTIALS field, including the ticket, is encrypted. A ticket is already an encrypted message. There is no reason to encrypt the ticket an additional time. (It had better not be necessary—tickets are later sent across the network unencrypted.)

An example of a field that was removed in Kerberos V5 because it was only slightly useful (if at all) was the name of the ticket target inside a ticket; that is, if Alice gets a ticket to Bob, then Bob's name is in the V4 ticket to Bob, but not in the V5 ticket.

11.8 CRYPTOGRAPHIC ALGORITHMS

Kerberos V4 assumes DES is the encryption algorithm. There are two problems with DES. One is that it is not secure enough for high-security environments. The other is that it is considered by the U.S. government to be too secure to export. Kerberos V5 is designed in a modular way which allows insertion of different encryption algorithms. When encryption is used, there is a type field allowing the receiver to know which decryption algorithm to use.

Since different encryption systems use different-length keys, and since some encryption systems allow variable-length keys, in V5 keys are tagged with a type and length.

DES continues to be used in all actual implementations of Kerberos (to our knowledge). Two cryptographic weaknesses in Kerberos V4 (modified Jueneman checksum, which was used for integrity protection without encryption, and PCBC, which was used for encryption and integrity protection) were repaired.

11.8.1 Integrity-Only Algorithms

The modified Jueneman checksum used in Kerberos V4, while never (publicly) broken, was not considered sufficiently secure (see §10.10 *Encryption for Integrity Only*). So in V5 it was replaced by a choice of algorithms.

Why did V5 not simply choose one known-to-be-secure integrity protection algorithm? No algorithm is ever known to be secure. It's just not known to be broken. So V5 selected a few algorithms, with the intent that if a serious cryptographic flaw was found in one of the algorithms being used, a different one could be substituted without changing the rest of the implementation. Unfortunately, if a recipient does not accept all defined algorithms, there is a possibility of non-interoperability (acceptable algorithms are not negotiated). Another problem with having a choice of algorithms is that Kerberos is really only as secure as the weakest algorithm the recipient will accept rather than the strongest. The reason for this is that if one algorithm is weak, then even if your implementation does not transmit it, a forger could use the weak algorithm to impersonate you to any implementation which accepts it.

If Kerberos V5 were designed today, the algorithms of choice would probably be DES-CBC and one or more of the MD algorithms computed on a concatenation of the secret key with the message. However, the idea of using MD(secret|message) as an integrity check wasn't well known at the time. Kerberos V5 does something probably equivalent in terms of security, but harder to explain. Much harder to explain, as a matter of fact. We agonized as to whether to bother you with the details. The algorithms are baroque and technically uninteresting. There never would be a reason to implement them except to be compatible with a Kerberos V5 implementation. But in the interest of completeness, we'll explain them here.

Kerberos V5 documentation refers to an integrity check as a *checksum*. We prefer the term MIC (message integrity code). The MICs specified in V5 are as follows, using the names in the Kerberos documentation. Three of them are required to be supported by implementations. The other two are optional.

- rsa-md5-des (required)

- des-mac (required)

- des-mac-k (required)

- rsa-md4-des (optional)

- rsa-md4-des-k (optional)

11.8.1.1 rsa-md5-des

This MIC is one of the required ones. The name is not particularly helpful, except that it's a combination of md5 and des. It has nothing to do with RSA other than that RSADSI (the company) owns rights to MD5, which is freely distributable provided that RSADSI is credited with every mention of it (or some such legalism).

The way the MIC is calculated is as follows:

1. Choose a 64-bit random number, known as a **confounder**

2. Prepend it to the message:

confounder	*message*

3. Calculate the MD5 message digest of the result, getting a 128-bit quantity.

4. Prepend the confounder chosen in Step 1 to the message digest:

64 bits	128 bits
confounder	*message digest*

5. Calculate a modified key by taking the KDC-supplied shared secret key and ⊕ing it with $F0F0F0F0F0F0F0F0_{16}$. Call the result K'.

6. Encrypt the result, using DES in CBC mode, using K' and an IV (initialization vector) of 0, resulting in a 192-bit encrypted quantity. That 192-bit quantity is the MIC.

How is this MIC verified? It's actually quite straightforward. You just reverse all the steps.

1. Calculate the modified key, by performing Step 5 above (⊕ing the KDC-supplied shared secret key with $F0F0F0F0F0F0F0F0_{16}$ to get K').

2. Decrypt the MIC, using K' in CBC mode, resulting in a 192-bit quantity. Let's call the first 64 bits of the decrypted quantity X, and the remainder Y.

64 bits	128 bits
X	Y

3. The first 64 bits of the result (X) should be the confounder. To verify that, append X to the message, and calculate the MD5 message digest of the result.

X	*message*

4. If the 128-bit result matches Y, then the MIC is verified as valid.

11.8.1.2 des-mac

This is another of the required MICs. To calculate it do the following:

1. Choose a 64-bit random number, known as a **confounder**.

2. Prepend it to the message:

confounder	*message*

3. Calculate the DES CBC residue of the result (confounder prepended to the message) using the unmodified KDC-supplied shared secret key K, and using an IV of 0. The result is a 64-bit quantity we'll call R, for the *Residue*.

4. Calculate the modified key $K' = K \oplus F0F0F0F0F0F0F0F0_{16}$.

5. Prepend the 64-bit confounder C to the 64-bit residue R, getting a 128-bit value.

6. Perform DES encryption in CBC mode on the 128-bit $C|R$ from the previous step, using K' as the key, and an IV of 0.

7. The result is the 128-bit MIC.

Verifying this MIC is straightforward (see Homework Problem 9).

11.8.1.3 des-mac-k

This is another of the MICs which are required. The MICs that end with "-k" in their name are the old-style ones, before it occurred to the Kerberos designers that using a modified key would be a good idea. These are no longer recommended, but need to be implemented for backward compatibility.

This MIC is calculated by doing a CBC-residue over the message using the original key K, and using K also as the IV. The MIC is verified the same way.

11.8.1.4 rsa-md4-des

This MIC is the same as rsa-md5-des, except that MD4 is used instead of MD5.

11.8.1.5 rsa-md4-des-k

This MIC is no longer recommended, and is only there for backward compatibility. Again, the "-k" in the name indicates that it was designed before the Kerberos designers realized it would be a good idea to use a modified version of the key for calculating the MIC.

This MIC is calculated as follows. First calculate MD4 of the message, yielding 128 bits (16 octets). Take the result and encrypt it using DES in CBC mode, with the unmodified session key K used as both the encryption key and the IV. The 128-bit result of the encryption is the MIC.

11.8.2 Encryption for Privacy and Integrity

The algorithms in this section provide encryption and integrity protection. The idea is to have an algorithm that not only encrypts the data, but allows Kerberos, when decrypting it, to detect if the message has been altered since being transmitted by the source.

The three algorithms are known in the Kerberos documentation as **des-cbc-crc**, **des-cbc-md4**, and **des-cbc-md5**. The basic idea is that a checksum is combined with the message, and then the message is encrypted with DES in CBC mode. The algorithms use the checksums CRC-32, MD4, and MD5, respectively. All the algorithms do the following:

1. Choose a 64-bit random number known in the Kerberos documentation as a **confounder**.

2. Create the following data structure, where the field CHECKSUM is filled with zeroes and is of the right length for the checksum algorithm of choice (32 bits for **des-cbc-crc** and 128 bits for the others):

confounder	*checksum*	*message*

3. Calculate the appropriate checksum over the above data structure.

4. Fill in the result in the CHECKSUM field

5. Add enough padding to make the data structure an integral number of 64-bit chunks:

confounder	*checksum*	*message*	*padding*

6. Encrypt the result using DES in CBC mode with an IV of 0.

11.9 HIERARCHY OF REALMS

In Kerberos V4, in order for principals in realm A to be authenticated by principals in realm B it was necessary for B's KDC to be registered as a principal in A's KDC. For full connectivity, this means that if there are n realms, the KDC in each realm has to be registered as a principal in each of the other $n-1$ realms. This is increasingly nightmarish as n gets large (see §7.7.4.1 *Multiple KDC Domains*).

In Kerberos V5, it is allowable to go through a series of realms in order to authenticate. For instance, a principal in realm A might wish to be authenticated by a principal in realm C. However, realm C might not be registered in A. But perhaps realm B is registered in A, and realm C is registered in *B*. A principal in *A* can get a ticket for something in *C* by first getting a ticket for *B*, and then asking *B* for a ticket to the KDC in *C*.

By allowing realm *B* to act as intermediary between realm *C* and other realms, we give the KDC at *B* the power to impersonate anyone in the world. Kerberos fixes this vulnerability somewhat by including in tickets a TRANSITED field which lists the names of all the realms that have been transited to obtain the ticket.

Why is the TRANSITED field useful? Suppose Woodward@Washington-Post.Com is contacted with a ticket that indicates the ticket was issued to the principal named Deep-Throat@WhiteHouse.gov, with the TRANSITED field indicating KGB.Russia. It is possible that Woodward should not assume the party using the ticket is really Mr. or Ms. Throat, since it would be in the interest of and the ability of the owner of the KGB realm's KDC to create a ticket that claims the source is anything. The KGB KDC can give such a ticket, along with the corresponding session key, to a confederate. Or the KDC can use the ticket and session key to impersonate the named source directly.

The only thing the KGB KDC cannot do is avoid being named inside the ticket, since a KDC will reject a ticket if the final entry in the TRANSITED field doesn't match the key with which the ticket is encrypted. If Alice gives Bob a ticket, Bob knows which KDC issued the ticket (it's the one with which he shares the key used to encrypt the ticket). But for all the other information in the ticket (like Alice's name and the other realms mentioned in the TRANSITED field), Bob has to trust the KDC which issued the ticket. And although the KDC which issued the ticket to Bob might be trustworthy, if there's any KDC in the path that isn't, all the earlier realms mentioned in the TRANSITED field and the original principal's name (Alice) are suspect.

The TRANSITED field in the ticket gives enough information for Bob (the service being accessed with the ticket) to know whether there are any realms on the path that Bob considers untrustworthy. A realm might be considered completely untrustworthy as a transit realm, but trustworthy when it claims to be acting on behalf of principals in its own realm. Each principal will have its own policy for which realms to trust.

You could say that by doing this, Kerberos is permitting maximum flexibility in possible policies. Or you could say that Kerberos is abdicating responsibility for this crucial decision by throwing it to the whim of application developers who will almost certainly get it wrong.

Either way, some sort of policy is necessary. One such policy—and a likely one at that—is to arrange realms into a tree such that each realm shares a key with each of its children and with its parent. The set of realms trusted for any authentication is the shortest path through the tree, i.e., the

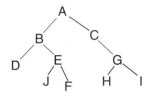

path that gets no closer to the root than the common ancestor lowest in the tree.

For example, in the above diagram, realm G shares a key with its parent realm (C) and each of its children (H and I). To get from realm I to realm H, you'd go through G. To get from realm F to realm D, you'd go through the lowest common ancestor (B), and to get there you'd have to go through E, so the path would be F–E–B–D.

It's especially convenient if the path of realms can be identified solely on the basis of the syntax of names. If realm names were just unstructured strings, it would be difficult to find a path. Luckily realm names in all current implementations of Kerberos are hierarchical, since they follow either internet or X.500 naming. For instance, assume Cat@Hat.Com wishes to access Dennis@Menace.Com. Cat@Hat.Com resides in realm Hat.Com. Dennis@Menace.Com resides in Menace.Com. The next level of hierarchy is simply called Com. If we create a realm named Com that shares a key with all realms with names of the form x.Com, it can then serve as an authentication intermediary. In general, to get from one realm to another, one travels upward to a common ancestor, and then downward to the destination realm.

It is likely that some administrative entity exists which would be a likely CA operator for the Com realm, because some such entity must ensure that there are no name collisions in the .Com space.

Sometimes it might be desirable to shortcut the hierarchy. This might be for efficiency reasons (so authentication between two realms distant in the naming hierarchy does not need to be done via a long sequence of KDCs), or for trust reasons (there might be KDCs along the naming hierarchy path that the two realms would prefer not to have to trust).

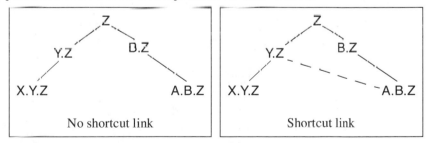

It is possible to have links between KDCs that wouldn't ordinarily be linked based on the naming hierarchy. Such links are usually called **cross links**. A safe rule with cross links is that when traversing the naming hierarchy to get to the target, cross links should always be used if they make the path shorter, because it means fewer KDCs need to be trusted.

There are two issues with realm paths. One is how the initiator finds a realm path to the target. As we've shown, if names are hierarchical and the path of realms follows the same hierarchy, with the possible addition of cross links, it is easy to find a path. The other issue is how the target decides whether the realm path used was acceptable. As we said, Kerberos leaves it up to the application.

The TRANSITED field lists the sequence of transited realms, omitting the source and destination realms. Realm names are listed separated by commas. Since the list of realms might get large, Kerberos permits various abbreviations. If the realm list is empty, no realms were transited. But if the realm list consists of a single comma, it means that the hierarchy of realms was transited in the normal way (parent to parent from the source up to the first common ancestor, then child to child down to the destination). Two consecutive commas in a list (or a leading or trailing comma) indicate that the hierarchy was transited in the normal way between the two realms surrounding the comma pair (or between source realm and first-listed realm, or between last-listed realm and destination realm). There are other abbreviation rules as well.

11.10 EVADING PASSWORD-GUESSING ATTACKS

With Kerberos V4, there is no authentication of the request to the KDC for a TGT. Anyone can send a cleartext message to the KDC requesting a TGT for user Pope@Vatican.Com, and the KDC will send back a ticket, encrypted according to Pope's master key. Since the function that maps a password string to a DES key is publicly known, an intruder can use the encrypted credentials for an off-line password-guessing attack to find Pope's password.

To avoid this attack, a mechanism has been added to Kerberos V5 in which information known as PREAUTHENTICATION-DATA can be sent along with the request for a TGT for user Pope which proves that the requester knew user Pope's master key. The preauthentication data consists of a current timestamp encrypted with user Pope's master key.

There's another opportunity for password guessing. Although the preauthentication data forces Alice to prove she knows user Pope's master key before she can obtain a TGT for Pope, she can use her own TGT or master key to ask for a ticket to the principal named Pope. She'll get back a quantity (the ticket to user Pope encrypted according to Pope's master key) which she can use for an off-line password-guessing attack to find Pope's password. Kerberos prevents this attack by marking database entries for human users (such as Pope), with a flag indicating that the KDC should not issue a ticket to this principal. This prevents someone from obtaining a ticket for something whose master key is derived from a password (and therefore vulnerable to password guessing). If, in the future, Kerberos is used for an application where it might make sense to create a ticket to a human user (for instance, electronic mail), then some other mechanism would need to be devised to prevent Trudy from guessing passwords based on tickets she requests (see Homework Problem 5).

This does not avoid password-guessing attacks completely. Someone can still guess passwords by constructing a request to the KDC for each password guess, and eventually one will be accepted. If passwords are even moderately well chosen, however, this is likely to be a very time-consuming task. Furthermore, a KDC could include code to record the frequency of wrong password guesses and lock the target account and/or alert an administrator should a threshold be exceeded. A more important attack is that an eavesdropper who sees the initial Kerberos login exchange can perform an off-line password guessing attack using either the preauthentication data provided by the user or the TGT sent in response.

11.11 KEY INSIDE AUTHENTICATOR

Suppose Alice wants to have two separate conversations with Bob. If she uses the same key (the Alice-Bob session key chosen by the KDC) for both conversations, then theoretically an intruder could swap the data from one conversation with the other, and confuse Alice and Bob. Alice could get two tickets for Bob, but instead, Kerberos allows Alice to choose a different key for a particular conversation and put that into the authenticator. If the authenticator has a session key that Alice inserted, Bob will use the Alice-Bob session key to decrypt the authenticator, but will use the session key Alice put into the authenticator in that conversation with Alice.

11.12 DOUBLE TGT AUTHENTICATION

Suppose Alice needs to access service Bob, but Bob does not know his master key. We'll assume Bob used his master key to obtain a TGT and session key, and then forgot his master key. Usually, if Alice asks for a ticket to Bob, the KDC will give her a ticket encrypted with Bob's master key. But Bob will not be able to decrypt the ticket, since Bob no longer knows his master key. If Bob is a user at a workstation, the workstation could at this point prompt Bob to type in his password again, but this would be inconvenient for the user.

Kerberos assumes Alice knows that Bob is the type of thing who is unlikely to know his own master key. In a method unspecified in Kerberos, Alice is supposed to ask Bob for his TGT. Alice then sends Bob's TGT as well as her own TGT to the KDC. (Hence the name **double TGT authentication**). Since Bob's TGT is encrypted under a key that is private to the KDC, the KDC can decrypt it. It then issues a ticket to Bob for Alice which is encrypted with Bob's session key rather than Bob's master key.

The application which inspired this bit of the design was XWINDOWS. XWINDOWS clients and servers are backwards from what one might have guessed. The XWINDOWS server is the process that controls the user's screen. XWINDOWS clients are applications that make requests to the server to open windows and display information. While the user of an XWINDOWS terminal may need to authenticate himself to some remote application in order to start it, that application must authenticate itself to the XWINDOWS server to get permission to display its output. The human, Bob, logs into a workstation. The workstation then gets a TGT and session key on behalf of Bob and then promptly forgets Bob's master key. The application which is writing onto Bob's workstation must authenticate itself to the workstation. Since the workstation has no credentials other than Bob's TGT and session key, only a double TGT authentication as described above can work.

11.13 KDC DATABASE

Each entry in the V5 KDC database contains the following information. The structure of the database is somewhat implementation-specific, but since all current implementations are derived from the MIT implementation, we describe the MIT implementation.

* *name*—name of principal

* *key*—principal's master key

* *p_kvno*—principal's key version number. If this principal has k different valid keys, there will be k database entries for this principal. This could have been done more compactly by allowing multiple ⟨*key, p_kvno, k_kvno*⟩ entries per database.

* *max_life*—maximum lifetime for tickets issued to this principal

* *max_renewable_life*—maximum total lifetime for renewable tickets to this principal

* *k_kvno*—KDC key version under which *key* is encrypted

* *expiration*—time when this database entry expires

* *mod_date*—time of last modification to this entry

* *mod_name*—name of the principal who made the last modification to this entry

- flags indicating the KDC's policy on various things; for instance, whether to require pre-authentication data, whether to allow certain types of tickets such as forwardable, renewable, proxiable, postdated, and so on

- *password expiration*—time when password expires. This is used to force the user to change passwords occasionally.

- *last_pwd_change*—time when user last changed password

- *last_success*—time of last successful user login (i.e., last AS_REQ with correct preauthentication data)

11.14 KERBEROS V5 MESSAGES

Given that the Kerberos V5 messages are defined in ASN.1 notation, it isn't useful to show exact message formats. We will instead just list the information in each of the messages.

11.14.1 Authenticator

The authenticator is not a free-standing message, but rather is contained in a TGS_REQ or an AP_REQ. The entire thing is encrypted, using the key in the ticket that always accompanies an authenticator. Assume the authenticator is being sent in a message transmitted by Alice. When decrypted, the authenticator contains the following fields:

AUTHENTICATOR-VNO	version number (5)
CNAME, CREALM	Alice's name and realm
CKSUM	(optional) checksum of application data that might have been sent along with the AP_REQ
CTIME, CUSEC	time at Alice (in seconds, microseconds)
SUBKEY	(optional) key Alice would like to use instead of the key in the ticket, for the conversation with Bob
SEQ-NUMBER	initial sequence number that Alice will use in her KRB_SAFE and KRB_PROT messages to Bob
AUTHORIZATION-DATA	application-specific data limiting Alice's rights

11.14.2 Ticket

A ticket is not a free-standing message, but is rather carried in messages such as TGS_REQ, AS_REP, TGS_REP, AP_REQ, and KRB_CRED. A ticket given to Alice for use with Bob looks like this:

MSG-TYPE	message type (1)
TKT-VNO	protocol version number (5)
REALM, SNAME	Bob's name and realm
The remainder of the fields are encrypted with Bob's master key (unless this ticket was obtained using Bob's TGT as in §11.12 *Double TGT Authentication*).	
FLAGS	FORWARDABLE, FORWARDED, PROXIABLE, PROXY, MAY-POST-DATE, POSTDATED, INVALID, RENEWABLE, INITIAL (ticket was issued using AS_REQ rather than TGS_REQ) PRE-AUTHENT (user authenticated himself to the KDC before the ticket was issued) HW-AUTHENT (user was authenticated before ticket issued, using something like a smart card)
KEY	key to be used when communicating with Alice
CNAME, CREALM	Alice's name and realm
TRANSITED	Names of realms transited between Alice's realm and Bob's realm
AUTH-TIME, START-TIME, END-TIME, RENEW-TILL	timestamps. START-TIME and RENEW-TILL are optional. Described in §11.4 *Ticket Lifetimes*.
CADDR	(optional) the set of addresses from which this ticket will be valid
AUTHORIZATION-DATA	application-specific data limiting Alice's rights

11.14.3 AS_REQ

An AS_REQ is used to request a TGT. It can also be used to ask for regular tickets, but tickets requested with an AS_REQ (as opposed to a TGS_REQ) will return credentials encrypted with the requester's master key. The TGS_REQ contains a TGT, and the credentials returned in response to a TGS_REQ are encrypted according to the session key in the TGT. Let's assume that the request is on behalf of Alice in Wonderland. Let's assume she's asking for either a TGT or a ticket to Bob.

MSG-TYPE	message type (10)
PVNO	protocol version number (5)
PADATA	(optional) preauthentication data—timestamp encrypted with Alice's master key
KDC-OPTIONS	flags—each flag indicates a request to set the corresponding flag in the ticket the KDC will return (see below)
CNAME	Alice's name (the "c" comes from "client")
SNAME	Bob's name (or the name krbtgt if the request is for a TGT)
REALM	realm in which both Alice and Bob reside
FROM	(postdated ticket) desired start-time
TILL	desired end-time, which is the expiration time in the ticket
RTIME	desired renew-till time (only in request for renewable ticket)
NONCE	number to be returned in the reply to prevent replay attacks (MIT implementation uses current timestamp as the nonce)
ETYPE	type of encryption Alice would like KDC to use when encrypting the credentials
ADDRESSES	network layer addresses to include in ticket—used in proxy or forwardable tickets, or when Alice has multiple network layer addresses

The flags that make sense in an **AS_REQ** are:

- FORWARDABLE—Please set the FORWARDABLE flag in the returned TGT (so that the TGT can later be sent back to the KDC to request a TGT with a different network layer address inside).

- PROXIABLE—Please set the PROXIABLE flag in the returned TGT (so that the TGT can be used to request a ticket with a different network layer address inside).

- ALLOW-POSTDATE—Please set the ALLOW-POSTDATE flag in the returned TGT (so that this TGT can be used to request postdated tickets).

- POSTDATED—Make the returned ticket or TGT postdated, using the START-TIME in the request. Note that the START-TIME is an optional field, and it probably would have been more elegant to merely assume, if the requester included a START-TIME, that the requester wanted the ticket to be a postdated ticket. But the way Kerberos is defined, if the requester includes a START-TIME and does not set the postdated flag, then the START-TIME is ignored and an ordinary, nonpostdated ticket is returned.

- RENEWABLE—Please set the RENEWABLE flag in the returned ticket or TGT.

- RENEWABLE-OK—The requester wants a ticket with a long lifetime. If the KDC is not willing to issue a ticket with that long a lifetime, the requester is willing to settle for a renewable ticket with an initial expiration time as far in the future as the KDC is willing to issue and renewable until the requested expiration time.

11.14.4 TGS_REQ

A TGS_REQ is used to request either a TGT or a ticket.

MSG-TYPE	message type (12)
PVNO	protocol version number (5)
PADATA	ticket and authenticator
KDC-OPTIONS	flags from AS_REQ, plus a few more explained above
SNAME	(or the name krbtgt if the request is for a TGT)
REALM	realm in which Bob resides (Alice might reside in a differerent realm in the case of a TGS_REQ)
FROM	(postdated ticket) desired start-time
TILL	desired end-time, which is the expiration time in the ticket
RTIME	desired renew-till time (only in request for renewable ticket)
NONCE	number to be returned in the reply to prevent replay attacks (MIT implementation uses current timestamp as the nonce)
ETYPE	type of encryption Alice would like KDC to use when encrypting the credentials
ADDRESSES	network layer addresses to include in ticket—used in proxy or forwardable tickets, or when Alice has multiple network layer addresses
AUTHORIZATION-DATA	application specific data to be copied into TGT and tickets requested using that TGT, intended to convey restrictions on use. Note that this field is encrypted and integrity-protected.
ADDITIONAL-TICKETS	Bob's TGT in the case where Bob does not know his master key (see §11.12 *Double TGT Authentication*)

The differences between a TGS_REQ and an AS_REQ are:

- The TGS_REQ contains a TGT or a renewable or postdated ticket (the AS_REQ does not).

- The TGS_REQ includes an authenticator in its PADATA field, proving the requester knows the key contained in the TGT or ticket in the request. The AS_REQ contains an encrypted timestamp in its optional PADATA field, proving the requester knows Alice's master key.

- The reply to a TGS_REQ is usually encrypted with the key inside the TGT or ticket enclosed with the request. However, if the authenticator contains a different key (called a subkey), the reply is encrypted with the subkey inside the authenticator. In contrast, the reply to an **AS_REQ** is always encrypted with the requester's master key.

- There are more flags that might be relevant in a **TGS_REQ**. All the flags applicable to an **AS_REQ** are applicable to a **TGS_REQ**. In addition, the following flags are applicable in a **TGS_REQ**:

  - FORWARDED—A list of addresses appears in the request which is different than the list of addresses (if any) that appears in the ticket. The list in the request should be included in the returned ticket, and the FORWARDED flag should be set in the returned ticket.

  - PROXY—Same as FORWARDED, except this flag is used when requesting a TGT.

  - ENC-TKT-IN-SKEY—Included in this request is Bob's TGT (see §11.12 *Double TGT Authentication*).

  - RENEW—Please renew the enclosed ticket.

  - VALIDATE—Please validate the enclosed postdated ticket.

- The **AS_REQ** contains the field CNAME, which does not appear in a **TGS_REQ**. It is not needed in the **TGS_REQ** because the KDC obtains the name of the requester from inside the ticket or TGT enclosed with the **TGS_REQ**.

- The **TGS_REQ** contains the field AUTHORIZATION-DATA, and the **AS_REQ** does not. This field is supposed to be copied from the request into the ticket or TGT returned with the reply. It's actually somewhat of a nuisance that Kerberos does not allow this field in an **AS_REQ**. If you want a TGT or ticket with AUTHORIZATION-DATA, then you have to first obtain a TGT without that field, and then use that TGT in a **TGS_REQ** to request a TGT with AUTHORIZATION-DATA. Note that in order to prevent an intruder from modifying AUTHORIZATION-DATA in the request on its way to the KDC, the field is encrypted and integrity protected with the key in the enclosed ticket or TGT, or if a subkey is present in the authenticator, then it's encrypted with that subkey. Note that AUTHORIZATION-DATA is treated differently than the other fields in the request, such as Bob's name, which are sent unencrypted and without integrity protection. Alice knows those other fields arrived intact because they are encrypted and integrity-protected when the KDC returns the credentials to Alice.

- The **TGS_REQ** also contains the field ADDITIONAL-TICKETS, which if ENC-TKT-IN-SKEY is set in the KDC-OPTIONS field in the **TGS_REQ**, contains Bob's TGT.

11.14.5 AS_REP

An AS_REP is the reply from the KDC to an AS_REQ. It returns a TGT or ticket.

MSG-TYPE	message type (11)
PVNO	protocol version number (5)
PADATA	(optional) salt to combine with the user's password in order to compute the master key derived from the user's password (see below)
CREALM	Alice's realm
CNAME	Alice's name. The purpose of Alice's name and realm is to help Alice's workstation figure out what key to use to decrypt the encrypted data.
TICKET	the ticket to Bob that Alice requested
ENC-PART	encrypted portion (see below)

In practice, PADATA is absent, indicating that the salt to be used is the user's name and realm. If a different salt is specified, it is not possible to transmit PADATA in the AS_REQ, because the user's master key would not be known.

Kerberos does provide mechanisms for recovery in case Alice's workstation does not know the proper value of salt. One plausible reason why Alice's workstation would not know the salt is that the realm name has changed since Alice last set her password. If the workstation has the wrong salt value, it will supply an incorrect value for PADATA in the request, and the KDC will return an error message. The error message returned by the KDC contains the proper salt value, and then Alice's workstation can try again, this time knowing the proper salt value.

The ENC-PART is encrypted with Alice's master key. When decrypted, it contains the following fields:

KEY	encryption key associated with the ticket enclosed in the AS_REP
LAST-REQ	a sequence of from 0 to 5 timestamps specifying such information as when Alice last requested a TGT, or last requested any ticket. The specification is vague about how these times are supposed to be synchronized across KDC replicas. Indeed, the MIT implementation (as of the writing of this book) does not implement any of these, and always returns no timestamps in this field.
NONCE	The nonce copied from the AS_REQ
KEY-EXPIRATION	(optional) time when user's master key will expire for the purpose of warning Alice to change her password
FLAGS	a copy of the flags that appear inside the ticket (so that Alice can check if the KDC granted all she requested in the request, and also allows her to detect malicious modification that might have been done to the AS_REQ)

AUTH-TIME, START-TIME, END-TIME, RENEW-TILL	timestamps; START-TIME and RENEW-TILL are optional (see §11.4 *Ticket Lifetimes*)
SREALM, SNAME	Bob's name and realm
CADDR	(optional) the set of addresses from which this ticket will be valid

11.14.6 TGS_REP

A TGS_REP is the reply from the KDC to a TGS_REQ. It is virtually identical to an AS_REP. The differences are:

- There is never a PADATA field in a TGS_REP, whereas it is optional in an AS_REP. (The PADATA field in an AS_REP contains the salt.)

- There is no KEY-EXPIRATION field in a TGS_REP, whereas it is optional in an AS_REP.

- The ENC-PART field is encrypted with the key in the TGT or ticket sent in the TGS_REQ; or if a subkey is included in the authenticator sent in the TGS_REQ, then the ENC-PART is encrypted with that subkey.

11.14.7 AP_REQ

An AP_REQ is the first message when Alice, who has obtained a ticket to Bob, actually attempts to communicate with Bob.

MSG-TYPE	message type (14)
PVNO	protocol version number (5)
AP-OPTIONS	flags, of which two are defined. USE-SESSION-KEY, which means the ticket is encrypted under the session key in Bob's TGT (rather than Bob's master key—see §11.12 *Double TGT Authentication*) MUTUAL-REQUIRED, which tells Bob mutual authentication is requested
TICKET	the ticket to Bob
AUTHENTICATOR	an authenticator, proving Alice knows the key inside the ticket

11.14.8 AP_REP

An **AP_REP** is Bob's reply to an **AP_REQ** from Alice.

MSG-TYPE	message type (15)
PVNO	protocol version number (5)
the rest is encrypted:	
CTIME	the time copied from the CTIME field of the authenticator in the **AP_REQ**
CUSEC	the low order bits of CTIME, since CTIME is expressed in seconds; this field specifies microseconds
SUBKEY	an optional field intended for Bob to be able to influence the Alice-Bob session key in an application-specific way
SEQ-NUMBER	starting sequence number for messages sent from Bob to Alice

The encrypted section (CTIME through SEQ-NUMBER) is encrypted with the key inside the ticket from the **AP_REQ**, unless a SUBKEY field is included in the AUTHENTICATOR from the **AP_REQ**, in which case it is encrypted with the subkey.

11.14.9 KRB_SAFE

A **KRB_SAFE** message transfers data between Alice and Bob with integrity protection.

MSG-TYPE	message type (20)
PVNO	protocol version number (5)
USER-DATA	whatever the application wants to send
TIMESTAMP	(optional) current time in seconds at the originator of the message, so the recipient can put messages in order, and can make sure the timestamp is within acceptable clock skew
USEC	(optional) the low-order bits (the microsecond portion) of the time, since TIMESTAMP is in seconds
SEQ-NUMBER	(optional) sequence number of this message, so the recipient can detect lost messages and put messages in order
S-ADDRESS	the network address of the sender of the message (the same address is presumably in the network layer header, but here it is cryptographically protected)
R-ADDRESS	the recipient's network address. Again, presumably it is equal to the destination address in the network layer header, but here it is cryptographically protected.
CKSUM	checksum on the fields USER-DATA through R-ADDRESS, using one of the checksum types defined in §11.8.1 *Integrity-Only Algorithms*

11.14.10 KRB_PRIV

A KRB_PRIV message is encrypted (and integrity-protected) data sent between Alice and Bob. It is encrypted with the key arranged for this conversation.

MSG-TYPE	message type (21)
PVNO	protocol version number (5)
the rest is encrypted:	
USER-DATA	whatever the applications wants to send
TIMESTAMP	(optional) current time in seconds at the originator of the message, so the recipient can put messages in order, and make sure the timestamp is within acceptable clock skew
USEC	(optional) the low order bits (the microsecond portion) of the time, since TIMESTAMP is in seconds
SEQ-NUMBER	(optional) sequence number of this message, so the recipient can detect lost messages and put messages in order
S-ADDRESS	the network address of the sender of the message (the same address is presumably in the network layer header, but here it is cryptographically protected)
R-ADDRESS	the recipient's network address. Again, presumably it is equal to the destination address in the network layer header, but here it is cryptographically protected.

11.14.11 KRB_CRED

A KRB_CRED message is used for passing credentials (a ticket and session key) for the purpose of delegation (see §11.3 *Delegation of Rights*). Assume Alice would like to delegate to Ted her right to access Bob. Alice would send Ted a KRB_CRED message containing a ticket to Bob, along with the session key corresponding to Bob's ticket. The encrypted portion of the KRB_CRED message is encrypted using a key that has been established between Alice and Ted, so the assumption is that Alice has already initiated a Kerberos protected conversation to Ted, and they now share a key.

MSG-TYPE	message type (22)
PVNO	protocol version number (5)
TICKETS	a sequence of tickets
	the rest is encrypted with the Alice-Ted conversation key:
TICKET-INFO	information corresponding to each ticket in TICKETS field, see below
NONCE	(optional) a number supplied by Carol to Alice, which Alice puts into the KRB_CRED message, when delegating to Carol, to reassure Carol that the KRB_CRED is not a replay transmitted by an intruder, and is indeed recently transmitted by Alice
TIMESTAMP	(optional) current time in seconds at the originator of the message, so the recipient can put messages in order, and make sure the timestamp is within acceptable clock skew
USEC	(optional) the low order bits (the microsecond portion) of the time, since TIMESTAMP is in seconds
S-ADDRESS	the network address of the sender of the message (the same address is presumably in the network layer header, but here it is cryptographically protected)
R-ADDRESS	the recipient's network address. Again, presumably it is equal to the destination address in the network layer header, but here it is cryptographically protected.

The TICKET-INFO field is a sequence of one or more repetitions of the following information:

KEY	encryption key associated with the corresponding ticket enclosed in the KRB_CRED
PREALM, PNAME	(optional) Alice's name and realm
FLAGS	(optional) a copy of the flags that appear inside the ticket
AUTH-TIME, START-TIME, END-TIME, RENEW-TILL	(optional) timestamps
SREALM, SNAME	(optional) Bob's name and realm
CADDR	(optional) the set of addresses from which this ticket will be valid

11.14.12 KRB_ERROR

In Kerberos V4 there were two types of error messages, one that would be returned by the KDC, the other returned by an application when authentication failed. In Kerberos V5 there is only one error message defined, and it is used for both purposes. None of the information in the error message is encrypted or integrity-protected. Let's assume that Alice has sent a message to Bob, and that Bob is returning the error message to Alice because of some problem with Alice's message.

MSG-TYPE	message type (30)
PVNO	protocol version number (5)
CTIME, CUSEC	(optional) CTIME and CUSEC fields copied from the message generated by Alice that caused the error
STIME, SUSEC	time at Bob when he generated the KRB_ERROR message
ERROR-CODE	the error code, indicating the type of error
CNAME, CREALM	(optional) Alice's name and realm
REALM, SNAME	Bob's realm and name
E-TEXT	additional information to help explain the error, in printable text.
E-DATA	additional information to help explain the error. Not guaranteed to be printable text.

Here are all the error codes. Error codes 1–30 come only from the KDC, in response to a AS_REQ or TGS_REQ. The others can come from either the KDC or an application, in response to an AP_REQ, KRB_PRIV, KRB_SAFE, or KRB_CRED.

code	reason
0	no error. (Really, it's in the documentation! I'm sure it's annoying to get an error message telling you that you *didn't* make an error but it's not going to do what you asked it to do anyway. In reality, this would never appear, and is probably listed in the documentation just to ensure nobody assigns error code 0 to a real error.)
1	Alice's entry in the KDC database has expired.
2	Bob's entry in the KDC database has expired.
3	The requested Kerberos version number is not supported.
4	The KDC has forgotten the key with which Alice's entry in its database was encrypted. (It was an old version number, and the KDC didn't save that key.)
5	The KDC has forgotten the key with which Bob's entry in its database was encrypted.
6	The KDC never heard of Alice.
7	The KDC never heard of Bob.
8	Either Bob or Alice appears in the KDC database multiple times. (Really, it would make more sense to check this when modifying the KDC database, or have a utility that checks this every once in awhile rather than checking this when requests are made.)
9	Either Bob or Alice's entry in the KDC does not contain a master key (see parenthetical remark for error 8).
10	Alice asked for a postdated ticket, but her TGT does not allow this.
11	The requested start time is later than the end time (maybe the KDC should just give Alice the useless ticket that she requested).

code	reason
12	KDC policy does not allow the request.
13	KDC cannot grant the requested option.
14	KDC doesn't support this encryption type.
15	KDC doesn't support this checksum type.
16	KDC does not support this type of PADATA.
17	KDC does not support the transited type. (The TRANSITED field has a type and a value. The type is one that the KDC does not understand.)
18	Alice's credentials have been revoked—the account is marked invalid in KDC, or Alice's TGT has been revoked.
19	Bob's credentials have been revoked.
20	TGT has been revoked.
21	Alice's entry is not yet valid—try again later.
22	Bob's entry is not yet valid—try again later.
23	Alice's password has expired.
31	Integrity check on decrypted field failed.
32	The ticket has expired.
33	The ticket is not yet valid.
34	The request is a replay.
35	This ticket isn't for us.
36	The ticket and authenticator don't match.
37	The clock skew is too great.
38	The network address in the network layer header doesn't match the network layer address inside the ticket.
39	The protocol version number doesn't match.
40	The message type is unsupported.
41	The checksum didn't check. (Yhe documentation describes this error as *message stream modified*, but we prefer not to place blame—there might be a perfectly innocent explanation.)
42	The message is out of order. In both encrypted and integrity-checked data, there is a sequence number. The network can certainly reorder messages, and such innocent reordering of messages should not generate an error. If the messages are being delivered with a reliable transport layer protocol, then this error would be generated because of some deliberate tampering with the message stream, which can be detected by Kerberos. If the messages are being delivered with a datagram service (like UDP), then since the sequence number is optional, it should not be used.
44	The specified version of the key is not available.
45	Bob doesn't know his key.

code	reason
46	Mutual authentication failed.
47	The message direction is incorrect. In V4 this was determined based on the D BIT. The D BIT no longer exists in V5, but instead, in integrity-protected and encrypted data, there is a SENDER'S ADDRESS and a RECEIVER'S ADDRESS field. If Bob receives a message from Alice and these fields are swapped, it indicates that an intruder is trying to trick them by mirroring messages back.
48	*alternative authentication method required.* For instance, Bob does not know his master key, but does have a TGT (see §11.12 *Double TGT Authentication*).
49	The sequence number in the message is incorrect.
50	*inappropriate type of checksum in message.* Presumably, this is because Bob doesn't support that checksum type. The wording in the documentation implies that Bob is making a value judgement on Alice's choice of checksum. For instance, if Alice were to choose CRC-32 as an integrity check instead of a message digest, Bob might sneeringly send this error message.
60	generic error. The description is in E-TEXT.
61	The field is too long for this implementation.

11.15 HOMEWORK

1. Suppose the Kerberos V5 password to key conversion function is identical to V4, but then takes the output that V4 would compute and ⊕s it with the realm name. This would produce a different key in each realm, as desired. What is wrong with this algorithm? (Hint: the reason it is good for your key to be different in different realms is so that if your key in one realm is known, it does not divulge your key in other realms.)

2. Consider the following variant of Kerberos. Instead of having postdated or renewable tickets, a server which notes that the start-time is older than some limit presents the ticket to the TGS and asks if it should believe the ticket. What are the tradeoffs of this approach relative to the Kerberos V5 approach?

3. The philosophy behind requiring renewable tickets to be renewed before they expire is that a KDC should not need to remember blacklist information indefinitely. But does that work for postdated tickets, given that a postdated ticket can be requested with a start-time arbitrarily far into the future?

4. Design a different method of Bob authenticating Alice when Bob does not remember his own master key, which places the work on Bob instead of Alice. In other words, Alice will act as

if Bob was an ordinary civilized thing that does remember its own master key, and Bob interacts appropriately with the KDC so that Alice will be unaware that Bob didn't know his own master key.

5. Suppose it was desired to use Kerberos for securing electronic mail. The obvious way of accomplishing this is for Alice, when sending a message to Bob, to obtain a ticket for Bob and include that in the email message, and encrypt and/or integrity-protect the email message using the key in the ticket. The problem with this is that then the KDC would give Alice a quantity encrypted with Bob's password-derived master key, and then Alice could do off-line password guessing. How might Kerberos be extended to email without allowing off-line password guessing? (Hint: issue human users an extra, unguessable master key for use with mail, and extend the Kerberos protocol to allow Bob to safely obtain his unguessable master key from the KDC.)

6. In the mutual authentication in the Needham/Schroeder protocol upon which Kerberos is based, the authenticator contained only an encrypted timestamp. The protocol is that Alice sends Bob the authenticator, and then Bob must decrypt the authenticator, add one to the value inside, re-encrypt it, and send it back to Alice. Why was it necessary for Bob to increment the value before re-encrypting it and sending it to Alice? Why isn't it necessary in Kerberos V5, in the **AP_REP** message? In Kerberos V4, it is the checksum field (which isn't really a checksum—see §10.10 *Encryption for Integrity Only*) that is extracted and incremented. Would it have been just as secure in V4 for Bob to send back the contents of the checksum field encrypted and not incremented?

7. In the **KRB_SAFE** message, there is both a timestamp and a sequence number. Presuming that both timestamp fields (TIMESTAMP and USEC) are sent, and that the application makes sure the timestamp increases on every message, does the sequence number provide any additional protection?

8. Prove that if there is a 64-bit value that works as a DES checksum, the value $\oplus$'d with $F0F0F0F0F0F0F0F0_{16}$ will also have a correct DES checksum.

9. Give the algorithm for verifying the MIC described in §11.8.1.2 *des-mac*.

PART 3

ELECTRONIC MAIL

12 ELECTRONIC MAIL SECURITY

This chapter gives an overview of the issues involved in making electronic mail secure. First we discuss non-security-related issues such as distribution lists and mail forwarders. Then we list various security features, and in the remainder of the chapter we describe how each of these features might be implemented. A lot of the techniques are equally applicable to encrypting or integrity-protecting any sort of data, such as files kept on a file server or data stored on backup media. In the following chapters we discuss three secure mail standards—PEM, PGP, and X.400.

12.1 DISTRIBUTION LISTS

Electronic mail allows a user to send a message to one or more recipients. The simplest form of electronic mail message is where Alice sends a message to Bob.

```
To: Bob
From: Alice

Care to meet me in my apartment tonight?
```

Usually, a mail system allows a message to be sent to multiple recipients, for example:

```
To: Bob, Carol, Ted
From: Alice

Care to meet me in my apartment tonight?
```

Sometimes it is impossible or inconvenient to list all recipients. For this reason, mail is often sent to a **distribution list**, a name that stands for a set of recipients. For instance, a message might be sent to Taxpayers. There are two ways of implementing distribution lists.

The first way involves sending the message to a site at which the list is maintained, and that site then sends a copy of the message to each recipient on the list. We'll call that the **remote exploder method**.

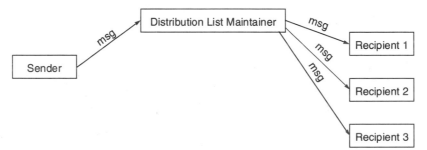

Figure 12-1. Remote Exploder

The second method is for the sender to retrieve the list from the site where it is kept, and then send a copy of the message to each recipient on the list. We'll call that the **local exploder method**.

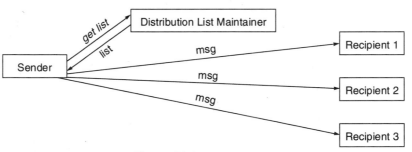

Figure 12-2. Local Exploder

Sometimes a member of a distribution list can be another distribution list. For instance, the mailing list Security Customers, used to advertise security products, might include law enforcers, bankers, Democratic National Committee, locksmiths, and members of organized crime. It is possible to construct a distribution list with an infinite loop. Suppose someone is maintaining a mailing list for cryptographers. Someone else is maintaining one for cryptanalysts. The cryptanalysts point out that they also want to hear the information sent to the cryptographers mailing list, so the distribution list Cryptanalysts is added to the Cryptographers mailing list. And for similar reasons Cryptographers is added to Cryptanalysts. The mail system must handle infinite loops in distribution lists in a reasonable manner, i.e. it must send each recipient at least one copy of each message but not an unreasonable number of copies of any. Loops like this effectively merge the mailing lists. (See Homework Problem 1.)

As we described above, there are two methods of implementing distribution lists. The advantages of the local exploder method are:

- It is easier to prevent mail forwarding loops.

- If there are multiple distribution lists, it is possible for the sender to prevent duplicate copies being sent to individuals on multiple lists.

- If the network billing is usage-based as opposed to flat-fee, it is easier for the sender to know in advance just how much bandwidth will be consumed to transmit the message.

There are several advantages to the remote exploder method:

- It allows you to send to a list whose membership you are not allowed to know. (*To U.S. spies living abroad from the IRS: friendly reminder—the tax deadline is April 15. Being caught or killed is not one of the grounds for automatic extension.*)

- If distribution lists are organized geographically, you need only send one copy of a message over an expensive link to a remote area. (*To Citizens of France from the U.S. government: Thanks for the big statue.*)

- When the distribution list is longer than the message, it is more efficient to send the message from the sender to the distribution list site than to send the distribution list to the sender. (*To people of planet earth: Greeting. Unless you stop transmitting reruns of the I Love Lucy show to us we will be forced to destroy your planet.*)

- When distribution lists are included on distribution lists, it would be time-consuming to track down the whole tree to get to all the individuals. Instead, the message can be making progress as it is sent to the various exploders. Parallelism is exploited.

12.2 STORE AND FORWARD

The simplest implementation of electronic mail consists of sending a message directly from the source machine to the destination machine. In order for a message to be successfully delivered under that scenario, it is necessary for both the source and destination machines to be running, and reachable from each other on the network. This might be especially inconvenient if the user machines are only occasionally connected to the network, for example a portable PC that dials into the network periodically. Thus came the concept of electronic post office boxes. Instead of sending mail directly to the user's workstation, the mail is instead sent to a machine which is more or less permanently on the network. When the user's workstation attaches to the network, it reads the mail from the appropriate mail storage machine.

In general, the **mail infrastructure** consists of a whole mesh of mail forwarders. X.400 calls them **Message Transfer Agent**s, or **MTA**s. The mail processing at the source and destination machines is done by a program known by X.400 as the **User Agent** or **UA**. Mail is not simply sent from the source machine to a mailbox machine for the destination. Instead, it gets forwarded from UA to MTA to … to MTA to UA.

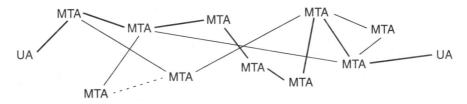

Figure 12-3. Mail Infrastructure Operation

Some reasons for needing multiple MTAs along a path from source to destination are:

- The path from source to destination might be intermittent. For instance, there might be portions of the network that are only occasionally connected, via some dial-up link.

- For security reasons, the MTAs might need to authenticate other MTAs as well as user machines. It might then be necessary to have a chain of MTAs to find a path from source to destination where each link is between a pair of MTAs that trust one another.

- For security reasons, a company might want a **security gateway**, a place through which all mail has to be forwarded. Usually the purpose of such a gateway is to prevent any access to the company's network except for mail. For instance, it would prevent people from logging in from a site external to the company's network.

- Different parts of the network might be using different protocol suites, for instance TCP/IP in some places and OSI in others.

There are interesting issues with how one supports routing with MTAs.

- How do MTAs find out about "neighbor" MTAs? This is usually done with manual configuration, though potentially they might be able to find each other in a directory service.

- How do MTAs compute a path to a destination, or at least find the next "closer" MTA? Again, this is usually done with manual configuration.

Good references for reading about electronic mail are [BIRR82, SCHR83, PISC93, PLAT91].

12.3 SECURITY SERVICES FOR ELECTRONIC MAIL

This section describes the kinds of security services one might desire for electronic mail. In following sections we describe how these features might be implemented. Most electronic mail systems do not provide most of these features. Even those designed specifically for security often only provide for some of these features.

- **privacy**—the ability to keep anyone but the intended recipient from reading the message. (see §12.5 *Privacy*)

- **authentication**—reassurance to the recipient of the identity of the sender. (see §12.6 *Authentication of the Source*)

- **integrity**—reassurance to the recipient that the message has not been altered since it was transmitted by the sender. (see §12.7 *Message Integrity*)

- **non-repudiation**—the ability of the recipient to prove to a third party that the sender really did send the message. This feature is also sometimes called **third party authentication**. The term *non-repudiation* means that the sender cannot later deny sending the message. (see §12.8 *Non-Repudiation*)

- **proof of submission**—verification given to the sender that the message was handed to the mail delivery system (the same basic idea as sending certified mail through the U.S. postal service). With certified postal mail you just receive proof that you sent something to a particular address on a particular date, but with electronic mail it is possible to have the mail system verify acceptance of the contents of a particular message, perhaps by signing the message digest of the contents of the message. (see §12.9 *Proof of Submission*)

- **proof of delivery**—verification that the recipient received the message. Postal mail has a similar feature (return receipt requested), but again it only verifies that something was delivered on a particular date to the recipient. With electronic mail it is possible to verify the contents, as we mentioned under proof of submission. (see §12.10 *Proof of Delivery*)

- **message flow confidentiality**—an extension of privacy such that Carol not only cannot know the content of the message Alice sent Bob, but cannot even determine whether Alice sent Bob a message. (see §12.11 *Message Flow Confidentiality*)

- **anonymity**—the ability to send a message so that the recipient can't find out the identity of the sender. (see §12.12 *Anonymity*)

- **containment**—the ability of the network to keep certain security levels of information from leaking out of a particular region. Methods for implementing this are in §12.13 *Containment*).

- **audit**—the ability of the network to record events that might have some security relevance, such as that Alice sent a message to Bob on a particular date. This would be fairly straightforward to implement, but is not mentioned in any of the secure mail standards, so we don't have a section on it.

- **accounting**—the ability of the mail system to maintain system usage statistics. In addition to providing clues for system resource management, this information allows the mail system to charge its clients according to their usage. For example, the system might charge by number of messages sent, as long as the system itself authenticates the source of each message to ensure that the proper party is billed. Again, there's not much to say about this, so we don't have a separate section on it.

- **self destruct**—an option allowing a sender to specify that a message should be destroyed after delivery to the recipient. This allows Alice to send a message to Bob that Bob cannot forward or store. The mail system will decrypt and display the message, but then delete it. (*Good morning Mr. Phelps...*). This can be implemented by marking the message as a *self-destruct* message, and having the mail program at the destination cooperate by deleting the message immediately after displaying it.

- **message sequence integrity**—reassurance that an entire sequence of messages arrived in the order transmitted, without any loss.

12.4 ESTABLISHING KEYS

Most security services are best provided by cryptographic means. But cryptography requires keys. If Alice wants to send a message to Bob, what keys does she have to know? How does she reliably and efficiently learn these keys? Who is involved in sending mail between Alice and Bob? Well, Alice and Bob, of course. But there's also the mail infrastructure. And there might be distribution list exploders. In some cases keys are shared between Alice and Bob. In other cases keys are shared between Alice and the mail infrastructure. In still others, it might be between Alice and the distribution list exploder, and between the distribution list exploder and Bob.

For now, we'll explain how Alice and Bob establish the proper keys between each other. The mechanisms depend on whether public keys or secret keys are being used. When we discuss specific services, we'll explain who needs keys.

12.4.1 Establishing Public Keys

There are many services (e.g. privacy), in which it would be very useful for Alice to know Bob's public key. How does Alice learn Bob's public key? Suppose Carol creates a ⟨public key, private key⟩ pair ⟨e, d⟩. If she can trick Alice into believing Bob's public key is e, then Carol can read Alice's messages to Bob (and Bob won't be able to read them). So it's important that Alice be assured that the key really does belong to Bob.

It could be that Alice physically visits Bob and he personally tells her his public key. Or Alice might be told Bob's public key by someone she trusts. Or Alice might telephone Bob and ask him his public key, which raises the interesting questions of how Alice is sure she has Bob's telephone number and not Carol's, and how Alice can be sure, even if she has the right telephone number, that it is Bob who has answered the phone and not Arnold Schwarzenegger doing an excellent voice impersonation.

These methods of obtaining Bob's public key become increasingly inconvenient as the population of the mail community grows. The commonly used method is to have Alice start by obtaining the public key of at least one thing she trusts, through one of the above mechanisms. Then she obtains other keys which have been signed by a key she trusts, with a message known as a **certificate** with content *x's public key is y*. Eventually she will have a chain starting from a public key she knows and trusts, then a sequence of certificates where each is signed by a public key that she trusts (due to the previous certificates in the chain) and vouches for another public key, until she gets a certificate vouching for Bob's public key. There are very different ways of doing this, as we will see in Chapter 13 *Privacy Enhanced Mail (PEM)* and Chapter 14 *PGP (Pretty Good Privacy)*. In order to send a message to Bob, Alice will need to have obtained a chain of certificates ending with Bob's public key. There are three interesting issues:

- How does Alice obtain the certificates?

- How does Alice know whether to trust the certificates?

- Assuming Alice has lots of certificates from which to choose, how does she select appropriate certificates to form a chain from a key she trusts to Bob's key? (See Homework Problem 2.)

Remember from §7.7.3 *Certificate Revocation* that in addition to certificates, there are probably going to be CRLs (certificate revocation lists). Therefore, Alice not only has to have a chain of certificates, but she also has to have the relevant CRLs so that she can determine that none of the public keys on which she is depending has been revoked. Alice has to somehow obtain the relevant CRLs. The mechanism for that could be the same as for obtaining certificates, or it could be different. The different mail standards we'll discuss do it in different ways.

12.4.2 Establishing Secret Keys

How can Alice and Bob establish a shared secret key? The simplest way is with some other means of private communication, for instance by meeting in person in a private place, or by talking on the phone (if they aren't paranoid about the phone being tapped). This strategy is OK for a few scattered private parties, but doesn't scale well at all.

A more scalable strategy is for Alice to obtain a ticket for Bob from a KDC (see §9.4 *Mediated Authentication (with KDC)*), and include that ticket with her first message to Bob.

12.5 PRIVACY

Most people think that electronic mail is private. But there are many ways in which inquiring minds can read your messages:

- An eavesdropper can listen to the message while it is being transmitted on the wire. Perhaps the network provides link encryption, in which case this one threat is avoided.

- Relay nodes (routers or mail forwarders) might have software to store messages and divulge them to people other than the intended recipients. The relay node might be doing that because it has been compromised by a bad guy, or it might be the intended function of the node. For instance the relay node might be a security gateway, and the owners of the network may want the ability to monitor mail to and from the outside.

There are often conflicting security needs. Alice wants to keep the contents of her message to Bob private. But Alice's employer might want the capability of monitoring her mail to ensure she isn't revealing company secrets. Another example is that citizens might want to be able to carry on private conversations, but their government might want to be able, under appropriate circumstances (of course), to monitor all communications.

12.5.1 End-to-End Privacy

Alice might want to send a message to Bob in such a way that only Bob can read it. She can't depend on the network keeping the message secret, but she can ensure that nobody but Bob can read the message by using cryptography to encrypt the message.

The natural assumption is that if Alice wants to send Bob an encrypted message, she encrypts it using Bob's public key (if public key technology is being used for keys) or by using the key she shares with Bob (if secret key technology is being used). However, this is not how mail encryption is generally done, for several reasons:

- If Alice has a long message to send to multiple recipients, the long message would have to be encrypted once for each recipient, producing a different version to be sent to each recipient.

- Public key encryption is far less efficient than secret key encryption. So it is desirable to encrypt the message with secret key encryption even if Bob's key is a public key.

- As described in §7.8 *Session Key Establishment*, it's not desirable to use a long-term key more than necessary. So to preserve the useful lifetime of the long-term key Alice and Bob share, it is preferable to encrypt as little as possible with a key that is expensive to replace.

So the way it is done is that Alice chooses a random secret key S to be used only for encrypting that one message. She encrypts the message with S, encrypts S with Bob's key, and transmits both quantities to Bob. Even if the message is being sent to multiple recipients, she only encrypts the message once, with key S. But she encrypts S once for each recipient, with the appropriate key, and includes each encrypted S with the encrypted message.

Let's assume Bob's key is K_{Bob}, Carol's key is K_{Carol}, and Ted's key is K_{Ted}. If public key technology is being used, then K_{Bob} is Bob's public key. If secret key technology is being used, then K_{Bob} is the key that Alice shares with Bob. The message Alice would like to send to Bob, Carol, and Ted is m. S is the secret key Alice chose specifically for encrypting m. (We'll write $K\{x\}$ to indicate x encrypted with key K.) The mail message Alice will send includes.

- Bob's name; $K_{Bob}\{S\}$

- Carol's name; $K_{Carol}\{S\}$

- Ted's name; $K_{Ted}\{S\}$

- $S\{m\}$

So, for example, the message Alice sends might look like this:

```
To: Bob, Carol, Ted
From: Alice
Key-info: Bob-4280234208034
```

```
Key-info: Carol-48235235344848488
Key-info: Ted-99349248
Msg-info: RJekcr283hkjsdf8ghn327&3489724&#$*92
```

In that way, each recipient can decrypt the appropriate encrypted version of the secret key, and each will use the same secret key to decrypt the message.

12.5.2 Privacy with Distribution List Exploders

Suppose Alice is sending a message to a distribution list which will be remotely exploded, and Bob is only one of the recipients. Assume the distribution list is stored at some node remote from Alice, and that Alice does not even know the individuals on the distribution list. We can't assume she has keys for all the members of the distribution list. Instead, she has a key only for the distribution list exploder. Alice does not need to treat the distribution list exploder any differently than any other recipient of a message. It is merely someone she shares a key with and sends messages to. The distribution list exploder will need keys for all the individuals on the list.

As described in the end-to-end case, Alice will choose a random per-message secret key S, and encrypt the message with S. The distribution list exploder will decrypt S (but it does not need to decrypt the message!), and re-encrypt S with the key for each recipient to whom it is forwarding the message.

Local exploding requires different mechanisms. Alice still has to trust the maintainer of the mailing list, since a bad guy could insert extra names into the distribution list. The distribution list is most likely just a list of names. Alice will not be able to send a secure message to a name without establishing a key for that individual.

12.6 Authentication of the Source

With traditional (unsecured) mail systems, it is possible for Carol to send a message to Bob where the FROM: field says Alice. Obviously this can cause great harm if Bob takes the message seriously. For instance, Alice might be Bob's manager, and the message Carol sends might say Urgent meeting with a customer in Juneau, Alaska; I've left; meet me there tomorrow.

It would be desirable for the message system to assure Bob that the message did indeed come from Alice.

12.6.1 Source Authentication Based on Public Key Technology

Assuming Bob knows Alice's public key, Alice can digitally sign the message, using her private key, which will assure Bob that Alice wrote the message. The method usually chosen to sign a message is for Alice to first compute a hash of the message (for instance using MD5), and then to sign the message digest, since computing a message digest is faster than public key operations, and the message digest is usually a smaller quantity to sign than the message.

This method extends easily to multiple recipients and distribution lists. If Alice is sending a message to multiple recipients, the same signature will work for all recipients.

If Alice does not know that Bob knows her public key, she could send the message anyway and let Bob fetch the public key (together with finding a chain of certificates to certify Alice's key) if he needs to. Or she could include the public key in the header of the message, together with a chain of certificates. Or she might guess that he already has a lot of the certificates in the chain, and she might just furnish what she thinks is likely to be the remainder.

Note that Alice doesn't even have to know whether Bob is crypto capable to send a signed message. Sometimes users send signed messages just to advertise the fact that they can. If the signature is formatted innocuously, it just looks like cybercrud in the mail header to non-crypto-capable recipients. Of course, added cybercrud sometimes annoys humans, even if it doesn't prevent them from deciphering the message. For example, the message

```
From: Alice
To: Bob
Subject: I got PEM working
... and I'm sending this message with PEM.
```

would look something like this when received by Bob:

```
To: Bob
Subject: I got PEM working
Date: Fri, 01 Apr 94 10:12:37 -0400
From: Alice

-----BEGIN PRIVACY-ENHANCED MESSAGE-----
Proc-Type: 4,MIC-CLEAR
Content-Domain: RFC822
DEK-Info: DES-CBC,31747476B4831B1D
Originator-ID-Asymmetric: MEMxCzAJBgNVBAYTAlVTMSYwJAYDVQQKEx1EaWd
 pdGFsIEVxdWlwbWVudCBDb3Jwb3JhdGlvbjEMMAoGA1UECxMDTEtH,02
MIC-Info: RSA-MD5,RSA,u1OHP1RwLqePAoaN5nPk9W7Q2EfjaP+yDBSaLyMcSgc
 MK2YicGSAqLz47Ol+TUR4YmMD/JnHMtsCJerV2QFtFQ==

... and I'm sending this message with PEM.
-----END PRIVACY-ENHANCED MESSAGE-----
```

12.6.2 Source Authentication Based on Secret Keys

If Alice has a shared key with Bob, then she can reassure Bob that she is Alice by proving she knows the shared secret key. She does this by performing some cryptographic computation on the message using the shared secret key. This quantity also serves as an integrity check, and is usually called a **MIC** (see §3.7 *Generating MICs* and §4.2.2 *Computing a MIC with a Hash*). Various possibilities for computing a MIC include:

1. The MIC is the CBC residue of the message computed with the shared secret key.

2. The MIC is the message digest of the shared secret appended to the message.

3. The MIC is the encrypted message digest, where the 128-bit message digest is encrypted with the shared secret key, for instance in ECB or CBC mode.

What if there are multiple recipients? Alice's shared secret with Bob will be different from Alice's shared secret with Ted. If the MIC method is 1 or 2 above, then Alice would have to do a computation-intensive cryptographic pass over the long message for each recipient. The third method is therefore preferable. Alice computes the message digest once, and computes the MIC on the message digest independently for each recipient.

12.6.3 Source Authentication with Distribution Lists

With public keys, source authentication is easy, even with distribution lists. Basically, the distribution list will merely forward the message without changing the authentication information. Alice's public key will authenticate the message. The distribution list exploder plays no part in the source authentication.

With secret keys it is more complicated. We can't assume Alice will share a secret key with every recipient, or even that Alice will know who the recipients are. The only choice is for Alice to share a key with the distribution list exploder. The distribution list exploder will be able to verify that the message came from Alice, but whatever authentication information Alice puts into the message will become meaningless after the distribution list exploder forwards the message. It must remove Alice's authentication information, and replace it with its own authentication information for each recipient. The recipients will know the message came from the distribution list exploder, but they will have to take the exploder's word that the message really did originate from Alice. When using mail exploders and secret key technology, it is vital that the mail exploder verify the source before forwarding the message, and include the name of the sender in the body of the message that the mail exploder cryptographically protects. PEM does not define a field to accomplish this, which would make it problematic to use secret key PEM with mail exploders. This problem is solved twice today:

- Nobody uses PEM-aware mail exploders.

- Nobody uses secret key PEM.

12.7 MESSAGE INTEGRITY

When Bob receives a message from Alice, how does he know that Carol did not intercept the message and modify it? For instance, she might have changed the message Fire Carol immediately to Promote Carol immediately.

It makes little sense to provide for authentication of the source without also guaranteeing integrity of the contents of the message. Who would care that the message originated with Alice, if the contents might have been modified en route? Indeed, all of the mail standards provide message integrity and source authentication together. They either provide both or neither. The mechanisms discussed in the previous section for source authentication provide message integrity as well.

12.7.1 Message Integrity Without Source Authentication

Might someone want to provide message integrity protection without source authentication? The only vaguely plausible example we could come up with for when this might be useful was a ransom note. The kidnappers would want to prove that they were the kidnappers, perhaps by extracting some secret information from the victim. The note would give the proof that they were the kidnappers, and include directions for dropping off the ransom money. They'd want to keep the message private, since they wouldn't want someone else to get that secret, convince the family they were the kidnappers, and collect the ransom. Nor would they want some third party to see the directions for dropping off the ransom money, since someone else might try to pick up the money. (Kidnappers are such suspicious people.) The message would be anonymous, so there would be no source verification.

Integrity protection would be somewhat important, to prevent someone from guessing that the first part of the message was the proof that they were the kidnappers, and substitute a different second part of the message, with different directions for dropping off ransom money.

In some sense in this example there is source authentication—it's just not done with cryptography by the mail system. Instead the contents of the message provide source authentication by humans. We know of no systems that provide this odd combination (message integrity without source authentication), and kidnappers represent such a small market that none is likely to be developed.

It's meaningless to provide integrity protection without source authentication if the message is unencrypted, because anyone can remove the message from the wire and construct a different message. It isn't possible to do message integrity without source authentication with secret key technology, since the sender must share a secret with the recipient, so the recipient will know who the message came from based on which secret key is used.

If the message is encrypted (where the sender knows the public key of the recipient), it is possible to do something that could be considered integrity protection without source authentication. It is still possible for someone to remove the entire message from the wire and substitute a different message. But what can be ensured with an encrypted message is that the entire message came from one source, although the source is anonymous.

12.8 NON-REPUDIATION

Repudiation is the act of denying that you sent a message. If the message system provides for **non-repudiation**, it means that if Alice sends a message to Bob, Alice cannot later deny that she sent the message. Bob can prove to a third party that Alice did indeed send the message. For instance, if Alice sends a message to the bank that she wishes to transfer a million dollars to Bob's account, the bank might not honor the transaction unless it is sent in such a way that not only can the bank know the message was from Alice, but they can prove it to a court if necessary.

It is not always desirable to have non-repudiation. For instance, Alice might be the head of some large organization and want to give the go-ahead to her underlings for some scheme like, say, selling arms to Iran to raise money to fund the Contras. The underlings must be absolutely certain the orders came from Alice, so it is necessary to have source authentication of the message, but Alice wants plausible deniability (what a great phrase!), so that if any of her underlings are caught or killed, she can disavow any knowledge of their actions.

With public keys, it is very natural to provide non-repudiable source authentication, and more difficult to provide repudiable source authentication. With secret keys, it is very natural to provide repudiable source authentication and very difficult to provide non-repudiable messages.

12.8.1 Non-repudiation Based on Public Key Technology

The usual method Alice uses to prove the authenticity of her message to Bob is to include her public key signature on the message digest of the message, using her private key. This method of source authentication not only reassures Bob that Alice sent the message, but Bob can prove to anyone else that Alice sent the message. Only someone with knowledge of Alice's private key could have signed the message digest with it. But anyone knowing her public key can verify her signature.

12.8.2 Plausible Deniability Based on Public Key Technology

How can Alice send a message to Bob in such a way that Bob knows it came from Alice, but Bob can't prove to anyone else that it came from Alice? Alice can send a public key based repudiable message m to Bob by doing the following.

First we'll review our notation. We use curly braces { } for encrypting something with a public key, with a subscript specifying the name of the individual whose public key we are using. We use square brackets [] for signing something with a private key, with a subscript specifying the name of the individual whose private key is being used.

1. Alice picks a secret key S, which she will use just for m.

2. She encrypts S with Bob's public key, getting $\{S\}_{Bob}$.

3. She signs $\{S\}_{Bob}$ with her private key, getting $[\{S\}_{Bob}]_{Alice}$.

4. She uses S to compute a MIC for m (for example, by using DES to compute the CBC residue of the message).

5. She sends the MIC, $[\{S\}_{Bob}]_{Alice}$, and m to Bob.

Bob will know that the message came from Alice, because Alice signed the encrypted S. But Bob can't prove to anyone else that Alice sent him m. He can prove that at some point Alice sent some message using key S, but it might not have been m. Once Bob has the quantity $[\{S\}_{Bob}]_{Alice}$ he can construct any message he likes and construct an integrity code using S.

12.8.3 Non-Repudiation with Secret Keys

It is surprising that it is possible to provide non-repudiation with secret keys. Let's say Alice is sending a message to Bob, and it has to be possible for Bob to prove later, to "the judge", that Alice sent the message. We'll need a notary N who must be trusted by Bob and the judge. (A **notary** is a trusted service that vouches for certain information.) Alice sends the message to N, and does source authentication with N so that N knows the message came from Alice. N does some computation on the message and Alice's name using a secret quantity S_N that N shares with nobody. We'll call the result of this computation N's **seal** on the message. (For instance N's seal might be the message digest of the concatenation of Alice, the message, and S_N.) Then the message together with the seal is sent to Bob. Bob can't tell whether N's seal is genuine, because that would require knowing S_N (which N shares with nobody). If Alice were dishonest and wanted to send a message to Bob that Bob would only accept if it were non-repudiable, then Alice could put in any cybercrud and pretend that it is authentication information from N,

There are two things we can do to assure Bob that the message was vouched for by N, and that therefore he can later prove to the judge that N vouched for the message.

- Bob and N could establish a shared key, and N could use it to generate a MIC for the concatenation of Alice, the message, and the seal. Bob can verify this MIC (since he knows the shared key) and thus verify the validity of the seal.

- Bob could, after receiving the message, send a request to N asking N if N's seal is genuine. This request would of course have to include Alice, the message, and the alleged seal.

Now let's assume at some later time Bob needs to prove to the judge that Alice sent the message. Bob sends Alice, the message, and the seal to the judge, who sends it to N in an integrity-protected conversation. N verifies the validity of the seal and reports that to the judge.

Note that N does not actually have to see the message, in case Alice and Bob want to keep the message private. Alice could instead just send the message digest to N, and N could compute the seal of the message digest.

12.9 PROOF OF SUBMISSION

When we send paper mail, the postal service allows us to send it *certified*, which means we pay extra money and get a piece of paper that verifies we submitted something on a particular date to a particular address.

Some electronic mail systems offer a similar service, but by using cryptography on the contents of the message, it turns out to be more powerful than the postal service certified mail concept.

The mail system can implement this by computing a message digest of the message concatenated with any other information that might be useful, like the time of submission, and then sign the message digest. The user could later use the receipt to prove that the message was sent (though not that it was delivered).

12.10 PROOF OF DELIVERY

This feature corresponds to the paper mail postal service *return receipt requested*. It can be implemented in electronic mail by having either the destination or the mail delivery service sign a message digest of the message concatenated with any other information that might be useful (like the time of receipt). If the mail service gives the proof of delivery, it would be done after transmitting the message to the destination. If the destination gives the proof of delivery, it would be done after the destination receives the message. In either case this requires the cooperation of the recipient. It obviously requires the cooperation of the recipient if the recipient returns the proof of delivery. But it also requires the cooperation of the recipient if the mail system returns the proof of delivery, since the recipient might refuse to acknowledge the last packet of the message (once the recipient realizes the message is an eviction notice, for instance).

Note that it is provably impossible to provide a receipt if and only if the recipient got the message. The problem is, if the recipient signs before the message is delivered, then the message can get lost, but the mail system has the signature. If the recipient signs after receiving the message, the recipient might not furnish a signature at that point, but yet have the message.

12.11 MESSAGE FLOW CONFIDENTIALITY

This feature allows Alice to send Bob a message in such a way that no eavesdropper can find out that Alice sent Bob a message. This would be useful when the mere fact that Alice sent Bob a message is useful information, even if the contents were encrypted so that only Bob could read the contents. (For instance, Bob might be a headhunter. Or Bob might be a reporter and Alice might be a member of a secret congressional committee who is leaking information to the press.) The X.402 standard hints that such a service might be provided and hints at mechanisms for providing it

If Alice knows that intruder Carol is monitoring her outgoing mail to look to see if she is sending messages to Bob, she can utilize a friend as an intermediary. She can send an encrypted message to Fred, with the message she wants to send to Bob embedded in the contents of the message to Fred. So the message Fred would read is This is Alice. Please forward the following message to Bob. Thanks a lot. followed by Alice's message to Bob. If Alice were sufficiently paranoid, she might prefer a service that is constantly sending encrypted dummy messages to random recipients. If Fred forwards Alice's message after a random delay, then even if Carol knows Fred provides this service, she cannot know to which recipient Alice was asking Fred to forward a message.

To be even more paranoid, a path through several intermediaries could be used. Alice does this by taking the (encrypted) message she'd like to send to Bob, enclosing that in an encrypted message to the last intermediary, enclosing that in an encrypted message to the penultimate intermediary, encloses that—you get the idea. Using the multiple intermediary technique, even if someone bribed one of the intermediaries to remember the directions from which it received and sent mail, Alice could not be paired with Bob. To discover that Alice had sent a message to Bob would require the cooperation of all the intermediaries.

12.12 ANONYMITY

There are times when Alice might want to send Bob a message, but not have Bob be able to tell who sent the message. One might think that would be easy. Alice could merely not sign the message. However, most mail systems automatically include the sender's name in the mail message. One could imagine modifying one's mailer to leave out that information, but a clever recipient can get clues. For instance, the network layer address of the node from which it was sent might be sent with the message. Often the node from which the recipient receives the message is not the actual source, but instead is an intermediate node that stores and forwards mail. However, most mail transports include a record of the path the message took, and this information might be available to the recipient.

If Alice really wants to ensure anonymity, she can use the same technique as for message flow confidentiality. She can give the message to a third party, Fred, and have Fred send the unsigned message on to Bob.

If Fred does not have enough clients, he can't really provide anonymity. For instance, if Alice is the only one who has sent a message to Fred, then Bob can guess the message came from her, even if Fred is sending out lots of messages to random people. Fred can have lots of clients by providing other, innocuous services, such as weather reports, bookmaking, or pornographic screen savers (where you are required to transmit a fixed-length, encrypted message in order to get a response), or by having the user community cooperate by sending dummy messages to Fred at random intervals to provide cover for someone who might really require the service. (We specified fixed-length messages to Fred so that people could not correlate the lengths of messages into and out of Fred—someone wanting to send a longer message would have to break it into multiple messages, and pad short messages.)

There's an amusing anecdote about anonymous mail. Someone does provide an anonymous mail service. The way it works is you send an ordinary mail message to the service, telling it to whom you'd like to send an anonymous message. It strips off your real address and substitutes a pseudonym for you. The first time you send a message it assigns you a pseudonym, but on subsequent messages it fills in the same pseudonym. So people won't know from whom the message came, but they'll know that different messages came from the same person. Mail sent to any of the pseudonyms assigned by the anonymity service will be directed to that service, which will substitute the real address instead of the destination's pseudonym (and incidentally, assign a pseudonym to the source and substitute that—this particular service didn't allow for non-anonymous mail to be sent to a pseudonym).

Anyway, one December day in 1993, someone decided to add him/herself to the IETF mailing list as the pseudonym assigned by the service. Then someone sent a message to the IETF mailing list (it happens). When the message was distributed by the mailing list, it was sent to all the members, including the pseudonym. When this pseudonym-addressed copy was received by the anonymous mail service, it assigned a pseudonym to the source (the mailing list) and sent an assignment message back to the mailing list, which of course got distributed to all the mailing list members:

```
To: ietf@nat-flnt{MHS:ietf@CNRI.Reston.VA.US}
From: 00000000 {MHS:"<@ns.novell.com:ietf-request@
 ietf.nri.reston.va.us>"@sjf-domain-hub.Novell}
Subject: Anonymous code name allocated.
Date: 12/28/93    Time:  9:08a

You have sent a message using the anonymous contact service.
You have been allocated the code name an60254.
You can be reached anonymously using the address
an60254@anon.penet.fi.

If you want to use a nickname, please send a message to
nick@anon.penet.fi, with a Subject: field containing your nickname.

For instructions, send a message to help@anon.penet.fi.
```

12.13 CONTAINMENT

This feature is modeled after nondiscretionary access controls (see §1.11.1 *Mandatory (Non-discretionary) Access Controls*). The idea is that the network would be partitioned into pieces that are capable of handling certain security classes. Each message would be marked with its security classification, and the message routers would refuse to forward a message to a portion of the network that didn't handle its security class.

12.14 ANNOYING TEXT FORMAT ISSUES

There is unfortunately no single standard for text representation. Some systems have <LF> (line feed, ASCII 10) as the line delimiter. Others have <CR> (carriage return, ASCII 13). Others have <CR><LF> (<CR> followed by <LF>). Some systems have line-length limitations. Others happily wrap lines. Some systems expect parity on the high-order bit of each byte. Others get upset if the high-order bit is on. Still others don't get upset, but calmly clear the bit. Some systems don't even use ASCII, but use some other encoding for characters, such as EBCDIC.

When sending a text message to someone on another system, we'd like the message to appear to the human on the other end about the way it looked to the human who sent it. This is a messy, boring problem. Your system can't really know what the conventions are at the remote site, and the destination might have difficulties translating appropriately because it would not know what the conventions were at the source. The usual method of solving problems like these is to define a canonical format. The data is translated at the source into canonical format, and at the destination out of canonical format into local format. This way, each system only needs to know how to convert its local format to and from canonical format (as opposed to needing to know how to convert its local format to and from each other possible format).

Unfortunately, there is no single standard canonical format. SMTP (Simple Mail Transport Protocol) is a standard for Internet mail, and it defines a canonical format. It is documented in RFC 822. Its canonical format uses <CR><LF> as the line delimiter. But there are non-SMTP mail systems, and messages can get modified in non-reversible ways as messages pass through various sorts of gateways. For instance, some mail gateways remove white space at the ends of lines (spaces immediately preceding the end of the line), add line breaks to lines that seem too long to fit on a screen, or turn the tab character into five spaces.

These sorts of transformations are mostly harmless when trying to send simple text messages from one user to another across diverse systems, but it causes problems when trying to send arbitrary data between systems. Certainly if you're trying to send arbitrary binary data, having all your high-order bits cleared or having <CR><LF> inserted periodically will hopelessly mangle the data. But even if you are sending text, security features can get broken by mail gateways diddling with the data. For instance, a digital signature will no longer verify if any of the message is modified. It's difficult to predict exactly what kinds of modifications an arbitrary mail gateway will make to your file in its attempt to be helpful.

Mail is not the only application which has this problem. File transfer also has the problem. It would be easy just to send the bits in a file and have them appear at the destination machine exactly as they were at the source machine, but that is often not what is wanted. Because of the different representations for text, a text file might not display intelligibly on a different system. (And of course there are other problems besides displaying text. A floating point number is represented differently on different machines. Maybe you'd even like your executable code to run on a different machine!) Most file transfer protocols give you the choice of whether you are sending binary data (in which case it won't muck with your data) or text (in which case it will attempt to do transformations on the data so that it will display properly).

SMTP made the assumption that the only thing anyone would ever want to mail was text, so there is no capability of sending arbitrary data. The mail infrastructure is always allowed to play around with your data in an attempt to be helpful.

12.14.1 Disguising Data as Text

People have long wanted to mail types of data other than simple text (for instance, diagrams, voice, pictures, or even text in languages with large character sets), and they have done so by coming up with an encoding that will pass through all known maulers ;-). The classic way UNIX systems did this was to run a program called *uuencode* on the data, mail the result, and have the recipient *uudecode* it. The encoding process accepts arbitrary octet strings and produces strings containing only "safe" characters with an occasional end-of-line delimiter to keep the mailers happy. There are obviously fewer than 256 safe values for a byte (otherwise, arbitrary binary data would work just fine). It turns out there are at least 64 safe characters, but not much more than that, so the encoding packs 6 bits of information into each character, by translating each of the possible values of the 6 bits into one of the safe characters, and adding <CR><LF> sufficiently often. This encoding expands the information by about 33%.

PEM and PGP both make the assumption that they have to work with a mail system such as SMTP that will assume their data is text, so they both have a convention similar to uuencode/uudecode for packing and unpacking 6 bits into a character. We will use the term **encode** to mean any similar mechanism, even if it isn't exactly the transformation that the UNIX utility provides. X.400 has a method of transmitting data unmodified, so it does not need to do this.

So there are two transformations of data. One is canonicalization, which is minor diddling such as changing the end-of-line character into <CR><LF>. The other is encoding, which is packing 6 bits per character, thereby making the data completely unintelligible to humans and expanding it by about 33%.

There is a troublesome consequence of encoding, in that you can't always assume that the recipient of the mail message has PEM or PGP. The recipient might have to read the message with an ordinary mail program. Obviously they would not be able to read an encrypted message with an ordinary mail program, but you'd want them to be able to read a message that is unencrypted but integrity-protected.

Suppose Alice sends the message Bob, your terminal is about to explode. You'd better quickly run out of your office. She decides to use PEM so that it will add an integrity check to the message, since she *really cares* that Bob gets the message without it getting garbled. PEM helpfully reformats the message so that it now looks like:

```
-----BEGIN PRIVACY-ENHANCED MESSAGE-----
Proc-Type: 4,MIC-ONLY
Originator-ID-Asymmetric: MEMxCzAJBgNVBAYTAlVTMSYwJAYDVQQKEx1EaWd
  pdGFsIEVxdWlwbWVudCBDb3Jwb3JhdGlvbjEMMAoGA1UECxMDTEtH,05
MIC-Info: RSA-MD5,RSA,ZHiLe5DJdd4fE1/w++csvPbpFG9K9PWkPwU3fSLh9I+
  ZNyFdZ7pBk1zPvXrya5+14XQcwIcb3Dcqk2RbnyzWzQ==

Qm9iLCB5b3VyIHRlcm1pbmFsIGlzIGFib3V0IHRvDQpleHBsb2RlLiAgWW91J2Qg
YmV0dGVyIHF1aWNrbHkgcnVuIG91dCBvZiB5b3VyIG9mZmljZS4NCg==
-----END PRIVACY-ENHANCED MESSAGE-----
```

The first five lines of cybercrud include information like the integrity check. The actual message is the bottom two lines:

```
Qm9iLCB5b3VyIHRlcm1pbmFsIGlzIGFib3V0IHRvDQpleHBsb2RlLiAgWW91J2Qg
YmV0dGVyIHF1aWNrbHkgcnVuIG91dCBvZiB5b3VyIG9mZmljZS4NCg==
```

Suppose Bob's mail program has not yet implemented PEM. It is reasonable to expect him to have problems understanding an encrypted message, but Alice did not encrypt the message. She merely requested an integrity check be added to the message. But PEM had to reformat the data, because the integrity check would fail if the text was modified in any way.

The human Bob will have trouble processing

```
Qm9iLCB5b3VyIHRlcm1pbmFsIGlzIGFib3V0IHRvDQpleHBsb2RlLiAgWW91J2Qg
YmV0dGVyIHF1aWNrbHkgcnVuIG91dCBvZiB5b3VyIG9mZmljZS4NCg==
```

It's not encrypted—it is easy to turn it back into human-readable text, if there is a utility at Bob's node to do this. Without such a utility, Bob will probably take longer than is prudent (given the contents of Alice's message) to read the message.

Because of this problem, both PEM and PGP have the capability of sending something without modification. When you use that mode, they will not modify the message. It's your problem if mail gateways modify the message and the integrity check no longer matches. The programs add an integrity check without encoding the message. The message would then look like this:

```
-----BEGIN PRIVACY-ENHANCED MESSAGE-----
Proc-Type: 4,MIC-CLEAR
Originator-ID-Asymmetric: MEMxCzAJBgNVBAYTAlVTMSYwJAYDVQQKEx1EaWd
  pdGFsIEVxdWlwbWVudCBDb3Jwb3JhdGlvbjEMMAoGA1UECxMDTEtH,05
MIC-Info: RSA-MD5,RSA,ZHiLe5DJdd4fE1/w++csvPbpFG9K9PWkPwU3fSLh9I+
  ZNyFdZ7pBk1zPvXrya5+14XQcwIcb3Dcqk2RbnyzWzQ==

Bob, your terminal is about to explode. You'd better quickly run out of
```

```
your office
-----END PRIVACY-ENHANCED MESSAGE-----
```

If Alice sends her message to Bob in this mode using PEM (or PGP, but we'll assume PEM for now), then it is possible that she'll be lucky and one of the following will be true:

- The message happens to be encoded in a way which no mail utility en route will feel obliged to modify. Bob's mailer has PEM and the integrity check will succeed.

- Bob's mailer does not have PEM, and the message does not get maliciously corrupted en route by some third party Carol. What Bob sees is the actual text of the message, plus some cybercrud for the signature and so on, which he ignores.

It is possible that she'll be unlucky (or rather, Bob will be unlucky in this case) and one of the following will happen:

- Bob's mail has PEM, and the message gets modified by a helpful mail utility in a "harmless" sort of way. The integrity check fails and Bob ignores the message.

- Bob's mailer does not have PEM, and bad-guy Carol modifies the message en route into something like, **Are you still free for tennis today after work?**

In either case, Bob gets blown to bits.

12.15 NAMES AND ADDRESSES

When sending a message to Alice, there are actually two different meanings of *destination*. One is as a way for the authentication system to know what key to use to encrypt the message. The other is for the mail delivery system to know where the receiving mailbox is. Unfortunately, for some of the standards, the names look different. For instance, PEM uses X.500 names for identifying users, but works with SMTP mail, which uses Internet addresses for finding mailboxes.
Internet addresses look like: Alice@Wonderland.Edu
X.500 names look like: /C=US/O=CIA/OU=drugs/PN='Manuel Noriega'
It would be really annoying if every time you wanted to send a PEM message, PEM made you type two names (especially if one of them was an X.500 name). However, PEM doesn't usually make you do that. Whenever you receive a PEM message, since both forms of source identification are in the message, PEM keeps a local database of mappings between Internet addresses and X.500 names. When you send a message to someone from whom you've received a PEM message, the Internet address suffices, since PEM will figure out the X.500 name.

PGP doesn't have a formal standard for what names look like. They could be simple text strings that people are familiar with, like **Radia Perlman**. Some people (like Radia Perlman) are cleverly named so that there are not likely to be many different people with their names. However, other people (like John Smith) did not have sufficiently imaginative parents. In order for names to hopefully be unique, PGP recommends that you include your internet mail address as a substring of your PGP-authenticated name, so your name would be something like **John Smith <Smith@cia.gov>**.

X.400 has the potential of being cleaner, since the name is X.500, and both the key and the mailbox are attributes of the name.

12.16 OLD MESSAGES

There are a lot of interesting issues that might arise with old messages. Keys get revoked. Keys get changed. How can one look at a five-year-old message and know whether the mail message was valid at the time it was sent? We'll discuss several scenarios and ways for coping with these circumstances, based on use of a notary (see §12.8.3 *Non-Repudiation with Secret Keys*). People have suggested all sorts of digital notary services, but we claim that all services can be accomplished with a notary that simply, given a pile of bits, will date and sign the pile of bits.

12.16.1 Case 1: The Dishonest Buyer

Suppose there is a company that allows electronic purchase orders. The deal is that you are responsible for any purchase orders signed with your key, unless you report your key stolen. From the time you declare the key stolen, all purchase orders signed with the key are invalid, but all purchase orders signed before that time are valid. Suppose Alice signed a purchase order with her private key a year ago. Then she decides she wants to renege on the deal, so she reports her key stolen. The company knows they received the purchase order a year ago, but how can they prove it? We can assume the purchase order has a date in it, which is integrity-protected with the signature, but anyone who has the private key can backdate a message.

One way the company can protect itself is to send each purchase order, when received, to a notary. Our version of the notary simply dates and signs the message, so the company can prove they received the message before the timestamp added by the notary. It will also be convenient for the company to store, with the purchase order, the certificates and certificate revocation lists (CRLs) it used originally to verify Alice's signature. Now if Alice denies having sent the message, the company can give a judge Alice's notarized message along with the certificates and CRLs, and the judge can determine that Alice's message was legally binding at the time it was received.

If the company is worried about Alice controlling a certification authority (CA), and therefore being able to fake dates on certificates or CRLs, then the company can have the notary also sign and date the certificates and CRLs. See Homework Problem 9.

12.16.2 Case 2: The Solution Looking for a Problem

The notary, as described above, can only prove that a message was generated before the date on which the notary signed it. Someone could hold a message for years, and then have the notary sign it.

Suppose you want to prove that a message was generated after a certain date. This can be accomplished by including in the message something that you could not have known until that date, for instance the winning lottery number in some daily lottery drawing with sufficiently large numbers, or a signed timestamp from a notary for that day.

We can't actually think of a plausible scenario for why anyone would want this feature. We'd love to hear any good ideas.

12.17 HOMEWORK

1 Outline a scheme for sending a message to a distribution list, where distribution lists can be nested. Attempt to avoid duplicate copies to recipients that are members of multiple lists. Discuss both the local exploder and remote exploder methods of distribution list expansion.

2. Suppose Alice has a lot of stored certificates with various things certifying public keys of other things. For instance she might have reliably received C's public key, and simply believe C's public key. Then she has some certificates signed by C regarding public keys for D, E, F, and G. Then she might have some public keys signed by E, some signed by F, and so forth. These keys in turn might sign certificates for other keys. Let's say Alice wants to know Bob's public key. What methods might be devised for reasonably efficiently finding a chain of certificates that lead to verifying Bob's public key?

3. Using tickets as in §12.4.2 *Establishing Secret Keys*, suppose Alice's KDC is different from Bob's KDC. Alice will have to use a chain of KDCs to get a ticket for Bob (see §7.7.4.1 *Multiple KDC Domains*). Does Alice need to include the entire chain of tickets or merely the final ticket to Bob? How is this different from use of certificates?

4. Suppose Alice sends an encrypted, signed message to Bob via the mechanism suggested in §12.8.2 *Plausible Deniability Based on Public Key Technology*. Why can't Bob prove to third party Charlie that Alice sent the message? Why are both cryptographic operations on *S* necessary? (Alice both encrypts it with Bob's public key and signs it with her private key.)

5. Assume we are using secret key technology. What is wrong with the following source authentication scheme? Alice chooses a per-message secret key *K*, and puts an encrypted version of *K* in the header for each recipient, say Bob and Ted. Then she uses *K* to compute a MIC on the message, say a DES-CBC residue, or by computing a message digest of *K* appended to the message. (Hint: it works fine for a single recipient, but there is a security problem if Alice sends a multiple-recipient message.)

6. Using the authentication without non-repudiation described in §12.8.2 *Plausible Deniability Based on Public Key Technology*, Bob can forge Alice's signature on a message to himself. Why can't he forge Alice's signature on a message to someone else using the same technique?

7. Which security features can be provided without changing the mail delivery infrastructure, i.e., by only running special software at the source and destination?

8. Which security features (privacy, integrity protection, repudiability, non-repudiability, source authentication) would be desired, and which ones would definitely not be used, in the following cases:

   • submitting an expense report

   • inviting a friend to lunch

   • selling illegal pornography over the network

   • running an (illegal) gambling operation on the network

   • sending a mission description to the Mission Impossible team

   • sending a purchase order

   • sending a tip to the IRS to audit a neighbor you don't like but are afraid of

   • sending a love letter

   • sending an (unwanted) obscene note

   • sending a blackmail letter

   • sending a ransom note

   • sending a resume to a headhunter

9. Suppose you are a judge trying to decide a dispute between a buyer and a supplier. The buyer claims not to have produced a particular email purchase order, while the supplier shows you the purchase order, and certificates and CRLs demonstrating that the purchase order was signed by the buyer, all signed by a notary. How would the dates on the various pieces of evidence influence your decision? What if only the purchase order was signed by the notary? Note that the security community continues to debate issues such as whether the CRL should be required to have a later date than the notary's signature.

13 PRIVACY ENHANCED MAIL (PEM)

13.1 INTRODUCTION

PEM was developed by the Internet community as a means of adding encryption, source authentication, and integrity protection to ordinary text messages. It is documented in four pieces. RFC 1421 describes the message formats. RFC 1422 describes the CA hierarchy. RFC 1423 describes a base set of cryptographic algorithms that can be used with PEM. RFC 1424 describes mail message formats for requesting certificates and for requesting or posting certificate revocation lists.

PEM was designed to work by having smart software only at the source and destination (as opposed to in the mail infrastructure, for instance in the mail gateways). PEM assumes that the message it wants to send will be carried by a mail infrastructure which might be based on some simple-minded mail transport protocol that can only send ordinary text, and a lot of PEM's complexity involves encoding information in such a way that it will pass unmodified through all the mailers known to the PEM designers (there's no guarantee that someone won't invent a mail gateway which will mangle data in new and innovative ways, though).

The design of PEM lets you base user keys on secret key or public key technology, but everyone assumes that only the public key variant will be widely deployed. (Message encryption is always done with secret key technology, even when user keys are based on public key technology—see §12.5.1 *End-to-End Privacy*.) Although PEM is designed to be independent of the actual cryptographic algorithms chosen, the only ones defined and deployed today are RSA for public user keys, MD2 and MD5 for message digests, and DES for secret user keys and for encryption.

13.1.1 Structure of a PEM Message

A mail message can contain pieces that have been processed in different ways by PEM. For instance, part of a message might be encrypted, and another part might be integrity-protected. PEM puts markers before and after such blocks so that the PEM at the destination will know which pieces need what processing. PEM marks a piece that it has processed in some way (for instance encrypted) with a text string before and after the piece. PEM will insert

`-----BEGIN PRIVACY-ENHANCED MESSAGE-----`

before and insert

`-----END PRIVACY-ENHANCED MESSAGE-----`

at the end of the piece of the message that PEM has processed.

Extra information needs to be sent along with the PEM-processed message, for instance the (encrypted) key used to encrypt the data, or the message integrity code (MIC). Instead of inserting all this information as pure cybercrud, PEM inserts a label for each piece of information attached to the piece of the message it has processed. There are various labels for various pieces of PEM information, for instance **Proc-Type**, **Originator-ID-Asymmetric**, and **MIC-Info**. The intention is that a human will ignore that stuff, so it wasn't necessary for PEM to make it semi-human-intelligible. The delimiting strings are indeed helpful to alert a human that might not have a PEM-capable mail reader as to why the message seems like junk. In §13.17 *Message Formats* we will walk through the PEM message syntax in its full glory, explaining exactly what each field means and which variations are allowed.

The different types of pieces PEM can combine into a message are

- ordinary, unsecured data

- integrity-protected unmodified data—An integrity check is added to the message, but the original message is included unmodified as part of the PEM message. The PEM terminology for this kind of data is **MIC-CLEAR**. The assumption is that the text will not be garbled in annoying ways along the route by meddling mail utilities. Otherwise the integrity check will not work. See §13.7 *Reformatting Data to Get Through Mailers*. (Note that, as with the types below, the integrity check also provides source authentication.)

- integrity-protected encoded data—PEM first encodes the message so that it will pass through all mailers unmodified. Then PEM adds an integrity check. PEM calls this **MIC-ONLY**. Since the encoded message is not readable by normal humans, the mail program at the destination must be able to convert the text back into human readable format.

- encoded encrypted integrity-protected data—PEM computes an integrity check on the message. PEM then encrypts the message and the integrity check with a randomly selected per-message secret key. The encrypted message, the encrypted integrity check, and the per-message key (encrypted by the interchange key—see §13.2 *Establishing Keys*) are each then encoded to pass through mailers as ordinary text. PEM calls this **ENCRYPTED**. Clearly in this case the mail program at the destination must be PEM-aware so that it can decrypt the message.

For example, let's assume the simple message

> From: Alice
> To: Bob
> Subject: Keep this proposition private!
> Care to meet me at my apartment tonight?

The MIC-CLEAR version would look like this:

```
To: Bob
Subject: Keep this proposition private!
Date: Fri, 01 Apr 94 10:12:37 -0400
From: Alice

-----BEGIN PRIVACY-ENHANCED MESSAGE-----
Proc-Type: 4,MIC-CLEAR
Content-Domain: RFC822
Originator-ID-Asymmetric: MEMxCzAJBgNVBAYTAlVTMSYwJAYDVQQKEx1EaWd
 pdGFsIEVxdWlwbWVudCBDb3Jwb3JhdGlvbjEMMAoGA1UECxMDTEtH,02
MIC-Info: RSA-MD5,RSA,u1OHP1RwLqePAoaN5nPk9W7Q2EfjaP+yDBSaLyMcSgc
 MK2YicGSAqLz47Ol+TUR4YmMD/JnHMtsCJerV2QFtFQ--

Care to meet me at my apartment tonight?
-----END PRIVACY-ENHANCED MESSAGE-----
```

The MIC-ONLY version would look like this:

```
To: Bob
Subject: Keep this proposition private!
Date: Fri, 01 Apr 94 10:15:02 -0400
From: Alice

-----BEGIN PRIVACY-ENHANCED MESSAGE-----
Proc-Type: 4,MIC-ONLY
Content-Domain: RFC822
Originator-ID-Asymmetric: MEMxCzAJBgNVBAYTAlVTMSYwJAYDVQQKEx1EaWd
 pdGFsIEVxdWlwbWVudCBDb3Jwb3JhdGlvbjEMMAoGA1UECxMDTEtH,02
MIC-Info: RSA-MD5,RSA,u1OHP1RwLqePAoaN5nPk9W7Q2EfjaP+yDBSaLyMcSgc
 MK2YicGSAqLz47Ol+TUR4YmMD/JnHMtsCJerV2QFtFQ==

G9yYXRpb24xDDAKBgNVBAsTA0xLRzESMBAGA1UEAxMJSm9obiBMaW5uMFcwCgYE
-----END PRIVACY-ENHANCED MESSAGE-----
```

The ENCRYPTED version would look like this:

```
To: Bob
Subject: Keep this proposition private!
Date: Fri, 01 Apr 94 10:10:31 -0400
From: Alice

-----BEGIN PRIVACY-ENHANCED MESSAGE-----
Proc-Type: 4,ENCRYPTED
Content-Domain: RFC822
DEK-Info: DES-CBC,31747476B4831B1D
Originator-ID-Asymmetric: MEMxCzAJBgNVBAYTAlVTMSYwJAYDVQQKEx1EaWd
 pdGFsIEVxdWlwbWVudCBDb3Jwb3JhdGlvbjEMMAoGA1UECxMDTEtH,02
Key-Info: RSA,Pv3W7Ds86/fQBnvB5DsvUXgpK7+6h5aSVcNeYf9uWtly9m2VHzC
 v2t7A6qgbXtIcf4kaMj1FL2yl9/N9mWpm4w==
MIC-Info: RSA-MD5,RSA,FUiVRM3x5Ku0aZveGIJ1hv/hi3Iowpm1iypd9VP7MGw
 PPQra+42TkbR/2jhnqXyVEXLaJ7BSyNhBh/9znIUj5uk0N7IXeBxX
Recipient-ID-Asymmetric: MEMxCzAJBgNVBAYTAlVTMSYwJAYDVQQKEx1EaWdp
 dGFsIEVxdWlwbWVudCBDb3Jwb3JhdGlvbjEMMAoGA1UECxMDTEtH,05
Key-Info: RSA,dpUp7/QoY9YOzzZCVcIwxIDMN0WbGCFAGN3T+xlV/0pBu2n5+x8
 PmBvMUN0NcBi5vtqBS4cfmgShiK0I4zu05Q==

21OHDuHTP5BABnlsqENz1WVerZxxWo2AsPHhm2SIz9qpLMvxT/x0+8UEf8dDsTDr
wbQo9/x+
-----END PRIVACY-ENHANCED MESSAGE-----
```

Not only can these types of data be combined in a message, but they can be nested inside one another. For instance, assuming public key based user keys, Alice might enclose an integrity-protected message from Fred in an encrypted message to Bob. (Bob, I received the following message from Fred. Should I alert the authorities?)

13.2 ESTABLISHING KEYS

Suppose Alice is sending a message to Bob. For an integrity check, or for encryption, PEM has to find appropriate cryptographic keys. The per-message key used to encrypt a message is just a randomly selected number. But there is also a long-term key which PEM refers to as an **interchange key**. When public keys are used, the interchange key is Bob's public key. When secret keys are used, the interchange key is a key Alice and Bob share.

The interchange key is used to encrypt the per-message key:

The key is 2582	encrypted with interchange key
data...	encrypted with message key (2582)

PEM gives no hint as to how to establish secret key based interchange keys. The assumption is that there is some out-of-band-mechanism for doing it, for instance calling someone on the phone and agreeing on a number. The PEM designers could have allowed fields for Kerberos-style tickets to be carried in the message, but interest in secret key based interchange keys for PEM is low, so there hasn't been a lot of thought on how to deploy secret key based PEM.

In the case of PEM based on public key technology, PEM defines a certification hierarchy based on the X.500 naming hierarchy. A hierarchical naming scheme means that names contain multiple components, like A/B/C/D, reflecting a tree structure where each successive component gives the next branch downwards. Having the certification hierarchy follow the naming hierarchy means that there is a CA named A/B/C that certifies all the names of the form A/B/C/*, and there's a CA named A/B that certifies all the names of the form A/B/* (including CA A/B/C). Alice can find Bob's public key through some service such as the directory service. It's not enough for Alice to be told Bob's public key. She needs a certificate vouching for it being Bob's key, and signed by a CA that Alice trusts. If the CA that can vouch for Bob isn't one that Alice knows about, then Alice needs a chain of certificates, where Bob's CA (CA_1) vouches for Bob, some other CA (CA_2) vouches for CA_1, CA_3 vouches for CA_2, ... back to a CA that Alice is willing to trust.

While it is hoped that eventually there will exist a global directory service in which all certificates can be stored to make them universally available, the PEM designers considered it important to be able to operate before such a directory service was deployed. For that reason, they specified how the header of a PEM message could contain certificates relevant to authenticating the sender of the message. This not only permits the receiver to verify the signature of a message without access to a directory service, it provides a convenient method for delivering certificates to someone who needs to know the sender's public key in order to send him an encrypted message.

Thus a convenient way for Bob to send Alice the necessary certificates is for Bob to use PEM to send Alice a message including all necessary certificates in the header. Note that even if Alice and Bob intend that all of their conversations be encrypted, the first message one of them sends the other must be unencrypted (since neither yet knows the other's public key). This will not be necessary if Alice can look up Bob's certificates in some directory service.

Note that certificates take up a lot of room, and they may not be necessary. Indeed, Alice may have cached Bob's certificates. In that case, there is no reason for Bob to send the certificates. Some PEM implementations allow the user to tell PEM to leave out the certificates for a particular message. If Bob sends a message without the certificates, but Alice really doesn't have them, then Alice can send Bob a message (or call him on the phone) and ask him to send a message with the certificates. Or perhaps she can retrieve them from the directory service.

13.3 SOME PEM HISTORY

The PEM Certificate Hierarchy is somewhat baroque, and to understand why it is the way it is, it helps to know some history. It got to where it is by a series of compromises, each one of which made sense in context. In fact, at the time of this writing the structure was still being fine-tuned.

The original vision for the PEM Certificate Hierarchy was to have a large number of independently operated Certification Authorities, each having responsibility for a subtree of the global namespace. Most X.500 names would list individuals as members of an organization, and it seemed natural for the organization to operate the CA for its own members. For instance, the organization CIA might have a CA called /C=US/O=CIA, and all the names of people in CIA start out with the string /C=US/O=CIA, for example /C=US/O=CIA/CN=Noriega. If an organization was large, it might create subsidiary CAs and delegate to them control of sub-parts of the organization's name space. For instance, there might be /C=US/O=CIA/OU=plumbers. Someone who worked in that organization would then have a name like /C=US/O=CIA/OU=plumbers/CN=Liddy. A single global root CA would certify the names and public keys of all the independent organizations. To be considered valid by the recipient, a certificate would have to follow the rule that the **issuer name** (the name of the CA that signs the certificate) be a prefix of the **subject name** (the name of the owner of the public key being certified). This would guarantee that a CA in one organization could not issue a valid certificate for a user in another. So for instance, with the certificate for Liddy, the issuer name would be /C=US/O=CIA/OU=plumbers and the subject name would be /C=US/O=CIA/OU=plumbers/CN=Liddy. (Note that PEM does allow a CA to certify anything in its subtree, so the CA for /C=US/O=CIA would be allowed to issue a certificate for /C=US/O=CIA/OU=plumbers/CN=Liddy.)

While PEM is today deployed in the free-wheeling internet community where it replaces a system with virtually no security at all and where security requirements are therefore not "military-grade", the vision was for PEM to open up new applications by offering a single uniformly high standard of authentication. It might, for example, be possible to sign purchase orders as PEM messages and consider them legally binding. And it should be possible to send an encrypted message to someone around the world with complete confidence that only the intended recipient would be able to read it. Such confidence requires faith in both the cryptographic mechanisms used and the operational procedures of the people who create certificates. If there are "sloppy" CAs around who will issue certificates to anyone with an honest face, how can you know who is really sending and reading your messages?

The original vision for PEM, therefore, set a uniformly high standard for the operational procedures of CAs. Since the compromise of a CA's key would be particularly disastrous, it would be required that CAs be implemented in specially packaged hardware that made it nearly impossible to extract the CA's private key from the hardware. Strict administrative rules would be followed in qualifying the people who could operate the CAs and in the procedures they would follow in ensuring that they issued certificates only to people who had adequately proven their identities.

The root CA would be particularly sensitive, since its compromise would render the entire PEM infrastructure useless (though it would not compromise the security of PEM unless the compromise were undetected and the attacker could sneak forged certificates into the system). The root CA would be operated by RSADSI (the organization that licenses the RSA patent) or an affiliate, and that organization would use draconian procedures to protect the integrity of its certificates.

This structure had a side effect that it made possible a licensing structure and mechanism for RSADSI to collect fees for use of the RSA patent. A user's certificate could represent not just proof of his public key but also a license to use RSA. The same CA hardware that protects the CA's private key could also act as a "postage meter" which keeps track of the number of certificates it issues and can require payment of a per-certificate fee to RSADSI. Collection of royalties is therefore distributed. RSADSI could enforce the use of metering hardware (or some alternative royalty arrangement) by refusing to certify an organizational CA until some accommodation was reached. Without such an organizational certificate, the certificates issued by a CA would not be accepted by "standard" PEM implementations.

This vision of the PEM certificate hierarchy was ultimately rejected by the IETF standards community for a number of reasons.

- Universities were not amenable to enforcing the same administrative procedures for authenticating their students as defense contractors were in authenticating their employees. No "one size fits all" compromise could be reached. It may have been discussions of mandatory drug testing for CA operators that pushed this over the edge.

- There were concerns about the availability and cost of the CA hardware. For several years, organizational certificates and the hardware remained "a few months" away.

- There was reluctance to trust RSADSI—or any single party—with the security of the entire system.

- There was a reluctance to expand the RSADSI monopoly. RSADSI was the sole licensing authority for the RSA algorithm, so it might seem that it was necessary to make peace with them in order to use PEM, but this was simplistic. The U.S. Government has rights to use the algorithm as it sees fit without payment of royalties. Several companies had already reached agreements with RSADSI and were afraid of having to "pay again". RSA is only patented within the U.S., and foreign concerns were afraid of having to pay for what they currently use for free. And after September 20, 2000, the RSA patent will expire, and people were not happy about the possibility of having to continue to pay RSADSI after that date in order to obtain certificates.

In any case, it was decided that this relatively straightforward solution to the certificate hierarchy was unacceptable, and the designers embellished it in the minimal fashion that worked—they added another layer to the hierarchy and explicitly allowed people to go into competition with RSADSI. The result is the hierarchy we're about to describe.

13.4 CERTIFICATE HIERARCHY

RFC 1422 recommends an organization of CAs. It recommends a single root CA, called the **IPRA**, which stands for **Internet Policy Registration Authority** and is managed by the Internet Society. Certified by the IPRA are CAs called **PCAs** (for **Policy Certification Authorities**), so named because each one has a written policy it will enforce in its issuance of certificates. The design envisions at least three kinds of policies that will be enforced. The names have not been standardized, so we'll arbitrarily name them for ease of explanation.

- High Assurance (HA)

A HA CA is meant to be super-secure. The rules aren't standardized, but some of the ideas are as follows.

A HA CA is supposed to be implemented on special hardware designed so that it is tamper-resistant (impossible to extract its private key even if you were to steal the whole box), and managed by people who have passed security checks and perhaps periodic drug tests or other procedures. Also, the people who run a HA CA have to have wonderfully paranoid criteria for authenticating you before issuing you a certificate. Furthermore, a HA CA will refuse to grant a certificate to any organization that doesn't have the same strict rules about how its CA is managed and how its CA grants certificates.

- Discretionary Assurance (DA)

A DA CA is intended to be well managed at the top level, but it doesn't impose any rules on the organizations to which it grants CA certificates (other than that they actually "own" the name listed in their certificate). The managers of a DA CA will make sure that when an organization, say the Chaos Computer Club, asks for a certificate for their CA, that they really are the Chaos Computer Club. However, the DA CA managers will not make any constraints on how the Chaos Computer Club manages its CA.

Note that technically the IPRA is of the DA type. It can't be of the HA type, because it will issue certificates to a DA CA and a NA CA (see below)

* No Assurance (NA)

A NA CA has no constraints except that it is not allowed to issue two certificates with the same name. It is expected that users certified by a NA CA will not in general use their real names and may in fact operate under **personas** (pseudonyms) like Rabid Dog. Even the issuing NA CA might not know the true identity of the users it certifies.

The rule in RFC 1422 is that there can only be a single path through the CA hierarchy to any individual. What that means is that if an organization, say MIT, decides it wants to be certified with a DA CA, then it cannot also be certified with a HA CA. It also means that cross certificates (see §11.9 *Hierarchy of Realms*) are not allowed. The CA hierarchy is a tree.

This rule makes it easy to know the proper chain of certificates to give to someone. The maximal set of certificates they can need is the chain of certificates beginning with the IPRA. There are disadvantages to the restrictions, however. Cross certificates are often useful, so that the chain of certificates can be shorter between two organizations with a lot of mail traffic. And sometimes the two organizations would trust each other's CAs more than they'd trust the entire chain of CAs to and from the IPRA.

Also the rule prevents an organization that would like to get certificates from a HA CA (or made that decision at some point in the past) from granting a certificate to some suborganization's CA that will be less strict than the HA rules demand. An organization can accomplish this by operating two CAs, one which will follow the HA rules, and another which is not constrained by those rules.

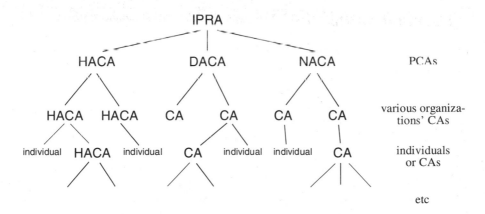

Figure 13-1. RFC 1422 Certification Authority Hierarchy

One could implement a PEM that followed the other PEM RFCs but not 1422, and base it on some other CA hierarchy. However, the hierarchy in RFC 1422 is the one being set up, and if you want to interoperate with other PEM implementations, you should follow the guidelines.

13.5 CERTIFICATE REVOCATION LISTS (CRLs)

Recall from §7.7.3 *Certificate Revocation* that although someone may have a valid-looking certificate, they are not necessarily a valid user, since the certificate might have been revoked. In order to really authenticate someone, we need not only the relevant certificates in the certificate chain, but timely CRLs to ensure that none of those certificates has been revoked.

It is possible for PEM users to obtain both certificates and CRLs without the aid of PEM, assuming some sufficiently sophisticated (and as yet undeployed) directory service. PEM wants to be useable even if such a directory service is for some reason unavailable, so it allows Bob to send Alice the relevant certificates for him by including them in the header of a PEM message he sends to her. PEM doesn't include a field in the header for CRLs, though. Instead PEM defines a CRL service that sends the latest CRLs as a mail message in response to receipt of a request in a mail message.

PEM defines two message types for the CRL service—CRL-RETRIEVAL-REQUEST and CRL. You send a CRL-RETRIEVAL-REQUEST message to the CRL service. The request is unencrypted and unsigned, and consists of a sequence of encoded X.500 names of CAs whose CRLs you want. The service responds with a CRL message containing (as text) the requested CRLs encoded, unencrypted, and unsigned, though each included CRL is signed by the CA that issued it. For each CA, the CRL service can send only the CA's most recently issued CRL that it knows about.

Note that you don't always want the latest CRLs. You really want the ones that were valid at the time a message was received. You might be checking the signatures (on every relevant certificate) for a message that had been forwarded to you months after it was originally received. PEM doesn't provide such a service. The original recipient would have had to obtain the relevant CRLs immediately upon receiving the message, and then kept them with the message. Alternatively, some sort of library service could be set up to archive all CRLs.

13.6 X.509 CERTIFICATES AND CRLS

PEM certificates and CRLs follow the X.509 standard.

A PEM certificate contains the following information:

- VERSION. There are currently two versions defined, version 1 for which the code is 0, and version 2 for which the code is 1.

- SERIALNUMBER. An integer that, together with the issuing CA's name, uniquely identifies this certificate.

- SIGNATURE. Deceptively named, this specifies the algorithm used to compute the signature on this certificate. It consists of a subfield identifying the algorithm followed by optional parameters for the algorithm. For PEM, only one algorithm has been defined, and it takes one parameter whose value is null. The algorithm identifier is 1.2.840.113549.1.1.2

- ISSUER. The X.500 name of the issuing CA.

- VALIDITY. This contains two subfields, the time the certificate becomes valid, and the last time for which it is valid. Times are specified as UTC (Coordinated Universal Time, formerly known as Greenwich Mean Time).

- SUBJECT. The X.500 name of the entity whose key is being certified.

- SUBJECTPUBLICKEYINFO. This contains two subfields, an algorithm identifer (itself containing two subfields, one identifying the algorithm and the other providing optional parameters for it), and the subject's public key (itself containing two subfields, the RSA modulus and the RSA public exponent). For PEM, there are two possible algorithm identifiers, both of which specify the same algorithm (RSA). One is 2.5.8.1.1 and takes one parameter, which specifies the number of bits in the RSA modulus. The other is 1.2.840.113549.1.1.1 and takes one parameter, which is null.

- ISSUERUNIQUEIDENTIFIER. Optional (permitted only in version 2). Uniquely identifies the issuer of this certificate.

- SUBJECTUNIQUEIDENTIFIER. Optional (permitted only in version 2). Uniquely identifies the subject of this certificate.

- ALGORITHMIDENTIFIER. This repeats the SIGNATURE field. This field is completely and utterly redundant and didn't need to be there.

- ENCRYPTED. Perhaps it would have been better to call this field *signature*. But that name was already taken. Anyway, this field contains the signature on all but the last of the above fields.

It follows PKCS #1 (see §5.3.6 *Public-Key Cryptography Standard (PKCS)*), using MD2 as the message digest and RSA for the signature.

The purpose of the optional UNIQUEIDENTIFIER fields is to eliminate the possibility of confusion when a name is reused. For example, John Smith might leave an organization and then the organization might hire another John Smith, assigning the new John Smith the same X.500 name.

> *The author of that poem is either Homer or, if not Homer, somebody else of the same name.* —Aldous Huxley

A PEM CRL contains the following information:

- SIGNATURE. Identical to the SIGNATURE field in certificates, this specifies the algorithm used to compute the signature on this CRL.

- ISSUER. Identical to the ISSUER field in certificates, this is the X.500 name of the issuing CA.

- THISUPDATE. This contains the time the CRL was issued, specified as UTC.

- NEXTUPDATE. (Optional field.) This contains the time the next CRL is expected to be issued, specified as UTC. A reasonable policy is to treat as suspect any certificate issued by a CA whose current CRL has a NEXTUPDATE time in the past.

The following two fields repeat as a pair once for each revoked certificate:

- USERCERTIFICATE. This contains the serial number of the revoked certificate.

- REVOCATIONDATE. This contains the UTC time the certificate was revoked.

- ALGORITHMIDENTIFIER. As for certificates, this repeats the SIGNATURE field.

- ENCRYPTED. This field contains the signature on all but the last of the above fields. It follows PKCS #1 using MD2 as the message digest and RSA for the signature.

13.7 REFORMATTING DATA TO GET THROUGH MAILERS

As discussed in §12.14 *Annoying Text Format Issues*, the mail infrastructure on which PEM depends for delivering messages might modify messages. PEM needs a reversible encoding of a message that will transit through all known kinds of mail gateways (and even those the PEM designers don't know about, hopefully) without having the gateways feel compelled to mess with the data. The theory is, if no "funny" characters are used, lines are a reasonable length, you don't care about the value of the high-order bit (the parity bit), and all lines are terminated with <CR><LF>, your data will be safe from helpful mail forwarders.

PEM packs 6 bits of information into each 8-bit character. It takes 24 bits of input and converts that into 32 bits (4 characters, each of which will be transmitted as 8 bits). If the data does not consist of an integral number of 24-bit chunks, it is padded with 0 bits to the next multiple of 24 bits, and each octet of pad bits is encoded by =. Actually, PEM packs 65 values into the 8 bits, since the padding gets converted to the = character, which is not one of the 64 characters used for encoding information. The encoding characters consist of the 26 upper-case (A–Z) and 26 lower-case (a–z) letters, the ten digits (0–9), +, and /. PEM uses the character = for the one or two possible padding characters necessary at the end of the data. For those who care, the table of encodings is as follows:

value	character	ASCII representation
0	A	101 octal
⋮	⋮	⋮
25	Z	132 octal
26	a	141 octal
⋮	⋮	⋮
51	z	172 octal
52	0	60 octal
⋮	⋮	⋮
61	9	71 octal
62	+	53 octal
63	/	57 octal
padding	=	75 octal

Figure 13-2. PEM 6-Bit Encoding

13.8 GENERAL STRUCTURE OF A PEM MESSAGE

(See also §13.17 *Message Formats*.) A PEM message is sent like an ordinary mail message. As a matter of fact, the PEM portion might only be a small piece inside an ordinary mail message.

If public key interchange keys are being used and Alice is sending a message to Bob, the PEM portion has the following structure:

marker indicating PEM-processed portion of the message follows: `-----BEGIN PRIVACY-ENHANCED MESSAGE-----`	
header, including information such as which of the three modes is being used (MIC-CLEAR, MIC-ONLY, ENCRYPTED)	
Initialization Vector (IV) for DES-CBC [field present only for ENCRYPTED message]	
certificate for Alice, signed by Alice's CA	optional (see below)
certificate for Alice's CA, signed by CA_2	
⋮	
certificate signed by IPRA	
Message Integrity Code (MIC), which is encrypted if the message is encrypted	
DES key used to encrypt the message, encrypted with Bob's public key [field present only for ENCRYPTED message]	
blank line	
message, either encrypted [if ENCRYPTED], merely mangled to fit into 6-bit canonical get-through-any-mailer format [if MIC-ONLY], or actually human-intelligible [if MIC-CLEAR]	
marker indicating PEM-processed portion of the message is finished: `------END PRIVACY-ENHANCED MESSAGE------`	

It is optional how many certificates in the chain to include. If Alice is pretty sure Bob has the remaining certificates, she can stop at some point before the IPRA. It is possible that no certificates appear explicitly, in which case what appears in their place is the serial number and issuer name of Alice's certificate.

If secret key interchange keys are being used, the structure is:

marker indicating PEM-processed portion of the message follows: `-----BEGIN PRIVACY-ENHANCED MESSAGE-----`
header, including information such as which of the three modes is being used (MIC-CLEAR, MIC-ONLY, ENCRYPTED)
Initialization Vector (IV) for DES-CBC [field present only for ENCRYPTED message]

DES key used to encrypt the message, encrypted with the interchange key shared by Alice and Bob   [field present only for ENCRYPTED message]
Message Integrity Code (MIC), encrypted using the interchange key shared by Alice and Bob.
blank line
message, either encrypted [if ENCRYPTED], merely mangled to fit into 6-bit canonical get-through-any-mailer format [if MIC-ONLY], or actually human intelligible [if MIC-CLEAR]
marker indicating PEM-processed portion of the message is finished: -----END PRIVACY-ENHANCED MESSAGE-----

13.9 ENCRYPTION

While PEM was designed to be relatively independent of the user's choice of encryption algorithms, and fields exist in the header to specify the encryption algorithm being used, the use of DES is expected to dominate for encryption of messages and is indeed the only algorithm named in the early specifications or implemented in the early prototypes.

For the encryption of message keys, an RSA-based public key encryption scheme is expected to dominate, but in fact three schemes are specified. One is RSA (when public key interchange keys are being used), and there are two variants of DES (when secret key interchange keys are being used): DES-ECB, where the key is encrypted using an ordinary interchange key; and DES-EDE, where the key is encrypted three times using a double-length interchange key. More types may be added in the future. Note that the per-message DES key is only 64 bits long, so cipher block chaining is not needed for encrypting it.

A message is encrypted using a per-message DES key, in CBC mode with a randomly chosen 64-bit initialization vector (IV). The per-message DES key is different from the interchange key, even when secret key interchange keys are used. Furthermore, if Alice sends two messages to Bob, each has a different per-message DES key. If Bob sends a message to Alice, he chooses yet another per-message DES key. Given that DES keys are chosen at random, it is theoretically possible that more than one message will be encrypted with the same DES key, but it is sufficiently unlikely that we're sure you can find better things to worry about (like a long-lost piece of the Skylab satellite falling on you).

The reason for using an IV in this case is very subtle. Ordinarily, the purposes of an IV are:

- to ensure that if two messages begin with the same text and are transmitted using the same key, a bad guy seeing the encrypted version will not be able to tell that the messages begin the same

- to prevent a bad guy who can supply messages to be encrypted from mounting a chosen plaintext attack against the key

With PEM, however, every message is sent with a different key, so these concerns do not arise. The reason PEM uses an IV is to make exhaustive attacks against per-message keys more difficult in the case where several messages are sent and the attacker happens to know they all begin with the same text and knows that text (e.g. "**Dear sir:**" or more likely " "). In that case, an attacker with a fast crypto engine could start encrypting that text with all 2^{56} keys and check whether the resulting block matched the first block of any of the captured messages. In 2^{56} encryptions, the attacker can crack all of the messages. With PEM's IV, however, the attacker has to try 2^{56} keys for each message, since the first blocks of text will be different after the IVs are $\oplus$ed.

Each message to be CBC-encrypted is padded with 1 to 8 bytes to make it a multiple of 8 bytes (even if it started out as a multiple of 8 bytes). The content of each of the pad bytes is the number of pad bytes. So a message that was already a multiple of 8 bytes would be padded with eight 8s. A message that was 2 more than a multiple of 8 would have 6 bytes of 6s.

13.10 SOURCE AUTHENTICATION AND INTEGRITY PROTECTION

Integrity protection is provided by calculating a MIC (Message Integrity Code) for the message. The defined types of MIC are MD2 and MD5. But a message digest by itself is not a MIC since anyone can modify the message and compute the message digest of the modified message. So the message digest has to be cryptographically protected. In the public key case, this is done by signing the message digest; in the secret key case, it is done by encrypting the message digest with the interchange key.

Assume Alice is sending Bob a message. With a secret key based interchange key the 128-bit message digest is encrypted with the interchange key using DES in ECB mode. With public key based interchange keys Alice signs the message digest, and if the message is encrypted, additionally encrypts the MIC. The signature is done using RSA as specified in PKCS #1. The encryption of the signed message digest is done with the per-message DES key, using DES in CBC mode with the same key, IV, and padding used for encrypting the message.

In the public key case, why must the MIC be encrypted when the message is encrypted? The reason is that the message digest can be computed from the MIC by using Alice's public key. Someone can guess the contents of the message, and then be able to verify it by checking the message digest of the guess against that of the message. For instance, if they guess the message will say either **attack** or **retreat**, they can compute the message digest on both guessed messages, and see whether either guess is correct. It's nice that the MIC doesn't need to be encrypted when the message is not encrypted. In that case a per-message key can be dispensed with entirely and the sender need not learn the public key of the recipient in order to send a signed message.

13.11 MULTIPLE RECIPIENTS

A signed but unencrypted message can be sent to any number of recipients without modification. PEM merely signs the message with the sender's private key:

-----BEGIN PRIVACY-ENHANCED MESSAGE-----
header, saying MIC-CLEAR or MIC-ONLY
MIC (message digest signed with Alice's private key)
unencrypted message
-----END PRIVACY-ENHANCED MESSAGE-----

To transmit an encrypted message to multiple recipients, PEM encrypts the message once (with, as usual, a randomly chosen key), and then separately encrypts the per-message key for each recipient:

-----BEGIN PRIVACY-ENHANCED MESSAGE-----
header, saying ENCRYPTED
MIC (message digest signed with Alice's private key and encrypted with message key)
Message key encrypted with Bob's public key
Message key encrypted with Ted's public key
encrypted message
-----END PRIVACY-ENHANCED MESSAGE-----

Note that the message is encrypted only once, but the per-message key must be encrypted once for each recipient.

It is possible to mix usage of public and secret keys. For instance, suppose Alice is sending a message to Bob and Carol, where Bob has a public key, but Carol has a secret key shared with Alice, and Carol's node cannot execute public key cryptographic algorithms (perhaps because Carol hasn't made the proper licensing arrangement). Alice picks a per-message secret key, encrypts the message with that secret key, and then encrypts the per-message key with Bob's public key (for Bob), and encrypts it with the key she shares with Carol (for Carol). The integrity check need only appear once to take care of all recipients capable of dealing with public keys. Alice merely signs the message digest with her private key. However, just because Alice has a public key does not mean that all the recipients can make use of it. For instance, those U.S. recipients who haven't licensed RSA cannot legally verify the signature. Alice needs to include a separate MIC for each recipient who cannot deal with her public key. For instance, for Carol, Alice will include the message digest encrypted with the secret key that Alice and Carol share.

-----BEGIN PRIVACY-ENHANCED MESSAGE-----
header, saying ENCRYPTED
MIC (message digest signed with Alice's private key and encrypted with message key)
Message key encrypted with Bob's public key
MIC (message digest encrypted with the key Alice and Carol share)
Message key encrypted with the key Alice and Carol share
encrypted message
-----END PRIVACY-ENHANCED MESSAGE-----

13.12 BRACKETING PEM MESSAGES

Bob has just received a message. How does his PEM processor know whether the message is a PEM message, or just an ordinary message? Even if PEM knows (somehow) that the message is a PEM message, it's not always obvious where PEM should start processing, and where to end processing. For instance, Alice might have sent a signed message to Bob, so that the entire message as transmitted by Alice should be processed by PEM, but mail gateways en route might add cybercrud to the beginning and/or end of the message. (Luckily most mail gateways are sufficiently well-behaved so that they don't add things to the middle of a message—if they did, PEM would not be able to cope.) By the time Bob receives the message his PEM processor might need to skip the first few lines, start processing at some point, and end at some other point in the message. As a matter of fact, it isn't strictly necessary for an entire message from Alice to be PEM-processed. She might just want to encrypt a small portion of the message. For example:

```
Hello Bob
This is to inform you that your raise has gone through and your new salary is
-----BEGIN PRIVACY-ENHANCED MESSAGE-----
```

header saying encrypted

afdsjklasdfjklas;f

```
-----END PRIVACY-ENHANCED MESSAGE-----
Once again congratulations on the good work.
Sincerely, Alice
```

That is why PEM marks the beginning of the PEM-processed portion of the message with the string
```
-----BEGIN PRIVACY-ENHANCED MESSAGE-----
```
and the end of the message with the string
```
-----END PRIVACY-ENHANCED MESSAGE-----
```
This might sound straightforward, but there are problems. A human being is perfectly capable of typing the above strings (we did, for instance). Suppose
```
-----END PRIVACY-ENHANCED MESSAGE-----
```
appears in the middle of a message. For instance, Alice might be transmitting a portion of this book (after getting written permission from the publisher, of course!).

Note that if the message is encoded (as a MIC-ONLY or ENCRYPTED message will be), then the string
```
-----END PRIVACY-ENHANCED MESSAGE-----
```
can't possibly appear inside the (encoded) body of the message (even if it was in the original message) because "-" is not one of the encode characters. But PEM does have to worry about disguising the PEM end marker in MIC-CLEAR messages.

Although the end marker is the only string that could confuse PEM, instead of only searching for
```
-----END PRIVACY-ENHANCED MESSAGE-----
```
PEM always modifies every line of the text of a MIC-CLEAR message that begins with a dash, just because RFC 934 did it that way for forwarded mail markers. When PEM sees a line that begins with a dash, it adds the two characters "- " (dash space) to the beginning of the line. So the string
```
-----END PRIVACY-ENHANCED MESSAGE-----
```
would appear as
```
- -----END PRIVACY-ENHANCED MESSAGE-----
```
if it appeared in the middle of a MIC-CLEAR message. Any other line that started with a dash

would also appear that way. For example,

`--Sincerely, Alice--`

would appear as:

`- --Sincerely, Alice--`

 Bob's PEM processor will most likely remove the extra characters before displaying the text of the message to Bob. However, if Bob does not have PEM, Bob will see the PEM cybercrud, and see the mysterious "- " added to the beginning of some of the lines of the text of the message.

 PEM really can't defend itself from being confused in all cases. For instance, Alice might have typed the following message and sent it with a non-PEM mailer.

```
To: Bob
     Have you heard about this new PEM standard? I don't
completely understand it, but it seems to imply that I can make my
message to you secret by adding the string
     -----BEGIN PRIVACY-ENHANCED MESSAGE-----
and some other stuff like MIC-INFO and RFC-1822 at the beginning
of the message and putting the string
     -----END PRIVACY-ENHANCED MESSAGE-----
at the end. I don't understand how this could prevent anyone from
reading the message, although maybe enough cybercrud on the
beginning of the message would convince them the message must be
hopelessly garbled and they might not even attempt to read it.
--Alice
```

If Bob's machine has PEM, it will see those markers and attempt to parse the message as a PEM message. It will probably notice that the message is ill-formed, though Alice could have typed something that happened to have all the text looking like correct fields. At that point it would probably notice that signatures would not verify or that it was lacking the proper certificates. If Alice did indeed manage to type in a completely correct PEM message, then PEM at Bob's node will not notice (Alice will have passed a warped form of the Turing test).

 Another issue is nested messages. It is permissible to have, for instance, an encrypted message inside a signed message, or Alice might be forwarding a signed message from Fred as an enclosure in a signed message to Bob (see §13.14.1 *Forwarding a Message*). The PEM processor at Bob's node presumably has to process the outer message, which might involve decrypting and/or decoding. Once the outer message is processed, the string

`-----BEGIN PRIVACY-ENHANCED MESSAGE-----`

might be uncovered, and PEM has the same problem as we mentioned before, which is to somehow determine whether that is really the beginning of a PEM message, or whether Alice just happened to have included that particular string in her message.

 The PEM protocol was designed so that it is conceptually possible to nest PEM processing, but it would require PEM processors far more sophisticated than anyone is likely to ever implement to deal with all possible cases, and furthermore the user interface would be horrible to contemplate. Current PEM processors don't automatically deal with nesting at all. (See Homework Problem 9.)

13.13 REMOTE DISTRIBUTION LIST EXPLODERS

The PEM specifications say nothing about distribution list exploders, but they were considered in the design process. We will explain possible implementations.

13.13.1 Remote Exploding Using Public Keys

First we'll look at public key based PEM. If you send an encrypted message through a PEM-capable distribution list exploder, you encrypt the per-message secret key with the distribution list exploder's public key. (There's really no useful way to send an encrypted message through a non-PEM-capable distribution list exploder.) The encrypted message does not need to be decrypted by the distribution list exploder. The only thing the distribution list exploder needs to do is to decrypt the per-message key and re-encrypt it, once for each recipient, using that recipient's public key. There's no way to prevent a curious distribution list exploder from decrypting the message, but it doesn't need to.

Signatures are trivial to forward—they don't get changed at all. Even if the message is encrypted, so that the signature is encrypted with the per-message key, the signature doesn't change—the only change to the message is the addition of the encrypted per-message key for each recipient. If the message is unencrypted (MIC-ONLY or MIC-CLEAR), there is no per-message key, so the entire message can be forwarded unchanged by even a non-PEM-capable distribution list exploder.

Let's say that Alice is sending an encrypted message to the distribution list D. The message as received by the distribution list exploder for D will contain

- D's name; per-message key encrypted with D's public key

- message digest of (unencrypted) message, signed with Alice's private key, then encrypted with per-message key

- message encrypted with per-message key

The distribution list exploder will decrypt the per-message key and, for each recipient, re-encrypt the key with that recipient's public key. Suppose D consists of Bob, Carol, and Ted. The message the distribution list exploder transmits will contain

- Bob's name; per-message key encrypted with Bob's public key

- Carol's name; per-message key encrypted with Carol's public key

- Ted's name; per-message key encrypted with Ted's public key

- message digest of (unencrypted) message, signed with Alice's private key, then encrypted with per-message key

- message encrypted with per-message key

13.13.2 Remote Exploding Using Secret Keys

With secret keys, the shared secret is between Alice and the distribution list exploder, not between Alice and the ultimate recipients. With secret keys, all security services (MIC-ONLY, MIC-CLEAR, as well as ENCRYPTED) require a PEM-capable distribution list exploder.

Encrypted messages work similarly to the public key case. The distribution list exploder does not need to decrypt the message. It only needs to decrypt the per-message key and re-encrypt it, once for each recipient, with the secret key it shares with that recipient. The exploder does need to decrypt the message if it wants to check the MIC. While not necessary, checking the MIC and discarding messages which fail the check can protect the exploder from garbage messages that anyone can send to it claiming to be a legitimate user.

Integrity protection does not really work with secret keys and remote distribution list exploders. The exploder has to decrypt the MIC (to obtain the message digest of the unencrypted message) and re-encrypt it with the per-recipient secret key, once for each recipient. The only assurance a recipient gets with this technique is that the message came from the exploder, not that it came from Alice. PEM defines no means for the exploder to assert the name of the original sender in an integrity-protected field, so an intruder can modify the unprotected FROM field to make the message appear to have originally come from someone else. Also, an untrustworthy exploder can forge messages from anyone it chooses. (See Homework Problem 10.)

So, let's say Alice is sending an encrypted message to D, where that expands to Bob, Carol, and Ted. The message Alice sends contains

- D's name; per-message key and message digest encrypted with key Alice shares with D

- message encrypted with per-message key

The message the distribution list exploder sends contains

- Bob's name, per-message key and message digest encrypted with the key D shares with Bob

- Carol's name, per-message key and message digest encrypted with the key D shares with Carol

- Ted's name, per-message key and message digest encrypted with the key D shares with Ted

Suppose we're not satisfied with this technique, because it does not allow the distribution list exploder to assert, in an integrity-protected field, that the message did come from Alice. If we want the distribution list exploder to add the name Alice to the message in an integrity-protected way, it would either have to separately compute a MIC for that field (which PEM's format does not accommodate), or it could forward a modified version of the message that has Alice's name prepended, and compute a MIC on the modified message, by doing the following:

- decrypt the per-message key with the key it shares with Alice

- decrypt the message with the per-message key

- compute the message digest of the message

- decrypt the MIC with the key it shares with Alice

- compare the decrypted MIC with the message digest (if they match, the exploder has verified that the message did indeed come from Alice)

- if the decrypted MIC does not equal the message digest, discard the message

- (assuming the decrypted MIC equals the message digest) add text to the message, to the effect that the exploder has verified the message came from Alice

- compute a message digest on the new message (old message plus Alice's name added by the exploder)

- use the message digest computed in the previous bullet as the basis for the per-recipient MICs, encrypting a copy of it for each recipient, according to the secret key the exploder shares with that recipient

- encrypt the new message with the per-message secret key (if the exploder is feeling creative, it can choose a new per-message secret key—doing so neither hurts nor helps)

- encrypt the per-message secret key with the secret key the exploder shares with each recipient

A service that did all the above does furnish some measure of integrity protection, but there are complications. For instance, what should the exploder assert as Alice's name? With secret keys, there's no agreed-upon global name. The name by which the exploder knows Alice might not mean anything to the ultimate recipient.

Another issue is that the scheme we outlined assumes that the message is text, to be processed by a human. If instead the message was encoded data, then the text that the distribution list exploder adds would probably either confuse the recipient or be ignored.

Luckily, nobody really cares about PEM with secret keys, so the fact that these issues have no good solution shouldn't keep you awake nights.

13.13.3 Mixing Key Types

An exploder can serve as a gateway between the public key world and the secret key world (at least to protect the privacy of a message). Again, all it needs to do is decrypt the per-message key using its key and then re-encrypt it with the appropriate type of key for each recipient. The end-to-end signature is preserved if the original sender and the ultimate recipient use public key (even if there are secret key intermediaries).

13.14 FORWARDING AND ENCLOSURES

Alice might want to forward to Bob a message she received from someone else, inside a message of her own:

```
    -----BEGIN PRIVACY-ENHANCED MESSAGE-----

  header, saying MIC-CLEAR

  MIC (message digest signed with Bob's private key)

    Bob—
    Get a load of the outrageous stuff Fred is sending me!
    - --Alice
    - ----BEGIN PRIVACY-ENHANCED MESSAGE-----

  header, saying MIC-CLEAR

  MIC (message digest signed with Fred's private key)

    Alice—
    The rhythm of your typing at the terminal is driving me insane.
    Either type completely rhythmically or completely unrhythmically.
    I will complain to upper level management if you don't adjust your
    typing.
    - - - --Fred
    - ----END PRIVACY-ENHANCED MESSAGE-----
    -----END PRIVACY-ENHANCED MESSAGE-----
```

13.14.1 Forwarding a Message

What should you do to a message from Fred before forwarding it to Bob so that Bob can verify Fred's signature? With non-PEM mailers, one often extracts text from one message and includes it in another. PEM certainly doesn't stop you from doing that, but if you don't send a message with the PEM information intact, there's no way for Bob to know that the original text was really from Fred (he has to take your word for it). With public keys, it is possible to usefully forward PEM signatures. But secret key based source authentication information cannot be usefully forwarded because such information cannot be verified by a third party. Therefore, in this section, we'll assume user keys are based on public key technology.

Suppose Alice is just forwarding a message from Fred to Bob without adding any annotations of her own, and in the same format as she received it (ENCRYPTED, MIC-CLEAR, or MIC-ONLY). In that case she processes the message like a distribution list exploder:

- In the case of a MIC-CLEAR or MIC-ONLY message, she just forwards it, without having to do any processing on it.

- In the case of an ENCRYPTED message, she decrypts the per-message key, reencrypts it with Bob's key, and adds the encrypted key and Bob's name to the header.

It could be that Alice wants to change the format of the message. The term **upgrading** means that she turns an unencrypted message into an encrypted message. The term **downgrading** means she turns an encrypted message into an unencrypted message. The PEM designers were careful to have the signature on a message apply to the unencrypted message, so that a message can be downgraded or upgraded without changing the signature.

For example, let's assume Alice has a MIC-ONLY message from Fred. It contains

- header, saying MIC-ONLY

- MIC (message digest signed with Fred's private key)

- message (encoded but unencrypted)

In order to encrypt it to send it to Bob, Alice picks a per-message key K in order to encrypt the message. Now, she can't simply encrypt the encoded message, since PEM mandates that encryption is based on an unencoded message. So she has to decode the message, encrypt the result, and encode the result of the encryption. So what she sends is

- header, saying ENCRYPTED

- K encrypted with Bob's public key

- encrypted MIC, consisting of the message digest signed with Fred's private key and encrypted with K. Note that Alice can't sign the MIC with Fred's private key, so she has to use the MIC she received. Since the MIC she received from Fred is encoded (to pass through mailers), she has to decode the MIC to obtain the actual message digest signed with Fred's public key. That is the quantity she encrypts and then encodes.

- message encrypted with K

Downgrading a message is just reversing the process. If Alice wants to annotate Fred's message before forwarding it, then she can enclose the complete message inside the text of her message, and then sign or encrypt her own message as she desires.

13.15 CANONICALIZATION

PEM puts messages into **canonical form** before encrypting them or computing message integrity codes. This is so that the encrypted or signed form will not depend on the local representation of the system on which the message originated, simplifying the verification task if the system on which the message is received has a different local format.

PEM's canonical form is modeled after the SMTP wire format, and uses <CR><LF> as the end-of-line delimiter and ASCII as the character set.

Why does PEM need to do this? To ensure that receiving mail agents do not have to be overly creative in picking a local representation for received messages.

Why does PEM need to canonicalize a MIC-ONLY message, which will be turned into the 6-bit representation, which certainly won't have any funny characters or long lines? It has to do it for the same reason that an ordinary mail program (one that doesn't do integrity checks or encryption) has to canonicalize. It is so that the receiver's computer can display the message without having to know the specific local format of the sender.

If PEM could somehow know that the contents of the message was not text, but rather some other data form for which sender and recipient would accept the same bytes, it could skip the canonicalization step and save a lot of trouble. The
```
Content-Domain: RFC822
```
line in the PEM header offers a convenient place to specify such options at some point in the future.

The PEM spec is rather vague about the specifics of canonicalization. This is because this is really an ugly boring problem.

13.16 UNPROTECTED INFORMATION

PEM only provides integrity protection or privacy on the contents of a message. There is other information in a message, however, and if people use PEM carelessly there are interesting security flaws that can be exploited. PEM does not protect the SUBJECT, TO, FROM, or TIMESTAMP field. How can a bad guy exploit the fact that PEM does not protect these fields?

Why would it be nice to cryptographically protect the subject line? A naive user might put private information into the subject line, and expose the information to an eavesdropper. Or suppose Alice sees a message from Fred, in which Fred suggests some outrageous idea. Alice forwards Fred's message, integrity-protected, with the subject line Fire this Bozo immediately, but someone modifies the unprotected subject line to Great idea! Implement this suggestion immediately. Since the subject line is not protected, the message will arrive signed by Alice, but having the subject line modified completely changes what she intended to say.

The TO and FROM fields cannot be encrypted because the mail infrastructure needs to see them. Theoretically they could be included in the integrity protection even though they couldn't be privacy-protected. PEM didn't do this because mailers tend to mangle these fields. PEM could have gotten around this by making a copy of that information and moving it inside the message.

It's unfortunate that PEM doesn't integrity-protect the TO field. For instance, Alice might send the signed message I agree to donate $1000 to your organization to organization Z, and the message might be copied and used by organization Y to fool Alice's underlings into sending them money also.

An example of where it is unfortunate that PEM didn't do something with the FROM field is where secret key based interchange keys are used and Alice sends a message to a distribution list located on a remote exploder. The remote exploder has to check Alice's MIC and then add its own per-recipient MIC. PEM does not provide any cryptographically protected method for the exploder to assert that it did indeed check and the message had come from Alice.

The other piece of header information that is not cryptographically protected is the timestamp. This doesn't seem too important. Even naive users would realize that if the time of sending a message were important, they should date the message in the text. Naive users would probably not even know that the mail infrastructure adds a time of posting.

Note that even if PEM protected all the header fields, it would be possible to misuse electronic mail. For instance, if Alice sends Bob the signed message I approve, Bob can't use the message later to prove that Alice okayed his action, since the message isn't explicit about what Alice was approving.

If Alice is careful, most of these PEM problems can be worked around. To protect the header information, Alice should include the header information in the text. The only problem we've described that has no PEM workaround is that a remote mail exploder cannot cryptographically assert that a message using secret interchange keys did originate with Alice.

13.17 Message Formats

The PEM message formats have fields that consist of text. Sometimes the fields are encrypted, and sometimes they are encoded (which looks encrypted to humans but isn't).

The types of messages are MIC-CLEAR, MIC-ONLY, and ENCRYPTED, and the format for each of these varies slightly depending on whether public or secret key cryptography is being used. We'll describe the public key and secret key variants separately. If some recipients use public key and some use secret key, then fields from both variants must be present.

Each field in the message has a label indicating what it contains. There are a few reasons for this label:

- To provide a visual clue to a human reader wondering what all the cybercrud is (but a civilized PEM mailer ought not show the cybercrud to the human)

- To identify the field—the position of the field in the message does not uniquely identify it because some fields are optional and/or repeated (e.g. CA CERTIFICATE)

13.17.1 ENCRYPTED, Public Key Variant

`----BEGIN PRIVACY-ENHANCED MESSAGE-----`	pre-encapsulation boundary
`Proc-Type: 4,ENCRYPTED`	type of PEM message (version,type)
`Content-Domain: RFC822`	message form
`DEK-Info: DES-CBC,` *16 hex digits*	message encryption algorithm, IV
`Originator-Certificate:` *cybercrud*	sender's encoded certificate (optional)
`Originator-ID-Asymmetric:` *cybercrud,number*	sender ID (present only if sender's certificate not present)
`Key-Info: RSA,`*cybercrud*	key-info for CC'd sender (if needed)
`Issuer-Certificate:` *cybercrud* ⋮	sequence of zero or more CA certificates (possibly whole chain from the sender's certificate to the IPRA's)
`MIC-Info: RSA-MDx,RSA,`*cybercrud*	message digest algorithm, message digest encryption algorithm, encoded encrypted MIC
`Recipient-ID-Asymmetric:` *cybercrud,number* `Key-Info: RSA,`*cybercrud* ⋮	for each recipient: recipient ID (encoded X.500 name of CA that signed certificate, certificate serial number); key-info for recipient
	blank line
cybercrud	encoded encrypted message
`----END PRIVACY-ENHANCED MESSAGE----`	post-encapsulation boundary

`-----BEGIN PRIVACY-ENHANCED MESSAGE-----`

PRE-ENCAPSULATION BOUNDARY. This is just to show that a PEM-processed portion of the mail message is about to begin.

`Proc-Type: 4,ENCRYPTED`

MESSAGE TYPE. The first subfield (4) specifies that this is version four of PEM. There are currently no other legal values for this field. The second subfield (ENCRYPTED) specifies that this is an encrypted message. The other legal values for this field are MIC-ONLY and MIC-CLEAR.

```
Content-Domain: RFC822
```

MESSAGE FORM. The intention is that there might eventually be lots of types of mail messages, such as PostScript, spreadsheet, bitmap, executable image for an XYZ processor, and so on. However, the only defined type is RFC822, which is an Internet standard for ordinary text messages.

```
DEK-Info: DES-CBC,0123456789ABCDEF
```

MESSAGE ENCRYPTION ALGORITHM, IV. The first subfield identifies the cryptographic algorithm used to encrypt the message. Currently the only "registered" algorithm is DES-CBC. The second subfield specifies the IV as 16 hex digits. So in the example above, the IV is $0123456789ABCDEF_{16}$.

```
Originator-Certificate: MIIBfzCCASkCAQIwDQYJKoZIhvcNAQECBQAwQzELM
 AkGA1UEBhMCVVMxJjAkBgNVBAoTHURpZ210YWwgRXF1aXBtZW50IENvcnBvcmF0a
 W9uMQwwCgYDVQQLEwNMS0cwHhcNOTIwOTA4MjAxODMzWhcNOTQwOTA4MjAxODMzW
 jBXMQswCQYDVQQGEwJVUzEmMCQGA1UEChMdRGlnaXRhbCBFcXVpcG1lbnQgQ29yc
 G9yYXRpb24xDDAKBgNVBAsTA0xLRzESMBAGA1UEAxMJSm9obiBMaW5uMFcwCgYEV
 QgBAQICAgADSQAwRgJBAMEom520pxxpN7Y+0e8nWsI2yVK4YPu30+meJEwH9w0Xu
 O3hmHTHowzrNwgdgFeic4SH1kFOwf1K7RrOgnTurQ0CAQMwDQYJKoZIhvcNAQECB
 QADQQBq/+L5hKVZvN/jtgsjeUE5eQBrMpSf3ND4kqyP65xj29OhFk5Mbh4DpfJ+7
 wOwJATwUjOERhzwVJm5WmIOoRs4
```

SENDER'S CERTIFICATE. BIG pile of cybercrud as specified in X.509. Since a certificate is ASN.1-coded information (as opposed to nice printable text strings), the certificate is encoded as per §13.7 *Reformatting Data to Get Through Mailers*. Certificates are described in §13.6 *X.509 Certificates and CRLs*.

```
Originator-ID-Asymmetric: MEMxCzAJBgNVBAYTAlVTMSYwJAYDVQQKEx1EaWd
 pdGFsIEVxdWlwbWVudCBDb3Jwb3JhdGlvbjEMMAoGA1UECxMDTEtH,216
```

SENDER ID. This field can replace the SENDER'S CERTIFICATE field to save space. It consists of the X.500 name of the CA that issued the sender her certificate, coded in ASN.1 and encoded 6 bits per character, followed by a comma, followed by the serial number of the sender's certificate in decimal using decimal digits. In the example above, the serial number is 216.

```
Key-Info: RSA,Pv3W7Ds86/fQBnvB5DsvUXgpK7+6h5aSVcNeYf9uWtly9m2VHzC
 v2t7A6qgbXtIcf4kaMj1FL2yl9/N9mWpm4w==
```

KEY-INFO. This is strictly necessary only if the sender CC's herself on the message. It is also useful when the mail system returns the message to the sender due to some error condition. The purpose of this field is to enable the sender to decrypt the message. The first subfield specifies the cryptographic algorithm used for encrypting the per-message key. The only defined public key algorithm is RSA. The second subfield contains the per-message key encrypted with the sender's public key and then encoded.

```
Issuer-Certificate: MIIBXzCCAQkCAQowDQYJKoZIhvcNAQECBQAwNzELMAkGA
1UEBhMCVVMxKDAmBgNVBAoTH1RydXN0ZWQgSW5mb3JtYXRpb24gU31zdGVtcyBQQ
0EwHhcNOTIwOTA4MTk0NTQzWhcNOTQwOTA4MTk0NTQzWjBDMQswCQYDVQQGEwJVU
zEmMCQGA1UEChMdRGluaXRhbCBFcXVpcG1lbnQgQ29ycG9yYXRpb24xDDAKBgNVB
AsTA0xLRzBXMAoGBFUIAQECAgIAA0kAMEYCQQDkwhgRGX6ScwOHTVk48NK07tiih
t9bBExsbxphdp7brUrypA4kZDYqZNVv9Ee5kHv5qn428Pc31bGH+z1S7bq/AgEDM
A0GCSqGSIb3DQEBAgUAA0EARfI+2huFXK9jsROeK+CaohcB23cBFjzqhslhI50UU
Y4rBx8QhcApY/g+mhXzBz1JPe/HANQMG567DHB3AJKaTQ==
```

CA CERTIFICATE. The certificate of one of the CAs in the chain from the sender to the IPRA. The first one certifies the sender's CA, the next one certifies the sender's CA's parent, ..., the last one certifies the IPRA. However, it is permissible to include in the message only an initial subsequence of this certificate chain (even an empty subsequence!), as long as no certificates are skipped.

```
MIC-Info: RSA-MD5,RSA,FUiVRM3x5Ku0aZveGIJ1hv/hi3Iowpm1iypd9VP7MGw
PPQra+42TkbR/2jhnqXyVEXLaJ7BSyNhBh/9znIUj5uk0N7IXeBxX
```

MESSAGE DIGEST ALGORITHM, MESSAGE DIGEST ENCRYPTION ALGORITHM, MIC. The choices for message digest algorithm are **RSA-MD2** and **RSA-MD5**. RSA-MD2 is merely MD2. RSA-MD5 is MD5. In both cases, RSA is included in the name to acknowledge that MD2 and MD5 were donated for use in PEM by RSADSI. The choices for message digest encryption algorithm are **RSA**. (Luckily RSA is a good choice). The MIC (the message digest encrypted with the sender's private key, then encrypted with the per-message key) is an encoded 512-bit number.

```
Recipient-ID-Asymmetric: MEMxCzAJBgNVBAYTAlVTMSYwJAYDVQQKEx1EaWdp
dGFsIEVxdWlwbWVudCBDb3Jwb3JhdGlvbjEMMAoGA1UECxMDTEtH,729
```

RECIPIENT ID. This is an identifier for a recipient's certificate. It consists of the X.500 name of the CA that issued this recipient's certificate, coded in ASN.1 and encoded 6 bits per character, followed by a comma, followed by the serial number of the certificate in decimal using decimal digits. In the above example, the serial number is 729. Note that identifying the recipient in this arcane manner, rather than simply by name, allows a recipient with multiple public keys to know which key to use to decrypt his KEY-INFO field:

```
Key-Info: RSA,dpUp7/QoY9YOZzZCVcIwxIDMN0WbGCFAGN3T+x1V/0pBu2n5+x8
PmBvMUN0NcBi5vtqBS4cfmgShiK0I4zu05Q==
```

KEY-INFO. This field provides the recipient (identified by the immediately preceding RECIPIENT ID field) with the per-message key. The second subfield contains the per-message key encrypted with the recipient's public key and then encoded. The first subfield specifies the cryptographic algorithm used for encrypting the per-message key. The only defined public key algorithm is **RSA**. Note that even if there were more choices, there would be no reason to specify the algorithm since the algorithm is whatever algorithm is specified for the key in the recipient's certificate. However, bit-bumming the encoding of mail messages did not seem to be a priority with the PEM designers.

```
21OHDuHTP5BABnlsqENz1WVerZxxWo2AsPHhm2SIz9qpLMvxT/x0+8UEf8dDsTDr
wbQo9/x+
```

ENCRYPTED MESSAGE. The message DES-CBC encrypted with the per-message key and then encoded.

```
-----END PRIVACY-ENHANCED MESSAGE-----
```

POST-ENCAPSULATION BOUNDARY. This is just to show that a PEM-processed portion of the mail message has ended.

13.17.2 ENCRYPTED, Secret Key Variant

`----BEGIN PRIVACY-ENHANCED MESSAGE-----`	pre-encapsulation boundary
`Proc-Type: 4,ENCRYPTED`	type of PEM message (version,type)
`Content-Domain: RFC822`	message form
`DEK-Info: DES-CBC,` *16 hex digits*	message encryption algorithm, IV
`Originator-ID-Symmetric:` *entity identifier, issuing authority, version/expiration*	sender ID
`Recipient-ID-Symmetric:` *entity identifier, issuing authority, version/expiration* `Key-Info: DES-ECB,RSA-MDx,` *16 hex digits, 32 hex digits* ⋮	for each recipient: recipient ID; key-info for recipient
	blank line
cybercrud	encoded encrypted message
`----END PRIVACY-ENHANCED MESSAGE-----`	post-encapsulation boundary

```
-----BEGIN PRIVACY-ENHANCED MESSAGE-----
```

PRE-ENCAPSULATION BOUNDARY. This is just to show that a PEM-processed portion of the mail message is about to begin.

```
Proc-Type: 4,ENCRYPTED
```

MESSAGE TYPE. The first subfield (4) specifies that this is version four of PEM. There are currently no other legal values for this field. The second subfield (ENCRYPTED) specifies that this is an encrypted message. The other legal values for this field are MIC-ONLY and MIC-CLEAR.

`Content-Domain: RFC822`

MESSAGE FORM. The intention is that there might eventually be lots of types of mail messages, such as PostScript, spreadsheet, bitmap, executable image for an XYZ processor, and so on. However, the only defined type is RFC822, which is an Internet standard for ordinary text messages.

`DEK-Info: DES-CBC,0123456789ABCDEF`

MESSAGE ENCRYPTION ALGORITHM, IV. The first subfield identifies the cryptographic algorithm used to encrypt the message. Currently the only "registered" algorithm is DES-CBC. The second subfield specifies the IV as 16 hex digits. So in the example above, the IV is $0123456789ABCDEF_{16}$.

`Originator-ID-Symmetric: Alice@Wonderland.edu,,`

SENDER ID. This field uniquely identifies the sender to the recipients. There are three subfields. The first subfield identifies the sender. The other two subfields are useless, but are there to make the sender ID have the same format as the recipient IDs. In practice, the two useless subfields are omitted (except for the delimiting commas). There is no standard for the format of any of the subfields, but RFC 1421 strongly recommends using an internet mail address for the first subfield.

`Recipient-ID-Symmetric: WhiteRabbit@Wonderland.edu,`
`  MadHatter@Wonderland.edu,1`

RECIPIENT ID. This field uniquely identifies the interchange key to be used by the recipient. There are three subfields. The first subfield identifies the recipient (so that the recipient knows this field and the immediately following KEY-INFO field are for him). The second subfield identifies the issuer of the shared key (in the event that multiple issuing authorities have assigned shared keys between the sender and recipient). The third subfield uniquely identifies the key (in the event that multiple keys have been issued between the sender and recipient by the same issuing authority). There is no standard for the format of any of the subfields, but RFC 1421 strongly recommends using an internet mail address for the first subfield.

`Key-Info: DES-ECB,RSA-MD5,0123456789ABCDEF,`
`  FEDCBA9876543210012356789ABCDEF`

KEY-INFO. This field provides the recipient (identified by the immediately preceding RECIPIENT ID field) with the per-message key and the MIC. The first subfield specifies the cryptographic algorithm used to encrypt the per-message key. The choices are DES-ECB (see §3.6.1 *Electronic Code Book (ECB)*) and DES-EDE (see §3.8 *Multiple Encryption DES*). DES-EDE is used when the shared interchange key is double length. The second subfield specifies the algorithm used to compute the message digest. The choices are RSA-MD2 (for MD2) and RSA-MD5 (for MD5). The third subfield is the per-message key encrypted with the interchange key, expressed as a 16-digit hexadecimal number. The fourth subfield is the MIC, which is the message digest encrypted with the per-message key in ECB mode, expressed as a 32-digit hexadecimal number.

```
21OHDuHTP5BABnlsqENz1WVerZxxWo2AsPHhm2SIz9qpLMvxT/x0+8UEf8dDsTDr
wbQo9/x+
```

ENCRYPTED MESSAGE. The message DES-CBC encrypted with the per-message key and then encoded.

```
-----END PRIVACY-ENHANCED MESSAGE-----
```

POST-ENCAPSULATION BOUNDARY. This is just to show that a PEM-processed portion of the mail message has ended.

13.17.3 MIC-ONLY or MIC-CLEAR, Public Key Variant

`----BEGIN PRIVACY-ENHANCED MESSAGE-----`	pre-encapsulation boundary
`Proc-Type: 4,MIC-ONLY` *or* `MIC-CLEAR`	type of PEM message (version,type)
`Content-Domain: RFC822`	message form
`Originator-Certificate:` *cybercrud*	sender's encoded certificate (optional)
`Originator-ID-Asymmetric:` *cybercrud,number*	sender ID (present only if sender's certificate not present)
`Issuer-Certificate:` *cybercrud* ⋮	sequence of zero or more CA certificates (possibly whole chain from sender to the root)
`MIC-Info: RSA-MDx,RSA,`*cybercrud*	message digest algorithm, message digest encryption algorithm, encoded MIC
	blank line
message	message (encoded if MIC-ONLY)
`----END PRIVACY-ENHANCED MESSAGE-----`	post-encapsulation boundary

The only differences between an ENCRYPTED public key PEM message and a MIC-ONLY or MIC-CLEAR public key PEM message are the following:

- The TYPE OF MESSAGE field specifies MIC-ONLY or MIC-CLEAR.

- The MIC is not encrypted, though it is encoded 6 bits per character.

- The message is not encrypted; for MIC-ONLY it is encoded 6 bits per character, while for MIC-CLEAR it is included unmodified (except for the insertion of a "- " before each beginning-of-line "-").

- The MESSAGE ENCRYPTION ALGORITHM, IV field is omitted.

- All the fields giving per-recipient information are omitted.

- The KEY-INFO field for giving information about the sender's key is omitted.

13.17.4 MIC-ONLY and MIC-CLEAR, Secret Key Variant

`----BEGIN PRIVACY-ENHANCED MESSAGE-----`	pre-encapsulation boundary
`Proc-Type: 4,MIC-ONLY` *or* `MIC-CLEAR`	type of PEM message (version,type)
`Content-Domain: RFC822`	message form
`Originator-ID-Symmetric:` *entity identifier, issuing authority, version/expiration*	sender ID
`Recipient-ID-Symmetric:` *entity identifier, issuing authority, version/expiration* `Key-Info: DES-ECB,RSA-MDx,` *16 hex digits, 32 hex digits* ⋮	for each recipient: recipient ID; key-info for recipient
	blank line
message	message (encoded if MIC-ONLY)
`----END PRIVACY-ENHANCED MESSAGE-----`	post-encapsulation boundary

The only differences between an ENCRYPTED secret key PEM message and a MIC-ONLY or MIC-CLEAR secret key PEM message are the following:

- The TYPE OF MESSAGE field specifies MIC-ONLY or MIC-CLEAR.

- The message is not encrypted; for MIC-ONLY it is encoded 6 bits per character, while with MIC-CLEAR it is included unmodified (except for the insertion of a "- " before each beginning-of-line "-").

- The MESSAGE ENCRYPTION ALGORITHM, IV field is omitted.

13.17.5 CRL-RETRIEVAL-REQUEST

`----BEGIN PRIVACY-ENHANCED MESSAGE-----`	pre-encapsulation boundary
`Proc-Type: 4,CRL-RETRIEVAL-REQUEST`	type of PEM message (version,type)
`Issuer:` *cybercrud* ⋮	for each CRL requested: the encoded X.500 name of the issuing CA
`----END PRIVACY-ENHANCED MESSAGE-----`	post-encapsulation boundary

13.17.6 CRL

`----BEGIN PRIVACY-ENHANCED MESSAGE-----`	pre-encapsulation boundary
`Proc-Type: 4,CRL`	type of PEM message (version,type)
`CRL:` *cybercrud* `Originator-Certificate:` *cybercrud* ⋮	for each CRL retrieved: encoded X.509 format CRL; encoded X.509 certificate of the CA that issued the CRL
`----END PRIVACY-ENHANCED MESSAGE-----`	post-encapsulation boundary

13.18 DES-CBC AS MIC DOESN'T WORK

Originally, PEM had an additional method of obtaining a MIC on a message, which was the DES-CBC residue. The PEM documentation referred to this form of integrity check as DES-MAC. Ironically, they included this because the MD functions were new and therefore cryptographically suspect. It is instructive to see how something as seemingly straightforward as an integrity check can have problems. The DES-MAC version of integrity checking has several interesting security problems:

- If Alice is using public key technology for interchange keys and uses DES-MAC as the integrity check when sending a message to Bob, Bob can thereafter send messages to anyone he wants, claiming to be Alice. Furthermore, if the message type is MIC-CLEAR or MIC-ONLY (as opposed to ENCRYPTED), anyone who eavesdrops on the message can thereafter send messages to anyone she wants, claiming to be Alice.

- If Alice uses secret key interchange keys and ever sends a message to multiple recipients, say Bob and Ted, then Bob can thereafter send DES-MAC integrity check messages (MIC-CLEAR, MIC-ONLY, or ENCRYPTED) to Ted, claiming to be Alice (and Ted can likewise send such messages to Bob claiming to be Alice). This is true regardless of the choice of integrity check (DES-MAC, MD2, or MD5) Alice chose when she sent the multi-recipient message.

We'll have to describe how DES-MAC is specified in the earlier PEM specification. Suppose Alice is sending a message to Bob and Ted. The algorithm for using DES MAC as the integrity check is as follows:

1. Choose a per-message key (this is the same key PEM would use if PEM was going to encrypt the message).

2. Modify the per-message key by $\oplus$ing it with $F0F0F0F0F0F0F0F0_{16}$ (to avoid the classic cryptographic flaw described in §3.7.1 *Ensuring Privacy and Integrity Together*).

3. Compute the 64-bit CBC residue with the modified per-message key.

4. Encrypt the residue. If secret key based interchange keys are used, encrypt the CBC residue with the interchange key associated with Ted, plus encrypt the CBC residue with the interchange key associated with Bob, and send both quantities along with the message. If public key based interchange keys are used, Alice signs the residue with her private RSA key.

The problem is that it is possible, given a 64-bit quantity x and a DES key k, to generate a message m such that the CBC residue of m with key k is x. (We'll demonstrate that later in this section.) Let's look at several cases:

- Alice sends a MIC-ONLY message to Bob, using public key interchange keys, using DES-MAC as the integrity check. Carol eavesdrops on the message. She can see that it came from Alice. She finds Alice's public key, extracts the signed DES-MAC from the message header, and reverses the signature on the DES-MAC, thereby retrieving the DES-MAC of the message. Carol now knows the quantity x (the DES-MAC) and the quantity y, which is Alice's signature on x. As we said, she can invent any key k and construct a message m with DES-MAC x (using key k). She can then send m to anyone she wants, say Ted, and claim that the message was from Alice, because she'll include y as the signed DES-MAC for m.

- Suppose instead that Alice sends an encrypted message to Bob. In this case only Bob knows the quantities x (the DES-MAC of the message) and y (Alice's signature on x) because PEM specifies that if the message is encrypted, the integrity check is encrypted with the key used to encrypt the per-message key. But that means that Bob can now send messages claiming to be Alice, just like any eavesdropper could have done in the previous example.

- Alice sends a message with DES-MAC integrity check to both Bob and Ted, using secret key interchange keys. So she shares a key K_{AB} with Bob, and shares a key K_{AT} with Ted. The DES-MAC is included twice, once encrypted with K_{AB} and once encrypted with K_{AT}. Furthermore the per-message key k is sent twice, once encrypted with K_{AB} and once encrypted with K_{AT}. An eavesdropper cannot discover the DES-MAC of the message even if the message isn't encrypted—she can't compute it because she doesn't know k, and she can't decrypt the encrypted DES-MAC because she doesn't know either K_{AB} or K_{AT}. However, Bob does know the DES-MAC x, and can see $K_{AT}\{x\}$. He also knows k and $K_{AT}\{k\}$. So after receiving this message from Alice, Bob can construct a message m with CBC residue x, send it to Ted using per-message key k, claim that Alice is sending it, and send $K_{AT}\{k\}$ as the encrypted per-message key and $K_{AT}\{x\}$ as the encrypted DES-MAC.

- Alice sends a message with MD5 integrity check to Bob and Ted, using secret key interchange keys. PEM specifies that each of the two 64-bit halves of the MD5 is encrypted with the interchange key of each recipient. Let's say that the halves are x_1 and x_2. So Alice will send $K_{AT}\{x_1\}$ and $K_{AB}\{x_1\}$ as well as $K_{AT}\{x_2\}$ and $K_{AB}\{x_2\}$. Now even though Alice wasn't using DES-MAC, Bob knows a 64-bit quantity (say x_2) and what that quantity looks like when encrypted with K_{AT}. He also knows the per-message key k and $K_{AT}\{k\}$. So Bob can construct a message m with CBC-residue x_2 and send it to Ted using per-message key k, claiming that it was from Alice and that DES-MAC was the integrity check used. Note that any of the quantities x_1, x_2, or k could have been chosen to be the per-message key and/or the DES-MAC of the forged message.

Now we'll show how, given a 64-bit value r and a key k, it is possible for Carol to construct a message m with r as the CBC residue (using key k) (see Figure 13-3). Carol can actually construct any message she wants. The only constraint on the message is that somewhere inside the message there has to a 64-bit block (8 characters) that must be filled with a value determined only by the rest of the message and r and k.

Let's assume that there's one 8-byte block of the message, say m_4, that Carol can fill with "garbage" without suspicion. She constructs the message she wants in the remaining plaintext blocks. She will be sending a message to Ted, signed by Alice. Ted might think it strange to have 8 bytes of crud in the middle of the message, but maybe Carol can cleverly write the message so that somewhere inside the message she says something like, *Hey, did I tell you about how I fixed my porch this weekend? It went well until I hit my thumb with the hammer. Then I said, "@f#!Ruoe"! Now, back to business ...*

Alternatively, mailers are so wonderfully user-friendly that cybercrud appears in them all the time. PEM headers certainly are ugly and would be ignored by a human. Even non-PEM messages often contain obscure-looking headers and postmarks. If Carol were to embed arbitrary cybercrud there it probably would not create suspicion.

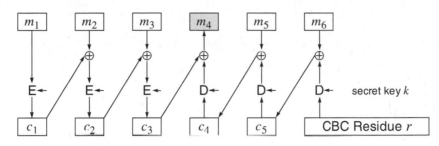

Figure 13-3. Generating a Message with a Given CBC Residue

Anyway, Carol works backwards from r. DES is reversible, so she can decrypt r and $\oplus$ that value with m_6 to discover what c_5 should be. She then decrypts c_5 and $\oplus$s it with m_5, to compute c_4.

Also, she works forward. She can encrypt m_1 to get c_1. Then she $\oplus$s c_1 with m_2 and encrypts the result to get c_2 and then $\oplus$s c_2 with m_3 and encrypts the result to get c_3. Now she has gotten to where the two ends of the computation meet. She $\oplus$s c_3 with the decryption of c_4 to get m_4.

Why don't the other types of MIC have the problems we've described in this section? The reason is that with message digests it is impossible for Carol to come up with another message with a particular message digest. So the PEM designers simply removed DES-MAC as a permissible integrity check.

13.19 HOMEWORK

1. Will the following work for an integrity check in electronic mail? When Alice sends a message to Bob, she computes a message digest of the message (for instance, MD5), and sends the message digest along with the message. Is any extra security gained by having Alice encrypt the message digest with Bob's public key?

2. Why doesn't the message portion of a PEM message need a label?

3. In the public key case of **ENCRYPTED** messages, there is a KEY-INFO field for each recipient (where the per-message encryption key is encrypted with that recipient's public key), plus a KEY-INFO field for the sender of the message, say Alice, where the per-message encryption key is encrypted with Alice's public key. The purpose of the KEY-INFO field for Alice is so that if she were later to see a copy of the encrypted message, she'd be able to decrypt it.) In the secret key case of **ENCRYPTED** messages, however, there is no such field for Alice

(though there is still one for each recipient). Why was it considered necessary to include a KEY-INFO field for Alice in the public key case and not in the secret key case?

4. Design a mechanism to allow Alice and Bob to establish a secret key cryptographic interchange key. Design a method using something like Kerberos KDCs (and remember, Alice and Bob are not necessarily registered with the same KDC). If Alice does not keep track of KDC-assigned interchange keys for people to whom she has previously sent messages, she really would need a KEY-INFO field now (in addition to the KEY-INFO field for each recipient) in order to later decrypt an encrypted message she had sent to Bob. What information would be in Alice's KEY-INFO field?

5. Why are the KEY-INFO fields not necessary in public key MIC-CLEAR and MIC-ONLY messages, whereas they are necessary in public key ENCRYPTED messages and in all secret key messages?

6. Suppose Alice sends a MIC-CLEAR or MIC-ONLY message. In the public key case, Alice encrypts the message digest with her private key. Why is it necessary for Alice to do this, given that anyone could compute the MIC? Furthermore, if Alice is sending an ENCRYPTED message, she first encrypts the message digest with her private key (as she would have done for a MIC-CLEAR or MIC-ONLY message), and then encrypts the message digest with the per-message secret key. Why was this last encryption considered necessary for encrypted messages and not for MIC-CLEAR or MIC-ONLY?

    Now assume Alice sends Bob a MIC-ONLY or MIC-CLEAR message with secret key based interchange keys. PEM requires her to encrypt the MIC with Bob's interchange key. Why is this necessary?

7. In §13.18 *DES-CBC as MIC Doesn't Work* we described how Carol, given a 64-bit value x and a key k, could construct a message m with DES-CBC x. Suppose Carol can't really send an arbitrary 8 bytes of garbage embedded in the message. For instance, suppose she wants to send the forged message MIC-CLEAR, so each byte is constrained to have one of only 64 valid values. Assume Carol is reasonably flexible about the message she'd like to send (for instance there might be two places in which crud could be embedded). Find a computationally feasible method for Carol to generate a message which will satisfy the constraint.

8. In §13.10 *Source Authentication and Integrity Protection* we described why the MIC for an encrypted message had to be encrypted in the public key case. Why is it not necessary with secret key based user keys?

9. Describe a plausible algorithm and user interface for a PEM processor at a receiver that deals with nested PEM messages, embedded strings that look like begin and end PEM markers, and

messages in which some of the PEM enclosures fail PEM processing due to signatures not verifying or certificates missing.

10. For remote exploding using secret keys, integrity protection is based on a shared secret between the originator and the exploder. (See §13.13.2 *Remote Exploding Using Secret Keys*.) How could a notary service be used to prevent the exploder from forging messages?

11. When a PEM message is both signed and encrypted, PEM computes the signature on the unencrypted message. What would be the problem with computing the signature on the encrypted message instead?

14 PGP (PRETTY GOOD PRIVACY)

14.1 INTRODUCTION

PGP is another secure mail protocol. It started out as a single public-domain implementation that was, in the words of Philip Zimmerman, the author of PGP, *guerrilla freeware*. It was the author's intention that it be distributed widely (anyone with a copy is invited to send copies to friends; copies can also be obtained from a bunch of Internet FTP sites). Unfortunately, both RSADSI, by enforcing the RSA patent, and government authorities, by enforcing export control of dangerous technologies like nuclear weapons and the ability to encrypt mail, caused PGP to start its life as contraband. Ironically, PGP has been, from the start, legal and freely available in many other countries because the RSA patent is U.S. only and other governments have different policies about the export, import, and use of privacy protection technology. For instance, there is a version of PGP available over the Internet from Finland. Finland is very liberal about cryptography (but is still snitty about selling nuclear weapons, we presume). The situation in the U.S. has improved. A commercial implementation of PGP is now available in the U.S., and a royalty-free non-commercial-use version is available from M.I.T. Neither is legally exportable.

The PGP documentation is delightfully conspiratorial and fun to read. Phil starts out by asserting that although we honest people don't really think we need to encrypt our email—we're not hiding anything—we should all start encrypting our mail so that in case someone needs privacy, the poor soul won't arouse suspicion by being the only one encrypting mail. Phil uses the analogy with paper mail. If the "standard" scheme were to write everything on postcards, and then only in unusual cases where you felt you didn't want the government or the next door neighbor reading your mail would you enclose it in an envelope, then a letter in an envelope would arouse suspicion and save the snooper time—every letter in an envelope would probably contain something interesting to the snooper.

> *If privacy is outlawed, only outlaws will have privacy.*
>
> —Phil Zimmerman

14.2 OVERVIEW

PGP is not just for mail. It performs encryption and integrity protection on files. Mail is not treated any different from ordinary files. Someone wishing to send a secure mail message could first transform the file to be mailed using PGP, and then mail the transformed file using a traditional mailer. Similarly, if one were to receive a PGP-encrypted mail message, one could treat the received message as a file and feed it to PGP to process. This is a bit inconvenient. So PGP source code comes with modifications for a number of common mail systems, enabling people to integrate PGP into their mail systems.

14.3 KEY DISTRIBUTION

PGP uses public key cryptography for personal keys. The biggest difference between PGP and PEM is how public keys are certified. PEM assumes a rigid hierarchy of CAs. PGP assumes anarchy. Each user decides which keys to trust. If Bob has talked in person to Alice, and Alice has written down her key for him, Bob can store Alice's public key and trust that it is hers. If he trusts Alice sufficiently, and Bob receives a certificate signed by Alice's key that says Carol's public key is P, then Bob can trust that P really does belong to Carol.

While with PEM the infrastructure decides whom you should trust to certify people, PGP leaves it up to you. This means PEM is potentially more convenient, while PGP is potentially more secure (if you're careful). It also means that PEM is unusable until you "hook into" an infrastructure. Deployment of PEM was held up for years trying to settle the details of how that infrastructure would work. PGP is easy to use "out of the box", but it's an open question whether it will be able to scale to large environments.

In the PEM model, finding a path of certificates is very simple. The certificate chain follows the naming hierarchy (approximately), and the path is simple—one simply goes down from the root (the Internet PCA Registration Authority).

Knowing whether to trust a path is simple in PEM. There is only one path and you are expected to trust it.

> *You can trust me.*   —used car salesman, Westboro, MA, April 4, 1993

With PGP, there might be several paths. For instance, you might have the following certificates:

| Carol's key is P_1 signed with P_2 |

Alice's key is P_2	signed with P_4
Carol's key is P_1	signed with P_5

It might even be the case that the last certificate instead said

Carol's key is P_3	signed with P_5

There are several issues:

- You might have a disorganized mass of certificates. How can you find a chain that leads from a key you know to Carol's key?

- There might be multiple chains, and some might lead to different keys for Carol.

- If you do find a chain, how much do you trust that chain?

In order to trust a chain of certificates you have to believe that the first public key in the chain really belongs to whom you think it does, and that you trust every individual in the chain. Should you trust a certificate signed by what you believe is Ted's key? Even if you're sure that Ted's public key is P_5, can you trust Ted not to certify anything in sight for a $100 bribe? Even if Ted is honest, can you trust him not to be sloppy about checking that the key really belongs to the named person? In other words, are Ted's pre-certification policies and procedures for authenticating users adequate?

Suppose Ted is honest and usually very careful about checking a key before signing a certificate. Suppose Carol is Ted's ex-spouse, from whom he had a bitter divorce. Should you then trust Ted's signature to certify Carol's public key?

PGP cannot answer these questions, of course. Not even people can really answer these questions. But PGP asks you for advice, and stores with each key a quantity indicating how much the key should be trusted as being legitimate and how much the owner of the key should be trusted in certifying other keys. With a particular signature (as in the case where you'd trust Ted to certify just about any key except Carol's), PGP also asks its user for advice and stores information about how much that particular signature should be trusted.

14.4 EFFICIENT ENCODING

To appreciate how clever PGP is, let's review inefficiencies of encoding in PEM.

Both PEM and PGP are designed to work in the environment where the contents of a message might be restricted by two problems. The first problem is that intermediate mail relays insist that the message contain only innocuous ASCII characters and limited-length lines. The second problem is that the representation of text at the destination machine may be different from the representation at the source machine. The solution to this problem is to turn the message into canonical format before encrypting or signing it. This includes converting the end-of-line indication, which might be linefeed only (<LF>) at the source, into <CR><LF> which is the SMTP standard. This may make the message a little bit bigger.

PEM expects to be handed ordinary text. If the message being sent with PEM is not in fact text consisting of innocuous ASCII characters, then in order to send it through PEM it must be encoded with a utility such as uuencode, which expands it by about 33%.

Then PEM does whatever processing it needs to do. For instance it might encrypt the (newly expanded) message. Once encrypted, the message has to get encoded by PEM so that it will consist of only innocuous ASCII characters with <CR><LF>s occurring sufficiently frequently. If the message started out as ordinary text, then only PEM will do the encoding and the message will expand by about 33%, but if the message needed to be encoded for submission to PEM, then the data will have been encoded twice, resulting in an expansion of about 78%. A message sent MIC-CLEAR will not need to be expanded even once. To summarize, there are four cases:

1. Text sent with PEM as MIC-CLEAR—the message does not get expanded at all.

2. Text sent with PEM as MIC-ONLY or ENCRYPTED—the message gets expanded once (33%).

3. Non-text sent with PEM as MIC-CLEAR—the message gets encoded before submittal to PEM, thus expanded once (33%).

4. Non-text sent with PEM as MIC-ONLY or ENCRYPTED—the message gets expanded twice (78%).

Since PEM is going to encode the message anyway, why do you need to encode the message before handing it to PEM? The reason is the canonicalization step that PEM insists on performing. If you have a file that would be damaged by the canonicalization, you have to encode it so that PEM won't damage it.

In contrast, PGP allows you to specify, when handing a file to PGP to process, whether the file is text or binary. (Though PGP checks up on you when you tell it you're giving it text—if it doesn't look like text, PGP will change the state of the flag associated with the file). If you tell PGP the file is binary, then PGP will not canonicalize it, and PGP will mark the PGP-processed message as binary so that the PGP at the receiver will know not to perform reverse canonicalization. By merely marking the file this way, PGP manages to avoid ever needing two encodings on a single message.

Furthermore, PGP does not always assume that the encrypted file needs to be encoded in order to get through mail relays. For instance, the file might be sent through a mail system (like X.400) that supports transparent transport of data. Or it might not be mailed at all, but merely transported via floppy disk. In some cases, PGP might know, based on the mail system into which it is integrated, whether the file needs to be encoded. In other cases, the user might explicitly tell PGP whether it should encode the output to prepare it for simple-minded mailers.

An additional trick that PGP does to conserve bits is to compress a file before sending it, whether it is binary or text. PGP uses the utility ZIP for compression. Typically, 50% compression is achieved, so even though PGP will need to do one expansion encoding after encrypting a file, what PGP actually has to transmit will often be smaller than the original file.

14.5 CERTIFICATE AND KEY REVOCATION

A certificate can be revoked by whoever signed the certificate. It does not necessarily mean that the key in the certificate is bad; it just means that whoever signed the certificate no longer wants to vouch for its authenticity. Given that anyone can issue a certificate for anyone, and then issue a revocation of the certificate, having a revoked certificate does not necessarily mean any thing bad about the individual certified. Otherwise, an enemy of yours could issue a certificate for you and then immediately revoke it, making everyone suspicious of you. (The reasoning might be: Why was the certificate revoked? Must be because the person had lied or something...) If a certificate is revoked, then whoever was relying on that certificate to authenticate you will no longer be able to authenticate you.

Certificates can optionally have a validity period, in which case they expire after the specified time period. They can be renewed by being reissued. The current custom in PGP is to issue non-expiring certificates (by omitting the VALIDITY PERIOD field).

Keys can be revoked too. My key can only be revoked by me (or someone who stole my private key—but gee, if the bad guy is so obliging as to tell the world he stole my key, I'm not worried about him forging a key revocation for my key). The idea is that I will issue a key revocation only when I think someone has discovered my private key. I'll presumably generate a new key for myself, and distribute the key revocation for the old key as widely as possible (perhaps by publishing it in *The New York Times* as a legal notice).

Key and certificate revocations are distributed informally, just as are public keys and certificates.

14.6 SIGNATURE TYPES

For each signed quantity, PGP indicates whether what is being signed is a message or a certificate. The reason for this is to guard against the remote possibility that you'd sign a message saying something like **Let's do lunch**, and the encoding of **Let's do lunch** could be parsed as a valid certificate. It's good practice whenever a key can be used for multiple things to explicitly say what kind of thing is being processed. This avoids any possibility of aliasing (in this case confusing messages and certificates).

One could argue that it's really ridiculously unlikely that a message could be parsed as a certificate, or vice versa, but PGP's SIGNATURE TYPE field is only one byte long, so why not?

14.7 YOUR PRIVATE KEY

If all you want to do is verify signatures on signed messages, you don't need a private key. However, if you want to sign your own messages, or if you want to receive encrypted PGP mail, you need a private key.

PGP will generate a private key for you. You can specify the size of the key. Then it asks you for a password, and it converts the string you type into an IDEA key by doing an MD5 message digest on it. Then it uses that IDEA key to encrypt the private key. Encryption is done with 64-bit CFB using a random IV which is stored with the encrypted private key.

14.8 KEY RINGS

A key ring is a data structure you keep that contains some public keys, some information about people, and some certificates. Usually this information is just stored locally, but some PGP users might share their key ring information, which would provide a quick method of building up your database of public keys.

PGP allows you to assert how much trust you place on different people. There are three levels of trust: none, partial, or complete. You might not trust Fred at all, so you would not trust a certificate signed by Fred, but you might want to keep Fred's public key around so that you can verify messages you receive from him, or be able to send encrypted messages to him.

PGP computes the trust that should be placed on certificates and public keys in your key ring based on the trust information you asserted on the people. A certificate signed by someone you indicated you don't trust at all will be ignored.

Whom or what you trust is a very private decision. You could have your own version of PGP that had arbitrarily complex trust rules. It does not have to be compatible with anyone else's. It could even always ask you to make the decision for each key and certificate, but give you the raw data (Carol and Ted both said this was Alice. You indicated before you have level 4 trust in Carol, level 6 trust in Carol's public key, level 5 trust in Ted, and level 2 trust in Ted's public key. How much trust would you like indicated for Alice's key?)

The public domain version of PGP gives you only three levels of trust (none, partial, or complete, as we said above). One completely trusted individual signing a certificate will yield a completely trusted certificate. Several partially trusted individuals signing certificates attesting to the same public key for Alice will yield a completely trusted public key for Alice. If you have a key for Alice that is not completely trusted, you can still verify messages from Alice, and send encrypted messages to Alice, but PGP will give you a warning.

14.9 ANOMALIES

14.9.1 File Name

PGP includes a FILE NAME field with any message (see §14.10 *Object Formats*). This field specifies the name of the file that was read to produce the PGP object so that the recipient can ask PGP to store the information using the same file name. We don't think this is very useful in the context of mail, although it can be helpful when PGP is used as a file encryption tool. But for mail, it means you have to be careful what you call the file on your machine (a name like TO-THE-DWEEB might offend the recipient, and you might have forgotten that PGP tells the recipient what you called the file on your machine).

Aside from being mostly useless, this feature is slightly dangerous. A careless user might be tricked into storing a received message that is actually a virus-containing executable with a file name (such as .login) that the system might understand and wind up executing. Admittedly, PGP warns you when it is about to overwrite an existing file, but the user might not have such a file, or might ignore the warning.

PGP also includes the time the file was last modified. As with FILE NAME, this can be useful for a file encryption tool, but its existence is probably a bad idea for mail, because again it's telling information that you may not realize it's divulging.

14.9.2 People Names

PGP allows you to choose any name you want. It does not enforce uniqueness or reasonableness. This causes an interesting problem. You can name yourself Richard Nixon (that might even be your name but you might not be *the* Richard Nixon). You might have lots of people willing to sign certificates as to your public key.

An unsuspecting person, say Julie, has a public key associated with the name Richard Nixon. She would completely trust the Richard Nixon she knows, but doesn't realize that the key she holds is yours, not his.

If I have two public keys, both indicating that the associated human is John Smith, I won't know which key to use when I send a message to one of the John Smiths. For this reason, it is helpful if the user identification string contains a little more information than just the name of the user, for instance, the user's email address. PGP recommends (but does not require) including Internet email addresses in the name.

14.10 OBJECT FORMATS

PGP reads and writes a variety of objects. Objects may contain a variety of fields, and some objects contain other objects. Each object can be represented in two formats—*compact* and *SMTP mailable*. The SMTP mailable format is computed from the compact format by performing the same encoding that PEM uses (see §13.7 *Reformatting Data to Get Through Mailers*) and adding a human-readable header and trailer so that a human (or a smart mail receiver) will know the cyber-crud between the header and trailer needs to be processed by PGP. The human-readable header is

```
-----BEGIN PGP MESSAGE-----
Version 2.2
```

and the human readable trailer is

```
-----END PGP MESSAGE-----
```

14.10.1 Message Formats

PGP messages are composed of a sequence of primitive objects (see §14.10.2 *Primitive Object Formats*). We'll describe the message formats in this section.

Encrypted Message.   PGP encrypts messages with the secret key algorithm IDEA using 64-bit CFB mode with a randomly chosen IV that is included with the message. The sending PGP chooses a random IDEA key for encrypting the message, and then encrypts that IDEA key with the public key of the recipient, placing the encrypted IDEA key in the header. If the message is being sent to multiple recipients, the IDEA key is individually encrypted with the key of each recipient, and all the encrypted keys are placed in the header.

IDEA key encrypted with recipient$_1$'s public key
IDEA key encrypted with recipient$_2$'s public key
⋮
IDEA key encrypted with recipient$_k$'s public key
message encrypted with IDEA key

When the final object is decrypted with the IDEA key, the result is either PLAINTEXT DATA or COMPRESSED DATA, depending on whether PGP decided the data was compressible. If PGP decided the data was compressible, then when the COMPRESSED DATA is uncompressed, the result is PLAINTEXT DATA.

Signed Message. This is likely to be COMPRESSED DATA. When uncompressed, the result is

signature
plaintext data

Encrypted Signed Message. This is just like an ENCRYPTED MESSAGE, but with the message replaced by a SIGNED MESSAGE.

IDEA key encrypted with recipient$_1$'s public key
IDEA key encrypted with recipient$_2$'s public key
⋮
IDEA key encrypted with recipient$_k$'s public key
signed message encrypted with IDEA key

When the final object is decrypted with the IDEA key, the result will probably be COMPRESSED DATA (unless PGP noticed that it was not compressible), which when uncompressed is a SIGNED MESSAGE.

Signed Human-Readable Message. Usually PGP modifies even an unencrypted message before mailing it, for two reasons. It compresses it for ecological reasons (saves bits), and it encodes it so it will have some hope of making it through mailers unmodified. This is nice but it means that if the recipient does not have PGP, the human at the other end will not be able to read the message (see §13.7 *Reformatting Data to Get Through Mailers*). So PGP allows you to tell it not to muck with

the message. You will hold PGP harmless if the message gets modified by mailers and the signature
then does not verify. This form of message is

| -----BEGIN PGP SIGNED MESSAGE----- |
| cleartext message |
| -----BEGIN PGP SIGNATURE-----
Version: 2.2 |
| signature |
| -----END PGP SIGNATURE----- |

Just like with PEM, we have to ensure that the string

`-----BEGIN PGP SIGNATURE-----`

does not appear in the text of the message. And just like PEM, PGP protects against such a mishap
by prepending '- ' to any line that begins with '-'. The PGP at the receiver is smart enough to strip
that off before attempting to verify the signature.

14.10.2 Primitive Object Formats

Primitive object formats are

| CTB | length | stuff |

where **CTB** stands for **cipher type byte** (aren't you glad you asked?) and specifies the PGP object
type and the length of *length*. We'll describe the interpretation of *stuff* for the various object types
in this section.

Certain object types contain one or more integers in their stuff field. Integers are encoded as a
length in bits (two octets, most significant first) followed by the binary integer with leading 0 bits
to pad to a multiple of 8 bits then packed into octets most significant first.

The CTB is interpreted bit by bit (most significant to least significant) as follows:

bit 7: 1

bit 6: reserved, i.e. set to 0 and ignored

bit 5–2: a 4-bit field indicating which type of object follows. The defined values are

0001—something encrypted using someone's public key (the only thing ever actually
encrypted this way is an IDEA key)

0010—signature

0101—private key encrypted with a password

0110—public key

1000—compressed data

1001—something encrypted with a secret key

101 —plaintext data plus a file name and mode (binary or text)

110 —key ring trust information

1101—user identification

1110—comment

bits 1–0: a 2-bit field indicating the length of the length field. The defined values are:

00—1-byte length field follows CTB

01—2-byte length field follows CTB

10—4-byte length field follows CTB

11—there is no length field (this can only occur for the last object in a message—the
length is to the externally determined end of data)

Key Encrypted under a Public Key (0001 in CTB).

field description

1 byte	version number (2)
8 byte	key ID (low order 64 bits of RSA modulus)
1 byte	algorithm ID (1 for RSA, no others defined)
Integer	IDEA key encrypted with RSA

IDEA key before RSA-encryption.   PGP follows the PKCS #1 standard, which defines how to
encrypt something with RSA, usually a key (see §5.3.6 *Public-Key Cryptography Standard
(PKCS)*). PGP encrypts a little more than just the IDEA key. PGP encrypts a 19-byte quantity consisting of a byte = 1, the 16-byte IDEA key, and a 2-byte CRC-16 of the IDEA key. The purpose of
the extra data is so that in case you accidentally decrypt with the wrong RSA key the contents will
not look right. So PGP encrypts, using RSA,

0	2	*n* random non-zero bytes	0	1	IDEA key	CRC

Signature (0010 in CTB).

field description

1 byte	version number (2)
1 byte	# of bytes before key ID field (5 if validity period missing, else 7)
1 byte	signature type (see below)
4 byte	time when signed
0 or 2 byte	validity period in days (0 means infinite)
8 byte	key ID (low order 64 bits of RSA key)
1 byte	public key algorithm (1 for RSA, no others defined)
1 byte	message digest algorithm (1 for MD5, no others defined)
2 byte	first two bytes of message digest, to reassure us that we decrypted with the proper key
integer	message digest signed with RSA (see below)

The defined signature types (written in hex) are

   00—signature on a binary message or document
   01—signature on a text message with <CR><LF> indicating EOL
   10—certificate with unspecified assurance
   11—key certification with no assurance
   12—key certification with casual assurance
   13—key certification with heavy-duty assurance
   20—key revocation (attempt to revoke key that signed this)
   30—certificate revocation (revokes a certificate signed with the key that signed this)
   40—signature of a signature (notary service)

The message digest is computed on

message to be signed	signature type	timestamp	validity period

The quantity signed using RSA is

0	1	n bytes of FF_{16}	0	$3020300c06082a864886f70d0205050004 10_{16}$	message digest

The 18-byte constant is ASN.1 cybercrud meaning MD5.

Private key encrypted with password (0101 in CTB).

	field description
1 byte	version number (2)
4 byte	time when key created
2 byte	validity period in days (0 means infinite)
1 byte	public key algorithm (1 for RSA, no others defined)
integer	public modulus
integer	public exponent
1 byte	algorithm encrypting private key (1 for IDEA, no others defined)
8 byte	random if key encrypted, else 0
integer	encrypted quantity

The encrypted quantity, before encryption, looks like

	field description
integer	private exponent
integer	p (the first prime, in format of integer)
integer	q (the second prime, in format of integer)
integer	information for speeding up the RSA operations (see §5.3.4.4 *Optimizing RSA Private Key Operations*)
2 byte	CRC-16 of preceding fields

Encryption is done using IDEA in 64-bit CFB mode (see §3.4 *International Data Encryption Algorithm (IDEA)* and §3.6 *Encrypting a Large Message*)

Public key (0110 in CTB).

	field description
1 byte	version number (2)
4 byte	time when key created
2 byte	validity period in days (0 means infinite)
1 byte	public key algorithm (1 for RSA, no others defined)
integer	public modulus
integer	public exponent

Compressed Data (1000 in CTB).   Any PGP object or sequence of objects can be compressed.

	field description
1 byte	compression algorithm (1 for ZIP, no others defined)
–	compressed data

Something Encrypted with a Secret Key (1001 in CTB).

	field description
–	encrypted data

Encryption is done using IDEA in 64-bit CFB mode with an IV of 0. The data being encrypted is

	field description
8 byte	random data
2 byte	last two bytes of random data
–	unencrypted data

The purpose of the random data is so that successive encryptions of the same unencrypted data will result in different ciphertext. The purpose of repeating the last two bytes of random data is to recognize that decryption worked properly.

Plaintext Data (1011 in CTB) .

	field description
1 byte	mode (ASCII b for binary, t for text)
1 byte	length of following field in bytes
	file name (ASCII string)
4 byte	time file last modified, or 0
–	message

Key Ring.   The key ring stores public keys and information about each key. The information about each key consists of the name of the human associated with the key (the user ID), the set of certificate signatures you've received vouching for the fact that that user has that public key, and trust information about each of the pieces of information. Key revocations and certificate revocations (see SIGNATURE object format) are also stored on the key ring.

So the key ring looks like

public key	trust	user ID	trust	signature	trust	...	signature	trust
public key	trust	user ID	trust	signature	trust	...	signature	trust

⋮

| public key | trust | user ID | trust | signature | trust | ... | signature | trust |

The trust information following the public key indicates how much that public key is trusted to sign things, and is manually set. If the key has been revoked, the key revocation is inserted immediately before the user ID. The trust information following the user ID indicates how much confidence is placed on the public key belonging to the user, and is computed from the trust information following the signatures. The trust information following each signature is copied from the trust information of the public key that did the signing. Certificate revocations are included with the normal signatures.

PGP encourages people to share the information in their key rings. However, users should make their own trust decisions. So when key ring information is transmitted, the trust information is removed.

Key Ring Trust Information (1100 in CTB).   Since this format is only used locally, we won't bother documenting its gory details, but we will say that it has two different interpretations depending on whether the previous item is a user ID or not.

	field description
1 byte	how much the preceding item should be trusted

User Identification (1101 in CTB).

	field description
–	ASCII string giving user's name, perhaps email address also

Comment (1110 in CTB).

	field description
–	ASCII string

15 *X.400*

X.400 is CCITT's electronic mail standard. ISO has also approved some of the documents in the series. PEM and PGP are complete specifications, in that someone can look at the documents and build an implementation that will interoperate with existing implementations. In contrast, many of the CCITT and ISO "standards" are not complete specifications. Instead they give a framework for an implementation. For instance, they might define a field called ENCRYPTION ALGORITHM, but then not give any assigned values to that field. Obviously, this isn't really a standard, since the whole purpose of a standard (according to our naive view of the world) is to be able to read the document and make an implementation that will interwork with an independently developed implementation. So, the next step is to have "implementors' workshops" in which implementors make the final decisions necessary to really lock down packet formats and anything else necessary to ensure interoperability.

Any time X.400 wants to leave a decision up to implementors, the field is encoded as an *object identifier* followed by optional parameters whose nature is defined by whoever assigns the object identifier. For instance, some implementor might decide to do message encryption with IDEA in OFB mode with a 27-bit IV. That implementor can obtain an object identifier, and write down the specifications for encryption according to that object identifier. The nice thing about object identifiers is that it's easy to obtain them. Therefore any committee can define its own techniques and ensure that if they were to send a message to someone who hasn't implemented those techniques (or who happens to have defined exactly the same technique, but assigned it a different object identifier), the recipient will not be confused by the message. But although the recipient will not misparse the message, it also will not be able to read the message—the presence of an unknown object identifier will tell it not to attempt to read the message.

Since object identifiers are hierarchically assigned, there is no single place to find all the assigned values, and therefore it is likely that some algorithms have been given multiple object identifiers. Certainly no object identifiers for encryption algorithms are specified in any of the X.400 series of documents. X.509 specifies a few object identifiers. The only object identifier it specifies for an encryption algorithm is RSA. However, it is underspecified, in that RSA alone is not enough information to interoperate with another implementation that uses RSA as the basis for encryption, since padding and other details must be also specified.

Much of the functionality of X.400 can be deployed in an interoperable way because of implementors' workshops. However, because of lack of interest in X.400 security, the work has not been done to completely specify the security parts of X.400. Because real standardization of X.400 security has not happened, we can only guess as to what the designers had in mind in providing certain fields. There is no assurance that, if and when real standardization occurs, the functionality will be provided the way we describe.

X.400 consists of a bunch of different documents. The X series documents are CCITT documents. The ISO series are 10021-*n*, where *n* varies between 1 and 7. There are minor wording differences between the ISO and CCITT documents. The drafts are kept aligned by having a common draft document with both sets of wording. The convention is when there is a difference in wording, the two choices are put into square brackets, separated by a bar, with the CCITT wording first. For instance, from version 5.5 of X.400, section 6:

> This [Recommendation|International Standard] is one of a set of [Recommendations|International Standards] and describes the system model and Elements of Service of the Message Handling System (MHS) and Services. This [Recommendation|International Standard] overviews the capabilities of an MHS that are used [by Administrations|] for the provision of [public|] MH Services to enable users to exchange messages on a store-and-forward basis.

While it is always a joy to read CCITT/ISO documents, this technique makes it even more fun to read the drafts.

The various documents are:

- X.400/ISO 10021-1, *System and Service Overview*

- X.402/ISO 10021-2, *Overall Architecture*

- X.403/(not an ISO document), *Conformance Testing*

- X.407/ISO 10021-3, *Abstract Service Definition Conventions*

- X.408/(not an ISO document), *Encoded Information Type Conversion Rules*

- X.411/ISO 10021-4, *MTS: Abstract Service Definition and Procedures*

- X.413/ISO 10021-5, *MS: Abstract Service Definition*

- X.419/ISO 10021-6, *Protocol Specifications*

- X.420/ISO 10021-7, *Interpersonal Messaging System*

X.400's design is reminiscent of post office mail. It has features equivalent to certified mail and return receipt mail. It's irrelevant for understanding security why X.400 is broken into so many documents, so we'll just generically refer to "X.400". The only thing that might be relevant to understanding security is that X.400 is a system for carrying messages, and interpersonal mail is only one of the types of messages that X.400 might carry. Mail is defined in X.420. Any security-related parameters defined in X.420 would be specific to mail and not applicable to other types of messages, unless the committees that defined those types of messages put equivalent parameters into their standard. But essentially all the security-related parameters are defined in the portion of X.400 applicable to all sorts of messages.

15.1 OVERVIEW OF X.400

There are certain acronyms one needs to digest in order to read any X.400 documentation. The model is that the mail system is a service known as the MTS (message transfer service). Mail is forwarded through a bunch of nodes known as MTAs (message transfer agents). A message starts out at a User Agent (UA) and is submitted to an MTA, and then is forwarded from MTA to MTA until it finally gets delivered to the destination UA. The actual user interacts with the UA rather than directly with an MTA.

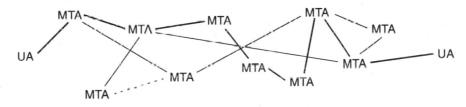

Figure 15-1. Message Transfer Service

There are various operations that may take place:

- message submission—A user (UA) of the message service hands a message to the message service for delivery (equivalent to putting a letter in a post office box).

- message delivery—The message service hands a message to a user (equivalent to having the postal deliverer put a letter in your home's mailbox).

- probe submission—A user asks the message service whether it would be able to deliver a letter with certain characteristics to a certain destination.

- report delivery—The message service gives a user some notification, for instance an explanation of why a message was not delivered, or proof that a message was delivered.

It is possible to write an entire book on X.400 [PLAT91]. But our book is on network security, so we will concentrate on the features of X.400 that have something to do with security.

15.2 SECURITY FUNCTIONS POSSIBLE WITH X.400

Let us assume Alice sends a message to Bob. The security features that might be provided by an X.400 implementation are:

- encryption of the message.

- message origin authentication. This is reassurance to Bob that the message came from Alice.

- non-repudiation of origin. Although similar to authentication of the source, this feature additionally allows Bob to prove to a third party, Carol, that it was indeed Alice who sent the message to Bob.

- report origin authentication. If there is anything the mail service needs to tell Alice about the delivery of her message to Bob, it is done by having the mail service send Alice a delivery or nondelivery report. The report origin authentication feature gives reassurance to Alice that it was indeed the mail system which sent the delivery/nondelivery report.

- probe origin authentication. If Alice wants to check whether a message with particular characteristics (such as security level) can be delivered to Bob without actually sending the message itself, she can send a probe. (For instance, the message might be very long and sending it would waste a lot of bandwidth.) Since the mail service doesn't want to divulge information to a third party, Carol, about what type of messages Alice can send to Bob, the probe origin authentication feature reassures the mail service that the probe was indeed sent by Alice.

- proof of delivery. This is reassurance to Alice that Bob received the message.

- non-repudiation of delivery. This is stronger than proof of delivery. It not only assures Alice that Bob received the message, but it allows Alice to prove to a third party, Carol, that Bob received the message.

- proof of submission. This is reassurance to Alice by the mail service that it received the message Alice is sending to Bob.

- non-repudiation of submission. This allows Alice to prove to a third party, Carol, that the mail service accepted the message from Alice.

- secure access management. This allows mail "neighbors" to authenticate one another. In other words, it allows a mail user to authenticate an MTA (mail transfer agent), and it allows an MTA to authenticate a mail user, and it allows adjacent MTAs to authenticate one another.

- content integrity protection. This reassures Bob that the single message he receives from Alice has not been modified since Alice sent it.

- message sequence integrity. This assures Bob that an entire sequence of messages from Alice has been received, without loss or duplication.

- message flow confidentiality. This is an attempt to prevent anyone from knowing that Alice is sending messages to Bob. This feature is not really supported, but suggestions as to how it might be implemented are given in X.400.

- message security labeling. This is an attempt to support non-discretionary access controls (see §1.11.1 *Mandatory (Nondiscretionary) Access Controls*). It is the ability to label a message as to the category and sensitivity in which it fits. MTAs on the boundary of a security domain check the message security label to ensure inappropriate messages do not leak out of the domain.

- message sensitivity level labeling. This is defined in X.420, which means it is specific for mail (i.e. it might not be provided for some other type of message carried by X.400). It gives information as to how the message should be handled at the destination. There are three defined values: company confidential, private, and personal. For example, private means the message should not be sent to anyone except those explicitly mentioned (for instance, mail for someone might ordinarily be forwarded to a secretary).

15.3 STRUCTURE OF AN X.400 MESSAGE

An X.400 message consists of an **envelope**, which is control information, and **content**. The content consists of a header followed by a sequence of **body parts**.

An envelope contains the same kind of information that you'd write on an envelope when mailing a postal letter. The mail infrastructure will only read and modify the envelope (just like you don't expect the postal service to look inside your envelope to see what's inside, but it's OK for it to do things to the envelope like add postmarks). The X.400 mail infrastructure not only doesn't read what's inside the envelope—it also doesn't modify it. This is in contrast to SMTP mail, where there isn't a clear distinction between the envelope and the header of the message, so SMTP adds status

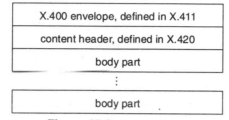

Figure 15-2. X.400 message

information to the beginnings and ends of messages. In X.400 all such information is segregated into the envelope.

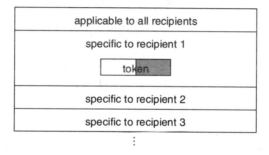

Figure 15-3. X.400 envelope

There are two types of X.400 envelope defined. One is a **message submission envelope**, and conveys information that the message sender needs to give to the mail service, for instance the complete list of recipients, and a request for proof of submission of the message. The other defined envelope is the **message delivery envelope**, which conveys information to the recipient of a message. When the message is handed to the mail service, the contents of the envelope are as defined for a message submission envelope. When delivered to the destination, the mail service has replaced the submission envelope with a delivery envelope. The information might be different from the information in the submission envelope. For instance, the list of other recipients might be absent in the message delivery envelope. And the proof of submission request is absent in the delivery envelope because it is irrelevant there.

The security features of X.400 are provided by fields that are part of the envelope. All security-related fields in X.400 are optional. The envelope has a portion for fields that only need to be listed once (as opposed to per recipient). It also has a portion for fields that are per-recipient. One of the per-recipient fields is known as the *token*. Part of the token is encrypted and part of it is unencrypted, but the entire token is integrity protected. So there are four places where a security-related field might be (see Figure 15-3):

• in the per-message part of the envelope (applicable to all recipients)

- in the per-recipient part of the envelope, but not inside the token

- in the unencrypted part of the token

- in the encrypted part of the token (gray area in the figure)

X.400 is somewhat confusing in that most of the fields can occur in any of those four places. This is because X.400 has been designed to be flexible enough to accommodate a large number of implementation options. For example, if you were using public key encryption, the integrity check would most logically be in the per-message part of the envelope, but if you were using secret key encryption, the integrity check would have to be computed separately for each recipient, and therefore it would have to occur in the per-recipient part.

In Figure 15-2 we've indicated an X.420 message inside the envelope. X.400 is defining other types of messages, such as EDI (Electronic Data Interchange, X.435). If one were sending an EDI message, then there would be an X.435 message inside the envelope. X.400 security is really provided in the envelope, and not in the X.420 portion. The only vaguely security-related function in X.420 is *sensitivity* (see §15.3.6 *Security Fields for X.420*).

Continuing our examination of Figure 15-2, the X.420 message contains several body parts. The idea is that a message might contain a piece that's text, another that's audio, another that's an included executable binary file, and so on. Some types of body parts are defined in X.420, though it's possible to define new ones by using an object identifier. In fact, there has been an object identifier defined for a PEM body part. Given that X.400 security has not been really deployed, a perfectly reasonable method of obtaining mail security with X.400 is to use the PEM body part, and use PEM for encryption, integrity protection, and source authentication.

There are disadvantages to doing secure mail by using a PEM body part instead of exploiting the security hooks provided by X.400. PEM has to encode messages (due to the assumption that the PEM message will be carried by SMTP mail, but when carried inside X.400 encoding is not necessary). And PEM is only for text. X.420 supports other things, such as voice, facsimile, and videotex. So if it were desired to send encrypted voice, for instance, there would have to be some convention invented for marking the PEM message as being voice. It is conceptually possible to do multimedia PEM by having PEM work on, say, MIME (an Internet standard for multimedia), but that adds an additional level of complexity, since the multimedia features are already available within X.400.

There are also advantages to doing secure mail as a PEM body part. It is conceptually simple and it works. X.400 security is not completely designed—the hooks are there to implement something, but that's different from being standardized and deployed. Another advantage of doing secure mail this way (using a PEM body part) is that it is possible to interoperate with non-X.400 implementations. It would be easy to build a gateway between the X.400 world and the SMTP world that simply extracted the PEM body part and transmitted it with SMTP.

15.3.1 Per-Message Security Fields

The security related fields which are listed once (as opposed to per recipient) are:

- originator certificate—This is a certificate giving the public key of the message source, as defined in X.509, though X.411 hints that other forms of certificates, or at least other key distribution techniques, may be defined in the future.

- content-confidentiality-algorithm identifier—This defines the algorithm used to encrypt the message, if the message is encrypted. This field consists of an object identifier which defines the algorithm followed by parameters which are specific to the selected algorithm.

- message-origin-authentication check—This is a digital signature of the content of the message, the message-security label, the content identifier (the subject line), and the message-origin-authentication-algorithm identifier. If the content of the message is encrypted, the standard specifies that it is the ciphertext that should be signed, rather than the plaintext. This has the advantage that the other protected fields can be checked by intermediate mail forwarders (MTAs), so that a bad guy cannot modify, for instance, the message-security label in order to circumvent mandatory access controls. (Note: we complained in §13.16 *Unprotected Information* that PEM does not protect the subject line of the message. X.400 does protect it.)

- message-security label—Four kinds of information may be included in this field:

    - security-policy identifier—an object identifier intended to define the policy to be used to deal with the security classification, privacy mark, and security categories fields

    - security-classification—an integer with six defined values:
      unmarked (0), unclassified (1), restricted (2), confidential (3), secret (4), and top secret (5)

    - privacy-mark—a printable string, for instance:
      IN STRICTEST CONFIDENCE

    - security-categories—X.400 suggests these take the form of a set of ⟨object identifier, parameters⟩ values, none of which is defined of course. This is clearly inspired by the compartments world common in defense departments.

- proof-of-submission request—This is an optional field, which when you specify it, gives you the opportunity to specify whether you meant it or not. In other words, if you don't include the field, it means you don't request proof of submission. If you do include the field, you can either specify the value yes, I really want proof of submission, or you can specify the value I don't want proof of submission, but thought I'd include the parameter just to make the header longer. There is a semi-plausible reason for allowing inclusion of the optional parameter in the case when the value would be the same as for leaving out the parameter. It's possible that it might be convenient for a program that generates messages to always include the same parameters and just vary the values of the parameters, rather than sometimes leave out parameters.

- content type—X.400 has standardized a few values, but allows object identifiers for content types not standardized by X.400. The values X.400 has standardized are:

  - 0—unidentified. This will be delivered to the recipient, and X.400 doesn't care what's inside. Hopefully the recipient and sender are sufficiently compatible that the recipient will know how to interpret the contents.

  - 1—external. This is there for interworking between 1984 and 1988 versions of X.400.

  - 2—1984 version of X.420

  - 22—1988 version of X.420 (there must be some wonderful story as to how they chose 22 rather than 3)

15.3.2 Per-Recipient Security Fields

The security-related fields which are individually listed for each recipient, in the X.400 envelope, are:

- content-integrity check—a MIC for the contents of the message. For some MICs, for instance secret key algorithms in which the recipients don't all share the same key with the originator, it is necessary to have a different integrity check for each recipient. When using a MIC where a single quantity can be verified by all recipients (as in a public key based digital signature), most likely this field would not be used, and instead the signature would appear in the message-origin-authentication check field, which is not a per-recipient field.

- proof-of-delivery request—an optional field with two values, one being I want proof of delivery to this recipient, and the other being I'm just letting you know I don't want proof of delivery to this recipient.

- message-token. Theoretically, X.400 allows one to specify any type of token. However, X.400 specifies one type, which it calls **asymmetric token**. The specified fields are all optional. Part of the token is encrypted and part is unencrypted, but the entire token is signed. X.400 refers to the unencrypted portion as **signed data** and the encrypted portion as **encrypted data**. X.400 security is very confusing since many fields can be put in any of several places: in the portion of the header that applies to all recipients; or, if in the per-recipient portion of the header, outside the token, in the unencrypted portion of the token, or in the encrypted portion of the token. If outside the token, it is neither encrypted nor integrity-protected, except for the fields which are explicitly included in the origin-authentication check (the content of the message, the message-security label, the content identifier, and the message-origin-authentication-algorithm identifier). If a field is chosen to be inside the token in the unencrypted portion, then it is integrity-protected but not encrypted. If it is desired for the field to be encrypted as well as integrity-checked, it is placed in the encrypted portion of the token.

15.3.2.1 Security Fields in the Token

The token is a field in the per-recipient portion of the message. The security-related fields in the token are

- recipient-name
- time (at which the token was created)
- signed data (i.e., the unencrypted part of the token)
- encrypted data

15.3.2.2 Unencrypted Part of the Token

The fields which may be included in signed data (the unencrypted part of the token) are:

- content-confidentiality-algorithm identifier—optional, but presumably included if and only if the message is encrypted.

- content-integrity check—a MIC of the contents of the message. This field could appear inside the token in either the encrypted portion or the unencrypted portion, and it can also appear outside the token, in the per-recipient part of the header. Indeed, it might be completely unnecessary, and therefore left out entirely, if the message-origin-authentication check appears. Presumably implementations would be smart enough not to include this information in lots of places for a single message.

- message-security label—a field that can also occur in the per-message part of the header. Allowing an implementation to put it inside the token allows one to specify a different value for the security label for each recipient, and allows the security label to be integrity-checked if the message-origin-authentication field is left out (for instance, because the implementation does not use public keys).

- proof-of-delivery request.

- message-sequence-number.

15.3.2.3 Encrypted Part of the Token

The fields which may be included in encrypted data in the token are

- content-confidentiality key—the encryption key used for encrypting the message

- content-integrity check

- message-security label—might want to be encrypted so as to not divulge to an eavesdropper that sensitive information is being sent

- content-integrity key

- message-sequence-number

15.3.3 Fields for Probe Messages

The X.400 envelope for probes contains the following security-related fields, all of which are optional:

- originator certificate

- probe origin-authentication check

- message-security label

15.3.4 Fields for Proof of Delivery

- proof-of-delivery-algorithm identifier—the signature algorithm used for the proof of delivery

- signed hash of the message (the message header, the message contents, the delivery time, the actual recipient name, and the originally intended recipient name)

Note that the decrypted content of the message is signed. This is possible because the destination generates the proof of delivery.

15.3.5 Fields for Proof of Submission

- proof-of-submission-algorithm identifier—the signature algorithm used for the proof of submission

- signed hash of the (encrypted) message, the message header, and the submission time

15.3.6 Security Fields for X.420

Security is also mentioned in X.420. One type of body part defined in X.420 is **encrypted body part**. It is defined as consisting of parameters and encrypted data. So far so good. However, in the words of X.420, *The parameters of such a body part, and the encryption technique that those parameters might identify and parameterize, are for FURTHER STUDY.*

Why would X.420 bother to start defining an encrypted body part, when X.400 already provides fields for encrypting a message? The answer is that there are advantages to doing encryption on a body part rather than the whole message. It gives the flexibility of encrypting part of the message and not others, and it allows someone to send an encrypted message without writing on the envelope *the contents of this message are encrypted.* Luckily, if anyone wants to have the feature of an encrypted body part, they can use the PEM body part which has been recently defined.

In the header portion defined in X.420, the only field defined that is vaguely security-related is sensitivity. That field is optional. If present there are three defined values:

- personal, meaning that the mail is supposed to be sent to the specified recipients as individuals, rather than as their job descriptions. For instance, a message complaining about a problem with some product might be sent to the manager of that product's implementation group, John Smith. If John Smith has since left the company and his successor is Jane Doe, then it would be reasonable to send the message to Jane Doe. However, if the mail is marked personal, it means it is something only of interest to the individual John Smith.

- private, meaning that the mail should not be sent to anyone except the people explicitly listed as recipients. For instance, if Jane Doe's mail is usually sent first to her secretary, a message marked private should not be handled that way.

- company-confidential, meaning that the mail should be handled according to whatever rules the company has for handling company confidential mail (for instance, after displaying the message on a terminal screen, the company policy might require the terminal to be shredded).

X.420 does not really specify exactly what one does with the sensitivity parameter. Rather it just allows you to mark messages. Interestingly, it only allows one marking. For instance a mail message cannot be marked both private and company-confidential.

16 A COMPARISON OF PEM, PGP, AND X.400

16.1 INTRODUCTION

You might think that making electronic mail secure would be quite straightforward. So it's surprising how different the three secure mail systems turned out to be.

16.2 CERTIFICATION HIERARCHY

As mentioned in §13.4 *Certificate Hierarchy*, PEM has a very rigid certification hierarchy. For any given name, there is only one certificate path to that name and all users of PEM are expected to trust it. PGP's philosophy is that individuals should make their own trust decisions. There might be many chains of certificates that would algorithmically certify something, but different users might trust different paths. For instance, you might not trust any path involving Ted. X.400 doesn't specify the trust rules for the certification hierarchy. Any system implementing X.400 would have to make its own decision. A PEM-like or PGP-like or yet another scheme would all be possible. A naive implementation might accept any certificate chain that algorithmically led to the target ⟨*name, key*⟩ pair.

> *We could do that, but it would be wrong. That's for sure.*
>
> —Richard Nixon

The problem is, anybody or anything that had a certificate could issue certificates for other things and complete the chain. For instance, Saddam Hussein might very well have a certificate stating his ⟨*name, public key*⟩ pair. The naive implementation would then believe a certificate signed by him that stated that some key belonged to the President of the United States.

X.400 does not explicitly state what its model is for the certification hierarchy. It could theoretically work with a PEM-like or PGP-like model. Until such details are written down, X.400 is not adequately specified to guarantee interoperability, especially between implementations.

16.3 CERTIFICATE DISTRIBUTION

PEM has a slot in the mail header for placing certificates. Certificates are rather large and it was the original intention of PEM that certificates be retrieved from the directory service. However, no widely deployed directory service existed on which PEM could depend, so a slot in the mail header was provided for certificate distribution. Using the mail header for certificate distribution is quite awkward. If Alice wants to send a signed message to Bob, it is not a problem—she will include her own certificates in the header, and she does not need to know Bob's public key. However, if Alice wants to send Bob an encrypted message, then before Alice can send the message to Bob, she needs to ask Bob to send her a signed message so that she can get Bob's certificates. The assumption is that once a good directory service gets deployed, it will be used instead of the mail header for certificate distribution.

PGP does not have a slot in the mail header. PGP assumes the certificates are distributed through some other means, for instance by copying them from a bulletin board, having them sent as the text of an electronic mail message, or being retrieved from a directory service. X.400 also has the optional mechanism for carrying certificates in the header, but the assumption is that X.400 will rely on the X.500 directory service.

16.4 ENCRYPTION

When encrypting files, PGP (like PEM and X.400) uses secret key cryptography for performance reasons. The secret key algorithm used is IDEA. Just as with PEM, the secret key used to encrypt the message is itself encrypted with the public key of the recipient. Also, as with PEM, if a message is to be sent to multiple recipients, it is encrypted once with a secret key randomly chosen by the sender, and that key is separately encrypted for each recipient, with the public key of the recipient.

PGP compresses the plaintext before encrypting it, if possible. PEM does not. X.400 doesn't say. PGP does not compress the message if it has already been compressed or (perhaps because it is not text but arbitrary binary data) does not compress well. Compression accomplishes several things. It speeds up the encryption and decryption steps (because the file is shorter), it makes cryptanalysis harder because the plaintext has fewer useable patterns, and it saves disk space and transmission time because the files are shorter.

16.5 ENCODING OF TRANSMITTED MESSAGES

All the mail systems support the following types of messages:

* unencrypted and signed

* encrypted and signed

PGP and X.400 support an additional type, which is encrypted but not signed.

PEM and PGP both support two versions of unencrypted and signed, which we call *human-readable* vs. *mailer-defensive*. The mailer-defensive version is noncryptographically encoded to be guaranteed to get through mailers unmodified. The other version is human-readable, which has the advantage that it can be read by the recipient even if the recipient has just an ordinary mail reader (i.e. not PEM or PGP). PGP has an additional version which we call *compact*. In the compact version PGP does not modify anything in order to protect against helpful mailers. The text of the message might have been compressed through the PKZIP[1] compression algorithm, the signature is sent without turning it into printable ASCII, and there are no delimiting banners such as

```
-----BEGIN PGP MESSAGE-----
```

to help a human parse the message. X.400 only has one type, since X.400 is designed to carry mail without having the mail be modified enroute.

Again, because X.400 always assumes it can carry arbitrary data through mailers, it does not need to support an encoded version of encrypted mail. PEM always encodes the encrypted message into innocuous ASCII with sufficiently short lines (which expands the message). PGP supports both—you can send the encrypted message unmodified, or encoded into innocuous ASCII.

16.6 CRYPTOGRAPHIC ALGORITHMS SUPPORTED

All three mail standards are designed to be cryptographic-algorithm-independent. However, in order for two implementations to interwork they need to both support the cryptographic algo-

---

1. PKZIP® is a registered trademark of PKWARE Inc.

rithm chosen for a particular message. If there are multiple algorithms supported, there must be a method of specifying which algorithm is being used.

Although all three theoretically support a choice of algorithm, PEM in practice only supports DES for encryption, and DES or RSA for permanent keys, depending on whether the secret key PEM variant or the public key variant of PEM is being used. And in practice, all the popular PEM implementations are based on public key.

PGP in practice only supports IDEA for encryption and RSA for permanent keys.

X.400 in practice doesn't support any cryptographic protocols to our knowledge.

16.7 RECIPIENTS WITH MULTIPLE KEYS

PEM identifies recipients not by name but instead by certificate (in the public key case) or by interchange key issuer and key sequence number (in the secret key case). Kerberos solves the problem of letting a recipient know which key to use by associating a version number with a key, and transmitting that along with anything that needs to be decrypted (see §10.8 *Key Version Numbers*). PGP solves the problem by sending along the low-order 64 bits of the key, and doesn't even give the name of the recipient, under the assumption that it is extremely unlikely that any two recipients of a given message will have valid keys with the same 64 bits (see §14.10.2 *Primitive Object Formats*).

16.8 MAIL-INTERMEDIARY-PROVIDED FUNCTIONS

PEM and PGP operate totally end to end. They need to defend themselves from helpful mailers, but they don't expect any actual services from them. X.400, on the other hand, requires the mail delivery infrastructure to provide all sorts of features, such as proof of submission.

PART 4

LEFTOVERS

17 MORE SECURITY SYSTEMS

A lot of systems have been deployed with security features, and it is rather surprising how different they can be from one another. In this chapter we give an overview of some of the systems we have found interesting. We do not go into as much detail with the systems in this chapter as we did with Kerberos, PEM, PGP, and the cryptographic algorithms, partially because these systems are likely to change quickly, and partially because the security aspects of most commercial systems have not been publicly documented in enough detail for us to do that. Why haven't they been fully documented in the public literature? One reason is that lack of documentation makes it harder for a relatively unsophisticated cracker to exploit security flaws that might exist. Sometimes it is because a company considers the technology a trade secret. Often it is just because careful documentation of the security features is a lot of work and has little commercial benefit.

Given that companies will keep coming out with new products, and new features in existing products, don't use this chapter as a product survey. The purpose of the chapter is just to introduce the personalities of some systems that happened to exist at the time we were writing the book, and that we found, for some reason or another, to have made interesting engineering trade-offs or introduced clever performance enhancements.

17.1 NETWARE V3

Novell's networking package is known as NetWare. This section describes the cryptographic security in Version 3. Version 4 security was enhanced to use public key cryptography. We describe Version 4 security in §17.2 *NetWare V4*.

Each server has a database consisting of information about each authorized client. The information includes the user's name, the salt, and the hash of the user's password with the salt. The salt is not actually a random number, but instead is a 32-bit user ID assigned by the server when the user is installed in the server database. The salt serves two purposes. It makes the hash of Alice's password server-dependent, so that if Alice uses the same password on multiple servers, the database at each server will, with high probability, store a different hash of her password. It also makes the hash of Ted's password different from the hash of Alice's password even if they have the same password. We'll use X to designate the hash of the password stored at the server.

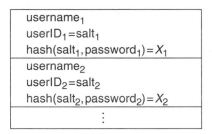

$$\begin{array}{|l|}
\hline
\text{username}_1 \\
\text{userID}_1 = \text{salt}_1 \\
\text{hash(salt}_1,\text{password}_1) = X_1 \\
\hline
\text{username}_2 \\
\text{userID}_2 = \text{salt}_2 \\
\text{hash(salt}_2,\text{password}_2) = X_2 \\
\hline
\vdots \\
\hline
\end{array}$$

Figure 17-1. Server Password Database

Alice tells her workstation her name, password, and the name of the server to which she'd like to log in. The workstation sends Alice's name to the server. The server sends the salt value and a random challenge R to the workstation. The workstation performs the hash of the password Alice typed with the salt, and now both the workstation and the server know the same secret value X (assuming Alice typed her password correctly).

Now the workstation and the server each computes hash(X,R) to get a value we'll call Y. The workstation transmits Y to the server, and if it matches hash(X,R), then the server considers Alice authenticated. At this point the workstation and the server each compute Z=hash$(X,R,$constant string$)$. Z is what they'll use as a secret session key.

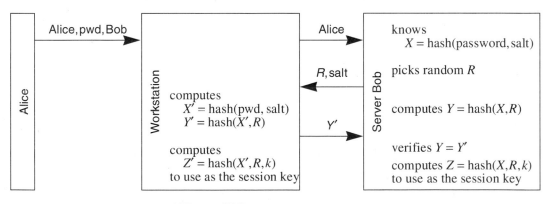

Figure 17-2. NetWare V3 Authentication

After the authentication exchange each packet is integrity-protected by performing a hash of the packet and Z. Once the workstation receives an integrity-protected packet from the server, mutual authentication has occurred, because the server has proven it knows Z.

Actually, for performance reasons, only the first 52 bytes of the packet are cryptographically checksummed. Checksumming the first 52 bytes of the packet is sufficient to answer the threats of eavesdroppers gaining information from the authentication exchange and intruders hijacking a session after the initial authentication exchange. It does not prevent an attacker from removing a packet in transit and substituting one with modified data after the first 52 bytes, but this is a far less realistic threat, particularly if the two communicating parties are on the same LAN.

Why did Novell choose 52 bytes rather than some nice power of 2? Because 52 bytes is long enough to protect all the information necessary to prevent hijacking, and there's additional information appended to those 52 bytes to form a single 64-byte message digest block. The extra information is the 4-byte packet length and the 8-byte secret.

Why does the server store the secret value X rather than simply the user's password? A workstation that knew the value X would be able to impersonate Alice without knowing Alice's password. But in terms of real-world threats, it is a lot more secure to store X than Alice's password. If Trudy were to steal the server's database and acquire X, she'd only be able to exploit X if she were able to acquire the client authentication code and modify it to use X rather than compute it from what the user types. In contrast, if the server stored the user's password directly, then if Trudy stole the server's database, she'd be able to impersonate Alice directly by typing her password at unmodified client code.

Storing X rather than the password will not prevent Trudy from doing an off-line password-guessing attack, but if Alice chose her password wisely, then an off-line password-guessing attack is unlikely to succeed.

Another reason it is more secure to store X than the user's password is because of the salt. Let's assume Trudy can modify the client code, and can therefore use X to impersonate Alice directly, and therefore X is as security-sensitive as Alice's actual password. Since X is very likely to be different at each server, even if Alice's password is the same, then Trudy will only be able to impersonate Alice at the server from which Trudy acquired the database.

17.2 NetWare V4

There were two major reasons for modifying security in Version 4 of NetWare. The first was to utilize public key cryptography, which has the potential to make theft of the server database less of a security issue. The other was to simplify management. Instead of having a database entry for Alice separately managed at each server Alice is authorized to use, NetWare Directory Services (NDS) stores Alice's security information, and servers retrieve the information from NDS.

Each user has an RSA key, but of course the user does not remember that. The user remembers a password. NDS stores Alice's private key encrypted with her password. To prevent off-line password guessing, Alice's workstation must prove knowledge of her password before NDS will transmit her encrypted private key. The pre-authentication phase, where her workstation proves it knows her password, is similar to NetWare V3. NDS stores a hash of Alice's password and salt. In V3 we said the salt was useful because it made the hash of Alice's password different on different servers. That case does not apply for V4 since Alice's entry is only stored in one place—NetWare Directory Services. But the salt is still useful, since it means that an intruder who reads the directory service database has to conduct separate dictionary attacks against each account.

First Alice logs into the workstation by typing her name and password. The workstation then authenticates on Alice's behalf to NDS in order to obtain Alice's private key. For security as well as performance, once the workstation acquires Alice's private key from NDS, it converts it into a temporary Gillou-Quisquater (GQ) key (see §17.2.1 *NetWare's Gillou-Quisquater Authentication Scheme*) and then forgets her password and private RSA key.

Authentication with GQ is public key authentication, but there are two important differences from authenticating with RSA.

- A private RSA key lasts forever. A GQ key, as NetWare uses it, expires—the workstation determines when the GQ key should expire when it creates the GQ key from the RSA key. If some untrustworthy software steals Alice's password or private RSA key, it can impersonate her forever (or until she notices what has happened and changes her long-term private key). Conversion to a GQ key limits the amount of time in which damage can be done. Note that this is the same reasoning that led the Kerberos designers to introduce the concept of a TGT and session key for the user rather than using the user's master key throughout a session.

- GQ authentication is faster than RSA for the client (Alice, the thing proving her identity) but slower for the server (Bob, the thing authenticating Alice). The NetWare designers envisioned slow PCs for clients and fast PCs for servers.

NetWare could have implemented the conversion of the long-term secret into a short-term secret differently. Rather than generate a GQ key pair, the workstation could choose a new RSA key pair, generate a certificate for it by signing it with the user's long-term private RSA key, and then forget the user's long-term secret. That is what DASS does, as we'll see in §17.5 *DASS/SPX*. But generating a temporary GQ key is much faster than generating an RSA key, so the NetWare scheme has higher performance during login.

Once the workstation has acquired a GQ key for Alice, it stores it for the duration of her session and uses it to authenticate on her behalf to any servers she accesses during her session.

If Alice asks to log into server Bob, then Bob must retrieve Alice's public RSA key from NDS. Alice's temporary GQ key works with her permanent public RSA key, in the sense that a signature generated with her temporary GQ key is verified using her permanent public RSA key.

To summarize, the information stored for Alice in NDS includes

Alice's name
hash(salt, password) = X
public RSA key
encrypted private RSA key

used to verify that Alice's workstation knows her password before NDS transmits her encrypted private RSA key

encrypted using a hash of Alice's password

Figure 17-3. NetWare V4 NDS Database Entry for Alice

Here is the protocol in which Alice's workstation obtains her encrypted private RSA key from NDS:

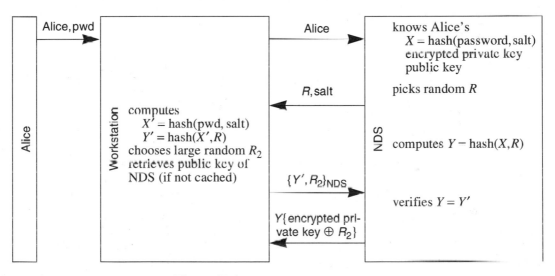

Figure 17-4. NetWare V4 Pre-authentication

First Alice logs in and her workstation communicates with NDS in order to obtain her private RSA key, which her workstation will use to generate a finite-lifetime GQ key for her:

1. Alice types her name and password to her workstation.

2. The workstation uses that to authenticate on Alice's behalf to NDS, in an authentication exchange nearly identical to NetWare V3, except for the final message of the pre-authentication. The final message in V3 consists simply of Y, which is hash(X,R), where R is the challenge transmitted by the server. In V4, in addition to transmitting Y, the workstation transmits

a large random number R_2 (chosen by the workstation), which will be used by NDS for concealing NDS's reply to the workstation from eavesdroppers. The entire message (Y and the random number R_2) is encrypted with the NDS's public key. Encrypting the message with NDS's public key means that an eavesdropper cannot use Y and R to verify password guesses off-line (as it could in V3).

3. Once NDS is assured that the workstation knows Alice's password, NDS transmits Alice's encrypted private RSA key to the workstation. To prevent off-line password guessing by eavesdroppers, the encrypted private RSA key is $\oplus$'d with the random number R_2 sent in the previous step, and then encrypted with Y.

4. The workstation decrypts Alice's private RSA key. It immediately turns it into a GQ key with an expiration time, and then forgets the password and private RSA key.

Here is what occurs when Alice accesses a network resource, say a server named Bob.

1. Alice asks to log into Bob.

2. Bob obtains Alice's public key from NDS.

3. Alice is authenticated in a public key authentication handshake in which the workstation uses Alice's GQ key and Bob uses her public RSA key.

4. A session key is also established as part of the authentication handshake between the workstation and Bob, and that session key is used to integrity-protect the initial portion of each of the packets of the Alice-Bob exchange (just like in V3).

17.2.1 NetWare's Gillou-Quisquater Authentication Scheme

NetWare V4 authentication is not based on RSA, but rather on a variant of an algorithm by Gillou and Quisquater. We'll call NetWare's variant **GQ**. GQ requires that each user have an RSA key pair. The user's private RSA key is used to generate a private GQ key with a temporary lifetime. Then the workstation forgets the user's private RSA key, and future authentication is done using only the GQ key and the user's public RSA key. The GQ key can only do signatures (it can't encrypt or decrypt). Signature verification uses the public RSA key.

This is how the workstation acquires a private GQ key for the user:

1. The workstation acquires the user's private RSA key.

2. The workstation generates a message, m_0, which includes the validity interval for the GQ key it is about to create.

3.   The workstation signs m_0 with the user's private RSA key. This signature of m_0 is the user's private GQ key, Q. The workstation must not divulge this quantity.

4.   The workstation forgets the user's private RSA key, but remembers m_0 (which is used, together with the user's public RSA key, to verify a GQ signature) and Q (the RSA signature on m_0).

This is how the GQ key is used to sign a message:

1.   To sign a message, say m, the workstation needs to know Q, m, and the user's public RSA key. These quantities are all fed into a magic function that outputs a signature. As used by NetWare, m is the challenge supplied by the server.

2.   The signature verification function requires as input m, the signature on m, m_0, and the user's public RSA key. With these inputs, the signature verification function decides whether or not the signature is valid.

The mathematics involved are ugly and unintuitive, but we'll document them here for completeness. We'll describe the mechanics, but to understand why it's secure, you should read [GUIL88].

- The user's RSA key pair is $\langle e,n \rangle$ for the public key, and $\langle d,n \rangle$ for the private key.

- $Q - m_0{}^d \mod n$ is the RSA signature on m_0.

To sign a message m, do the following:

1.   Generate eight random numbers $r_1, \ldots r_8$ in the range $[2, n-2]$.

2.   Compute eight quantities $x_1, \ldots x_8$, where $x_i = r_i{}^e \mod n$.

3.   Compute MD4$(m|x_1|x_2|\ldots|x_8)$.

4.   Break the 128-bit message digest computed in the previous step into 8 16-bit quantities and call the pieces $c_1, \ldots c_8$.

5.   Compute eight quantities $y_1, \ldots y_8$, where $y_i = r_i Q^{c_i} \mod n$.

6.   The GQ signature of m consists of $x_1, \ldots x_8$, and $y_1, \ldots y_8$.

To verify the GQ signature of m, do the following:

1.   Receive m_0, m, $x_1, \ldots x_8$, and $y_1, \ldots y_8$.

2.   Reliably find the user's public key $\langle e,n \rangle$.

3.   Compute MD4$(m|x_1|x_2|\ldots|x_8)$.

4. Break the 128-bit message digest computed in the previous step into 8 16-bit quantities and call the pieces $c_1, \ldots c_8$.

5. Accept the signature if for each i, $y_i{}^e = x_i m_0{}^{c_i} \bmod n$.

Why does this work?

$y_i = r_i Q^{c_i} \bmod n$ (this is how y_i got computed in the signing algorithm)

$y_i{}^e = (r_i Q^{c_i})^e = r_i{}^e (Q^e)^{c_i} \bmod n$

$r_i{}^e = x_i \bmod n$ (this is how x_i got computed in the signing algorithm)

$Q = m_0{}^d \bmod n$, so $Q^e = m_0 \bmod n$

$y_i{}^e = (r_i Q^{c_i})^e = r_i{}^e (Q^e)^{c_i} = x_i m_0{}^{c_i} \bmod n$, which is what is being tested

17.3 KRYPTOKNIGHT

KryptoKnight was developed at IBM. Its product name is NetSP (Network Security Program). We really like the name KryptoKnight, so we'll use that rather than the probably more correct term NetSP. It is a secret key based authentication and key establishment system similar to Kerberos. There are several papers describing the concepts behind it [MOLV92, BIRD93, HAUS94, BIRD95, JANS95].

Ways in which KryptoKnight is similar to Kerberos:

- They both use KDCs, though KryptoKnight calls them **Authentication Servers**.

- There can be multiple realms, which KryptoKnight refers to as **domains**.

- There can be replicated KDCs within a single realm.

- Upon first login, the user's password is converted into a long-term key, which is used to obtain a TGT from the KDC, and then both the password and long-term key are forgotten by the workstation.

- Like Kerberos V5, to prevent an intruder from simply asking the KDC for a TGT for Alice and then using that TGT to mount an off-line password-guessing attack, Alice's workstation needs to prove to the KDC that it knows her password before the KDC will transmit a TGT.

KryptoKnight differs from Kerberos in the following ways:

- KryptoKnight uses message digest functions rather than DES for authentication and even for encryption of tickets. Using message digest functions rather than DES in authentication offers performance advantages and may make it easier to comply with export controls.

- With Kerberos, Alice must obtain a ticket to Bob before initiating a conversation. In Krypto-Knight, there is the option for Alice to alert Bob directly that she would like to converse, and have Bob do the handshaking with the KDC(s). One example where this functionality is vital is where Bob is a firewall and prevents Alice from accessing anything inside the network, including the KDC, until Alice has been authenticated by Bob. Another example is where it is less expensive for Bob than Alice to communicate with the KDC, for instance if Alice has a very-low-bandwidth link into the network.

- Like Kerberos V4 but unlike Kerberos V5, interrealm authentication between Alice and Bob is only allowed when Alice's KDC and Bob's KDC have been administratively set up with a shared key; i.e., transit realms are not allowed.

- KryptoKnight does not rely on synchronized clocks, and can instead use random number challenges.

- The KryptoKnight designers were very careful to minimize the number of messages, lengths of messages, and amount of encryption (for example, Kerberos V4 unnecessarily encrypts an already-encrypted ticket). Ironically, in some cases KryptoKnight uses more messages than Kerberos, but this is because of not relying on synchronized clocks and therefore requiring an extra message to transmit a challenge.

- Other than pre-authentication, KryptoKnight does not bother with any of the features that got added to Kerberos V5, such as delegation, authorization data, postdated and renewable tickets, and hierarchical realms.

17.3.1 KryptoKnight Tickets

In Kerberos, when Alice asks for a ticket to Bob, she is given a quantity, encrypted with Bob's key, containing the session key Alice and Bob will share and other information such as Alice's name and the expiration time of the ticket.

In a ticket, the only information that requires encryption is the session key, but the rest of the information has to be protected from modification. KryptoKnight tickets are rather elegant. Indeed in a KryptoKnight ticket, the only thing that is encrypted is the session key. And it is encrypted using a message digest function, rather than by secret key encryption.

The most important fields in a ticket are Alice's name, the expiration time, and the encrypted session key. The session key is encrypted by $\oplus$ing it with a quantity that Bob and the KDC, but no one else, can compute. That quantity is the message digest of the concatenation of the secret Bob shares with the KDC, Alice's name, and the expiration time of the ticket. If someone were to modify the name or expiration time in the ticket, then when Bob computes the message digest of his secret|Alice|expiration time, he'll get a totally different value, and the ticket will decrypt to something totally unpredictable, and therefore useless to an intruder. So this encryption method for encrypting the session key also serves as integrity protection for the unencrypted fields in the ticket.

17.3.2 Authenticators

During the authentication handshake, Alice and Bob send each other something functionally equivalent to Kerberos authenticators. The Kerberos authenticator is a timestamp DES-encrypted with the shared secret. In KryptoKnight, it is instead a nonce, generated by the other side as a challenge. Alice "signs" Bob's challenge by prepending the secret she and Bob share and returning the message digest of the result. Similarly, Bob signs Alice's challenge. KryptoKnight provides all Kerberos V4 functionality (except encryption of user data) using message digest functions rather than secret key cryptography.

17.3.3 Nonces vs. Timestamps

We said before that KryptoKnight does not require synchronized time. Actually, the authentication protocols can use either timestamps or nonces. There is a trade-off between nonces and timestamps. Timestamps require somewhat-synchronized clocks. If time is only used to indicate expiration time, it doesn't need to be very accurate. But if an encrypted timestamp is sent as part of the authentication handshake, then time synchronization is more critical. Relying on timestamps also raises another security vulnerability, since the timekeeping mechanism has to be kept secure (or else an intruder can accomplish bad things by setting the clocks back a month or so). The disadvantages of using nonces instead of timestamps are that nonces require additional messages, and they do not allow Alice to hold onto a ticket to Bob and use it multiple times (see below).

Because sometimes one mechanism is preferable to the other, KryptoKnight tickets contain both a nonce and an expiration time, though usually only one of the fields will be security-relevant in any given exchange. Authenticators can also be based on time or nonces.

How does KryptoKnight work when it uses nonces instead of timestamps in the authentication handshake? The timestamp in a ticket to Bob assures Bob that Alice has obtained the ticket recently, because the expiration time has not yet occurred. In order to use a nonce instead of an expiration time, Alice needs to ask Bob for a nonce before she can request a ticket to Bob. She sends Bob's nonce to the KDC and it puts it into the ticket. Bob has to remember the nonce he gave to Alice, and make sure that the ticket is based on his nonce.

Actually the nonce does not need to be transmitted as part of the ticket. The nonce, instead of being explicitly in the ticket, is just one of the fields (along with Alice's name and the secret that Bob and the KDC share) which get input into the message digest that the KDC ⊕s with the session key.

With the nonce mechanism, once Alice is removed from the KDC database, she is unable to obtain more tickets. With the expiration time mechanism, once Alice obtains a ticket there is no way to revoke it until the expiration time occurs.

17.3.4 Data Encryption

Once a session is set up, if encryption is desired, the data is encrypted with a secret key cryptographic scheme. The prototype used DES. The current product (as of this writing) uses a weakened secret key algorithm with a 40-bit key, which was the price IBM paid to make the product freely exportable from the U.S.

17.4 SNMP

SNMP, which stands for Simple Network Management Protocol (see glossary for definition of *simple*), is a protocol standardized by the IETF for controlling systems across a network. It lets you set and read parameters, and lets systems generate and transmit traps, which are special event notifications that the system thinks someone might want to know about, like that the printer has run out of paper or the building is on fire.

Certain parameters are security-sensitive, such as *operational status*. It isn't desirable to let just anyone send an SNMP message to your nuclear power plant to tell it to shut off its cooling system. So SNMP allows read/write access to different subsets of parameters depending on which group you're in (they call it a **community**). Version 1 has you assert which community you're in by stating the community name in the SNMP message. This only provides security if community names are used like passwords, i.e., they aren't really easy to guess, and there are no eavesdroppers.

Enhanced security was one of the primary goals behind the design of version 2 of SNMP. Each SNMPv2 message can be source-authenticated and integrity-protected using a shared secret configured into the system being managed and the system doing the management. This is done cryptographically by prepending the secret to the message, taking the MD5 message digest of the result, and transmitting the message digest along with the message (without sending the secret, of course). In addition, a second secret can optionally be configured, and used for encrypting the

SNMP message using DES. (The spec mentions the possibility of using other algorithms, including public key algorithms, but in practice the algorithms used are DES and MD5.)

SNMP has an interesting model of operation. Individual humans talk to a thing known as an enterprise manager, and the enterprise manager, instead of talking to the device directly using SNMP, may communicate with an element manager, and it is the element manager that sends the management commands to the device. There can in fact be arbitrarily deep hierarchies of automated management entities.

What is the purpose of the element manager? It would seem simpler to send SNMP commands directly to the device, but originally the assumption was that a lot of devices would be manufactured with their own management protocols. The element manager hid the complexities of all the management protocols from the rest of the world, since it spoke SNMP to the thing attempting to manage the device, and spoke the native management protocol to the actual device. Another reason the element manager might be necessary is that in some cases the device-specific management protocol was unroutable (built directly on the data link layer rather than a network layer), so whatever was managing the device had to sit on the same LAN as the device.

But SNMP caught on as a standard, and most devices indeed now speak SNMP. However, even if all devices speak SNMP, the element manager is still very convenient because of SNMP security. A device such as a line printer or a toaster is likely to have limited memory for configuring information such as secrets for each community, or authorization information specifying what specific parameters each community is allowed to access. So all this information can be configured into the element manager. The device only needs a single secret which it shares with the element manager, and it allows the element manager access to anything. The element manager keeps the database of secrets and authorization information. It receives an SNMP command, verifies the source, decrypts the message if necessary, checks if the source is authorized for that command for that device, and if so, the element manager sends the request, wrapped in the element manager's security information, to the device. When the device replies with the parameter's value (in the case of a read) or the status of the request (in the case of a write), the element manager rewraps the message with the security information for the source, and transmits it to the manager server.

What is the purpose of enterprise managers? The reason is scalability. Having enterprise managers rather than individuals (their workstations of course) talk directly to the element managers saves configuration. Rather than configuring the element manager with a key (and other information) for each individual human who is authorized to set parameters on a particular device, the element manager configures security information per enterprise manager. If many humans are authorized to use a particular enterprise manager, then the enterprise manager keeps the individual security information, and once it has verified someone is in the community, the enterprise manager issues the commands, using the key established between that enterprise manager and that element manager. There can actually be hierarchies of enterprise managers, just like a human management chain in an organization. An individual, Alice, talks to her boss, Bob, who keeps track of all the individuals for whom he is responsible. If Alice has something to say she says it to Bob, who says it to his boss, Carol. Carol doesn't know anything about Alice, but Bob is authorized to talk to Carol.

17.5 DASS/SPX

DASS stands for Distributed Authentication Security Service. It was deployed as SPX, pronounced Sphinx, and nobody has come up with an acronym expansion for SPX. It was developed at Digital Equipment Corporation and documented in RFC 1507 and [TARD91]. SPX is technically the product name, whereas DASS is the architecture, rather like NetSP and KryptoKnight. We'll use the term DASS because we think it is the more commonly used term for it in the security community, though we haven't done any official polls.

17.5.1 DASS Certification Hierarchy

DASS is based on public keys. There's a certification hierarchy that follows the naming hierarchy. Conceptually there's a CA responsible for each node in the naming hierarchy. Each CA signs a certificate for its parent and for each of its children. These are known as up certificates and down certificates, respectively. DASS also allows cross certificates, where a CA can sign a certificate for any other CA, so that authentication can short-circuit the hierarchy for performance or security reasons. Also, there does not need to be a distinct CA for every node in the tree. One CA could be responsible for many parts of the naming tree.

DASS uses X.509 syntax for certificates and originally envisioned storing certificates in an X.500-style directory service, but since one was not deployed, the DASS designers invented their own certificate distribution service, which they called a CDC, for Certificate Distribution Center. It not only stores certificates, but also stores encrypted private keys. Certificates are publicly readable. Encrypted private keys require a password-based authentication exchange.

17.5.2 Obtaining the User's Private Key

Each user and each network resource has an RSA key pair. To save the human user from having to remember a private RSA key, the private key is stored in the CDC, encrypted with a password the human is capable of remembering. Like Kerberos V5 and NetWare V4, the user's workstation has to first prove it knows the user's password before the CDC will transmit the user's encrypted private key to the workstation. People think of a directory service as something that just stores information and either allows you to see it or does not, based on the access control status of the information. This business of requiring you to do a secret handshake before it allows you to access something is not generally thought of as part of a directory service. But it's not unreasonable to combine the functionality of a CDC and a directory service as NetWare V4 and DASS do.

Like NetWare V4, the pre-authentication handshake is cryptographically protected to prevent eavesdroppers from capturing a quantity with which to do password guessing. In DASS it is done by having Alice choose a DES key, and transmit the DES key, the hash of her password, and a time-stamp to the CDC, in a message encrypted with the CDC's public key. The CDC decrypts the received message, verifies the hash of Alice's password (which the CDC stores in addition to Alice's encrypted private RSA key), checks that the message is within acceptable clock skew, and then transmits Alice's encrypted private RSA key, encrypted with the DES key Alice provided. Having Alice put a timestamp into her message is actually unnecessary, since replay of her message is not a security threat.

17.5.3 Login Key

Once the workstation retrieves the user's private key P, it immediately chooses what DASS refers to as a *login* RSA key pair and then generates a certificate, which we'll call the **login certificate**, signing it with P, stating the user's login public key and an expiration time. Then it forgets P and remembers only the login private key and the login certificate. This is similar to obtaining a TGT in Kerberos, or obtaining a GQ key in NetWare V4. The DASS method is lower-performance during login than the NetWare method because it takes more computation to generate an RSA key pair than a GQ key. During authentication the DASS method is lower-performance on the client side because RSA signature generation is slower than GQ signature generation. But the DASS method is higher-performance on the server side, because with small public exponents, RSA signature verification is faster than GQ signature verification. The DASS designers envisioned a world where workstations had cycles to burn while servers were overburdened. The NetWare designers envisioned the opposite.

17.5.4 DASS Authentication Handshake

Let's say user Alice accesses resource Bob. We won't distinguish between Alice's workstation and Alice. Obviously it's Alice's workstation that is performing the cryptographic operations, but we'll refer to the two ends of the conversation as Alice and Bob. The initial authentication handshake is a mutual authentication handshake based on public keys. Alice knows Bob's public key by looking up and verifying his certificate in the CDC. Bob knows Alice's long-term public key by looking up her certificate in the CDC (and verifying the certificate signature). But the key in

Alice's certificate is not the key Alice will be using. Alice has to transmit her login certificate to Bob, and Bob, after following the certificate chain, now knows Alice's public key for this login session.

In the process of doing an authentication handshake, Alice and Bob establish a shared secret key. Future cryptographic operations, such as encryption of the conversation, are done using that shared secret key. For performance reasons, DASS is designed so that subsequent authentication exchanges between the same two parties can also be done without any public key operations, using only the shared secret key.

It is interesting how the secret key is established between Alice and Bob. Alice (her workstation of course) chooses a DES key $S_{Alice-Bob}$ at random, encrypts $S_{Alice-Bob}$ with Bob's public key, and signs the result using her login private key (for integrity protection). We'll use X to designate the encrypted signed $S_{Alice-Bob}$.

Alice sends her login certificate and X to Bob, along with an authenticator proving she knows the key $S_{Alice-Bob}$. Bob then does the following:

- gets Alice's long-term public key, by retrieving and verifying her certificate from the CDC

- verifies Alice's login certificate by using her long-term public key

- extracts Alice's login public key from her login certificate

- reverses Alice's signature on X by using her login public key

- reverses the encryption of X using his own private key, getting $S_{Alice-Bob}$

- verifies the authenticator by decrypting it using $S_{Alice-Bob}$ and checking whether the time is valid

- encrypts the timestamp using $S_{Alice-Bob}$ and returns it to provide mutual authentication

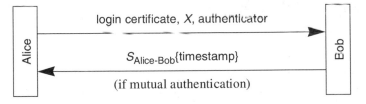

Figure 17-5. DASS Authentication

For performance reasons, both Bob and Alice cache both $S_{Alice-Bob}$ and X. If Alice accesses Bob again, Alice will transmit X again, with a new authenticator. So why does Bob need to remember X? The reason he does is to save himself the trouble of cryptographically unwrapping X again in order to obtain $S_{Alice-Bob}$. Alice might have forgotten $S_{Alice-Bob}$ and chosen a new secret. So Bob has to check if the X he receives is the same as the one he has cached, but if they match he can assume he's using the same key as before with Alice. If they don't match, or if Bob has forgotten the cached information, the authentication handshake works just fine. It just involves the extra computation of Bob cryptographically unwrapping X.

Why does Alice need to cache X? Since Alice does not know whether Bob has cached $S_{\text{Alice-Bob}}$, she has to send X again so that the authentication handshake can proceed whether or not Bob has cached $S_{\text{Alice-Bob}}$. Since she has to perform cryptographic operations in order to regenerate X, it saves her time if she caches X.

An interesting feature of DASS is that the authentication handshake is designed to work in a single message in the case of one-way authentication, and two messages in the case of mutual authentication. The price it pays to reach this theoretical minimum number of messages is that it requires roughly synchronized clocks, like Kerberos.

17.5.5 DASS Authenticators

When Alice initiates a connection to Bob, she sends an authenticator. When mutual authentication is required, Bob sends an authenticator back to Alice. The authenticator is very different in the two directions. In the Alice→Bob direction, Alice sends Bob an unencrypted timestamp and a MIC. The MIC is computed by doing a DES CBC residue using the secret key $S_{\text{Alice-Bob}}$ and an IV of 0, computed over the timestamp and the network layer source and destination addresses extracted from the network layer header. The authenticator Bob sends back to Alice is the timestamp encrypted with $S_{\text{Alice-Bob}}$.

17.5.6 DASS Delegation

DASS is designed so that if Alice wants to delegate to Bob in addition to performing an authentication handshake with him, the delegation can be piggybacked on the authentication handshake.

Recall that during the authentication handshake (without delegation), Alice sends Bob her login certificate, the magic quantity X, and an authenticator. Remember that X is the session key $S_{\text{Alice-Bob}}$ encrypted with Bob's public key and signed with Alice's login key.

If delegation is being done as well as authentication, there's one less public key operation, because instead of sending X (which is the session key encrypted with Bob's public key and then signed with Alice's private key), Alice just sends the session key encrypted with Bob's public key. In order to delegate to Bob, she sends Bob her login private key encrypted with $S_{\text{Alice-Bob}}$. As in the non-delegation case, she also sends an authenticator proving she knows $S_{\text{Alice-Bob}}$. It takes some thought as to why, in the delegation case, it isn't necessary to sign the encrypted session key, whereas it is necessary in the non-delegation case. The DASS designers really enjoyed standing on their heads to minimize public key operations (see Homework Problem 1).

17.5.7 Saving Bits

While DASS was intended to work with a variety of protocols, and was only actually deployed with TCP/IP, the DASS designers wanted to integrate their protocols with DECnet Phase IV, which introduced some interesting constraints. They could only piggyback the security information on existing transport layer connection messages if the additional information did not make the transport layer connection messages longer than an Ethernet packet (approximately 1500 bytes). Alice initiates contact with Bob with a **connect request** message. Bob replies with a **connect confirm** message. There were only 16 spare bytes in a **connect confirm**, and DASS managed to only use 8 of them. DASS needed more space in a **connect request**, because Alice sends her login certificate, X, and an authenticator. Luckily, there was enough room. But there would not have been enough room if the DASS designers didn't spend a lot of time doing clever compression of the data they needed to send.

The exact packet formats are not important, but the most dramatic encoding trick they played was the encoding of Alice's login private key when she transmits it to Bob for delegation. Recall that an RSA public key consists of $\langle e,n \rangle$, where n is the modulus and e is the public exponent. An RSA private key consists of $\langle d,n \rangle$. Alice's login certificate contains $\langle e,n \rangle$. You'd expect Alice to send d in order to give Bob her login private key. But instead, she sends p, which is the smaller of the factors of n, and will be about half as big as d (so it will be about 256 bits instead of 512). Bob has to divide n by p to get q, and then use Euclid's algorithm to calculate d (given that he knows e and n from her login certificate). Actually, when doing delegation it's friendly to pass more than just d, since if Bob knows n's factorization he can do private key operations more efficiently. Given p, Bob can compute all the information that would have been good to send him. If instead, Alice were to pass all the information so that Bob didn't need to do any computation, it would take about 2½ times the size of the modulus (so about 1300 bits). The DASS method makes Bob do some work up front, but then he can sign efficiently on Alice's behalf.

DASS does use ASN.1 encoding, which might seem surprising since its designers were so worried about encoding efficiency. But they were very careful to avoid sending redundant information, and they were clever in their use of ASN.1 syntax. By using **IMPLICIT** and other tricks they avoided the size explosion found in Kerberos V5 and X.509.

17.6 LOTUS NOTES SECURITY

Lotus Notes has a security system without a cute name, or really any name at all. Lotus just implemented it and shipped it. There are three versions out there, with the clever names *version 1*, *version 2*, and *version 3*. As of the writing of this book, Lotus is working on something they plan on calling *version 4*. The chief difference between them is that version 3 has hierarchical names, whereas the earlier versions had flat names. Hierarchical names are clearly better for scalability, but for small networks and ease of use, flat names have appeal. Lotus hopes that earlier versions will eventually go away in favor of version 3 (or higher), but nothing ever really goes away, especially if it's extremely simple to use.

Like the other systems we've discussed, Lotus Notes security provides for mutual authentication and establishment of a shared session key. It also provides for electronic mail security. It is public key based, though just like all security systems, it uses public keys in conjunction with secret keys for encryption. The algorithms it uses are RSA, MD2, RC2, and RC4 (see glossary).

17.6.1 ID Files

An ID file contains the sort of user-specific security information that most other deployed schemes would store in a directory service. Lotus Notes security assumes that a user Alice will carry her ID file on a floppy or smart card, or have it stored in nonvolatile memory on her workstation. Because an ID file might be stolen or lost, the ID file is encrypted with Alice's password.

There are interesting tradeoffs between the ID file scheme and a directory service based scheme. The advantages of storing the user's security information in a directory service are:

- It is more convenient. If ID files are kept on floppies or smart cards, users have to carry something around, and if they lose it or forget it they can't log into the network. If ID files are kept on a workstation, then the user is restricted to using that workstation. It is possible to store a given user's ID file on more than one workstation, but it becomes infeasible in some environments to maintain a user's ID file on every possible workstation that that user might use. And operations like password changes become very awkward.

- It might be more secure. A directory service based scheme, if properly designed, can make it difficult for an intruder to capture a quantity with which to do password guessing. If an ID file is on a floppy, someone who steals the floppy can do an off-line password-guessing attack. If the ID file is stored on a workstation, anyone who can physically access the workstation can read out the information and do off-line guessing. In the case of a smart card, however, it is possible to design a smart card that will refuse to divulge its contents, and which will limit the number of password guesses by disabling itself after too many incorrect guesses.

The advantages of the ID file scheme are:

- It might be more secure, because it provides "two-factor authentication", based on both *what you have* and *what you know*.

- It requires less of the network to be operational. Sometimes the environment is quite primitive, such as when the network itself is mostly broken and you need security for network management in order to fix the network, or when directory service replicas need to authenticate one another, or when a bunch of people with laptops show up at a meeting and want to form a private little network.

- It might be more secure because someone who had physical access to a directory service replica could read the directory service database and do off-line password guessing. With ID files, very careful users can keep their information out of the enemy's hands, whereas with a directory service solution, the users have to trust someone else to protect the directory service replicas.

Lotus Notes security does depend on the directory service for encrypting mail, finding cross certificates, and revoking certificates, but basic authentication works even if the directory service is unavailable.

17.6.2 Coping with Export Controls

It is amusing to see what lengths Lotus had to go to in order to satisfy export criteria, and yet provide reasonable security where legal. Each user has two public key pairs, a long one (on the order of 512 bits) and a short one (on the order of 400 bits). Bulk encryption, as you'd expect, is done using secret key cryptography. Again, to satisfy the export rules at the time Lotus asked for a license, there are two key lengths for secret keys, a short one (on the order of 40 bits) and a long one (on the order of 64 bits). The long keys are used within the U.S. The short ones are used for encryption when (at least) one of the participants is outside the U.S.

In Lotus electronic mail, as in PGP and PEM, public keys are used for authentication and for encryption of per-session secret keys that are used for message encryption. To satisfy export criteria, if either participant is outside the U.S., a short secret per-message key is used. And it is encrypted with the short public key. But the signature on the message is computed using the sender's long public key, whether or not the participants are within the U.S. This means that the signature on the message is secure even against an adversary capable of breaking the shorter RSA keys and secret keys used for encrypting the message.

It isn't clear why the export control people insisted on requiring use of a short public key to encrypt a short secret key. If they can break short (400-bit) RSA keys, then they can extract the secret key, no matter how long, providing it is encrypted with a short RSA key. And if they can break short (40-bit) secret keys, they can decrypt any message encrypted with a short key even if that key is encrypted with a long RSA key.

If you are designing a system and want it to be exportable, don't assume that what you've read in this section will apply to your system at the time you seek export approval and for the particular government person with whom you negotiate. But this section is indicative of the sorts of contortions you may have to make if you want to maximize security, interoperability, and exportability all at the same time.

17.6.3 Certificates for Flat Names

With hierarchical names, it's fairly easy to choose a chain of certificates that authenticates Alice to Bob, assuming the CA hierarchy follows the naming hierarchy. Flat names, by definition, don't have any structure. With flat names we could assume (like PGP) that applications will somehow find an appropriate chain of certificates. The flat-name version of Lotus does not use chains of certificates. Instead, Alice is responsible for obtaining certificates for herself from different CAs. If she has enough certificates from enough different CAs, then when she attempts to communicate with Bob, it is likely she'll have a certificate from a CA that Bob knows and trusts. Lotus certificates aren't X.509-encoded, but they contain basically the same information. In the flat name version, Alice starts out having one certificate, created by the administrator that created her account and ID file, and then she obtains other certificates as needed.

The non-hierarchical version of Lotus Notes assumes there are numerous CAs, and each has been configured to know some of the other CAs' public keys. If Alice has a certificate from CA_1, she can obtain a certificate from CA_2 if CA_2 has been configured with a public key for CA_1 and if Bob, the human who is managing CA_2, decides he wants to give Alice a certificate. The semi-automated method for Alice to get a certificate is to send a signed message to Bob asking him to give her a certificate. The signed message contains all of Alice's certificates. The mail program verifies Alice's signature and informs Bob of the list of CAs that have vouched for Alice's public key. Bob makes a policy decision based on Alice's name and the CA names. If he thinks Alice's name is reasonable, and he trusts at least one of the CAs from which Alice has a certificate, he creates and mails back a certificate with Alice's name and public key signed by CA_2.

In this way Alice collects a bunch of certificates from some set of CAs. Lotus allows Alice to specify, for the CA corresponding to each of her certificates, whether Alice trusts that CA or not. If Alice marks a CA as being untrustworthy, then she will not necessarily believe a certificate signed by that CA. But even if she personally has nothing but contempt for some CA, say CA_d, she might need a certificate from CA_d in order to communicate with someone who does respect CA_d.

When two things, say Alice and Bob, authenticate, they each send the other a list of CAs they'll trust, and then each of them (hopefully) finds a certificate the other will believe and sends it to the other. For example, say Alice has certificates from CA_1, CA_2, and CA_3, and marks CA_2 and CA_3 as trusted. Suppose Bob has certificates from CA_1, CA_2, and CA_4, and marks CA_1 and CA_4 as trusted. Early in the authentication handshake, Alice sends the list of CAs she trusts, namely $\{CA_2, CA_3\}$ to Bob, and Bob sends $\{CA_1, CA_4\}$ to Alice. Alice has a certificate Bob will believe, namely the one signed by CA_1, so she sends that one to Bob. Bob also happens to have a certificate Alice will believe, the one from CA_2, and he sends that certificate to Alice.

It might have been nice to allow Alice to maintain a list of CAs she trusts rather than having the trust information be a flag on certificates, since then Alice could accept certificates from a CA that hasn't granted Alice a certificate.

17.6.4 Certificates for Hierarchical Names

Lotus Notes hierarchical names are fairly straightforward. A user is given a certificate by the CA responsible for that portion of the naming hierarchy. (Actually, the user has two certificates, one for a long key and one for a short key, but we'll ignore that in our discussion.) There's also a chain of certificates from the root of the name space down to the user, and it is that chain of certificates that a user presents for authentication (see §17.6.5 *Lotus Notes Authentication*). In order to authenticate Alice, Bob needs the chain of certificates from a common ancestor of Alice and Bob down to Alice.

But there may not be a common ancestor. The name tree for Alice may be disjoint from the name tree for Bob. For instance, they might be in different companies, and there may be no common root level with a CA jointly managed by the two companies. In this case, the only way for Bob to authenticate Alice is through a cross certificate. Some ancestor of Bob has to have created a certificate for some ancestor of Alice.

Cross certificates are stored in the directory service. When Bob wants to authenticate Alice, he searches the directory service for a cross certificate from one of his ancestors to one of Alice's ancestors. If no such cross certificate exists, then Bob and Alice cannot authenticate. In any case in which Bob needs a cross certificate for Alice, Alice will likewise need to find a cross certificate for Bob in her directory service.

How does Alice know the chain of certificates from her root down to herself? They are stored in her ID file. In other systems, like DASS, each CA in the naming hierarchy issues an up certificate for its parent CA, in addition to issuing down certificates for each of its child CAs. These certificates are stored in the corresponding directory. The DASS scheme is actually more convenient in the case where the key of a CA changes. With the DASS scheme, all that is necessary is for each child CA to reissue its up certificate, and the parent CA of the changed CA to issue a new down certificate. With the Lotus Notes scheme, if the key of a CA high up in the name space changes, a change has to be made to the ID file of each user. There is currently no automated method of doing this. On the other hand, the Lotus scheme has a lesser dependence on the directory service and can therefore be used when more network components are not functioning.

17.6.5 Lotus Notes Authentication

The authentication handshake in Lotus Notes is similar to DASS, in that it allows caching of state from one connection to another. If both parties have cached the state, they can eliminate the step where they exchange and verify certificates.

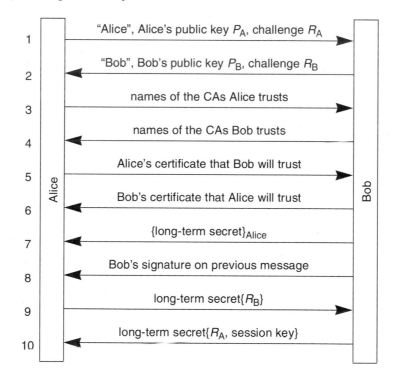

In the first two messages, Alice and Bob tell each other their public keys and give each other a challenge. In messages 3 through 6, Alice and Bob tell each other the list of CAs each trusts, and then reply with a certificate the other will accept, based on the received list of trusted CAs. In messages 7 and 8, Bob sends Alice their long-term shared secret, encrypted with Alice's public key (to foil eavesdroppers) and signed with Bob's private key, to prove it's Bob sending the message (Alice takes Bob's word for it on their shared secret key).

There's a clever performance reason why messages 7 and 8 are sent as two quantities rather than having Bob send the signed encrypted long-term secret as one quantity. The reason is so that the computation-intensive private key operations, the one where Alice decrypts the long-term secret and the one in which Bob signs the encrypted long-term secret, can proceed in parallel. Remember that RSA public key operations can be made faster than private key operations by using a small public exponent (§5.3.4.3 *Having a Small Constant e*).

In message 9, Alice proves her identity. She needed to know her private key in order to extract the long-term secret, which she then uses to encrypt Bob's challenge.

In message 10, Bob proves his identity and securely sends Alice a session key they will share for this one conversation.

The reason Alice and Bob send the unsigned public keys in the beginning is for performance reasons. If the parties have, on a previous connection, exchanged and verified each other's certificates, then the step of exchanging and verifying the certificates can be skipped. In the case where they've maintained state, messages 3 through 8 are skipped.

The certificate exchange we described was based on the non-hierarchical version. That version is used if either Alice or Bob has a non-hierarchical name. If both have hierarchical names, then messages 3 and 4 are skipped, and instead of sending a single certificate, each of Bob and Alice send the complete set of certificates from their root down to them. In the case where Bob and Alice are in disjoint name trees, and therefore there is no common ancestor of their names, each of Alice and Bob has to find a cross certificate in their directory service to one of the certificates they received.

Note that some of these messages might be longer than a single packet. The authentication handshake is actually implemented on top of a reliable transport layer protocol, so it is possible for any of the messages in the handshake to consist of multiple physical packets.

17.6.6 Authentication Long-Term Secret

In a DASS authentication, both Alice and Bob may retain a cache, and if they remember information from a previous Alice-Bob exchange, they can save themselves some processing. The Lotus scheme as we described it in the previous section would seem to have the same property. However, the Lotus scheme is even more clever, since Bob does not need to keep any state!

Note that in message 7, Bob chooses the long-term secret and sends it to Alice encrypted with Alice's public key. The clever idea (devised by Al Eldridge, who designed Lotus Notes security) is that Bob does not choose a random number for the long-term secret, but rather computes it as a cryptographic hash of Alice's name and a secret known only to Bob. If Alice authenticates a second time, Bob will choose the same long-term secret.

If Alice has cached the long-term secret from a previous authentication, she can skip messages 3 through 8 and send message 9, which is Bob's challenge (from message 2) encrypted with the cached long-term secret. Bob computes the long-term secret based only on Alice's name and his own secret.

Why is this secure? Bob doesn't know what CA, if any, is vouching for Alice. But Bob does know that on some previous exchange he was impressed enough with Alice's certificates that he was willing to tell her a long-term secret.

Bob is allowed to change his own hashing secret and in fact does so periodically for security reasons. If Bob has changed his hashing secret since Alice's previous authentication, then Alice will have the wrong long-term secret. In that case her authentication will fail and she will revert to the unabridged authentication handshake, and this time (assuming Bob still likes her certificates) she'll get the new long-term secret.

17.6.7 Mail

The authentication handshake described in the previous section requires Alice and Bob to be actively communicating with each other. With electronic mail, however, Alice will compose a message to be transmitted to Bob, and Bob will eventually receive the message. He might be completely disconnected from the network at the time Alice composes and transmits the message, so Alice has to be able to accomplish message signing and message encryption without shaking hands with Bob.

Lotus Notes mail allows you to encrypt, sign, both encrypt and sign, or do no cryptographic protection of a message. Alice includes her certificates in any message she signs. The hierarchical model is much more straightforward for electronic mail than the flat model. In the hierarchical model, she includes the complete chain of certificates from her root down. In the flat model, Alice wouldn't know which CAs Bob trusts, so she has to send all her certificates.

17.6.8 Certification Revocation

Since Alice sends Bob her certificates as part of authentication, certificate revocation is awkward in Lotus Notes security. There is no such thing as a certificate revocation list. Instead, a user's certificate is revoked by removing it from the directory service. The theory is, if Bob is paranoid he can check the directory service to ensure Alice's certificate is there when Alice logs in, or he can remember when he last looked up Alice's certificate so that he doesn't need to do it if he's done it recently. If Bob is not paranoid, he does not need to check the directory service, increasing availability and performance at the expense of security. For instance, workstations do not check for certificate revocation of servers.

17.7 DCE SECURITY

> *I declare this thing open—whatever it is.*   —Prince Philip

DCE stands for *Distributed Computing Environment*. It is an OSF (Open Software Foundation) product. OSF is a multivendor consortium. DCE security has been incorporated into a number of products from a variety of vendors. DCE security is conceptually similar to Kerberos, and indeed uses Kerberos V5 as one of its components. DCE has a modular design. Kerberos V5 is used for authentication although alternative mechanisms can in principle be substituted. Authentication, authorization, and encryption mechanisms are architecturally separate.

Recall that Kerberos uses KDCs and Ticket Granting Servers, and in the Kerberos chapters we called both things the KDC, since they have to share the same database and same keys and therefore really are the same thing. DCE adds **Privilege Servers** and **Registration Servers**. In practice a Privilege Server and a Registration Server come packaged with a KDC. Privilege Servers and Registration Servers are on-line trusted entities, like KDCs. The purpose of a Privilege Server is to get the principal's UUID (universal unique ID), and the groups (see §7.9.1 *Groups*) to which that principal belongs, to be included in a Kerberos ticket in a secure way. The purpose of a Registration Server is to provide a combined database for a KDC and corresponding Privilege Server. The KDC uses a master key for each principal, along with other stuff that's less interesting. The Privilege Server uses, for each principal, a UUID and the set of groups to which that principal belongs.

ACLs (access control lists) exist outside the context of DCE and in many of the operating systems that support DCE. ACLs could list principals by name, but names are long and subject to change. So in most implementations, ACLs list UIDs (user IDs) and GIDs (group IDs) instead. In Kerberos the principal's name is in a ticket, and Kerberos gives no help in translating from name to UID or in looking up the set of GIDs associated with a principal. Furthermore, Kerberos does not standardize UIDs and GIDs. Different platforms have different forms of UID and GID. For example, most UNIX systems have 32-bit UIDs and GIDs. Some really old UNIX systems have 16-bit UIDs and GIDs. Kerberos assumes systems will translate names to UIDs in some platform-specific way.

DCE standardizes group and user UUIDs at 128 bits long and standardizes DCE ACLs containing those UUIDs. Additionally, DCE does the translation from name to UUID, which is convenient for the applications but makes it difficult for them to use the native ACL format with DCE. The DCE designers, knowing that a UID field of 32 bits was really insufficient, hoped that they'd inspire the operating systems to migrate to their standard of 128 bits. In the meantime most DCE implementations use 32-bit UIDs and GIDs padded out with a constant to look like 128-bit UUIDs.

A UUID in an ACL can belong to either a principal or a group. A user Alice will in general not need to know her own UUID, but usually is capable of remembering her own name, so the login exchange is based on her name.

A user should be authorized to access something if the user's UUID is in the ACL, or if a group to which the user belongs is listed in the ACL. DCE wanted an efficient method of knowing to which groups a user belongs, and this was done by including group information in the ticket.

It is interesting how the DCE designers managed to get this information to be included in Kerberos tickets without modifying Kerberos. It would have been a small change to Kerberos to have the KDC maintain UUID and group membership with each principal, and put that information into the ticket. But instead, they designed elaborate mechanisms so they could work with an architecturally pure Kerberos. They still can't use unmodified KDCs, however, because they access the KDC using DCE RPC instead of UDP datagrams, and because management depends on being able to modify data through the Registration Server.

Kerberos V5 has a field known as AUTHORIZATION DATA. Kerberos does not interpret the contents of this field. Rather it allows a user (say Alice), when requesting a TGT, to specify a value for that field. Kerberos just copies the requested value into the AUTHORIZATION DATA field of the TGT, and then copies that field into the AUTHORIZATION DATA field of any tickets issued based on that TGT. Alice's workstation requests TGTs and tickets on Alice's behalf, but does not maintain the database of Alice's UUID or group memberships. Even if it has that information, it can't be trusted to supply it. So Alice's Privilege Server supplies that information. The Privilege Server reads the database of user name/UUID/group membership from the Registration Server.

With DCE, Alice logs in just like in Kerberos (see Figure 17-6). Alice's workstation gets an ordinary Kerberos TGT with Alice's name inside. The workstation then requests a ticket to the Privilege Server, which to the KDC is just another principal in the realm. The workstation then contacts the Privilege Server. The Privilege Server extracts Alice's name from the ticket, looks up Alice's UUID and group membership, and requests a TGT from the KDC with the Privilege Server's name in the CLIENT NAME field, and Alice's UUID and group membership in the AUTHORIZATION DATA. This TGT is referred to in DCE as a **PTGT**, for **Privilege Ticket Granting Ticket**. The Privilege Server then, in an encrypted message, gives Alice's workstation the PTGT and the corresponding session key (the one encrypted inside the PTGT). Alice's workstation uses the PTGT and corresponding key instead of the original TGT. Note that the above description is architectural—since the Privilege Server and KDC are packaged together, the messages between them might not actually occur.

Now let's say that Alice asks to talk to server Bob. The workstation sends the PTGT to the KDC, along with the request for a ticket to Bob. The KDC will return to Alice a ticket to Bob with the AUTHORIZATION DATA field copied from the PTGT (so that it will contain Alice's UUID and group membership), and with the CLIENT NAME field equal to the Privilege Server's name. The ticket does not contain Alice's name, but it is not needed, since ACLs list Alice's UUID or use group UUIDs.

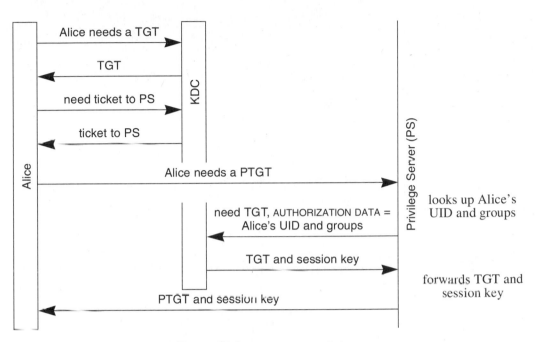

Figure 17-6. Obtaining a PTGT in DCE.

A DCE application, Bob, refuses to honor Kerberos tickets unless the Privilege Server's name is in the CLIENT NAME field. Once Bob checks to make sure the Privilege Server's name is in the ticket, Bob uses the AUTHORIZATION DATA field to discover Alice's UUID and group membership. Since the only way for Alice's workstation to obtain such a ticket (and corresponding session key) is through following the proper procedure, Bob can be assured that the UUID and group information in the ticket is correct. Bob checks this against the ACL of the resource Alice is asking to use.

Multirealm DCE is similar to multirealm Kerberos. Suppose Alice is in realm A and Bob (the resource Alice would like to access) is in realm B. Furthermore, assume B is not a principal in A, so that it is necessary to go through transit realm C. (See Figure 17-7.)

Alice (her workstation) uses her PTGT to request from her KDC a ticket to Bob. Her KDC knows that Bob is not local, so instead gives her a ticket to the KDC in realm C. The AUTHORIZATION DATA and CLIENT NAME will get copied from the PTGT into the ticket to C, so the ticket to the KDC in realm C will still contain A's Privilege Server as CLIENT NAME, and Alice's UUID and groups in AUTHORIZATION DATA. Alice uses the ticket to the KDC in C to ask for a ticket to the Privilege Server in Bob's realm (B). C's KDC will return a ticket to the KDC in B. CLIENT NAME will still be A's Privilege Server. AUTHORIZATION DATA will still be Alice's UUID and groups. The TRANSITED field will contain C. Alice then uses the ticket to B's KDC to ask the KDC for a ticket to B's Privilege Server. The reason she needs to do this is to get a ticket with B's Privilege Server's

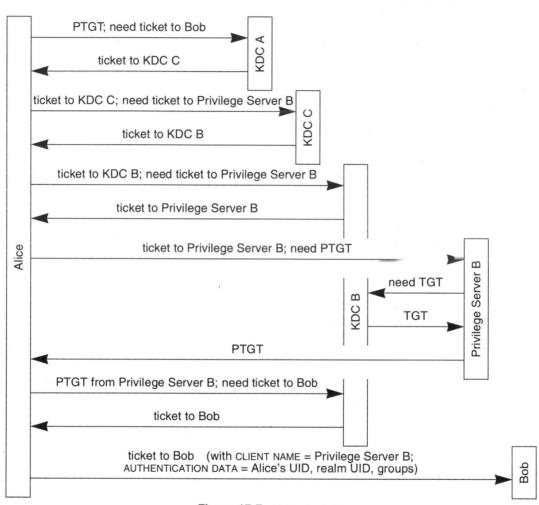

Figure 17-7. Multirealm DCE

name in the CLIENT NAME field, since Bob will not honor a ticket unless the CLIENT NAME is the name of the Privilege Server in Bob's realm. Alice then contacts B's Privilege Server.

B's Privilege Server checks the ticket for legality. Since the ticket is coming from outside the realm, B's Privilege Server will reject it if the CLIENT NAME is not the standard text string that denotes Privilege Server. B's Privilege Server also checks the TRANSITED field for acceptability. The recommended policy for an acceptable transit path is traversal of the tree implied by the hierarchical names, going up to the least common ancestor and then down, though with a single cross-link allowed on the path. With DCE security it is only Privilege Servers that check the TRANSITED field. In fact, once a Privilege Server returns a PTGT, the transit information is gone. DCE made the decision that it was more practical for the Privilege Server to check the transit information. Kerberos, remember, leaves it up to each application.

Assuming B's Privilege Server accepts the transit information, it requests a ticket from B's KDC that contains **Privilege Server B** as CLIENT NAME, and Alice's UUID, group information, and realm UUID as AUTHORIZATION DATA. That's a PTGT just like the original PTGT, except now it has B's Privilege Server's name instead of A's. Alice uses that PTGT to request, from B's KDC, a ticket to Bob. Finally she gets a ticket to Bob, with CLIENT NAME **Privilege Server B** and AUTHORIZATION DATA equal to her UUID, group membership, and realm UUID.

Because of the way that DCE did groups, a user can only be in groups maintained by the Privilege Server of the user's realm. It is possible to put groups and individuals from other realms into a DCE ACL, since each ACL entry effectively consists of a pair of UUIDs: the UUID of either the individual or the group, and the UUID of the realm in which the group or individual resides.

Once Alice and Bob have mutually authenticated, DCE does not use the Kerberos integrity-protected or encrypted data exchanges. Instead, DCE has its own mechanisms for integrity protection, or integrity plus privacy protection within its RPC protocol, using the session key Kerberos does provide. As with Kerberos, the protocols are designed to allow multiple different cryptographic algorithms, but today DCE uses MD5 and DES.

17.8 MICROSOFT SECURITY

LAN Manager comes equipped with a simple, straightforward cryptographic authentication protocol between client and server based on shared secrets. Each server that a user is entitled to access is configured with security information about that user, including a hash of the user's password. When a user Alice wishes to access a server, she types her name and password at her workstation, which contacts the server, sending Alice's name. The server sends a challenge, which the workstation encrypts using the hash of the user's password. Some applications (like RPC) continue cryptographic protection beyond the initial handshake using the user's hashed password to establish a session key.

This protocol is very similar to NetWare V3. In both protocols, the fact that the server stores a hash of the user's password rather than the actual password does not theoretically make the scheme more secure. A modified version of the client software could impersonate the user if it directly used the hash of the password rather than hashing the string the user types. But it would be a lot more convenient and practical for an intruder Trudy if she could capture the actual password rather than the hash of the password, since then Trudy could type the password at unmodified client code. One difference between the protocols is that the LAN Manager scheme does not use salt.

That means that if the user uses the same password on multiple servers, and an intruder captures one server's database, the intruder can impersonate the user at other servers.

For NT, the scheme was extended in a way that was transparent to client machines. *Transparent* means that the new scheme works with the old client code and in fact a client machine cannot tell based on the protocol whether the server is using the old protocol or the new protocol. In the NT protocol, instead of keeping the security information at each server, security information is stored in a trusted on-line entity called a *domain controller*. This has the following advantages:

- Management is simplified, since user security information only needs to be configured into a single location, the domain controller.

- It is more user-friendly, since a user will have a single password that will work on all servers the user is entitled to use. In the old scheme, a user could certainly use the same password on all servers, but when the user Alice changed her password, she'd have to remember to change her password at all the servers.

The NT scheme works like the authentication facilitator node we discussed in §7.1.2 *Storing User Passwords*. The domain controller (which is what we called the authentication facilitator node), stores a secret for each server in the domain, which enables a server in the domain and the domain controller to communicate securely. The domain controller also stores security information for each human user in the domain, including a hash of the user's password, a list of groups to which the user belongs, when to prod the user to change her password, and the hours she's allowed to log in. When a user wishes to log into a server in the user's domain, that server sends a challenge to the user's workstation, which then generates a cryptographic response based on the user's password and the challenge (see Figure 17-8). Since the server does not store any security information for the user, it cannot evaluate the response. Instead, in an encrypted conversation to the domain controller, the server forwards its challenge and the workstation's response. The domain controller answers yes or no in the encrypted reply to the server. If the answer is yes, the domain controller also sends information about the user, such as to which groups the user belongs, and the user's hashed password. (This information, like all the sensitive information between the domain controller and the server, is encrypted.) The hashed password is transmitted so that the server can use it to compute a session key for protection of the remainder of the client-server conversation.

It is possible for a client in one domain D_1 to be authenticated by a server in another domain D_2 provided that D_1 and D_2 have been preconfigured to trust each other. There is no transitivity, i.e., if Alice is in domain D_1 and Bob is in domain D_2, they can communicate if D_1 and D_2 have a trust relationship. It is not possible to transit through domain D_3 in the case where D_1 and D_3 trust each other and D_3 and D_2 trust each other but D_1 and D_2 do not trust each other. This is similar to Kerberos V4.

Names include a domain name, for example D_1\Alice and D_2\Bob. When Alice's workstation contacts Bob, it transmits Alice's name (D_1\Alice). Bob contacts Bob's own domain controller, as

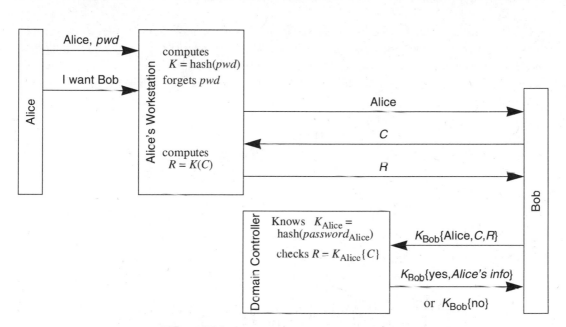

Figure 17-8. Microsoft Windows NT Authentication

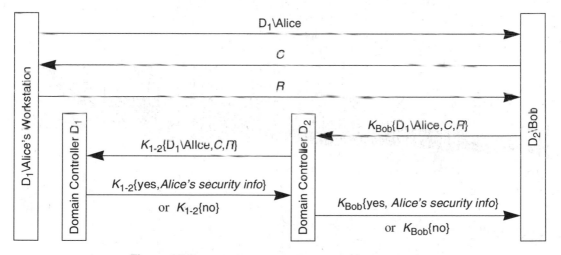

Figure 17-9. Microsoft Windows NT Interdomain Authentication

in the single domain protocol. But Bob's domain controller can't make the decision since D_2 has no information stored for $D_1 \backslash$Alice. But D_2 can communicate securely with D_1, and so D_2 forwards the information ($D_1 \backslash$Alice, C, R) to D_1, which replies to D_2 with **yes** (plus group information, Alice's hashed password, and so on) or **no**, and then D_2 relays this information to Bob (see Figure 17-9).

The cryptographic aspects of the protocol are straightforward. RC4 is used to encrypt the conversation between the server and the domain controller. The domain controller has a long-term secret key stored for each server in the domain, and uses that to establish initial mutual authentication with the server, but as a side-effect of the authentication they establish a session key, and use that to encrypt subsequent communication. The session key for the conversation with the domain controller is obtained by adding the two challenges used in the mutual authentication and encrypting the result with the long-term secret. There is an authenticator in every packet that proves the message is in proper sequence, which prevents session hijacking, but is not used to provide integrity protection of the contents of the message. Encryption is only used on select fields in the packet, i.e., only where necessary.

17.9 NETWORK DENIAL OF SERVICE

The scheme in this section has not been commercially deployed, but it is being built on an experimental basis. It was devised by Radia Perlman and written up in [PERL88].

Routing in today's networks depends on the cooperation of all the routers. If a router were to generate confusing routing messages, or simply flood the network with enough garbage data to saturate the links, it can make a network inoperative. To some extent a network can be designed so that pieces are reasonably independent. For instance in a hierarchical network, although a rogue router in one piece can disable that piece of the network, if routing is properly designed the disruption will remain in that one section of the network. Some routing protocols are being enhanced with authentication information to ensure that only routing messages from authorized routers are accepted. However, such a network would still be disabled by a saboteur corrupting a legitimate router.

A fail-stop failure is one in which a computer is working perfectly one moment and then reverts instantaneously to halting. In real life, failures are not usually so civilized. Often a node starts acting erratically due to software failure, hardware failure, or misconfiguration. Without the help of saboteurs, many of today's networks have suffered collapse due to a sick node. It is only a matter of time before the vandals that have delighted in designing and deploying viruses expand their exploits into network sabotage.

But it is possible to design a network that will continue to function even when being attacked by saboteurs. Our scheme will guarantee that two nodes will be able to converse provided that some path of properly functioning routers and links connects the two nodes. (If no such path exists, then there is no scheme that could possibly work.) So with this scheme, a network can operate properly even with several corrupted routes.

The first part of the scheme involves robust broadcast, in which each message generated by a router is delivered to all the other routers. The robust broadcast mechanism will be used to distribute public key information for all the routers, so that routers need to start out knowing only a single public key. It will also be used to distribute routing information. The second part of the robust network design involves robust data packet delivery, in which a message generated by a node is delivered only to the specified destination.

17.9.1 Robust Broadcast

Flooding is a simple routing mechanism in which a router that receives a message forwards the message on each link except the one from which the message was received. Flooding has the basic property we want—a message is guaranteed to get delivered as long as at least one properly functioning path exists—but with one serious problem. Flooding will only work if we assume that the routers have infinite storage for buffered messages and the links have infinite bandwidth. Few networks have such characteristics, so simple flooding will not solve our problem.

The basic idea behind robust broadcast is that each router guarantees a fraction of its memory and bandwidth resources to each other router. Each router keeps a database of messages to be forwarded, and reserves a portion of the database, say one buffer, for each other router. The messages are transmitted over each link, round robin, so each router's message will have a chance to be delivered over each link.

How do we ensure that the buffer reserved for a given router will be holding a message generated by that router? We do that with public key signatures. Each router signs each message it generates, and only a message with a valid signature can occupy a buffer.

How do we ensure that it is the most recently generated message from a router that occupies the buffer? We do that by using a sequence number. Let's say router R_1 receives a message with source R_2, a valid signature, and a higher sequence number than the message stored for R_2. Then R_1 overwrites the message it had for R_2.

How does R_1 know R_2's public key, so that R_1 can verify R_2's signature? We could use a standard off-line CA. Each router would know the public key of the CA. Each router could include its certificate in each message. But that would make revocation difficult. Another possibility is to have the CA on-line, and have the CA generate and broadcast a list of nodes and public keys whenever the list changes.

What happens if node R_2 is malfunctioning, and generates a message with the highest possible sequence number (assuming the sequence number is a finite-sized field)? In that case, R_2 cannot generate any more messages until it gets a new public key and registers that new public key with the CA. At that point, R_2 can start over again with sequence number 1.

For efficiency, it would be nice to stop transmitting a particular message over a particular link once the neighbor on that link has received the message. This is done by marking each message in the database with an indication, for each neighbor, specifying whether that message needs to be transmitted to that neighbor or whether an acknowledgment for that message needs to be transmitted to that neighbor. When a message (with valid signature and new sequence number) with source R_2 is received by R_1 from neighbor N, R_1 stores the message in the database, marking it as needing to be acknowledged to N, and needing to be transmitted to all the other neighbors. If a duplicate message is received from neighbor N, then that message is marked as needing to be acknowledged to N (and not needing to be transmitted to N). If an acknowledgment for a message is received from neighbor N, that message is marked as not needing to be transmitted or acknowledged to N. When the link to N is available, the next marked message is transmitted, while the database is traversed in round-robin order. If the message is marked as needing to be transmitted, then the message is transmitted. If the message is marked as needing to be acknowledged, then an acknowledgment for that message is transmitted to N.

		N_1	N_2	N_3	N_4
message source	R_1	transmit	ack	ack	OK
	R_2	OK	OK	OK	OK
	R_3	transmit	transmit	transmit	ack
	R_4	ack	ack	OK	OK

The table above shows a database with messages from four different sources: R_1, R_2, R_3, and R_4. The node keeping this database has four neighbors: N_1, N_2, N_3, and N_4. Each message is marked, for each neighbor, with transmit if the message needs to be transmitted to that neighbor, ack if an acknowledgment needs to be sent, or OK if neither needs to be sent. The database is scanned round robin per link, and messages are transmitted as marked.

17.9.2 Robust Packet Delivery

Now we know how to robustly broadcast messages. We could use broadcast for delivery of data messages, but it would be inefficient. Instead we will use the robust broadcast mechanism to reliably deliver routing information, and use the routing information to compute routes. Once a route is computed, it is set up with a special cryptographically protected route setup packet, but then data packets can be forwarded without any cryptographic overhead.

The type of routing protocol we will use is known as a **link state protocol**. In a link state protocol, each router is responsible for figuring out who its neighbors are and generating a packet known as a **link state packet** (**LSP**), which gives the identity of the source router and the list of neighbors of that router. Each LSP is broadcast to all the other routers, and each router is responsible for maintaining a database of the most recently generated LSP from each other router. Given this database, it is possible to efficiently compute routes. For details on routing protocols, see [PERL92].

Now assume that source S computes a path to destination D. Assume S is lucky enough to compute a properly functioning path (all the routers and links along the path are working properly). S transmits a special route setup packet, cryptographically signed and with a sequence number, that causes all the routers along the path to remember, for source/destination pair S/D, from which link they should expect to receive packets and to which link they should forward packets. The route setup packet has a sequence number, and a router R is only required to remember the highest numbered route from S to D. With that rule, we bound the maximum number of routes a router will need to maintain to n^2, where n is the number of nodes. In practice, it would probably suffice to have a router remember some much smaller number of routes; if a router were asked to remember a route when it had run out of resources, it could complain and force the source to generate a route which did not include that router.

In conventional route setup, a router only needs to remember the outbound link for a particular source/destination pair. We are requiring the router to also remember the link from which it should expect to receive packets for that source/destination pair. If a router checks to make sure that a packet was received from the proper link, then as long as the source was lucky enough to choose a properly functioning path, there is nothing a node off the path can do to disrupt communication on that path. And data packets do not need to be cryptographically protected.

If S is not lucky enough to choose a correct path, it has a complete map of the network, and can therefore choose an alternate path. There isn't any completely satisfactory way of doing this, since there are an exponential number of possible paths between any pair of nodes. But in practice, since there are unlikely to be more than one or two corrupted routers, a source can start getting suspicious of routers that appear on paths that don't work, and avoid them. And in the worst case, if a source were to try a lot of paths, it could revert to broadcasting the packet, which would guarantee delivery provided any path exists.

We were vague about the difference between a *node* and a *router*. It is possible to only have the routers participate in the cryptographic protection, and have each router generate and sign route setup packets on behalf of the endnodes serviced by that router.

17.10 CLIPPER

Telephones are easy to tap, and cellular telephones make eavesdropping even easier. Because of this, people have developed encrypting telephones, which so far have been too expensive to catch on, but today it is technically feasible to make encrypting telephones inexpensively. This makes the Government nervous because criminals are sometimes convicted using evidence gathered through wiretaps. To fill the need for encryption without the U.S. government giving up the ability to wiretap (with legitimate reason and through a court order), the U.S. government has proposed the Clipper chip. The Clipper proposal offers high-grade encryption while preserving the ability of the U.S. government to wiretap.

The politics of Clipper are at least as exciting as the technical aspects. We discuss the politics in §1.8 *Key Escrow for Law Enforcement*. Here we concentrate on the technical aspects.

Technically the concept of Clipper is reasonably simple. Each Clipper chip manufactured contains a unique 80-bit key and a unique 32-bit ID. For each key K, an 80-bit random number K_1 is selected, and then $K_2=K\oplus K_1$ is computed. Neither quantity K_1 nor K_2 gives any information about K, but if you know both K_1 and K_2, you can compute K easily, since it is $K_1\oplus K_2$. K_1 (and the unique ID) is given to one federal agency, and K_2 (and the unique ID) is given to a different federal agency. It hasn't been decided which agencies they'll be, but they should be agencies that everyone trusts, like the IRS, and that are independent of one another without likelihood of collusion, like the Army and the Navy.

Let's say that Alice, using a telephone containing a Clipper chip, wants to talk to Bob, who has a similar device. Alice's chip has been registered with the two agencies (as has Bob's). Let's say Alice's chip has unique ID ID_A and secret key K_A. With a court order, the government can obtain the two components of Alice's chip's key and then reconstruct K_A. Without a court order, K_A remains secret.

What key will Alice and Bob use for communicating? It can't be K_A or K_B (Bob's chip's secret key) because neither side wants to reveal its secret key. So Alice and Bob use some mechanism, unspecified in the Clipper standard, to produce a shared secret key S. A reasonable choice is Diffie-Hellman (see §5.4 *Diffie-Hellman*), which in fact has been implemented in the current crop of Clipper phones. Alice feeds S to her Clipper chip and Bob feeds S to his Clipper chip. The chips use S to encrypt and decrypt the data. So where does K_A come in, and how would the government, knowing K_A, be able to decrypt the conversation? Also, how does the government know the unique ID of Alice's chip in order to obtain (with court order) K_A? It would be an administrative nightmare for the U.S. government to try to keep track of who owns each Clipper chip.

The information the government needs is in a field known as the **LEAF**, for **Law Enforcement Access Field**, that Alice's and Bob's Clipper chips transmit along with the encrypted data. Although Bob's chip does not utilize any of the information in the LEAF it receives from Alice's chip, Bob's chip refuses to communicate unless it receives a valid-looking LEAF. The central challenge in the design of Clipper is preventing someone from building a device that uses a Clipper chip for secure communication but substitutes garbage for the LEAF before transmitting the data.

The Clipper design is very clever. The LEAF that Alice transmits to Bob contains ID_A, $K_A\{S\}$, and a checksum C. The field ID_A enables the government to retrieve K_A and then decrypt the field $K_A\{S\}$ to obtain S. Since the same key S is used in both directions, the government only needs one of the keys K_A or K_B in order to decrypt the entire conversation.

How does Bob's chip know whether the LEAF is valid? Bob's chip can't know whether ID_A is the correct value and it can't decrypt $K_A\{S\}$ to check if it's the correct encrypted key. Bob's chip makes its decision based on the value of the field C. C is basically some sort of message digest of the other fields in the LEAF (ID_A and $K_A\{S\}$) and the key S. Bob's chip computes the message digest of the values in the received LEAF for ID_A and $K_A\{S\}$, along with S (which Bob's chip knows). If the computed checksum matches the received C, then the entire LEAF is assumed to be valid.

The message digest algorithm used to compute C need not be secret, so what's to prevent someone from foiling the government's ability to wiretap by modifying the quantity $K_A\{S\}$ (or ID_A) and sending the matching C? To prevent modification of the LEAF, all Clipper chips share an 80-bit secret **family key**, F. The quantity $ID_A|K_A\{S\}|C$ is encrypted with F. Since Bob's chip knows F, it can decrypt the LEAF to extract ID_A, $K_A\{S\}$, and C. It can't verify that either ID_A or $K_A\{S\}$ is correct, but knowing S, it can compute C. If the C in the LEAF doesn't match the computed C, the chip will refuse to decrypt the conversation.

With the LEAF thus guaranteed, the government can (with a valid court order) tap Alice's line, read ID_A from the LEAF, and then retrieve K_A. Then it can read $K_A\{S\}$ from the LEAF and decrypt it to obtain S. At this point, it can decrypt the recorded conversation.

It is rather astonishing that all Clipper chips will know the value F, and yet the expectation is that the value will remain secret. Clipper chips are carefully manufactured so that it should not be possible, by taking one apart, to obtain F. The encryption algorithm (known as **SKIPJACK**) is also supposed to be kept secret, and the same technology that prevents someone from reverse-engineering the encryption algorithm will protect F.

How much of a disaster would it be if someone discovered F? It would not make Clipper-protected conversations less secure. However, it would mean someone could build a device that inter-operated with Clipper devices and foiled wiretapping by generating garbage for $ID_A|K_A\{S\}$, computing the proper value for C based on the garbage and the session key S, and encrypting it all with F.

It has been pointed out that people could, with less effort, build a device that encrypted the data before transmitting it to the Clipper chip. Provided the receiver had a compatible device (Clipper plus the extra encryption device), the output stream would look like normal Clipper output, until someone, under court order, decrypted the conversation and realized they were obtaining ciphertext.

If you had a device capable of encrypting conversations, why would you bother going through the extra step of sending the encrypted stream through a Clipper chip? Perhaps you don't have complete faith in your cryptographic algorithm. Another reason surfaces if it becomes illegal or suspicious to use non-Clipper encryption. If you send your encrypted stream through a Clipper chip, the government would not know that you were using your own encryption, until after it obtained the court order and decrypted your conversation. One wonders what penalties could be associated with using non-Clipper encryption that would deter the sorts of people who are worried about being wiretapped.

> Prosecutor: *Did you murder your wife?*
> Defendant: *No.*
> Prosecutor: *Do you know the penalty for perjury?*
> Defendant: *No, but I bet it's less than the penalty for murder!*
>
> —classic joke

If someone discovered *F* and built a Clipper-compatible device, then Alice, with that device, could foil wiretapping while talking to Bob, who had an ordinary Clipper device. If the government had Alice under suspicion, and therefore had obtained her Clipper key, it would still need to get a court order for Bob's Clipper key before it could decrypt the Alice-Bob conversation. If both Alice and Bob had one of these Clipper-compatible devices, then the government would discover, only after court order, that Alice and Bob were not using real Clipper devices, just as it would discover if Alice and Bob were using an extra encryption step before the Clipper chip.

Matt Blaze [BLAZ94] discovered an interesting property of the Clipper design that makes it possible for Alice, with a lot of effort, to forge a LEAF in a way that Bob will accept, but will prevent government wiretaps. The problem is that the quantity *C* is only 16 bits long. Remember that Bob's chip cannot verify that either of the quantities ID_A or $K_A\{S\}$ is correct. All the chip can do is verify that *C* is based on those quantities and the proper key *S*.

The LEAF is 128 bits long, consisting of 32 bits of ID, 80 bits of encrypted key, and 16 bits of checksum. Bob's chip will accept any sequence of bits for the ID and the encrypted key just so long as those fields, plus the Alice-Bob session key, produce the correct 16-bit checksum. The implication of this is that if Alice were to send a 128-bit random number, it would have 1 chance in 2^{16} of having the correct checksum, when decrypted with the family key *F*.

Now we get to Matt Blaze's attack. Alice can use any Clipper chip as a tester. She tells it she wants to converse using the key she's agreed upon with Bob. Then she feeds it random 128-bit LEAF values. On average she'll only have to try 2^{15} random numbers before one will wind up with the correct checksum.

Now that she knows a LEAF value that will be accepted by Bob's chip for the key she's sharing with Bob, she needs a special piece of hardware that takes the output stream from her Clipper device, removes the LEAF values it transmits, and substitutes the one she found. Bob's device won't know there's a problem, and the problem will only be detected when the government attempts to wiretap.

Matt Blaze's attack is not important in practice, since it would either take a lot of parallel hardware or cause an unacceptable delay in conversation startup, but the discovery was useful in embarrassing the designers for having missed such an "obvious" flaw.

17.10.1 Key Escrow

The Clipper chip has become synonymous with key escrow in the public debate, and has given key escrow a bad name. But there are good reasons other than keeping Big Brother employed for wanting to back up keys.

It's certainly important to keep secret the key with which you encrypt your data. It's possible to be really careful about that. It could be that the only copy of your key is on your smart card, and the smart card is carefully engineered so that it is impossible to obtain the key from the smart card. Then one day your three-year-old finds it and flushes it down the toilet. Is it OK with you to accept that all your work is irretrievably gone? Maybe not.

A similar problem occurs with house keys. When you arrive home during a blizzard, and discover you've lost your key, you really don't want to sit outside until some other member of your family gets home. Typically you've hidden a key under the WELCOME mat (which is equivalent to having a key hung from a chain from the doorknob), or you've given a copy of the key to a neighbor, who hopefully won't break in but will be home when you need the key.

What can you do with your cryptographic key to ensure you can retrieve the key if you forget or lose the key? You could write it on a piece of paper and stick it in an obscure drawer at home, or you could lock it in your safe deposit box.

There are various mechanized approaches that don't involve obsolete technology like paper and safe deposit boxes. One possibility is to store your key on some sort of server. If you're paranoid someone will break into that server you could break your key into pieces, like the Clipper proposal does, where all the pieces need to be $\oplus$'d in order to recover the key. Then you could store each piece on an independent server.

Contacting all the servers to give them their pieces of your key might be some trouble. An elegant solution is to take each piece, encrypt it with the public key of the server to which you'd like to give that piece, and store it on your own machine. Then if you lose the key you can give the corresponding quantities to the corresponding servers and recover it.

17.11 HOMEWORK

1. In §17.5.6 *DASS Delegation* we describe how Alice manages to simultaneously establish a session key with Bob, pass along her login private key to Bob, and authenticate to Bob. Analyze the protocol as described. Why can't an eavesdropper discover Alice's login private key? Why can Bob discover Alice's login private key? How can Bob be sure that the authenticator came from Alice? In the non-delegation case, he knows that only Alice knows the session

key (that encrypted the authenticator) because the session key, when passed to Bob, was signed with Alice's private key. But the signing step is omitted in the delegation case.

2. Propose an alternative design for Clipper where each chip knows only a public key and the government holds the corresponding private key, and where each party sends the session key encrypted under the public key as part of its transmission. How might Bob verify that the LEAF in your design is correct? What would the advantages and disadvantages of this scheme be over Clipper?

BIBLIOGRAPHY

ALAG93   Alagappan, K., *Telnet Authentication: SPX*, RFC 1412, January 1993.

BALE85   Balenson, D., "Automated Distribution of Cryptographic Keys Using the Financial Institution Key Management Standard", *IEEE Communications*, Vol 23 #9, September 1985, pp. 41–46.

BALE93   Balenson, D., *Privacy Enhancement for Internet Electronic Mail: Part III: Algorithms, Modes, and Identifiers*, RFC 1423, February 1993.

BELL74   Bell, D. E. and LaPadula, L. J., *Secure Computer Systems: Mathematical Foundations and Model*, M74-244, Mitre Corp., Bedford, Massachusetts, October 1974.

BELL90   Bellovin, S. M. and Merritt, M., "Limitations of the Kerberos Authentication System", *Computer Communications Review*, Vol 20 #5, October 1990, pp. 119–132.

BELL92a   Bellovin, S. M. and Merritt, M., "Encrypted Key Exchange: Password-Based Protocols Secure Against Dictionary Attacks", *Proceedings of the IEEE Computer Society Symposium on Research in Security and Privacy*, Oakland, California, May 1992, pp. 72–84.

BELL92b   Bellovin, S. M., "There Be Dragons", *UNIX Security Symposium III*, Baltimore, MD, September 1992, pp. 1–16.

BELL93   Bellovin, S. M. and Meritt, M., "Augmented Encrypted Key Exchange", *Proceedings of the First ACM Conference on Computer and Communications Security*, November 1993, pp. 244–250.

BIBA77   Biba, K. J., *Integrity Considerations for Secure Computer Systems*, ESD-TR-76-372, USAF Electronic Systems Division, Bedford, Mass., April 1977.

BIHA91   Biham, E., and Shamir, A., "Differential Cryptanalysis of DES-like Cryptosystems", *Journal of Cryptology*, Vol 4 #1, 1991, pp. 3–72.

BIHA92   Biham, E., and Shamir, A., "Differential Cryptanalysis of Snefru, Khafre, REDOC-II, LOCI, and Lucifer", *Advances in Cryptology—CRYPTO '91 Proceedings*, Springer-Verlag, Berlin, 1992.

BIHA93   Biham, E., and Shamir, A., "Differential Cryptanalysis of the Full 16-Round DES", *Advances in Cryptology—CRYPTO '92 Proceedings*, Springer-Verlag, Berlin, 1993.

BIRD93   Bird, R., Gopal, I., Herzberg, A., Janson, P., Kutten, S., Molva, R., and Yung, M., "Systematic design of a family of attack-resistant authentication protocols", *IEEE Journal on Selected Areas in Communications*, Vol 11 #5, June 1993, pp. 679–693.

BIRD95   Bird, R., Gopal, I., Herzberg, A., Janson, P., Kutten, S., Molva, R., and Yung, M., "The KryptoKnight family of light-weight protocols for authentication and key distribution", to appear in *IEEE Transactions on Networking*, 1995.

BIRR82   Birrell, A., Needham, R., and Schroeder, M., "Grapevine: An Exercise in Distributed Computing", *Communications of the ACM*, Vol 25 #4, April 1992.

BIRR84   Birrell, A. D., *Secure Communication Using Remote Procedure Calls*, CSL-TR 84-2, Xerox Corporation, Palo Alto Research Center, September 1984.

BIRR86   Birrell, A. D., Lampson, B. W., Needham, R. M., and Schroeder, M. D., "A Global Authentication Service without Global Trust", *Proceedings of the 1986 IEEE Symposium on Security and Privacy*, IEEE Computer Society Press, Oakland, CA, April 1986, pp. 223–230.

BLAZ94   Blaze, M., "Protocol Failure in the Escrowed Encryption Standard", *Proceedings of the Second ACM Conference on Computer and Communications Security*, November 1994.

BLUM86   Blum, L., Blum, M., and Shub, M., "A Simple Unpredictable Pseudo-Random Number Generator", *SIAM Journal on Computing*, Vol 15 #2, 1986.

BORM93a Borman, D., *Telnet Authentication Option*, RFC 1416, February 1993.

BORM93b Borman, D., *Telnet Authentication: Kerberos Version 4*, RFC 1411, January 1993.

BRAD89   Braden, R., *Requirements for Internet hosts—communications layers*, RFC 1122, October 1989.

BRAD94   Braden, R., Clark, D., Crocker, S., and Huitema, C., *Report of IAB Workshop on Security in the Internet Architecture*, RFC 1636, February 1994.

BURR90   Burrows, M., Abadi, M., and Needham, R. M., "A Logic of Authentication", *ACM Transactions on Computer Systems*, Vol 8 #1, February 1990, pp. 18–36.

CHES94   Cheswick, W., and Bellovin, S., *Firewalls and Internet Security: Repelling the Wily Hacker*, Addison-Wesley, Reading. Mass., 1994.

COME88   Comer, D., *Internetworking with TCP/IP: Principles, Protocols, and Architecture*, Prentice Hall, Englewood Cliffs, New Jersey, 1988.

COOP89   Cooper, J. A., *Computer and Communications Security: Strategies for the 1990s*, McGraw-Hill, New York, 1989.

CORM91   Corman, Leiserson, and Rivest, *Introduction to Algorithms*, MIT Press & McGraw-Hill, 1991.

CROC82   Crocker, D., *Standard for the format of ARPA Internet text messages*, RFC 822, August 1982.

DATA77   *Data Encryption Standard*, FIPS PUB 46, National Bureau of Standards, U.S. Department of Commerce, Washington, D.C., January 1977.

DAVI78   Davis, R. M., "The Data Encryption Standard in Perspective", *IEEE Communications Society Magazine*, Vol 16 #6, 1978, pp. 5–9.

DAVI84a   Davies, D. W. and Price, W. L., *Security for Computer Networks*, John Wiley and Sons, New York, 1984.

DAVI84b   Davis, D., Ihaka, R., and Fenstermacher, P., "Cryptographic Randomness from Air Turbulence in Disk Drives", *Advances in Cryptology—Crypto '94*, Springer-Verlag Lecture Notes in Computer Science #839, 1984.

DENB89   Den Boer, B., "Cryptanalysis of FEAL", *Advances in Cryptology—Eurocrypt 88*, Lecture Notes in Computer Science, Vol 330, Springer-Verlag, Berlin, 1989.

DENB92   Den Boer, B. and Bosselaers, A., "An Attack on the Last Two Rounds of MD4", *Advances in Cryptology—Crypto '91 Proceedings*, Springer-Verlag, Berlin, 1992, pp. 194–203.

DENN76   Denning, Dorothy E. R., "A lattice model of secure information flow", *Communications of the ACM*, Vol 19 #5, May 1976, pp. 236–243.

DENN81   Denning, D. E., and Sacco, G. M., "Timestamps in key distribution protocols", *Communications of the ACM*, Vol 24 #8, August 1981, pp. 533–536.

DENN82   Denning, Dorothy E. R., *Cryptography and Data Security*, Addison-Wesley Publishing Company, Reading, Massachusetts, 1982.

DENN90   Denning, P. (ed)., *Computers Under Attack: Intruders, Worms, and Viruses*, ACM Press/Addison-Wesley, Reading, MA, 1990.

DEPA85   *Department of Defense (Dod) Trusted Computer System Evaluation Criteria (TCSEC)*, [Orange Book], DoD 5200.28-STD, December 1985.

DES81   *DES Modes of Operation*, FIPS PUB 81, National Bureau of Standards, U.S. Department of Commerce, Washington, D.C., 1981.

DESM86   Desmedt, Y. and Odlyzko, A. M., "A chosen text attack on the RSA cryptosystem and some discrete logarithm schemes", *Advances in Cryptology—CRYPTO '85 Proceedings*, Vol 218 of Lecture Notes in Computer Science, Springer-Verlag, Berlin, 1986, pp. 516–521.

DIFF76a   Diffie, W. and Hellman, M. E., "A critique of the proposed Data Encryption Standard", *Communications of the ACM*, Vol 19 #3, 1976, pp. 164–165.

DIFF76b   Diffie, W. and Hellman, M. E., "New directions in cryptography", *IEEE Transactions on Information Theory*, Vol 22 #6, 1976, pp. 644–654.

DIFF77   Diffie, W. and Hellman, M. E., "Exhaustive cryptanalysis of the NBS Data Encryption Standard", *Computer*, Vol 10 #6, 1977, pp. 74–84.

DIFF79   Diffie, W. and Hellman, M. E., "Privacy and Authentication: An Introduction to Cryptography", *Proceedings of the IEEE*, Vol 67 #3, March 1979, pp. 397–427.

DIFF88   Diffie, W., "The first ten years of public-key cryptography", *Proceedings of the IEEE*, Vol 7 #5, May 1988, pp. 560–577.

DIRE88   *The Directory—Authentication Framework*, CCITT Recommendation X.509, 1988.

EAST94   Eastlake, D., Crocker, S., and Schiller, J., *Randomness Requirements for Security*, Internet RFC 1750, December 1994.

EBER92   Eberle, H., *A High-speed DES Implementation for Network Applications*, Digital Systems Research Center, Technical Report #90, Palo Alto, California, September 1992.

ELGA85   Elgamal, T., "A public key cryptosystem and a signature scheme based on discrete logarithms", *IEEE Transactions on Information Theory*, Vol 31, 1985, pp. 469–472.

FARR91   Farrow, R., *UNIX System Security: How to Protect Your Data and Prevent Intruders*, Addison-Wesley, Reading, MA, 1991.

FEIG87   Feige, U., Fiat, A., and Shamir, A., "Zero-Knowledge Proofs of Identity", *Proceedings of the ACM Symposium on the Theory of Computing*, ACM Press, New York, 1987, pp. 210–217.

FELD89   Feldmeier, D. C., and Karn, P. R., "UNIX Password Security—Ten Years Later", *Advances in Cryptology—CRYPTO '89 Proceedings*, Springer-Verlag, Berlin.

FINA82   *Financial Institution Message Authentication*, American National Standard X9.9, American National Standards Institute, 1982.

FINA85   *Financial Institution Key Management (Wholesale)*, American National Standard X9.17, American National Standards Institute, 1985.

FORD94   Ford, W., *Computer Communications Security: Principles, Standard Protocols, and Techniques*, Prentice Hall, Englewood Cliffs, New Jersey, 1994.

GAIN56   Gaines, H. F., *Cryptanalysis*, Dover, New York, 1956.

GALV93   Galvin, J. and McCloghrie, K., *Security Protocols for version 2 of the Simple Network Management Protocol (SNMPv2)*, RFC 1446, April 1993.

GASS76   Gasser, M., *A random word generator for pronounceable passwords*, Mitre Corp, Bedford, Mass., Report MTR-3006, November 1976.

GASS88   Gasser, M., *Building a Secure Computer System*, Van Nostrand Reinhold, New York, 1988.

GASS89   Gasser, M., Goldstein, A., Kaufman, C., and Lampson, B., "The Digital distributed system security architecture", *Proceedings of the 12th National Computer Security Conference*, NIST/NCSC, October 1989, pp. 305–319.

GASS90   Gasser, M., McDermott, E., "An Architecture for Practical Delegation in a Distributed System", *1990 Symposium on Security and Privacy*.

GUIL88   Guillou, L., and Quisquater, J., "A Practical Zero-Knowledge Protocol Fitted to Security Microprocessor Minimizing Both Transmission and Memory", *Advances in Cryptology—EUROCRYPT '88*, Springer-Verlag, Berlin, 1988.

HAPG73   Hapgood, F., "The Computer Hackers", *Harvard Magazine*, October 1973, pp. 26–29 and 46.

HAUS94   Hauser, R., Janson, P., Molva, R., Tsudik, G., and Van Herreweghen, E., "Robust and secure password/key change method", *Proc. of the Third European Symposium on Research in Computer Security (ESORICS)*, Lecture Notes in Computer Science, Springer-Verlag, Berlin Germany, November 1994, pp. 107–122..

HELL78   Hellman, M. E., "An overview of public-key cryptography", *IEEE Transactions on Communications*, Vol 16 #6, November 1978, pp. 24–32.

HELL79   Hellman, M. E., "DES will be totally insecure within ten years", *IEEE Spectrum*, Vol 16, 1979, pp. 32–39.

HELL81   Hellman, M. E., and Merkle, R. C., "On the security of multiple encryption", *Communications of the ACM*, Vol 24, 1981, pp. 465–467.

HOLB91   Holbrook, J. and Reynolds, J., *Site Security Handbook*, RFC 1244, July 1991.

ISO87   ISO/IEC 8825: *Information Technology—Open Systems Interconnection—Specification of ASN.1 Encoding Rules*, 1987. (Also ITU-T X.690 series Recommendations).

ISO88   ISO/IEC 9594-8: *Information Technology—Open Systems Interconnection—The Directory—Authentication Framework*, 1988 (revised 1993). (Also ITU-T Recommendation X.509).

JANS95   Janson, P. and G. Tsudik, G., "Secure and minimal protocols for authenticated key distribution", *Computer Communications Journal*, 1995. to appear.

JUEN84   Jueneman, R. R., Matyas, S. M., and Meyer, C. H., "Message Authentication with Manipulation Detection Codes", *Proceedings of the 1983 Symposium on Security and Privacy*, IEEE Computer Society Press, 1984, pp. 33–54.

JUEN85   Jueneman, R. R., Matyas, S. M., and Meyer, C. H., "Message Authentication", *IEEE Communications*, Vol 23 #9, September 1985, pp. 29–40.

KAHN67   Kahn, D., *The codebreakers: the story of secret writing*, Macmillan, New York, 1967.

KALI88   Kaliski, B. S., Rivest, R., and Sherman, A., "Is the Data Encryption Standard a Group? (Results of Cycling Experiments on DES)", *Journal of Cryptology*, Vol 1, 1988, pp. 3–36.

KALI92   Kaliski, B., *The MD2 Message-Digest Algorithm*, RFC 1319, April 1992.

KALI93   Kaliski, B., *Privacy Enhancement for Internet Electronic Mail: Part IV: Key Certification and Related Services*, RFC 1424, February 1993.

KAUF93   Kaufman, C., *DASS—Distributed Authentication Security Service*, RFC 1507, September 1993.

KENT93   Kent, S., *Privacy Enhancement for Internet Electronic Mail: Part II: Certificate-Based Key Management*, RFC 1422, February 1993.

KNUT69   Knuth, D. E., *The Art of Computer Programming: Seminumerical Algorithms*, Volume 2, Addison-Wesley, Reading, Massachusetts, 1969.

KOHL93   Kohl, J. and Newman, C., *The Kerberos Network Authentication Service (V5)*, RFC 1510, September 1993.

KONH81   Konheim, A., *Cryptography: A Primer*, John Wiley & Sons, 1981.

LAMP73   Lampson, B., "A Note on the Confinement Problem", *Communications of the ACM*, Vol 16 #10, October 1973, pp. 613–615.

LAMP74   Lampson, B., "Protection", *ACM Operating Systems Review*, Vol 8 #1, January 1974, pp. 18–24.

LAMP81   Lamport, L., "Password authentication with insecure communication", *Communications of the ACM*, Vol 24 #11, November 1981, pp. 770–772.

LAMP91   Lampson, B., Abadi, M., Burrows, M., and Wobber, E., "Authentication in Distributed Systems: Theory and Practice", *Proceedings of the 13th ACM Symposium on Operating System Principles*, October 1991.

LEE94   Lee, R. and Israel, J., "Understanding the Role of Identification and Authentication in NetWare 4", *Novell Application Notes*, Vol 5 # 10, October 1994, pp. 27–51.

LEVY84   Levy, S., *Hackers—Heroes of the Computer Revolution*, Doubleday, New York, 1984.

LINN90   Linn, J., "Practical Authentication for Distributed Computing", *IEEE Symposium on Security and Privacy*, Oakland, California, May 1990.

LINN93a   Linn, J., *Privacy Enhancement for Internet Electronic Mail: Part I: Message Encryption and Authentication Procedures*, RFC 1421, February 1993.

LINN93b   Linn, J., *Generic Security Service Application Program Interface*, RFC 1508, September 1993.

LINN93c   Linn, J., *Common Authentication Technology Overview*, RFC 1511, September 1993.

MADR92   Madron, T., *Network Security in the '90s: Issues and Solutions for Managers*, John Wiley & Sons, New York, 1992.

MERK78   Merkle, R., "Secure communication over insecure channels", *Communications of the ACM*, Vol 21, April 1978, pp. 294–299.

MERK90   Merkle, R., "A fast software one-way hash function", *Journal of Cryptology*, Vol 3 #1, 1990, pp. 43–58.

MEYE82   Meyer, C. and Matyas, S., *Cryptography: A New Dimension in Computer Data Security*, Wiley, New York, 1982.

MILL87   Miller, S., Neuman, B., Schiller, J., and Saltzer, J., *Kerberos Authentication and Authorization System*, Project Athena Technical Plan, Section E.2.1, MIT Project Athena, Cambridge, MA, December 1987.

MIYA88   Miyaguchi, S., Shiraishi, A., and Shimizu, A., "Fast data encryption algorithm Feal-8", *Review of Electrical Communications Laboratories*, Vol 36 #4, 1988, pp. 433–437.

MOLV92   Molva, R., Tsudik, G., Van Herreweghen, E., and Zatti, S., "KryptoKnight authentication and key distribution system", *European Symposium on Research in Computer Security*, 1992, pp. 155–174.

MORR79   Morris, R. and Thompson, K., "Password Security: A Case History", *Communications of the ACM*, Vol 22, November 1979, pp. 594–597.

NATI91   National Research Council, System Security Study Committee, *Computers at Risk: Safe Computing in the Information Age*, National Academy Press, Washington, D.C., 1991.

NEED78   Needham, R. M., and Schroeder, M. D., "Using encryption for authentication in large networks of computers", *Communications of the ACM*, Vol 21, December 1978, pp. 993–999.

NEED87   Needham, R. M., and Schroeder, M. D., "Authentication Revisited", *Operating Systems Review*, Vol 21 #1, January 1987, pp. 7.

OTWA87   Otway, D, and Rees, O., "Efficient and Timely Authentication", *Operating Systems Review*, Vol 21 #1, January 1987, pp. 8–10.

PASS85   *Password Usage*, FIPS Pub 112, National Bureau of Standards, Washington, D.C., May 1985.

PERL88   Perlman, R., *Network Layer Protocols with Byzantine Robustness*, MIT Laboratory for Computer Science Technical Report #429, October 1988.

PERL92   Perlman, R., *Interconnections: Bridges and Routers*, Addison-Wesley, Reading, Mass., 1992.

PFLE89   Pfleeger, C. P., *Security in Computing*, Prentice Hall, Englewood Cliffs, NJ, 1989.

PISC93   Piscitello, D., and Chapin, A. L., *Open Systems Networking: TCP/IP and OSI*, Addison-Wesley, Reading, Mass., 1993.

PLAT91   Plattner, B., Lanz, C., Lubich, H., Muller, M., Walker, T., *X.400 Message Handling: Standardes, Interworking, Applications*, Addison-Wesley, Reading, Mass., 1991.

POME81   Pomerance, C., "On the distribution of pseudoprimes", *Mathematics of Computation*, Vol 37 #156, 1981, pp. 587–593.

POST82   Postel, J., *Simple Mail Transfer Protocol*, RFC 821, August 1982.

RABI79   Rabin, M. O., *Digitized signatures and public key functions as intractable as factorization*, MIT Laboratory for Computer Science, Technical Report 212, January 1979.

RABI80   Rabin, M. O., "Probabilistic algorithm for primality testing", *Journal of Number Theory*, Vol 12, 1980, pp. 128–138.

RIVE78   Rivest, R. L., Shamir, A., and Adleman, L., "A method for obtaining digital signatures and public-key cryptosystems", *Communications of the ACM*, Vol 21 #2, February 1978, pp. 120–126.

RIVE91a   Rivest, R. L., "The MD4 message digest algorithm", *Advances in Cryptology—Crypto '90 Proceedings*, Lecture Notes in Computer Science 537, Springer-Verlag, 1991, pp. 303–311.

RIVE91b   Rivest, R., letter to NIST dated 26 October 1991 circulated on the Internet.

RIVE92a   Rivest, R., *The MD4 Message-Digest Algorithm*, RFC 1320, April 1992.

RIVE92b   Rivest, R., *The MD5 Message-Digest Algorithm*, RFC 1321, April 1992.

RUSS91   Russell, D. and Gangemi, G. T., *Computer Security Basics*, O'Reilly & Associates, Inc., Sebastopol, CA, July 1991.

SAND91   Sandler, C., Badgett, T., and Lefkowitz, L., *VAX Security*, John Wiley & Sons, Inc., New York, 1991.

SCHN94   Schneier, B., *Applied Cryptography: Protocols, Algorithms, and Source Code in C*, John Wiley & Sons, Inc., New York, 1994.

SCHR83   Schroeder, M., Birrell, A., and Needham, R., "Experience with Grapevine: The Growth of a Distributed System", *ACM Transactions on Computer Systems*, Vol 2 #1, February 1984.

SEBE89   Seberry, J. and Pieprzyk, J., *Cryptography: An Introduction to Computer Security*, Prentice Hall, Englewood Cliffs, New Jersey, 1989.

SECU93   *Secure Hash Standard*, National Institute of Science and Technology, Federal Information Processing Standard (FIPS) 180, April 1993.

SHAM81   Shamir, A., *On the Generation of Cryptographically Strong Pseudo-Random Sequences*, Department of Applied Mathemenatics, The Weizmann Institute of Science, Rehovot, Israel, 1981.

SHAN48   Shannon, C., "A Mathematical Theory of Communication", *Bell System Journal*, Vol 27, 1948, pp. 379-423 and pp. 623-656.

SHIM88   Shimizu, A. and Miyaguchi, S., "Fast Data Encipherment Algorithm FEAL", *Advances in Cryptography—Eurocrypt 87*, Lecture Notes in Computer Science, Vol 304, Springer-Verlag, Berlin, 1988.

SOLO77   Solovay, R., and Strassen, V., "A Fast Monte-Carlo test for Primality", *SIAM Journal on Computing*, Vol 6., March 1977, pp. 84–85.

SPAF88   Spafford, E. H., *The Internet Work Program: An Analysis*, Purdue Technical Report CSD-TR-823, Purdue University, November 1988.

STEI88   Steiner, J. G., Neuman, C., and Schiller, J. I., "Kerberos: An authentication service for open network systems", *Proceedings of the USENIX Winter Conference*, February 1988, pp. 191–202.

STER92   Sterling, Bruce, *The Hacker Crackdown: Law and Disorder on the Electronic Frontier*, Bantam Books, New York, NY, 1992.

STOL89   Stoll, C., *The Cuckoo's Egg: Tracing a Spy Through the Maze of Computer Espionage*, Doubleday, New York, 1989.

STUB92   Stubblebine, S. G. and Gligor, V. D., "On Message Integrity in Cryptographic Protocols", *IEEE Symposium on Research on Security and Privacy*, Oakland, California, May 1992, pp. 85–104.

STUB93   Stubblebine, S. G. and Gligor, V. D., "Protecting the Integrity of Privacy-enhanced Electronic Mail with DES-Based Authentication Codes", *PSRG Workshop on Network and Distributed Systems Security*, San Diego, California, February 1993.

TANE87   Tanenbaum, A., *Operating Systems—Design and Implementation*, Prentice Hall, Englewood Cliffs, New Jersey, 1987.

TANE88   Tanenbaum, A., *Computer Networks*, Prentice Hall, Englewood Cliffs, New Jersey, 1988.

TARD91   Tardo, J. J., and Alagappan, K., "SPX: Global Authentication using Public Key Certificates", *Proceedings of the 1991 IEEE Symposium on Security and Privacy*, May 1991, pp. 232–244.

TRUS87   *Trusted Network Interpretation (TNI) of the Trusted Computer System Evaluation Criteria (TCSEC)*, [Red Book], NCSC-TG-005 Version 1, 1987.

WRAY93   Wray, J., *Generic Security Service API: C-bindings*, RFC 1509, September 1993.

GLOSSARY

access control—a mechanism for limiting use of some resource to authorized users.

access control list—a data structure associated with a resource that specifies the authorized users.

access control set—a synonym for access control list; some people make the distinction that the order of entries an access control set cannot be significant, while the order of entries in an access control list might be.

ACL—see *Access Control List*.

ANSI—one of several organizations that develop and publish standards for computer networking. It stands for American National Standards Institute.

ASCII—a mapping between text characters and numbers. It stands for American Standard Code for Information Interchange.

ASN.1 (Abstract Syntax Notation 1)—an ISO standard for data represenation and data structure definitions. We can hardly wait to see ASN.2.

asymmetric cryptography—public key cryptography.

Athena—a project conducted at the Massachusetts Institute of Technology that developed a number of interesting technologies including the Kerberos cryptographic authentication system.

ATM—automatic teller machine. (Though in a book on computer networking, you'd probably expect this to have something to do with Asynchronous Transfer Mode, a high performance networking technology.)

audit—keep a record of events that might have some security significance, such as when access to resources occurred.

authenticate—to determine that something is genuine. In the context of this book, to reliably determine the identity of a communicating party.

authentication—the process of reliably determining the identity of a communicating party.

authorization—permission to access a resource.

background authentication—authentication that takes place automatically when a user requests a service without the user having to do anything.

bad guy—someone who is trying to defeat a cryptographic or other security mechanism. (No moral implications here; some of our best friends are bad guys.)

batch job—a process run on behalf of a particular user while the user need not be physically present at any terminal and no terminal is associated with the process. The user will presumably return later and harvest the results.

biometric device—a device that authenticates people by measuring some hard-to-forge physical property, like a fingerprint or the strokes and timing of a signature.

block encryption—scrambling, in a reversible manner, a fixed-size piece of data into a fixed size piece of ciphertext.

bucket brigade attack—getting in between two legitimate users, relaying their messages to each other, and thereby spoofing each of them into thinking they are talking directly to the other.

CA—certification authority. Something that signs certificates.

call back—a security mechanism for dial-in connections to a network whereby a user calls in, requests a connection, and hangs up. The computer system then calls him back and thus reliably knows the telephone number of the caller.

caller ID—a relatively new service offered by the telephone system whereby the recipient of a call is reliably informed of the number of the phone originating the call.

captive account—an account on a timesharing system that allows someone who uses that account to run only a single program which carefully controls access to system resources.

CBC (cipher block chaining)—a method of using a block encryption scheme for encrypting an arbitrary-sized message.

CBC residue—the last block of ciphertext when encrypting a message using cipher block chaining. Since it is difficult to find two messages with the same CBC residue without knowing the key, CBC residue is often used as an integrity-protecting checksum for a message.

CCITT—a standards organization dominated by European telephone companies known as PTTs, where PTT stands for Postal, Telephone, and Telegraph Authority, and CCITT stands for something or other in French. (If you insist, it's Comité Consultatif International de Télégraphique et Téléphonique.) CCITT publishes standards for computer networking, including the X.400 series of documents concerning electronic mail and the X.500 series of documents concerning directory services. Its name is now ITU.

CDC (certificate distribution center)—the name the DASS system gives to their on-line system that distributes certificates and user private keys.

certificate—a message signed with a public key digital signature stating that a specified public key belongs to someone or something with a specified name.

certification authority (CA)—something trusted to sign certificates.

certificate revocation list (CRL)—a digitally signed data structure listing all the certificates created by a given CA that have not yet expired but are no longer valid.

CFB (cipher feedback)—a method of using a block encryption scheme for encrypting an arbitrary-sized message.

challenge—a number given to something so that it can cryptographically process the number using a secret quantity it knows and return the result (called the response). The purpose of the exercise is to prove knowledge of the secret quantity without revealing it to an eavesdropper. This is known as challenge/response authentication.

Chaos Computer Club—a loosely knit organization centered in Germany that made the news by staging some high-profile break-ins to computer networks.

checksum—a small, fixed-length quantity computed as a function of an arbitrary length message. A checksum is computed by the sender of a message and recomputed and checked by the recipient of a message to detect data corruption. Originally, the term checksum meant the specific integrity check consisting of adding all the numbers together and throwing away carries. Usage has extended the definition to include more complex non-cryptographic functions such as CRCs, which detect hardware faults with high probability, and cryptographic functions such as message digests, which can withstand attacks from clever attackers.

CIA (Central Intelligence Agency)—the arm of the United States government responsible for spying, and hence a convenient target for our lame jokes.

classified—an adjective describing something the government does not want divulged for national security reasons. There are various categories of classified, including CONFIDENTIAL, SECRET, and TOP SECRET.

cleartext—a message that is not encrypted.

Clipper—the name by which the U.S. government's scheme for encrypting telephones is known. The scheme allows high-grade encryption while allowing wiretapping with a court order. (The name will change due to trademark violation, but that's the name it's known by now.)

client—something that accesses a service by communicating with it over a computer network.

CLNP (Connectionless Network Protocol)—An OSI standard network layer protocol for sending data through a computer network.

COCOM—A treaty among many leading Western nations that coordinated export control regulations on technologies of military significance, including cryptography. The treaty is no longer in force, but similar export regulations in many countries remain as its legacy.

compromise—in common English usage, to give up some things in order to reach agreement on something; this usage rarely arises in the security community. In the context of security, to invade something by getting around its security. A person who has been compromised might be someone who has accepted a bribe. A computer that has been compromised might be one that has had a Trojan horse installed.

confidentiality—the property of not being divulged to unauthorized parties.

confinement—not allowing information of a certain security classification to escape from the environment in which it is allowed to reside.

cracker—a person who uses other people's computers for criminal purposes. It's not a very good word, but we hope people will use it instead of "hacker" so as not to sully the true spirit in which the word "hacker" was invented (see *hacker*).

CRC (cyclic redundancy code)—a form of noncryptographic integrity check popular as error detection.

CRC-32—a particular CRC that produces a 32-bit output.

credentials—secret information used to prove ones identity in an authentication exchange.

CRL (Certificate Revocation List)—a digitally signed message that lists all the unexpired but revoked certificates issued by a particular CA. It is similar to the book of stolen charge card numbers that stores receive frequently to enable them to reject bad credit cards.

cryptanalysis—the process of finding weaknesses or flaws in cryptographic algorithms.

cryptographic checksum—an integrity check with the property that it is infeasible to find a valid checksum for a message unless you know some secret.

cryptography—mathematical manipulation of data for the purpose of reversible or irreversible transformation.

CSMA/CD (Carrier Sense Multiple Access with Collision Detect)—a LAN technology using contention for sharing the wire. Examples are 802.3 and Ethernet.

cybercrud—mostly useless computer generated gibberish that people either ignore or are intimidated and annoyed by.

DASS (Distributed Authentication Security Service)—a public key-based authentication protocol defined in RFC 1507.

DCE (Distributed Computing Environment)—a group of programs and protocols standardized by the Open Software Foundation built atop a cryptographically protected remote procedure call protocol.

decipher—to decrypt.

decrypt—to undo the encryption process.

delegation—giving some of your rights to another person or process.

daemon process—a process that runs on a computer with no associated user, usually to carry out some administrative function.

DES (Data Encryption Standard)—a secret key cryptographic scheme standardized by NIST.

Diffie-Hellman key exchange—a method of establishing a shared key over an insecure medium, named after the inventors (Diffie and Hellman).

directory service—a service provided on a computer network that allows one to look up addresses (and perhaps other information) based on names.

discrete logarithm—An integer x satisfying the equation $y = a^x \bmod p$ for given y, a, and p.

discretionary access controls—a mechanism allowing the owner of a resource to decide who can access the resource. Outside the military environment, they are usually simply referred to as *access controls*.

download—to send a program over the network to be loaded and executed, typically by a special purpose device like a printer or router.

DNS (Domain Name System)—the naming convention defined in RFC 1033. DNS names are often referred to as *internet addresses* or *internet names*.

DSS (Digital Signature Standard)—a public key cryptographic system for computing digital signatures (i.e., it does not do encryption).

eavesdrop—to listen in on a conversation without the knowledge or consent of the communicating parties.

EBCDIC—IBM's encoding of characters. It serves the same purpose as ASCII, but is incompatible with ASCII. Stands for Extended Binary Coded Decimal Interchange Code.

ECB (electronic code book)—a method of using a block encryption scheme to encrypt a large message. It's the most straightforward method, consisting of independently encrypting each plaintext block.

EDE (encrypt/decrypt/encrypt)—a method of making a secret key scheme more secure using multiple keys. The technique is to first encrypt the message with one key, then do a decryption with a different key on the resulting ciphertext, and finally encrypt the result with either the first key used, or a third key.

El Gamal—a public key cryptographic system whose security depends on the difficulty of computing discrete logarithms. It is best known for its method of computing digital signatures, though the specification includes a technique for encryption as well. Named after its inventor (El Gamal, in case you couldn't guess).

encipher—to encrypt. Used in international standards documents instead of *encrypt* because the French interpret *encrypt* to mean to put some body into a crypt; *decrypt* would presumably mean to retrieve them.

encrypt—to scramble information so that only someone knowing the appropriate secret can obtain the original information (through decryption).

escrow—to hold something in safe-keeping. Most uses of the word actually mean keeping the something safe from the owner as opposed to providing any safety for the owner.

Euclid's algorithm—an algorithm to find the greatest common divisor of two numbers. It can also be used to compute multiplicative inverses in modular arithmetic.

execute—in the case of a program, to run the program.

exploder—a component of an electronic mail system that takes a single message addressed to a distribution list and turns it into many mail messages to the individual recipients

FIPS (Federal Information Processing Standard)—one of a series of U.S. government documents specifying standards for various aspects of data processing, including the Data Encryption Standard (DES).

form factor—the outward appearance of a function, for instance the number and size of the inputs and the number and size of the outputs.

gcd—greatest common divisor.

good guy—someone using a cryptographic or other security system in the manner in which its designers intended (see *bad guy*).

greatest common divisor—the largest integer that evenly divides each of a set of provided integers.

group—(in the context of this book) a named collection of users, created for convenience in stating authorization policy.

hacker—someone who plays with computers for the pure intellectual challenge. The proper use of the word is as applied to the kind of extraordinarily talented and dedicated people who , if given an opportunity to spend six weeks on the beach, would build a computer out of sand and write the operating system and all utilities. Unfortunately, the media has taken to using the term *hacker* to apply to people who use computers for criminal purposes. The most malicious thing a true hacker would ever do is sneak their own bicycle into the building after management has issued an anti-bicycle edict, or refuse to bathe.

hash—a cryptographic one-way function that takes an arbitrary-sized input and yields a fixed-size output.

hop—a direct communication channel between two computers. In a complex computer network, a message might take many hops between its source and destination.

IDEA (International Data Encryption Algorithm)—a secret key cryptographic scheme gaining popularity.

IETF (Internet Engineering Task Force)—a standards body whose focus is protocols for use in the Internet. Its publications are called Internet RFCs (Requests For Comments).

initialization vector (IV)—a number used by the CBC, OFB, and CFB encryption techniques to initialize the first round. Subsequent rounds use the results of the earlier rounds.

integrity—correctness. A system protects the integrity of data if it prevents unauthorized modification (as opposed to protecting the confidentiality of data, which prevents unauthorized disclosure).

Internet—When not capitalized, it means a connected collection of computer networks. I_2've always hated the term since I_2'd define a network as the collection of nodes that have connectivity between them. Once you interconnect a bunch of networks, the result is one big network! But the world uses the term. When capitalized, *the Internet* refers to the large and still growing network that started as the ARPANET, a research network funded by the US department of defense.

intermediary—something that facilitates communication between parties that wish to communicate.

IRS (Internal Revenue Service)—the universally beloved branch of the United States government that rightfully, equitably, and fairly collects taxes. And they have a wonderful sense of humor and won't mind when we occasionally poke fun at them in this book.

ISO (International Standards Organization)—an international organization tasked with developing and publishing standards for everything from wine glasses to computer network protocols. In this book, references to ISO are to its standards for computer networking known as Open Systems Interconnect (or OSI).

ITAR (International Trafficking in Arms Regulation)—the collection of laws in the United States that regulate the export of dangerous technologies like nuclear weapons and personal mail encryption.

IV—initialization vector.

KDC—see *Key Distribution Center*.

Kerberize—(Don't you hate it when people verbify a noun?) to enhance an application to use Kerberos for authentication and/or encryption.

Kerberos—a DES-based authentication system developed at MIT as part of Project Athena and subsequently incorporated into a growing collection of commercial products.

key—a quantity used in cryptography to encrypt or decrypt information.

Key Distribution Center (KDC)—an on-line trusted intermediary that has master keys for all principals and which generates conversation keys between principals when requested.

KGB—Russian equivalent of the CIA.

LAN (Local Area Network)—a method of interconnecting multiple systems in such a way that all transmissions over the LAN can be listened to by all systems on the LAN.

LEAF (law enforcement access field)—the field that must be transmitted by one Clipper chip to the Clipper chip at the other end of the conversation. Without it, the receiving Clipper will refuse to decrypt the conversation. The LEAF field enables law enforcement to decrypt the conversation, after a court order to obtain the sending Clipper's unique key.

logarithm—The base b logarithm of x is the exponent to which b must be raised to get x, so $b^{\log_b x}$ = x. The security of most public key cryptographic algorithms depends on the difficulty of computing discrete logarithms (i.e. finding integer x such that $b^x = a \bmod p$ given large integers a, b, and p.

logic bomb—a piece of code maliciously added to a program that specifically is designed to lay dormant until some event occurs, such as a specific date being reached or a user typing some command. The classic example of a logic bomb is a piece of code inserted into a critical program by a disgruntled employee in order to cause trouble long after the employee is gone.

MAC—see *message authentication code* or *mandatory access controls*. (And if that isn't enough, it also stands for *medium access control* in data link layer networking jargon, where it has nothing to do with the security sense of *access control*.)

mandatory access controls—an access control mechanism where the owner of data does not have full control over who may access the data. For example, a system may keep track of the fact that a file contains TOP SECRET data and deny access to that data to a user without the proper clearance even if the creator of the data wishes to grant access.

masquerade—to pretend to be X when you are not X, and without X's permission.

message authentication code (MAC)—a synonym of message integrity code (MIC).

message digest—an irreversible function that takes an arbitrary sized message and outputs a fixed length quantity. MD2, MD4, and MD5 are message digest algorithms documented in RFCs 1319, 1320, and 1321.

message integrity code (MIC)—a fixed-length quantity generated cryptographically and associated with a message to reassure the recipient that the message is genuine. The term is most often used in connection with secret key cryptography, since a public key MIC is usually called a digital signature.

MIC—see *message integrity code*.

Minesweeper—an addictive game bundled with Windows^{TM} in a ploy by Microsoft to reduce productivity in the rest of the industry. It would be more appropriately named *Mindsweeper*.

MS/DOS—a primitive operating system used by most personal computers.

mutual authentication—when each party in a conversation proves its identity to the other.

NIS—Network Information Service, formerly known as YP, Sun Microsystem's Directory Service.

NIST—National Institute of Standards and Technology, formerly known as NBS (National Bureau of Standards).

nonce—a number used in a cryptographic protocol that must (with extremely high probability) be different each time the protocol is run with a given set of participants in order to ensure that an attacker can't usefully inject messages recorded from a previous running of the protocol. There are many ways of generating nonces, including suitably large random numbers, sequence numbers, and timestamps.

non-discretionary access controls—same as *mandatory access controls*.

non-repudiation—the property of a scheme in which there is proof of who sent a message that a recipient can show to a third party and the third party can independently verify the source.

nonvolatile memory—storage that maintains its state without external power, for example, magnetic disks and core memories.

OFB—see *output feedback mode*.

on-line server—something that provides a service and is generally available on the network (i.e. it can run unattended).

one-time pad—an encryption method where a long string known to sender and receiver is ⊕'d with plaintext to get ciphertext and ⊕'d with ciphertext to recover plaintext. This extremely simple encryption method is proveably secure for keeping a message confidential if the string used is truly random, known only to the communicating parties, and any given string is only used for encryption once.

one-to-one mapping—a function that assigns an output value to each input value in such a way that each input maps to exactly one output, and no two inputs map to the same output.

Open—1. Open is supposed to mean that the thing described was developed by a committee from which no interested party was excluded, the thing is documented in sufficient detail to enable independent interworking implementations based on documentation alone, and there are no patent, copyright, or trade secret impediments to its deployment. 2. A marketing term meaning *good*.

OSF (Open Software Foundation)—an organization founded as an industry consortium to develop and license open software (see *open*). It is best known for OSF/1, a UNIX variant, and DCE, a family of protocols centered around a secure RPC and distributed file system.

OSI (Open Systems Interconnect)—the name of the computer networking standards approved by ISO. In the networking community, the terms "OSI" and "ISO" tend to be used interchangeably, annoying the purists. We tend to use them interchangeably.

out of band—by some mechanism separate from the transmission of data. An out-of-band mechanism for key distribution would be something other than sending messages across the network, for example by having people talk on the phone to each other or give each other pieces of paper or floppies.

output feedback mode (OFB)—a method of turning a secret key block cipher into a stream cipher. OFB effectively generates a pseudo-random one-time pad by iteratively encrypting the previous block, starting with an IV.

Ovaltine—some combination of sugar and chemicals sold as a milk additive.

overrun—in the security community the term *overrun* means taken over by a bad guy. A common goal is to minimize the damage done if a single node in a system is overrun and its secrets revealed.

pad—additional bits added to a message to make it a desired length, for instance an integral number of bytes. This meaning of pad has no relation to the word *pad* in the phrase *one-time pad*, or the word *pad* in the phrase *PostIt*® *Pad*.

password—a supposedly secret string used to prove one's identity.

PC (personal computer)—We use the term interchangeably with *workstation*. In common usage, a PC is an inexpensive device with an inadequate operating system while a workstation has neither of these properties. Sometimes PC is intended to refer exclusively to IBM-compatible personal computers, but that distinction is never intended in this book.

permutation—a method of encryption where parts of the message are rearranged. Encryption by permutation is not very secure by itself, but it can be used in combination with substitution to build powerful ciphers like DES.

PIN (Personal Identification Number)—a short sequence of digits used as a password.

PKCS (Public-Key Cryptography Standard)—a series of documents produced and distributed by RSA Data Security, Inc., proposing techniques for using public key cryptographic algorithms in a safe and interoperable manner.

PKZIP™—a software package for data compression and backup from PKWare, Inc.

plausible deniability—a situation in which events are structured so that someone can claim not to have known or done something, and no proof exists to the contrary. Whenever this term comes up, the person in question is almost certainly guilty.

PostIt® **Pad**—the original brand of those yellow sticky things you write notes on and leave on people's doors, chairs, etc in offices

PostScript®—a write-only programming language created by Adobe Systems Inc. to describe printed pages.

preauthentication—a protocol for proving you know your password before you are allowed access to a high quality secret encrypted with that password. Preauthentication is there to prevent an intruder from easily obtaining a quantity with which to do off-line password guessing.

principal—a completely generic term used by the security community to include both people and computer systems. Coined because it is more dignified than *thingy* and because *object* and *entity* (which also mean thingy) were already overused.

privacy—When we use the term, it means protection from the unauthorized disclosure of data. Security purists use confidentiality for this because the word privacy has been coopted by the lawyers to mean approximately the opposite: privacy legislation consists of laws requiring governments and businesses to tell people what information those organizations are storing about them.

private key—the quantity in public key cryptography that must be kept secret.

privileged user—a user of a computer who is authorized to bypass normal access control mechanisms, usually to be able to perform system management functions.

protected subsystem—a program that can run at a higher level of privilege than the user of the program is entitled to, because it has very structured interfaces that will not allow any but security-safe operations.

public key—the quantity in public key cryptography that is safely divulged to as large an extent as is necessary or convenient.

public key cryptography—also known as *asymmetric cryptography*, a cryptographic system where encryption and decryption are performed using different keys.

RC2—a proprietary secret key encryption scheme marketed by RSADSI. It's a block encryption scheme with 64-bit blocks and a varying length key. It reportedly stands for *Ron's Cipher #2*, and we believe you can guess who Ron is.

RC4—another proprietary secret key encryption scheme marketed by RSADSI. It's a stream encryption algorithm that effectively produces an unbounded length pseudorandom stream from a varying length key. The stream is $\oplus$'d with the data for encryption and decryption.

rcp—a UNIX command for copying a file across the network.

realm—a Kerberos term for all of the principals served by a particular KDC.

recursion—see *recursion*.

rlogin—a UNIX command for logging into a machine across the network.

Reference Monitor—a piece of code in a computer system that oversees all security-related activity such as resource access.

reflection attack—an attack where messages received from something are replayed back to it.

replaying—storing and retransmitting messages. The word is usually used when implying that the entity doing the replay of messages is mounting some sort of security attack.

repudiation—denying that you did something or made some statement.

revocation—taking back privileges, either from a person who is no longer trusted (as when an employee quits) or from a secret (when its rightful owner believes it may have been divulged).

RPC—remote procedure call.

RSA—a public key cryptographic algorithm named for its inventors (Rivest, Shamir, and Adleman) that does encryption and digital signatures.

RSADSI—an abbreviation for RSA Data Security, Inc., the company that licences the RSA technology.

rsh—the UNIX remote shell command, which executes a specified command on a specified machine across the network.

salt—a user-specific value cryptographically combined with that user's password to obtain the hash of that user's password. Salt serves several purposes. It makes the hash of two users' passwords different even if their passwords are the same. It also means that an intruder can't precompute hashes of a few thousand guessed passwords, and compare that list against a stolen database of hashed passwords. The salt can be a random number which is stored, in the clear, along with the hash of the user's password, or it could consist of the user's name or some other user-specific information.

secret key—the shared secret quantity in secret key cryptography that is used to encrypt and decrypt data.

secret key cryptography—also known as *symmetric cryptography*, a scheme in which the same key is used for encryption and decryption.

security kernel—the part of an operating system responsible for enforcement of security. Usually used in the context of an operating system constructed with such functions partitioned from the rest of the O/S to minimize the chances of security-relevant bugs.

self-synchronizing—(as used in this book) an encryption scheme in which, if some of the ciphertext is garbled by the addition, deletion, or modification of information, some of the message will be garbled at the receiver, but at some point in the message stream following the ciphertext modification, the message will decrypt properly.

server—some resource available on the network to provide some service such as name lookup, file storage, or printing.

sign—to use your private key to generate a digital signature as a means of proving you generated, or approve of, some message.

signature—a quantity associated with a message which only someone with knowledge of your private key could have generated, but which can be verified through knowledge of your public key.

Simple—the first word in the name of many protocols in the Internet suite.

Simple Network Management Protocol (SNMP)—a protocol for controlling systems across a network, standardized by the IETF.

Simple Mail Transport Protocol (SMTP)—a protocol for sending electronic mail across a network, standardized by the IETF.

SKIPJACK—a secret key encryption algorithm using 64-bit blocks and 80-bit keys. It is embedded in Clipper chips, and is classified by the U.S. government (meaning they won't tell you what it is).

smart card—a credit-card-sized object used for authentication that contains nonvolatile storage and computational power. Some smart cards are capable of performing cryptographic operations on the card.

SMTP—see *Simple Mail Transport Protocol*.

spoof—to convince someone that you are some entity X when you are not X, without X's permission. Synonyms are *impersonate* and *masquerade*.

stream encryption—an encryption algorithm that encrypts and decrypts arbitrary sized messages.

strong—A cryptographic algorithm is said to be strong if it would take a large amount of computational power to defeat it.

strong authentication—authentication where someone eavesdropping on the authentication exchange does not gain sufficient information to impersonate the principal in a subsequent authentication.

substitution—an encryption algorithm where a one-to-one mapping is performed on a fixed-size block, for example where each letter of the alphabet has an enciphered equivalent. Substitution ciphers are not very secure unless the block size is large, but they can be combined with permutation ciphers in a series of rounds to build stong ciphers like DES.

superuser—an operating system concept in which an individual is allowed to circumvent ordinary security mechanisms. For instance, the system manager must be able to read everyone's files for the purpose of doing backups.

symmetric cryptography—secret key cryptography. Called *symmetric* because the same key is used for encryption and decryption.

TGT—see *ticket granting ticket*.

ticket—a data structure constructed by a trusted intermediary to enable two parties to authenticate

ticket-granting ticket (TGT)—a Kerberos data structure which is really a ticket to the KDC. The purpose is to allow a user's workstation to forget the user's long-term secret soon after the user logs in.

tiger teams—groups of people hired by an organization to defeat its own security systems in order that the organization can learn weaknesses.

totient function—$\phi(n)$, the number of positive integers less than n which are relatively prime to n.

trap door function—a function that appears irreversible, but which has a secret method (a *trap door*) which, if known, allows someone to reverse the function.

trusted intermediary—a third party such as a KDC or CA that permits two parties to authenticate without prior configuration of keys between those two parties.

trusted server—something that aids in network authentication.

trusted software—software that has been produced in a way that makes you confident that there could be no Trojan horses (or even security relevant bugs) in the code.

Trojan horse—a piece of code embedded in a useful program for nefarious purposes, for instance to steal information. Usually the term *Trojan horse* is used rather than *virus* when the offending code does not attempt to replicate itself into other programs.

Turing test—a test proposed by Alan Turing for testing whether a computer had achieved artificial intelligence. The test was that a person would communicate by keyboard to either the computer or to a human, and if the tester couldn't tell which was the human and which was the computer, then the computer had passed the Turing test.

UA—see *user agent*.

user agent—the first layer of software insulating the user from the vagaries of the electronic mail infrastructure.

uudecode—a UNIX utility for reversing the effects of uuencode.

uuencode—a UNIX utility for encoding arbitrary binary data as harmless printable characters by encoding 6 bits of binary data per character.

verify a signature—perform a cryptographic calculation using a message, a signature, and a public key to determine whether the signature was generated by someone knowing the corresponding private key signing the message.

virus—a piece of a computer program that replicates by embedding itself in other programs. When those programs are run, the virus is invoked again and can spread further.

VMS (Virtual Memory System)—a Digital Equipment Corporation proprietary operating system.

work factor—an estimate of the computational resources required to defeat a given cryptographic system.

workstation—a single-user computer such as a PC. Sometimes the term workstation implies the computer is running Unix, but for the purpose of this book the specific hardware and specific operating system of the user's computer is irrelevant.

worm—a self-contained program that replicates by running copies of itself—usually on different machines across a computer network.

X.400—A CCITT standard for electronic mail.

X.500—A CCITT standard for directory services.

X.509—A CCITT standard for security services within the X.500 directory services framework. The X.509 encoding of public key certificates has been widely adopted; the other protocol elements of X.509 have not.

YP—Yellow Pages, a directory service part of Sun Microsystems distributed environment.

zero knowledge proof—1. a scheme in which you can convince someone you know a secret without actually divulging the secret. You know a secret, they know something equivalent to a public key. You answer questions, and the answers convince the other that you know the secret without giving them any information that will help them find the secret. 2. what you write when you're faking an answer on a math test.

INDEX